COLLEGE ENGLISH AND COMMUNICATION
FOURTH EDITION

Marie M. Stewart, Ph.D.
Former Head of the
Business Education Department
Stonington High School
Stonington, Connecticut

Kenneth Zimmer, Ed.D.
Professor of Business Education
and Office Administration
California State University
Los Angeles, California

Gregg Division
McGraw-Hill Book Company
New York   Atlanta   Dallas   St. Louis   San Francisco   Auckland
Bogotá   Guatemala   Hamburg   Johannesburg   Lisbon   London
Madrid   Mexico   Montreal   New Delhi   Panama   Paris
San Juan   São Paulo   Singapore   Sydney   Tokyo   Toronto

Sponsoring Editor: Joseph Tinervia
Editing Supervisor: Timothy Perrin
Design Supervisors: Nancy Ovedovitz and Howard Brotman
Production Supervisor: Laurence Charnow

Cover Illustrator: Jorge Hernandez
Technical Studio: Burmar Technical Corp.

Photo Credits: American Management Association: 440; Martin Bough, Studios, Inc.: 17, 20, 33, 148, 154, 236, 242, 270, 322, 358, 485, 536; Ken Karp: viii, 136; Lensman: 12 (Gordon Beall); Kay Reese & Associates: 38 (Lynn Pelham), 480 (Arthur Levine).

Library of Congress Cataloging in Publication Data

Stewart, Marie M., date
  College English and communication.
  Includes index.
  1. English language—Rhetoric. I. Zimmer,
Kenneth, date.   II. Title.
PE1408.S763 1982   808'.066651021   81-6015
ISBN 0-07-072846-1   AACR2

COLLEGE ENGLISH AND COMMUNICATION, Fourth Edition

   12 13 14 15 DODO 8 9 8 7 6

ISBN   0-07-072846-1

PREFACE

The business world of the 1980s is highly competitive and performance-oriented. Each year, companies across the country spend millions of dollars to find the best qualified prospective employees and to upgrade their present employees, all in an effort to improve productivity and profitability. To get the job you want, then, you may need one or more special job-related skills, such as the ability to type, develop computer programs, write shorthand, or operate data processing machines or other office machinery. In addition, you will also need another skill: the ability to communicate effectively during an interview and on the job.

Why do employers demand communication skill as a basic need for *all* employees? The reason is simple: experienced executives and managers are aware that most business workers spend the greater part of each workday communicating—writing, listening, speaking, and reading. They know that workers who write poorly, listen inattentively, or read slowly will impede progress. Of course, such employees are not considered valuable—especially in today's competitive, performance-oriented business world.

THE *COLLEGE ENGLISH AND COMMUNICATION* PROGRAM

The Fourth Edition of *College English and Communication* provides a comprehensive program to help you develop the proficiency in writing, listening, speaking, and reading that you will need for career success. It is especially designed to help you master the fundamental principles of communication, and it achieves this goal through its carefully planned, step-by-step presentation.

Chapter 1: Communicating Effectively. Because understanding the communication process is fundamental to effective writing, listening, speaking, and reading, Chapter 1 offers an overview of the communication process. This introductory chapter also describes many of the communication media used in business.

Chapter 2: Developing Listening and Reading Skills. As a follow-up to the introduction to communication in Chapter 1, Chapter 2 helps you develop your listening and reading skills—skills that are as important on the job as they are in the classroom. In Chapter 2 you will begin a long-range program for improving your listening and reading skills.

Chapter 3: Understanding Language Structure. Chapter 3 provides a detailed discussion of the principles of grammar that you must apply if you wish to write and speak effectively. Throughout the chapter, principles of grammar are simplified whenever possible, and many examples are offered to illustrate proper usage. Often, "Memory Hooks" are presented to give special attention to difficult points of grammar, and "Twilight Zones" explain aspects of language usage that are in a state of transition. In addition, many "Checkup" exercises provide immediate reinforcement and practice in applying the principles presented in the chapter.

Chapter 4: Applying the Mechanics of Style. In Chapter 4 you will master the style for expressing numbers and for using punctuation, capitalization, and abbreviations in written communications. Because a consistent application of writing style helps the reader to interpret messages correctly, Chapter 4 is an especially important preparation for writing business letters, memos, and reports. As in Chapter 3, many "Checkup" exercises are provided for immediate reinforcement and practice.

Chapter 5: Using Words for Greatest Effect. The effective communicator must, of course, be able to use words skillfully both in writing and in speaking, and *College English and Communication*, Fourth Edition, provides a continuing program to expand and refine your vocabulary. Chapter 5 will introduce you to the reference tools that will make your writing less difficult and, at the same time, more effective. In this chapter you will learn techniques for using words precisely and for achieving variety in word usage. In addition, Chapter 5 offers some basic methods for improving spelling.

Chapter 6: Establishing Writing Skill. Understanding the rules of grammar and having a wide vocabulary do not, of course, guarantee effective writing. Letters, memos, and reports must be planned if they are to achieve their goals, and Chapter 6 presents the techniques for planning and organizing messages. This chapter also discusses human behavior and advanced writing techniques that will help transform average writing into forceful communication.

Chapter 7: Writing Business Memos and Letters. Chapter 7 offers you the opportunity to apply all the writing techniques presented in the first six chapters. This chapter treats each category of business letter and memo individually—requests, claim and adjustment letters, sales letters, and so on. By giving each type of communication special emphasis in a separate section, the text provides ample opportunities to learn about and to write each kind of letter and memo.

Chapter 8: Preparing Reports and Special Communications. Reports are important, commonly used business communications, and they are treated in detail in Chapter 8. Besides memorandum reports and long reports, this chapter discusses progress reports, minutes of meetings, and agendas.

Chapter 9: Communicating Orally. Speaking to co-workers, customers, and others is an important part of the business day for most people, and Chapter 9 presents the basic information that you must know to speak effectively in one-to-one situations and in group dicussions, as well as what you must know to prepare and deliver a formal speech. Also included in this chapter is a discussion on enunciation and pronunciation.

Chapter 10: Communicating for Career Success. During employment interviews and on the job, the communication skills that you have developed will be tested. In Chapter 10 you will discover how you can apply your communication skills to find a job and to make your interviews more effective. In this chapter you will also learn techniques for handling your communication duties on the job.

As mentioned above, the text offers "Checkup" exercises within the sections in Chapters 3 and 4; in addition, it offers a variety of "Communication Projects" at the end of each section:

- *Practical Application* exercises reinforce the principles presented in each section and review principles covered in previous sections.

- *Edition Practice* exercises help you acquire the ability to detect—and to correct—errors in English usage.

- *Case Problems* generally emphasize the human relations aspects of successful business communication. They will help you develop your ability to make sound judgments and decisions in typical on-the-job situations.

SUPPLEMENTARY MATERIALS

Besides the text, the *College English and Communication* program includes two other publications:

For the student. A comprehensive book of skill-building activities entitled *Communication Problems Correlated With College English and Communication*, Fourth Edition, provides additional exercises to improve your communication skills. The exercises provide excellent reinforcement of the text principles section by section, as well as periodic reviews of preceding sections.

For the instructor. Instructor's Guide and Key for College English and Communication, Fourth Edition, is a valuable source of information for planning and presenting a successful communications course. This guide includes (1) general teaching suggestions for each of the ten chapters, (2) 32 pages of test masters that the instructor may duplicate for classroom use, (3) a complete key to all text exercises, (4) a facsimile key of all pages in *Communication Problems*, and (5) a facsimile key of all 32 test pages.

CONTENTS

CHAPTER 1

COMMUNICATING EFFECTIVELY

1 THE COMMUNICATION PROCESS

The purpose of this book is to help you communicate more effectively. In order to achieve this goal, you must become familiar with the many aspects of the communication process. You must develop an understanding of (1) the components of the communication process, (2) the goals of effective communication, (3) those factors that influence the effectiveness of communication, and (4) the importance, to you and to everybody else, of being an effective communicator.

COMPONENTS OF COMMUNICATION

Simply defined, communication is the process of transmitting a message from one source to another.

SENDER → message → RECEIVER

Notice that this definition involves three components: a sender, a message, and a receiver.

The Sender

The sender of a message may be a *person* representing himself or herself, representing someone else, or representing a group of individuals (a business firm or a corporation, for example); or the sender may be a *machine*, such as a computer. The purposes of the sender usually are to inquire, to inform, to persuade, or to develop goodwill.

INQUIRE—"May I have an appointment on January 5?"
INFORM—"Our sale will begin on August 1."
PERSUADE—"This stereo receiver is a *good* buy at $275."
GOODWILL—"We value your business, so we have extended your credit limit."

The Receiver

The receiver of a message, likewise, may be a *person* receiving the message for himself, for another individual, or for a group; or it may be a *machine*. The receiver of a message may respond to a message in the manner requested by the sender, may alter the response to suit his or her own needs, or may not respond at all.

The Message

The heart of a communication is the message. Often the message is intended to provide the receiver with facts or ideas not already possessed by the receiver or to add to or alter those facts or ideas already possessed. On the other hand, a message may be sent for the purpose of seeking information from the receiver. In any event, the message should affect the receiver's behavior in some way, influencing him or her to act or not to act as the sender of the message requests.

Sending Media   Messages may be sent in the form of pictures (photographs, drawings, or motion pictures), but most frequently messages are in the form of written or spoken words.

Receiving Media   Messages are received either by reading or by listening. Although these skills are just as important as the writing and speaking skills, reading and listening are often overlooked in communication courses. The most effective letter writer will exert little influence over a reader who has a poor command of the language. An outstanding speaker will have little influence over an audience whose vocabulary level is considerably lower than that used by the speaker.

To both sender and receiver, therefore, a knowledge of words—their spelling, their pronunciation, their meaning, and their implications—and a knowledge of language structure are necessary skills if there is to be effective communication.

Data Communication

When a message is sent from one machine to another machine, this type of communication is called data communication. In data communication, machine language or symbols may substitute for words. Since data communication is widely used today, it is discussed more thoroughly in Section 2.

Nonverbal Communication

Very often a message may be sent or received without an exchange of words. A facial expression, such as a frown or a raised eyebrow, or a body gesture, such as shrugged shoulders, may convey a message even more effectively than words. Silence, the absence of any words, may also convey a message. The message probably is, "I don't have any interest in what you are saying, so I am not responding." These forms of communication that do not involve the use of words or pictures are referred to as nonverbal communication, and the term "body language" has been popularized by some writers to designate this form of communication.

GOALS OF EFFECTIVE COMMUNICATION

To further our knowledge of what contributes to effective communication, we need to know *why* we communicate. Earlier, we defined communication simply as a sender transmitting a message to a receiver. However, this simplified definition is really not sufficient for most purposes. It does not give any indication that the message was received, that it was received exactly as the sender intended it to be received, or that it affected the receiver's thinking or behavior in any way. To determine the effectiveness of communication, we must determine first the goals of communication and second whether these goals have been met.

Precise Interpretation

The first goal of effective communication is to convey a message that the receiver perceives exactly as the sender intends, with no difference in meaning in the minds of the two parties. In other words, the interpretation of the message by both the sender and the receiver should be identical. To achieve precise interpretation, therefore, it is the responsibility of the sender to make certain that the message is perfectly clear and that it is complete. The receiver has the responsibility of reading or listening to the message carefully. Whenever the receiver's interpretation of the message differs from that of the sender, regardless of whose fault it is, we have a breakdown in communication. Can breakdowns in communication be avoided?

Communication breakdowns can be avoided by the use of a technique called "feedback." In the process of transmitting a message, the sender uses devices to determine if the receiver is interpreting the message correctly. In face-to-face oral conversation, feedback is more easily achieved. The receiver frowns or says, "I don't understand," thereby signaling the sender that the message is not being received clearly. The sender can then reexplain or ask questions in order to clarify the message. The sender can ask questions during the process of sending the message, questions that will provide the feedback to determine whether the message is being received precisely.

Feedback is not achieved so easily in written communication until there has been some kind of response from the receiver of the message. The wrong response from the receiver, questions asked by the receiver, silence on the part of the receiver—all may indicate that there has been a temporary breakdown in communications. However, the fact that there has been some feedback gives the sender an opportunity to mend the breakdown in communication by providing additional information or by correcting a wrong interpretation of the message.

Favorable Response

We have already briefly mentioned the second goal of effective communication: to obtain a favorable response from the receiver of the message. It is not always possible to determine whether this second goal of effective communication has been achieved. The receiver may make no response for a long period of time because he or she may be reflecting on the message or may not be in a position to take action immediately. However, we can claim success whenever a favorable response is obtained, whether immediately or at some time in the future.

Favorable Relations

As we have indicated, it is not always possible to achieve the second goal of effective communication, a favorable response. However, regardless of the kind of response obtained from the receiver, the message should always help to develop favorable relations between the sender and the receiver. With favorable relations, the door is left open for future communication that may result in a favorable response at a later time.

Without favorable relations, the door may close and the process of communication may cease.

FACTORS THAT INFLUENCE EFFECTIVE COMMUNICATION

Although the sender of a message knows the goals he or she seeks to achieve, the sender must keep in mind that there are a number of factors that influence the communication either favorably or unfavorably. Senders who are aware of the factors control them so that they will have a favorable effect on the communication process. Among the major factors that influence the communication process are (1) the background of the receiver, (2) the appearance of the communicator or the communication, (3) the communication skills of the sender and the receiver, and (4) distractions.

The Background of the Receiver

Background refers to the following four elements:
1. The *knowledge* already possessed by the receiver as related to the facts, ideas, and language used in the message.
2. The *personality* of the receiver, particularly the emotions, the attitudes, and the prejudices that are likely to exert influence on the message.
3. The *experiences* the receiver has had related to the message content.
4. The *interest and motivation* of the receiver regarding the subject of the message.

These background factors play an important role in determining the reaction of the receiver to the message. For example, suppose you receive a letter urging you to buy diamonds. The writer of the message says diamonds are an excellent investment. You have no *knowledge* about the value of diamonds for investment purposes. Thus your reaction to this message will be quite different from that of the person who is very knowledgeable about diamond investments. Your *personality* is one of extreme conservatism; you seldom take risks. This personality characteristic will also affect your reaction to the message. In addition, last year you invested in a supposedly "safe" investment and lost a lot of money. This *experience* has a negative effect on your view of diamonds as an investment. If, instead, you had made a considerable gain, your reaction might be quite different. The thought of owning diamonds for their sheer beauty interests you, and this *interest* might motivate you to look further into the possibility of making an investment in diamonds.

Obviously the writer who weighs all these factors before preparing the message stands a greater chance that the message will be accepted than the writer who ignores these factors.

Appearance of the Communicator or Communication

A disheveled-looking speaker or salesperson, a rasping, unclear telephone voice, a sloppy letter filled with erasures—all these would certainly "turn off" the receiver of a message. Therefore, it is extremely important to make a favorable visual and aural impression if a positive reaction is desired, and such a reaction is, of course, the goal of every communication.

Communication Skills of Sender and Receiver

The tools of language include selecting words accurately to express meaning and spelling and pronouncing them correctly. How well the sender of a message uses these tools and how well the receiver interprets their use are major determinants of the effectiveness of the message. Using the wrong word, making a major grammatical error, or misusing a mark of punctuation may change the intended meaning of the message. Even if the receiver understands the message, the receiver's opinion of the sender of the message is certain to suffer.

Although each of these tools of language is discussed much more thoroughly in later sections of this book, at this point you should be aware that there is a very definite relationship between these tools and reading, listening, and speaking—and not just a relationship to writing. If the communication process is to be successful, the sender of a message must be an effective writer and speaker, and the receiver must be an effective reader and listener. Since all of us are sometimes senders and sometimes receivers, we must strive for efficiency in using the basic tools of language for reading, writing, listening, and speaking.

Distractions

Under what environmental conditions is the written or oral message received? Is the room noisy? Too warm or too cold? Poorly lighted? Is the receiver of the message more concerned about some personal event at the time the message is received? All of us are subject to distractions that draw our attention away from what we are reading or listening to. As we read or listen, many thoughts may pass through our minds. Sometimes these thoughts are triggered by something we read or hear or see. Whatever the reason, the result is that we do not concentrate on the message and may miss important data that can cause us to reach erroneous conclusions.

Some distractions can be prevented by the sender, particularly in an oral communication situation where the environment can be controlled. But even in the case of written communication, the sender can prevent certain distractions. A sloppy-looking letter, for example, may distract the reader.

NEED FOR EFFECTIVE COMMUNICATION

Effective communication is essential for the success of every activity, whether it is an individual or a group activity. Every individual requires effective communication for a happy and successful home life, school life, and vocational life. A breakdown in communication can lead to serious problems in our personal lives as well as in our business lives.

Effective communication is equally necessary for success in government, in business, and in personal activities. Although this book is concerned primarily with effective communication in the world of business, you should keep in mind that improving your communication techniques will favorably affect *all* aspects of your life—not just your business life.

YOU AS A BUSINESS COMMUNICATOR

To ensure personal success, as well as the success of the company in which you are employed, you and every other employee must be skilled business communicators. No matter how extensive or elaborate a communication system may exist, effective communication still depends upon each individual who functions within the organization. What are the requirements of a skillful business communicator that you should strive to acquire?

Language Facility

Because every business employee is involved in some form of communicating, you must have facility in using the language to both send and receive messages. A skilled communicator must be able to communicate facts, ideas, opinions, and instructions with a minimum of effort and with clarity, confidence, and knowledge. Therefore, you must know how to use language correctly. You must command a broad vocabulary, which involves not only the ability to spell and pronounce words but also the ability to select words precisely. You must be able to speak and write without error, with as much clarity and in as few words as possible. Not only must you be familiar with the many media available for communication, but you must also have the ability to select the best medium to convey a particular message. Also, you must be able to read and to listen with understanding.

In recent years, business people and the general public have become increasingly aware of the need for improving every business worker's communication skills—particularly the skills of workers who come in contact with the public. Today, courses in effective speaking and writing, as well as in reading improvement, are offered not only by colleges and universities but also by companies themselves. Businesses know that the time and money spent to improve the communication skills of their employees represent dollars saved in time and understanding in day-to-day business operations.

Acquiring Knowledge and Using It

To be a skilled business communicator, you must be well-read and well informed about your field of work, your company, and your particular function in that company. You must learn how to acquire information by using research techniques, and you must learn how to send information to others. To send messages, you must know how to outline, draft, and perfect each message so that it fits your purpose and suits your medium.

Understanding Human Relations

No matter how well you develop the first two requirements of a skillful communicator, unless you understand and practice good human relations, you will have great difficulty in achieving success in business, not just in communicating but in all aspects of your job. Human relations involves the ability to understand and to deal with people in such a way that a favorable relationship is maintained. Skill in human relations cannot be learned mechanically as can structure and usage or vocabulary and spelling. Although these mechanics contribute to skill in human relations, they are only basic tools for making communication in any human relations situation more effective.

Employees who are skilled in human relations have learned to consider carefully each situation in which they are dealing with others, taking time to consider the feelings and goals of those with whom they are dealing. They remember that every person believes that his or her own opinion is founded on good reasons. They give instructions clearly and carefully, taking time to make sure that they are correct. We might say that they practice "business diplomacy."

Sales representatives dealing with irate customers hear the customers out and then try to satisfy both the customers and their companies by understanding both sides of the issue. Employers dealing with employees who have a grievance try to show the workers that they understand their problems, and they remember to give reasons for the company policies they must uphold. Supervisors who must change the jobs of employees let the workers know why they are being given a different kind of work. In all phases of activity today, the business community is interested in improving human relations. That is why studies of personnel relations, labor relations, management relations, and public relations are being given a great deal of attention.

COMMUNICATION SKILLS AND YOUR FUTURE

Perhaps the way you can best prove your ability to accept leadership responsibilities is through communication. By your facility in expressing ideas, you can convince others of your merits.

As you study the material presented in this book and obtain valuable practice in building your communication skills, keep in mind the important role that communications can play in helping you achieve a successful future in the business world. And remember, too, that every hour of study is time spent in working for yourself, for your own personal advancement.

COMMUNICATION PROJECTS

Practical Application

A. As you are writing these practical applications, make a list of the distractions that are occurring.

B. Think back to some recent situation in your life in which you had trouble communicating with someone.

1. Who was the individual with whom you had difficulty communicating?
2. What was the cause of the difficulty in communicating?
3. How could the difficulty have been avoided or corrected?

C. Your instructor will identify an object for each member of the class to observe. Write a brief but complete description of that object. Each member of the class will read his or her description. Is all members' perception of that object the same? What are the probable reasons for any differences?

D. Give an example showing how each of the following factors may cause a difference in perception: age, sex, race, religion, educational background, financial status, physical handicap.

E. Every communication requires a sender and a receiver, and both must have the same perception of the message. Are you able to receive the following messages? If not, use the dictionary to determine the meaning of the word that prevents you from receiving the message precisely. Explain each message.

1. The lawyer prepared his brief.
2. His joie de vivre was catching.
3. The electrical appliance was grounded.
4. The will was probated.
5. Do you like ecru?

Editing Practice

Sound Alikes   In the following sentences, replace each incorrectly used word with the correct word that sounds like it.

1. The land was least by Mr. Yates.
2. What is the principle river in your state?
3. My library book is overdo.
4. You chose a lovely sight on which to build your house.
5. Good speakers should use plane, concise words.

Case Problem

Office Grooming   Don Vitt was quite concerned when Ruth Conrad, his secretary, arrived at the office with her hair in curlers and a scarf over her head. There has always been an unwritten rule that both men and women in his office dress in a manner acceptable for business.

1. What should Don say to Ruth?
2. Should Don send Ruth home as a disciplinary measure? Under what conditions?

2 COMMUNICATING IN THE BUSINESS WORLD

One of the primary goals of the first section of this chapter was to convince you of the importance of effective communication in every aspect of your life, including the vocational aspect. If you have not already embarked upon a career in business, you will soon do so. Whatever your aspiration—accountant, secretary, sales representative, management trainee, or some other business position—you will need to acquire a thorough *knowledge* of your particular field and those *skills* that may be necessary to perform your duties. You will also need to develop the kind of *personality* that is essential for success in your chosen field. Then, with practical *experience*, you will progress within your field. But there is one additional vital requirement you must meet if you want to further assure your business success: the ability to communicate effectively.

Everyone who works in an office must excel in communicating in order to carry out the day-to-day activities of the job. How well these day-to-day activities are performed serves as an important basis for evaluating your performance on the job. Eventually your accumulated performance record determines whether or not you should receive an increase in salary, a promotion, or both. An inability to communicate effectively will make your performance less effective. Therefore, now is the time to remedy any communication deficiencies you may possess.

Skill in all communication media is important to every office worker, because a large part of everyone's business day is spent in communicating. Office workers must *write* memos and letters; must *speak* to co-workers, customers, and clients; must *read* memos, letters, reports, invoices, and instructions; and must *listen* to managers and executives, co-workers, and customers.

On your first job, it will be even more important that you reveal your skill in communicating. If you want to advance to higher positions, you must master the principles of writing, reading, listening, and speaking. Your initial performance will reveal to your supervisors and managers whether you have the potential to succeed in a higher position. The goal of this book is to help you acquire and develop these needed communication skills; the book will also guide you in using these skills most effectively.

THE SCOPE OF BUSINESS COMMUNICATION

Communication is the lifeline of every business. Millions of words are spoken and listened to, written and read, every business day. These daily communications are directed to or from those outside the company to or from those within the company, and the range of these communications is very wide.

Communication *outside* the company usually is very broad in scope; many channels of communication—from direct mail campaigns to press releases—are available. Outside the company, communication is directed to other companies, to government agencies, to stockholders, to suppliers, to customers, to the press, and to the general public.

Communication *within* the company is also broad in scope, taking the form of departmental meetings, interdivisional conferences, memorandums, reports, and other written and oral messages of many kinds. Without such communication, there would be no advertising campaign, no sales program, no marketing plan, no budget. In fact, there would be little or no business at all without communication, and certainly there would be no growth.

The scope of any company's communication system depends on both the size of the company and the nature of its business. While there are many obvious differences from company to company in operations, functions, and purposes, what is essential to all companies—whether large or small, local or international—is a system of communication that is effective.

COMMUNICATION MEDIA IN BUSINESS

Communication today is carried out through many sophisticated media, but originally communication was limited to face-to-face conversation. The earliest written communication took the form of symbols or drawings that illustrated the message, rather than spelling it out in words. As languages developed, and with them writing systems, patterns of written communications evolved. These patterns, or forms, of writing have been refined and added to over the centuries, so that today we have a wide choice of media for transmitting the written message. We may send our written messages anywhere in the world, choosing from among a number of methods of transmission. Our message can travel via slow ship or speedy airplane or by such faster methods as wire, wireless radio, or electronics so sophisticated that data can be sent to and from central storage areas instantly.

Even means of transmitting oral messages have become more sophisticated. The telephone, of course, has for a long time been a basic piece of equipment in every office; today it is a very versatile instrument, capable of providing many different services suited to today's changing needs. Using a satellite, Telstar, both oral and visual messages are transmitted around the world almost instantaneously.

You can see that we have an almost unlimited choice, whether we wish to communicate in print, by sound, or through an audiovisual combination. Sophisticated communication media allow us to send a message to the farthest spot on the globe as easily as we have always been able to send a message around the corner.

Using Oral Communication Media

Face-to-Face Contact   Face-to-face communication is particularly important in dealing with customers, with sales representatives, and with co-workers. Often face-to-face conversation is taken for granted and treated as if communicating orally requires little or no skill. As a matter of fact, this method requires an exceptional amount of skill if the message is to be transmitted clearly and convincingly.

The Telephone   The telephone is used by every business worker to communicate

with others both inside and outside the business office. The use of the telephone facilitates receiving messages from outside the office and sending messages to other locations speedily and almost effortlessly.

The Speakerphone utilizes a microphone and a speaker so that several people may participate in a telephone conversation as a group. The Picturephone adds a viewing screen to the audio equipment, so callers can see each other and show diagrams, blueprints, products, and other items while discussing them. The Magicall dialer is only one of several kinds of automatic dialers that store phone numbers on magnetic or motorized tape or on prepunched plastic cards, to be used to dial numbers automatically.

When great distances are involved, the use of the telephone is expensive, and the communicator must determine whether the cost is justified. When a great many calls are placed between various branch offices of one firm or between two or more separate firms, direct telephone lines may be installed to connect the callers. Calls placed on direct lines do not have to be transmitted through the telephone office. As a result, such calls are generally less expensive.

Interoffice Communication Devices   Although the telephone is frequently used for interoffice communication, other devices are available. Loudspeaker systems enable a speaker to address a group rather than each individual separately. Some interoffice communication systems are designed to connect two or more offices in the same building.

Meetings   Meetings or conferences are an integral aspect of every business office. Meetings are used to orient new employees, to train both new and experienced personnel, and to provide information on new policies and products. Sometimes they are used for "brainstorming," a technique often used for developing new ideas. Because business leaders must often lead conferences as well as participate in them, they should be familiar with discussion-leading techniques and parliamentary procedure. These techniques can save valuable time and make conferences more productive.

Speeches   Though not all business workers are called on to give formal speeches, many of them are required to do so at one time or another. This activity is not limited to the top executives of a business firm; secretaries, sales representatives, accountants, and others are sometimes invited to address school groups, professional and civic organizations, and church and social groups. Even the fields of radio and television are within the realm of possibility. A businessman or businesswoman must remember that when he or she speaks to a group, the firm—not the individual—is being represented. Often members of the audience will have little or no other contact with the company; therefore, they will judge the firm by the impression given by the speaker. Here is a valuable public relations opportunity. People who make the most of this type of opportunity are almost certain to enhance their chances for success in business.

Dictation Devices   Electronic dictating equipment is usually thought of as a means of recording dictation that a stenographer will later transcribe as a letter or a report. Today, however, the recording itself may be mailed directly to the correspondent. Since this technique is most informal, it should be used only within a company or with business associates with whom the dictator is well acquainted. Furthermore, this technique provides no written record of the message; therefore, the technique is not suitable for communications that may require future reference.

Television   Television serves as more than an entertainment medium. Closed circuit television and video recordings are becoming popular methods for conducting meetings and for providing employee instructional programs. For example, several large companies make extensive use of video recordings for training sales representatives. In addition, stores telecast video recordings to attract shoppers and communicate a sales-promotion message.

Using Written Communication Media

Memorandums   A memorandum is actually a form of letter or report, even though it differs in appearance from either of these forms of communication. Memorandums are usually neither so formal nor so long as either the business letter or the report, but this fact does not decrease their importance as a medium of communication. Memorandums are the most frequently used form of interoffice communication.

Letters   Letters are used for every conceivable type of business communication. They are used to communicate with those who buy from a firm and with those who sell to a firm. They are used for sales promotion, for giving or requesting information, for requesting credit, for granting (or refusing) credit, for requesting payment on overdue accounts, and for social-business purposes. A complete list of the purposes served by business letters would be almost endless. Letters may be written and prepared individually, or they may be written in a form-letter style designed for a mass mailing.

Telegrams   Domestic and international telegrams are used when speed is essential in transmitting written messages. Another advantage of the telegram is that it attracts more attention than other types of messages.

The Desk-Fax or Telefax is a compact unit that permits the sending and receiving of telegrams in a particular business office without having to contact Western Union. Businesses with large volumes of telegraph messages usually have their own special equipment, such as a telex teleprinter and the Desk-Fax, to handle telegraphic messages within the company.

A mailgram is a combination letter and telegram that provides overnight service within the continental United States. Mailgrams are sent by electronic devices to a teleprinter at a post office near the destination of the message. Here each Mailgram message is teleprinted, placed in a special envelope, and delivered by letter carrier to the addressee.

International messages are sent either as cablegrams or as radiograms. Cablegrams are transmitted through wires across the ocean floor, while radiograms are sent by wireless systems from aircraft or ships. Telex service is a worldwide direct-dial system that links one company's teleprinter with others around the world. Through telex, messages are transmitted immediately, so that it is possible to have a two-way written "conversation."

Since the cost of domestic and international telegraphic messages is based on the number of words used, special skill in writing highly condensed, yet clear, messages is required.

Reports   The modern business world depends heavily on reports to present facts or to report progress to business owners and to individuals at various operating levels. The length and formality of a report will vary with its purpose. One report may be a hundred pages long; another may be only one page long. The skillful writer must know the form and style most suitable for each particular report. There are several types of reports that business workers may have to prepare, but one special type of report with which they should be familiar is the report of what transpires at meetings, usually referred to as "minutes."

Business Literature   Books, newspapers, magazines, and pamphlets provide excellent opportunities for creative business writers to express their views on various phases of business. Employee newsletters and house organs (booklets or magazines for customers of the company) are widely used by large businesses of all types. Some of these publications depend entirely upon the contributions of employees for the articles they publish.

News Releases   A business likes to keep its name before the public. One way of doing so is to inform the public about changes in personnel, new products or service innovations, participation of its personnel in business or civic activities, and other such newsworthy items. For such events, news releases are written and sent to newspapers and radio and television stations. Naturally, news releases will receive more favorable attention if they are prepared in a style acceptable to the medium to which they are sent.

Advertising Copy   Advertising copy for newspapers, magazines, radio, television, pamphlets, folders, and sales letters accounts for an enormous volume of business communications. Such material is usually prepared by people especially trained for this kind of writing, although business workers in the fields of advertising, marketing, or sales are very frequently given this responsibility. Even if they do not actually prepare the copy, such employees must evaluate the material prepared by others.

SELECTING THE BEST MEDIUM

As you can see, there are many types of communication media available to the business worker for transmitting messages. Of all the media available, one is usually clearly better suited for meeting the goal of a specific message. How does the business worker determine which medium is best? The following are primary considerations in selecting the medium that is best suited to achieve your goal.

What type and size of audience do you want to reach? Are they located close to you and to each other or spread all over the world? Will an oral message serve your purpose, or will the written message serve it better? What is the length of your message? Your answers to these questions will help you in making your selection, but there are additional factors to consider as well.

Time Factor

How important is it that the receiver acquires the message immediately? If speed is essential and the message would be suitable in oral form, then perhaps you should telephone the message. If, on the other hand, the message should be written, then the best means of transmitting the message quickly would be one of the wire services.

Legal Factor

If there are legal implications involved in a message, such as an offer being made or accepted on the sale of real estate, then the sender must satisfy the legal requirement of using a written form of communication.

Cost Factor

There will be some cost involved in transmitting a message regardless of the type of medium used. Even face-to-face conversation involves time on the part of both the sender and the receiver, and in business, time is money. While cost should be neither the primary nor the only consideration in selecting communication media, it must not be ignored. To exist in today's competitive marketplace, business must be profit-conscious. Since communication costs decrease the profit a business makes, it is essential to keep communication costs to a minimum. When a less expensive medium will meet the goal of your message as effectively as a more costly medium, there should be no doubt as to which one to select.

The cost of preparing and actually transmitting a message is a small one compared with the high cost in loss of business if the message contains errors that lead to misunderstandings, loss of sales, or loss of goodwill. Therefore, all business workers must make every effort to make certain that each message transmitted, regardless of the type of medium used, be correct in every aspect. The cost of communication may be high, but if an effective communication results in increased business, then the cost is justified.

DATA COMMUNICATION

Data communication is widely used today by businesses that are automated and have electronic data processing systems. How does data communication differ from other types of communication?

First of all, the information that is to be transmitted must be translated into a special code, of which there are over sixty in use today. This code, called "language," takes the place of words we use in spoken or written messages. Thus the code represents the language of the machine, just as words represent the language of people. English may be your language, while COBOL may be a machine's language.

The second distinguishing characteristic of data communication is that data is transmitted between two computers by some electronic means such as a telephone line. One computer serves as storage or data bank, storing information that is sent to it for future retrieval. Another computer, or terminal, sends information to the storage computer or receives information that is already in storage. For example, when you want to make a flight reservation, you can telephone one of the offices of the airline of your choice. That office will key into its terminal the information regarding the flight

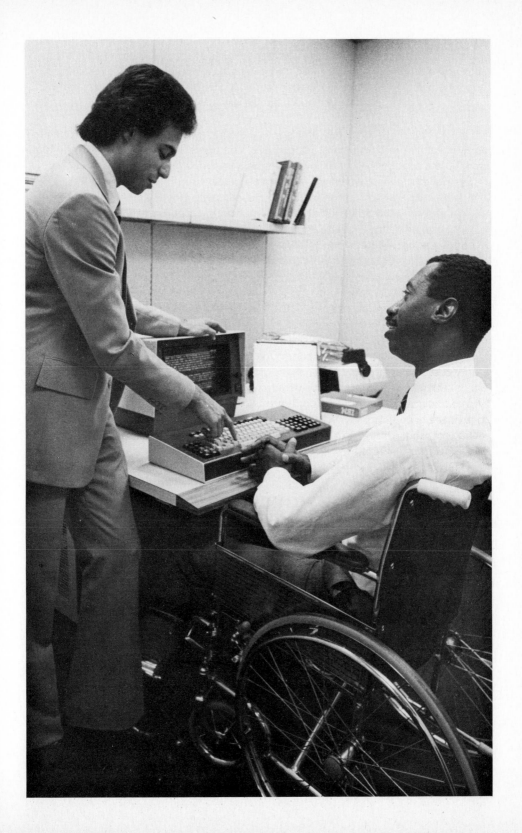

you wish to take. The terminal is connected to a central computer that will find out from the information it has stored whether space is available for you. If space is available, your name will be transmitted to the central computer, and your reservation will be immediately confirmed. All the communicating can be completed within a matter of one or two minutes. Here are some other examples of data communication at work in business today:

On the first of each month, the sales manager receives a report of last month's sales of each item by quantity and by price. The report is transmitted from the company's data processing center by means of a teleprinter service.

The Holiday Inn in Omaha confirms an executive's room reservation in Mexico City by its direct teleprinter communication (Holidex) with Holiday Inn's central office.

Using a computer terminal, a teller at your bank branch office finds out from the bank's main office the exact balance in your account. The branch notifies the main office that you are withdrawing $100 today.

Data communication makes it possible to store vast amounts of information in one place and to select and rapidly transmit this information to another place. The information that is stored, therefore, must be accurate and must also be clear to the user. Otherwise, costly mistakes may result. If Holiday Inn makes a reservation for an executive when there actually is no space available, ill will and the loss of that company's future business may be the outcome.

The effectiveness of any data communication system depends upon accuracy and clarity at the time the information is programmed, as well as at the time the information is retrieved. Undoubtedly, the person who needs the information wants it in order to make some important decision that must be put into writing, probably in the form of a report. Therefore, the business worker should be familiar with business report writing and should be able to communicate data in a manner that will be understood by the reader. One of the functions of this book is to teach you how to write such reports.

STARTING YOUR PERSONAL COMMUNICATION DEVELOPMENT PROGRAM

Thus far, you have acquired some basic knowledge of the role played by communication in helping business employees do their jobs successfully, including knowledge of the various media used by business employees as they participate in the communication process. With this background, you are ready to start your own personal communication development program. You will need to acquire skill in all aspects of communicating—reading, listening, writing, and speaking. You will begin, in the next chapter, with the development of reading and listening skills.

COMMUNICATION PROJECTS

Practical Application
A. For your chosen career field, list the knowledges and the skills required and the personality factors that contribute to success.

B. Explain this statement: "Everyone who works in an office must excel in communicating in order to carry out the day-to-day activities of the job."

C. For your chosen career field, give one specific example of how you might use the following communication skills:

writing   speaking   reading   listening

D. Evaluate your ability in each of the above communication skills (Practical Application C). What improvements do you feel you should make in each of these skills? Which skill do you feel you will use most in your job?

E. What are some nonverbal communication signals that students may give to a lecturer as they sit in a class?

F. If you have access to a company magazine or newspaper, please bring a copy to class. Class members will have an opportunity to look through these publications and discuss their merits.

Editing Practice

Test Your Word Knowledge   In the following paragraph, identify those words that are incorrectly used. Rewrite the paragraph, substituting the correct words.

> We will accede our quota in access of $450. We are adverse to believe we can continue at this pace and are already to set up a different basis for figuring quotas. May we count on your cooperation?

Case Problem

The Unfulfilled Promise   Joe's boss says to him, "Joe, I want you to prepare a report on expected increases in office costs and have it for me not later than June 1. I would like you to get an outline to me by May 1 so that I can suggest any modifications I would like to make. I'll get the modified outline back to you within a few days, and that will allow you sufficient time to prepare the report."

The outline is submitted on May 1. On May 10, Joe reminds his boss who says, "I've been so busy. You'll have your outline back in a day or two—promise!" May 15 arrives and still no outline.

1. Is the boss being fair to Joe?
2. What should Joe do?

CHAPTER 2

DEVELOPING LISTENING AND READING SKILLS

Communication is a two-sided process: it involves both the sending and the receiving of a message. A message sent but not received has not been communicated. A letter or memorandum, no matter how well written, communicates nothing if it goes unread. And a spoken message, no matter how clear, loud, or thoughtful, communicates nothing if it goes unheard.

THE NEED FOR LISTENING SKILL

No one doubts the importance of reading skill in contemporary life. Every stage in the life of an individual requires written records: birth certificate, school diplomas, driver's license, marriage license, and so on. Business records, of course, must also be in written form: bills, checks, receipts, licenses, patents, and contracts. When so many vital communications are in writing, the importance of reading skill is clear.

It may surprise you to learn that listening skill is equally important. Surveys show that *the majority of business people spend most of their communication time in listening.*[1] The average business employee spends approximately 70 percent of the workday in spoken communication. Nearly half of this time is spent listening. But research indicates that most of us listen with only about 25 percent efficiency.[2]

ACTIVE VERSUS PASSIVE LISTENING

Listening can be active or passive. When we listen passively, we absorb just enough of the speaker's words to keep the conversation going but understand little of what is being said. We know from the speaker's inflection and tone of voice when we should nod or smile or shake the head or say, "Oh, really?" In this way we attempt to reassure the speaker that he or she has our attention (though not much of it). With friends and relatives, passive listening sometimes meets the demands of social conversation—but not always. Remember, however, that a nod here and a smile there can sometimes show unintentional agreement!

The world of business requires much more of a listener. It requires *active* listening. Business conversation is sprinkled with facts—names, dates, places, and prices, and they all matter. The salesclerk must remember the customer's wishes; the bank teller must remember amounts and denominations of bills; the airline reservation agent must remember where a traveler wishes to go and when.

Business situations require hearing and absorbing as much as possible, and this requires active listening. Active listening means concentrating on what is being said

[1] William F. Keefe, *Listen, Management,* McGraw-Hill Book Company, New York, 1971, p. 9.
[2] Ralph G. Nichols and Leonard A. Stevens, *Are You Listening?,* McGraw-Hill Book Company, 1957, pp. ix, 6, 8.

and participating in it mentally. How can the listener participate mentally? By summarizing in his or her own mind what the speaker is saying.

HOW TO IMPROVE YOUR LISTENING SKILL

When reading, we can sometimes let our attention wander from the page, knowing that we can return later to read what we missed. Imagine how different the world would be, however, if the written word vanished immediately after being read! We could never return for a second reading. All that would survive from our reading would be in our own memories.

The spoken word, of course, really does vanish immediately. We cannot afford to let our attention wander when listening, because we get only one chance to absorb the speaker's words. Yet it seems even easier for the listener's attention to wander than for the reader's. One major reason is that the average person speaks between 125 and 150 words a minute, but a good listener can comprehend about 300 words a minute.[3] Perhaps the listener's mind realizes that it is necessary to listen only half the time and therefore does so. Unfortunately, missing even a single sentence can destroy or change the meaning of a long speech or conversation. Since the listener never knows when the most important parts of a message will come, the listener must concentrate on every word.

Whatever the reasons for poor listening, listening is a skill that can be improved. Listening-improvement programs are joining reading-improvement programs in high schools and colleges. Many businesses are also providing listening-improvement programs for their employees.

Determine Your Listening Strengths and Weaknesses

Everyone has listening strengths and weaknesses. The first step toward improving your listening skill is to find out what your weaknesses are. Your answers to the following questions will help you decide where to begin your listening-improvement program.

1. Have you recently had your hearing tested?
2. Do you try to screen out distracting outside sights and sounds when you listen to someone speak?
3. Do you make it a point not to interrupt before a speaker finishes a thought?
4. Do you avoid doing something else (reading, for example) while trying to listen?
5. When people talk to you, do you concentrate on what they are saying rather than think of other things at the same time?
6. Do you listen for ideas and feelings as well as for facts?
7. Do you look at the person who is talking to you?
8. Do you believe that other people can contribute to your knowledge?
9. If something is not clear to you, do you ask the speaker to repeat or reexplain the point?

[3]Ibid., p. 78.

10. Do you avoid letting the speaker's words and phrases prejudice you?
11. When someone is talking to you, do you try to make the person think that you are paying attention even if you are not?
12. Do you judge by a person's appearance and manner whether what he or she says will be of interest to you?
13. Do you turn your attention elsewhere when you believe a speaker will not have anything interesting to say to you?
14. Do you have to ask the speaker to repeat because you cannot remember what was said?
15. If you feel that it takes too much time and effort to understand something, do you try to avoid hearing it?

You should have answered "Yes" to the first ten questions and "No" to the last five. Even if you had a perfect score, the following suggestions may still help you improve your listening skills.

Adopt a Positive Attitude

To be a good listener, you must want to hear what the speaker has to say. It can be difficult to want to hear a speaker when you expect the speaker's views to contradict your own. But you cannot know for certain what someone is going to say until you hear it. You must know the speaker's views without ever having heard the reasons for those views, but it is irrational to pass judgment without hearing the speaker's arguments. Even if the speaker's views and your own are opposed, you must respect the speaker's right to have a point of view. Moreover, listening carefully may help you to organize a better argument against an opposing view.

Usually it is easy to find reasons for adopting a good listening attitude. The main purpose of a lecture or a class discussion is to learn; if students want to learn, they will also want to listen. The stenographer wants to listen when taking dictation in order to record accurately all that is said. The supervisor who wants to have a productive staff wants to hear about the workers' problems and needs. The employee who wants to do a good job and earn a promotion wants to hear all of the supervisor's instructions. Even when reasons for listening are less apparent, the good listener tries to find something of interest in the speaker's message and tries to sustain this interest until the speaker has finished.

Finally, a good listener does not judge what a speaker has to say based on the speaker's mannerisms, voice, speech patterns, appearance, or other personal characteristics. The good listener will notice all these incidental details but will focus on the *words* and *ideas*.

Prepare Yourself Physically for Effective Listening

Listening is a combination of physical and mental activities. The mental part of listening is more complex, but we must also remember and deal with the physical part. We cannot listen to what we cannot hear. Our listening ability improves when we watch the speaker, especially the speaker's lips. The sense of sight helps the sense of hearing.

Here are some suggestions to follow in physically preparing yourself to listen effectively:

> If you have trouble hearing, have a doctor test your hearing and suggest any necessary corrective measures. (A reputable hearing-aid distributor may test your hearing free.)
>
> Try to sit or stand in a place with no distracting sights or sounds.
>
> Keep your eyes on the speaker from start to finish.
>
> Choose a comfortable, well-ventilated, and well-lit place if possible; physical discomforts can distract you.
>
> Be prepared: keep a small pad and pencil with you. Business people often need to jot down notes on personal and business conversations as well as on formal speeches and lectures.

Prepare Yourself Mentally for Effective Listening

Effective listening is not an accident. It results from (among other things) mental preparation. For example, effective listeners have developed a wide vocabulary, which equips them to understand what they read and hear. The vocabulary learned in high school and college is not enough. Listeners must also master the special vocabulary of the field in which they work.

Every field has its special vocabulary. On entering a new field, set out at once to learn its special terms. Ask people to recommend books on the field, and write down and look up every unfamiliar word that you encounter, whether in reading or in conversation. Until the vocabulary is mastered, problems are sure to result. If a secretary asks an office clerk, for example, to bring a *ream* of typewriting paper, the clerk may return from the storeroom empty-handed because all the packages are labeled "500 Sheets" rather than "One Ream." When possible, it is best to ask the speaker to explain unfamiliar words.

The same policy applies when the speaker uses a familiar word without making clear which of several possible meanings is intended. Since the English language has many words with multiple meanings, the listener often faces this problem. In an office, for example, someone may ask a secretary to *duplicate* a letter. The secretary may not know whether to use carbon paper, a photocopier, or a fluid or stencil duplicator. A simple question will remove the secretary's doubt: "Would you like five photocopies?"

Develop Techniques of Concentration

Concentration means more than wrinkling your forehead or gritting your teeth. Concentration requires effort, of course, but effort alone is not enough. Like any other complex activity, concentration requires learning certain techniques. Skilled swimmers have learned how to coordinate arm and leg movement and how to breathe. Skilled typists have learned how to strike each key, how to keep their eyes on the copy, and how to sit before the keyboard. And skilled listeners have learned techniques of concentration.

As mentioned earlier, we can comprehend words at least twice as quickly as most people speak. To some people, this extra time is a hindrance, because they waste it by allowing their thoughts to wander from the subject. On the other hand, active listeners use this free time to concentrate on the speaker's words; therefore, they can better understand what is being said. Specifically, the effective listener can use this free time to:

> Identify the speaker's ideas and their relationships.
> Evaluate the correctness or validity of the message.
> Summarize the main points.
> Take notes.

Identify Ideas and Their Relationships As you begin to grasp the speaker's ideas, look for the relationships among them. Which idea is most important? Do the other ideas support the most important one? Is the speaker leading up to something? Can you anticipate what the speaker is going to say next? Is the speaker giving you cues that show the relationships among the speaker's ideas?

Consider the speech excerpt below.

> *Two major costs in operating a modern business are absenteeism and tardiness.*
>
> For instance, if an office with a thousand employees averages fifty absences a month and the average daily rate of pay is $50, the company loses $2,500 dollars a month or $30,000 a year. Such a loss takes a big bite out of company profits.

Note that the first sentence, the italicized words, is the main idea. The word *major* is a cue to the first sentence's importance. The speaker also uses the words *for instance* as a cue to indicate that what follows will support the main idea. Speakers use many other verbal cues: "first," "second," and "third"; "another important consideration"; "on the other hand"; "the most important thing"; "in summary"; and so on. Speakers also use many nonverbal cues: pauses; changes in volume or tone of voice; gestures such as pounding the table and shaking the head. All these cues help the listener to identify the speaker's ideas and see the interrelationships of these ideas.

Evaluate Correctness and Validity At some point as you summarize the speaker's message and see the structure of the speaker's ideas, you will probably find yourself beginning to agree or disagree with the speaker. Try to trace your agreement or disagreement to the speaker's reasoned arguments. Do the speaker's arguments really lead to the speaker's conclusions? Is the speaker trying to convince you with reason or to persuade you by pleading, coaxing, or insisting? Make sure that you are not in favor of the speaker's views strictly because they were presented with humor, enthusiasm, or charm. In the same way, make sure that you are not against a speaker's views because you dislike the speaker's personal characteristics.

Summarize When you listen, rephrase the speaker's ideas in your own mind. Try to put the speaker's ideas into the simplest, clearest, and most direct words possible. This process should reduce the speaker's message to its most basic terms and help you to understand and remember what you hear. The following example shows what you might be thinking while the speaker is talking.

What the Speaker Is Saying

I have read many books on selling. There are books that bring up every possible selling situation and give you ways and means to meet those situations—several hundred of them perhaps. But when you get in the presence of a prospect, you cannot recall any of them. However, you *can* remember this formula: ask yourself the simple question, "Just what does this prospect *want?*" If you cannot find out any other way, ask him. It is often that simple. Too many salesmen think they must do *all* of the talking. Avoid it. Listen at least half the time and ask questions. It is only in this way you can uncover unsatisfied wants.[4]

What You Are Saying to Yourself

You can't memorize ways of meeting every selling situation presented in books. You should find out what the prospect wants. Ask him what he wants, if necessary. You don't need to do all the talking—listen half the time, and ask questions.

Take Notes   Taking notes is, of course, an excellent way of keeping information for future reference. But pad and pencil are more than aids to memory. They are also tools that help the listener concentrate on the speaker's message. Since the listener cannot write down everything, the listener must decide what to include and what to leave out. As the listener makes such decisions, the process of summarizing begins. Furthermore, a skilled note taker uses underscores, indentions, arrows, and brackets to show the relative importance of the speaker's ideas. The structure of the speaker's message becomes visible on paper.

Here are some suggestions for taking notes:

1. Bring enough paper and an extra pen or pencil.
2. Listen for the speaker's cues as to what is most important, and number all the important ideas.
3. Abbreviate whenever possible. Use "1," not "first"; use "e.g." for "for example"; and so on. If you take shorthand, do not write *everything* the speaker says!
4. Use underscores, indentions, arrows, and brackets to highlight your notes. For example, underscore main ideas, indent supporting ideas, and put brackets around examples.
5. Read over notes promptly after the speaker has finished. Add any necessary clarification.
6. Label and date notes so that you can identify them later without difficulty.
7. Compare notes with a friend who listened along with you.

Make Habits of Good Listening Techniques

Good listening, like good reading or good typing, is a skill, and skills require practice. Take every opportunity to practice the listening techniques described above. Opportunities come more often than you may think. When a public figure gives a speech or

[4]William Phillips Sandford and Willard Hayes Yeager, *Effective Business Speech*, McGraw-Hill Book Company, 1960, p. 176.

a news conference, for example, you can often listen to a live or taped broadcast. The next morning you can compare your notes with reports in the newspaper. You can also hold discussions with a friend on any topic of mutual interest; afterward, compare your summaries with each other.

COMMUNICATION PROJECTS

Practical Application

A. Reexamine the questions used to determine your listening strengths and weaknesses (pages 23 and 24). Indicate the reason for the "Yes" or "No" answer to each question.

B. Your instructor will read a selection to you. Listen very carefully, but do not take notes. After the reading, your instructor will ask you to answer several questions about the selection.

C. A good listener is able to distinguish facts from opinions. On a separate sheet of paper indicate which of the following statements are opinions and which are facts.

1. The film we saw on pollution control was very thought-provoking.
2. He was offered $500 for his old car.
3. The owner of a car parked on the street after midnight is likely to be given a parking ticket.
4. A business executive should not wear casual clothes to work.
5. Some service stations are limiting gasoline sales to their customers.
6. Your choice of a Nu-Day home freezer is the wisest decision you ever made.
7. We will have fun at the party this weekend.
8. This clock will run for 40 hours without rewinding.
9. No other car has such a beautiful design as this one.
10. They will have a wonderful time at the family reunion.

D. Your instructor will give you a set of directions. Listen to them very carefully but take no written notes. Then follow the directions given.

E. List twenty words that cause you to feel strong emotions, such as delight, sadness, satisfaction, or horror. Be prepared to discuss the following questions:

1. Why do certain words affect people's emotions?
2. Why do words of this type have different shades of meaning for different people?

Editing Practice

Speaking Contextually   Some of the following sentences contain words that are out of context. Correct each sentence that contains a contextually incorrect word. Write OK for any correct sentence.

1. The alleged murderer is to be arranged in court next Monday.
2. They accused the company of infringing their patent rights.
3. Any discrimination of confidential information is prohibited.
4. Our fund-raising plans required the continued corporation of everyone.
5. Personality is a very important fact in securing and holding a job.

Case Problem

The Careless Clerk   Tom Williams was a reservation clerk for Westcoast Airlines. One afternoon he answered the telephone in his usual way by asking, "May I help you?" Mrs. Natasha Tiomkin introduced herself and told him that she wanted to make a reservation on a flight to Seattle, Washington, that would get her there in time for a 5 p.m. dinner meeting with an important client. Tom checked the flight bookings for the date and time requested and found that the only space available was on a flight leaving at 7 a.m. the same day. There was a 2:10 p.m. flight, arriving in Seattle at 4:15 p.m., but all seats had been booked. Mrs. Tiomkin had to attend a meeting that morning and could not leave before noon.

Tom said he would put Mrs. Tiomkin's name on the waiting list for the 2:10 flight and would notify her if there were any cancellations. He told Mrs. Tiomkin that there was a good chance of getting a seat on the 2:10 flight, since her name would be the first one on the waiting list. Mrs. Tiomkin thought this arrangement would be fine, gave Tom the necessary information about contacting her, and hung up. Just as soon as Tom hung up, the customer standing in front of him started asking for information regarding other flights, and Tom neglected to record Mrs. Tiomkin's name on the proper waiting list.

When Mrs. Tiomkin had not received word about her reservation by the day before the flight, she asked her secretary to check with the airline. The clerk who answered the telephone checked the waiting list but, of course, did not find Mrs. Tiomkin's name among the ten listed. With so many names already on the waiting list, chances were poor that a seat could be found for Mrs. Tiomkin. Mrs. Tiomkin's secretary passed along the news. Mrs. Tiomkin was furious. She telephoned the general manager of the airline and lodged a complaint.

1. Was Mrs. Tiomkin justified in her complaint? Why or why not?
2. What should the general manager say to Mrs. Tiomkin in order to smooth out the situation?
3. What advice should the general manager give Tom Williams?

4 DEVELOPING READING SKILLS

The ability to read is indispensable for anyone entering business. Typists must be able to read copy accurately and quickly. Secretaries must be able to proofread letters and to identify papers. Executives must be able to absorb the contents of the stream of letters, reports, periodicals, and books that cross their desks. Accountants must be able to check one set of figures against another and make sure that each group of figures is posted under the correct heading. Supervisors and managers must read production reports, forms, memos, schedules, evaluations, and requisitions.

Your ability to read may well determine how successful you will be on the job. Time spent now to improve your reading skill will bring rewards later at every stage of your career.

MEASURES OF READING SKILL

Although everyone in business must be able to read, no business employs people solely for the purpose of reading. Employees earn their livings for taking action based on what they read. The action taken may be sending a requested product, writing a reply, forwarding a message to the appropriate department, correcting an error, filing according to subject, and so on. The faster the employee can read, the more work the employee may be able to handle. Because reading speed affects how much work the employee can do, it helps determine the employee's value to the business. Reading speed, then, is an important measure of reading skill.

But speed counts for nothing if the reader does not *understand.* Reading well requires more than moving your eyes rapidly over words on paper. The reader must comprehend the ideas that the words represent. For this reason, reading comprehension is a second important measure of reading skill.

Do you fully comprehend the material that you read? As a student, have you had to spend every evening and weekend in order to complete reading assignments that other students complete in an hour or two a day? If so, then this should be cause for concern, but not for embarrassment or despair. With study and practice, you *can* improve both reading speed and reading comprehension.

Many people have benefited from reading-improvement courses offered by schools, business organizations, and private institutes. The results are often well worth the time and the money. If you are interested in enrolling in one of these reading programs, ask your instructor for advice. In the meantime, however, you can do several things on your own to improve your reading skill.

GUIDES TO READING IMPROVEMENT

Study the four-step program for improving reading skill that follows on pages 31 through 34.

Check Physical Factors

Poor vision and eye discomfort can hamper reading proficiency. You must be able to read comfortably, without difficulty or strain. In any case, you should have your eyes checked regularly by an eye specialist, particularly if you wear glasses, have blurred vision or smarting eyes, or need to hold copy either very close to your eyes or at arm's length.

Lighting conditions affect the ease with which you read. Natural light is best, of course, and indirect light is the best artificial light to read by. The light should fall on the copy, not on your eyes, and there should be no glaring or shiny spots before you.

In addition, your physical comfort will affect your ability to concentrate and read. You should sit comfortably in a well-ventilated room kept at a moderate temperature. The room should be free of distracting sights and sounds.

Whether or not you wear glasses, you should practice good eye hygiene. Here are some suggestions:

> Rest your eyes every half hour or so either by looking into the distance or by closing them for a few minutes.
>
> Exercise your eyes, especially when you are doing close work and your eyes begin feeling tired. One good exercise for strengthening the eye muscles is to rotate the eyeballs slowly without moving your head. Try to see far to the right; then to the left; then up; and finally, down.
>
> Avoid reading when you are in bright sunlight or while you are riding in a vehicle.
>
> Have eye injuries or sties attended to immediately by a physician.

Adjust Reading Rate to Material and Purpose

You should adjust your reading speed to the material you are reading and to your purpose for reading it.

Reading for Pleasure   When you are reading novels, magazine articles, newspaper items, and the like, you do not need to absorb every detail or remember many specific facts. Therefore, you should be able to read quite rapidly, at a rate of around 400 words a minute.

Reading for Specific Data   When you are looking for a specific name, date, or other item of information, you should be able, by skimming a page, to locate the item without reading every word. When you wish to determine the principal ideas in reading matter, perhaps in order to decide whether or not to read it, skim each page and stop only to read significant phrases.

Reading for Retention or Analysis   This kind of reading includes textbook reading or other study reading requiring either the memorization of facts or a thorough understanding of the meaning so that you can interpret, explain, or apply it to other situations. Reading for retention or analysis calls for active participation by the reader and may require a slower reading rate. Active participation in reading is discussed on page 34.

Copying and Checking This kind of reading includes proofreading typewritten or printed copy, checking invoices, copying material to prepare punched cards or tapes, and so on. Checking one copy against another or one column of figures against another calls for great concentration, because an error of one digit, one letter, or one syllable can change the meaning and the accuracy of a document. Such reading must be carefully done, with full concentration and attention to meaning and accuracy. One undetected error may be very costly! Unless the following were read for meaning, the error would go undiscovered.

The principle of $324 must be paid by January 5. (*Principal* is the proper word.)

Increase Reading Speed

Reading-improvement programs cannot make you read complicated textbooks as fast as you read light novels, but you can improve your speed at both types of reading. Here are six suggestions that will help you to read all kinds of materials faster.

Add to Your Vocabulary Enlarging your vocabulary will help you read faster and understand better. You will not stop to look up unknown words so often or spend so much time interpreting words that have several possible meanings.

Read in Thought Units Read in thought units rather than word by word. Remember that all words are not of equal importance. Develop your visual span by forcing your eyes to take in more words at each pause. With fewer pauses on each line of print, you naturally read faster. For example, read the following lines:

1. t m l q w z
2. books chair driver down
3. read in thought units

Certainly you had no difficulty in reading each of these lines, but each succeeding line should have been read faster. In the first line, you had to read individual letters; in the second, you read individual words; but in the third, your eyes could take in and read the whole phrase with one glance.

You should be able to read a line in a newspaper column with only one or two eye pauses and to read a book-width line with not more than four or five pauses. Read the following sentence, and notice the difference in speed when you read word by word and when you read in thought units.

Word by Word Good / readers / are / more / likely / to / understand / and / remember / what / they / read / if / they / actively / participate / in / what / they / are / reading.

Phrases Good readers / are more likely / to understand and remember / what they read / if they actively participate / in what they are reading.

Keep Your Eyes Moving From Left to Right Do not allow yourself to go back and read a phrase a second time. These backward movements of the eyes, called *regressions*, slow the reader and are often habit-forming. Force yourself to concentrate and to get the meaning of a phrase the first time. To do so demands practice, discipline, and the elimination of all distractions that might interfere with your reading.

Avoid Vocalization Don't spell or pronounce the words you are reading, not even silently. Such vocalization limits you to reading only as fast as you can read aloud.

Read Only Word Beginnings Many words can be identified by reading only the beginnings. For example, you can easily identify the complete words, from these first syllables: *remem—, sepa—, funda—, catal—, educa—.* You can tell from the rest of the sentence whether the exact ending of each word should be *remembering* or *remembrance; separate, separately,* or *separation;* and so on. For example: *Did he remem—(remember) to sepa—(separate) the old catal—(catalogs) from the new catal—(catalogs)?*

Practice Rapid Reading By exercising your willpower and by continually practicing rapid reading, you are certain to increase your reading speed. Reading, like any other skill, will improve with proper practice.

Improve Reading Comprehension

Even more important than reading speed to the student and business worker are comprehension (understanding) and retention (remembering). Many of the suggestions made for increasing reading *speed* will also contribute to greater *comprehension.* Some additional aids follow.

Scan or Preview the Material Before beginning a careful reading, look over the material, noting main headings and subheadings, looking at illustrations, and reading captions and numbered passages. This preliminary survey should not take much time, but it will help you to determine your own purpose in reading and will also let you see at once the importance that the author attached to different parts of the material. Then, after completing a careful reading of the whole piece, you will have read the most important points twice. This will reinforce your memory of the material.

Participate Actively in Your Reading Reading is, of course, the *receiving* of written communications. We also speak of *absorbing* the content of written materials. But this does not mean that reading is like being a mailbox or a sponge. Reading is an active process. Your mind must *work* both to get information from what you read and to understand that information. In other words, the reader must *extract* the content, like a miner digging for precious stones. This means studying the illustrations, reading the footnotes, and considering the author's examples. The author offers all of these as aids to the understanding of the author's ideas. Skipping these aids may make it more difficult for you to understand the text and may force you to spend more time in the long run extracting the knowledge that you need.

Take Notes If you own the book or magazine you are reading, you may wish to underline or otherwise mark key words or phrases. You may also want to make marginal notes. If the publication is not yours, you may take notes in a notebook that you can refer to later.

How do you select the essential material for note taking? By recording main ideas and related ideas. Never take verbatim notes, even if you know shorthand.

How do you find the main ideas? Usually, writers convey only one idea per paragraph. Often this main idea is in the first sentence, but sometimes it may be in the last sentence. Occasionally there may be two central ideas expressed in a key phrase or sentence within the paragraph. If you have difficulty finding a central idea, you may need to read the paragraph carefully two or three times. In addition to the central idea, you should also note facts, examples, and other ideas that explain, support, and develop the main idea.

Reread and Review How often you reread or review material will depend on its difficulty and on the use you plan to make of the information it contains. Often a quick skimming or rereading of your notes will be adequate for review if the first reading was done carefully.

If you will follow the suggestions made in this section and immediately begin a definite plan for reading improvement, you will find that not only will you be able to read more in the same amount of time, but also you will get more from what you read.

COMMUNICATION PROJECTS

Practical Application

A. To test your reading speed, have someone time you with a stopwatch (or a watch with a second hand) as you read the following selection.

Word processing changes the way office tasks are performed. For many years a secretary reported only to one manager or to a small number of managers. In a word processing office, however, the secretary is no longer expected to be a jack-of-all-trades who handles typing, filing, dictation, copying, computing, and various other tasks. The word processing employee works as part of a team, handles tasks for a number of managers, and specializes in nontyping or typing tasks.

Two kinds of workers are usually found in offices organized into word processing office systems—administrative secretaries and correspondence specialists. Nontyping tasks such as copying, computing, taking shorthand, and answering the telephone are handled by administrative secretaries. Typing assignments such as reports, statistical tables, letters, and memorandums prepared from handwritten drafts or machine dictation are handled by correspondence specialists.

Another feature of the word processing office is the use of automated typing equipment. This equipment was initially developed at the International Business Machines (IBM) World Trade Corporation in Germany. Automated equipment enables a typist to type (or record) a document, correct and revise it without retyping, and save it for use at a later time. In the word processing office, the correspondence specialist is usually trained to operate automated equipment.

Word processing represents a challenge for the worker who enters the business world. It provides an opportunity to learn new skills, use existing skills, and explore new careers. The word processing office has been called the office of the future. The future is now![1] (254 words)

How long did it take you to read the selection? Use the following chart to compute

[1]Bettie Hampton Ellis, *Word Processing: Concepts and Applications*, Gregg Division, McGraw-Hill Book Company, New York, 1980, p. 21.

your reading speed. Because the selection is 254 words long, your speed is 254 words a minute if you took 1 minute, 127 words a minute if you took 2 minutes, and so on.

15 seconds	1,016 wpm	$1\frac{1}{2}$ minutes	169 wpm	3 minutes	85 wpm
30 seconds	508 wpm	2 minutes	127 wpm	$3\frac{1}{2}$ minutes	72 wpm
1 minute	254 wpm	$2\frac{1}{2}$ minutes	101 wpm	4 minutes	64 wpm

B. One good reading habit that will help you gain speed is to look only at the beginnings of familiar words rather than at the entire words. Test your ability to do this by reading as rapidly as possible the following paragraph, in which the endings of some familiar words have been omitted.

The right atti__ makes all the diff__ in the out__ expres__ of your pers__: atti__ toward your work, tow__ your emp__, tow__ life in gen__. You reveal your atti__ tow__ people in the way you resp__ to sugg__. You can reject them in a self-right__, almost indig__ manner. Or you can adopt an indiff__, "don't care" atti__. These are both neg__ resp__. The pos__ resp__ is to accept sugg__ and crit__ thought__ and graciously. Then you can act upon them acc__ to your best judg__, with resul__ self-impr__.

C. Secretaries, typists, clerical workers, copy editors, and advertising copywriters must learn how to proofread carefully. Proofreading calls for the reading of each word not only for spelling but also for its meaning within the sentence. Proofread the following letter, and on a separate sheet of paper make a list of all the errors. Then rewrite the letter so that it is free from error.

In accordance with our telephone conservation, we are senting you corected specifacations. Note that instalation of a two-way comunication systems is now required. Also, the thermastat is to be re-located to the upstair hall.

Please send us your revise bid, propperly typed on your company stationary, not latter then Oct. 1.

D. Checking amounts of money and other figures often results in errors because of reading carelessness. Compare the following two lists. Indicate which pairs of items do not agree.

List A	List B
1. 838754B	838754B
2. 2243887	2243387
3. $4697.54	$46979.54
4. 6833T79	6833T79
5. SM178871	SM178187
6. 654V133	645V133
7. WTRZK	WTZRK
8. January 17, 1946	January 17, 1964
9. 115 dozen at $61\frac{3}{4}$¢	115 dozen at $63\frac{1}{4}$¢
10. T168V142L987	T168V142L897

Editing Practice

Digesting a Letter   Secretaries and administrative assistants often read all incoming letters for their employers. When employers are especially busy, they may ask their assistants or secretaries to prepare a short digest (or summary) of each letter so that their employers won't have to read the entire message. Using incomplete sentences, write a digest of the following letter.

> Dear Mr. Halsy:
>
> Your check for $868 is overdue in payment of additional repairs we have already completed in the remodeling of your offices.
>
> You will remember that when we found structural weakness in the corridor walls, we pointed this out to you as a violation of the building code. You authorized us to proceed with the necessary strengthening of the walls. We did so and notified you that the additional charges totaled $868, which was not covered in the original contract.
>
> May we have your check by return mail.
>
> Very truly yours,

Case Problem

The Talkative Visitor   Sally Bowman is receptionist and switchboard operator at the Lincoln Electrical Supply Company. One afternoon Michael Graham, who had an appointment to discuss a new product with Sally's boss, arrived at the office. However, because Sally's boss was in conference and would not be available for about ten minutes, Sally asked Mr. Graham to be seated until her boss was free. For a minute or two, Mr. Graham thumbed through one of the magazines lying on the table in the reception room. Then he started talking to Sally, who was not occupied at the switchboard at that moment. Soon, however, the board lit up, but Mr. Graham continued talking to Sally. The flashing of the lights indicated that the calling parties were getting impatient because of the delay, but Sally did not know how to get Mr. Graham to stop talking to her so that she could attend to her duties.

1. What could Sally say to Mr. Graham so that he would not be offended when she interrupted him?
2. Suppose Mr. Graham continued talking. What should Sally do?

CHAPTER 3

UNDERSTANDING LANGUAGE STRUCTURE

5
THE WORLD
AROUND US

The world around us is an ever-changing world. On a daily basis, we read and hear about advances in technology, science, medicine, and business; and each step forward changes the world around us, affecting both our personal and our business lives.

Advances in computer technology, for instance, have affected every aspect of our lives. In business, of course, computers are now commonly used for a great many information storage and retrieval needs. (Even those companies that cannot afford to buy their own computers can take advantage of time-sharing, a system that accommodates the small company's need for computer services.) Voice-activated computers make it possible to call in an order without speaking to a person. Word processing equipment has made the "office of the future" a reality today for many businesses, enabling one person to do the work of many through the use of computers. So common are computers today that personal computers are available for home use, allowing us to balance our checkbooks by computer! As you can see, then, the world of the 1980s is very different from the world of the 1970s; by 1990 we will surely see as many more changes in the world around us.

As our environment changes, so does the language we use to describe our environment. New terms are being increasingly introduced into our language. But one thing has not changed: *the need to know and to use standard English in all business communications.*

STANDARD ENGLISH

The now common use of computers and word processing equipment has emphasized the need to use standard English in the business world. Because the amount of information processed in the office is doubling every ten years, business executives are insisting more than ever before on accurate, effective communications. Every business day, office workers write and read reports, letters, memorandums, news releases, and other business messages; and they speak and listen to co-workers, clients, customers, suppliers, and others. Their dependency on the four language skills—reading, writing, speaking, and listening—is obvious. Therefore, the degree to which they can use standard English will greatly affect their ability to achieve results—profits, promotions, and success.

Standard English adopts a practical approach to language. It is not a stiff, scholarly approach to English. Standard English shuns outdated usage and, instead, opts for the modern, practical language of the 1980s. As presented in this textbook, standard English avoids out-of-date usage and attempts always to be up to date and acceptable.

Out-of-Date Usage

Some of the rules that were passed down to us from previous generations are clearly outdated and are therefore omitted in this discussion. For example, a long-standing rule was that an infinitive should not be "split." According to this rule, it is incorrect to say "She asked us to *quickly* check these invoices," because the word *quickly* splits the infinitive *to check*. But saying "to quickly check" is certainly natural; moreover, it is often awkward to avoid such constructions. Therefore, the split infinitive rule is not included in this presentation on standard English.

Also excluded are some "nitpicking" distinctions that were demanded for so many years. One such rule concerned the use of *as . . . as* and *so . . . as.* According to the rule, *as . . . as* should be used in positive comparisons:

> Martha is *as* interested in the seminar *as* Bill is.

But *so . . . as* should be used in negative comparisons:

> Martha is not *so* interested in the seminar *as* Bill is.

Clearly, such distinctions are not critical to clear, effective business writing and do not deserve your special attention.

Up-to-Date Usage

Some of the principles of our language are in the process of changing. For example, the word *data* was originally used only as a *plural* noun: "These data *are* conclusive." Slowly, over many years, it is being accepted as a singular noun: "This data *is* conclusive." To many people, *data* as a singular noun is an example of up-to-date usage. However, this use of *data* as a singular noun is not universally accepted, and the business writer should be aware of this fact.

In this book, principles that are in the process of change are identified as Twilight Zone uses. They are in the "twilight zone" because they are neither here nor there. Twilight is a period of transition between day and night, and the Twilight Zone notes will remind you of principles that are in transition—are not fully accepted yet. Pay special attention to Twilight Zone uses—especially in your writing.

NONSTANDARD ENGLISH

In many ways, standard English emphasizes the practical approach to language, but it does not mean "anything goes." Knowing the accepted standards of language is critical to effective business communication. The business world places a premium on the ability to write and to speak standard English because the audience should pay attention to the writer's or the speaker's message, not to his or her grammar. Standard English, the language of business communication, is least likely to call attention to itself and away from the message. Mastering standard English is, consequently, essential to business success.

SUCCESS IN YOUR CAREER

Your college training will help you not only to get a job but also to advance on the job. Your ability to communicate well in speaking, writing, reading, and listening will be a key factor in your on-the-job success because job performance greatly depends on communication skills.

This chapter will give you a solid foundation in language structure and modern English usage. As you know, you will be learning the essential principles of modern language use, not out-of-date or unnecessary rules. The Twilight Zones will serve to warn you of rules in the process of change, so be sure to use these rules carefully.

COMMUNICATION PROJECTS

Practical Application

A. Read the following paragraphs to find any violations of the rules of standard English. (This exercise previews the principles that are presented in the remaining sections of this chapter.)

1. All of us appreciate you giving us a demonstration of your new word processing equipment last Monday. Your A-111 model is indeed an impressive machine and will probably meet our needs satisfactory. Thank you for showing Mrs. Revere and I the features of the A-111. We enjoyed your presentation.
2. Beginning June 13, all of we agents will be using the new computer to make all guest reservations. Therefore, we are scheduling a series of training sessions for agents to learn how to operate the new equipment. In addition, we are scheduling a series of meetings to discuss the new procedures for handling customer's requests for reservations and for confirming there reservations.
3. The estimates for the new brochure is enclosed for you to review. As you will see, the cost of paper has raised about 15 percent in the passed year, and the increase is reflected in them estimates. Also, each of the printers have guaranteed that they can deliver 100,000 copys of the brochure with only 10 days' notice.

B. Correct any spelling errors.

> As you know, our regional meetings for next year will be held in Huston, Los Angeles, Atalanta, and New York. We have allready arranged for accomodations for all our staff at a hotel in each of these citys. Each sales representative who attends one of the regional meetings will receive an envelop filled with new-product information and motivational materials (see sample attached). If you have any suggestions or recomendations concerning our plans for these meetings, please do let us know.

Editing Practice

The Right Word   Select the correct word for each of the following sentences.

1. As soon as we can (collaborate, corroborate) the price, we will place our order.
2. Marion suggested that we place the contracts in the safe so that we do not (loose, lose) them.
3. All the district managers submitted (there, their, they're) revised budgets to the vice president.

4. Our supervisor, Ms. Henson, suggested a (fare, fair) method for determining sales credit.
5. Sales for the first six months of the year convince us that we should be able to (accede, exceed) our estimated budget by as much as 25 percent.
6. Helen and Ray are now in San Francisco, but (there, their, they're) scheduled to return to the office by next Monday.
7. Our store manager is trying to (device, devise) a way to reduce inventory losses.
8. Embassy Manufacturing Company has sales offices in several cities, but (it's, its) plant is in Knoxville, Tennessee.
9. One of the (principal, principle) reasons for delaying the project is that the cost of silver has risen so sharply.
10. To test the market for these products, we will conduct a nationwide (poll, pole) of men and women between the ages of 19 and 35.

Case Problem

Embarrassing Moment   Raymond Mullins belongs to one of the local civic clubs and attends its meetings regularly. During the social hour at one of the meetings, one of his best customers greets Mr. Mullins by name. However, Mr. Mullins has to return the greeting without mentioning the customer's name—he cannot remember it. During the conversation with the customer, another member of the organization, Frank Whelan, approaches both men. "Hello, Ray; it's good to see you again—and I'd like to welcome your guest to our meeting." Now Mr. Mullins must introduce the two men, and he still cannot remember the name of the customer whom Frank Whelan has mistaken for his guest.

1. What should Mr. Mullins say?
2. What might the customer have said, when he first appeared, to protect Mr. Mullins from being embarrassed?
3. What is a good way to remember names?

6 THE SENTENCE

The sentence is the basic unit of thought we use to express ourselves. The better we understand how to form and use sentences, therefore, the more effectively we can communicate our thoughts to others.

To use your powers of communication to your fullest ability, you must understand the basics of sentence use explained in this section.

DEFINITION

The traditional definition of a sentence has been, "A sentence is a group of words that express a complete thought." The key words here are "a *complete* thought." One common error is to join words together and use them as a sentence even though they do not express a complete thought. To avoid writing incomplete sentences—called "fragments"—apply the shortcut presented in the following Memory Hook.

■ Memory Hook

If a group of words makes *No Sense*, then it is *No Sentence*. Note how the *No Sense—No Sentence* principle helps to distinguish between a complete sentence and a fragment.

> When Mrs. Vickers arrives, we will begin the meeting. (These words make sense—together they express one thought. This is a sentence.)
>
> When Mrs. Vickers arrives. We will begin the meeting. (The first group of words is not a sentence; it makes no sense. What will happen "When Mrs. Vickers arrives"? The word *when* leads us to expect more. "When Mrs. Vickers arrives" should be part of the second group of words because it is not a sentence.)
>
> Mr. Owens reduced the price 10 percent because the customer paid cash. (This group of words makes sense; it is a sentence. The next example shows how some people incorrectly write such a sentence.)
>
> Mr. Owens reduced the price 10 percent. Because the customer paid cash. (The words *Because the customer paid cash* do not make sense by themselves. The word *because* leads us to expect more: What happened "because the customer paid cash"?)

Besides the words *when* and *because,* there are other words that "lead us to expect more": *since; whenever; while; although;* and others. (See the complete list on page 145.)

SUBJECTS AND PREDICATES

The subject of a sentence is the part that names (1) the person speaking, (2) the person spoken to, or (3) the person or thing spoken about.

1. *I* asked Ms. Lee for a copy of the last issue. (*I* is the complete subject of the sentence, the person speaking.)
2. *You* already have a copy. (*You* is the subject of the sentence, the person spoken to.)
   Send this magazine to Mrs. Trilling. (Here, *you* is understood to be the subject; *you* is the person spoken to.)
3. *The issue on my desk* is not the latest issue. (The complete subject here is several words long: *The issue on my desk,* the thing spoken about.)
   The woman on the cover of that issue is my sister. (The complete subject of the sentence is *The woman on the cover of that issue,* the person spoken about.)

Now, what is a *predicate?* After you select the subject, you will know that the rest of the sentence is the predicate.

In this chapter and the next, checkup exercises will help you apply the rules that have been presented. Use the results of the checkup exercises to pinpoint the areas in which you may need additional study.

Indicate whether the following groups of words are sentences or fragments. Then rewrite each fragment to make it a complete sentence.

1. Although we mailed the contract last Friday.
2. Dr. Ives is attending a seminar in Houston.
3. Every telephone in our office.
4. Because she is out of town, we canceled the meeting.
5. All our old files are stored in the basement of our building.
6. She requested three bids on the project.
7. Since Miss Klein joined our company.
8. Stanley was at the production meeting this morning.
9. When we receive the estimates.
10. After Stanley had called, Mr. Pembroke arrived.

SIMPLE SUBJECTS AND COMPOUND SUBJECTS

The *simple subject* is the main word in the complete subject.

> The *reason* for the delays is that the truckers are on strike. (The complete subject is *The reason for the delays*. The main word in the complete subject is *reason*.)
>
> Nine *accountants* in our firm are teaching courses in a business college. (The complete subject is *Nine accountants in our firm*. The main word in this complete subject is *accountants*.)

By knowing that the simple subject in the first example is *reason*, the writer will not fall into the trap of saying, "The reason for the delays *are* . . . . " Because the subject is *reason*, the verb must be *is*, not *are*. Likewise, by knowing that the simple subject in the second example is *accountants* (not *firm*), the writer will not make the mistake of saying, "Nine accountants in our firm *is* teaching . . . . "

Compound subjects are two or more equal subjects joined by a conjunction such as *and, but, or,* or *nor.*

> The *men and women* in our department have formed a softball team. (The complete subject is *The men and women in our department*. The main words in the complete subject are *men* and *women*, which are joined by the conjunction *and*. The compound subject is *men and women*.)
>
> *Foods* containing salt or *liquids* containing sugar were restricted by the doctor. (The complete subject is *Foods containing salt or liquids containing sugar*. The main words in the complete subject are *foods* and *liquids*, which are joined by the conjunction *or*. The compound subject is *foods or liquids*.)

SUBJECT FIRST, THEN PREDICATE

The normal order of a sentence is complete subject first, then complete predicate.

> Our entire department worked overtime to complete the project on schedule. (The complete subject is *Our entire department.* Because it precedes the complete predicate, the sentence is in normal order.)
>
> To complete the project on schedule, our entire department worked overtime. (Now part of the predicate precedes the subject *our entire department.* Therefore, the sentence is not in normal order; it is in *inverted* order.)

Most statements are written in normal order, but most questions are written in inverted order.

> Doesn't Mr. Ewes have the key to the stockroom? (This question is in inverted order. Why? Because the subject is *Mr. Ewes,* and part of the predicate precedes the subject. Normal order: *Mr. Ewes doesn't have the key to the stockroom?*)

Now let's see the kinds of errors that are commonly made in sentences that are in inverted order. Consider the sentence: "Where's the folders that Ms. Syms sent us?" The normal order is, "The folders that Ms. Syms sent us *is* where?" In normal order, "The folders . . . *is*" stands out as an obvious error. We must say, "The folders . . . *are.*" Therefore: "Where *are* the folders . . . ?"

By putting the following sentence in normal order, the writer would have quickly spotted the error: "In the enclosed catalog is a great many special bargains for you!" In normal order, this sentence reads: "A great many special bargains *is* in the enclosed catalog." "Bargains *is,*" of course, is wrong; the sentence should be: "In the enclosed catalog *are* . . . ."

☐ Checkup 2

For each of the following sentences, identify the complete subject. Then underline the simple subject or the compound subject. (**Hint:** If a sentence is inverted, change it to normal order before you make your choices.)

1. All airlines and travel agents recommend that travelers buy their tickets early.
2. Have you heard of the term "no-shows"?
3. This term describes people with airline reservations who do not show up for their flights.
4. To account for "no-shows," the airline companies accept more reservations for each flight than can be seated on that flight.
5. This nationwide policy attempts to fill each flight and therefore make each flight more profitable.
6. Travel agents and airline companies recommend that everyone reconfirm his or her reservation by phone.
7. Do you know what happens when more passengers show up than can be seated?
8. Some of the passengers must be placed on other flights.

9. The smart traveler knows that he or she may be entitled to a hotel room and meals under certain circumstances.
10. Have you written to the Civil Aeronautics Board for its free booklet?

COMMUNICATION PROJECTS

Practical Application

A. Read each of the following statements. For each fragment, write a complete sentence. For each inverted sentence, write the sentence in normal order. Then, for all sentences, identify the complete subject and underline the simple or compound subject.

1. When Miss Grady came to the office this morning.
2. In the enclosed booklet are many discounts for the sharp shopper.
3. What is your opinion of the new policy?
4. Milk and crackers is still my favorite snack.
5. Although Mr. Sullivan is on vacation.
6. Everyone in the Accounting Department and the Advertising Department.
7. Must this form be signed by Ms. Dykstra?
8. Since we opened our store in 1980.
9. A supervisor or a regional manager must approve all local advertisements.
10. Applicants for this job will be interviewed during the week of May 5.
11. Dr. Kinkaid said her book would be published early next month.
12. In our department, the accountants and their secretaries cooperate with one another to complete their projects on schedule.
13. A seminar on time-management principles is being conducted on the twenty-ninth floor.
14. Only Miss DePaul and her assistants.
15. Early retirement benefits are explained in our company manual.

B. Correct any errors in the following sentences. Write *OK* if a sentence has no error.

1. Attached are the sample you requested.
2. On her desk was the contracts we were looking for.
3. Is there any good suggestions in that report?
4. Have you replied to Ms. Bancroft's letter?
5. How profitable is the new products?
6. In the envelope on my desk is the requests for free samples.
7. You or Mr. Welty should receive copies of all status reports.
8. Seven names of customers who complained about this product is listed below.
9. Mrs. Friede or Mr. Owens will preside at the meeting.
10. Doesn't Karen and Mike have copies of the agreement?
11. Several executives are on vacation this week.
12. Where's the keys to the store room and the conference room?
13. The changes in the contract is listed on this sheet.
14. Marian and Daniel are in a meeting.
15. Is the green cardboard boxes to be used for storing old files?

Editing Practice

Proofreading for Errors   There are several errors in the following paragraph. Can you find them?

> Thank you for returning you completed form for our upcoming convention. We are glad to hear that six executives from you company is planning to attend. Because we know that this year's turnout will be the largest ever.

As a Matter of Fact . . .   Writers and typists proofread their copy not only for errors in grammar and spelling but also for inconsistencies and contradictions of facts. Can you find any such errors in the following excerpt from a memo?

> Last September 31, we signed an agreement to pay Robert Benson a fee of $100 a month for consultation on product development. The one-year agreement will expire next month.
>
> All of us agree that we have certainly received good value for our money. Therefore, we would like to increase Roberta's monthly fee 25 percent for the next contract—to a total of $25 a month.
>
> Do we have your permission to issue a new contract for the amount stated?

Case Problem

Making Introductions   At a special dinner with company executives, Adam Williams would like to introduce his wife Gladys to his boss, Louise Syms, Executive Vice President.

1. How should Adam make this introduction?
2. If he were not sure, what reference would you recommend to him?

7
VERBS

Many of the errors made in speaking and writing are errors in the use of verbs. By paying special attention to the principles of verb usage in this section and the next, you will be sure to avoid most of the common verb errors.

DEFINITION

A *verb* is a word that describes an action, a condition, or a state of being. Because verbs identify actions, they often spark sentences into motion, as the following examples show:

My supervisor *planned* a two-week ski trip last December. Unfortunately, she *canceled* her plans because of her promotion. (To understand the full impact of verbs, read these sentences *without* the verbs *planned* and *canceled*. Do you see how these verbs spark the sentences to life?)

Danielle and her assistant *were* at the production meeting. Walter *was* also at the meeting, but he *left* early. (The verbs *were*, *was*, and *left* spark these sentences. Without these verbs, the sentences would be meaningless.)

The first step toward using verbs expertly is to be able to identify verbs accurately. The following checkup will provide you with valuable practice in identifying verbs.

☐ Checkup 1

Identify the verbs in the following sentences.
1. Who typed the report for Ms. Howell?
2. Brian asked Pauline for the new vacation schedule.
3. We invited Miss Barclay to the luncheon next Sunday.
4. Only Owen, our manager, attends the data processing conventions.
5. Loren easily justified her reasons for the delay.
6. Mr. Henry, not Ms. Arnold, checks the inventory figures.
7. Our guest arrived at 10:30 this morning.
8. Mr. Pulaski was the only attorney on the panel.
9. Mrs. LaRue exceeds her sales goals every month.
10. They conducted a market survey last spring.

Now notice that the following groups of words are lifeless. Because they have no verbs, they tell of no action, no condition, no state of being. They need verbs.

Irma an expert on corporate finance. (A verb would bring these words to life: Irma *wants* an expert, Irma *is* an expert, Irma *hired* an expert, Irma *is becoming* an expert, and so on.)

Mrs. Banks a new car. (Lifeless. Verbs are needed: Mrs. Banks *bought*, *rented*, *sold*, *borrowed*, a new car.)

☐ Checkup 2

The following groups of words need verbs. Supply a verb for each group where the (?) appears.
1. Our vice president (?) the meeting.   *WAS AT*
2 Miss Taylor (?) the contract.   *HAS*
3. Several accountants (?) at the seminar.   *WERE*
4. During the discussion, we (?) the agenda.   *made*
5. Mr. Mendoza (?) all our questions.   *heard*
6. A revised sales report (?) on your desk.   *IS*

VERB PHRASES

Many verbs can be combined with other verbs to form a verb phrase. Verb phrases such as *am going, were planning, have been working, should have been corrected,* and *will have noticed* permit speakers and writers to pinpoint very precisely the meaning of a verb in a sentence. As you can see, then, a verb phrase may have two words or more than two words. The last verb in the phrase is called the *main* verb (or the *principal* verb), and the verb or verbs before the main verb are called *helping* verbs (or *auxiliary* verbs).

Helping Verb	Main Verb
is	typing
are	paying
do	permit
will	be
will be	permitted
had been	trying
did	attempt
should have	gone
might have been	listed
has been	hired
will have	been
will have been	completed

Note, again, that the main verb is the last verb in each phrase and that the other verbs are helpers. Let's use two examples in sentences:

> Anthony *will be* here at noon. (The verb phrase is *will be. Be* is the main verb; *will* is the helper.)
>
> Smoking *will be permitted* only in restricted areas. (The verb phrase is *will be permitted.* The main verb is *permitted*; the helpers are *will* and *be.*)

As you see, in one case *be* is the main verb. In the other, it is a helper. To tell when a verb is a helper and when it is the main verb, just look to see whether it is the *last* verb in the phrase.

Now, note how a verb phrase is split in many questions:

> *Has* Mr. VanDam *called* yet this morning? (The verb phrase *has called* is split by the subject, *Mr. VanDam.* The normal order would be "*Mr. VanDam has called....*")
>
> *Is* Miss Nussbaum *planning* to join us Friday afternoon? (The verb phrase *is planning* is separated by the subject, *Miss Nussbaum.*)

Some adverbs also split verb phrases:

> She *has* already *completed* her report to the marketing manager. (The verb phrase *has completed* is split by the adverb *already.*)

Watch carefully for split verb phrases as you look for main verbs and helping verbs.

☐ Checkup 3

Identify the verb phrases in the following sentences. Then underline the main verbs in each phrase.
1. All the specifications should have been revised by last Tuesday.
2. Do you have a duplicate copy of the committee's report?
3. Dr. Swenson has approved our budgets.
4. How many responses have we received to our special May ad?
5. Mr. Lawrence's flight has been delayed.
6. By November, Ms. Wilson will have sold nearly $250,000 worth of merchandise.
7. According to the procedures manual, you should have requested at least three cost estimates.
8. Trent has been making all the reservations for our sales representatives.
9. Mrs. D'Amico has been reelected mayor of our city, according to the news report.
10. Yes, the regional managers are meeting tomorrow morning in the conference room.

PRINCIPAL PARTS OF VERBS

The principal parts of verbs are used to express the time, or action, of a verb. The four principal parts are the present tense and the past tense, and the present participle and the past participle. For example, *talk, talked, talking,* and *talked* are the parts of the verb *talk.*

Depending on how a verb forms its principal parts, it may be classified as a *regular* verb or an *irregular* verb.

Regular Verbs

Most verbs in our language form their past tense and past participles by adding *d* or *ed* to the verb: *type, typed, typed; talk, talked, talked;* and so on. The present participles are formed simply by adding *ing* to the verb: *type, typing; talk, talking;* and so on.

There are so many regular verbs, and we use them so often, that correct use of regular verbs is almost automatic. We rarely make errors in the use of regular verbs.

Irregular Verbs

Irregular verbs have no usual way of forming their principal parts. In fact, they frequently change to a different word, as you will see in the list on pages 52 and 53. No rules will provide easy ways to remember the principal parts of irregular verbs. They must be memorized.

■ Memory Hook

Remember that the past tense of a verb *never* has a helper and that participles *always* have helpers. By remembering this, you will never make the mistake of using a past tense with a helper.

Has she wrote the monthly bulletin yet? (Obviously incorrect, because the verb phrase *has wrote* combines a helper with the past tense instead of the required past participle of the verb. *The past tense never has a helper.*)

Has she written the monthly bulletin yet? (Correct. The verb phrase *has written* ends with the past participle *written*.)

She is writing the bulletin now. (Correct. The present participle *writing* is used with the helper *is* in the verb phrase *is writing*.)

☐ Twilight Zone

Lend and *Loan*   Increasingly, the word *loan* is being used as a verb ("Will you please loan me your calculator?"), even though *lend* is a verb and *loan* is (or *was*) a noun. Do you distinguish between *lend* and *loan* in your speech and your writing? Many authorities still insist that we should.

Principal Parts of Irregular Verbs

Present	Past	Past Participle	Present Participle
am	was	been	being
bear	bore	borne	bearing
begin	began	begun	beginning
bid (to command)	bade	bidden	bidding
bid (to offer to pay)	bid	bid	bidding
bite	bit	bitten	biting
blow	blew	blown	blowing
break	broke	broken	breaking
bring	brought	brought	bringing
burst	burst	burst	bursting
catch	caught	caught	catching
choose	chose	chosen	choosing
come	came	come	coming
do	did	done	doing
draw	drew	drawn	drawing
drink	drank	drunk	drinking
drive	drove	driven	driving
eat	ate	eaten	eating
fall	fell	fallen	falling
fight	fought	fought	fighting
flee	fled	fled	fleeing
fly	flew	flown	flying
forget	forgot	forgotten	forgetting
freeze	froze	frozen	freezing
get	got	got	getting
give	gave	given	giving
go	went	gone	going

regular verb (ed)

☐Checkup 4

Find and correct each principal-part error in the following sentences. Indicate your correction as shown in the example below. Write *OK* if a sentence is correct.

> **Example:** Mrs. Gleason had went before we arrived at her office.
> **Correction:** had *gone* (Because *went* uses no helper; *went* is a past tense of the verb *go*; *gone* is the past participle.)

1. Do you know who has ~~took~~ *taken* the Anderson file from my desk?
OK 2. Apparently, the bookends simply fallen off the shelf from the vibrations of the machines.
3. John ~~come~~ *came* early yesterday to get a head start on his project.
4. We had ~~began~~ *begun* checking our inventory before Mrs. Acosta asked us to.
5. Carla and Frederick have ~~wrote~~ *written* many successful ads for our clients.
6. Only Miss Tribuno ~~known~~ *knew* about the planned merger from the beginning.

Principal Parts of Irregular Verbs *(Continued)*

Present	Past	Past Participle	Present Participle
grow	grew	grown	growing
hang (to put to death)	hanged	hanged	hanging
hang (to suspend)	hung	hung	hanging
hide	hid	hidden	hiding
know	knew	known	knowing
lay	laid (*not* layed)	laid (*not* layed)	laying
leave	left	left	leaving
lend	lent	lent	lending
lie	lay	lain	lying
pay	paid (*not* payed)	paid (*not* payed)	paying
ride	rode	ridden	riding
ring	rang	rung	ringing
rise	rose	risen	rising
run	ran	run	running
see	saw	seen	seeing
set	set	set	setting
shake	shook	shaken	shaking
sing	sang	sung	singing
sit	sat	sat	sitting
speak	spoke	spoken	speaking
steal	stole	stolen	stealing
strike	struck	struck	striking
take	took	taken	taking
tear	tore	torn	tearing
throw	threw	thrown	throwing
wear	wore	worn	wearing
write	wrote	written	writing

7. Yes, Miss Lincoln, we have spoke to the department head. *spoken*
8. Whom have they chose to succeed Elaine? *chosen*
9. While we were eating, we met Ms. Phillips, our vice president. *ok*
10. Leonard been on vacation all week. *has*

WERE INSTEAD OF WAS

After *if, as if, as though,* and *wish,* use *were* where ordinarily *was* would be used.

> We wish it *were* possible to exchange the merchandise, but state laws prohibit us from doing so. (It is not possible; therefore, "We wish it *were*"—not *was*—is correct.)
>
> John sometimes acts as though he *were* at a party instead of at work. (But he is not at a party; therefore, "as though he *were*"—not *was*—is correct.)
>
> If I *were* Mrs. Clarke, I would invest in real estate. (But I am not Mrs. Clarke; thus "If I *were*"—not *was*—is correct.)

The reason that *were* is used in such cases is that the statement describes something contrary to fact, something that simply is not true, or something that is highly doubtful or impossible. Of course, when the statement *is true* or could be true (as sometimes happens following *if*), then do *not* substitute *were* for *was*.

> If Mr. Vareen *was* already here, the receptionist probably gave him the package. (He may indeed have already been here, so this statement could be true. Thus we do not substitute *were* for *was*.)

☐ Checkup 5

Correct any errors in the following sentences. If a sentence has no error, write *OK.*
1. Miss Paulson often acts as though she was the only person in our department. *ok*
2. Mr. Olivier said, "If I were younger, I would try to become a professional musician." *ok*
3. As though coming in late every day was not enough, Mark had the audacity to ask for the afternoon off! *ok*
4. Several people noticed that Caroline sometimes behaves as if she was the only *were* sales representative for our company.
5. "Bill," said Mrs. Ogilvy, "I would take advantage of this once-in-a-lifetime opportunity if I were you." *ok*

COMMUNICATION PROJECTS

Practical Application

A. Identify the verbs and verb phrases in the following sentences. For each verb phrase, underline the main verb. If a sentence has no verb, supply a verb.
1. Yes, the package should have been mailed yesterday.
2. Has Ms. Burton seen the revised sketches for the ad?
3. Whom have they hired as Francine's assistant?
4. The original copy must have been misplaced.

5. We are filing a countersuit.
6. She has written a best-seller on consumer habits.
7. Last week Ms. Cox the sales record.
8. Dr. Peterson is conducting a nationwide survey.
9. New machines have been ordered for the mailroom.
10. Professor Haney, a marketing consultant, will arrive in New York tomorrow.
11. The renovation of the building is nearly completed.
12. Evelyn a good account executive.
13. More copies of the manual have been reprinted already.
14. The dark background will definitely be better.
15. Vera has been on the telephone with a client since 10 o'clock.
16. According to the study, the cost of living is rising more rapidly than wages.
17. Dr. Poole has prepared her speech for the upcoming conference.
18. By the end of October, we will have reached our sales goals for the year.
19. Two of our executives will attend a private luncheon at the governor's mansion tomorrow.
20. Three applicants have been interviewed this morning.

B. Correct any errors in the following sentences. (Complete a group of words that do not form a sentence.) If a sentence has no error, write *OK*.

1. Has the bell rung yet, Nancy?
2. Apparently, Steven been interested in nutrition for a long time.
3. Anne has loaned me her car for my trip this weekend.
4. On his desk was the brochures that we wanted.
5. Although we are out of stock. we will give rain checks.
6. Mrs. Jarvis is in Europe. If she was here, however, I know that she would approve your suggestion.
7. We should have chose a modern-looking cover for this catalog.
8. The chef does not buy meats that have been froze.
9. Only Miss Holland seen the new price list.
10. Either Mr. Trask or Ms. Corleone has went to our Dallas office recently.
11. As Mr. Raye requested. We are shipping the order by airfreight.
12. If you need a calculator, I will lend you mine.
13. The carpet in this office is completely wore out.
14. He drunk his coffee quickly before he started to outline his speech.
15. "Where is the swatches that the manufacturer sent us?" asked Carole.

Editing Practice

Editing for Vocabulary Errors   Correct any vocabulary errors in the following excerpt from a press release.

> Beverly K. Flaubert, president of GNC Enterprises, formerly announced today that GNC will move its corporate headquarters to the West Coast early next year. A specific sight has not yet been named, but according to inside company sources, it will probably be Los Angeles. GNC is one of the nation's principle manufacturers of electronic equipment.

Case Problem

The Straw That Broke the Camel's Back   Bob Haynes is the supervisor of one office section in which tardiness is a serious problem. Bob's boss was so disturbed by the excessive tardiness in this section that he suggested that Bob call a meeting of his people to see what could be done about the problem. Bob called the group together, explained the situation to them, and together they set up a plan to control the tardiness. They agreed that anyone who was tardy would remain at work twice the amount of time of the lateness. In addition, each member of the group pledged to be at work on time. The very next morning following his meeting, Mildred Anson, one of the clerks in Bob's section, was fifteen minutes late. When Bob talked to Mildred and reminded her that she was to remain thirty minutes after the regular time, Mildred explained that she lived beyond the bus line and had to ride with someone who worked for another company and who was on a different time schedule. Consequently, she said, she was not responsible for being late.

1. What should Bob Haynes do about this situation?
2. What should he say to Mildred?

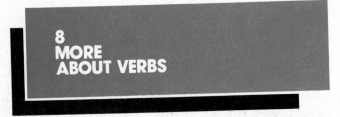

8
MORE ABOUT VERBS

Of all the thousands of verbs in the English language, none causes more difficulty for writers and speakers than these few verbs: *lie* and *lay*, *sit* and *set*, and *rise* and *raise*. Because these verbs are so often misused, you will at one stroke improve your writing and speaking skills by mastering their usage.

CLASSIFICATION OF VERBS

Understanding and using the correct forms of *lie-lay*, *sit-set*, and *rise-raise* is greatly simplified by understanding first the general classification of verbs and second where these six verbs fit in this classification. Verbs may be divided into three classes: (1) "being" verbs, (2) transitive verbs, and (3) intransitive verbs.

"BEING" VERBS

The "being" verbs are the different forms of the verb *to be*:

> *am, is, are, was, were*
> *be* with a helper: *shall be, will be, may be, can be, would be, might be,* and so on

been with a helper or helpers: *has been, have been, had been, shall have been, will have been, could have been, might have been,* and so on

being with a helper: *am being, is being, are being, was being, were being*

These are the eight "being" verbs. Because they are so often used, all eight must be memorized, preferably in this order: *am, is, are, was, were,* helper *be,* helper(s) *been,* helper *being.*

Remember: In a verb phrase (a verb that consists of two or more words), the last verb is the main verb. "Being" verbs are often used as helping verbs in verb phrases, but a verb phrase is not considered a "being" verb unless the *main* verb is a "being" verb.

Both supervisors *are* in the conference room. (*Are* is the only verb. It is obviously the main verb and a "being" verb.)

We *should have been* here earlier. (The complete verb phrase is *should have been.* Therefore, because *been* is the main verb, this verb phrase is a "being" verb.)

Several customers *were annoyed* at the new policy. (*Were* is definitely a "being" verb, but it is not the main verb in the verb phrase *were annoyed.* The main verb is *annoyed; were* is a helper. Thus *were annoyed* is not a "being" verb.)

Ms. Wascher *is planning* a trip to Chicago. (*Is,* of course, is a "being" verb, but it is not the main verb. *Planning* is the main verb; *is* is a helper. Thus *is planning* is not a "being" verb.)

☐ Checkup 1

Underline the verbs and verb phrases in the following sentences. Write "B" for each "being" verb.

1. Joanne Camp, our director of personnel, is responsible for our company's career opportunity program.
2. The program has been in effect since 1980.
3. It has been called "the most innovative program of its kind."
4. Employees are obviously benefiting from the career-opportunity program.
5. Through the program, several have been promoted to management-level jobs.
6. Some employees have indicated a preference for one of our branch offices.
7. Of course, our Hawaii office is the most popular branch office.
8. Two supervisors were transferred to Honolulu within the past two months.
9. Are you familiar with this program?
10. For more information, you should call the personnel department.

TRANSITIVE AND INTRANSITIVE VERBS

A verb that has an object is called a *transitive verb.* A verb that does not have an object is called an *intransitive verb. Lay, set,* and *raise* are transitive verbs; they always have objects. *Lie, sit,* and *rise* are intransitive verbs. Now, use the following memory hook to learn how to find objects of verbs. When you can find objects of verbs, you will be able to use *lie-lay, sit-set,* and *rise-raise* correctly.

■ Memory Hook

A transitive verb has an object. To find that object, say the verb plus the question "What?" or "Whom?" The answer to the question is the object. Read the following examples, then note the three-step procedure below each example:

Example 1: Her manager accepted her recommendation.

1. Say the verb.   *Accepted.*
2. Ask the question "What?" or   Accepted *what?*
"Whom?"   Accepted *recommendation.*
3. The answer to the question is the
object; the verb, therefore, is transi-   *Recommendation* is the object of
tive. If there is no answer, there is no   *accepted;* therefore, *accepted* is a
object; the verb is intransitive.   transitive verb.

Example 2: Leroy invited Carole to the dinner.

1. Say the verb.   *Invited.*
2. Ask the question "What?" or
"Whom?"   Invited *whom?*
3. Answer? (*Yes* = transitive.   Yes. Invited *Carole.*
No = intransitive.)   *Carole* is the object of *invited;* thus
                                                     invited is a transitive verb.

ALWAYS TRANSITIVE

Some transitive verbs are so easy to spot that no special procedure is needed to find them. Whenever you see a past participle that has a "being" verb as a helper, that verb is *always transitive.* The reason is that a "being" verb plus a past participle always makes the subject the receiver of the action, as the following examples illustrate:

The meeting *should have been can-*   "Being" verb (*should have*
celed.   *been*) + past participle (*can-*
                                                                   celed) = transitive verb. (**Rea-**
                                                                   son: The subject, *meeting,* re-
                                                                   ceives the action of the verb.)

Notice the difference between these similar sentences:

Mrs. Clarke *fired* Mr. Hanley.   Who receives the action of the verb
                                                       fired? Mr. Hanley.
Mrs. Clarke *was fired* by Mr. Hanley.   Now who receives the action of *was*
                                                       fired? The subject, *Mrs. Clarke.*

Note, however, that this rule applies only to "being" verbs plus *past* participles:

Ms. VanPelt has been negotiating this contract for several months. (*Negotiating* has a "being" verb helper, but it is a *present participle.* Thus the subject does *not* receive the action. Has been negotiating *what?* Answer: *contract. Contract* is the object; *has been negotiating* is a transitive verb.)

☐ **Checkup 2**

Underscore the verbs or verb phrases in the following sentences. Then, identify each as *B* for "being", *T* for "transitive", or *I* for "intransitive." (Watch for any past participles that have "being" verb helpers.)

1. Mrs. Carlin, our regional manager, will be on vacation next week.
2. The broadcast will be televised next Tuesday at 9 p.m.
3. Has anyone seen Mr. Persoff this afternoon?
4. The union delegates are demanding higher wages.
5. Perhaps Miss Finnegan has left already.
6. Obviously, both of the supervisors arrived very late.
7. The credit department manager has hired two part-time typists.
8. Two part-timers were hired by the credit department manager.
9. Anne DaCosta has been promoted to district supervisor.
10. The head of our medical department is Dr. Lugo.

LIE, LAY; SIT, SET; RISE, RAISE

Now that you can tell the difference between a transitive verb and an intransitive verb, you will find it easy to use *lie* and *lay*, *sit* and *set*, and *rise* and *raise* correctly. The reason is that in each pair, one verb is transitive and the other is intransitive.

The following memory hook will help you to recognize the correct verb instantly.

■ Memory Hook

The verbs *lie*, *sit*, and *rise* are intransitive. To remember this, note that the second letter in *lie*, *sit*, and *rise* is the letter *i*, and *intransitive* starts with the letter *i*.

intransitive
lie
sit
rise

Obviously, if *lie*, *sit*, and *rise* are intransitive, then *lay*, *set*, and *raise* are transitive verbs. Now pay special attention to the principal parts of these verbs:

Present	Past	Past Participle	Present Participle	Infinitive
lie	lay	lain	lying	to lie
lay	laid	laid	laying	to lay
sit	sat	sat	sitting	to sit
set	set	set	setting	to set
rise	rose	risen	rising	to rise
raise	raised	raised	raising	to raise

Note: Do not confuse the present tense *lay* with *lay* the past tense of *lie*. In the following sentence, which past tense form is correct, *lay* or *laid*?

Yesterday Bart (lay, laid) cartons on the floor.

Which is needed here, a transitive verb or an intransitive verb? Answer: *transitive*. Why? Because *cartons* is the object of the verb, the verb must be transitive. Laid *what*? Laid *cartons*. Here is another example:

After dinner, I usually (lie, lay) down for a short nap.

What is the object? There is no object; therefore, an intransitive verb—*lie*—is correct.

The shades were (risen, raised) slightly.

If you remembered that a "being" verb helper plus a past participle is *always transitive*, then you chose *raised*, a transitive verb.

☐ Checkup 3

Choose the correct verb in each of the following sentences. Label each choice *T* for "transitive" or *I* for "intransitive," and tell why your choice is correct.

1. The sales reports were (lain, laid) on the top shelf.
2. Please (sit, set) both display units near the front of the room.
3. These platforms must be (risen, raised) about 3 inches higher.
4. For this manuscript, (sit, set) your margins for 15 and 70.
5. The minimum salaries for most grade levels have been (risen, raised).
6. When the water level (rises, raises), this pump switches on automatically.
7. Matthew generally (sits, sets) in this office to compose new advertisements.
8. If you do not feel well, you may (lie, lay) down in the medical department.
9. All of us are helping to (rise, raise) money for handicapped children.
10. She has (lain, laid) in the sun too long.

COMMUNICATION PROJECTS

Practical Application

A. Underline the verb or verb phrase in the following sentences. Then label each *B* for "being," *T* for "transitive," or *I* for "intransitive."

1. She has been writing that article for several weeks.
2. Ms. Stimpson creates most of our direct mail brochures.
3. The messenger should have been here by now.
4. Has the design for this been approved yet?
5. Only two of our stores are in this area.
6. This price should have been corrected immediately.
7. My train has been late several times this week.
8. Ms. Quicker is planning the marketing strategy for our new product.

9. Are the new procedures being followed carefully?
10. To whom is the letter addressed?
11. Have you asked Mr. Fitzgerald for an agenda?
12. Yes, we product managers have completed our sales forecasts.
13. Dr. Suriano's survey forms have been mailed.
14. Are you buying a new car, Charles?
15. The reason for the delays is explained in this report.

B. Correct any errors in the following sentences. If a sentence is correct, write *OK*. (In Sections 8 through 28, Practical Application B reviews material from earlier lessons as well as from the current lesson.)

1. All the reports were laying on her desk when she arrived.
2. After the long trip home, we decided to lay down to rest.
3. On my desk is last year's brochure and this year's brochure.
4. You should set the alarm for 6 a.m.
5. At every meeting, he has risen that same objection to our marketing plan.
6. The map was lain out on the table so that we could trace our route.
7. The outstanding balance must be payed by the 15th of next month.
8. The machine has lain idle for several months.
9. Our Birmingham office sets on a hilltop.
10. Please lie that package on the table.
11. Make sure that the fence has been set securely.
12. In the manual is some interesting techniques for decorating an office.
13. Last night, I lay down to rest for one hour after dinner.
14. Mr. Merriam left his briefcase laying on the floor in my office.
15. As far as we know, no objection has been raised.
16. Will you please loan me your calculator?
17. Kevin has lain his plan out for all of us to see.
18. Does Versailles lie southeast of Paris?
19. Her salary has been raised twice this year.
20. The wallet that all of us were looking for was laying on my desk.

Editing Practice

Spelling Alert!   Check the following paragraph for spelling errors. How many can you find?

> As a service to our community, our company produced a special film on nutri-
> tion and distirbuted it—free—to schools thoughout our state. Among the
> topics dicsussed in the film is the role of nutrition to help fight the effects of
> emotional stress. For more information about this film, write the Community
> Services Department of the Em-Kay Corporation.

Case Problem

The Helpful Employee   Carolyn Proust recently gave notice of her intention to resign from her position as accounts receivable manager in the Armstrong Manufacturing

Company's office. Her replacement is coming in tomorrow, two days before Carolyn will be leaving, to be oriented to the new position. Carolyn has decided that a brief, typed summary of her duties would be helpful for the replacement.

1. Why would such a summary be helpful, even though Carolyn will be spending two days with the person who is to replace her?
2. What should the summary contain?

9 NOUNS: SINGULARS AND PLURALS

In spoken English, many of the difficulties of our language are unnoticed. For example, although *attorneys, attorney's* and *attorneys'* are three different forms of a word used for three different purposes, the pronunciation of all three words is the same. Therefore, we do not think about the spellings of these words as we say them. Even the person who does not know the differences can still use the words correctly in speaking.

In writing, however, the difficulties of our language surface, and we are forced to choose: Which is correct for a particular sentence—*attorneys, attorney's,* or *attorneys'*? They are not interchangeable; only one can be correct for a given sentence.

Whenever we are forced to choose, we must, of course, know what the choices are. The writer who knows the general ways in which plurals and possessives are formed will have no problem choosing *attorneys, attorney's,* or *attorneys',* whichever is correct for a particular sentence. But the writer who does not know the rules cannot make the correct choice.

This section and the next one will help you to master the use of plurals and possessives and therefore to solve some of the most common spelling problems. This section emphasizes forming noun plurals correctly. It will (1) review the general rules for forming most plurals, (2) present simple solutions for forming the most difficult plurals, (3) make you aware of those plurals for which you should consult a dictionary, and (4) analyze plurals that often cause grammatical errors. Let's begin.

PLURALS—THE BASIC RULES

The following rules for forming plurals are generally well known, but review them to make sure that you always apply them correctly.

Plurals of Common Nouns

Most common nouns form their plurals by adding *s* to the singular form:

nation	nations	employee	employees
office	offices	benefit	benefits
seminar	seminars	magazine	magazines

But nouns that end in *s, sh, ch, x,* and *z* form their plurals by adding *es* to the singular form:

lens	len*ses*	tax	tax*es*
rash	rash*es*	topaz	topaz*es*
church	church*es*		

Plurals of Proper Nouns

Most proper nouns or *names* form their plurals by adding *s* to the singular form. Those proper nouns which end in *s, sh, ch, x,* and *z* form their plurals by adding *es*—just as common nouns ending in these letters form their plurals.

farmer	farmers	Palmer	the Palmers
carton	cartons	Barton	the Bartons
brass	brasses	Ellis	the Ellises
dish	dishes	Walsh	the Walshes
branch	branches	Stritch	the Stritches
fox	foxes	Wilcox	the Wilcoxes
chintz	chintzes	Schlitz	the Schlitzes

Plurals of Compound Nouns

A compound noun is one noun that consists of two or more words. Compound nouns may be spelled with a hyphen or with a space between the words. However the compound noun is spelled, remember this rule: In a compound noun, make the main word or most important word plural.

bulletin board	bulletin boards
brother-in-law	brothers-in-law
vice president	vice presidents
general manager	general managers
major general	major generals
editor in chief	editors in chief
chief of staff	chiefs of staff

Plurals of Nouns Ending in Y

Singular nouns ending in *y* may form their plurals in one of two ways. If the *y* is preceded by a vowel, add *s* to form the plural. If the *y* is preceded by a consonant, change the *y* to *i* and add *es*. Study these examples:

attorney	attorneys	company	compan*ies*
toy	toys	subsidiary	subsidiar*ies*
valley	valleys	facility	facilit*ies*

Note: This rule does not apply to proper names ending in *y*. Proper names ending in *y* form their plurals by adding *s*:

Avery	the Averys	Bentley	the Bentleys
Brady	the Bradys	Mary	two Marys

☑ Checkup 1

Correct any errors in the following sentences. Make sure that you can justify your corrections. Write *OK* if a sentence is correct.

1. A concerned citizen donated the money to buy new park benches.
2. Two assistant district attornies were explaining the procedure to the complainant.
3. Several brigadier generals were at the court-martial.
4. People who live in New Jersey communitys and work in New York must pay taxes to both states.
5. In our camera store, 135-millimeter lens's are very popular.
6. We invited Elaine and Brad Benson to tonight's press party, so come to the party if you want to meet the Bensones.
7. The purchasing department has already ordered new bulleting boards and other supplys for the conference room.
8. The Bradies (Freda Brady and her husband Jonas) should arrive tonight at 7 p.m.
9. When she and her husband retired, they sold their business to their three son-in-laws.
10. Have you heard that Elvera and Conrad have been promoted to editor in chiefs?

SPECIAL PLURALS

The plurals of certain special forms—for example, the plurals of titles such as *Mr.* and *Mrs.*—cause problems for many writers. As the following explanations show, these problem areas are not really tough to understand.

Plurals of Titles With Names

When referring to two or more people with the same name and the same courtesy title, you may make either the name plural or the title (not both).

Singular	Plural Title	Plural Name
Mr. Martin	Messrs. Martin	the Mr. Martins
Ms. Havermeyer	Mss. Havermeyer	the Ms. Havermeyers
Mrs. Dublin	Mmes. Dublin	the Mrs. Dublins
Miss Spence	Misses Spence	the Miss Spences
Professor Abernathy	Professors Abernathy	the Professor Abernathys

Both plural forms given above are correct. Remember to make only the title *or* only the name plural—not both. (**Note:** *Messrs.* is the abbreviation for *Messieurs,* the French word for *Misters.* *Mmes.* is the abbreviation for *Mesdames,* the French word used for the plural of *Mrs.*)

Plurals That Require Apostrophes

Few plural forms require apostrophes. Specifically, an apostrophe plus *s* is used to form the plural of lowercase letters and abbreviations. In addition, an apostrophe is used for capital letters when there is possibility of confusion (as in *A's* and *I's*, which without apostrophes could be confused with *As* and *Is*).

In the following examples, note the use of an apostrophe plus *s* for *g's* and *f's* and for *c.o.d.'s.*

> All *c.o.d.'s* must be paid for at our receiving desk.
> This typewriter blurs some letters, especially the *g's* and *f's.*

Note, too, that modern usage does *not* require an apostrophe in any of the following terms:

> Our financial reports have certainly had *ups* and *downs* over the past two years.
> The temperature today was in the *80s.*
> Here is a list of *dos* and *don'ts.*

Plurals With Special Changes

Some very commonly used plurals are formed by changing the singular word in a radical way. For example, the singular *mouse* and the plural *mice* are obviously very different-looking words. The plural *mice* is *not* formed by simply adding an *s* (or *es*) to the singular form; the word is changed internally. Here are some other singulars that form their plurals by vowel changes or by adding letters other than *s* to the singular form:

man	men
woman	women
child	children
goose	geese
wolf	wolves
ox	oxen

Note: Not all words that end in *man* form their plurals by changing *man* to *men.* Some form their plurals by adding *s* to the singular form:

German	Germans
ottoman	ottomans

Plurals With Two Different Meanings

A few nouns have two different plural forms, each plural with its own meaning. Here are three examples:

brother	brothers (blood relatives)
	brethren (members of a society)
staff	staffs (personnel)
	staves (sticks, poles)
index	indexes (to books)
	indices (symbols)

☑Checkup 2

Study the following sentences. Then correct any errors.

1. The Mrs. Marxes (Helen Marx and her two daughters-in-law) will arrive on Thursday evening.
2. All the childs must be accompanied by their parents.
3. Although the temperature was in the 40's, the snow hardly melted.
4. Last semester she received two I's for incomplete courses; all her other grades were A's.
5. The Mr. Martin are interested in purchasing the property.
6. Be sure to ask the Misses Smiths whether they want a limousine to pick them up.
7. On the copies of the invoices, the p's indicate that the totals were paid; the x's indicate that the totals were not paid.
8. In the 1960's, our firm had its greatest growth period.
9. In September she will begin teaching a writing course especially designed for CPA's.
10. In this airline schedule, the a's and l's are abbreviations used to indicate arrival and leaving times.

DICTIONARY ALERTS

Whenever you are not sure of the spelling of a plural (or of any word), you should consult a dictionary. The plurals of singular nouns ending in *o*, *f*, and *fe*, for example, vary greatly. Therefore, you should memorize the plurals of commonly used words ending in *o*, *f*, and *fe*. For the others, be sure to consult a dictionary, because these plurals are tricky.

Plurals of Nouns Ending in *O*

Singular nouns ending in *o* preceded by a *vowel* form the plural by adding *s*. Some nouns ending in *o* preceded by a *consonant* form the plural by adding *s;* others, by adding *es*. Do not guess at the correct spelling of the plural of a noun ending in *o* when that *o* is preceded by a consonant; look it up in a dictionary.

It is interesting to note that nouns that relate to music and end in *o* always form their plurals by adding *s;* for example, *piano, pianos; alto, altos; oratorio, oratorios.*

Some examples of plurals of nouns ending in o are given below. Make a habit of consulting a dictionary to determine the correct plurals of nouns ending in o.

Final o preceded by a vowel:

studio	studios	cameo	cameos
folio	folios	ratio	ratios

Final o preceded by a consonant, adding s for the plural:

domino	dominos	zero	zeros
dynamo	dynamos	lasso	lassos
tobacco	tobaccos	albino	albinos

Final o preceded by a consonant, adding es for the plural:

mosquito	mosquitoes	cargo	cargoes
potato	potatoes	echo	echoes
motto	mottoes	hero	heroes
volcano	volcanoes	veto	vetoes

Plurals of Nouns Ending in *F* or *FE*

Some nouns ending in *f* or *fe* change the *f* or *fe* to *v* and add *es* to form their plurals; others simply add *s*. The plural of a noun ending in *f* or *fe*, therefore, should be recognized as a spelling hazard. Study the following illustrations and observe that there is neither a rule nor a pattern for these plurals.

Final *f* or *fe*, changing to *v* and adding *es*:

shelf	shelves	self	selves
life	lives	knife	knives
half	halves	leaf	leaves
loaf	loaves	thief	thieves

Final *f* or *fe*, adding *s*:

handkerchief	handkerchiefs	safe	safes
plaintiff	plaintiffs	gulf	gulfs
roof	roofs	grief	griefs
belief	beliefs	chef	chefs
proof	proofs	strife	strifes
bailiff	bailiffs	chief	chiefs

☑ Checkup 3

Study the following sentences. Then correct any errors.

1. Vitamin C is available in many foods, including tomatoes.
2. Husbands and wifes of employees are covered by the new dental plan.
3. The Loomis Company manufacturers radioes and televisions.
4. During lunch hour, Ms. Farrell will play piano concertos in the auditorium.
5. We have hired several art studioes to prepare our advertising brochures.

6. We will need several shelfs to store all those books and pamphlets.
7. The United Way works to improve the lifes of people in our community.
ok 8. The cargoes that these ships carry are usually perishable items.
ok 9. The chiefs of our South American offices will speak at this afternoon's meeting.
10. The zeroes in the last column should be aligned.

PLURALS FOR CORRECT GRAMMAR

Mastering the plural forms discussed so far will improve your spelling. But mastering the following rules will help you to avoid errors in grammar. For example, when you know that the word *news* is always singular, you will never write or say "The latest news *are* interesting." When you know that *scissors* is always plural, you will never write or say "Your scissors *is* sharp."

To speak and write correctly, therefore, you must know which nouns (1) have the same form in both the singular and the plural, (2) are always singular, (3) are always plural, or (4) follow the foreign spelling in the plural form.

Always Singular

The following nouns are always singular. Be sure to use a singular verb to agree with these nouns:

statistics (science)	molasses	economics (science)	milk
mathematics	civics	news	music

Always Plural

The following nouns are always plural. Use a plural verb to agree with these nouns:

statistics (facts)	auspices	premises	riches
scales (for weighing)	trousers	scissors	antics
credentials	proceeds	tidings	goods
belongings	winnings	thanks	tongs

One Form for Singular and Plural

Some nouns have only one form, a form that may be used in either a singular sense or a plural sense:

Chinese	deer	odds	sheep
cod	Japanese	politics	vermin
corps (pronounced "korz" in the plural)	moose	salmon	wheat

When modified by another number, the following nouns usually have the same form to denote either a singular or a plural number:

three *thousand* orders	four *score* years
six *hundred* chairs	two *dozen* replies

Foreign Nouns

When nouns of foreign origin were brought into use in English, both the singular and the plural forms of the nouns were usually adopted. Thus we have many singular-plural forms such as *alumnus-alumni* and *basis-bases*. Some of these foreign nouns eventually developed another plural form—a plural that was formed by adding *s* or *es* to the singular, as most nouns in our language form their plurals. Thus for a singular noun such as *curriculum* there are two plurals, *curricula* (the original, or foreign, plural) and *curriculums*. When there is a choice between two plural forms for foreign nouns, the foreign forms are generally used in formal, technical, or scientific writing.

Many of the foreign words were taken from Greek and Latin. In Latin, some common singular and plural endings were as follows:

Singular Ending	Plural Ending
um (candelabrum)	a (candelabra)
is (thesis)	es (theses)
us (stylus)	i (styli)
a (alumna)	ae (alumnae)

Words of Greek origin like *criterion* and *phenomenon* take the plural ending *a*—*criteria, phenomena*.

Keeping singular and plural endings in mind, study the following illustrations of plurals of foreign nouns:

Singular	Foreign Plural	English Plural
addendum	addenda	
alumna	alumnae	
alumnus	alumni	
analysis	analyses	
axis	axes	
basis	bases	
crisis	crises	
criterion	criteria	criterions
curriculum	curricula	curriculums
datum	data	
formula	formulae	formulas
hypothesis	hypotheses	
index	indices	indexes
medium	media	mediums
memorandum	memoranda	memorandums
nucleus	nuclei	nucleuses
oasis	oases	
parenthesis	parentheses	
stadium	stadia	stadiums
stimulus	stimuli	
terminus	termini	terminuses
vertebra	vertebrae	vertebras

■ Twilight Zone

Data, the plural of *datum,* is now frequently used as a singular idea with a singular verb (for example, "The data *supports* our theory."). This singular usage is considered correct by many people, but some writers continue to prefer the distinction between *datum,* singular, and *data,* plural. Thus they will say, "These data *support* our theory."

☑Checkup 4

Study the following sentences. Then correct any errors.
1. Please type all the page numbers in parenthesis.
2. All the alumni is supporting the school's construction project.
3. We received nearly two thousands requests for free samples.
4. For Gordon, mathematics are the most interesting subject.
5. Both consultants provided exhaustive analysis of the problems.
6. The proceeds of our charity drive are to be given to a children's hospital.
7. We estimated that about two dozens people would attend.
8. Ms. Adams has written a book describing several crisis she experienced as a newspaper correspondent.
9. The victim's belongings was held by the police officer.
10. The President suggested several stimuluses to help check inflation.

COMMUNICATION PROJECTS

Practical Application

A. Correct any errors in the following sentences. Write *OK* if a sentence is correct.
1. According to the news bulletin, the Schultz's have sold their cosmetic firm for a record sum.
2. In a federal park, the deers, as well as all the other animals, are protected from hunters.
3. Three of our corporate attornies are assigned to the lawsuit.
4. When we called Mrs. Kelly, she confirmed that all the Kellies will be at the reception.
5. Which one of the Fitchs did you speak with, Anna or Mark?
6. The Caravelle Company manufactures several thousands kinds of home products.
7. These machines have large knifes that cut the paper after it has been folded.
8. Many communitys have protested the new regulation.
9. The Joneses, who have managed the firm for three generations, have sold their stock to a conglomerate.
10. Emerson and Moore are noted designers of churchs throughout the country.
11. The district manager reorganized the territorys of three sales representatives.
12. Are there any news about the truckers' strike?
13. This storeroom is specially built to prevent vermins from reaching the food.
14. The goods that the manufacturer delivered was damaged.

15. The press release from Armor Publishing Company announced the promotion of two editors in chief.
16. The bidding for the construction of the new facilitys will begin next Monday, June 19.
17. Perhaps the Mrs. Wallaces will join the committee.
18. Salary schedules were discussed in detail at the meeting of personnel managers.
19. With the help of her daughters-in-law, Mrs. Godfrey is compiling a book of famous mottoes.
20. This reference has two main indices—an alphabetical index and a chronological index.

B. Correct any errors in the following sentences. Write *OK* if a sentence is correct.
1. In the front row was seated Ms. Barnes, the president of our company, and Mr. MacDougle, a senior vice president.
2. The mock-up model of the engine was lain on the table for all to inspect.
3. By March 1987, we will have payed the entire mortgage on our store.
4. We expect to have all the costs estimated and approved before the Anderson's return from the West Coast.
5. Please ask Jeffrey to help us sit this overhead projector on the conference room table.
6. Since January we have been lying plans for next year's budget.
7. Most of our magazines are aimed at a special market—namely, at woman between the ages of 18 and 49.
8. According to the Internal Revenue Service, winnings of any kind is taxable.
9. She wishes that she was able to attend the opening-day celebration, but she has other commitments.
10. Andrew Gibson been in charge of our Miami office since 1979.
11. The value of the stock has rised from $11 a share to $18 a share in just a few months.
12. The annual premiums have been raised; therefore, we must notify the Davis's immediately.
13. Do you think that Ms. Purdue known about the merger plans?
14. On Herman's desk is the inventory reports that you will need.
15. After she had spoke to us about the price increases, she spoke to the marketing manager.

Editing Practice

As a Matter of Fact . . . Writers and typists must check their work not only for spelling and grammatical errors but also for inconsistencies and contradictions of facts within the copy. Read the following statements to find any inconsistencies. Write *OK* if a statement has no inconsistencies.

1. Because Mrs. Hanson insisted that she had paid her bill, we double-checked our records. We found that Mr. Hanson was indeed correct.
2. The bill for the merchandise was $100 plus a $10 delivery charge. Therefore, we sent the supplier a check for $101.

3. We are temporarily out of stock on model 19-A432. May we substitute model 19-A432 instead?

4. Miss Anne B. Kingsley is our supervisor. Perhaps Anna will be able to answer your questions.

5. Ace Furniture Corporation has supplied all our office furniture for years. Thus, we highly recommend Acme Furniture for quality products.

Homonyms, Anyone? Correct any homonyms (or pseudohomonyms) that are misused in the following excerpt. (Before you begin, make sure you know what a *homonym* is.)

> To settle the dispute, we decided to meat with the supplier to discuss the costs. After several hours of negotiations, all of us finally agreed to a fare settlement, which the supplier excepted in full payment.

Case Problem

The Correspondence Consultant You have been hired by Kingston, Inc., to study its correspondence and to make recommendations for improving letters written by its personnel. List the details of the preliminary planning that would be necessary to do a top job.

10
NOUNS AND PRONOUNS: POSSESSIVE FORMS

Many of the most common—and the most easily noticeable—errors in writing are errors in using possessives. Often, the problem lies in the use of the apostrophe with possessive forms. As you'll see in this lesson, there are easy ways to master the use of possessive nouns and pronouns. The principles are few, so study them and practice them in the exercises provided.

BASIC USE OF THE APOSTROPHE

To immediately solve half the problems of using possessives, remember this: An apostrophe is *always* used with a noun to show possession, but an apostrophe is *never* used with a personal pronoun to show possession.

To show possession, the apostrophe is used with nouns as follows: *members' votes* (the votes of the members), *women's fashions* (fashions for women), and *the customer's decision* (the decision of the customer).

Follow these three rules in using apostrophes with nouns to show possession:

1. For a noun that does not end in s, add an apostrophe plus s.
   The *man's* suggestion was excellent.
   The *men's* suggestions were excellent. (Because neither *man* nor *men* ends in s, add an apostrophe plus s to show possession.
   This rule applies to all nouns—singular or plural—that do not end in s.)
2. For a plural noun that does end in s, add only the apostrophe.
   The *executives'* conference room is on the twenty-ninth floor.
   Ladies' coats and jackets are on sale this week.
   They need two *weeks'* time to complete the brochure.
   The *Joneses'* mortgage was approved by our mortgage department.
3. For a singular noun ending in s, add an apostrophe plus s if the possessive form is pronounced with an added syllable.
   The *witness's* statement was easily corroborated.
   His *boss's* approval is required. (The possessive *boss's* has one more syllable than *boss*, just as *witness's* has one more syllable than *witness*. Therefore, an apostrophe plus s must be added to each noun.)
4. For a singular noun ending in s, add only the apostrophe if the possessive form is pronounced *without* an added syllable. (This applies mostly to proper names that would sound awkward with the extra syllable.)
   Mr. *Hastings'* payment is due on the 15th. (The pronunciation of *Hastings's* would be awkward.)

Occasionally, writers place the apostrophe (or the apostrophe plus s) on the wrong word. Study the following memory hook to make sure that you can always identify the ownership word.

■ Memory Hook

Remember that the possessive word always precedes the object of possession.

> the *manager's* request (the request of the manager)
> my *assistant's* briefcase (the briefcase belonging to my assistant)
> a *customer's* complaint (a complaint of a customer)

By changing the phrase using *of* or *belonging to*, you can accurately identify the ownership word. In the above examples, the objects of ownership are *request*, *briefcase*, and *complaint*. In each case, then, the word before the object is the possessive word—the word that gets the apostrophe plus s: *manager's*, *assistant's*, and *customer's*.

Now let's look at a few more examples.

> All *secretaries'* salaries are being raised 7.5 percent. (Salaries of secretaries. Because *secretaries* is a plural that ends in s, only an apostrophe is added.)
> Our firm manufactures *children's* apparel. (Apparel for, or belonging to, children. Because *children* doesn't end in s, an apostrophe and s are added.)

Note: In official names of organizations, the apostrophe is generally omitted: *Lions*

Club, *Teachers College,* and so on. However, words that end in *men* still retain the apostrophe: *the McGraw-Hill Women's Club.*

☑Checkup 1

Add apostrophes as needed in the following sentences.
1. This free booklet gives valuable information on women's nutritional needs.
2. Are all members' recommendations included in this report?
3. Our representatives' cars are leased; they are not owned by the company.
4. Several applicants' résumés were received in the mail this morning.
5. Are you sure that Ms. Jacobson's flight is scheduled to arrive at 7:15 p.m.?

Now correct any errors in the use of possessives in the following sentences. Write *OK* if a sentence has no error.
6. Do you know when Karen's assistant will return from vacation?
7. Andrew left our company to manage his mother's business.
8. If Mr. Martin's analysis is correct, our sales will increase dramatically in the next few years.
9. Have you asked Mrs. Riley's' secretary for a duplicate of the government report?
10. Morton, who is a professional writer, is now working on a famous actress' biography.

ADDITIONAL USES OF THE APOSTROPHE

The basic rules for using the apostrophe, the rules just studied, apply to most of the possessives that you will write. The following rules cover additional uses of the apostrophe to show possession.

Possessive of a Compound Noun

To form the possessive of a compound noun, add an apostrophe plus *s* to the last word in the compound. However, if the last word in the compound ends in *s*, add only the apostrophe.

> His *sisters-in-law's* clothing store is a very successful business. (Store belonging to his sisters-in-law. *Law,* the last word, does not end in *s.*)
> Are you planning to borrow *someone else's* car for the trip? (Car belonging to someone else. *Else* does not end in *s.*)
> Both *assistant district attorneys'* offices are on the nineteenth floor. (Offices belonging to both assistant district attorneys. *Attorneys,* the last word, does end in *s.*)

Joint Ownership or Separate Ownership

To show *joint ownership,* add the apostrophe (or the apostrophe plus *s*) to the last part of the compound.

Mark and Owen's father is a janitor in our office building. (The father of Mark and Owen. Note the singular noun *father* and the singular verb *is.*)
Ralph and Sarah's appliance store is on First Avenue. (Appliance store belonging to Ralph and Sarah. Note the singular noun *store* and the singular verb *is.*)

To indicate *separate ownership,* add the apostrophe (or the apostrophe plus *s*) to each part of the compound.

Ralph's and Sarah's appliance stores are on First Avenue and Tenth Avenue, respectively. (The appliance store belonging to Ralph and the appliance store belonging to Sarah. Note the plural noun *stores* and the plural verb *are.*)
Mark's and Owen's fathers are janitors in our office building. (The father of Mark and the father of Owen. Note the plural noun *fathers* and the plural verb *are.*)

Possessive Case Before a Gerund

A *gerund* is a verb form that ends in *ing* and is used as a noun. For example: "*Proofreading* this long report is very tedious." "*Designing* the prototype is Howard's assignment." A noun or pronoun that precedes a gerund must be in the possessive case **(Reason:** because the gerund is the object of ownership).

All of us enjoyed *your* joining us for dinner. (Possessive *your*—not *you*— before the gerund *joining.*)
We were not aware of *Ingrid's* leaving early. (Possessive *Ingrid's*—not *Ingrid*— before the gerund *leaving.*)

Appositive Showing Possession

An *appositive* is a word or a group of words that explains or gives additional information about the word or phrase that comes before the appositive. When a noun that would ordinarily be in the possessive case is followed by an appositive, note that the *appositive* must then be in the possessive case.

Apparently, this is Mrs. Hess, our *supervisor's,* calculator. (Note that *supervisor,* not *Hess,* is made possessive.)

☑ Checkup 2

Correct any errors in the use of possessives in the following sentences. Write *OK* if a sentence has no error.
1. Christine and David's wedding is scheduled for next March 13.
2. Ms. Donne insisted on us checking the figures a second time.
3. Obviously, the two vice presidents reports are confidential.
4. Raising the price was somebody else' suggestion, not mine.
5. Fred's and Rosemary's daughter is attending law school.

6. We are having a party to celebrate our fathers-in-laws's retirement; they will both retire next month.
7. She certainly appreciated him *his* sending her a check for the full amount.
8. Roberta's and Kenneth's new apartment is on Riverside Drive.
9. As you probably know, Ellen and Tony's jobs are quite different.
OK 10. Vincent's helping us to complete the project was surely a nice gesture.

POSSESSIVE FORMS OF PERSONAL PRONOUNS

The possessives of personal pronouns are *never* formed with apostrophes. As you will see in the following list, none of the possessive personal pronouns has an apostrophe:

Personal Pronouns	Possessive Forms
I; we	my, mine; our, ours
you	your, yours
he; she; it; they	his; her, hers; its; their, theirs

Now study the following example sentences:

Joan asked *her* secretary to make reservations for Friday. (*Her* is a possessive personal pronoun—no apostrophe.)

This calculator is *ours*; that one is *theirs*. (*Ours* and *theirs*, both possessive personal pronouns, are never written with apostrophes.)

May I please use *your* typewriter? *Mine* is being repaired. (*Your* and *mine* are possessive personal pronouns; neither one has an apostrophe.)

Problems in Choosing the Correct Possessive Form

The possessive forms above are easy to understand, but their use sometimes becomes confusing because of their similarity to other words. Study the following homonyms to make sure that you will always use possessive pronouns correctly.

Its The possessive pronoun *its* means "belonging to it" or "of it," as in "This calculator is inexpensive, but *its* printout is too small to read." This possessive *its* is sometimes confused with the contraction *it's*, which means "it is."

It's surprising to hear that Freemont's has closed *its* largest store. (*It is* surprising . . . store belonging to it.)

Their The possessive form *their* is pronounced exactly like *there* and *they're*, so you can see why some people may confuse these three spellings. *They're* (like *it's*) is a contraction; it means "*they are*." *There* (see the word *here*?) identifies a place. And *their*, of course, is the possessive of *they*, and it means "belonging to them."

They're ready to begin *their* conference. (*They are* ready . . . the conference belonging to them.)

We should be there no later than 4:30 p.m. (*There* is an adverb that indicates a place; it answers the question Where? *There*.)

Theirs The possessive *theirs* and the contraction *there's* are pronounced the same. *There's* means "there is" or "there has," and *theirs,* of course, means "belonging to them."

> *There's* the folder we've been long looking for. (There is . . . .)
> Is this equipment *theirs*? (Equipment belonging to them.)

Your *Your,* a possessive pronoun, is pronounced exactly the same as *you're,* the contraction meaning "you are."

> As soon as *you're* ready, we'll begin working on *your* project. (As soon as *you are* ready, we will begin the project belonging to you.)

Our Clearly enunciated, the possessive *our* and the "being" verb *are* do not sound the same. Some people, however, incorrectly pronounce *our* as if it were *are.*

> *Our* supervisor and *our* manager *are* now planning budgets for next year.

Whose *Whose,* a possessive pronoun, should not be confused with the contraction *who's* meaning "who is" or "who has."

> *Who's* the person *whose* telephone must be repaired? (*Who* is . . . telephone belonging to *whom.*)

✓Checkup 3

Correct any errors in the following sentences. Write *OK* if a sentence has no error.
1. Because ~~there~~ *their* early, we will start the meeting at 2:30.
2. Do you know ~~who's~~ *whose* briefcase this is, Gregory?
OK 3. As Miss Finch explained, it's certainly worthwhile teaching consumers to make wise choices.
4. Sean and Tara said that we should let them know whenever we need ~~there~~ *their* help.
5. We cannot make the seating arrangements until we know whose planning to attend.
6. I am positive that this table is ours; therefore, that one must be there's.
7. She said that she will be at the airport by 8:15 a.m. and that she will meet us there.
8. I like this room because it's large and because its ceiling is high.
OK 9. Who's at the reception desk this morning, James or Marcia? ~~Whose~~
10. Theirs only one problem: ~~Who's~~ *Whose* going to pay for this?

COMMUNICATION PROJECTS

Practical Application
A. Correct any errors in the following sentences. Write *OK* if a sentence has no error.
1. Miss Carter's' promotion to vice president was no surprise.
2. We had already heard about ~~him~~ *his* rejecting the union's demands.
3. This machine is very expensive, but it's efficiency makes the price reasonable.
OK 4. While Edna is on vacation, whose going to handle the invoices?

5. Linda and Evelyn's husbands work for the same company.
6. Does the bookstore across the street have a childrens' section?
7. Will anyone's else secretary be on vacation next week?
8. As you know, their is very little difference between these two products.
9. Does anyone else know about you working part-time for another company?
10. Please let me know whether your interested in more information on this pump.
11. Ms. DeWitt's and Mr. Grasso's importing business is very successful.
12. She said, "Of course its possible to beat inflation, but all of us must work hard to do so."
13. Mr. Schultz's attorney will meet with us tomorrow afternoon.
14. Phyllis and Mike Bass will be married next month; we plan to have the Bass's office party on March 29.
15. The manager agreed that the womans' complaint was justified.
16. Each employees' bonus depends on his or her salary.
17. Mrs. Dartmouth, whose an excellent training director, will teach the course personally.
18. Did you know that the Joneses' daughters are CPAs?
19. My companys' medical benefits cover all employees and their families.
20. Each account executives' report must be signed and dated before it is submitted.

B. Correct any errors in the following sentences. Write *OK* if a sentence has no error.

1. Although Sara and Gregg Black are now out of town, we expect the Black's to return in time for the convention.
2. From my office I could clearly hear the mens' voices.
3. The reason for all the postponements is that Miss Anton is in the hospital.
4. We expect to complete the project within four weeks time.
5. When you went to my office, did you see whether any messages were laying on my desk?
6. Olsen & Johnson is a well-known manufacturer of boy's clothing.
7. As you can see, the Davis's are eager to sell their property.
8. Because there are three James Kelly's in our company, the telephone operators often have difficulty.
9. At yesterdays' meeting, we laid the strategy for our negotiations.
10. Is there an extra chair in anyone elses office?
11. All of us appreciated Jack helping us to proofread the annual report.
12. The actress's role was demanding—very demanding.
13. Ms. Halston said that she been to California a number of times.
14. As soon as the bell had rang, we left the room.
15. The Misses York, two of our sales representatives, are not related to each other.
16. The judge ordered that the company's assets be froze immediately.
17. Mr. Torino and Mr. Klein's attitudes toward the proposed sales plan were entirely different.
18. We will probably need about two dozen more chairs.
19. The members agreed that Miss Mendoza's credentials is impressive.
20. The only analysis that made sense was yours.

Editing Practice

Call an Editor!   Read the following excerpt from a memorandum. Then edit it to make the necessary corrections.

> After you and I had spoke about us including an article on nutrition in our September issue of *Consumers' World*, I asked Frances and Albert Castro to develop a 10,000-word article. The Castro's, as you know, are noted nutritionists, and they have wrote an excellent article. I have enclosed two copys for you.
> Because I know that your eager to meat the Castro's, I know that you'll be pleased to here that their coming to our office next Wednesday morning.

The Word Processing Supervisor   The following paragraph is part of a report that was submitted to you by one of the employees in your department. Read the paragraph to correct any spelling errors that you may find.

> We have enclosed sevral photoes that we recomend for our magazine advertizements and for our special sails promotion brochures.
> Because these photoes emphasize childrens' satisfaction with our products, they should be especially usefull.

Case Problem

The Correspondence Consultant   In Section 9, you outlined your preliminary plan for improving letters written by the personnel of Kingston, Inc. One phase of that plan was to study samples of letters currently being written. What are some of the weaknesses you expect to find?

11 PRONOUNS: NOMINATIVE AND OBJECTIVE FORMS

There was a time, not too long ago, when many top business executives proudly proclaimed themselves "self-made" successes—men and women who, despite little or no formal education, achieved great success in business.

Today's top business executives are men and women whose backgrounds may vary greatly, but almost all have had a formal education. More than ever, therefore, the modern business worker must write correctly, because errors in his or her communications will surely be noticed.

One of the ways in which you will be sure to eliminate some common, irritating errors from your letters and memos is to master the use of pronoun case forms. A business worker who must write often—and most business workers do—must choose correct pronouns expertly, so pay special attention to the following section.

CASE FORMS FOR PRONOUNS

Nouns and pronouns have three case forms: nominative, objective, and possessive. You have already studied possessive forms of nouns and pronouns, so we must concentrate here only on nominative and objective forms.

For nouns, nominative and objective forms are the same; we cannot make a mistake in their use. Therefore, as you will see, the only other case forms that you must study are the following nominative and objective pronoun forms:

Nominative:	I	he	she	we	they	who
Objective:	me	him	her	us	them	whom

Learn which are the nominative forms and which are the objective forms, and you will have no difficulty in selecting the correct pronoun quickly and accurately every time.

NOMINATIVE CASE

Only these three rules are needed to use the nominative forms of pronouns correctly.

Subject of a Verb *I, HE, She, WE, THEY, who.*

All pronouns that are subjects of verbs must be in the nominative case:

> *I* will leave at 3:30 p.m. promptly. (Why not "*Me* will leave . . . ."? Because the nominative form *I* must be the subject of the verb *will leave.*)
>
> *He* and Beverly are planning the banquet. (Not "*Him* and Beverly are planning . . . ." *He* is correct because it is part of the compound subject *He and Beverly.*)
>
> Lorraine does not know *who* has the October sales report. (*Who* is the subject of the verb *has*; thus the nominative form *who* is correct.)

Predicate Nominative

A *predicate nominative* is a noun or a pronoun that completes the meaning of a "being" verb. The "being" verbs, as you know, are *am, is, are, was, were,* helper *be,* and helper(s) *been.* Any pronoun that follows and completes the meaning of any one of these "being" verbs must always be in the nominative case.

> It must have been (they? them?) who ordered these pamphlets. (*Must have been* is a "being" verb, because the main verb is *been.* Thus the nominative case *they* is correct.)
>
> If I were (she? her?), I would report the error to Mrs. Franklin immediately. (*Were* is a "being" verb. A pronoun that completes the meaning of a "being" verb must be in the nominative case. Thus *she* is correct.)

Complement of the Infinitive *To Be*

Any pronoun that follows and completes the meaning of the infinitive *to be* when *to be* has no subject of its own is in the nominative case. To apply this rule correctly, you must understand that (1) the rule applies only to the infinitive *to be* and must not be used in any other situation, and (2) the infinitive *to be* has a subject of its own only if a noun or a pronoun immediately precedes it.

Study the following illustrations. In each example, note the reason for choosing the correct pronoun.

> Have you ever wished to be (she? her?)? (As soon as you see *to be*, look for a noun or pronoun directly before it. Is there a noun or pronoun before it? No. Then *to be* has no subject of its own in this sentence, and the nominative pronoun *she* is correct.)
>
> When she picked up the phone, Carolyn thought Richard to be (I? me?). (Is there a noun or pronoun directly before *to be*? Yes—*Richard*. Then *Richard* is the subject of *to be*, and the objective *me* is correct.)
>
> The customer thought the clerks to be (we? us?). (Is there a noun or pronoun directly before *to be*? Yes—*clerks*. Then *clerks* is the subject of *to be*, and the objective form *us* must follow *to be*.)

■ Memory Hook

For a Memory Hook on which to hang the *to be* rule, make this connection:

> NO subject—NOminative case

NO is the word to remember, and *NO* starts the word *NOminative*. Hooking up the two *Nos* results in immediate, correct application of the rule.

☑ Checkup 1

Correct any errors in the use of pronouns. Write *OK* if a sentence has no error. (Be prepared to give your reason for each nominative-case choice only.)

1. The most successful sales representatives are them who plan their time carefully.
2. If you were me, Betty, would you include a return card with this letter?
3. Our manager, Ms. Purefoy, is often taken to be her.
4. Did Mr. DiMaggio say that it must be me who signs these vouchers?
5. Who knows the latest election results?
6. No, I wouldn't want to be him.
7. Whenever a caller asks for you, you should answer "This is her."
8. Mrs. LoPinto and Miss Goode look very alike—in fact, Mrs. LoPinto is often thought to be her.
9. I am not certain whom has the key to the audiovisual room.
10. As you probably heard, Mr. Emery thought my brother to be I.

OBJECTIVE-CASE FORMS OF PRONOUNS

If you know when the nominative-case forms are correct, you will know that the objective-case forms are correct in all other situations. However, you will apply all the pronoun case rules with greater understanding if you know the following principles for using the objective-case forms.

Use the objective-case forms *me, us, him, her, them,* and *whom* when they are:

1. Objects of verbs, prepositions, or infinitives.

   Dr. Perez gave *us* a free copy of the book. (*Us* is the object of the verb *gave.*)
   Unfortunately, we cannot extend credit to *them* any longer. (*Them* is the object of the preposition *to.*)
   Mrs. Mantle should be able to hire *him* in January. (*Him* is the object of the infinitive *to hire.*)

2. Subjects of infinitives.

   We expected *them* to arrive early. (*Them* is the subject of the infinitive *to arrive.*)

3. Complements of the infinitive *to be* when *to be* has a subject of its own.

   The police were wrong in suspecting the thief to be *him.* (Note that *to be* has its own subject, *thief.* Thus *him* is the complement of *to be.*)

SPECIAL PRONOUN CASE PROBLEMS

There are a few special usage problems concerning pronouns, and these problems deserve special attention. Master the uses of pronouns in the three situations described below. Then, in the next section, you will study the last pronoun-usage problems.

Gregg and I or *Gregg and Me?*

Compound subjects or compound objects are nouns or pronouns joined by *and* or *or.*

Gregg and *I* gave . . .	. . . for Gregg and *me*
Miss Loo or *he* has . . .	. . . hired Miss Loo or *him*
she and *I* will bring . . .	. . . invited *her* and *me*
Kevin and *he* have written . . .	. . . written by Kevin and *him*
you and *she* know . . .	. . . between you and *her*

The compound subjects in the left-hand column are all subjects of verbs. The compound objects in the right-hand column are all objects either of prepositions or of verbs. Errors often arise in choosing the pronouns in such compounds. When is it "Gregg and *I*," and when is it "Gregg and *me*"? The following Memory Hook will help you decide.

■ Memory Hook

To choose the correct pronoun in a compound subject or object, simply omit everything in the compound except the pronoun. Then say the sentence aloud, and the correct answer will be obvious.

Dr. Chin and (I? me?) will arrive at 8:30 p.m. (By omitting *Dr. Chin and,* the answer becomes obvious: "*I* will arrive at 8:30 p.m.," not "*Me* will arrive at 8:30 p.m.")

Please make reservations for Ms. Baranski and (I? me?). (Again, omit *Ms. Baranski and,* and the answer becomes obvious: "Please make reservations for . . . *me.*")

They reserved two rooms for Mr. Flanagan and (I? me?). (Omit *Mr. Flanagan and:* "They reserved two rooms for . . . *me.*")

We Translators or *Us Translators*?

Writers and speakers who must choose between *we translators* and *us translators, we interviewers* and *us interviewers,* and *we technicians* and *us technicians* frequently find the choice confusing. Yet the choice is very simple! Read the following Memory Hook.

■ Memory Hook

To make the correct pronoun choice in expressions such as *we translators* and *us translators* (called "restrictive appositives"), simply omit the noun and use the pronoun alone. You will quickly see which pronoun is correct.

> (We? Us?) translators have our offices on the fourth floor. (When you omit the noun *translators,* you readily see that *We* is correct: "*We* . . . have our offices on the fourth floor." *We* is the subject of the verb *have.*)
>
> The judge asked (we? us?) translators for our opinions. (Again, omit *translators,* and the correct pronoun becomes obvious: "The judge asked *us* . . . for our opinions." *Us* is the object of the verb *asked.*)

✓ Checkup 2

The following sentences will test your mastery of the Memory Hooks that were just presented. Correct any errors in the use of pronouns. Write *OK* if a sentence has no error. (Whenever you choose a nominative pronoun, quote the rule for making your choice.)

1. Perhaps it was us who quoted the wrong price.
2. Please be sure to let Henry or I know what time the conference will start.
3. I agree that us managers should establish our own expense budgets.
4. Was that Scott or he in Mrs. Cofsky's office?
5. Only us technicians are permitted to handle these X-ray machines.
6. Would you like we auditors to help you complete the project?
7. She is confident that Laurel or her will be nominated.
8. Is there a chance that it was her?
9. Yes, you should have asked Ms. Pembroke or I before you proceeded.
10. The announcement was sent to only two of we supervisors.

Than I or Than Me?

The words *than* and *as* are often used in comparisons, such as "Clark has more experience than (I? me?)." Because the words following *than* or *as* usually represent an incomplete clause, you must complete the clause to find the correct pronoun: "Clark has more experience than I *(have experience)*." By completing the clause, you readily see that *I* is correct because it is the subject of the understood verb *have*. Thus the sentence should be "Clark has more experience than *I*." Here is another example: "These delays bother Mary Jo as much as (I? me?)." Again, complete the clause: "These delays bother Mary Jo as much as *(they bother) me*."

Beware: Sometimes either choice can make sense. "Mr. Jacobs is as impressed with Miss Gleason as (I? me?)." Two meanings are possible: (1) "Mr. Jacobs is as impressed with Miss Gleason as *(he is impressed with) me*," or (2) "Mr. Jacobs is as impressed with Miss Gleason as *I (am impressed with Miss Gleason)*." Either can make sense; the writer must be careful, then, to choose the correct pronoun.

☑ Checkup 3

Correct any errors in the use of pronouns. Write *OK* if a sentence has no error. (Whenever you choose a nominative pronoun, quote the rule for making your choice.)

1. Dr. Levesque works much faster than me.
2. She surprised we assistants by her decision.
3. None of we employees favors the merger.
4. Apparently, either Ms. Hildegard or him has given permission to proceed with the survey.
5. Do you think that Ross or me should reschedule next week's roundtable discussion?
6. I am convinced that Allison is a better sales representative than him.
7. As you can see, either Peter or me will have to give the presentation in Ms. Greco's absence.
8. Over the years, Shelley has brought in more new accounts than I.
9. When you meet with Ms. Paige and he, be ready to discuss current sales.
10. Most of the speakers were obviously not as well prepared as her.

COMMUNICATION PROJECTS

Practical Application

A. Correct any errors in the following sentences. Write *OK* if a sentence has no error. Whenever you select a nominative-case pronoun, give the reason for your selection by labeling your answer as follows: *sov* (subject of the verb), *pn* (predicate nominative), or *tbns* (to be—no subject of its own).

1. They should let us designers attend the monthly production meetings.
2. Are you now convinced that Eleanor is more creative than him?

3. Do you think that the account executive for this client is her? *she*
4. Dr. Perrin scheduled us men for appointments next Thursday.
5. Was it Daniel who wrote this press release, or was it her? *she*
6. No one believes that us women have finally lost a game! *we*
7. Both interviewers said that Annette shows greater potential than him. *he*
8. At a glance, I mistakenly thought your assistant to be she. *her*
9. He canceled the reservations for Ms. Wysocki and I. *me*
10. It was probably him whom you saw in the lobby. *he*
11. All us full-time employees are enrolled in the company's medical and dental plans. *we*
12. The vice president asked us women to explore the potential of this new market. *we*
13. Ask Katherine or he to explain the new bonus plan at Monday's meeting. *him*
14. Unfortunately, both the shift supervisor and me were out of the room when the machine malfunctioned. *I*
15. The head of the department complimented we committee members for our efforts to improve safety procedures. *us*
16. All of us admit that Roy writes better than us. *we*
17. They are both attorneys, but his sister is more widely known than him. *he*
18. Sometimes her and Albert argue needlessly over politics. *she*
19. Mrs. Deane said, "I would like to invite you and he to the dinner honoring Professor Pierce." *him*
20. For a moment, I thought the women on the elevator to be Elizabeth and she. *her*

B. Correct any errors in the following sentences. Write *OK* if a sentence has no error.

1. Ask William to double-check the Joneses' credit rating before he replies to their request.
2. The photographer submitted color prooves from which we selected the photos for the brochure. *proofs*
3. Is it true that us secretaries will receive a cost-of-living increase retroactive to January 1? *we*
4. Do you know whether the Ellis's are still in Phoenix?
5. Both of Mr. Martins contracts have been sent to the legal department.
6. If he were I, he would surely view the situation more objectively.
7. As soon as there ready to discuss the specifications, they should call the production manager.
8. Yes, Francine is planning to take her assistant and I to Las Vegas for the annual sales conference.
9. In your opinion, can Allen handle this assignment as well as she? *OK*
10. Ms. Delaney and us other store managers suggested curtailing our hours on weekends. *we*
11. The designers are now lying plans for the fall fashions.
12. Us auditors agreed that the bank manager was not to blame for the error. *We*
13. Has Mrs. Helms been a vice president as long as him?
14. Please ask Miss Cumberland whether this new cabinet is our's.
15. Her or Marvin will coordinate the press conference.

16. Each employees' wife or husband is fully covered under this new policy.
17. Are you certain that it was her who wrote the script for this commercial?
18. If Mr. Speers and her approve our hiring part-time help, we will complete the project well ahead of schedule.
19. After Ms. Sterne had spoke she answered many questions from the audience.
20. I suspected that the client was she, but I was not certain.

Editing Practice

Plurals and Possessives   Correct any error in the use of plurals or possessives. Write OK if a sentence has no error.

1. The vice presidents' offices are on the sixth floor.
2. The committee rejected Steven's proposal, but it accepted her's.
3. Whenever there prepared to discuss the schedule, they should call Suzanne, our production manager.
4. No, the Barneses have not yet sold their chain of stores.
5. Mr. Trachman often complains about the tax's that he pays to federal, state, and local governments.
6. Ms. Vernon buying lunch for us was a very thoughtful gesture.
7. As Nancy said during the session, "This ad is eye-catching, but it's message is too vague."
8. Both of our supervisors' recommended that we have a third shift starting at midnight.
9. Mrs. DeCamp and her daughter-in-laws opened two new women's clothing stores.
10. Of all the departments in the company, our's received the highest rating.

Proofreading for Spelling Errors   The person who typed the following memo misspelled one word. Can you find that word?

The attached sheet itemizes the estimated costs for reprinting some of our promotional brochures. As you will see, the printer offered us a special price for reprinting all the brochures during his slow business season (July and August). Because we can save aproximately $500 for brochures that we must reprint anyway, I suggest that we take advantage of this special offer.

aproximately

Case Problem

The Correspondence Consultant   Now that you have completed your study of the letters written by the staff of Kingston, Inc., you should be ready to make recommendations for improvement. What are your recommendations?

AM, ARE, IS, WERE, WAS BEING
BE, BEING, BEEN VERBS

12 PRONOUNS: ADDITIONAL USAGE PROBLEMS

The preceding section has prepared you to use *who* and *whom* correctly. *Who* is nominative case, and *whom* is objective case, and you have already mastered the uses of the nominative and objective cases. Therefore, as you complete this section, you will find that the once puzzling problem of choosing between *who* and *whom* will be a very simple choice—not at all puzzling.

Another stumbling block in using pronouns is the correct use of *myself*, *yourself*, and other pronouns that end in *self*. As you see, this is a minor problem; it will never trip you once you are aware of the simple rule governing the use of *self* pronouns.

SELF-ENDING PRONOUNS

The *self*-ending pronouns are *myself*, *yourself*, *himself*, *herself*, *itself*, *ourselves*, *yourselves*, and *themselves*. When used correctly, these pronouns serve two functions: (1) to emphasize or intensify the use of a noun or another pronoun or (2) to refer to a noun or pronoun that has already been named in a sentence (called "reflexive use").

Intensive Use

Self-ending pronouns can provide needed emphasis in statements such as these:

> Mrs. Rader *herself* told me the news. (Much more emphatic than "Mrs. Rader told me the news.")
> I asked Mr. Alexis *himself* to confirm the reports. (Much more emphatic than "I asked Mr. Alexis to confirm the reports.")

Reflexive Use

The second use of *self*-ending pronouns is to refer to a noun or pronoun that has already been named in the sentence.

> The legislators voted *themselves* another salary increase!
> Mrs. Rosen had forgotten to include *herself* in the total count.

Errors in the Use of Self-Ending Pronouns

Now that you have seen how *self*-ending pronouns should be used, note how they are commonly *misused*:

> When I asked the janitor for his advice, he said that he prefers spray-painting himself. (*Spray-painting himself* is probably not what the man prefers. The sen-

tence should be "When I asked the janitor for his advice, he said that he *himself* prefers spray-painting.")

Larry Naldi and *myself* will be available if you should have any problems. (To whom does *myself* refer? A *self*-ending pronoun must always have a clear antecedent—someone to whom it refers. This sentence should be: "Larry Naldi and *I* will . . .")

As you can see, then, you will always use *self*-ending pronouns correctly if you make sure that each has a clear antecedent within the sentence and that each is positioned correctly within the sentence.

CHOOSING PRONOUNS IN APPOSITIVES

An *appositive* is a restatement—a group of words used to explain a word or a phrase or to give more information about that word or phrase. Note the following appositives (in *italics*):

Two vice presidents, *Mrs. Garcia and Mr. Hamilton*, will speak at the luncheon tomorrow.

We asked our West Coast representatives, *Allen Dale and Betty Jo Tunney*, to give us their opinions.

Anna Compo, *a senior vice president of our firm*, has been named to the board of directors.

In each case, the appositive is a restatement of the word or words that immediately precede it. (Note the use of commas before and after the appositives. The commas are needed because these appositives are *nonrestrictive*; they give extra information.)

Appositives cause problems mainly when they include a compound containing a pronoun. Which case should the pronoun be?

Two vice presidents, Mrs. Garcia and (he? him?), will speak at the luncheon tomorrow.

We asked our West Coast representatives, Allen Dale and (she? her?), to give us their opinions.

■ Memory Hook

To choose the correct pronoun in compounds such as those above, follow this procedure:

Two vice presidents, Mrs. Garcia and (he? him?), will speak at the luncheon tomorrow. (Drop the words that the appositive renames and you will get: "Mrs. Garcia and (he? him?) will speak at the luncheon tomorrow." Then drop *Mrs. Garcia and* (as you learned in the Memory Hook on pages 82 and 83) and you are left with this choice: (he? him?) will speak at the luncheon tomorrow." Obviously, *he* is correct; *he* is the subject of the verb *will speak.*

Again:

We asked our West Coast representatives, Allen Dale and (she? her?), to give us their opinions. (Drop the words that the appositive renames and you get:

"We asked Allen Dale and (she? her?) to give us their opinions." Then drop *Allen Dale and* and the correct choice is obvious: We asked (she? her?) to give us . . . ." The answer, of course, is *her*: "We asked our West Coast representatives, Allen Dale and *her*, to give us their opinions.")

☑ Checkup 1

Correct any errors in the following sentences. Write *OK* if a sentence is correct.

1. She asked two people, Kevin Smith and myself, to serve as Fire Wardens for our floor.
2. Our department supervisors, Garr Stephenson and she, have developed an audiovisual presentation to teach people how to detect consumer fraud.
3. Patricia and myself wrote an article entitled "Executive Fitness" for our company newspaper.
4. "If you wish," said Mrs. Chin, "my two assistants, Harold and her, will help you prepare the brochure."
5. Are you sure that Mrs. Hanes wants to ship herself?
6. His best sales representatives, Brenda and she, will be out for the month of June.
7. Both Ms. Dancer and myself are convinced that radio advertisements would be most cost-effective.
8. The owners of this store, Miss Stapleton and him, are considering a very high bid from a national chain.
9. The only film editors who worked on this project were Lana and myself.
10. Do you know whether our guests, Mrs. Wilson and him, will need transportation from the airport?

WHO AND WHOM; WHOEVER AND WHOMEVER

The pronouns *who* and *whoever* are nominative-case forms, and *whom* and *whomever* are objective-case forms. Therefore, use *who* and *whoever* as you would use other nominative forms—that is, as subjects of verbs and as predicate nominatives. Use *whom* and *whomever* as you would use other objective forms—as objects of verbs and objects of prepositions.

To make the correct choice easier, study the following Memory Hook.

■ Memory Hook

To test whether *who* or *whom* is correct in a sentence, substitute *he* or *him*, as shown in the following examples. When *he* can be substituted, then *who* is correct (**Reason:** both *he* and *who* are nominative forms). When *him* can be substituted, then *whom* is correct (**Reason:** both *him* and *whom* are objective forms). Study these examples.

> The engineer (who? whom?) Brian mentioned is Jonah West. (Make the substitution: *Brian mentioned (him)*. The correct pronoun is *whom because him* can be substituted.)

We don't know (who? whom?) Ms. Sills selected. (Make the substitution: *she selected (him)*. The correct pronoun is *whom* because *him* can be substituted.)
Daniel doesn't know (who? whom?) Mr. Jones is. (Make the substitution: *Mr. Jones is (he)*. The pronoun *who* is correct because *he* can be substituted.)

Who or *Whom* in Interrogative Sentences

~(QUESTION!)

Questions containing *who* or *whom* are generally in inverted order. First, change the order from inverted to normal. Then substitute *he* or *him*, as explained in the Memory Hook above.

(Who? Whom?) is the sales representative in Marshall's office? (Normal order: *The sales representative in Marshall's office is (he)*. *Who* is correct because it is a predicate nominative.)
(Who? Whom?) did they deliver the packages to? (Normal order: *They did deliver the packages to (him)*. *Whom* is correct because *him* can be substituted.)

When a question is already in normal order, simply substitute *he* or *him*.

(Who? Whom?) has been assigned to the Randolph case? (Make the substitution: *(He) has been assigned to the Randolph case*. *Who* is correct because *he* can be substituted. *Who* is the subject of the verb.)
(Whoever? Whomever?) would reject such an interesting assignment? (Make the substitution: *(He) would reject. . . . Whoever* is correct because *he* can be substituted. *Whoever* is the subject of the verb.)

✓ Checkup 2

Correct any pronoun errors. Use the Memory Hook to check your choices. Be prepared to tell why each choice is correct.
1. Do you know whom *HE* is in charge of our Paris office?
2. Whom did Ms. Rusk recommend to replace Miss Olsen?
3. Who has been named vice president of finance?
4. Who have they assigned to the task force?
5. Who, is the production manager for Duffy Plastics?

Who and *Whom* in a Dependent Clause

Most *who, whom* errors are made when *who* or *whom* is used in a dependent clause. To avoid these common errors, follow this two-step procedure carefully.
Step 1 Isolate the dependent clause, starting with the word *who, whom, whoever,* or *whomever*. The case form depends on the use of the pronoun *within that clause*.

Miss Atkinson personally trains (whoever? whomever?) she hires for the customer relations department. (Isolate the clause: *(whoever? whomever?) she hires for the customer relations department*.)

Meg doesn't realize (who? whom?) that customer is. (Isolate the clause: *(who? whom?) that customer is.*)

Step 2   If an isolated clause is in inverted order, change it to normal order. If only the *who* pronoun is before the verb, then the clause is in normal order. But if a noun or another pronoun appears before the verb (in addition to the *who* pronoun), then the clause is *not* in normal order. Let's consider the clauses that were isolated in Step 1.

(Whoever? Whomever?) she hires for the customer relations department. (The *who* pronoun plus the pronoun *she* appear before the verb *hires*. This clause, therefore, is out of order. The normal order is *she hires (him) for the customer relations department.* Thus *whomever* is correct because *him* can be substituted.)

(Who? Whom?) that customer is. (The *who* pronoun and the noun *customer* both appear before the verb *is*, so this clause is inverted. The normal order is *that customer is (he)*. *Who* is correct because it is a predicate nominative.)

☑ **Checkup 3**

Using the two-step procedure described above, select the correct *who* pronouns. Be able to justify each selection.

1. The only manager (who? whom?) I have met is Emily VanHorn.
2. (Whoever? Whomever?) drafted this media plan did an excellent job.
3. Our former supervisor, (who? whom?) is now director of marketing, recently completed her master's degree in business administration.
4. Do you know (who? whom?) the main speaker will be?
5. Assign the Weems account to (whoever? whomever) has the most experience with electronics companies.
6. Yvette Sparks, (who? whom?) we recommended for promotion, is one of the finalists for the district manager job.
7. The Energy Commission is empowered to fine (whoever? whomever?) violates the new energy-conservation policies.
8. Mark Jaderstrom, (who? whom?) we consider the finest public relations director in the country, will join our staff in May.
9. Do you know (who? whom?) Carolyn asked for permission to reprint this article?
10. The person (who? whom?) you heard on last night's news is Sharon Rodgers, vice president in charge of our London office.

Clause Within a Who Clause   Parenthetical clauses such as *I think, she says, you know,* and *we believe* sometimes interrupt a *who* clause. To choose the correct pronoun, simply omit the interrupting clause, as shown in this example:

The person (who? whom?) I think we should write to is J. D. Turner. (Step 1. Isolate the clause: *(who? whom?) I think we should write to.* Step 2. Omit the parenthetical *I think,* and put the clause in normal order: *we should write to (him). Whom* is correct because *him* can be substituted.)

Note, however, that the choice is just as simple even when the parenthetical clause is not omitted:

> I think we should write to (who? whom?). (Again, *whom* is correct because *him* can be substituted.)

☑ Checkup 4

Correct any errors, and explain each correction.

1. Mr. Elson is the supervisor whom she said will coordinate the new procedures manual.
2. In this space we'll print a picture of whoever they name as the new vice president of finance.
3. Does he know whom they will name to head the committee?
4. Mr. Ekland promoted Rowland, whom we know will be an excellent account executive.
5. Send a free sample to whoever asks for one.
6. Send a free sample to whomever you want to send one to.
7. Give this prize to whomever you think deserves it most.
8. I am one of the people whom my boss credited for meeting our sales goals.
9. All of us are waiting to hear who they selected to succeed Mrs. Bartlett.
10. Anna Lasky, whom I am sure would know how to handle these certificates of deposit, is on vacation all week.

COMMUNICATION PROJECTS

Practical Application

A. Correct any errors, and explain each correction.

1. Whom did you say she is?
2. The letter was addressed to us, Helena and myself.
3. Who does Ms. Simms want us to ask to attend the seminar?
4. The two best sales representatives are Joy and him.
5. Occasionally, Mrs. Fern asks Rosemary and myself to help with the monthly billing.
6. Where are the two speakers, Lisa and he?
7. Please ask whomever has the key to open the conference room door.
8. We asked the newest trainees, Martha and he, to attend a special session on customer relations.
9. Whom did you say is the most likely candidate?
10. The Chicago and the Denver office managers, Sharon and him, will transfer to the West Coast early next year.
11. Renata appointed Gene and myself as our company's representatives at the convention.

12. We treat all our customers fairly, but we give extra service to those whom have *[handwritten: HE or has]* been long-time customers. *[handwritten: the]*

13. Janette is the only person whom I am sure would know the price of this product. *[handwritten: her]*

14. Who is the more experienced designer, Caryl or him? *[handwritten: he]*

15. Let's ask your assistants, Mark and she, to help us complete this paperwork. *[handwritten: Him]*

16. Whomever told you that this machine is on sale was incorrect. *[handwritten: HE]*

17. Either of my assistants, Susan or he, can help you operate this machine. *[handwritten: him]*

18. Whomever estimated the costs of producing these 60-second commercials *[handwritten: HE]* omitted certain items. *[handwritten: I me]*

19. Perhaps Sandra and myself will be able to help you convert these foreign sales into American dollars. *[handwritten: I myself]*

20. Three of us—Dave, Andrea, and me—agreed to the terms suggested by Mr. Lance.

B. Correct the following sentences. If a sentence is correct, write *OK.*

1. Two of the research assistants, Dorothy and he, are handling the consumer survey.

2. The person who you saw on the elevator this morning is Vanessa Lamour, head of our Chicago office. *[handwritten: Him]*

3. The duplicating machine operators are Curt and she. *[handwritten: HE]*

4. Ask whomever you consider the best graphic artist to design this. *[handwritten: Him]*

5. Do you know whose in charge of this account? *[handwritten: Him]*

6. Barry said that we must get written approval from Mrs. Comstock or he. *[handwritten: him]*

7. She is convinced that she and myself will be asked to coordinate the first session.

8. I have not worked on magazine ads as long as him. *[handwritten: HE]*

9. The office in the southeast corner is mine; the one next to it is her's.

10. Michele went with Gregory and I to the automobile show at the Coliseum, where our company was exhibiting its products. *[handwritten: me]*

11. According to the study, our sales representative's salaries are above the national average.

12. If I was you, Margaret, each payday I would buy a savings bond or put some money in a savings account.

13. Is Marie the person whom you think is responsible for hiring part-time help? *[handwritten: HE]*

14. The assistant personnel managers, Mr. Wembley and her, are recruiting on *[handwritten: HE]* campus this week. *[handwritten: she]*

15. Mrs. Nancy Brand, who has been our production manager since 1979, is considered an expert on the stock market. *[handwritten: HE]*

16. He is the person who we think should be promoted to director of public relations. *[handwritten: HE]*

17. No one knows who will succeed Ms. Lennon; however, I am sure that whomever *[handwritten: HE]* is selected will also be a CPA.

18. The sales manager should have asked we field representatives for our opinions.

19. Who's calculator is this? *[handwritten: me]*

20. When Miss Borden asked Carol and I to attend the hearings in Washington, D.C., we were both surprised and delighted.

Editing Practice

Spelling and Possessives   Correct any errors in spelling or in the use of possessives. Write *OK* for any correct sentence.

1. According to company policy, all employee's salaries must be reviewed at least once a year.
2. After six months on the job, you will be eligible for one weeks' vacation; after one year, two weeks' vacation.
3. Whenever there ready, we'll begin discussing the sales for October and November.
4. Carol Ducey's suggestion was to prepare a special catalog for the holiday season.
5. Our offices are on the fifteenth and nineteenth floors; their's are on the nineteenth and twentieth floors.
6. The judge fined both companys for "deliberately mislabeling" their products.
7. Our company manufactures medicine bottles that are specially designed for childrens' safety.
8. His sister-in-law's store is located in the new shoping mall on Main Street.
9. As Miss DuPont said, "Its obvious that we must increase our promotion efforts for all our new products."
10. When your prepared to mail the contracts, notify Miss Laine.

The Word Processing Department   The following excerpt is from a memorandum that was submitted to you by one of the employees in your department. Does it contain any errors?

> This morning we received a letter of intent from June Carlisle, attorney for Pruett Foods, Inc., in which Ms. Carlisle excepts our offer to buy Pruett's Detroit warehouse. Therefore, we should be able to sign a formal agreement by the end of November and begin using the warehouse by next January.

Case Problem

Creating the Wrong Impression   Fred Hancock was being interviewed by Janet Miller, general manager, for a position as office supervisor with the Economy Printing Company. In the interview, Ms. Miller asked about two important points: (1) the formal training in supervision that Fred had and (2) Fred's experience as a supervisor. Fred proudly mentioned his ten years of work experience and emphasized the value of this phase of his background for the office supervisor's job. He casually told Ms. Miller that he had no formal training in supervision but that his work experience taught him all he needed to know.

Later on, Ms. Miller asked Fred for his philosophy of supervision. Fred replied tartly: "I believe a supervisor's job is to keep close tabs on everybody so that they get their work done and don't get out of line. It is certainly not necessary to let them in on everything. What they don't know doesn't hurt them."

A few days after the personal interview with Ms. Miller, Fred received a letter from the Economy Printing Company thanking him for making application with them, but indicating that someone else had been hired for the position. Naturally, Fred was disappointed and tried to determine whether something had gone wrong in the interview, since his experience was exactly what the company wanted.

1. What went wrong in the interview that cost Fred this job?
2. What might Fred have said regarding training in supervision that might have helped him get this job?

13 PREDICATE AGREEMENT

In an effort to capture everyday speech and real-life emotions in their lyrics, writers of popular music often disregard the rules of grammar. Rock 'n' roll, country and western, and other types of popular songs try to tell a story, deliver a message, or just offer enjoyment. For example, the writer of popular music may write "he don't" because it sounds better than "he doesn't" for a particular situation, despite the fact that "he don't" is wrong, of course. A popular song is judged by its beat, its rhythm, its sound—anything but its grammar!

The only harm to all this is that listeners who hear "he don't" and other similar errors often enough start to believe that they are *correct*. The errors that we most commonly hear in popular music are the same errors that many people make in their everyday writing and speaking—mostly errors in predicate agreement, which is the subject of this and the next section. Pay special attention to the rules presented in this section, because your writing—especially your business writing—*will* be judged by its grammar.

BASIC AGREEMENT RULE

The basic rule of agreement for all sentences is: A predicate must agree with its simple subject in number and *in person*. The predicate always includes a verb, and that verb must agree with the simple subject. If the predicate also includes a pronoun that refers to the simple subject, that pronoun, too, must agree with the subject. Study the following rules and the examples illustrating them.

Agreement of Subject and Verb

Note how these verbs agree with their subjects:

> Mrs. Murray, one of our supervisors, (has? have?) the revised list. (The simple subject, *Mrs. Murray,* is singular; therefore, the singular verb *has* is correct.)

Two managers in our company (has? have?) been transferred to our office in St. Louis. (The simple subject is *managers,* which is plural; therefore, the correct verb is the plural *have.*)

As you already know, most plural nouns end in *s* or *es,* but verbs that end in *s* or *es* are singular:

> **Singular Noun and Verb:** The *company wants* to increase its profits. (*Company* and *wants* are singular forms.)
> One *person knows* the combination to the safe. (*Person* and *knows* are singular forms.)
> **Plural Noun and Verb:** The *companies want* to increase their profits. (*Companies* and *want* are plural.)
> Two *persons know* the combination to the safe. (*Persons* and *know* are plural forms.)

Agreement of Pronoun With Subject

If the predicate includes a pronoun that refers to the subject, the pronoun must agree with that subject.

> Mrs. Murray wants to take (his? her? its? their?) vacation in July. (*Mrs. Murray* is singular and feminine; therefore, the pronoun *her,* which is singular and feminine, is correct and agrees with *Mrs. Murray.* Note that the singular verb *wants* also agrees with *Mrs. Murray.*)
> Two managers said that (he? she? it? they?) prefer having (his? her? its? their?) production meetings once a week. (The simple subject, *managers,* is plural, and the pronouns *they* and *their* agree with the plural *managers.* Note that the plural verb *prefer* also agrees with *managers.*)
> Our store is having (his? her? its? their?) best year. (The simple subject, *store,* is singular and neuter; the pronoun that agrees with store is *its.* Note the singular verb *is having.*)
> Mr. Henson, an account executive in our Houston office, has announced that (he? she? it? they?) will not renew (his? her? its? their?) contract. (The simple subject, *Mr. Henson,* is singular and masculine; therefore, the pronouns that agree with *Mr. Henson* are *he* and *his.* Note the singular verb *has announced.*)

☐ Checkup 1

Choose the correct verbs and pronouns.

1. The Johnston Advertising Agency (is? are?) known for (his? her? its? their?) creative television campaigns.
2. Both partners said that (he? she? its? they?) (expects? expect?) this year's revenues to exceed last year's.
3. Mary Alice (submits? submit) all (his? her? its? their?) assignments on time.
4. Mrs. Rutherford frequently (travels? travel?) to Europe to meet (his? her? its? their?) clients.

5. Mr. Van Orden (has? have?) canceled (his? her? its? their?) vacation plans because of the strike threat.
6. My brother (wants? want?) to open (his? her? its? their?) own business.
7. All six managers (is? are?) planning to bring (his? her? its? their?) assistants to the convention.
8. The G&M Company (does? do?) not usually publicize (his? her? its? their?) financial statements.

AGREEMENT PROBLEMS

Four common agreement problems concern the verbs and pronouns selected to agree with (1) subjects in inverted sentences, (2) subjects that are separated from their verbs, (3) subjects that are common-gender nouns, and (4) indefinite-word subjects.

Inverted Sentences

As you saw in Section 6, in inverted sentences the subject follows the verb. As with normal-order sentences, the correct verb choice depends on identifying the subject.

> On the bookshelf (is? are?) the printouts that you need. (Careless writers and speakers see *bookshelf* and choose a verb to agree with it—*is*. But the subject of the sentence is *printouts*, not *bookshelf*; therefore, the verb *are* is correct.)

Sentences or clauses beginning with *there*—*there is, there are, there has been, there have been,* and so on—are in inverted order. Such sentences are very commonly written incorrectly.

> Her assistant said that there (is? are?) only three applicants for the position. (The simple subject of the clause is the plural noun *applicants.* Therefore, the verb *are* is correct.)
>
> There (is? are?) the photographs for the new brochure. (Changing the sentence to normal order shows that the subject of the sentence is the plural noun *photographs.* Therefore, the plural verb *are* is correct.)

Intervening Phrases and Clauses

Words that separate a subject from its verb may deceive the writer or speaker. Be sure to find the simple subject and you will be sure of choosing the correct verb to agree with it.

> The reason for the delays (is? are?) that the truckers are on strike. (The subject is the singular *reason;* therefore, the correct verb is *is.* But many people incorrectly see *delays* as the subject; *delays* is part of the prepositional phrase *for the delays.*)
>
> Our manager, who must approve any price increases recommended by her assistants, (has? have?) set 6.5 percent as the maximum increase this year. (The

subject is the singular *manager;* therefore, the correct verb is *has.* But many people incorrectly see *assistants have* as the words that should agree.)

☐ Checkup 2

Correct the following sentences. If a sentence is correct, write *OK.* Then identify the subjects and verbs that agree (use the form shown in the example).

> **Sentence:** On the shelf there is a few copies of the instruction booklet.
> **Answer:** *are—copies*

1. The <u>shipment</u> of spare parts have [has] not yet been received.
2. As you know, there is several good <u>reasons</u> for canceling this contract.
3. The entire <u>block,</u> with all its buildings, are to be auctioned next month.
4. All of us agree that there are many <u>alternatives</u> from which we may choose.
5. At the top of the stairs are the <u>book</u> that you wanted.
6. Are you sure that there is no more <u>invoices</u> to be processed?
7. Did you know that there is about four regional <u>meetings</u> scheduled for February?
8. Among the firms that have submitted bids there are only <u>one</u> located in our city.
9. <u>One</u> of the women in our department has already received her end-of-year bonus.
10. Near the duplicating machines are the special <u>paper</u> that you must use.

Pronoun Agreement With Common-Gender Nouns

Whenever the gender of a simple subject is clearly masculine or feminine, choosing the correct pronoun is no problem. Many simple subjects, such as *employee, citizen,* and *nobody,* could be either masculine or feminine. Which pronoun is correct?

The "traditional" rule was to choose *he* whenever the simple subject could be either masculine or feminine, a rule that ignored women. But in actual practice, writers would choose *he* to agree with simple subjects such as *executive, doctor,* and *treasurer,* and *she* to agree with simple subjects such as *nurse, secretary,* and *receptionist,* a practice that typecast men and women into very definite, limited roles. This practice is perhaps worse than ignoring women!

To avoid (not solve) this problem, use *he or she* or a similar combination of pronouns to refer to a simple subject that could be either masculine or feminine.

> An executive must depend on *his or her* assistants for accurate information.
> A secretary must be able to transcribe *his or her* shorthand precisely.

When *he or she* or similar combinations are used too often, the message will be difficult to read. In such cases, the above examples, for instance, might be revised as follows:

> Executives must depend on *their* assistants for accurate information.
> Secretaries must be able to transcribe *their* shorthand precisely.

Indefinite-Word Subject

The following words are always <u>singular</u>: *each, either, neither, everyone, everybody, someone, somebody, anyone, anybody, no one,* and *nobody.* When these words are used as subjects, therefore, their predicates must be singular.

> Each of us employees (has? have?) (his or her? our?) private locker. (*Has* and *his or her* agree with the singular subject *each.*)
> Anyone who (wishes? wish?) to return merchandise must bring (his or her? their?) receipt with (him or her? them?). (*Anyone* is singular; therefore, *wishes, his or her,* and *him or her* are correct.)

These words may also be used to modify other subjects, but when they do so, the subjects that they modify are still singular.

> Each employee (has? have?) (his or her? their?) private locker. (The subject is *employee; has* and *his or her* agree with the singular subject *employee. Each* modifies the subject.)

☑ Checkup 3

Correct the following sentences, using the answer form shown below. If a sentence is correct, write *OK.*

> Sentence: A good manager know how to get the most out of his staff.
> Answer: *knows, his or her—manager*

1. Everyone have been asked to show their discount coupon to the salesclerk.
2. An executive must train his assistant carefully.
3. Each of the parents has already given his or her donation.
4. Anyone who have their price list with them should be able to answer your question.
5. A manager should develop his human relations skills if he wants to succeed.
6. Neither store have the new model in their stockroom.
7. Anyone who want to pay by check should have their check approved at the customer service desk.
8. Each of the clerks have been instructed to get additional approval for credit card purchases over $500.
9. Nobody in our departments have completed their report yet.
10. Everyone who are on our mailing list will receive their free copy of this catalog by June 15.

COMMUNICATION PROJECTS

Practical Application

A. Correct the following sentences, using the answer form shown below.

> Sentence: Each <u>employee</u> have submitted their dental plan forms.
> Answer: *has, his or her—employee*

1. There's the sales reports that we were looking for.
2. Four copies of this letter has been distributed.
3. Do you know whether there is any extra looseleaf binders in the supply room?
4. In her office is the duplicate copies of the Adams contract.
5. According to the report, there was only two accidents in our plant last year.
6. Each customer should bring their receipt with them whenever they wish to return merchandise.
7. Although we stock many brands of household appliances, there is only a few that sell well.
8. Mr. DeJohn insists that there is some good reasons for adopting the new plan.
9. The report stated that there is more than 570 billion credit cards in the United States!
10. In this catalog is many different styles of office furniture.
11. The president of our company, as well as the executive vice president, is predicting that we will break our sales records this year.
12. Every executive in the country has been polled for their opinions.
13. Perhaps one of our secretaries are willing to work late to complete this report.
14. On the second floor of this building is the offices of a new plastics manufacturing company.
15. Don't Ms. Warden have the Ford Foundation report in her office?

B. Correct the following sentences. If a sentence is correct, write *OK*.

1. Is there extra copies that we can distribute at the meeting?
2. Mrs. Kramden said that these invoices were your s.
3. Mr. Leslie and me will be leaving on Tuesday, April 1, from O'Hare International Airport.
4. Every one of the women was asked to give their candid opinion of the idea.
5. Our company has had it's headquarters in Seattle since 1945.
6. A special government study showed that there is certainly enough jobs in the paper industry.
7. Whenever your looking for general statistical information, use an almanac.
8. Every one of we reporters attended the three-day conference.
9. Each employee should complete their questionnaire and submit it to their supervisor by December 13.
10. Karen and John Howard have managed their own business since 1975, but the Howard's are now eager to sell.
11. Please be courteous to whomever wants to exchange merchandise.
12. Sometimes Allen acts as if he was the sales manager rather than a sales representative.
13. All the secretaries in our department knows how to operate the automatic typewriter.
14. Every customer should receive their new credit card by January 15.
15. The Friendly Company is one of the best-known manufacturers of childrens' clothing.
16. Ms. Elizabeth Trask has been chose to head the mayor's committee.
17. Didn't they know that there is still more orders to be processed?

18. Under the new plan, a sales representative who meets their quota will receive a special bonus.
19. On my desk is the applications that I received this morning.
20. The B&G Company distributes foreign-made radioes, televisions, and cameras to American stores.

Editing Practice

Homonyms, Anyone? Correct any homonyms (or pseudohomonyms) that are misused in the following excerpt from a memorandum. (**Remember:** Homonyms are words that sound alike but have different meanings. Pseudohomonyms sound somewhat alike but have different meanings.)

> As you know, both our Data Processing Department and our Personal Department need more office space. Therefore, we have least the entire fifteenth floor to provide these departments with ample room for there needs.
> On March 1, the entire staff of Data Processing will be moved to the fifteenth floor. At a latter date, the Personnel Department staff will be moved, accept for Employee Benefits, which will remain on the fourteenth floor.

Case Problem

The Perplexed Secretary Linda Sears is private secretary to an executive. One day her boss, Mrs. Merriwether, indicated that she had to work all day on a speech she had to give the following day. "Do not disturb me under any circumstances," Mrs. Merriwether cautioned Linda. Just one hour later the telephone rang and a voice asked to speak to Mrs. Merriwether. "May I ask who is calling?" Linda inquired. In a slightly angered tone, the voice indicated that it was Mr. Lambert, Mrs. Merriwether's boss, and that he wanted to speak to Mrs. Merriwether immediately.

In view of Mrs. Merriwether's instructions, what should Linda say to Mr. Lambert? Give a reason for your answer.

14 PREDICATE AGREEMENT WITH SPECIAL SUBJECTS

The basic rule of agreement holds true for all cases of subject and verb agreement: *The predicate must agree in number and in person with the simple subject.* However, there are a few types of subjects that cause problems, and these subjects are given special attention in this section.

COLLECTIVE-NOUN SIMPLE SUBJECT

A collective noun is one that refers to a group or a collection of persons or things, for example, *class, jury, audience, company, committee,* and *herd.* Because a collective noun may be singular or plural, its correct number may not be easily recognized. Use the following Memory Hook to simplify your using collective nouns correctly.

■ Memory Hook

To make sure that your predicate agrees with a collective-noun simple subject, test whether the members of the group act as one or as a whole. When they act as one, the noun is considered singular. (Remember: *One* is singular.) When they act as individuals, the noun is considered plural. (Remember: *Individuals* is a plural word.)

> In a complicated case, a jury (does? do?) not usually give (its? their?) verdict quickly. (*Jury* is a collective noun; in this sentence, the jury is acting as a whole, as one unit. Therefore, *does* and *its* are the correct choices to agree with *jury.*)
> The jury (is? are?) arguing vehemently. (To argue, more than one person is needed. Here, the plural *are* is correct because the jury members are acting individually.)

☑ Checkup 1

Choose the correct verbs and pronouns in the following sentences.
1. Our class (meets? meet?) once a week.
2. The committee (is? are?) discussing the proposals among (itself? themselves?).
3. The Board of Directors will meet next Tuesday. The Board (is? are?) expected to give (its? their?) approval to the merger.
4. The faculty (was? were?) assigned to (its? their?) new offices in the Hudson Building.
5. The jury (has? have?) reached a decision and will therefore render (its? their?) verdict tomorrow.

FOREIGN-NOUN SUBJECT

As you already know, not all plurals are formed by adding *s* or *es* to the singular form. Some plurals of foreign nouns are formed by changing the ending; for example, *alumna, alumnae; alumnus, alumni; analysis, analyses; basis, bases; crisis, crises.* Look at the ending of foreign-noun simple subjects to determine whether they are singular or plural; then choose the predicate that agrees.

> The basis for her statements (was? were?) unsound. (*Basis* is singular; therefore, the predicate must be singular. *Was* is correct.)
> The bases for her statements (was? were?) unsound. (*Bases* is plural; therefore, the predicate must be plural. *Were* is correct.)

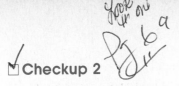

☑ Checkup 2

Correct any errors in the following sentences. Write *OK* if a sentence has no error.

1. The criteria for selecting candidates is explained in the brochure.
2. Does their analyses of past sales show any interesting patterns or trends?
3. The media that has been most effective for advertising our products is television, radio, and magazines.
4. The hypotheses is carefully explained in this press release.
5. The recent crisis has received special attention from the President and the Secretary of State.
6. The memoranda, which is on your desk, clearly explains the new procedures.
7. The newspapers reported on the stimuli that are being used by the government to spur our sluggish economy.
8. Parentheses is used to enclose references and directions.

PART, PORTION, OR AMOUNT SUBJECT

Some simple subjects refer to a part, a portion, or an amount of something, such as *all*, *some*, *half*, *two-thirds*, and *none*. Such subjects may be singular or plural, as shown in the following examples:

> Some of the house (has? have?) been painted. (The singular *has* is correct, because *some* refers to a singular, *house*.)
> Some of the houses (has? have?) been painted. (Here, *some* refers to the plural *houses*; therefore, the plural *have* is correct.)

Note that to determine each answer, you must answer the questions Part of what? Portion of what? Amount of what? In other words, in these cases the number of the predicate is determined by the complete subject, not by the simple subject alone.

Note, too, that although *none* may be singular or plural in informal usage, it is considered only a singular in formal usage.

☑ Checkup 3

Choose the correct words in the following sentences. Then indicate the word that influenced your choice. Follow the example. (For the pronoun *none*, assume that the use is informal.)

> **Sentence:** Nine-tenths of the forest (has? have?) been restored to (its? their?) original beauty.
> **Answer:** has, its—forest

1. All the machines (needs? need?) to have (its? their?) belts checked for wear.
2. Half the area (has? have?) been rented to an import-export firm.
3. None of the drivers (knows? know?) where the dispatcher went.
4. Two-thirds of the voters (is? are?) in favor of establishing a special agency to protect (its? their?) rights.

5. Two-thirds of the city (was? were?) affected by the blackout.
6. Part of the building (was? were?) recently leased to a savings bank.
7. (Is? Are?) some of the packages ready to be shipped?
8. Most of the homes in this new development (has? have?) been sold.
9. Some of the motors (was? were?) not inspected before (it? they?) (was? were?) shipped to customers.
10. Apparently, none of the inventory (was? were?) damaged by the flood.

A NUMBER, THE NUMBER SUBJECT

A *number* always has a plural meaning and takes a plural predicate. *The number* always has a singular meaning and takes a singular predicate.

> A number of cashiers (is? are?) on vacation this week. (Because *a number* is plural, the plural verb *are* is correct.)
>
> The number of cashiers on vacation this week (is? are?) greater than usual. (Because *the number* is always singular, the singular verb *is* is correct.)

Note that an adjective before *number* has no effect on the choice:

> A great number of responses to our recent ad have already been received. (The plural *have* is correct because *a number* is always plural.)

■ Memory Hook

To remember the above principle quickly and accurately, picture the following:

> **Plural:**   a
> **Singular:**   the

As you see, *plural* is shorter than *singular*, and *a* is shorter than *the*. So use this to remember that *a number* is plural and that *the number* is singular.

☑ Checkup 4

Correct any errors in the following sentences. Write *OK* if a sentence has no error.
1. Did you know that a number of new secretaries have recently been hired?
2. Because the number of people interested in this product are large, we know that we can sell it very successfully.
3. Mrs. Powers said that the number of unemployed people have increased within the past two months.
4. According to the government findings, a number of citizens are becoming increasingly concerned about the economy.
5. The number of registered voters in this district have increased almost 15 percent since last year.
6. The number of products that we manufacture have jumped to approximately 80.

COMMUNICATION PROJECTS

Practical Application

A. Correct any errors in the following sentences. If a sentence has no error, write *OK*.

1. She said that three-fourths of her time are spent in research.
2. The diagnosis for these patients has been confirmed by an orthopedic specialist.
3. Her accurate analyses of the chemicals was of great help.
4. The lab technician reported that the bacteria were harmless.
5. The large number of absences have delayed productions.
6. "Some of our clients," said Mrs. Johanson, "has requested long-term contracts in an effort to hold down prices."
7. Until the trial ends, the jury is staying at the Dover Hotel and the Trent Hotel.
8. Some of our warehouse space have been rented to a West Coast firm.
9. The supervisors proposed the addenda that is on your desk.
10. The company bowling team are playing its last match tomorrow evening.
11. Because a number of people has complained, we are changing the date for the meeting.
12. Most of the dispatchers prefers using this report form.
13. The number of orders we received this morning are surprising.
14. Nearly half of the shipments to the East Coast has been delayed by the airline strike.
15. Mr. Simpson said that two-thirds of this year's revenue have come from foreign sales.

B. Correct any errors in the following sentences. If a sentence has no error, write *OK*.

1. Because none of our trucks have any refrigeration equipment, we cannot ship perishables.
2. For your child's safety, every one of our products are tested carefully before they are packed and shipped.
3. Her wallet was laying where she had left it—on her desk.
4. Did you know that the Schultzes are planning to move their business to St. Louis?
5. Everyone are expected to arrive promptly at 9 a.m.
6. Neither of the supervisors have yet received the new product code sheet.
7. The new billing system gives each customer an itemized invoice showing their purchases for the month.
8. Nearly three-fourths of the merchandise was unacceptable.
9. Don't Mr. Godfrey know when Ms. Lucas is coming to our office?
10. Let's ask Roland and she to prepare a summary of their findings.
11. Because the number of accidents have been reduced drastically, the insurance company lowered our annual premiums.
12. On the bulletin board is the promotion notices for this month.
13. Generally, crises in the financial community raises the price of gold.
14. Yesterday, Ms. Allison and me negotiated new contracts with some of our suppliers.

15. Mrs. Pulaski said that the reason for the errors are that incorrect prices had been fed into the computer.
16. To be eligible for this increased insurance, an employee must submit their completed form no later than June 15.
17. None of the furniture for these rooms have been delivered yet.
18. Everybody has been asked to send their vacation request to Personnel by December 10.
19. Is she the person who you want to hire?
20. The shipping department supervisor informed us that there is no more large cartons in the warehouse.

Editing Practice

The Word Processing Supervisor   Can you find any spelling errors in the following paragraphs?

> Thank you for your recent request for information about the Dover Hotel. To answer your questions about our convention facilities, we have enclosed our latest brochure.
>
> As the brochure explains, the Dover Hotel can accomodate groups with from 15 to 515 people with equal ease—and with the same high-qualty service that has made the Dover famous for generations.
>
> Once you have read our brochure, Ms. Anna Jenkins, our Convention Manager, will be happy to answer any questions that you may have. You may call her at this toll-free number: 800-555-7000.

Case Problem

The Beginning Dictator   Shirley Howe has been recently promoted to a supervisory job where, for the first time, she is responsible for writing letters to customers. She has been assigned a part-time stenographer. Rather than dictate letters to the stenographer, Shirley writes them out in longhand and asks the stenographer to type them in letter form.

1. Do you think this is an efficient procedure? Why or why not?
2. What would you suggest?

To complete our study of subject and predicate agreement, we must tackle one more kind of subject—the compound subject. We are concerned only with those subjects joined by *and, or,* or *nor.* As you will see, there are two rules to be mastered: one for compound subjects joined by *and;* another for compound subjects joined by *or* or *nor.*

In addition, in this section we tackle one more predicate agreement problem. Because so many people err in matching the correct predicate with the relative pronouns *who, that,* and *which,* we will pay special attention to predicate agreement in relative-pronoun clauses.

SUBJECTS JOINED BY *AND*

Because a compound subject joined by *and* is a plural subject, it takes a plural verb.

> Harold *and* Beth *are* on their way to Australia. (The compound subject *Harold and Beth* is a plural subject; thus the plural verb *are* is correct.)
>
> A manager *and* an assistant manager *have* been asked to plan the seminar. (The compound subject joined by *and* is a plural subject; therefore, the plural verb *have* is correct.)

There are two exceptions to the rule that subjects joined by *and* are plural subjects. First, when two nouns joined by *and* refer to the same person or thing, that subject is considered singular:

> My agent *and* business adviser *is* Elvera, my wife. (Here, *agent and business adviser* refers to one person, not to two different persons, and is therefore considered singular. The verb *is* is correct.)
>
> Pie *and* ice cream *is* my favorite dessert. (This is one dessert; it consists of a scoop of ice cream on a slice of pie. Thus *pie and ice cream* takes a singular verb *is.*)

Of course, the writer who wished to specify two different people or two different desserts would write:

> My agent *and* my business adviser *are* Elvera and Jack. (Two different people are referred to; the plural verb *are* is correct.)
>
> Pie *and* ice cream *are* my favorite *desserts.* (Here, two different desserts are mentioned: one is pie; the other is ice cream. Note the plural verb *are* and the plural noun *desserts.*)

← SINGULAR ALL THE TIME.

Here is the second exception: When two subjects joined by *and* are modified by *each, every,* or *many a,* a singular predicate is correct.

> *Each* man, woman, *and* child in this area *is* eligible to receive this vaccine free from his or her physician. (The singular verb *is* and the singular *his or her* are

both correct because the compound subject *man, woman, and child* is modified by *each*.)

Many a father *and* mother has donated his or her time to helping the needy in this community. (The compound subject joined by *and* is modified by *many a*; thus the singular verb *has donated* is correct.)

☑ Checkup 1

Correct any agreement errors in the following sentences. If a sentence has no error, write *OK*. Explain why each sentence is or is not correct.

1. The letter and the envelope shows two different addresses.
2. Each manager, assistant manager, and supervisor were asked to attend the meeting next Friday.
3. Is Martha and her sister graduates of the same law school?
4. Accuracy and speed is both important for professional proofreaders.
5. Ham and eggs is my favorite breakfast.
6. Many an attorney and accountant have given their time to this charity drive.
7. The end and aim of the proposed legislation are to provide the elderly with adequate dental services.
8. As you know, each clerk, typist, and bookkeeper are going to receive an end-of-year bonus.
9. On tonight's show, a senator and a cabinet member is being interviewed.
10. Many a police officer and firefighter has protested the new law.

SUBJECTS JOINED BY *OR* OR *NOR*

Compound subjects joined by *or* or *nor* will cause no problem if you study this Memory Hook.

■ Memory Hook

When the parts of a compound subject are joined by *or* or *nor*, match the predicate to the subject that follows the *or* or *nor*.

> The manager *or* her assistants (has? have?) duplicate copies of the government regulations. (Because we have a compound subject joined by *or*, we must find the part of the subject that follows *or*—*assistants*. Then we must make the predicate match *assistants*; thus we choose the verb *have: assistants have*.)
>
> The assistants *or* the manager (has? have?) duplicate copies of the government regulations. (Now the part of the compound subject that follows *or* is *manager*, a singular noun. Therefore, the correct verb choice here is *has: manager has*.)
>
> Neither the account executives *nor* she (knows? know?) how much the prices will be raised. (Which subject follows *nor*? *She*, a singular pronoun. Thus the singular *knows* is correct.)
>
> Either Lucy *or* her partners (is? are?) going to represent (her? their?) company

at the workshop. (Which subject follows *or*? *Partners*, a plural noun. Thus *are* and *their* are the correct choices.)

Either her partners *or* Lucy (is? are?) going to represent (her? their?) company at the workshop. (Now the subject that follows *or* is *Lucy*, a singular noun; so *is* and *her* are the correct choices.)

☑ Checkup 2

Select the correct words. Give your reason for each selection.

1. Neither Miss Gottlieb nor her associates (agrees? agree?) that the discounts should be increased.
2. Perhaps Mr. Gilroy or Mrs. McCoy (has? have?) already ordered these parts.
3. The managers or their assistants (is? are?) responsible for making (his or her? their?) own schedules.
4. Ms. DeVito or her accountants (has? have?) forgotten (her? their?) payroll charts in the conference room.
5. Either Dr. Furst or the nurses (is? are?) on duty now.
6. An experienced bookkeeper or junior accountant (has? have?) been sought since January.
7. Either her accountants or Ms. DeVito (has? have?) forgotten (her? their?) payroll charts in the conference room.
8. Neither Leroy nor his associates (has? have?) prepared (his or her? their?) (speech? speeches?) yet.
9. Apparently, Mrs. Humboldt or her managers (has? have?) submitted (her? their?) suggestions to the Personnel Department.
10. Yes, either his clients or Mr. Greco (prefers? prefer?) changing (his? their?) media schedules.

RELATIVE-PRONOUN CLAUSES

The relative pronouns *who*, *that*, and *which*, are often used as subjects of relative clauses. They are called *relative* pronouns because they *relate* back to other words called *antecedents*. The predicates chosen to agree with these relative pronouns must actually agree with their antecedents, as shown below:

Mrs. DeWitt is one of those executives *who* train their assistants very carefully. (Do you see a relative pronoun? The relative pronoun is *who*. How do you know that it is a relative pronoun? Because it relates back to an antecedent, *executives*.)

A Sampson vacuum is one of those machines *that* simplify household work. (Do you see the relative pronoun *that*? How can you check that it is a relative pronoun? By finding its antecedent, *machines*.)

Remember that *who*, *that*, and *which* are not always relative pronouns; they don't always refer to an antecedent.

Who is the senior vice president of sales? (*Who* has no antecedent; it is not a relative pronoun.)

I didn't know *that* Danielle moved to Chicago. (*That* has no antecedent.)

Do you know *which* company is sponsoring this luncheon? (*Which* has no antecedent.)

■ Memory Hook

Whenever you see a relative pronoun introducing a clause, omit the pronoun and use the antecedent as the subject of the clause. In this way you will be sure to make the predicate agree with the antecedent.

> Ms. Ellison is one of those copywriters who (does? do?) (her? their?) best writing when under pressure. (If you omit *who* and start with the word *copywriters*, your choices are obvious: *copywriters do their*.)
>
> Mr. Monroe believes that the best worker is the one who (comes? come?) to work early to complete (his or her? their?) work. (Omit *who* and your choices must agree with *one*: *comes* and *his or her*.)
>
> She prefers one of those offices that (has? have?) traditional furniture in (it, them?). (By omitting *that*, the choices must obviously agree with *offices*: *have* and *them*.)

Note: Exceptions are clauses preceded by "*the only* one." Such clauses must take singular predicates.

> Myrna is the only one of the managers who *has* submitted *her* budget. (The meaning here is, "the only one who *has* submitted *her* budget is Myrna." Thus *has* and *her* are correct.)

☑ Checkup 3

Correct any errors in the following sentences. Write *OK* if a sentence has no error.

1. James is one of those administrators who does everything "by the book."
2. Lauren, the copy-desk chief, is one of those reporters who is always looking for a story.
3. We are bidding on one of those warehouses that are for sale in Union County.
4. Apparently, Miss Bacall is one of those designers who completes her work quickly and accurately.
5. All of us prefer working in one of those buildings that is in the midtown area.
6. She suggested that we close one of the four plants that is now operating inefficiently.

COMMUNICATION PROJECTS

Practical Application

A. Correct any errors in the following sentences. If a sentence has no error, write *OK*.

1. Not every man and woman in our department are in favor of the changes.
2. The invoices for the month of January is in this folder.

(who, which, that)
Look Before

3. Obviously, neither you nor he want to handle the new account.
4. Unfortunately, the report has several errors that is readily noticeable.
5. She estimates that two small rooms or one large room are enough for our meetings.
6. In the new mall is a beautiful restaurant and a well-known men's clothing store.
7. Either Mrs. Wallace or Mr. Preston are giving the speech tomorrow afternoon.
8. Every bottle and jar on the truck were broken in transit.
9. As you know, either the data processing supervisor or the keyboard operators on duty is supposed to schedule each project.
10. Our sales manager is one of those people who always meets her monthly quotas.
11. A block and tackle are a great tool for construction workers.
12. Everyone knows that Mr. Fitzgerald is one of those people who is always late in keeping his appointments.
13. Each clerk and typist in this office are now working on our new government contract.
14. Every estimate and schedule that we prepare are carefully checked by the production department.
15. Mercury or alcohol are needed to make this compound.
16. Many a mayor and governor have tried to revive this housing project.
17. Their new book is one of those that is expected to make the best-seller list.
18. Later today we should receive both packages, which are being shipped by Air Express.
19. A free sample or a discount coupon are usually effective in promoting sales.
20. Every newspaper and magazine in the state has praised the governor's handling of the crisis.

B. Correct any errors in the following sentences. Write *OK* if a sentence has no error.

1. Have the Rosses' answered their invitation yet?
2. Did either Louise or Mary Jo submit their report?
3. The number of orders we received today is surprisingly high.
4. Did you know that neither Larry nor Greg have returned from the conference?
5. Mrs. Woodward now works in one of those office buildings that was built last summer.
6. Their sales territorys are in the northern part of the state.
7. Most of us have chose August 12 as the best date for the day-long conference.
8. Admittance slips or other identification are required to enter this area of the chemical plant.
9. Nearly two-thirds of the shipment were lost in the railroad accident.
10. The staff was arguing for hours over the new procedures.
11. Barbara Schlein is the only one in our division who have a law degree.
12. Neither Sarah nor the other partners has told us her opinion.
13. We production managers did as much to complete the project on time as them.
14. There is a purchase order and an estimate form to be included with this letter.
15. The Messrs. Franklin are considering selling their shares to a conglomerate.
16. Every catalog and price list are carefully filed for future reference.
17. Where is the contract and the addendum that our attorney approved?

18. Miss Evans asked us, Pamela and ~~myself~~, *me* to review the proposal and report to her.

19. Mr. Lurie, our manager, ~~don't~~ *doesn't* give ~~us~~ *the* copywriters too many "emergency" projects.

20. *OK* The person who I think will be named as Miss Geer's replacement is Evelyn Belov.

Editing Practice

Plurals and Possessives   Correct any errors in the following sentences. If a sentence is correct, write *OK*.

1. The Rosses', Loretta and Steve, are considering accepting another offer.
2. Adrienne visited several communitys to talk with store owners.
3. A convention of police chief's is being planned for next spring.
4. Only one of the Davis's showed up at the trial.
5. Her company imports knifes, boots, tents, and other camping equipment.
6. His credentials for the general manager's job are excellent.
7. These two crises have occupied the President's time almost exclusively.
8. Daniel's and Frank's father-in-laws are partners in an accounting firm.
9. As a public service, our company provides schools with free brochures on nutrition for childrens.
10. Several years ago, she wrote an excellent article on womens' rights for *Today's Woman* magazine.

Case Problem

The Emergency   Ellen Burton and Irene Day are assistants in the Accounts Receivable Department of Baxter and Allen, Certified Public Accountants. Ellen is responsible for monthly billings to clients, and Irene is responsible for maintaining the correspondence files. All billings to customers are supposed to be mailed by the second day of each month. Ellen was absent from work for a week in late April because of illness and returned to the office April 29. Today is May 1, and the bills are far from ready to be mailed. The supervisor is away, and the problem must be resolved by Ellen.

1. Should Ellen ask Irene for help with the billing? Why or why not?
2. If she asks Irene for help, what should Ellen say to her?
3. What might be done by the department supervisor to avoid such bottlenecks?

16 ADJECTIVES

Verbs and nouns give us excellent black-and-white pictures. They can tell us, clearly and specifically, who did what to whom. But adjectives give us full-color pictures. They provide us with a way of describing nouns and pronouns vividly, interestingly, and accurately. Without adjectives, our written and spoken sentences would be dull and lifeless.

We generally make few errors in using adjectives; you will study how to avoid those few errors. Moreover, you will learn to use adjectives *expertly*.

IDENTIFYING ADJECTIVES

Any word that modifies or describes a noun or a pronoun is an adjective:

> Miss Moore sent *expensive* gifts to *several* customers. (*Expensive* modifies the noun *gifts*; *several* modifies the noun *customers*.)
>
> Miss Moore is *generous*. (Generous completes the "being" verb *is*; it modifies the noun *Miss Moore*.)
>
> She is *generous*. (Again, *generous* completes the meaning of the "being" verb *is*; here, it modifies the pronoun *she*.)

1. The words *a, an,* and *the* are adjectives. (They are usually called *articles*.)

> *The* attorney gave *a* speech on *an* issue of importance to all of us. (*The* modifies *attorney*; *a* modifies *speech*; and *an* modifies *issue*.)

2. Possessive adjectives (*my, your, his, her, its, our,* and *their*) and possessive nouns modify nouns.

> *Our* supervisor left *Jack's* proposal on *her* desk. (*Our, Jack's,* and *her* are possessive adjectives modifying *supervisor, proposal,* and *desk*, respectively.)

3. Numbers and words that tell "how many" or "in what order" can be used as adjectives:

> *Eight* representatives voted against the *first two* proposals. (*Eight* tells how many representatives; *two* tells how many proposals. *First* tells in what order.)
>
> *Each* employee had *many* suggestions. (*Each* modifies *employee*; *many* modifies *suggestions*.)

4. Proper nouns, too, serve as adjectives when they modify other nouns. Ms. DePaul, an *Illinois* congresswoman, announced that she will join a *Washington* law firm when her term expires. (*Illinois* and *Washington* are proper nouns when they stand alone; they are proper adjectives when they modify other nouns, as they do here.)

5. Compound adjectives are two or more words joined as one thought:

> She signed a *one-year* contract with a *well-known* company. (*One-year* is a compound adjective modifying *contract*; *well-known* is a compound adjective modifying *company*.)

6. Perhaps the most commonly used adjectives are descriptive adjectives—adjectives that describe or tell "what kind of."

> In a *strong, clear* voice, Miss Helms rejected the *irresponsible* policies some firms had used to gull *poor* consumers into buying *worthless* products. (*Strong, clear, irresponsible, poor,* and *worthless* are descriptive adjectives.)

□ Checkup 1

Circle each adjective in the following sentences. Remember: An adjective must describe or modify a noun or pronoun.

1. Our firm is negotiating a long-term contract with a European manufacturer.
2. His sister is a well-known designer for a West Coast company.
3. Send these packages to our New York office.
4. All employees must submit their requests within two weeks.
5. Our department is now conducting a noontime exercise for all employees who are interested.
6. Many people requested free samples of our new detergent.
7. Three trainees began working in her department this week.
8. One good reason for delaying this project is that we do not yet have Karen's estimates for manufacturing these products.
9. We are initiating a special program to help consumers budget their money.
10. Two Los Angeles retailers have already agreed to be our West Coast distributors for this new model.

COMPARISON OF ADJECTIVES

The qualities that adjectives describe can often be compared. For example, the adjectives *strong* and *clear* can be compared to show degrees of strength and clarity; *strong, stronger,* and *strongest; clear, clearer,* and *clearest.* These three forms of comparison are called the positive, the comparative, and the superlative degree.

> *Strong* and *clear* are positive degree forms; they are used to express the strength or clarity of one person or thing.
> *Stronger* and *clearer* are comparative degree forms; they allow us to compare strength or clarity between *two* persons or things and therefore to identify which of the two has more strength or clarity.
> *Strongest* and *clearest* are superlative forms; they allow us to compare the strength or clarity of three or more persons or things by telling which person or thing has the highest degree of strength or clarity.

Now let's see how we form the three degrees of comparison of adjectives.

noun = person, place, thing

Forming Adjective Comparisons

Adjectives may be compared in any one of the three following ways:
1. By adding *er* to the positive to form the comparative degree and *est* to the positive to form the superlative degree.

Positive	Comparative	Superlative
quick	quicker	quickest
happy	happier	happiest
late	later	latest

2. By inserting the word *more* or *less* before the positive to form the comparative degree, and *most* or *least* before the positive to form the superlative degree.

Positive	Comparative	Superlative
patient	more (less) patient	most (least) patient
punctual	more (less) punctual	most (least) punctual
responsible	more (less) responsible	most (least) responsible

3. By changing the form of the word completely.

Positive	Comparative	Superlative
much, many	more	most
little	less	least
good	better	best
bad	worse	worst

Selecting the Correct Forms

Adjectives of only *one* syllable are compared by adding *er* or *est* to the positive degree. Adjectives of *three* or more syllables add *more* or *less* or *most* or *least*. Adjectives of *two* syllables vary: some add *er* or *est*; others add *more* or *less* or *most* or *least*. However, these two-syllable adjectives are easy to compare because an error would be obvious, as shown here:

Marsha's suggestions were more useful than the other supervisors' suggestions. (*Usefuler* is obviously wrong; it offends our ears.)
When he heard the announcement, Charles was the happiest person in the room. (*Not most happy.*)

Avoiding Double Comparisons

The three forms of adjective comparisons should not be "mixed"—that is, of the three ways in which adjectives may be compared, only one should be used at a time.

First we discussed the issue that was of *greatest* concern to all of us. (*Greatest* is correct; not *most greatest*.)
Andrew recommended a *better* approach. (Not *more better*.)

Using Absolute Adjectives

Some adjectives (called *absolute adjectives*) describe qualities that cannot be compared. For example, a glass of water cannot be *fuller* or *fullest* or *most full* or *very full*. *Full* is already tops. Other adjectives that cannot be compared are:

accurate	dead	perfect	supreme
complete	empty	perpendicular	unanimous
correct	immaculate	round	unique

However, we can show differences in degrees by using the terms *more nearly* (or *less nearly*) full and *most nearly* (or *least nearly*) full.

> This container is *more nearly full* than that container. (Neither of the two containers is full, but one is closer to being full than the other, and *more nearly full* helps to express this.)

An advertising copywriter, of course, would prefer selling "the *most complete* encyclopedias" because "the *most nearly* complete encyclopedias" sounds lackluster. However, you should be aware that absolute adjectives cannot logically be compared. **Note:** Before you complete the following checkup, make sure that you remember to use the comparative degree to compare *two* persons or things; use the superlative degree only for *three or more* persons or things.

> Both samples are good, but we agree that this one is better. (*Better* is correct because *two* things are compared.)
> All the samples are good, but we agree that this one is *best*. (Three or more things compared.)

☒Checkup 2

Correct any error in adjective use in the following sentences. If a sentence is correct, write *OK*.

1. Which humidifier has the greatest capacity, Model 2-432B or Model 8-746D?
2. Now that these shelves have been reinforced, they are more strong than ever.
3. Without a doubt, her suggestion is a most unique one.
4. Daniel is the ambitiousest person in our department.
5. The new insulation and paneling make this room quieter and restfuler.
6. One of the most commonest complaints we've heard is that this vacuum cleaner makes too much noise.
7. Which room is largest, the family room or the living room?
8. Bob is a lot more happier now that his promotion has been announced.
9. Which sales representative is more successful, Harriet or Mark?
10. We thought that we had enough of this chemical, but the container was very empty.

ADJECTIVE PITFALLS

Study these few adjective pitfalls to make sure that you can avoid each.

Other, Else, and *All* in Comparisons

When comparing a particular person or thing with other members of the group to which it belongs, use the words *other* or *else* with the comparative degree. Compare the following sentences:

> Jack is *more* dependable than *any* member of our staff. Jack is *more* dependable than *any other* member of our staff. (Without the word *other,* the first sentence suggests that Jack is not a staff member but an outsider who is being compared with staff members. The word *other* makes it clear that Jack belongs to the staff and is being compared with the rest of the staff.)
>
> Selma is *more* imaginative than *anyone else* in our class. (The word *else* is required here to show that Selma is part of the class.)

With the superlative degree, however, use the word *all,* not *any.*

> Jack is the *most* dependable of *all* the correspondents on our staff.

Omission of the Modifier

When a modifier such as *a, the,* or *my* is repeated before each noun in a series, two or more persons or things are clearly indicated. If the modifier is not repeated, only one person or thing is meant.

> My accountant and attorney (was? were?) formerly with the district attorney's office. (Because the adjective *my* is not repeated, accountant and attorney is one person. Thus *was* is the correct verb.)
>
> My accountant and my attorney (was? were?) formerly with the district attorney's office. (By repeating *my,* the writer shows that there are two different people here. The verb *were,* therefore, is correct.)

Compound Adjectives

We have already seen that compound adjectives (two or more words combined before a noun to form one adjectival idea) are generally hyphenated.

first-quality product	air-conditioned office
well-ventilated room	800-meter race
no-fault insurance	up-to-date methods
pollution-conscious group	coast-to-coast telecast
duty-free goods	fund-raising efforts

After years of use, some compound adjectives have become so familiar that they no longer need hyphens. Such exceptions to the rule for hyphenating compounds are the following:

life insurance policy	real estate office
high school course	social security benefits

Some terms are no longer hyphenated when they follow the noun because they are no longer one-idea adjectives:

> Before the noun: Marvin has written a well-known book.
> After the noun: Marvin's book is well known.

But terms that retain the meaning of a one-idea adjective *do* retain the hyphen when they follow the noun.

> Our community is pollution-conscious.
> All our offices are air-conditioned.

☑ Checkup 3

Apply the rules just presented by correcting the following sentences. If a sentence has no error, write *OK*.

1. After her speech, there will be a 30-minute question-and-answer period.
2. We are convinced that the best way to promote our products is through word-of-mouth advertising.
3. Mrs. Tilden is a three-time winner of the coveted award.
4. Two court-appointed guardians, Miss VanCleef and Mr. Lambert, were asked for their advice.
5. Tracy, our senior account executive, handles more clients than anyone in our office.
6. Ms. Cole's suggestion is the best of any that we have received.
7. My friend and neighbor has volunteered to drive me to the airport tonight.
8. Erica, my assistant, has more experience than anyone in our department.
9. A center is usually the tallest of all the players on the team.
10. A center is usually taller than any player on the team.

This (These), That (Those)

The adjectives *this* and *these* indicate nearness to the speaker; *that* and *those* indicate distance from the speaker. Never use the pronoun *them* as an adjective to replace *these* or *those*.

> Did you deposit *those* checks for Mr. Barr? (Not *them checks*.)
> Are you finished working with *these* files? (Not *them* files.)

This (These), That (Those) With Kind(s) or Sort(s)

Kind and *sort* are singular nouns; *kinds* and *sorts,* plural nouns. A singular noun is modified by a singular adjective; a plural noun, by a plural adjective. Study the following illustrations:

> Mrs. Owens insists that (this? these?) kinds of problems will not recur. (*Kinds* is plural; thus the plural adjective *these* is correct.)

(That? Those?) sort of carton is definitely better for shipping breakable items.
(The singular adjective *that* should modify the singular noun *sort*).

Note: The expressions *kind of* and *sort of* should not be followed by the article *a* or *an*.
Say "kind of problem," not "kind of *a* problem."

☐ Checkup 4

Correct any errors in the following sentences. If a sentence has no error, write *OK*.

1. Those kind of discussions should be tabled until we have more time.
2. Remember to send them copies to Miss Thomas and Mr. Hewitt.
3. The new computer will not make this sort of an error.
4. Our advertising director said that these kind of brochures will probably be very effective.
5. When all of them invitations are ready for mailing, call the messenger service and ask for a pickup.
6. Most of us at the meeting preferred these kind of graphic displays.
7. Which kind of a keyboard do you think is easiest to use?
8. Please do not forget to ask Marilyn to help you process all them invoices.

For Added Polish

The following rules are not directly related to adjective use; however, they will help you to make correct choices when referring to two or more than two persons or things.

Each Other, One Another

Use *each other* when referring to two in number; use *one another* when referring to more than two in number.

> Fred and Jim enjoy working with *each other*. (Two in number.)
> All the accountants must be ready to check *one another's* figures. (More than two in number.)

Either, Neither; Any, Any One, No One, Not Any, None

Either and *neither* refer to one of two persons or things. *Any* or *any one, no one, not any*, and *none* should be used to refer to one of three or more persons or things, such as:

> *Either* of the stenographers will take your dictation. (Since *either* is used, there must be only two stenographers.)
> *Any one* of the stenographers will take your dictation. (Since *any one* is used, there must be more than two stenographers.)

✓ Checkup 5

Correct any errors in the following sentences. If a sentence has no error, write OK.

1. All our bookkeepers often work on each other's accounts.
2. You may ask either of those three copywriters to help you prepare your catalog.
3. As you know, neither of the five applicants will be able to come for interviews tomorrow.
4. Carmen and Michael help one another with big projects when necessary.
5. Of all the typists in our department, none will be available to help us on the Anderson project.
6. Merlin, Elaine, and Rebecca share each other's equipment.

COMMUNICATION PROJECTS

Practical Application

A. Correct any errors in the following sentences. If a sentence has no error, write OK.

1. Will all these kinds of appliances be on sale next week?
2. Yes, Mr. Darrin, you will be given full credit for all them returns you sent us.
3. Some historians have rated the late President Truman better than any President in this century.
4. Although all these personal-use computers are interesting, neither is exactly what I wanted.
5. Which of your parents is the oldest?
6. Ours is the building nearest the subway entrance.
7. After carefully examining both calculators, I recommend buying the least expensive model.
8. Both supervisors, Marion and Bernadine, cooperated with one another to finish the government project.
9. Of all our branch offices, the one that sells more than any is our Seattle office.
10. All them registration forms should be sent to our legal department.
11. Most people assume that this model is more better than the others.
12. No door-to-door soliciting is permitted in this building.
13. This is the same kind of an advertisement we used last year.
14. Each participant has been asked to prepare a 10-minute presentation.
15. International travelers may purchase duty-free goods at the airport.

B. Correct any errors in the following sentences. If a sentence has no error, write OK.

1. The three managers on this floor often meet with each other to discuss specific problems.
2. He should not have taken them contracts with him to the meeting.
3. The new procedure went into effect without anyone noticing it.
4. The ones who developed the first draft for the sales conference were Helen and I.
5. All the memoranda on your desk is on the same subject—our sales budget.
6. Which machine is heaviest, this one or that one?
7. All desks—especially receptionist's desks—should be neat and clean.
8. Her report made our sales strategy more clearer to all of us.

9. Which do you think is better—the Sampson, the Freemont, or the Bently air conditioner?
10. Please give this draft copy to whomever has the time to retype it.
11. One-half the invoices in this pile were received only this morning.
12. Everyone who needs help in completing their assignment should discuss the problem with their supervisor.
13. If you don't feel well, you should lay down for a few minutes in the medical department.
14. The accountant explained how we might profit from tax-exempt bonds.
15. Ms. Dannon asked Fred, Gloria, and I to check one another's estimates.
16. Neither Harold nor his assistants wants to revise the agenda for our meeting.
17. My friend and neighbor spends much of her time in community work.
18. Margaret receives a higher commission than anybody in the company.
19. Conrad said, "Between you and I, I see no reason for postponing this promotional campaign."
20. There is a few interesting job openings listed on the bulletin board.

Editing Practice

Plurals and Possessives Correct errors in the use of plurals or possessives. If a sentence has no error, write *OK*.

1. My neighbors' wife recently opened her new store in the Greenwood Mall.
2. As soon as the employee's vote, we will know who the new union delegate will be.
3. Please let me see there reports when you receive them.
4. In who's office will the meeting be held?
5. I appreciate Ms. Perrin interviewing me for the assistant manager's job.
6. I am sure that there very pleased with these low estimates.
7. Do you think its a good suggestion to establish a task force to study the problem?
8. Dorothy and Jacob Lamb are former university professors; the Lamb's will be joining our research and development department next month.
9. Ellen and Vernon's new store will open on March 15.
10. The editor in chiefs' office is next to mine.

The Word Processing Department Proofread the following excerpt from a procedures manual to make sure that it is error-free.

> For mailing purposes, file categorys are to be set up according to ZIP Codes. The post office requires that all bulk mailing be separated into bundles, each of which contains mail that goes to one particular ZIP Code number. In this office, then, address files must be kept in ZIP Code numeric order, not alphabetic order.

Case Problem

A Tactful Correction When Robert Whiting, a clerk, filled out a cash sales slip for a customer, he entered the total as $7 instead of $9. The customer took the slip to the cashier, Edith Lake, for payment; and Edith discovered the error.

1. What should Edith say to retain the customer's goodwill?
2. What should Edith say, if anything, to Robert about his error?

17 ADVERBS

Adverbs, like adjectives, describe or modify. As you have seen, adjectives modify nouns or pronouns. Adverbs cannot modify nouns or pronouns, yet many writers (and speakers) incorrectly choose adjectives when adverbs are needed.

DEFINITION

An adverb is a word that modifies, explains, or limits an adjective, a verb, or another adverb. Adverbs give shape to the words they modify by answering questions such as "Why?" "When?" "Where?" "How?" "How much?" "To what extent?"

Many adverbs are formed by adding *ly* to adjectives. (In fact, most words that end in *ly* are adverbs; however, not all adverbs end in *ly*, as we will see shortly.)

Adjective	Adverb
clear	clearly
frequent	frequently
hasty	hastily
immediate	immediately
perfect	perfectly
quiet	quietly

Adverbs that are derived from adjectives can be compared, just as adjectives can be compared: *clearly, more clearly, most clearly; quietly, more quietly, most quietly;* and so on.

TYPES OF ADVERBS

Two types of adverbs are discussed below: simple adverbs and conjunctive adverbs. In addition, adverbial clauses are discussed. Let's look first at simple adverbs.

Simple Adverbs = SA

Simple adverbs are those used as modifiers only. Besides all the many *ly* adverbs such as *clearly, immediately, frankly,* and *expensively,* the following adverbs are very commonly used:

also	never	soon
always	now	then
hard	often	there
here	quite	too
much	right	very

In the following sentences, note how adverbs are used to answer questions such as

"How?" "When?" "Where?" "Why?" "How little?" "How much?" and "To what extent?"

Adverbs modify adjectives:

This is a *very* good car. (The adverb *very* modifies an adjective, *good*. How good? Answer: *very* good.)

Amco Toys are *clearly* superior products. (The adverb *clearly* modifies the adjective *superior*. How superior? *Clearly* superior.)

Adverbs modify verbs:

Allen *immediately* called his accountant. (*Immediately* is an adverb; it modifies the verb *called*. Called when? Called *immediately*.)

Marisa estimated *precisely* the first-year unit sales for both these new products. (The adverb *precisely* modifies the verb *estimated*. Estimated how? Estimated *precisely*.)

Adverbs modify other adverbs:

These products are selling *much* better since we advertised them on radio. (The adverb *better*—the comparative form of *well*—modifies the verb *are selling*. Are selling to what extent? Are selling *better*. Better to what extent? *Much* better.)

Ms. Diggs did *very* well on her exam. (*Well* is an adverb; it modifies the verb *did*. Did how? Did *well*. And *very* is an adverb modifying *well*. How well? *Very* well.)

✓Checkup 1

Correct any adverb errors in the following sentences. Write *OK* if a sentence has no error.

1. Joe worked to hasty on the Glendale project.
2. Mrs. Hadle estimated the complete costs quite precisel4
3. Suzanne sketched the plans for the new complex very meticulous.4
4. All the invoices were processed quick by Martha and Jenny.
5. Carlton was waiting nervous for news of the vice president's decision.
6. When I spoke with Louise, she said that she was <u>nearly</u> finished with the purchase orders.

Conjunctive Adverbs

In addition to the simple adverbs discussed above—adverbs that modify adjectives, verbs, and other adverbs—there is another class of adverbs called conjunctive adverbs:

accordingly	likewise	then
consequently	moreover	therefore
furthermore	nevertheless	thus
however	otherwise	yet

Conjunctive adverbs are adverbs that connect two independent clauses. You will need to recognize them in order to punctuate properly.

Our marketing manager suggested a list price of $6.50; *however*, our sales representatives argued successfully in favor of a $5.95 list price.

Mr. Edelson does not agree that sales will increase next year; *moreover*, he believes that sales will definitely decrease.

Note that both examples have two *independent* clauses. Each clause could stand alone as a sentence.

3. Adverbial Clauses = AC

Adverbial clauses are dependent clauses that function as adverbs in sentences. They modify an adjective, a verb, or an adverb in the main clause.

Mr. Poole will leave when Ms. Adamson arrives. (The adverbial clause *when Ms. Adamson arrives* modifies the verb *will leave* in the main clause.)

This product will surely be successful *if the price is competitive*. (The adverbial clause *if the price is competitive* modifies the adjective *successful*.)

A subordinating conjunction introduces the dependent clause and joins that clause to an independent clause. Some commonly used subordinating conjunctions are:

after	before	unless
although	for	until
as	if	when
because	since	while

After we discussed salary increases, we reviewed potential incentive-compensation plans. (Note that the dependent clause cannot stand alone.)

Although Ms. Haney is against the idea, she is obviously willing to compromise.

✓ Checkup 2

Identify the simple adverbs, conjunctive adverbs, and adverbial clauses in the following sentences. (Note the punctuation used in each case.)

1. We must complete our proposal and submit it by Friday; therefore, our manager has approved our working overtime.
2. Call me if you need more information about this brochure.
3. The candidates will be interviewed after Ms. Greene returns from her vacation.
4. The meeting was longer than we expected; however, we accomplished all our goals during that three-hour session.
5. She has been working 12 hours a day since she opened her new store.
6. Since she opened her new store, she has been working 12 hours a day.
7. After Ms. Greene returns from her vacation, the candidates will be interviewed.
8. If you need more information about this brochure, call me.
9. We must complete our proposal and submit it by Friday; our manager, therefore, has approved our working overtime.

10. Although the meeting was longer than we expected, we accomplished all our goals during that three-hour session.

BAD OR BADLY?

Choosing between *bad* and *badly* is difficult for many writers and speakers. *Bad* is an adjective, and *badly* is an adverb. The key to the choice between *bad* and *badly* and other similar adjective-adverb pairs is the verb that precedes the choice:

> Dr. Jordan felt (bad? badly?) when he heard the announcement.
> Francine sketched the design (bad? badly?).

When the writer or speaker can identify linking verbs, such choices are very easily made.

Linking Verb or Not?

Adverbs, we have seen, can modify verbs. But they can modify only *action* verbs: finished *quickly*, called *immediately*, estimated *accurately*, waited *patiently*, and so on. Verbs that do not show action—let's call these no-action verbs "linking verbs"—generally join the subject to an adjective.

> Maria is angry. (The "being" verb *is* joins the subject to the adjective *angry*.)
> The women were patient. (The "being" verb *were* joins the subject to an adjective, *patient*.)

Besides the "being" verbs (*am, is, are, was, were, be, been, being*), other verbs can sometimes serve as no-action verbs: *seem, appear, look, feel, sound, taste,* and *smell,* for example. When they show no action, these verbs are linking verbs, and they are followed by adjectives (not adverbs).

> Maria appears angry. (No action. *Appears* is a linking verb. Note the similarity to "Maria *is* angry.")
> The women seem patient. (No action. *Seem* is a linking verb. Note the similarity to "The women *were* patient.")
> Maria spoke angrily. (*Spoke* is an action verb, and it is modified by the adverb *angrily*.)
> Maria appeared suddenly. (Here, *appeared* is an action verb, and it is modified by the adverb *suddenly*.)
> Dr. Jordan felt carefully for a possible break. (Here, *felt* is an action verb. Dr. Jordan is feeling with her hands.)

Adjectives are used after linking, or no-action, verbs. After action verbs, adverbs are used (to describe the action). The following Memory Hook will help you to remember this rule.

■ Memory Hook

Use the letter *j* in adjective and in subject to remind you that adjectives are joined to subjects by linking verbs.

Adjectives
    o
    i
    n
    e
    d   to subjects by linking verbs

☑Checkup 3

Choose the adjective or the adverb, whichever is correct. Remember that adjectives and subjects are joined by linking verbs.
1. In the laboratory, we could smell the gas (distinct? distinctly?).
2. The fire engine appeared (sudden? suddenly?) before us.
3. Did she look (careful? carefully?) through her files for the misplaced contract?
4. The chef's salad at Martha's Restaurant tastes very (good? well?).
5. Doreen said that this fabric feels too (rough? roughly?) to use for clothing.
6. Mrs. Marsh feels (bad? badly?) whenever she must reject an application.
7. Both detectives looked (careful? carefully?) for any sign of forced entry.
8. George felt (stealthy? stealthily?) along the floor for the small jewel.
9. Mrs. Loomis sounds (critical? critically?) of the plan to expand our offices.
10. The sun was shining (bright? brightly?) as we walked to the hotel.

FIVE PITFALLS

In speaking and writing, many people violate five principles of adverb use. These principles are neither tricky nor difficult, so you will be sure to avoid these pitfalls if you study them.

1. Position of the Adverb

Place an adverb as close as possible to the word that it modifies. Sometimes the meaning of a sentence can be changed by the position of the adverb.

> Only Miss Berenson has a computer terminal in her office. (No one else has one.)
> Miss Berenson has only a computer terminal in her office. (She has nothing else in her office, only a computer terminal.)
> Miss Berenson has a computer terminal only in her office. (She has one no where else but in her office.)

2. Double Negative

Adverbs that have negative meanings (*scarcely, hardly, only, never,* and *but*) should not be used with other negatives.

Sean *has scarcely* any money left in his advertising budget.
(**Not:** Sean *hasn't scarcely.*)
From the back of the room, Pamela could hardly hear the speaker.
(**Not:** Pamela *couldn't hardly.*)
Alicia *couldn't help suggesting* an alternative plan.
(**Not:** Alicia *couldn't help but suggest.*)

☑ Checkup 4

Correct each error in adverb usage in these sentences. Write *OK* if a sentence has no error.
1. As of yesterday, we hadn't but one response to our invitations.
2. My sister, who works for a mortgage company, says that buyers can't hardly find mortgage money.
3. Miss Peters only promoted John, not Edward or Helen.
4. We couldn't help but agree to Morton's suggestion.
5. As you know, there wasn't but one security guard on duty last night.
6. Agnes and Leo couldn't help but reject Nancy's estimate.

3. *Never* or *Not*?

Never or *not* are both adverbs, and both have negative meanings. *Not* expresses simple negation, but *never* means "not *ever.*" Note the word *ever.* Use *never* only when an appropriately long time is intended.

Charlotte has *not* called me yet this week. (Never would be incorrect because the meaning "not ever ... this week" would be wrong.)
I have *never* been to Australia. (*Never,* meaning "not ever," is correct in this sentence.)

4. *Where* for *That*

The subordinating conjunction *that* (not the conjunctive adverb *where*) should be used in expressions such as the following:

I read in a magazine *that* the Diamond Battery Company has been sold.
(**Not:** I read in a magazine *where* ....)
We saw in the newspaper *that* the mayor has endorsed Mrs. Simmons for governor. (**Not:** We saw in the newspaper *where* ....)

5. *Badly* or *Worst Way* for *Very Much*

Too often, we hear people say *badly* or *in the worst way* when they really mean *very much.* Study these illustrations:

Janice said that she wanted a vacation *very much.* (**Not:** wanted a vacation *badly* or wanted a vacation *in the worst way.*)

☑Checkup 5

Correct any errors in the following sentences.
1. Did you read in the annual report where *that* our company is predicting a 25 percent increase in earnings next year? *no†*
ok 2. Ms. Gilmore said that she never received the letter I sent her last month. *very much*
3. Because she wanted to save money in the worst way, Marjorie signed up for the bond-a-month savings program.
4. Yesterday, I read in an editorial where *that* most business executives are supporting the President's anti-inflation program.
5. Cynthia is taking a management-training course because she wants a promotion badly. *very much* .

ADJECTIVE AND ADVERB CONFUSION

The selection of adjective or adverb is especially troublesome for some people faced with the choice between *real* and *really*, *sure* and *surely*, *good* and *well*, *some* and *somewhat*, and *most* and *almost*. In each pair the first word is an adjective; the second, an adverb.

Sure, Surely; Real, Really

Sure and *real* are adjectives; *surely* and *really* are adverbs (note the *ly* endings). This Memory Hook will help you use them correctly.

■ Memory Hook

To test whether the adverbs *surely* or *really* are correct, substitute another adverb—for example, *very* or *certainly*.

> Mrs. Parsons was (real? really?) happy that we completed all the billing by December 31. (Substitute the adverb *very* or *certainly*: Mrs. Parsons was *very happy* or *certainly happy* makes sense. Thus the adverb *really* is correct.)
> You (sure? surely?) were correct: Louis is to be named regional manager next week. (Substitute the adverb *certainly*: You *certainly were correct* makes sense; thus the adverb *surely* is also correct.)

Good, Well

Good is an adjective, and *well* is an adverb. Therefore, *good* can modify nouns and pronouns; *well* can modify adjectives, verbs, or other adverbs.

> Pedro always submits *good* designs. (The adjective *good* modifies the noun *designs*.)
> Pedro always designs brochures *well*. (The adverb *well* modifies the verb *designs*. Notice that *well* answers the question "Designs how?" *Designs well*.)

Exception: *Well* can also be an adjective, *but only when referring to health.*

> Charles did not feel *well,* so he left earlier today. (Here, *well* is an adjective referring to health.)

Think of the term <u>*well-being*</u> and you'll remember that *well* is an adjective when it refers to <u>health</u>.

Some, Somewhat

Some is an adjective; *somewhat* is an adverb. Use this Memory Hook to use *some* and *somewhat* correctly.

■ Memory Hook

When you can substitute the words *a little bit* then *somewhat* is correct.

> Dr. Jones was (some? <u>somewhat?</u>) critical of the new procedure. (*Dr. Jones was a little bit critical* makes sense; thus *somewhat* is correct.)
> Dr. Jones has (<u>some?</u> somewhat?) criticisms of the new procedure. (Here, *a little bit criticisms* makes no sense; thus the adjective *some* is correct.)

Most, Almost

Most is an adjective, the superlative of *much* or *many,* as in *much, more, most. Almost* is an adverb meaning "not quite" or "very nearly."

> We have (most? <u>almost?</u>) enough data for our statistical report. (We have *not quite* or *very nearly* enough. *Almost* is correct.)
> (<u>Most?</u> Almost?) managers have registered for our Fundamentals of Accounting course. (Substituting *very nearly* makes no sense. *Most* managers does make sense.)

☑ Checkup 6

Correct any errors in the following sentences.
1. She was sure justified in approving overtime for her staff.
2. Because you don't feel well, I am asking Otto to drive you home.
3. Gloria was somewhat hesitant to ask for more instructions.
4. The government's anti-inflation program is not working as well as was expected.
5. Our vice president was sure angry when she heard about the delay.
6. Most anyone can learn to do this job well—if he or she has patience.
7. For all of us in the sales department, the sudden decrease in consumer buying is real alarming.
8. Mr. Bushman was some reluctant to approve the extra expense.

COMMUNICATION PROJECTS

Practical Application

A. Correct any adverb errors in the following sentences. Write *OK* if a sentence has no error.

1. Dolores has been late so frequent that Ms. Drury no longer believes her excuses. [*frequently*]
2. You never told me that Mr. Van Buren is waiting for me in the reception area. [*DIDN'T TELL*]
3. Because she injured herself when she fell, Ms. Abernathy needed help in the worst way. [*reely much*]
4. Mr. Hudson seemed confident as he delivered his speech to all the managers. [OK] [*what*]
5. Our foreign sales decreased some last month. [*what*]
6. Marion prepared the agenda very good. [*well*]
7. All of us felt bad when we heard that Dr. Jennings plans to retire next month. [OK] [*ly*]
8. Miss Grant hasn't never been to Europe, has she?
9. To prepare your speech good, you should follow these tips. [*well*]
10. From my office, across from St. Patrick's Cathedral, I can hear the church bells clear. [*ly*]
11. Why does this maple syrup taste so bitterly? [*bitter*]
12. Unfortunately, their report hasn't scarcely one new idea in it.
13. "The chances of our getting the Murphy contract sure look good!" said Mrs. DeMille. [*ly*]
14. Christine, our advertising copywriter, does her best work in a real quiet office. [*ly*]
15. Do you agree that we can't afford to increase our marketing budget this year? [*hardly*]
16. Mrs. Jefferson wants to get the Smith-Lambert account in the worst way. [*reely much*]
17. Andrew and I agree that her new idea should sure work well. [*ly*]
18. I only know that Miss Yardley will be promoted; no one else knows about her promotion.
19. When I read in the papers where homeowners' taxes would be increased, I wrote to my state senator. [*THAT*]
20. This dish smells deliciously, but I'm on a special diet. [*delicious*]

B. Correct any errors in the following sentences. Write *OK* if a sentence has no error.

1. Is Sonia doing good as a sales representative for the S&S Company? [*well*]
2. Focus the camera carefully so that your pictures will be more sharper.
3. Mr. Rogers sure doesn't like to be late for his appointments. [*ly*]
4. Janet is a conscientious worker, but she badly needs to take a course in office procedures. [*very much*]
5. Perhaps you would prefer one of those typewriters that uses cartridge tapes.
6. For many years, Edna and Jerry have worked diligent to build up their wholesale clothing business. [*ly*]
7. Ellen once had eight employees in her department, but now she hasn't but one assistant.
8. Miss Trump, Paul's manager, said that Paul works most as well as Larry. [*al*] [*p.p NOT*]
9. Keith's estimates were due last Friday, but because he was so busy, Keith never completed them.

10. Do you think that those kind of decorations would be appropriate for the office?
11. A womens' consciousness-raising course is being offered after work by our company's Office Training Center.
12. As I mentioned yesterday, I would be happy to help Ralph and Natalie complete these them forms.
13. Mr. Barcelona's new stores' cater to the suburban shopper.
14. With better lighting in this room, these proofs would probably look much more clearer than they do now.
15. Where's are your gloves? Did you leave them in the restaurant?
16. Mr. Fredricks, our district manager, don't know how such an error could have occurred.
    oK 17. Jeffrey usually does very good work in controlling inventory sales, but lately he hasn't been feeling well.
18. Because the Smiths' have lost their license to sell in this state, they are selling their warehouse at a bargain price.
19. Here is all the product descriptions that you asked for, Mrs. Evans.
20. To rush Mr. Conrad's supplies to him as quickly as possible, Barbara and myself will fill the order ourselves.

Editing Practice

Editor, Editor!   Rewrite the following letter, correcting whatever errors it contains.

Dear Mrs. Gibson:

FRUITY-BLEND is a most refreshing drink. It tastes deliciously and has all those kind of nutrients that dietitians recommend.

FRUITY contains less sugar than any soft drink on the market. It is tested regular for caloric content by our up to date research department. Your diet is safe with FRUITY.

If you have not yet tried FRUITY-BLEND, your first sip will make you wish you had tried it sooner. Act quick and buy the drink that is absolutely the best of any beverage of it's kind!

Cordially yours,

The Word Processing Supervisor   One of your staff members has been working on a brochure for the Office Training Department. The brochure will be sent to all employees in your company, and the following memorandum will accompany it. Read the memorandum carefully to make sure that it is error-free.

In answer to the many requests we have recieved, the Office Trianing Center has expanded the number of courses that will be avialable to employees begining next Febuary.

As you will see in the enclosed brochure, we are offering many more professional-development courses (such as "Understanding Finance" and "Principles of Effective Management") as well as personal-growth courses (such as "Conversational Spanish" and "Music Appreciation").

Register now for the course(s) of your choice!

Case Problem

Introducing Yourself   You have arrived at a reception for new students given by the college president. You meet the members of the faculty who are in the receiving line and then help yourself to some refreshments. The students and various faculty members who arrived earlier are clustered in many small groups around the room, and you do not know whether to stand by yourself until someone comes over to you or whether to approach one of the groups.

1. What do you think you should do? Why?
2. If you decided to approach one of the groups, what would you say?
3. If you were responsible for arranging this reception, what would you do to make it easier for a newcomer to mix with others?

18
PREPOSITIONS

Prepositions are very commonly used words—so commonly used, in fact, that writers and speakers often include more than one preposition in a sentence. This section will explain some of the errors that are made in using prepositions and, therefore, will help you to avoid making such errors.

DEFINITION

A *preposition* is a connecting word. It is always connected to a noun or a pronoun, and, together, the preposition and the noun (or pronoun) make up a *prepositional phrase*. Here are some commonly used prepositions and some examples of prepositional phrases:

Prepositions			Prepositional Phrases
about	but*	off	*above* the shelf
above	by	on	*among* the managers
after	except	over	*between* you and me
among	for	to	*by* the front door
at	from	under	*from* them
before	in	up	*into* the new conference room
below	into	upon	*of* the committee
beside	like	until	*on* the elevator
between	of	with	*with* Ms. Nelson and Mr. Fitch

*When it means "except."

The noun or pronoun that follows the preposition is called the *object* of the preposition. The phrase *between you and me* has a compound object: *you and me*. A prepositional phrase also includes words that modify the object: for example, in the phrase *into the new conference room*, *into* is the preposition and *room* is its object; *the*, *new*, and *conference* modify the noun *room*.

PREPOSITIONAL PHRASES MAY CLOUD VERB CHOICE

A prepositional phrase is connected to some word in the sentence. You have already seen sentences in which prepositional phrases fall between the subject and its verb, clouding correct verb choice.

> The reason *for these meetings* is to revise our agenda. (Because *meetings* is plural, some people would incorrectly choose the verb *are*. But the subject of the sentence is *reason*, and the verb *is* is correct. The prepositional phrase *for these meetings* modifies *reason* and separates the subject from its verb.)
>
> The employees *on the committee* are in favor of the proposal. (Seeing the singular word *committee*, some people would tend to write or say "committee *is*," but the prepositional phrase *on the committee* separates the subject *employees* from the correct verb, *are*.)

☐ Checkup 1

Correct any errors in the following sentences. Write *OK* if a sentence has no error.
1. Only one of the supervisors wants to attend next month's convention.
2. All the women on the task force is on vacation this week.
3. Did you know that the invoices in this pile was all received just this morning?
4. One of the supervisors have hired part-time typists.
5. The executives on our floor is in a meeting in the conference room.
6. Perhaps one of the books on that shelf is the book that you want.

WORDS REQUIRING SPECIFIC PREPOSITIONS

Years of use have made some expressions "correct" even though there may be no logic to this "correct" usage. Such usage, called *idiomatic* usage, governs many expressions in our language.

The use of specific prepositions with certain words is idiomatic—that is, long-accepted use has made it correct to use these prepositions as follows:

abhorrence *of*
abhorrent *to*
abide *by* a decision
abide *with* a person
abounds *in* or *with*

accompanied *by* (attended by a person)
accompanied *with* (attended by something)
acquit *of*

adapted *to* (adjusted to)
adapted *for* (made over for)
adapted *from* a work
affinity *between*
agree *to* a proposal
agree *with* someone
agreeable *to* (*with* is permissible)
angry *at* a thing or condition
angry *with* a person
attend *to* (listen)
attend *upon* (wait)
beneficial *to*
bestow *upon*
buy *from*
compare *to* the mirror image (assert
   a likeness)
compare *with* the reverse side (analyze
   for similarities or differences)
compliance *with*
comply *with*
confer *on* or *upon* (give to)
confer *with* (talk to)
confide *in* (place confidence in)
confide *to* (entrust to)
conform *to* (in conformity *to* or *with*)
consist *in* (exists in)
consist *of* (made up of)
convenient *for* (suitable for, easy for)
convenient *to* (near)
conversant *with*
correspond *to* or *with* (match; agree with)
correspond *with* (exchange letters)
credit *for*
deal *in* goods or services
deal *with* someone
depend or dependent *on* (but
   independent *of*)

derogatory *to*
different *from* (not *than* or *to*)
disappointed *in* or *with*
discrepancy *between* two
   things
discrepancy *in* one thing
dispense *with*
employ *for* a purpose
employed *at* a stipulated
   salary
employed *in, on,* or *upon* a
   work or business
enter *into* (become a party to)
enter *into* or *upon* (start)
enter *in* a record
enter *at* a given point
exception *to* a statement
familiarize *with*
foreign *to* (preferred to *from*)
identical *with*
independent *of* (not *from*)
inferior or superior *to*
need *of* or *for*
part *from* (take leave of)
part *with* (relinquish)
plan or planning *to* (not *on*)
profit *by*
in regard *to*
with regard *to*
as regards
retroactive *to* (not *from*)
speak *to* (tell something to
   a person)
speak *with* (discuss with)
wait *for* a person, a train, an
   event
wait *on* a customer, a guest

☐ Checkup 2

Fill in the correct preposition for each of the following sentences.
1. Are you sure that this model is identical (?) that one?
2. Do you know which hotels are convenient (?) the convention center?
3. As you know, we must be sure to comply (?) the government regulations.

4. While she was waiting (?) Ms. Schwartz, my supervisor assembled all the correspondence she needed for the meeting.
5. Each of us checked our monthly totals carefully, yet Helen's totals do not correspond (?) mine.
6. To no one's surprise, Anthony was disappointed (?) the results.
7. Although we will appeal, we must abide (?) the decision until it is overturned.
8. Jay takes exception (?) my statement about the reasons for inflation.

Because some of the expressions listed above are used (and misused) more often than others, they are given special attention below.

Agree With, Agree To

Use *agree with* when the object of the preposition is a person; use *agree to* when the object is not a person, such as:

> Does Harold *agree with* Martha concerning the handling of the Freemont account? (Because the object of the preposition is a person, the preposition *with* is correct.)
>
> Does Harold *agree* to Martha's suggestion concerning the handling of the Freemont account? (Here, the object of the preposition is *suggestion*. Because the object is not a person, the preposition *to* is correct.)

Angry With, Angry At

Use *angry with* when the object of the preposition is a person; use *angry at* when the object is not a person, such as:

> Karen appeared to be *angry with* Frances when they discussed their schedule yesterday. (*With* is correct because the object of the preposition is a person.)
>
> Karen appeared to be *angry at* the suggestions made at yesterday's meeting. (*At* is correct because *suggestions*, the object of the preposition, is not a person.)

Part From, Part With

Part from means "to take leave of"; *part with* means "to relinquish, to give up." *Part from* is generally used when the object of the preposition is a person; and *part with*, when the object is not a person.

> When I *parted from* George at the airport, I immediately returned to the office. (*From* is correct; the meaning is "to take leave of.")
>
> Mr. and Mrs. Henderson obviously did not want to *part with* the property, which they had owned since the 1950s. (*With* is correct; the meaning is "to relinquish, to give up.")

Discrepancy In, Discrepancy Between

Use *discrepancy in* when the object of the preposition is singular; use *discrepancy between* when the object denotes exactly *two* in number.

> The *discrepancies in* Maria's sales analysis were simply errors in addition. (*Analysis* is singular; therefore, *in* is correct.)
> The *discrepancy between* Maria's analysis and Pauline's analysis was quickly resolved by our auditor. (There are two analyses—Maria's and Pauline's; therefore *between* is correct.)

In Regard To, With Regard To, As Regards

These three phrases are equally correct, but *regards* cannot be used with *in* or *with*. Whenever *regards*, the word ending in *s*, is used, it must be paired with *as*, the word that also ends in *s*.

> Sherri has already notified all the participants (in? with? as?) regard to the time change. (Either *in* or *with* can be used because *regard* does not end in *s*.)
> As *regards* medical insurance, you may discuss your coverage with Mrs. Lupus, manager of our benefits department. (*As* must be used with *regards*.)

Different From, Identical With, Plan To, Retroactive To

The correct prepositions to be used after *different, identical, plan,* and *retroactive* should be memorized. These expressions are used so frequently that you should not need to continually check a reference manual. Study the following illustrations:

> Please let me know whether your total is *different from* mine. (Not *different than*.)
> Is the coverage available from Mutual Systems Insurance *identical with* the coverage available from A&A Life? (Not *identical to*.)
> When are you *planning to meet* with Mrs. Horton? (Not *planning on meeting*.)
> Naturally, Catherine was delighted to hear that her raise would be *retroactive to* July 1. (Not *retroactive from*.)

☐ Checkup 3

Correct any errors in the following sentences. Write *OK* if a sentence has no error.

1. When you get your broker's license, do you plan on opening your own insurance agency?
2. The Trent Company asked to speak with us in regards to our proposal for developing the Trent property in the southern part of the city.
3. Matthew parted with Frank at the train station.
4. As I read her detailed analysis, I found several discrepancies in it.
5. Although Barbara's proposal was rejected, she was not angry at her manager.

6. Although the new model looks identical to the old model, it is not; the new model has several engineering features that make it much more advanced.
7. Do you agree with Kenneth's recommendation concerning the reorganization of the accounting and auditing staffs?
8. Would you please explain to me specifically how this tool is different than that one?
9. Our vice president, Mrs. Davidson, said that our firm has no definite plans as regards a merger.
10. We wasted too much time trying to resolve the discrepancy between Mr. Aaron's figures and Miss Alcott's figures.

PITFALLS AND ILLITERACIES

Choosing correctly between certain prepositions—*between* and *among*, for example—traps many writers and speakers. In addition, people either add extra prepositions when they are *unnecessary* and leave out prepositions when they *are* necessary. To avoid such pitfalls, study the following guide to correct preposition usage.

Between, Among

Between is commonly used when referring to two persons, places, or things; *among* when referring to more than two.

> The entire project is to be divided *between* the circulation department and the accounts receivable department. (Because there are two departments, the preposition *between* is correct.)
> The entire project is to be divided *among* the circulation department, the accounts receivable department, and the accounts payable department. (Here, three departments are mentioned, so *among* is correct.)

Between may also be used to express a relationship of one thing to each of several other things on a one-to-one basis.

> A new contract was signed *between* the teacher's union and each of the seven school districts in the county.

Beside, Besides

Beside means "by the side of," *besides* means "in addition to." Study the following illustrations:

> Who is the person seated *beside* Ms. Caruthers? (*Beside,* meaning "by the side of" Ms. Caruthers, is correct.)
> Who was invited to the dinner *besides* Carolyn Bains? (Meaning "in addition to Carolyn Bains.")

Inside, Outside

The preposition *of* is not used after *inside* or *outside*. When referring to time, use *within*, not *inside of*.

> My office is the first one *inside* the main entrance. (Not *inside of*.)
> We should keep these boxes *outside* the supply room. (Not *outside* of.)
> Annemarie should have her market analysis completed *within* the week. (Not *inside of*.)

All, Both

Use *of* after *all* or *both* only when *all* or *both* refers to a pronoun. Omit *of* if either word refers to a noun.

> All the members agreed to postpone the hearing until March 15. (*Of* is not needed.)
> All of them agreed to postpone the hearing until March 15. (*All of* is followed by the pronoun *them*.)

At, To; In, Into

At and *in* denote position; *to* and *into* signify motion.

> She arrived *at* our office before 9 p.m. and went immediately *to* the conference room. (*At* for position; *to* for motion.)
> We went *into* the building and met our attorneys *in* the lobby. (*Into* for motion; *in* for position.)

Note: When either *at* or *in* refers to a place, use *in* for larger places and *at* for smaller.

> My sister Martha, who lives in California, works at Disneyland.
> (*In California*, the larger place; *at Disneyland*, the smaller place.)

Behind, Not In Back Of

Use *behind*, not *in back of*. *In front of*, however, is correct.

> Temporarily, please place these boxes *behind*, not *in front of*, the desk. (*Behind*, not *in back of*.)

From, Off

From is generally used with persons; *off* is used with things. *Off* can be used with persons only when something that is physically resting on them is being lifted away.

Never use *of* or *from* after *off*.

> Perhaps you may borrow a calculator *from* Alice.
> Please take those cartons *off* the credenza.
> As Dr. Hamilton took his hand *off* my shoulder, I felt the pain disappear.

Should Of

Of is a preposition; *have* is a verb. Writing *of* for *have* is a very serious error that may be charged to poor diction. "Shuduv" is often heard instead of "should have"; consequently *should of* is often written instead of *should have*. Study this illustration:

> You should have asked for a receipt for your income tax records. (Not *should of*.)

Where . . . At; Where . . . To

Adding *at* or *to* to *where* is an illiteracy.

> Do you know *where* Jessica is? (Not *where Jessica is at*.)
> *Where* did Mrs. Preston go? (Not *Where did Mrs. Preston go to?*)

Help From

Another illiteracy is the use of *from* after the word *help*.

> Yvette couldn't *help* questioning the reasons for the delays. (Not *help from*.)

Opposite To

Do not use the word *to* with *opposite*.

> The Childress Building is *opposite* ours. (Not *opposite to ours*.)

Like For

Like for is incorrect; omit the *for*.

> We should *like* you to be our guest at the annual convention. (Not *like for you*.)

☐ Checkup 4

Correct any preposition errors in the following sentences. Write *OK* if a sentence has no error.
1. She put all of the papers in her briefcase before she left.
2. The woman seated besides Mrs. Pool is the new director of marketing.
3. Ask the driver to pull the car in the garage.

4. Over $5,000 in incentive compensation was shared between Mr. Lloyd and Ms. Bentley.
5. According to company policy, we must do our free-lance work outside of office hours.
6. Let's go in the conference room to continue this discussion.
7. Her new store is opposite to the train station, isn't it?
8. Where have Edna and Brett gone to?
9. As you know, Joanne can't help from talking about sales at every production meeting.
10. If you know where the new brochures are at, would you please get some for me?

COMMUNICATION PROJECTS

Practical Application

A. Correct any errors in the following sentences. Write *OK* if a sentence has no error.

1. Mr. Gregg made only one statement in regards to the merger: "No comment."
2. James was angry at his office manager until she explained why she changed his schedule.
3. Did you really find a discrepancy between your July sales total and mine?
4. In answer to the reporters' questions, we could not help from giving direct answers.
5. No, the French Shack Restaurant is not opposite our store.
6. Do you know who, beside Grace, is going to be transferred to St. Louis?
7. Mr. Treat dislikes parting with any of the antiques in his collection.
8. Yes, Mrs. Young, you can expect to receive your merchandise inside of three weeks.
9. More than half the work in this department is shared among only three people—Martin, Christopher, and Elizabeth.
10. Mr. Calderone's solution is identical to Miss Owen's, yet they had not discussed this problem before this morning.
11. Mr. North, we should like for you to be our guest speaker at our fund-raiser for handicapped children.
12. Bernadette plans on working in our Paris office as a foreign correspondent.
13. Write to Mrs. LaRosa to explain that her name was taken off of our mailing list accidentally.
14. Please help us take all these machines off of the table.
15. Please help Jerry and me place all these boxes in back of those curtains.
16. Does anyone know where Ms. Campbell has gone to?
17. Beside all the people in our department, you should send this report to the chiefs of other departments.
18. With the help of part-time typists, we should easily be able to submit the entire medium-range report inside of two weeks.
19. Do you know what Mrs. Vernon plans to do in regards to the security problem in her department?

20. As you probably know, the high-impact plastic used to manufacture this cassette is different from the plastic used for that one.

B. Correct any errors in the following sentences. Write *OK* if a sentence has no error.

1. The owner of these stores and factories are planning to sell his holdings to a large corporation.
2. If you were the head of this department, who would you select to head this task force?
3. Ask the Kents' to sign both copies of this contract, keep one for their files, and return one to us.
4. In your opinion, who would you say is most dependable in regard to completing assignments on schedule, Roy or Albert?
5. As soon as the judge announced that the defendant was acquitted from the charge, the reporters ran from the room.
6. Everyone in our community did their best to raise money for a community center for the elderly.
7. Peggy sure enjoys working with the new computer.
8. I feel good now that I take vitamins and avoid junk foods.
9. Frankly, Annette proofreads more accurately than him.
10. Do these new specifications conform with the government's regulations?
11. Because our supplies are so low, you should reorder them items by telephone as soon as possible.
12. Ms. Havel said that a bonus would be given to you and I if we complete this advertising campaign on time.
13. Among our department's most experienced writers are Charles McKinley, a senior copywriter.
14. Each branch office has their own branch manager, of course, but some branches have vice presidents in addition to branch managers.
15. My assistant, who you met last week, will assemble all the information you need.
16. Don't Jocelyn have the key to the computer room?
17. Yes, you may depend on Allen and I to complete your project on time and within the budgeted costs.
18. Does anyone know whose in charge of the Freeman account?
19. I must admit that Mr. Grant works much longer hours than me.
20. A number of complaints about this stereo has been received—mostly in regard to its speaker system.

Editing Practice

Using Business Vocabulary   From the list below, select the word that best completes each of the blanks. Write the corresponding letter in the space provided.

a. comptroller	f. irreparable
b. cumulative	g. miscellaneous
c. enumerate	h. monopolize
d. hesitant	i. negligible
e. inexhaustible	j. unscrupulous

1. At this morning's meeting we discussed _____(?)_____ topics.
2. The insurance adjustor agreed that the damage is _____(?)_____ and, therefore,
3. Michelle appeared somewhat _____(?)_____ to discuss the plans to reorganize our departments.
4. Fortunately, the amount of smoke damage to the supplies in the storeroom was _____(?)_____ .
5. The committee should not allow any one person to _____(?)_____ the discussion.
6. To make this agenda clearer, you should _____(?)_____ the topics in list form.
7. The first monthly column lists January sales; each succeeding column lists _____(?)_____ sales for the preceding month.
8. Mr. Mobley, the _____(?)_____ of our company, completed the requirements for an M.B.A. degree in June.
9. She wrote a best-selling exposé of excessive profiteering by _____(?)_____ companies during the oil shortage.
10. Our supply of this metal is virtually _____(?)_____ , but mining it is very expensive.

Writing Sentences   Each of the following words is a "must" for your vocabulary and your spelling lists. Do you know the meaning of each word? Can you spell each one correctly?

Write a sentence using each word.

1. accommodate
2. campaign
3. dissatisfied
4. equivalent
5. exorbitant
6. guarantee
7. necessary
8. omission
9. potential
10. questionnaire

Case Problem

A Case of Ethics   There is a rule at the Burns Office Equipment Company that personal mail may not be sent through the company's postage meter machine. Jack Thompson, who is in charge of the mail room, receives a batch of mail from Brad Parton, a sales assistant, that contains some obviously personal letters written by Brad. Jack is not sure whether Brad inadvertently placed his personal mail among the company correspondence or whether Brad was trying deliberately to slip his personal letters in with the other letters.

1. What should Jack do about the situation? Why?
2. What should Jack say to Brad?

19 CONJUNCTIONS

A word that is used to *connect* words, phrases, or clauses within a sentence is called a *conjunction*.

> A printer *and* a binder have already submitted their bids for this project. (In this sentence, the conjunction *and* joins two words, *printer* and *binder*.)
>
> Do you know whether Miss Bilger is in her office *or* at a meeting? (The conjunction *or* connects the phrases *in her office* and *at a meeting*.)
>
> Mr. DiPalma has already left for the airport, *but* he said that he would call the office as soon as he arrived in Detroit. (The conjunction *but* connects the two main clauses.)

The rules of punctuation and sentence structure will be easier to learn once you have reviewed all the uses of conjunctions. This section on conjunctions considers first the classification of conjunctions, then pitfalls in conjunction usage, and finally, parallel structure.

CLASSIFICATION OF CONJUNCTIONS

Conjunctions are classified as coordinate, correlative, and subordinate. The first two types—coordinate and correlative conjunctions—connect two or more items of equal rank. The last type—subordinate conjunction—connects a subordinate clause to a main clause.

Coordinate Conjunctions

The coordinate conjunctions are *and, but, or,* and *nor.* They connect only *like* elements of grammar—two or more words, two or more phrases, or two or more clauses. Coordinate conjunctions cannot be used to connect two or more *un*like elements of grammar.

> The Anson Company publishes newspapers and magazines. (The conjunction *and* connects the words *newspapers* and *magazines*.)
>
> Mr. Buckley has been on the telephone *or* in a conference for most of the day. (The conjunction *or* connects the prepositional phrases *on the telephone* and *in a conference*.)
>
> Mrs. Tillman approved the cover design for this brochure, *but* she rejected the colors suggested. (The conjunction *but* connects two independent, or main, clauses.)

Correlative Conjunctions

Correlative conjunctions are *pairs* of conjunctions; they, too, are used to connect *like* grammatical elements. The most commonly used correlative conjunctions are listed below. Note that *either* and *or* go together and that *neither* and *nor* go together.

both . . . and   not only . . . but also
either . . . or   whether . . . or
neither . . . nor

These correlatives are used to connect words, phrases, and clauses, just as coordinate conjunctions are used. In the first sentence below, for example, note the coordinate *and* means "in addition to" or "also"—the same meaning as *not only . . . but also*. But note how the second sentence conveys a slightly different meaning, a slightly different emphasis.

The defendant *and* the plaintiff disagreed with the judge's ruling. *Not only* the defendant *but also* the plaintiff disagreed with the judge's ruling.

Subordinate Conjunctions

Subordinate conjunctions join clauses of *unequal* rank. A subordinate conjunction introduces a subordinate (or dependent) clause and connects it to a main (or independent) clause.

Although the builder had been far ahead of schedule, the sudden snowstorms delayed completion of the homes for several weeks. (*Although* is a subordinate conjunction; it introduces a subordinate clause, *although the builder had been far ahead of schedule,* and connects this subordinate clause to the main clause.)

Please call Dorothy Manley *if* you plan to attend the seminar. (The subordinate conjunction *if* introduces the subordinate clause *if you plan to attend the seminar,* and it connects this subordinate clause to the main clause.)

As you may have noticed, in the first example above, a comma separates the subordinate clause from the main clause. But no comma is used in the second sentence, where the subordinate clause follows the main clause. Comma use with subordinate clauses is discussed in greater detail in a later section, but you must first be able to identify such clauses if you are to punctuate them correctly. So that you will be sure to identify subordinate clauses, study the following list of commonly used subordinate conjunctions.

after	before	provided that	when
although	even if	since	whenever
as	for	so that	where
as if	how	than	wherever
as soon as	if	that	whether
as though	in case that	unless	while
because	in order that	until	why

☐ Checkup 1

Identify the conjunctions in the following sentences. Classify each as coordinate, correlative, or subordinate.

1. Did you mail both the application form and the check?
2. The manager of our Detroit office and the assistant manager of our Denver office will be in town this week.
3. When you get the estimates from the production department, please let me know the unit costs for each item.
4. Mail the completed form today if you want to receive the April issue.
5. Yes, Karen, either Carlos or Vera has a copy of the agenda.
6. You can save 10 percent by enclosing your payment now, unless you prefer to be billed at a later date.
7. Mrs. Gilmore knows that the list price has been increased.
8. She plans to buy new luggage before she leaves for vacation next month.
9. While we were negotiating a new contract with Wilson & Denton, we heard about the strike threat.
10. We will discuss our marketing strategy for these new products as soon as our regional managers arrive.

CONJUNCTION PITFALLS

The major conjunction pitfalls are (1) choosing a conjunction that does not best convey the intended meaning and (2) choosing a preposition when a conjunction is required. The following discussion emphasizes the selection of the correct conjunction whenever you are faced with these pitfalls.

But or And?

The conjunction *and* simply *joins* elements, while the conjunction *but* provides a contrast between two elements that *and* does not provide.

> This less expensive model sells very well, *but* the more expensive model is probably the better value. (*But* for contrast.)

Who, Which, or That?

Use *who* to refer to persons and *which* to refer to objects. Never say or write *and who* or *and which.*

> Deliver this package to Mrs. Bromley, *who* is the new director of financial planning. (*Who* refers to a person.)
> She is now planning a special promotion campaign, *which* will include television, radio, and newspaper advertisements. (*Which* refers to an object. Not *and which.*)

That may be used to refer to persons, animals, or objects.

> The man *that* you heard is our director of operations, Mr. Francis. (Here, *that* refers to a person. *Whom* could also have been used.)
> The racehorse *that* she bought is insured for more than $1,000,000. (Here, *that* refers to animals.)
> Among the magazines *that* our executives subscribe to is *Business Week*. (Here, *that* refers to objects.)

Since or *Because* (not *Being That*)

There is no such conjunction as *being that;* its use is incorrect. Instead, *since* or *because* will convey the correct meaning.

> *Because* Ms. Gleason is on vacation, we decided to postpone our discussion of employee benefits. (*Because,* not *being that.*)

That (not *Because* or *Like*)

The word *that* is correct in the terms *the reason is that* and *pretend that.* Do not say or write *the reason is because* or *pretend like.*

> The *reasons* for the price increase *are that* the cost of the raw materials has risen 25 percent and *that* shipping costs have increased 15 percent. (Not *reasons are because.*)
> Sometimes Miss VanBuren seems to *pretend that* this problem is minor. (Not *pretend like.*)

☐ Checkup 2

Make any needed corrections. Write *OK* if a sentence is correct.
1. Her new job is very demanding, and she enjoys it very much.
2. Apparently, the reason for cancelling the flight is because the plane is now snow-bound in Chicago.
3. Sheila intends to stay late this evening being that she wants to work on the Lambert account.
4. The primary reason for discussing this problem is because we are eager to hear our employees' suggestions.
5. Edna interviewed two applicants, which were referred to us by the DePaul Employment Agency.
6. Jerry bought a new car, and he doesn't like it as much as his old car.
7. This organization cares for stray animals, whom it shelters in modern facilities.
8. She recommended several attorneys which are located here in this building.

Unless (not *Without* or *Except*)

Without and *except* are prepositions, and a preposition always introduces a prepositional phrase (a preposition plus its noun or pronoun object and any modifiers). Yet many people incorrectly use these prepositions as substitutes for the subordinate conjunction *unless*.

> Do not mail this check *without* Henry's signature. (*Without Henry's signature* is a prepositional phrase: *signature* is the object of the preposition *without*, and *Henry's* modifies *signature*.)
>
> Do not mail this check *unless* you get Henry's signature. (Do not say *without you get Henry's signature. You get Henry's signature* is a clause, and it cannot be introduced by a preposition. It must be introduced by the conjunction *unless*.)

As, As If, or As Though (not *Like*)

The word *like* is one of the most overused and *misused* words in our language. Be sure to remember that *like* is a preposition, and as you know, a preposition cannot introduce a clause. Use *as, as if,* or *as though*—not *like*—in sentences such as these:

> You looked *as if* you were angry, but I knew that you were not. (Not *like you were angry. You were angry* is a clause, and a clause cannot be introduced by a preposition, such as *like*.)
>
> I certainly wish that I owned a business *like* his. (The preposition *like* is correct in this sentence. It introduces the prepositional phrase *like his*.)

☐ Checkup 3

Make any needed corrections. Write *OK* if a sentence is correct.
1. Sometimes Peter acts like he were in charge of the entire project!
2. Anne, please do not open this safe except I tell you to do so.
3. Be sure not to send this copy to the printer without you get the approval of the advertising director.
4. John said, "It seems like business is picking up substantially in the last two quarters."
5. Order clerks are not supposed to give discounts without getting approval.
6. Order clerks are not supposed to give discounts unless they get approval.
7. Please don't leave without you sign this check.
8. Howard should not just sit there like he had no work to do.

PARALLEL STRUCTURE

A well-trained communicator observes the rules of parallel structure. As you will see, ideas of equal importance or of equal weight should be expressed in parallel form—that is, they should be treated similarly.

The new machine works quietly and quickly. (The conjunction *and* joins two parallel words—two adverbs.)

The new machine works quietly and with speed. (The same ideas are expressed in this sentence, but they are not expressed in parallel form. The conjunction *and* joins an adverb, *quietly*, to a prepositional phrase, *with speed*. An adverb and a prepositional phrase are not parallel; they are *unlike* elements.)

Now let's see how parallel structure should be achieved when using coordinate conjunctions and correlative conjunctions.

With Coordinate Conjunctions

Coordinate conjunctions connect like elements: an adjective with an adjective, an adverb with an adverb, a prepositional phrase with a prepositional phrase, and so on. Thus the elements before and after the coordinate conjunctions should match.

The committee members seem objective and (to be impartial? impartial?) in listening to each case. (The adjective *objective* appears before the coordinate conjunction *and*, so an adjective should follow *and*. The answer that achieves parallelism is *impartial*.)

As a recruiter, your duties will include speaking to seniors, screening likely candidates, and (to interview? interviewing?) applicants. (The parallel items before the coordinate conjunction *and* are *speaking* and *screening*—two gerunds. Therefore, a gerund must follow *and*; *interviewing* is correct.)

☐ Checkup 4

Balance the following sentences to make them parallel.
1. This machine requires monthly maintenance and yearly overhauling.
2. These plastic sheets can be bent, rolled, or are even immersible in water.
3. You may request a loan by mail, by telephone, or come in person.
4. Both applicants seem to be personable and have courtesy.
5. Eating the proper foods is important, but to exercise is also important.
6. This book will help you understand the basics of finance and applying the basic rules to your job.

With Correlative Conjunctions

Correlative conjunctions, as you know, are used in pairs. For parallelism, the element that follows the first conjunction must match the element that follows the second member in the pair.

Pauline usually asks either *Albert* or *me* to sit in on the monthly production meeting. (The elements that follow each of the paired conjunctions *either...or* are (1) *Albert* and (2) *me*—a noun and a pronoun. Nouns and pronouns are considered like elements because pronouns are noun substitutes; thus the phrase *either Albert or me* is parallel.)

All sales items are available *not only* in any of our stores *but also* through our shop-at-home service. (The structure is parallel because the correlative conjunctions *not only...but also* join two prepositional phrases: *in any of our stores* and *through our shop-at-home service.*)

Not only did Mrs. Edwin complete her project ahead of schedule, *but* she *also* came in under budget. (The correlative conjunctions *not only...but also* join two independent clauses. Thus the structure is parallel. Do not be mislead by the inverted order of the first independent clause.)

☐ Checkup 5

Balance the elements joined by correlative conjunctions so that they are parallel.

1. To save fuel, our staff members are trying to either form car pools or to use public transportation.
2. The announcement was written either by Mr. Lancaster or his assistant.
3. Mrs. Quimby likes both hiking and to go fishing when she is on vacation.
4. Either the press release was prepared by Charles or by his assistant, Marjorie.
5. Our supervisor hasn't decided whether Joanne will be selected or Harold.
6. She neither agreed with Miss Olsen nor with Mrs. Lloyd.

COMMUNICATION PROJECTS

Practical Application

A. Correct any errors. Write *OK* if a sentence is correct.

1. Such large discounts are neither given to large-volume buyers nor to small-volume buyers.
2. Our company will show an increased profit this year unless consumer buying is suddenly curtailed.
3. The reason she arrived late is because her original flight had been canceled.
4. Mr. Harrison gives away free products like they cost the company nothing.
5. Our supervisor feels that neither overtime nor a third shift is the answer to our production backlog.
6. According to well-informed sources, it looks like the contract will be let to Jacoby & Arno.
7. Finally, after several hours, they not only agreed on the list prices but also on the discounts for these products.
8. Bank policy states that an unemployed person cannot secure a loan without a co-signer.
9. Bank policy states that an unemployed person cannot secure a loan unless he or she has a cosigner.
10. This book is both well written and has colorful illustrations.

11. Our deadline is noon tomorrow, and we have plenty of time to complete the assignment.
12. Writing the first draft is easy, but to edit it is more difficult.
13. Catherine said that when she speaks to large audiences, she always pretends like she were talking to a few close friends.
14. The reason sales decreased last quarter is because five sales representatives left at the same time.
15. Do not order more equipment without you are sure that the expense is budgeted.
16. Mr. Nelson claimed both that our Minneapolis store and our Seattle store were among the top ten in our company.
17. Which job do you prefer—typing, filing, or to take dictation?
18. Being that Miss Hopkins was ill, our department had more work than we were able to handle.
19. These machines must be checked carefully and with regularity.
20. The agenda for the conference will either be prepared by Sarah or by Nathan.

B. Correct any errors. Write *OK* if a sentence is correct.

1. I wish that I had an extra income like Paul and you.
2. Don't plan on buying new equipment until the budget is approved.
3. We read in the paper where the First Bank and Trust has elected new officers.
4. Being that Angelo is in charge of corporate trust accounts, he should be able to answer your questions.
5. Generally we prefer to ignore them kinds of suggestions.
6. Unfortunately, we have neither the time or the money to waste on such impractical schemes.
7. The Knapps' have bought the controlling interest in the Winthrop Corporation.
8. To complete the typing on time, Ellen suggested that we divide all the reports among the two of us, Ellen and me.
9. Don't Mrs. Brandon supervise the warehouse in California?
10. He neither completed the forms correctly nor submitted them to us before the deadline.
11. I tried to call Mrs. Simpson all day yesterday, but I never received an answer.
12. Frankly, I thought that the speaker appeared like he was poorly prepared.
13. Helen will be promoted to senior reporter next month, and she does not know about the promotion yet!
14. We have no information in regards to the new government contract.
15. The questionnaires on the table in the lobby was received only this morning.
16. Miss Denton asked Mary Jo and I to visit our branch manager in San Francisco while we were there.
17. Our supervisor recently bought one of those personal computers that sells for under $5,000.
18. Apparently, the Patton's are eager to sell all their property.
19. There seems to be some differences of opinion about which recommendation is best.
20. From 9 a.m. until noon, a number of applicants was interviewed for the Kansas territory.

Editing Practice

The Word Processing Supervisor   Correct any errors in the following excerpt from a sales letter.

The next time you plan to advertise your products to todays' homeowner, be sure to find out about *Today's Home*, the magazine for modern men and women who are interested in improveing the quality of their homes and their lives. Many advertisers have found that *Today's Home* is the best way to reach that $40 billion home-improvement market. Perhaps you will too.

To find out about advertising rates for *Today's Home*, call this toll-free number: 800-555-9679.

Plurals and Possessives   Correct any errors in the following sentences. Write *OK* if a sentence has no error.

1. The Professors Smith, tonights' guest speakers, will discuss the effect of the fuel shortage on our economy.
2. Marias' new home is only a ten-minute drive from the center of town.
3. Some of the ratioes given in this table are obviously typographical errors.
4. Many of the cameras and televisions that we import are manufactured by the Japaneses.
5. When typing a table, be sure to align the periods and the zeroes in each column.
6. All the designs showed creativity and flair, but the one that I prefer is her's.
7. Ella's and Audrey's new store is located on the south side of Fifth Avenue.
8. Your sister-in-laws and your brothers are co-owners of this property, aren't they?
9. One of the best children's schools in our area is the Milford School on West Tenth Street.
10. The only people who did not attend the celebration were the Carltons'.

Case Problem

The Pool Supervisor   Executives of the Hammett Company who use stenographers from the pool are complaining that their letters have to be retyped because of errors in spelling. What steps would you take to remedy the situation?

CHAPTER 4

APPLYING THE MECHANICS OF STYLE

20
PERIOD,
QUESTION MARK,
EXCLAMATION POINT

Good speakers pause, change the pitch of their voices, and gesture to help their listeners interpret the message accurately and quickly. In the same way, good writers use punctuation marks to help their readers better understand a message.

The period, question mark, and exclamation point are the three marks of punctuation used to end sentences. But they also have other uses, as we will see in this section.

PERIOD

To simplify the presentation on the period, we will divide the discussion into three main topics: when to use a period, when not to use a period, and pitfalls in using periods.

When to Use a Period

Use a period (1) to end a declarative or an imperative sentence and (2) to end a request that is phrased as a question simply for the sake of courtesy.

After Declarative and Imperative Sentences A declarative sentence makes a statement; an imperative sentence orders or entreats someone to action.

> You should enclose a check with your order. (Declarative sentence) Enclose a check with your order. (Imperative sentence)

After Requests Phrased as Questions To avoid the abrupt sound of an order or command, a request or a suggestion is often phrased as a question. Obviously, a question has a more polite sound than a command or order.

> Will you please send us your check immediately. (This sentence doesn't really ask for an answer. Because it requests the reader to do something, not to answer a question, we omit the question mark after such sentences.)
>
> Will you be able to ship the materials to us by September 12? (This is a real question, not a request. The writer wants a "Yes" or "No" answer.)
>
> May we have the materials by September 12. (Not really a question; the writer is saying "Send us the materials by September 12"—but is saying it politely.)

☐ Checkup 1

Which of the following sentences should end with periods?

1. Rush our order to our warehouse as soon as possible, Mr. Hall
2. May I have your payment by the end of the week
3. I asked Leroy if he wanted to come with us
4. May Joan and I leave early today

5. May we have your revised estimate by Monday, October 9
6. Miss Donaldson has been leading all our sales representatives for several months now
7. Please mail your report to the district office by the end of the week
8. Has Peggy had these invoices checked
9. When do you expect to receive the manufacturer's samples
10. May I use your calculator

When Not to Use a Period

Do not use periods for sentences other than declarative and imperative sentences and requests phrased as questions. Therefore, do not use periods in the following instances.

After a Sentence Ending in an Abbreviation   Do not add a second period to the end of a sentence if the last word in the sentence is an abbreviation that already ends in a period. Only one period is needed.

> The invitation specifically said 8 p.m. (Not *8 p.m..*)
> All orders to Kramer and Thornton should be shipped c.o.d. (Not *c.o.d..*)

After a Heading or Title; After a Roman Numeral   A period should not follow headings set on separate lines (that is, headings not run-in with the text). Also, no period should follow a roman numeral used with a name or a title.

> Chapter Four: The Mechanics of Style (Chapter heading)
> Principles of Financial Management (Heading in a book)
> Joseph Henry III was founder of this company. (Not *Joseph Henry III. was . . . .*)

After Numbers or Letters Enclosed in Parentheses   Do not use periods with numbers or letters enclosed in parentheses.

> In long-term international trade transactions, there are three major problem areas for exporters: (1) losses, (2) delayed payments, and (3) political risks. (Numbers enclosed in parentheses)

When such numbers or letters are not in parentheses, then periods are used:

> We will discuss three major problem areas:
> 1. Losses
> 2. Delayed payments
> 3. Political risks

After Items in Tabulated Lists or in Outlines   Do not use a period after short phrases unless the phrases are essential to the grammatical completeness of the statement introducing the list. *Do* use a period after independent clauses, dependent clauses, or long phrases appearing on separate lines in a list. If the list includes both short and long phrases, use periods.

> These two volumes discuss the following topics:
> 1. Fundamentals of finance
> 2. Developing expense budgets

These two volumes discuss:

1. The fundamentals of finance.
2. How to develop expense budgets.

Remember these points:

1. Every manager must know the fundamentals of finance.
2. Every manager must know how to develop expense budgets.

After Even Amounts of Dollars Except in tabulations (when it is important to align all numbers), do not use periods or zeros in even dollar amounts.

> Thank you for your $50 check, which we received this morning.
> (Not $50., not $50.00)

☐ Checkup 2

Find the errors and make the needed corrections. Write *OK* if a sentence is correct.
1. Our questionnaires were sent to three groups of employees:
   a. Exempt employees
   b. Nonexempt employees
   c. Free-lance workers
2. Our new Heater-Miser will cut your fuel bills substantially, and it's yours for only $49.00.
3. Miss Marsh carefully explained (1.) the life insurance plan, (2.) the medical insurance coverage, and (3.) the optional dental plan.
4. Former Senator George T. Harrison III. has been elected to our Board of Directors.
5. Last week we signed a two-year shipping agreement with Cross County Trucking, Inc..
6. If you qualify, you can receive a five-year renewable term policy worth $65,000. for only $214. a year.

Period Pitfalls

The careful business writer avoids these two common traps in using periods: (1) using a period to end an incomplete thought and (2) using a comma when a period is needed. Master the following guides so that you will avoid these pitfalls.

The Period Fault Using a period at the end of an incomplete thought is called a "period fault." Because the incomplete thought is not a sentence, it cannot stand alone. Often, joining this incomplete thought to a main clause will solve the problem.

> We are not shipping orders this week. Because our warehouse is currently taking yearly inventory. (The second group of words cannot stand alone. This dependent clause should be joined to the first clause as follows: *We are not shipping orders this week, because our warehouse is currently taking yearly inventory.*)

Note that condensed expressions are not considered incomplete sentences. A condensed expression may be an answer to a question that precedes the expression or a statement that logically follows from it.

> In the survey, what did our women employees name as their primary goals? Fair play and equal opportunities for advancement. (By itself, the second statement would not ordinarily be considered a complete sentence and would not end in a period. But here it is obviously an answer to the question that precedes it, so it is correctly treated as a complete sentence, followed by a period.)

The Comma-for-Period Fault   A comma should not join two separate sentences; on the contrary, a period should separate the sentences. Note these examples:

> Orders for CB radios will be filled at the end of next month, we are currently out of stock. (The comma is incorrect. Because these are two separate, distinct thoughts, each should be written as an independent sentence.)
> Mrs. Milich will leave for Atlanta tomorrow, she will be attending a data processing convention. (Again, two separate, distinct thoughts should be written as separate sentences. The comma is incorrect.)

☐ Checkup 3

Are there any period faults or comma-for-period faults in the following sentences? Make any corrections that are necessary.

1. We hope that you will be able to join us for lunch on Monday, we will meet in Dining Room B at 12:30.
2. Our new catalog is enclosed, an up-to-date price list will be sent to you within the next two weeks.
3. Ms. Ho is exploring the benefits of computer time-sharing; she believes that time-sharing will prove economical for our company.
4. Although the strike has officially ended. We do not expect to resume production until the first of next month.
5. The Stanton Company is not planning to expand its sales force. Because it expects sales of consumer goods to plunge sharply for the next two years.
6. As you will see from the enclosed résumé. I worked in the Word Processing Department for Barton Chemicals, Inc., for two years.

QUESTION MARK

Use a question mark after a *direct* question, after a short direct question following a statement, and in a series of questions.

After a Direct Question

A direct question always ends with a question mark.

> Have you ever heard of management by objectives (MBO)?
> Miss Parks, do you have time to help us process these invoices?
> Did she say "Cancel the Cummings order"?
> Mr. O'Leary asked, "What is the suggested retail price of Model 12-56B?"

After a Short Direct Question Following a Statement

A sentence that begins as a statement but ends as a question is considered a question. Therefore, use a question mark at the end of such sentences.

> John mailed the package to Ms. Vereen, didn't he? (The question that ends this sentence—*didn't he?*—must have a question mark.)
>
> Erica is scheduled to be the first speaker, isn't she? (Again, a question ends the sentence; thus a question mark is needed.)

In a Series of Questions

When a sentence contains a series of questions, each question in the series may have its own question mark, unless the items in the series are joined by conjunctions and commas. Compare the following pairs of sentences.

> Does the research director plan to conduct a marketing survey in New York? in Boston? in Los Angeles? (Note that each item begins with a lowercase letter, not a capital letter, and that each item ends with a question mark.)
>
> Does the research director plan to conduct a marketing survey in New York, in Boston, or in Los Angeles? (Here, the items in the series are joined by commas and the conjunction *or*, and only *one* question mark is needed—at the end of the sentence.)
>
> Who will speak first—the president? the vice president? the director of personnel?
>
> Who will speak first—the president, the vice president, or the director of personnel?

Question Mark Pitfall

Many questions include the word *ask*, *why*, or *how*—so many, in fact, that some writers automatically use a question mark to end any sentence that includes one of these words. But not every sentence with *ask*, *why*, or *how* is a direct question. These words are also used in *indirect* questions, which are statements that end in periods, not question marks.

> No one asked why the price is so high. (A statement, not a question) Miss DeKalb asked us why we revised the schedule. (Not a question; the period is correct.)

☐ Checkup 4

Are periods and question marks used correctly? Make any necessary corrections.
1. When will you complete your sales analysis of these products, Helen?
2. We are often asked whether we need part-time help?
3. Did you send this report to the president of the company? the vice president of finance? the budget director?
4. Ask Helen when she will complete the sales analysis of these products?

5. Miss Hadle asked Miss Palmer for help with the end-of-month statements?
6. All the videotape cassettes are in the cabinet, aren't they.
7. Mrs. Halloran asked when we plan to submit our proposal for reorganizing the two departments?
8. Mr. Kyoto does not like any of the names suggested for our latest men's cologne, does he.

EXCLAMATION POINT

Everyone recognizes the exclamation point as the mark of strong emotion or feeling. We often see signs and advertisements that say "Special Sale! One Day Only!" or "Hurry! This offer is limited!" However, in routine business writing, including sales letters, the exclamation point is not used as often as in signs and advertisements.

By saving the exclamation point for special situations, writers give the exclamation point special impact. Do not overuse the exclamation point. Note that it is especially effective after a single word or a short phrase.

> Mark exceeded his sales goals by 45 percent!
> Oh! What wonderful news this is!
> Congratulations! We are happy to hear that you have been promoted to National Sales Manager.

Sometimes the exclamation point may substitute for the question mark if a strong statement is intended, rather than an answer to a question.

> What happened to our order? (The question mark shows that the writer wants an answer to the question.)
> What happened to our order! (The exclamation point shows that the writer wants to express irritation or anger.)

☐ Checkup 5

Are exclamation points used correctly in the following sentences? Make the necessary corrections.
1. Oh! What have I done?
2. Great. We completed the entire project one month ahead of schedule.
3. Guess who won the annual sales contest.
4. How happy I am to hear about your appointment.
5. Good work. Your research study will save the company thousands of dollars.
6. What a relief? After a dangerous flight, she landed her plane safely.

COMMUNICATION PROJECTS

Practical Application
A. Make any needed corrections in the use of periods, question marks, or exclamation points. Write *OK* for each correct sentence.
1. Our subscription will expire next month, we should renew it now.
2. Will you send us your check for $49.75 by the end of next week.

3. Radios are selling very well, we can hardly meet the demand.
4. Congratulations. All of us are happy to hear that you have been named Regional Manager.
5. Miss Berenson asked whether we had interviewed anyone for the assistant manager's position?
6. Donna, you do plan to attend next Monday's planning session, don't you.
7. Each new sales representative was given:
    1. A sales-training kit.
    2. Several catalogs.
    3. Product information sheets explaining each product.
    4. An up-to-date price list.
    5. Customer-profile cards.
8. Miss Wilson does not have the authority to sign requisitions over $500, only Mrs. Mendez can sign such requisitions.
9. Do you know whether these specification sheets have been approved by George Divine? By Olga Petrov? By Phyllis DeMarco?
10. We were offered $4,500.00 as a trade-in on this machine, which we purchased five years ago for $15,000.00.
11. Is funding for this educational project available under Title II.?
12. Ms. Weinstein, our supervisor, is scheduled to return from Houston on Friday. On the 6:15 flight.
13. This plastic is very, very expensive. Although the quality is obviously excellent.
14. Did you ask Fred whether he has seen this month's expense report.
15. Mrs. Jenkins has been active in community affairs for many years, hasn't she.
16. Michael asked Diana to explain the new procedures to her staff?
17. Should we invite Carole, Bob, Scott, and Bernice?
18. Ask them to (1.) ship all four cartons first class, (2.) bill us for the delivery cost, (3.) send us an itemized invoice, and (4.) charge the entire amount to account B179-1945.
19. We are now looking at word processing equipment from different manufacturers. So that we may see the advantages and disadvantages of each machine.
20. May we have your complete payment by March 15?

B. Correct any errors in the following sentences. Write *OK* if a sentence is correct.
1. Perhaps we should have ordered an additional 100 copys of the brochure for distribution at tomorrow's meeting.
2. Mr. Martin asked us whether we need additionnal typists to work on the Jamison account.
3. At the sale price of $49.00, this clock radio is a genuine bargain.
4. Each customers' credit card number is listed on these sheets in alphabetical order.
5. Here is one of the announcements that is to be listed on the bulletin board.
6. The assistant manager asked whether these appliances are also on sale?
7. Mrs. Everett appreciates us helping her with the monthly audit.
8. Whom do you think Mr. McConnell will name as his new assistant?
9. I am sure that she said to send all these packages c.o.d..

10. Correcting all the copies was more harder than we thought it would be.
11. The deadline for completing all the forms is tomorrow, and she completed them several days early.
12. This new brochure should be more effective than any brochure we have ever mailed to our customers.
13. Submit your application form as soon as possible, the deadline is September 1.
14. Will you please ship the entire order by airfreight by November 15.
15. These televisions will be reduced to $399 next Monday. Which is the first day of our special sale.
16. Please do not send these contracts to Central Filing without Mr. Turner sees them first.
17. It seems like this week will never end.
18. The reason she left early is because she has a 10:15 a.m. flight.
19. To make sure that we finish typing all the contracts on time, let's divide them between the four of us.
20. Our supervisor has assigned two more assistants to Brenda and I.

Editing Practice

Editor Needed! Are there any agreement errors in the following sentences?

1. Either Janet or Veronica are to take over the Owens account.
2. Every man and women in our branch offices have already completed their questionnaire.
3. Dependability and initiative is important for advancement to management positions.
4. The number of customers who complained about the new billing procedures are surprisingly high.
5. Some of the area have been purchased by the government.
6. Here is the microphone and the slide projector that you requested.
7. All tax records prior to 1978 has been discarded.
8. Mr. Granger said there is only a few people who know about the tentative merger.
9. On the top shelf is the latest government regulations concerning the use of preservatives in children's foods.
10. Every customer has the right to see his credit history file.

Proofreading for Spelling Errors Are there any misspelled words in the following excerpt from a sales letter? Give the correct spellings.

You are cordially invited to Glendale's annual one-day warehouse clearance sale! Each year, Glendale's well-known sale attracts hundreds of shoppers from the metropolitan area, shoppers who know that they will find genuine bargains in fine-quality furniture.

Sofas, recliners, dining room sets, and many other peices of furniture—all name brands—will be available at sizable savings for the discriminating shopper. Be sure to mark the date and time on your calender: Saturday, February 12, from 9 a.m. until 9 p.m.

Case Problem

Retaining Goodwill Fred James is supervisor of the adjustment department of a large department store. In reviewing the carbons of letters sent to customers by some of his correspondents, Fred found the following two statements: (1) "Really, Mrs. Whitehouse, you can't blame us if you don't follow the instructions included with each mixer." (2) "You should know that we can't allow a refund unless you return the merchandise within a reasonable time."

1. Do you find anything wrong with either of these statements?
2. If so, what would you have written?

21 SEMICOLON, COLON, DASH

The period, question mark, and exclamation point are used predominantly to end sentences, as you have seen in the preceding section. On the other hand, the semicolon, colon, and dash are used *within* sentences; they are tools that tell the reader to pause before completing the sentence. Thus all three marks—semicolon, colon, and dash—hold the reader temporarily, but each has its own specific function, as you will see in this section.

SEMICOLON

The semicolon forces the reader to pause and helps the reader to understand the message clearly. A common use of the semicolon is (1) to indicate the omission of a conjunction. In addition, the semicolon is used (2) before an introductory word that begins the second clause in a sentence and (3) before explanatory or enumerating words.

To Indicate Omission of a Conjunction

A compound sentence is a sentence that contains two or more independent clauses. In such a sentence the clauses are usually connected by a comma and a conjunction.

> The enclosed Super-Card is for your use only, but you may order additional cards for other members of your family by completing the enclosed request form. (This is a compound sentence; it has two independent clauses connected by a comma and the conjunction *but.*)

The conjunction in a compound sentence may be omitted and a semicolon may be used in its place.

> The enclosed Super-Card is for your personal use only; you may order additional cards for other members of your family by completing the enclosed request form. (Here, the semicolon joins the two independent clauses.)

Before a Second Clause Starting With an Introductory Word

In some compound sentences, the second clause starts with an introductory word such as:

accordingly	consequently	moreover
again	furthermore	nevertheless
also	however	otherwise
besides	indeed	therefore

In such sentences, the semicolon serves to separate the two clauses; at the same time, the introductory word tells the specific relationship between the two clauses, making the meaning easier to comprehend.

> The United States consumes more fuel each year than it produces; consequently, it is dependent upon imported fuel to meet its demands. (The semicolon separates the two independent clauses, and the introductory word *consequently* describes how the two clauses are related. *Consequently* tells the reader that the second statement is a result of the first statement.)
>
> Mrs. Milland will retire on the first of next month; however, she will continue to serve as a consultant to the executive committee. (Again, the semicolon separates the two independent clauses and tells the reader to pause. The introductory word *however* then tells the reader that a contrasting statement will follow.)

Note: The introductory word is not always the *first* word in the second clause.

> The United States consumes more fuel each year than it produces; it is dependent, *consequently,* upon imported fuel to meet its demands.
>
> Mrs. Milland will retire on the first of next month; she will, *however,* continue to serve as a consultant to the executive committee.

Before Explanatory or Enumerating Words

Writers often use terms such as *for example, for instance,* and *that is.* Use a semicolon before such terms when they introduce an independent clause, an enumeration, or an explanation that is incidental to the rest of the sentence.

> Ms. Spinka is trying hard to reduce the cost of direct-mail advertising; for example, she has negotiated long-term paper contracts to hedge against the rising cost of paper. (*For example* introduces an independent clause.)
>
> Mitsy suggested several ways to cut expenses; for instance, leasing delivery trucks, buying cartons in large quantities, and using less-expensive packing materials. (*For instance* introduces an enumeration.)

Besides the three uses of the semicolon discussed above, three other uses are discussed in Section 22. These concern the use of the semicolon as a substitute for the comma in certain cases.

☐ Checkup 1

Make any necessary corrections in the following sentences.

1. In the summer, Ann and I go to the shore, in the winter, we go to the mountains.
2. Transportation costs have increased nearly 25 percent during the past year, consequently, we were forced to raise the price of our products.
3. We use no sugar in any of the children's foods that we manufacture; besides, government regulations forbid us to do so.
4. Our company wants all our customers to know the ingredients of our products, therefore, we provide detailed labels on every bottle of vitamins we sell.
5. She opened her second sports shop in Los Angeles recently, she has had a store in San Francisco for nearly five years.
6. Ray and Sheila's presentation was interesting, moreover, it taught many people how to become wise shoppers.
7. Miss Fitzsimmons stressed the need to get competitive bids, accordingly, we now ask at least three suppliers to bid on each project.
8. The warehouse will be closed for inventory next week, nevertheless, the warehouse manager and her assistants will be at work.

COLON

A colon also stops the reader, but it does so for a specific purpose: to focus on something that follows the colon.

Colon Before Listed Items

Expressions such as *the following, as follows, this, these,* and *thus* are the terms most commonly used to introduce a list of items. When they do, they are often followed by a colon. The list itself may follow on the same line as the colon, or each item may be typed on a new line.

> In long-term international trade transactions, these are the three major problem areas for exporters: (1) losses, (2) delayed payments, and (3) political risks.
>
> In long-term international trade transactions, there are three major problem areas for exporters:
>
> 1. Losses
> 2. Delayed payments
> 3. Political risks

When the words *the following, as follows,* and so on, do not directly lead into the list (as, for example, when an "interrupting" sentence appears between the lead-in sentence and the list), then a period, not a colon, should be used. Note these examples.

> Note that the schedules have been changed as follows. A revised completion date is listed next to each product. (A period, not a colon, is used after *as follows* because the actual list does not follow directly. A sentence separates the lead-in *as follows* and the actual list.)
>
> The following techniques will help you to use your time more effectively. Read them carefully; then read the examples of how to apply each technique. (Again, the first sentence does not directly lead into the listing, so the sentence ends in a period, not a colon.)

Colon Instead of Semicolon

You have learned that a semicolon is used before expressions as *for example* and *that is* when these expressions introduce an independent clause, an enumeration, or an explanation that is incidental to the rest of the sentence. However, when the explanation or enumeration is anticipated, a colon is used instead of a semicolon.

> Mr. Cronkite mentioned two specific reasons for rejecting the suggestion: namely, the net operating profit was too low (under 9 percent) and the break-even point would not be reached until the fourth year of sales.

Colon to Emphasize

Probably the most important reason for using a colon as a sign for the reader to pause is to emphasize, to point up, a thought that the writer considers important. Study the following illustrations:

> Please try to remember that you must let us know by March 16 the audiovisual equipment you will need for your speech.
>
> **Remember:**   Let us know by March 16 the audiovisual equipment you will need for your speech. (Do you see that this sentence emphasizes the idea more than the preceding sentence does?)

Capitalizing After Colon

The first word of a complete sentence following a colon should be capitalized if (1) the sentence requires special emphasis or (2) the sentence states a formal rule.

> The new policy affects only two groups of employees: those who earn a commission and those who are paid on an hourly basis. (Not a complete sentence; the first word is not capitalized.)
>
> Here is one good reason for adopting this new procedure: It will save us as much as $15,000 a year. (Complete sentence; the first word is capitalized because the sentence requires special emphasis.)
>
> The first step is the most important: Outline your ideas before you begin writing. (Complete sentence; the first word is capitalized because the sentence states a formal rule.)

☐ Checkup 2

Correct any errors in colon use in the following sentences.

1. Among the misspelled words in this report are these: *Accommodate, separate,* and *believe.*
2. The Acme Company offers the following benefits to its employees paid vacations, complete major medical coverage, and free life insurance worth up to one year's salary.
3. She gave these reasons for canceling the contract. Each is explained in detail in her March 4 letter.
4. The committee has requested the following monthly budgets to complete its report: An itemized budget for each month is enclosed.
5. The security guard gave us the reason why the alarm had sounded: the power had been cut.
6. Only two people will speak during the morning session: We urge you to attend this session. One of the speakers is Bill Timmins; the other is José Lopez.

DASH

The dash shares some of the features of the semicolon and the colon: All three stop the reader, but the dash does so much more forcefully. Compare, for example, the different impact in each of the following examples. Notice how the dash provides greater impact than either the semicolon or the colon.

> Your advertising dollar will bring you the greatest return if you buy time on OKTV; this is the television network that statistics prove is tuned in by most viewers in this area. (A good sentence, but not a forceful one.)
>
> For the best return on your advertising dollar, do this: Buy time on OKTV, the television network that statistics prove is tuned in by most viewers in this area. (This is a better sentence; a more forceful one.)
>
> Your advertising dollar will bring you the greatest return if you buy time on OKTV—the television network that statistics prove is tuned in by most viewers in this area. (The dash snaps off the main thought and thereby adds power to the rest of the message. This is the most forceful sentence.)

The semicolon provides the needed pause between clauses, but the colon provides more than a pause: It promises that something important will follow. The dash goes even further by drawing special attention to what follows the dash. Therefore, the dash makes the third example the strongest of the three. These three punctuation marks allow the writer to guide the reader through the message. At the same time, they allow the writer to provide variety and interest to the message.

Forceful Summarizing, Forceful Repetition

When you are writing, you will sometimes summarize the main points of your message to make sure that your readers remember these key points. Besides summarizing, you will often deliberately repeat a key point to make a stronger impression on your readers. (The same is true when you are speaking, of course.) When you are summarizing or repeating, use a dash to separate the summary of the repetition from the rest of the sentence.

> An agenda, a name badge, a directory of hotel services, a notebook, a list of places of worship and restaurants within walking distance of our hotel—all will be provided to each AMA conventioneer at check-in. (The dash is used for forceful summarizing.)
>
> On the last day of the convention, a gala banquet will be held at La Plaza—not *The Plaza*, which is also close to the hotel, but *La Plaza.* (Forceful repetition; the writer repeats the name of the restaurant to distinguish it from a similar name.)

The Dash With an Afterthought

Good writers often plan their afterthoughts. By doing so, they may add variety to their writing, arouse the reader's curiosity, soften a statement that might otherwise be offensive, or provide special emphasis to a statement.

> Be sure to join us for our banquet on the last day of the convention—a surprise guest speaker will add to your enjoyment. (To add variety in style and to arouse the reader's curiosity)
>
> As you see, then, we cannot send you all the samples you requested—but we have enclosed some representative samples that will surely help you make your selection. (To soften a refusal)
>
> Remember, please, that this offer is for a limited time only—reserve your signed edition by returning the enclosed order card today. (To provide special emphasis)

☐Checkup 3

Add dashes where needed.

1. We are eager to tell you more about our New-Look luggage but before we do, let us tell you about the synthetic materials commonly used for luggage today.
2. Send for your examination copy but do so today.
3. A garment bag, an overnight case, a three-suiter all are included in this special price.
4. We are unable to take advantage of your offer at least, not for now.
5. The plans seem to be taking shape but more about this later.
6. Hotels, restaurants, car rental agencies, department stores these are some of the many places that will honor your new Super-Card.

Punctuating Words Set Off by Dashes

At the End of a Sentence   To set off words at the end of a sentence, only one dash is needed. The dash is placed before the words to be set off; a period, question mark, or exclamation point then ends the sentence.

The Rollo-125X has all the features you want in a camera—fast shutter speed, changeable focusing screen, lightweight construction. (The dash precedes the words to be set off, then a period ends this declarative sentence.)

Note that no punctuation is used with the dash unless an abbreviation or quotation precedes the dash.

The first session will begin at 9 a.m.—please be on time! (The period before the dash belongs to the abbreviation. An exclamation point ends the sentence.)

Within a Sentence To set off words within a sentence, two dashes are needed. Again, no punctuation is used with the first dash unless an abbreviation or quotation precedes the dash. The second dash may have a question mark or an exclamation point *before* it, but only if the words set off require a question mark or an exclamation point.

The new director of advertising—what is her name?—will be teaching the Fundamentals of Advertising course sponsored by the Office Training Center. (The dashes set off a question; thus a question mark precedes the second dash.)
Mr. Hayes—after only one year!—has set a new sales record for our company. (The words set off require an exclamation point.)
Several of the supervisors—Janet Gaines and Richard Morton are among them—are now attending a three-day Management for Results seminar. (No period before the second dash.)

Whether a group of words is at the end of the sentence or within the sentence, commas may be used in the usual way. No comma appears before or after either dash.

Several of the supervisors—Janet, Richard, and Nina are among them—are now taking a three-day Management for Results seminar. (No comma before or after either dash.)

☐Checkup 4

Correct any punctuation errors in the following sentences.
1. It will probably be the Owens Printing Company—don't you agree—that submits the lowest bid.
2. Tomorrow's meeting will begin at 8:30 a.m.—but you'd better be there earlier, since you're the first speaker.
3. The price, the warranty, the service contract, the guaranteed delivery date,—these are the reasons we recommend buying Lowry trucks and vans for our delivery fleet.
4. Please wire these prices and specifications to Mr. Antal—he's in Belgium now, isn't he—before he leaves for Paris.
5. Ms. Burnette awarded each of us an extra bonus—it amounted to almost $2,000 a person—for our work in winning the Taste Great Coffee account.

6. Friendly service, modern facilities, reasonable prices,—these are just a few of the reasons the Sunview Motel has become a "Skier's Paradise" for so many people.

COMMUNICATIONS PROJECTS

Practical Applications

A. Correct any errors. Write *OK* for any correct sentence.

1. Three credit cards—Visa, MasterCard, and Diner's Club—are accepted by this restaurant.
2. The customer relations department is trying to improve our service in the following areas: Acknowledging orders, informing customers of delays, and billing customers promptly.
3. Mrs. Allen is a delightful speaker,—delightful and very informative too.
4. I am sure that our guests will be interested in: seeing a Broadway play, attending a concert at Lincoln Center, and shopping on Fifth Avenue.
5. Rather than pay a high interest rate—18 percent annually!—on all her charge accounts, Ms. Jakway decided to get a bank loan at 12 percent to consolidate her debts.
6. Our Peoria store—have you been there recently—has been very profitable since it was renovated.
7. The Credit Union can help you to save money in several ways: for example, it allows you to transfer money automatically from your paycheck directly to your savings, and it offers you car loans and other loans at reasonable interest rates.
8. Camera News will bring you the latest information on: new techniques, the latest equipment, photography shows, and much more.
9. The rule is clear: no one is permitted to smoke in the laboratory.
10. We have no steel-belted snow tires—all other snow tires are in stock.—but we should receive a shipment within two weeks.
11. The press proofs were originally due on March 19, however, the printer now "guarantees" delivery by April 1.
12. The following changes in the pension plan will become effective on November 15: Note that only employees under the age of 45 are affected by these changes.
13. Among the items that our firm imports are these delicacies: truffles from France, marmalade from England, and shortbread from Scotland.
14. Some employees are in favor of the four-day workweek, however, most of those whom we polled prefer the five-day workweek.
15. The manager of our Miami store is Grace Pembroke, the manager of our Seattle store is Alvin Stein.
16. To save energy, we ask you to turn off all lights before you leave the office, however, do leave on hallway lights and stairway lights.
17. Here is the new policy: we shall not accept credit-card payment for purchases under $5.
18. The Office Training Center offers a variety of courses for personal enjoyment and professional development, we encourage all our employees to take advantage of these offerings.

19. All tickets for the May 3 performance have been sold, however, the ticket office will call us if there are any cancellations.
20. The Marcus Company imports handicrafts from Norway, the Fiore Company imports leather goods from Italy.

B. Correct any errors in the following sentences. Write *OK* for any correct sentence.

1. Try to discourage customers from charging purchases under $5. Because the time it takes to handle the paperwork makes such small charge sales unprofitable.
2. There concern is that one sales representative may not be able to cover the entire state.
3. A few of the items were indeed damaged, the others have been returned to inventory.
4. Now that fishing season has begun, we are selling many fiberglass rods, in fact, our White Plains store alone sold 150 rods last week.
5. The Grillo Agency buys these kind of forms from us in large quantities.
6. Why don't the plant manager receive a copy of this monthly report?
7. If you have extra copies of these inventory statements, please send one to Ms. Bouchard and I.
8. Beside the property that she owns in New York State, Danielle also owns property on the West Coast.
9. Does Mr. Gregory plan on taking Dr. Carlisle to dinner?
10. I am positive that Louise already seen the new layout for the twenty-third floor.
11. Apparently, Mr. Todd couldn't hardly wait to leave for Memphis.
12. The secretaries' in our office are indispensable to all of us sales representatives; thus we gladly recommend that they be included in the end-of-year bonus.
13. You should not accept them figures as correct until you've verified them yourself.
14. Mrs. Serafian is one of those managers who helps employees to advance on the job.
15. Mr. Ward said that anyone who wants to join the pension plan must submit their completed form to the Benefits Department no later than Monday, July 19.
16. Call me whenever your ready to leave for the airport.
17. Here is the sketches for the cover of next year's catalog.
18. Miss D'Amico said that there are plenty of opportunities for Barbara and I to advance in the Sales Department.
19. The person who you spoke with is probably Mr. Irving, the comptroller of our division.
20. The trucking firm claimed that the entire shipment would be delivered within one weeks' time.

Editing Practice

The Word Processing Supervisor A correspondent in the Sales Department overuses the italicized words in the following sentences. Supply two synonyms for each word.

1. We are fully *cognizant* of your sales promotion difficulties.
2. This statement is not intended to be *dogmatic.*

3. Evans was never known to *shirk* his responsibilities.
4. The increased fringe benefits will have a *terrific* effect on morale.
5. Please let me know how you feel about the *matter*.
6. A sales representative's card should indicate his or her *line*.

Using Business Vocabulary   Fill in the blanks with the correct word from the list below.

a.	allocated	f.	grievance
b.	efficiency	g.	itemize
c.	eliminate	h.	permissible
d.	foreign	i.	persuasive
e.	fragile	j.	resources

1. The union and management both agreed to establish a (?) committee to hear employees' complaint charges.
2. All these items are breakable, so be sure that the boxes are marked (?)
3. Our tax attorney told us that it is (?) to deduct such expenses on our income tax statement.
4. Clearly, we do not have the (?) needed to complete this vast project in only two years.
5. Please ask each supplier to (?) the costs, not merely to submit a total bill.
6. In our business, we must deal with domestic and (?) banks.
7. Ms. Loomis said that this sales letter is well written but must be more (?) if it is to be effective.
8. Our comptroller (?) the capital expenses carefully to each department.
9. In an effort to reduce expenses, we are trying to (?) some of the unnecessary handling of products before they are shipped to stores.
10. The study shows that we can work at greater (?) if we have newer, faster, machinery.

Case Problem

Addressing Your Boss   John Teller was recently hired as junior accountant in the office of the Boswell Manufacturing Company. There is an air of informality in the office, and John notes that his co-workers refer to the president, James J. Castle, as Jim. John has been saying "Mr. Castle" whenever speaking to him or referring to him in any way.

1. Should John call the president by his first name or continue to use "Mr. Castle"?
2. Under what circumstances do you think employees should call their co-workers by their first names and under what circumstances by a courtesy title, such as *Mr.* or *Miss?*

22
THE COMMA

The effective speaker knows precisely where to pause so that the listener is easily able to grasp, and then connect, idea after idea after idea. In a similar way, the effective writer uses commas to separate elements within a sentence, showing the reader the logical places to pause before continuing to read.

> Mary set the priorities carefully. (A simple declarative sentence.) Mary, set the priorities carefully. (An imperative sentence. The comma indicates the normal pause after someone's name when we are speaking directly to that person.)
>
> When Mark returns the reports that he needs will be on his desk. (Without the needed comma, the sentence is muddled and ambiguous. Should the reader pause after the word *returns*? the word *reports*? The next example shows the proper punctuation.)
>
> When Mark returns, the reports that he needs will be on his desk. (Note how the comma—the natural pause—helps the reader to understand the meaning immediately.)

In writing, as in speaking, we pause often and for many different reasons. Therefore, commas are used for a variety of situations. This section and the next two sections cover all the uses of commas that you must know.

IN A COMPOUND SENTENCE

Two or more independent clauses can be joined in one sentence—a *compound* sentence. When they are joined by a conjunction such as *and, but, or,* or *nor,* a comma is used before the conjunction. The following Memory Hook will help you to determine specifically when this rule applies.

■ Memory Hook

Remember the four conjunctions *and, but, or* and *nor*. When they join two independent clauses, then each clause can stand alone—that is, the clause before the conjunction and the clause after the conjunction can stand alone. Therefore, to test whether a sentence is indeed a compound sentence, simply try to use the clause after the conjunction as an independent sentence. If the clause can be used independently, then the original sentence is a compound sentence, and a comma must be used before the conjunction.

> The damage was reported only this morning, but it will be repaired by the end of the day. (Do you see the conjunction *but*? Now test whether what follows the conjunction is an independent clause by using it as a sentence: *it will be*

repaired by the end of the day. Yes, it can stand alone; it is independent. Thus a comma is needed before the conjunction *but.*)

The damage was reported only this morning but will be repaired by the end of the day. (Again, test whether the words that follow the conjunction *but* can be used independently: *will be repaired by the end of the day.* No, these words cannot stand alone because they have no subject; they are not an independent clause. Therefore, no comma is needed before the conjunction in this sentence.)

To put it simply, the rule is No Subject—No Comma. If the words following the conjunction do not have a subject, they are not independent and no comma should precede the conjunction.

There are only two exceptions to this rule concerning the comma before the conjunction in compound sentences: (1) when the two clauses are very short or very long and (2) when a misreading is possible because one of the clauses already includes a comma.

Very Short or Very Long Clauses

Note the reasons that a comma is not needed when the independent clauses are unusually short or unusually long.

Very Short Clauses   The comma may be omitted when the clauses are very short because no pause may be needed.

> She sent a check but we haven't received it. (The clauses are short; no comma is needed.)
> Marcia writes the ads and Jack designs them.

Very Long Clauses   As we have seen, the brief pause that a comma provides may not be needed when two clauses are very short; on the other hand, this brief pause may not be enough when the two clauses are very long. A semicolon may be needed between two long clauses.

> The findings of our research chemists clearly point to the possible effectiveness of polyvinyl chloride (PVC) as a replacement for the more expensive materials we are now using; and we fully support the need to fund further research to explore the uses of PVC for our entire line of products.

Possible Misreadings

If either clause of a compound sentence already contains a comma (or more than one comma), a misreading may be likely. If so, use a semicolon, not a comma, to separate the two clauses. But if no misreading is likely, use a comma.

> The goal of the week-long seminar is to improve our skills in writing business letters, memos, and informal reports; and formal reports, too, will be covered if time permits. (The semicolon provides a stronger break and prevents this possible misreading: *informal reports, and formal reports . . . .*)

☐ Checkup 1

Correct these sentences.

1. Janet suggested that we invite Karen, Maureen, and Steve; and Kenneth requested that his assistants, too, be invited.
2. The specifications, which we received today, are clear, and potential problems have been resolved.
3. Miss Dostal corrected the invoices this morning, and returned them to Jacob this afternoon.
4. Joanne attended, but Mike did not.
5. Mr. Anthony explained some of the causes for the delay in the production of the long-overdue materials; and he outlined three key steps that he believes can help us to compensate for the time lost.
6. The Frankel Printing Company prints all our brochures, pamphlets, and leaflets, and catalogs are printed by Delmar Printers and Binders.

IN A SERIES

A series consists of three or more items in sequence. The items may be words, phrases, or clauses. Use commas to separate the items in a series as shown here:

> Shorthand, typewriting, and bookkeeping courses are offered by our Office Training Center. (A series of words; notice that the commas are used only with the items that precede the conjunction.)
>
> The line of customers extended down the aisle, past the counter, and out the door. (A series of phrases)
>
> Marlene wrote the specifications, Luis checked them, and Barry submitted them to Mrs. Graye. (A series of clauses)

Now note what happens when the abbreviation *etc.* ends a series.

Etc. Ending a Series

Etc. means "and so forth"; therefore, never write *and etc.* because the *and* is already included in *etc.* When *etc.* ends a series, it must be set off by a comma before and after it (unless, of course, *etc.* ends the sentences).

> At the meeting we discussed budgets, expenses, sales, salaries, *etc.* (A comma before *etc.* Here, it ends a sentence.)
>
> We discussed budgets, expenses, sales, salaries, etc., at the meeting. (A comma before and after *etc.*)

Semicolon Instead of Comma in Series

A comma slows; a semicolon "holds." Logically, then, if the items in a series are long independent clauses or if they already contain commas, a semicolon should be used to separate these items.

We should like you to do the following: arrange our goods into shipping units; transport them to the place where they are to be consumed; store them there if storage is necessary; and obtain a signed receipt showing the time of delivery and the condition of the goods. (You can see that a long pause is needed between the items.)

During our vacation trip last year, we stopped at the following places: Oil City, Pennsylvania; Ann Arbor, Michigan; Gary, Indiana; Kansas City, Missouri; and Santa Fe, New Mexico. (A semicolon to separate the parts of the series holds the reader long enough for him or her to grasp the meaning immediately.

When Not to Use a Comma

Do not use a comma in the following situations.

At the End of a Series   Do not use a comma after the last item in a series, the item following the conjunction (unless the sentence structure requires one). Only the items before the conjunction are separated by commas.

> Larry, Trent, and Rosemary have been appointed to the task force. (A comma after *Rosemary*, the last item in the series, would be incorrect.)
> Larry, Trent, and Rosemary, who are supervisors in our finance department, have been appointed to the task force. (Here, the sentence structure, not the series itself, requires a comma after *Rosemary*.)

With Repeated Conjunctions   When the conjunction is repeated between the items in a series, no commas are needed.

> We will certainly discuss these goals on Wednesday or Thursday or Friday. (The conjunction *or* is repeated between the items in the series.)

In Certain Company Names   When a company name consists of a series of names joined by an ampersand (&), no comma is used before the ampersand.

> Ms. Forman is now a partner with Myers, Lily, Bristol & Campbell.

☐ Checkup 2

Check the following series carefully. Correct any errors.
1. Dean's duties include recruiting, interviewing, training, and etc.
2. Hawkins, Greco, DePaul, & Smith is the new law firm on the fifth floor of our building.
3. Ms. McGarry listed housewares, furnishings, camera equipment, etc. as the sale items for this weekend.
4. Among the references that every writer should have at hand are a comprehensive dictionary, a thesaurus and a dictionary of synonyms.
5. This heater can be used in the home, at the office or on a camping trip.
6. Natalie is responsible for the agenda, Al will coordinate the printing of the handouts and Arthur will rent all the audiovisual equipment needed for the conference.

7. Ask Betty, Frank and Jonathan to double-check this outline, and then ask them to give the final copy to Gregory.
8. Mr. Harrison, the manager of our store, said that you may pay by check, cash, or money order or if you prefer, we will bill you for these items.

FOLLOWING AN INTRODUCTORY WORD, PHRASE, OR CLAUSE

A comma follows an introductory word, phrase, or clause to signal the reader to pause. The pause prevents a possible misinterpretation or confusion of the meaning.

Introductory Word

A comma follows an introductory word at the beginning of a sentence or clause. Among the most commonly used introductory words are these:

consequently	meanwhile	now	theoretically
finally	moreover	obviously	therefore
first	namely	originally	yes

Naturally, we will review the estimates carefully to make sure that each is complete and accurate. (Comma after the introductory word, which is at the beginning of the sentence.)

We have revised the job description; originally, we had asked for someone with at least three years' experience in product management. (Comma after the introductory word, which introduces the second clause in the sentence.)

The current price is only $7.69 a pound; we know, however, that low production will increase the demand for, and the price of, this metal. (Comma before and after *however*, which interrupts the second clause in this sentence.)

However high the price, we must purchase several tons before the end of the month. (Here the word *however* is not an introductory word. It is essential to the message—*However high the price*—and, therefore, is not followed by a comma.)

Introductory Phrase

Commas are often required after infinitive phrases, participial phrases, and prepositional phrases, as explained below.

After Infinitive Phrases   An infinitive phrase that introduces a sentence is followed by a comma unless the phrase is the subject of the sentence.

To proofread accurately, you need more than a command of spelling rules and grammar rules. (The infinitive phrase introduces the sentence; it modifies the subject *you*.)

To proofread carefully requires more than a command of spelling rules and grammar rules. (Here the infinitive phrase is the subject of the sentence.)

After Participial Phrases A participial phrase is always followed by a comma.

> Knowing that the price would soon increase, Maryanne doubled the usual order of chemicals. (Comma after participial phrase)
> Raised from the floor, the valuable stock was safe from flood damage and therefore insurable. (Introductory participial phrase)

Do not confuse a participial phrase with a gerund phrase. A gerund phrase at the beginning of a sentence is always a subject. A participial phrase is never a subject; it is an adjective and must be followed by a comma.

> Knowing the prices of chemicals is the purchasing manager's responsibility. (The gerund phrase *Knowing the prices of chemicals* is the subject of the sentence.)

After Prepositional Phrases Use a comma after long prepositional phrases and prepositional phrases that include verbs.

> In one of the ad campaigns for Able Electronics, Horace used a laser-light photograph that won a graphic arts award. (Long prepositional phrase)
> After checking the budget figures, Joan met with our comptroller. (Prepositional phrase containing a gerund, *checking*)

Do not use a comma if the prepositional phrase is short or if it flows directly into the main thought of the sentence.

> At noon tomorrow we will meet to discuss next year's budget. (The prepositional phrase *At noon tomorrow* is short and flows into the sentence.)

Introductory Clause

A comma is needed after a subordinate clause that precedes the main clause. The comma provides a needed pause to slow the reader before the main thought.

> As Mary Lou repeated, the announcement will not be released to the press until May 15. (Without the comma, the reader might treat *As Mary Lou repeated the announcement* as one group. The comma makes the reader pause after *repeated*.)

To apply this comma rule, you must of course be able to identify the words and phrases that commonly begin introductory clauses. To remember the following list better, try using each word or phrase to introduce a clause.

after	even if	provided	until
although	for	since	when
as	how	so that	whenever
as if	if	supposing	where
as soon as	inasmuch as	then	whereas
as though	in case	till	wherever
because	in order that	though	whether
before	otherwise	unless	while

☐ Checkup 3

Correct any comma errors in the use of introductory words, phrases, and clauses.

1. If you prefer the bill can be paid upon delivery.
2. To compute the compounded interest rate use the following chart.
3. The entire entertainment budget has already been spent; consequently, we must charge these expenses to another budget.
4. As soon as our plans are completed we will submit the sketches to the committee.
5. Finally Mr. Lawrence will summarize the speeches at 4:45.
6. To succeed in business, requires drive, intelligence, and good personal skills.
7. As though we copywriters do not have enough work, we now have another "rush" project.
8. Proofreading the new price lists, Karen and Earl worked almost the entire morning.
9. Proofreading the new price lists took Karen and Earl most of the morning.
10. At 10 a.m. next Tuesday and 11 a.m. next Thursday Vincent will give a one-hour presentation on sales goals for next year.

COMMA PITFALLS

Here and in the next two sections, certain comma pitfalls are presented. The first rule for avoiding comma pitfalls is this: Use two commas, never just one, to separate any words that interrupt the parts of a compound subject, compound object, or compound verb. If no words interrupt the compound, use no comma.

> Estelle or Henry can help us complete these statements. (No words interrupt the compound subject *Estelle or Henry;* therefore, no commas are needed.)
>
> Estelle or Henry, both of whom are working overtime tonight, can help us to complete these statements. (Here the interrupter does not separate the two parts of the compound subject.)
>
> Estelle, who was transferred to our department last week, or Henry can help us complete these statements. (Two commas separate the interrupting words *who was transferred to our department last week* from the compound subject.)
>
> In this course we will discuss stocks and bonds. (No words interrupt the compound object *stocks and bonds;* therefore, no commas are needed.)
>
> In this course we will discuss stocks, which are interesting to most investors, and bonds. (The words that interrupt the compound object are separated by *two* commas.)
>
> You must sign the renewal card and mail it to us by March 1. (No words interrupt the compound verb phrases *sign the renewal card* and *mail it to us by March 1.*)
>
> You must sign the renewal card, which is enclosed, and mail it to us by March 1. (The words that interrupt the compound verb are separated by *two* commas.)

COMMUNICATION PROJECTS

Practical Application

A. Correct the following sentences. Write *OK* for any correct sentence.

1. DeWitt, Hanson, & Merritt will audit our inventory.
2. Our New York store will be open on Friday nights until 9 o'clock, and will feature a new gourmet foods department.
3. After Miss Hall speaks will we have a coffee break?
4. We can ship the appliances by truck, or send the entire shipment airfreight.
5. Miss Everett explained the uses of bank checks, certified checks and cashiers' checks.
6. As soon as the reorganization is effective Mr. Erickson will move to our New Orleans office.
7. Either Cynthia, or Lisa should have a copy of the promotion plans for next year.
8. The new offices will be ready for occupancy in April however we will not move into the offices until June.
9. While Ms. Barker is on vacation, Mr. Unger, her assistant, will approve all invoices.
10. The corporate donations were as follows: Jonas Chemicals, $5,000; Rand Productions, $7,500; and Bartlett Paints, $6,000.
11. The Interstar Corporation designs and manufactures toasters, blenders, waffle irons, and etc.
12. On Friday we will distribute all these materials at our company-wide meeting.
13. The heads of the Accounting Department, the Legal Department and the Finance Department will conduct the three-day seminar.
14. Waiting patiently Mr. Harris sat in the lobby for nearly two hours.
15. To prepare accurate estimates, is essential to the success of this proposal.

B. Correct any errors in the following sentences. Write *OK* if a sentence is correct.

1. You may find the following books helpful: They provide many methods for conserving energy.
2. We recommend that you store these and all other drugs in a safe place, that is, you should keep them out of the reach of children.
3. To complete this project by May 15 we will work overtime for the next two weeks.
4. We need more paint, turpentine, masking tape etc.
5. Do you have any sample swatches that we may use to make our selections.
6. As explained in Section XXV., each taxpayer must file for this rebate.
7. Ms. Hanly plans to start a management consulting firm by the end of this year; moreover she expects to have offices in Washington and in New York by the end of next year.
8. Our office training center offers courses in typewriting, shorthand, office practices, and etc.
9. Among the companies that agreed to attend the hearings is Klein, Jonas & Madison; Treat and Brokaw, Inc.; and Wallace Industries.
10. The costs of water, heat, and electricity, are itemized individually.

11. This machine is not economical to operate nor does it use standard-size paper.
12. Anne's proposals are always very well written, thus she is often asked to help other account executives.
13. Mr. Harris and him will probably conduct the first session.
14. There's all the materials we will need for tomorrow's meeting.
15. Mortgage rates are now very high, and are increasing drastically each year.
16. You may pick up these parts at our downtown store or you may have them delivered to your home.
17. Our office manager asked us whether we had discussed the problem with the fire warden?
18. When Miss Simpson arrives please ask her to join us in the conference room.
19. One of the supervisors—Gregory or Helen or Manuel—has the latest price list.
20. Angelo and Francine, will be attending a sales convention for most of next week.

Editing Practice

A Matter of Agreement   Correct any agreement errors in these sentences.
1. Carl don't have his tickets for his flight to Detroit yet.
2. Where is all the invoices that must be processed?
3. Either Miss Martino or Mr. Wayne conduct the weekly production meeting.
4. Among our department's most experienced copywriters is Margaret Daly.
5. Miss Wong explained that there is ten accounts that need special attention.
6. Every employee has been asked to submit their completed pension forms to the Personnel Department by May 17.
7. Where's Janet and Catherine staying in Houston?
8. Most of the orders for Model 19-B12 has been filled.
9. There seems to be at least three good reasons for canceling our order.
10. The number of requests for product information was surprisingly high last week.

The Word Processing Department   As you are proofreading copy on the video screen of your word processing equipment, you read the following excerpt from a memorandum. Does it contain any errors? Make the necessary corrections.

> Car-leasing rates from the top three agencies in our area varied very slightly. As the enclosed chart shows, the rates for compareable six-cylinder cars ranged from $23.95 a day (from Able Cars and Vans) to $25.95 a day (from Dependable Auto Rental).
>
> We recomend that we use Able for all our rental needs not only because Able offers the lowest daily rate but also because Able permits us to return rented cars to any of their locations. The other agencies specify that cars must be returned to the same place from which they were rented; otherwise, the low rates quoted do not apply.

Case Problem

Telephone Technique   Criticize the following telephone conversation. Then rewrite it to avoid the types of errors you criticized.

> *Person answering.* Hello
> *Caller.* Who is this?

Person answering. Who do you want?
Caller. I was trying to get the credit department.
Person answering. This is the credit department.
Caller. Is George Becker there?
Person answering. Yes, he is.
Caller. May I speak with him, please?

23
THE COMMA
(CONTINUED)

Words that are not essential to the clarity of the message are set off by commas. On the other hand, words that *are* essential to the clarity of the message are not set off. In this section you will learn to distinguish between essential groups of words and nonessential groups of words; consequently, you will learn how to make your meaning clear to the reader in all cases.

SUBORDINATE CLAUSE FOLLOWING MAIN CLAUSE

We have already seen that a subordinate clause preceding a main clause is always set off by a comma.

> As we explained in our June 4 memo, the customer cards will be filed in alphabetic order. (Comma after subordinate clause that precedes a main clause)

When the subordinate clause follows the main clause, a comma may or may not be needed to separate the two clauses. The answer depends on whether the subordinate clause is essential to the meaning of the complete sentence. Note these examples:

> The customer cards will be filed in alphabetic order, as we explained in our June 4 memo. (The words *in alphabetic order* tell precisely how the cards are to be filed; the words *as we explained in our June 4 memo*, therefore, provide extra information. Because the words *as we explained in our June 4 memo* are not essential to the meaning of the sentence, they are set off by a comma.)
> The customer cards will be filed as we explained in our June 4 memo. (Without the words *in alphabetic order*, the sentence is changed. Now the words *as we explained in our June 4 memo* are essential to the meaning of the sentence; they alone tell how the cards will be filed. No comma should set off this subordinate clause.)

INTERRUPTING, PARENTHETIC, AND EXPLANATORY ELEMENTS

Interrupting

Because an interrupting element does not provide essential information, it is set off by commas:

> Our fast delivery, moreover, is free to all charge customers. (*Moreover* is an interrupting word; it can be omitted from the sentence without affecting its clarity.)
>
> The manager insisted, consequently, that we should close the store at 9 p.m. (*Consequently* is set off by commas because it interrupts the meaning of the sentence.)

Parenthetic

A parenthetic element is an extra comment that qualifies or amends the message. Parenthetic statements may be words, phrases, or clauses intended to soften a harsh statement or emphasize a contrast.

> The government regulation, as I see it, is subject to different interpretations. (The expression *as I see it* is a parenthetic comment that is not essential to the sentence. It should be set off by commas.)
>
> The Los Angeles Warehouse, but not the store, is to be sold to another company. (The parenthetic statement *but not the store* emphasizes the contrast; it is set off by commas.)

Explanatory

Although an explanatory element gives additional information, the information is not essential to the meaning and is therefore set off by commas.

> The manager, realizing his error, offered the customer a refund. (The explanatory element is a participial phrase, *realizing his error*. In reading this sentence aloud, note that you would pause before and after the explanatory statement. In writing, you set off such explanatory elements with commas.)
>
> Alice Ulster, who is the senior vice president of public relations, will chair the committee. (Here the explanatory element is the clause *who is the senior vice president of public relations*. Again, in reading this sentence aloud, you would pause before and after this explanatory statement. In writing, you set off the explanatory element with commas.)

If the clause is essential to the meaning of the sentence, however, it is not set off by commas.

> Our firm has four regional managers. The regional manager who suggested this new procedure is Ken Philbin. (The clause *who suggested this new*

procedure does not provide additional information. Because it is essential to the meaning of the sentence, it is not set off by commas. Note that in reading this sentence aloud, you would not pause before and after this clause.)

☐ Checkup 1

Are commas used correctly in these sentences? Make any necessary corrections.
1. The person, whom you should ask for help, is Marlin Dunn.
2. Mr. Clark, expecting an urgent call waited patiently in his office.
3. The best approach as we discussed yesterday is to offer a special discount on large orders.
4. His mother who is our tax attorney explained the new IRS regulations to us.
5. The president of our company eager to end the month-long strike agreed to most of the employees' demands.
6. The interest charge but not the shipping cost is an acceptable tax deduction.
7. The most effective plan we think is to increase our sales representatives' incentive-compensation program.
8. The safety course is mandatory, therefore, for all warehouse personnel.
9. We will schedule the meeting for next Friday, unless you will not be available then.
10. The person, who is responsible for publicity releases, is Mr. Love.

APPOSITIVES AND RELATED CONSTRUCTIONS

The rules for using commas with appositives and with three closely related constructions can be grouped for this discussion. Studying these rules as a unit will aid in learning, in retaining, and in using them correctly.

Appositives

An appositive is a word or a group of words that gives more information about a preceding word or phrase. When an appositive is not essential to the message, it is set off by commas.

> The director of marketing services, Allen B. Fine, will review our budgets next Friday. (The appositive, *Allen B. Fine*, offers additional information and is set off by commas.)
> The president of our company, a well-known college professor, is an expert in corporate finance.

When the appositive is very closely connected with the noun that precedes it, no commas are used to separate the appositive.

> Her husband Richard is also an attorney for March, Patton & Wells. (The appositive *Richard* is very closely connected to the noun preceding it; therefore, no commas are needed.)
> The year 1995 will mark the 100th anniversary of our firm. (Here, *1995* is essential to the meaning of the sentence. It is not set off by commas.)

Degrees, Titles, and Other Explanatory Terms

Several commonly used abbreviations offer additional information about the names that precede them. For example, *M.D.* following a person's name tells that he or she is a doctor of medicine, and *Inc.* following a company name tells that the firm has been incorporated.

Abbreviations such as *M.D.*, *Ph.D.*, and *D.D.S.* are always set off by commas.

> Bradford W. Kelly, M.D., is the head of our company's medical department.
> Alice O. Bruno, Ph.D., is the director of research and development for the Chemical Division of Allied Products.

The abbreviations *Inc.* and *Ltd.* may or may not be set off with commas, depending on the preference of each individual company. Always follow the style shown on a company's letterhead.

> Send checks to Owens & Rusk, Inc., at its Memphis office. (*Owens & Rusk, Inc.*, is the official company name.)
> Ms. MacGrath works for Time Inc. in New York. (*Time Inc.* is the official company name.)

Like *Inc.* and *Ltd.*, the abbreviations *Jr.* and *Sr.* may or may not be set off with commas. Follow the preference of each individual when writing *Jr.* and *Sr.* or roman numerals after a person's name.

> William D. Achison Jr. has been named to the Board of Directors. (Mr. Achison prefers no commas setting off *Jr.*)
> Henry Dawson, III, is a senior partner of Reynolds, Wimby, and Feld. (Mr. Dawson prefers commas setting off III following his name.)

Note that when commas are used to set off abbreviations such as *M.D.*, *Inc.*, or *Jr.* they are used in pairs. Do not use a single comma to set off such abbreviations.

Calendar Dates

In month/day/year dates, the year is set off with two commas. In month/year dates, the commas are generally omitted because they are not needed.

> On September 6, 1981, we signed a long-term lease agreement with Normandy Realtors.
> In September 1981 we signed a long-term lease agreement with Normandy Realtors.

States, Cities

Two commas also set off the name of a state when it follows the name of a city.

> Our office in Rochester, Minnesota, is headed by Shirley Adzick.

□ Checkup 2

Are there any comma errors in the following sentences? Make the necessary corrections.

1. Mrs. Mendoza has lived in Tempe Arizona since 1976.
2. Elizabeth Janowski Ph.D. is conducting the marketing research for two of our new products.
3. Two of our attorneys, Paul Ulster and Gail Fenton suggested that we reject the offer.
4. Kenneth Vereen, Jr. has been appointed assistant director of advertising.
5. One of our reporters, Jane P. Smith, recently received an award for excellence in political reporting.
6. On December 31, 1988 our ten-year leasing agreement with Empire Automobiles will end.
7. Ward & Stroud, Inc. is now selling at $21 a share.
8. Carol Jenkins discussed a unique advertising concept in the April 1982 issue of *Business Future* magazine.
9. Our Canton Ohio plant consistently has the best safety record of all our plants.
10. One of the research chemists for our company, Dr. Helen T. Kim was named Chemist of the Year by *Chemistry* magazine.

THAT AND *WHICH*

Clauses that are not necessary to the meaning of a sentence should be introduced by *which* and, of course, set off by commas. Clauses that are necessary to the meaning of a sentence are introduced by *that*. They are not set off by commas.

> Only the inventory that is damaged will be sold at a 50 percent discount. (No commas separating a "that" clause)
> The damaged inventory, which includes radios and stereos, will be sold at a 50 percent discount. (The "which" clause gives additional information and is correctly set off by commas.)

COMMA PITFALLS

Here are two more comma pitfalls that trap many writers: (1) using a comma to separate a subject from its predicate and (2) using a comma to separate a verb or an infinitive from its object or complement.

Comma Separating Subject from Predicate

Never separate a subject from its predicate by a single comma.

> The prices listed on the enclosed sheet, are effective July 1. (Incorrect. No comma should separate a subject from its verb.)
> The prices listed on the enclosed sheet, which has been distributed to all order clerks, are effective July 1. (Correct. Two commas separate a clause that gives additional information.)

Comma Separating Verb or Infinitive from Object or Complement

Never separate a verb or an infinitive from its object or complement by a single comma.

> For many years Adrian Bouchard has been, the top sales representative for Crowley and Simpson. (Incorrect. A single comma should not separate the verb *has been* from its complement.)
>
> Ms. Sachs was obviously happy to hear, that the insurance policy would cover damage by flood. (Incorrect. A single comma should not separate the infinitive from its object.)

☐ Checkup 3

Find and correct the errors in the following sentences.

1. The enclosed catalog, which we are sending you free, will describe many of the items that are now on sale.
2. The results of the recent independent survey show, that the modern consumer is indeed price-conscious.
3. An item, that is on sale, cannot be returned for a cash refund.
4. The employees on the safety committee, are holding a special session next Tuesday.
5. Our New York store which is one of our largest stores in the northeast has more than 150 full-time employees.
6. We agreed to pay the shipping charge, which amounts to $48.

COMMUNICATION PROBLEMS

Practical Application

A. Correct any errors in the following sentences. Write *OK* for any correct sentence.

1. Please return to Mrs. Rodgers, the contract folder and the correspondence file.
2. Have you heard that James Chu, has been named assistant treasurer?
3. The announcement, that the sales-incentive plan would be revised was greeted with cheers.
4. On October 12, 1981 Miss Quimby filed her first patent claim.
5. The economy which has been sluggish for the past three years is the major subject in all business newspapers and magazines.
6. Robert's sister Tara, is also a chemical engineer.
7. All suggested price increases according to the president of our company will be reviewed by an impartial panel.
8. One of her most recent articles, received praise from *The Wall Street Journal*.
9. Ms. Jaworski asked Gregory Myers Esq. to serve as our counsel.
10. The estimates prepared by Dr. Brower, were accepted as the most realistic estimates.

11. Dina Perelli has been a copywriter for Prentice and & Gladstone, Inc. for nearly twenty years.
12. The quantity discount however is limited to purchase of more than 100 copies.
13. We will draw up the contract, after we have confirmed the details.
14. Gary Stephenson who is the director of data processing has hired four new employees this week.
15. Adam is now the manager of our Cincinnati, Ohio office.
16. The mayor asked Elaine Perrine, Ph.D. to head the task force.
17. The reason for the delays in shipping merchandise is, that the truckers have been on strike for several weeks.
18. Our goal is to add to, not detract from the marketing advantages we now enjoy.
19. The parts, that we ordered today, are scheduled to be delivered no later than August 19.
20. On Tuesday May 5 we will submit our cost estimates for the Casler project.

B. Make the necessary corrections in the following sentences. Write *OK* if a sentence is correct.

1. Here is the revised specifications for the new warehouse.
2. Mark has already submitted his suggestions to the committee, hasn't he.
3. It seems like we are easily going to surpass last year's excellent sales record.
4. As soon as Mrs. Loomis and him arrive, please ask them to join us in the conference room.
5. Apparently, she wants to speak with us in regards to our expense budgets.
6. We were surprised that our manager hadn't only one change to suggest.
7. Ms. Camp said that Ronald is doing very good in his new position.
8. Each customer will receive their itemized invoice by the 15th of every month.
9. She invited both vice president's to attend the discussion next Wednesday.
10. There is several programmers who have volunteered to work on our new project.
11. Mr. Schmidt is one of the consultants who you met at our recent convention.
12. Either Diane McCabe or Gary Elrod is the supervisor of the 12-to-8 shift.
13. Between you and I, I am positive that the merger will not be approved.
14. Whenever your ready to meet with Ms. Ruppert, please call her secretary for an appointment.
15. The Jones's submitted their proposal last month, but we have not yet voted on it.
16. If you wish, you may use the looseleaf binders that are laying on the floor of the stockroom.
17. Both the mens' lounge and the womens' lounge are being moved to the nineteenth floor.
18. When we saw Miss Gilbert, she had already went to the monthly managers' meeting.
19. On display in the showroom were minicomputers, calculators, electronic games, and etc.
20. Our newest stores are those in Gary, Indiana, Kansas City, Kansas, and Santa Fe, New Mexico.

Editing Practice

Homonyms   Read the following excerpt carefully, paying special attention to homonyms. Make any necessary corrections.

> You're May 4 order will be shipped to you no later than May 19. As you requested, the entire cost of this order ($576.89) plus the cost of shipping ($29.75) will be charged to your account.
>
> Because your order totaled more than $500, you will find a special discount coupon enclosed. This coupon entitles you to a $25 discount on any future order of $100 or more.
>
> Thank you for buying from Jackson & Roth. Its our pleasure to serve you.

Plurals and Possessives   Correct any errors in the use of plurals and possessives in the following sentences. Write *OK* if a sentence has no error.

1. The Harnett Corporation has manufactured childrens furniture for more than three generations.
2. A special sale on ladies' clothing will begin next Monday, September 6.
3. Janet and Suzanne opened there new restaurant in the Midtown Mall.
4. As you know, Mr. Truscott disapproves of us leaving early.
5. The Harrisons' partners have agreed to sell their shares to the Harrisons for a total of $2 million.
6. All the sales representatives' will receive their bonus checks by March 1.
7. Ms. Arness claims that their are plenty of appliances in inventory for the upcoming sale.
8. We expect to complete the entire report within three weeks time.
9. Are you sure about David requesting a transfer?
10. I do not know whose attaché case this is, but I am positive that it is not her's.

Case Problem

Correcting the Boss   Ethel Nelson, secretary to Mirriam McChesney, placed a set of letters on her employer's desk for signature. In glancing over the letters, Ms. McChesney reads the following sentence in one of the letters: "We will mail the package before January 6, 19__, so that you will have it in time."

Ms. McChesney takes her pen and draws a line through the comma following "19__" and tells Ethel that the comma does not belong there.

1. Who is correct? Why?
2. What should Ethel do about the situation?
3. How should Ms. McChesney make corrections so that the entire letter does not have to be retyped?

This third section on the use of commas concludes all the principles that you must know regarding this commonly used punctuation mark. As you can see by the fact that the comma requires three sections in this text, the comma is both a versatile and an important tool for the business writer. Study these last few rules so that you will master the use of the comma in business correspondence.

WITH MODIFYING ADJECTIVES

When two or more adjectives separately modify a noun, a comma is used to separate the adjectives.

> Ms. Lorimer gave an informative, lively speech. (Each of the adjectives, *informative* and *lively,* modifies the noun *speech:* an informative speech, a lively speech. A comma is used because each adjective separately modifies the noun.)
>
> Collins & Verona is the most prestigious, most profitable, most respected brokerage firm in the financial community. (Because each of the adjectives separately modifies the noun *firm,* commas are used to separate the adjectives.)

This rule is easy to apply so long as one is able to determine that the adjectives *separately* modify the noun. Use the following Memory Hook to apply this rule correctly.

■ Memory Hook

To test whether a comma is needed between adjectives, place the word *and* between the adjectives. If *and* cannot be correctly inserted between the adjectives, no comma is needed. If *and* can be correctly inserted, then a comma is needed.

> Eleanor is considered a brilliant, reliable, accurate accountant. (The commas are correct because you can say "brilliant *and* reliable *and* accurate." There is no comma after *accurate,* of course, because you would not say "accurate *and* accountant.")
>
> Judith Marz discussed modern financial analysis with the members of the committee. (No comma is used here. You would not say "modern *and* financial analysis." The first adjective, *modern,* modifies the unit *financial analysis,* which consists of the second adjective plus the noun.)

☐ Checkup 1

Insert commas as needed between adjectives in the following sentences. Think about inserting *and* between the adjectives to help make your decisions.

1. Curtis Fabric Company manufactures lightweight thermal blankets.
2. Our broker recommended a few conservative financial investments.
3. This morning Mr. Truman sat through several lengthy production meetings.
4. Sharp clean legible copies are available from our duplicating center.
5. A recent new acquisition has spurred profits for the Thurston Corporation.
6. Mr. Carson is known as a slow methodical effective copywriter.
7. The latest scientific discoveries are reported each month in *Twentieth Century Science.*
8. Her new best-selling book has made her an overnight celebrity.

FOR OMISSIONS, WITH REPEATED EXPRESSIONS, AND IN DIRECT ADDRESS

The comma is also used to save time and words, to emphasize an important thought, and to set off names and terms in direct address. These are the uses discussed in this section.

Omissions

Sometimes writers can use the comma to avoid repeating words that have already been stated in the sentence. The comma makes the reader pause long enough to mentally supply the omitted word. Note these examples:

> Production meetings are held once a week; inventory meetings, once a month. (The words *are held* are not repeated in the second clause. The comma indicates this omission and slows the reader long enough to supply the missing words.)
> Starting on June 15, Mr. Hart will be in charge of the Bennett account; Ms. Dirkins, the Hastings & Ames account; Ms. Ellison, the Barker Chemical account; and Mr. Donnelly, the Henderson Trucking account. (Rather than repeat the words *will be in charge of* three times, the writer uses a comma after each name to tell the reader to pause long enough to supply these words.)

Repeated Expressions

Repetition is one of the most effective ways to emphasize an important point. Repetitions, of course, must be planned if they are to be effective, and the repeated words must be separated by a comma.

> The manual says, "Never, never accept credit charges for amounts under $25." (Note the comma that separates the repetition *Never, never.*)

Direct Address

In writing, when we address people directly, we set off their names (or similar terms) with commas.

> As you requested, Mrs. Greene, we are sending you two copies of our latest catalog.
> Thank you, friend, for supporting our charitable organization.

☐ Checkup 2

Do the following sentences correctly illustrate use of commas for omissions, for planned repetition, and for direct address? Make any needed corrections.

1. Ms. Gardner said that Ed is working very very hard on the upcoming sales meeting.
2. The first regional sales conference will be held on July 15; the second on July 30; and the third on August 15.
3. We ask you, ladies and gentlemen, for your continued support for the Cancer Fund.
4. Janet verified that the report was correct absolutely correct.
5. She bought her first store in 1978; her second in 1981.
6. The newspapers reported that Addison & Wells contributed $10,000 to Senator Carson's campaign; Premier Electronics, $5,000; and Smith, Dent & McCoy, $7,500.
7. Only in rare rare instances does the treasurer preside at our monthly status meetings.
8. We sincerely appreciate your helping us Ms. Franco.

IN NUMBERS AND BETWEEN UNRELATED NUMBERS

Use a comma to separate thousands, hundred thousands, millions, and so on, in numbers of four or more digits. This function of the comma prevents misreading of numbers.

> Our company payroll exceeded $1,500,000 last year and is estimated to be $1,800,000 this year.

When unrelated numbers are written together, a comma should separate them.

> As of December 31, 750 employees had signed up for the optional insurance plan. (The comma slows down the reader and makes each number distinct.)

COMMA PITFALLS

Now that you know all the important uses of the comma, be sure to master the last principles for *not* using a comma.

In Numbers

Never use commas in the following numbers, regardless of the number of digits: years, page numbers, house and telephone numbers, ZIP Code numbers, serial numbers, and decimals.

in 1985	1191 Hunter Avenue	Dallas, Texas 75201	12.75
page 1318	(201) 555-2184	RD 14315789	

In Weights, Capacities, Measurements

Never use a comma to separate the parts of *one* weight, *one* capacity, or *one* measurement.

> The broadcast lasted exactly 1 hour 25 minutes 15 seconds. (No commas to separate the parts of *one* time measurement)

☐ Checkup 3

Did the writers of the following sentences fall into any of the comma pitfalls described above? Correct any errors.

1. By 1988 500 employees will have received their college degrees through our firm's tuition-assistance program.
2. Surprisingly, the question-and-answer period lasted 2 hours, 45 minutes.
3. The discussion on pages 1,445 and 1,446 explains the procedures for getting government aid.
4. In 1982 she moved her store to 1,870 Rockland Street.
5. As you will see on Invoice 17-19853, 14 items were shipped, not 15.
6. My copy of Policy 80,876 is in my safe-deposit box.
7. The display cabinet is precisely 9 feet, 7 inches high.
8. Her deposit, which totaled $1700, will be refunded to her if the item is out of stock.

Communication Projects

Practical Application
A. Correct any incorrect sentences. Write *OK* for each correct sentence.

1. Thank you Ms. Schwartz for sending your check so promptly.
2. In her calm unemotional way, Gloria listened to both sides of the story and then settled the argument.
3. Everyone mentioned that you gave a good presentation, a very good presentation.
4. This year, Irving's merit increase will be about $2,000; Barbara's $2,500; Sandra's $2,300; and Allen's $2,100.
5. The latest, government tax regulations are fully described in this book.

6. My travel and entertainment budget for this year is $5000.
7. Because the materials weighed 25 pounds, 10 ounces, we shipped them ahead to the hotel.
8. The Sunview Motel offers warm modern spacious rooms and friendly helpful employees.
9. We recommend the strongest toughest cartons for packing and shipping these delicate items.
10. Please be sure to sign the copies, all three copies.
11. The switch on this pump has been specially designed to give fast efficient trouble-free service for many years.
12. If you would prefer returning the merchandise for credit Miss Conover, we should be happy to have you do so.
13. No, Jack, that isn't Mr. Everett. Mr. Everett is a tall slim friendly-looking man.
14. Early in 1982 14 of our stores were sold to the Harper Retail Corporation.
15. Because she is an informative energetic speaker, Dr. Manley is often asked to appear at conventions.

B. Correct any errors in these sentences. Write *OK* for each correct sentence.

1. We leased the car, parked in the driveway, from ABC Car Rentals.
2. Mr. Berenson is a creative writer a very creative writer.
3. By the end of 1988 5,000 foreign cars will be sold each month in our city alone.
4. The month before Mr. Wilson retired from our company after 25 years with the firm.
5. Remember Mrs. D'Acosta you have a meeting at 10 a.m.
6. All the executives, who work for our company, are considered dynamic men and women.
7. As you reported Geraldine our competitor is planning to develop a new speaker system that will compete more effectively against ours.
8. While Ms. Fremont is on the phone let's make copies of the agenda for this morning's meeting.
9. Mr. Norris, a native of Warren, Ohio, will join our company next month.
10. At the booths we will need order forms, catalogs, price lists, and etc.
11. Myrna, Olga, and William, deserve the credit for the fine exhibit.
12. We itemized the merchandise clearly and proofread the order form accurately, nevertheless, we received three incorrect items.
13. She returned the damaged radio to us, we credited her account for $39.95.
14. Through our company's buying service, employees can enjoy discounts on refrigerators, televisions, stereos etc.
15. Any supervisor, who has not yet received the new manual, should pick up a copy at the reception desk in the lobby.

Editing Practice

The Word Processing Supervisor   The president of your company is sending a personal letter to all 750 technicians and engineers employed by the company to thank them for a special achievement. Read the following excerpt from the president's letter. Does it contain any errors? Make any necessary corrections.

> Many of you have already seen the article in the August issue of *Consumer World* magazine naming our television number one in each of the ten categories tested. Never before has any appliance been rated first in all ten test categories. Needless to say, I am exceptionally proud of this accomplishment, and I congratulate all our service technicians and engineers for achieving this singular honor.
>
> Precisely how did we accomplish this goal? Through expert communication. Our sales representatives and our service technicians accurately communicate to our engineers the wants and needs of our customers. And our engineers, in turn, are designing our products not only with the customer in mind but also with the service technician in mind. The result: a better product, an easier-to-service product.

Case Problem

The Mumbling Dictator Jean Walker recently has been hired as a secretary in the law firm of Beatty and Barnes. Mrs. Barnes does most of her dictating to a recording machine, and Jean transcribes the dictation as soon as possible. Although Mrs. Barnes's voice is loud enough, Jean has difficulty understanding her; many of her words are garbled. Jean suspects that Mrs. Barnes dictates with a hard candy in her mouth, but she is not really sure.

1. How should Jean handle this situation?
2. If you were Mrs. Barnes, would you object to Jean's criticizing your dictation technique?

25 QUOTATION MARKS, PARENTHESES, APOSTROPHES

As we have seen, punctuation marks enable the writer to present a message that is clear and unambiguous and help the reader to understand the message quickly. Most of the punctuation marks presented thus far serve to tell the reader when to stop and when to pause. Now we will study three different marks of punctuation—quotation marks, parentheses, and apostrophes. We will see that quotation marks are primarily used to identify for the reader the exact words that someone used. Parentheses may be used in some of the same ways in which commas and dashes are used; however, although they share some functions in common, commas, dashes, and parentheses are not always interchangeable. Apostrophes are, as you already know, used to indicate possession. But they may also be used to form the plurals of certain letters, signs, and symbols.

Both as writer and reader you must be able to use these marks expertly if you are to master the tools of communication. Study their uses in this section.

QUOTATION MARKS

All of us know that quotation marks are primarily used to specify the precise words of a writer or speaker. But there are other common uses of quotation marks; the most important uses are discussed below.

Direct Quotations

A direct quotation is the word-for-word record of something that has been said or written, and quotation marks are the symbols that signal a direct quotation. In most instances, a comma precedes a direct quotation that comes at the end of the sentence.

> Before she left, Caroline said, "I will stay at the Hilton in Chicago on Thursday evening." (Note the comma before the direct quotation.)
> The contract says, "The entire shipment must be received no later than August 12." (The quotation marks give the exact wording found in the contract. Note the comma before the direct quotation.)

When a quotation is introduced by an independent clause, a colon replaces the comma before the quotation.

> The contract reads as follows: "The entire shipment must be received no later than August 12."

A colon (not a comma) should be used when the quotation is long or consists of several sentences.

> Caroline said: "I will stay at the Hilton in Chicago on Thursday evening. On Friday afternoon, I will leave for Los Angeles, where I will be at the Sheraton. Ask my secretary for a copy of my itinerary."

When a question is quoted, the question marks fall inside the second quotation mark. When an exclamation is quoted, the exclamation mark falls inside the second quotation mark.

> "May I meet with you on May 3?" she asked. (In a quoted question, the question mark goes before the closing quotation mark.)
> "What a remarkably low price!" he exclaimed. (In a quoted exclamation, the exclamation mark goes before the closing quotation mark.)
> "Leo will send you a new catalog," said Mr. Moore. (Note that when a sentence begins with a declaration, a comma, rather than a period, is placed before the closing quotation mark.)

Note: When *etc.* is used at the end of a quotation, the *etc.* should be placed outside the quotation mark.

> "We the people of the United States," etc., is the beginning of the Preamble to the Constitution of the United States.

Indirect Quotations

Indirect quotations are not word-for-word repetitions; therefore, they are not enclosed in quotation marks. Often, indirect quotations are introduced by *that*.

> Mr. Moore said that Leo will send you a new catalog. (This is an indirect quotation. No quotation marks are needed.)

Interrupted Quotations

A direct quotation may be interrupted, but only the quoted words are enclosed in quotation marks.

> "If the price is $2 or less a pound," said Miss Sandford's memo, "we should order at least one year's supply of the chemical." (The commas set off the interruption, and the quotation marks show Miss Sandford's exact words.)

In an interrupted quotation, if a semicolon or period would ordinarily end the first part of the quotation, hold that semicolon or period so that it follows the interrupting words.

> "We expect to win the Bradford contract," said Ms. Tillma; "moreover, we expect to be at least $25,000 under the next lowest bid."
> "Ask Edward to help you complete this inventory report," said Mrs. DeHaven. "If he's busy, then ask Gloria to help you."

Quotation Within a Quotation

Use single quotation marks for quotations within other quotations.

> Harold asked, "Did Miss Frankel say '16 days' or '60 days'?"

The period or comma that ends a quotation within a quotation is placed within both the single and the double quotation marks, as follows.

> "We disagree, of course, that their offer was 'reasonable,'" said Mr. Iovino.
> She said, "Please be sure to mark the invoice 'Paid in Full.'"

☐ Checkup 1

Correct any errors in the following sentences.
1. "Is the new price effective as of January 1" she asked?

2. Here is the exact wording on the invoice, "All payments are due within 30 days. Payments received within 10 days are subject to a 2 percent discount."
3. "What a great site for a convention" exclaimed Ms. Johnston!
4. "As of June 20, we are about $150,000 short of our sales budget," said Mr. Reavis, "however, we expect to make up for this within the next few months."
5. Miriam said, "We will have all these backorders processed no later than tomorrow afternoon".
6. "I recommended buying this stock when it sold for $15 a share," said Ms. Conroy, "and now it's selling for $75"!
7. "Mr. Derrick has a copy of the contract," said James, "but he took it with him to Detroit."
8. "Has Mr. Marlowe approved our buying a new computer?" asked Andrew.

Quoting Terms and Expressions

Writers often signal their readers that certain expressions or terms are particularly significant by enclosing the significant words in quotation marks. The first word within the quotation marks is capitalized if the expression is a complete sentence or, of course, if the word would be capitalized normally. Following are some of the ways quotation marks are used to denote expressions and terms having special significance.

For Explanations, Definitions, and Unusual Terms Words and phrases used as definitions or introduced by such expressions as *so-called*, *known as*, *marked*, and *signed*, are enclosed in quotation marks.

> In the printing trade, a *widow* is simply "a short last line of a paragraph." (The definition is in quotation marks; the word being defined is in italics. Note that underscoring in typewritten copy is equivalent to italics in printed copy.)
> Working regularly at a second job is known as "moonlighting."
> It was signed "Laura B. Sheng."

Terms that may be unfamiliar to the general reader or that are unusual when used in certain contexts should be set off so that the reader is prepared to recognize them. In the next examples, the signals are the quotation marks around the rather commonplace words *flat* and *pull* since each is used in a rather uncommon way.

> The photo-offset printer corrected the "flat" before reprinting this book. (Technical term that may be unfamiliar to the reader)
> For our upcoming direct-mail advertising campaign, we tested three sales letters to see which one would have the strongest "pull." (Unusual use of term)

For Translation of Foreign Words

The translation of a foreign word or expression is enclosed in quotation marks. (Note that the foreign word or expression is in *italics*.)

> Next to each paragraph, Mr. Petrovich wrote *da*, which is Russian for "yes."

For Slang, Humor, or Poor Grammar

To add punch to a message—for example, to a sales letter or newsletter—a writer may use a slang expression, a funny comment, or a deliberate grammatical error. Such uses, when carefully limited, can attract attention and help to make a point. To show that the use is intentional, the writer encloses the expression in quotations.

> To prove to you that we're "pushovers," we are offering you a 50 percent discount to renew your subscription to *SportsWorld*. (Slang expression)
> Next week, Mr. Miguel Esposito will make his "debut" as sales manager. (Humorous expression)
> All you sales representatives are doing very well in this month's contest, but it "ain't over yet!" (Deliberate grammatical error)

☐ Checkup 2

Are quotation marks used correctly in the following sentences? Correct any errors.
1. The so-called panel of experts apparently knew very little about data processing.
2. Because we've exceeded our sales goals by 60 percent, we should be permitted to do some horn-tooting.
3. Although the packages were marked Fragile, our messengers handled them carelessly.
4. The check was signed "Frederick P. Lister," but the teller wisely compared the signature to the one on file.
5. A simple definition of *laissez-faire* is noninterference.
6. The so-called bargains were merely overpriced imitations.

Quoting Titles

The titles of parts or chapters of books are enclosed in quotation marks, but the titles of books are underscored.

> Read Chapter 12, "Preparing Budgets," in Principles of Finance. (The chapter title is enclosed in quotations; the book title is underscored.)

Also enclosed in quotation marks are the titles of lectures, articles, essays, sermons, mottoes, paintings, poems, and sculptures and the names of ships.

> Last year, we cruised for two weeks on the "Queen Elizabeth II."
> Sarah's latest article, "Setting Career Goals," appeared in Management Monthly.

Besides book titles, the titles of complete, separately bound works such as newspapers, magazines, booklets, and long poems should also be underscored. In addition, the titles of plays, operas, and movies should be underscored. Again, note that underscoring in typewritten copy is equivalent to *italics* in printed copy.

Her new book was reviewed favorably in <u>The New York Times</u> recently.

The title of this book is <u>College English and Communication</u>.

My supervisor's son is now appearing in the Broadway production of <u>A Chorus Line</u>.

Words such as *preface, introduction, index,* and *appendix* are not enclosed in quotations. When they refer to parts of a specific book, they are capitalized.

You'll enjoy the Preface to <u>Sell for Success</u>.

Punctuating at the End of Quoted Material

Question: Where are punctuation marks placed at the end of quotations? Study the answers below.

1. Periods and commas are *always* placed within the closing quotation mark. "All Sales representatives," according to the newsletter, "must cut their travel expenses by 15 percent next year."
2. Colons and semicolons are always placed *outside* the closing quotation mark.

   She disagrees that these stocks are "blue chips": American Metals, Inc.; Paige Industries; Clemson Rubber Company; and Verona Plastics.

   Mr. DuPont, too, believes that the construction estimates we received are "flagrantly excessive"; however, he has little hope of getting lower estimates from other bidders.

3. Question marks and exclamation points may be placed either inside or outside the closing quotation mark. Follow these rules to decide.
   a. If the quoted words make up a question, then the question mark belongs with those quoted words. Place the question mark *inside* the closing quotation mark.

   Mrs. Early asked, "Do you think that next year's sales budget is too high?" (Only the quoted words make up the question; thus the question mark belongs with the quoted words—*inside* the closing quotation mark.)

   Treat exclamations the same way.

   Mr. Wynn said, "I don't believe these prices!" (Only the words in quotations make up the exclamation; thus the exclamation point belongs with those words—*inside* the closing quotation mark.)

   b. If the quoted words do *not* make up a question (that is, if the quotation is *part of* a question), then the question mark belongs to the entire sentence. Place the question mark *outside* the closing quotation mark.

   Do you agree with Mr. DuPont that these construction estimates are "flagrantly excessive"? (The entire sentence is a question; the quotation is only *part of* the question. The question mark belongs *outside* the closing quotation mark.)

Treat exclamations the same way.

> Imagine calling these stocks "blue chips"! (The entire sentence is an exclamation; the quoted words are only *part of* the exclamation. The exclamation point belongs *outside* the closing quotation mark.)

☐ Checkup 3

In the following sentences, correct any errors in the use of quotation marks.
1. The title of her article is "Understanding Business Contracts".
2. Each contestant was awarded a miniature reproduction of a famous sculpture, The Thinker, by Rodin.
3. You will find the "Index" to the book *A Guide to Stock Investments* both thorough and comprehensive.
4. An oil tanker named Ocean Carrier was involved in an accident off the coast of Florida.
5. At the beginning of her speech, she read Robert Frost's well-known poem, "The Road Not Taken."
6. Are you sure that Mrs. Fielding specifically said "25 percent discount?"
7. No one should accept these "excuses!"
8. Ms. Erickson said her client was "absolutely innocent;" moreover, she said that she would prove it.

PARENTHESES

As we already noted, commas, dashes, and parentheses share certain common uses. However, they are not interchangeable. Just as words that have similar meanings still have subtle distinctions, so, too, do commas, dashes, and parentheses have distinctions. The careful business writer is aware of these distinctions. Study the use of parentheses discussed below.

For Words That Give Additional Information

Commas, dashes, and parentheses may be used to set off words that give additional information. The words set off by commas may be omitted, but they generally add something to the main thought. The words set off by dashes are often given additional emphasis by the dashes. But the words set off by parentheses are clearly deemphasized; they may be omitted.

> Adam Fonda, our chief financial officer, explained the new system. (The words set off by commas may be omitted, but they do add something to the main thought.)
> Last year, four representatives in our region—including Anne Morrow, a new representative—won the Million Dollar Sales Award. (The words set off by dashes may be omitted; however, the writer deliberately uses dashes to draw attention to these words.)

In the past year, we lost only one account (Benson Plastics, which had small billings for the past three years). (The words in parentheses are extraneous; they contribute little to the main thought.)

For References

Parentheses are very useful for enclosing references and directions.

> The Bibliography (see page 539) includes an up-to-date listing of magazines and periodicals that may be of interest.
> Add water slowly to the powder (be sure that the room is well ventilated), and stir carefully.

Punctuation With Words in Parentheses

Parentheses may be used to enclose words within a sentence, or they may be used to enclose an entire independent sentence.

Parentheses Within a Sentence   No punctuation mark goes *before* the opening parenthesis within a sentence. Whatever punctuation would normally be used at this point is placed *after* the closing parenthesis.

> When we meet next Thursday (at the weekly planning meeting), we will discuss the new salary schedules. (The comma that is needed after the clause *When we meet next Thursday* is placed *after* the *closing* parenthesis, not *before* the *opening* parenthesis.)
> Ms. Drury suggests that we keep the list price low (under $5), and Mr. Richards assured her that we could easily do so. (The comma needed to separate the two independent clauses is placed *after* the *closing* parenthesis, not *before* the *opening* parenthesis.)
> Kilgore Electronics estimated a total unit cost of $1.26 (see the itemized statement enclosed); however, this applies only to manufacturing 100,000 units or more. (The semicolon is placed *after* the *closing* parenthesis.)

Note that these rules do not affect any punctuation needed *within* the parentheses. Study the following examples:

> As soon as we decide where we will hold our next product information meeting (probably Chicago, Illinois, or Washington, D.C.), we must immediately reserve 100 rooms for our sales representatives.
> Let's visit their main office (is it on the East Coast?) and give them a formal presentation on our services.

If an independent clause in parentheses within a sentence is a question or exclamation, the question mark or exclamation mark is included within the parentheses. If the independent clause is a declaration, however, no period is used within the parentheses. Note too, that when parentheses are included within a sentence, the first word in parentheses is not capitalized (unless, of course, the first word is a proper noun) even if the words in parentheses are an independent clause.

> Be sure to ask Bob Trout (he's in charge of our word processing center) to review this report.

Parentheses for Complete Sentences   When the words enclosed in parentheses are entirely independent (that is, that they are not part of another sentence), the first word in parentheses is capitalized and normal end punctuation is used before the closing parenthesis.

> As you requested, we have amortized these costs over a five-year period. (Please see Appendix A page 105.)
>
> At this special price, our supply won't last long. Thus we urge you to send in your order form now. (Can you afford *not* to?)

☐ Checkup 4

Edit the following sentences for correct use of parentheses.
1. If Ellen accepts the offer to manage the Chicago office (We think that she will.), she will be the youngest general manager in our company.
2. Louis said that all invoices (all!) must be paid by Friday.
3. Do you know whether he would prefer the deluxe model (it's only $2 more?).
4. The new monthly inventory form, (see the attached sample) is easy to complete.
5. The shelves in this cabinet can be easily adjusted (see page 12); the only tool required is a screwdriver.
6. The Jakway Corporation, (formerly known as the Jakway Manufacturing Company), is now on the New York Stock Exchange.
7. Ms. DeVries was formerly with the J&R Electronics (she was responsible for J&R's Equal Employment Opportunity Program).
8. The specifications require a 2-inch-thick fireproof insulation around the entire furnace (see the diagram on page 17.)

APOSTROPHES

The primary use of apostrophes is to show possession. A secondary use is to form the plurals of letters, signs, symbols, and words used as words. Those uses have already been discussed.

In addition, apostrophes may also be used to form contractions and to show the omission of figures. These additional uses are discussed below.

For Contractions

An apostrophe is used to show a shortened form of one or more words. Some well-known contractions are *o'clock* (for "of the clock"), *don't* (for "do not"), *won't* (for "will not"), *I've* (for "I have"), *we'd* (for "we had"), *they're* (for "they are"), and *it's* (for "it is" or "it has").

For Omission of Figures

In year dates, an apostrophe may be used to show that the first two digits have been omitted. For example, *'78* and *'79* for *1978* and *1979*.

☐ Checkup 5

Do the following sentences have any errors in the use of apostrophes? Make the necessary corrections.
1. Although Ms. Stimson was graduated from law school in '74, she began practicing law only this year.
2. Are you certain that he doesnt suspect that the party is for him?
3. Maria shouldn't have used all her vacation time so quickly.
4. Mr. Karolak and Ms. Landers both graduated in 78.
5. Dont Andrew and Betty know about the meeting tomorrow?

COMMUNICATION PROJECTS

Practical Application

A. Correct any errors in the use of quotation marks, parentheses, or apostrophes. Write *OK* for each correct sentence.
1. Karen admitted that she had made an error (shes always very honest).
2. To find more about consumers' rights, be sure to read Chapter 9, Personal Finance and the Consumer, in Margaret Hatta's new book, *Consumer Fraud.*
3. Until the authorities can prove otherwise, the fire will be officially considered an "accident".
4. Regina Logan, the political commentator on WNEW 1120 on your dial, will interview Mayor Franklin at 9 a.m. tomorrow.
5. About 95 percent of our representatives responded to the survey. (Most of the respondents returned their completed questionnaire within three days).
6. At the end of the tape, the narrator said, "supplies are limited, so please hurry"!
7. Several signs, each with "Special Sale"! in large letters, were placed in the window of the store.
8. Mr. Brown insists "that we should delay building the new factory until the engineers are satisfied that the environment will be protected."
9. The new regulation (its been approved by the board) will go into effect next January 1.
10. "As you know," said Miss McVay, "the Cleveland warehouse is one of our most efficient operations."
11. The attorney carefully explained that *nolo contendere* means "no contest".
12. He asked me, "Do you plan to insure this package"?
13. Marilou gave the same answer to all three questions: "Definitely!"
14. For several decades, the Fasano Food Company has identified its products with this slogan: "The best of the best".

15. Richard said, "Please be sure to mark each carton 'Fragile.'"
16. No, they havent submitted their weekly reports yet.
17. A customer wants to know "whether the discount applies to sale items?"
18. She asked to take these contracts to Mr. Hicks (is he still on the second floor) as soon as Mrs. Flores signs the contracts.
19. When she finished engineering school, (she was graduated with the class of '79), she joined the firm of Hardgood and Cranston.
20. As Ms. Evans later explained, "The so-called 'experts could not explain why the machinery had broken down."

B. Correct any errors in the following sentences. Write *OK* if a sentence is correct.
1. Pauline K. Hargrove (she's the editor of *Today's Woman*) will give the keynote address.
2. For several years, Ms. Bruno sold advertising space on the East Coast (from Key West, Florida, to Eastport, Maine,) but she became national sales manager in 1981.
3. Connie asked, "What's a *non sequitur*?" Maureen answered, "A *non sequitur* is 'a statement that does not follow."
4. The complete addresses of the major industrial organizations are given in Appendix D (see page 1,131).
5. "I am not interested in the offer," said Mr. Portera, "moreover, it is clearly a conflict of interest."
6. Among the topics that will be covered at the seminar are these: (1.) time management, (2.) decision making, and (3.) human relations.
7. For an interesting article on personnel relations, read Personnel Relations and Corporate Success, which appeared in a recent issue of *The Modern Executive*.
8. Mr. Steele said, "Although I been in the fashion industry for more than 20 years, I have met no designer more creative or more gifted than Colleen Gregus."
9. The list is $550.00, but we are sure that we will be able to get at least a 15 percent discount.
10. In our lobby are reproductions of many of the world's greatest paintings, including perhaps the best reproduction of the Mona Lisa.
11. Dr. Jenners believes that, we should be able to complete the project about two months early.
12. Once a month, we check the switches, cables, wires, and etc.
13. It was Peters idea to use a Roaring Twenties motif for the window displays.
14. For more information on the enclosed media schedule, call Diana Quicker (extension 3175.)
15. The first-prize winners will receive a two-week cruise on the "America", a beautiful ocean liner.
16. Apparently, the reason for all the delays is because the executives are on vacation.
17. The announcement specifically stated, "All employees must submit their completed forms to the Personnel Department no later than March 15".
18. An estimate form and a schedule should be included in the folder. (See pages 112 and 113 for examples of a completed estimate form and a completed schedule.)

19. "In all cases" according to the procedures manual, "a teller must verify the signature for any check over $500."
20. Our headquarters building was built in 1978; our warehouse in 1981.

Editing Practice

The Editing Desk   Correct any verb errors in the following sentences.

1. Marion said that she been to Puerto Rico twice within the past year.
2. Although a number of applicants were interviewed today, we have not yet hired anyone for the position of manager of data processing.
3. Don't Mr. Edgar want to keep a duplicate copy of all invoices that we receive?
4. More than a million dollars was raised for the new firehouse.
5. "The increasing number of careers open to women is encouraging," said Dr. Benedict.
6. Has Beatrice already went to the seminar at the Advertising Club?
7. The teller found checks and cash laying on the floor.
8. Have Carla and Jerome wrote their reports yet?
9. Where is the new catalog and the price list that we received this morning?
10. Surprisingly, the number of people who requested free samples were very, very low.

Case Problem

Solving Problems by Discussion   The small-group discussion technique is often used to solve problems. Shared ideas and experiences of a group often provide better solutions to problems than the limited ideas and experiences of an individual. Here is the way this technique works: (1) Divide the group into small sections of four, five, or six. (2) Make certain everyone in each group is acquainted. (3) Elect a chairperson and a recorder for each group. The recorder will take notes and will later report the major points of the discussion to the entire class. (4) Make certain that everyone understands the problem to be discussed. (5) Be sure that everyone enters into the discussion.

Here is the problem: What are the most important subjects (besides those "majored in") for business students? Why?

26
CAPITALIZATION

The rules of capitalization help the writer to make words distinctive, to emphasize words, and to show that certain words are of greater importance. Some of the rules for capitalization cause writers no problems because they are very well-known, long-established rules. These rules are reviewed briefly in this section. Other capitalization rules do cause problems, and these pitfalls are fully discussed in this section.

FIRST WORDS

Always capitalize the first word of:

1. A sentence or a group of words used as a sentence:

> The lease expires at the end of this year. (Complete sentence)
> Yes, *this* year. (Group of words used as a sentence)

2. Each line of poetry:

> I advocate a semi-revolution
> The trouble with a total revolution
> (Ask any reputable Rosicrucian)
> Is that it brings the same class up on top.
> —Robert Frost

3. Each item in an outline:

> The committee recommended that:
> 1. We double the budget for the project.
> 2. We notify all our customers of the temporary changes.
> 3. We assign full-time personnel to handle the project.

4. A sentence in a direct quotation:

> The attorney specifically said, "Be sure to get permission from the copyright holder to reprint this excerpt."

5. A complete sentence after a colon when that sentence is a formal rule or needs special emphasis:

> Her long-standing rule is this: There is no "sure thing" when it comes to investments. (Rule)
> Time-management experts always stress this point: Spend your time on high-priority tasks only. (For emphasis)

Also capitalize the first word after a colon when the material that follows consists of two or more sentences:

> She discussed fully the two main reasons for increasing prices: First, the

truckers' strike has substantially increased shipping costs. Second, the cost of importing the raw materials has doubled in the past ten months.

6. A complimentary closing:

Sincerely yours,

☐ Checkup 1

Do the following sentences capitalize first words correctly? Make any necessary corrections.

1. I think that "very respectfully yours" is too formal a closing for this letter.
2. How many people will be transferred to our Houston office? only two or three.
3. Karen came to my office and said, "Hurry! We've got to be at the airport in one hour."
4. As our accountant always says, "keep receipts for all business expenses."
5. She gave two reasons for requesting a transfer to our headquarters office: she believes that she will have more opportunities for advancement at headquarters. in addition, she wants to attend New York University, which is near our headquarters office.
6. Among the promotion materials we created are:
   1. direct mail letters.
   2. fliers and brochures.
   3. posters.
   4. miscellaneous handouts.

HEADINGS AND TITLES OF PUBLICATIONS

In headings and in titles of publications, the main words are always capitalized. Words that are *not* capitalized are articles, conjunctions, and short prepositions (that is, prepositions of three or fewer letters), unless they are the first words or last words in the title.

> She wrote the article "The Season for Success," which was published in *The Advertising and Promotion Magazine*. (*The* is capitalized because it is the first word in both titles. *For* is a short preposition, and *and* is a conjunction.)
> You should read "The Job I'm Looking For," the first chapter in *Finding a New Job*. (Capitalize *The*, the first word in a title, and *For*, the last word in a title. Do not capitalize the article *a*.)

Hyphenated expressions follow the same rules.

> The title of his column is "Up-to-Date Methods for Investing: A Resource for Brokers." (Do not capitalize *to* in the hyphenated compound. Note that the article *A* is considered the first word when it follows a colon.)

PROPER ADJECTIVES

A proper adjective is an adjective formed from a proper noun; for example, *Mexican, South American, Lenten, Victorian*. Proper adjectives are capitalized.

Note: Through long use, certain adjectives are no longer capitalized because they have lost their association with the proper nouns from which they were derived; for example, *venetian* blind, *turkish* towel, *india* ink, *panama* hat. Always consult a dictionary to decide whether or not to capitalize such adjectives.

Seasons of the Year

Seasons of the year are not capitalized; for example, the *spring* styles, our *fall* opening, sales during the *winter* months.

☐ Checkup 2

Correct any errors in these sentences. Write *OK* for each correct sentence.
1. She wrote a biting satire of our society called "It's Un-american To Be Poor."
2. Because our business is seasonal, sales always drop in the Winter months.
3. He created a huge banner that read, "Once-In-A-Lifetime Savings At Our Fourth Of July Sale!"
4. Her well-known book, "Women In Business: a Guide For Today's Executive," has made her an overnight celebrity.
5. Next Spring we will open a new store called Fashions For The Entire Family.
6. They wrote a book entitled "Teaching English to Spanish-speaking Students."

NAMES OF PERSONS, PLACES, AND THINGS

Writers use capital letters to say: "This is the name of a specific person, place, or thing. This name is the exclusive property of this particular person, place, or thing."

> My friend Roberta works for County Bank here in New York City. (*Roberta* is the name of a specific person. *County Bank* is the name of a specific bank. *New York City* is the name of a specific city.)
> My friend works for a bank here in the city. (Here *bank* and *city* are not capitalized because they are not part of the exclusive name of a particular bank or a particular city.)

Names of Persons

To each of us, the sound of our own name is sweet music. Therefore, a mistake in spelling or in capitalizing someone's name may jeopardize goodwill. Names should be written *as the owners wish them to be written*, regardless of the rules. Only if there is no way of finding out the specific spelling that a person prefers are the following rules to be used.

O', Mc, Mac   The prefixes *O'* and *Mc* are followed by a capital letter without spacing; for example, *O'Brien, McCaffrey.* The prefix *Mac* may or may not be followed by a capital, as: *MacMillan, Macmillan.*

D, Da, De, Della, Di, Du, La, Le, Lo, Van, Von These prefixes are capitalized only when the surname is written alone, without a first name, title, or initials; for example, *De Frias, Van Hoven, Du Mont*. When a first name, an initial, or a title appears with the surname, the prefix is not capitalized unless the individual person prefers a capital letter.

> We enjoyed La Follette's speech. (*La* is capitalized because only the surname is written.)
>
> Did you enjoy Senator la Follette's speech? (*La* is not capitalized because a title is written with the surname.)
>
> We always enjoy Von Hoffman's lectures. (*Von* is capitalized because only the surname is written.)
>
> Are you registered for any of Professor von Hoffman's classes? (Because a title is written with the surname, *von* is not capitalized.)
>
> I voted for De Luca. (*De* is capitalized because only the surname is written.)
>
> In her victory speech, Governor-elect de Luca vowed to continue her fight for judicial reform. (Because a title is written with the surname, *de* is not capitalized.)

Names of Places

Capitalize names of geographical localities, streets, parks, rivers, buildings, and so on, such as *South America, Main Street, Bryant Park, Delaware River, Medical Arts Building*.

Capitalize the word *city* only when it is a part of the corporate name of a city: *Dodge City*, but the *city* of Boston.

Capitalize the word *state* only when it follows the name of a state: *Kansas State*, but the *state of Kansas*.

Capitalize the word *the* in names of places only when *the* is part of the official name: *The Hague*, but *the Maritime Provinces*.

NAMES OF THINGS

Capital letters identify official names of companies, associations, committees, bureaus, buildings, schools, course titles, clubs, government bodies, historical events and documents, and so on.

> Several employees are taking Typing at County Business School. (*Typing* is the official course title; *County Business School* is the official school name.)
>
> Several employees are taking a typing course at a nearby business school. (No capitals)
>
> Ms. Dimitrios is a consultant for the Hamilton Investment Company, which has offices here in the Fairchild Building. (Capitalize the official name of the company and the building.)
>
> She is a consultant for an investment company in this building. (No capitals)

Capitalize the names of the days of the week, the months of the year, religious days and holidays, and imaginative names of eras and periods: *Tuesday, Wednesday; March, June; Easter, Passover; the Roaring Twenties, the Middle Ages.*

☐ Checkup 3

Are the names of places, persons, and things capitalized correctly in these sentences? Make any necessary corrections.

1. In 1980, Mount St. Helens erupted and caused widespread damage throughout the State of Washington.
2. Mount McKinley, in the State of Alaska, is the highest Mountain in the United States.
3. Ms. Anita Von Fischer is the owner of several hotels in the Catskill mountains, a famous resort area in New York State.
4. While we were in Las Vegas, we visited the Grand canyon.
5. Our company is planning a fourth of july sale that will surely be a tremendous success.
6. The national education association is exploring the possibility of purchasing the Herald building.
7. van Dam, a well-known writer of popular history books, is now completing a two-volume study of the Inquisition.
8. All this merchandise must be shipped to our Dodge city store as soon as possible.

CAPITALIZATION PITFALLS

Writers often face choices in capitalizing words such as *west* and *east, president* and *governor,* and *company* and *government.* The following discussion presents logical solutions to using such terms and, therefore, will help you to avoid capitalization pitfalls.

Points of the Compass

North, south, east, and *west* are capitalized whenever they refer to specific sections of the country and, of course, when they are part of proper names. They are not capitalized when they refer merely to direction.

> We need a warehouse in the West in order to solve our present shipping problems and lower our shipping costs. (Specific part of the country)
> She filmed the commercial in South Dakota. (*South* is part of a proper name.)
> Fortunately, the airport is only 15 miles east of our office. (Here, *east* simply indicates direction.)

Substitutions

Many official names have substitutes or nicknames that may be used to replace them. Capitalize substitutes for official names of persons or places. Do not use substitutes unless they are well known.

She denied rumors that the company was planning to move from the Windy City. (*Windy City* is a well-known substitute for *Chicago.*)

John Aliano, who is presently writing a book on Joe DiMaggio, will discuss the Yankee Clipper on Sports Extra tonight at 8:30. (To sports fans, *Yankee Clipper* is a well-known nickname for *Joe DiMaggio.*)

Short Forms

Writers often substitute one word for the complete name of a person, place, or thing. Such substitutions are capitalized when they are intended to indicate a specific person, place, or thing.

> The most recent biography of the Admiral is entitled *Nimitz in the Pacific.* (Here, *Admiral* obviously refers to a specific person.)
>
> She has written a biography about an admiral who was famous in World War II. (Because *admiral* does not refer to a particular person, it is not capitalized.)
>
> When the engineers had completed inspecting the Lincoln Tunnel, they concluded that the Tunnel was completely safe. (Capitalize *Tunnel,* because it refers to a specific thing.)
>
> None of our engineers has ever worked on a tunnel. (No capitalization. No specific tunnel is intended.)

The words *company, association, school, college,* and so on, are not usually capitalized when they stand alone, even though they may substitute for the official name of a specific organization.

> Her company is considering a merger with Fitch & Sellers.
>
> We visited the college when we were in Los Angeles recently.

Writers will usually capitalize the names of departments or divisions within their own companies when the department name is preceded by *the.* When preceded by *your, our, their,* and so on, the department name is not capitalized. Names of departments in other companies are also not capitalized.

> The Advertising Department recommended that we run a full-page ad in <u>Business Week</u>. (Capitalize the department name within your own company when the name is preceded by *the.* But: Our advertising department recommended . . . .)
>
> The Manufacturing Division estimates that our unit cost will be under $10. (Capitalize division name within your own company when the name is preceded by *the.* But: Our manufacturing division estimates . . . .)
>
> Their credit department has approved a $5,000 credit line for us. (Do not capitalize the name of a department in another company.)

However, for special emphasis the names of departments, divisions, and committees may be capitalized whether they are names within the writer's company or not.

> I am eager to find out more about the position you advertised in your Purchasing Department. (Capitalize department name for emphasis or to show special importance.)

The terms *government* and *federal government* are not capitalized. *Federal* is capitalized, of course, when it is part of an official name, such as *Federal Communications Commission.*

☐ Checkup 4

Correct any errors in the use of capitals in these sentences.
1. Janet bought a home in the South.
2. Send a duplicate copy to our accounting department.
3. Is the General in his office now?
4. Next summer, Jack and I will drive East to New York.
5. When we went to Panama, I took excellent pictures of the canal.
6. The federal Bureau of Investigation has a regional office here in our building.
7. Grace lives in a suburban community just 10 miles North of Atlanta.
8. Their Sales Department sent us a new catalog and a revised price list.

Commercial Products

Distinguish carefully between a proper noun that is part of the official name of a product and a common noun that names the *general* class of the product. For example, you would write *Arch Saver shoes,* not *Arch Saver Shoes,* because the official brand name is *Arch Saver.* Note the following:

Kleenex tissues	Xerox machine
General Electric appliances	Goodrich tires

Personal and Official Titles

Always capitalize a title written before a name.

> The speakers were General Smyth, Professor Kirsch, and Ensign York.

A title written after a name or without a name is capitalized when (1) it is a very high national or international title or (2) it is part of an address.

> Kurt Waldheim, the Secretary General of the United Nations, is scheduled to speak on tonight's broadcast. (Always capitalize this internationally known title.)
>
> In yesterday's column, she discussed the President's economic policies. (*President*—referring to the President of the United States—is always capitalized.)
>
> Erica Godfrey, president of Godfrey Electronics, announced the acquisition of a major European manufacturing company today. (Do not capitalize *president* in such situations.)
>
> Ms. Erica Godfrey, President
> Godfrey Electronics, Inc.
> 1500 College Avenue
> Racine, Wisconsin 53403
> (Capitalize a title that is part of an address.)

When joined to titles, *ex-* and *-elect* are not capitalized. Also, *former* and *late* are not capitalized.

> Among the dignitaries invited to the dinner was former Mayor Wagner.
> The late President Johnson is the subject of this short documentary film.
> Governor-elect Helms said that she would make our transportation system one of her top priorities.
> Next semester, ex-Senator Seeley will teach a course on political science.

☐ Checkup 5

Find and correct any capitalization errors in the following sentences.

1. Diana is currently working on the Folger Coffee account.
2. Please make two Xerox Copies of this agenda.
3. Arnold Hart, President of Mercury Aviation Corporation, announced his retirement earlier this week.
4. Warren Burger, chief justice of the Supreme Court, wrote the majority opinion.
5. Harry S Truman became President in April 1945.
6. Beth test-drives General Motors Cars.

COMMUNICATION PROJECTS

Practical Application

A. Correct any capitalization errors in the following sentences. Write *OK* for any sentence that is correct.

1. The Senator said that he would not seek re-election next year.
2. Marisa Gomez, president of the Chamber of Commerce, is expected to announce her candidacy soon.
3. Use "cordially" or "cordially yours" for less formal closings.
4. Joan Franklin is our representative in the State of Kansas.
5. Next week we will advertise our new Fall styles.
6. The policy is this: always get approval for purchases over $500.
7. All our stores are closed on New Year's day.
8. Our Company has won the contract to paint City Hall.
9. The Corn Belt includes the States of Iowa, Nebraska, and Illinois.
10. Ms. Christie recently leased a Chevrolet Sedan.
11. Flight 191 leaves from O'Hare Airport at 7:15 this evening.
12. "Buying And Selling Stocks" is a very interesting article.
13. The Metropolitan Opera house and Lincoln center are in New York City.
14. Before she became our Manager, Jennifer was a representative on the west coast.
15. Miss Nichols is coauthor of a book titled *Fundamentals of Advertising*.
16. Our largest warehouse is about 30 miles south of Atlanta.
17. Although Mr. Hammond was born in the south, he spent most of his life in the State of Maine.
18. Our Company signed a contract giving us exclusive distribution rights to the new movie.

19. Lorraine McDaniels is a former President of the Advertising Club.
20. Mrs. Williams is now serving her third term in congress.

B. Correct any errors in the following sentences. Write *OK* if a sentence is correct.

1. The railroads are pressuring the Government to approve the increase in fares.
2. We must complete these letters, memos and reports by the end of the day.
3. Vera is studying American History at Central Community College.
4. Don't Mr. Rinaldo know that the computer is now being repaired?
5. Almost everyone in our Department has been assigned to this project.
6. Most of the customers whom we surveyed, are in favor of the new procedure.
7. The details of the Federal Insurance Contributions act, known as FICA, are explained in this brochure.
8. Margaret Jamison, former President of the Retail Jewelers Association, has been named to the Mayor's committee.
9. Each of the supervisors have been invited to the discussion.
10. Danielle Warner, who you met at this morning's meeting, is the head of our advertising department.
11. Do you know where Frank and Maureen are at?
12. The personnel manager asked, "What is the salary range for this new position"?
13. Model T-141 has been one of our best-sellers since it was introduced in January 1981, moreover, we expect it to continue to sell well for several more years.
14. The person who is sitting besides John is the supervisor of our data processing department.
15. The poster that you're looking for is in back of the file cabinet.
16. Helen could not help from pointing out that the sales estimates were unrealistic.
17. There is the production report and the inventory chart that you wanted.
18. Although this machine does indeed work very good, it costs almost 40 percent more than its closest competitor.
19. Mrs. Ellison said that we could expect delivery of all the merchandise inside of two weeks.
20. Ed is an assistant supervisor, but he sometimes acts like he was the executive vice-president.

Editing Practice

The Word Processing Supervisor   Edit the following sentences to correct any errors they may contain. Write *OK* if a sentence contains no error.

1. Being that we did not pay the bill within ten days, we cannot deduct the 2 percent discount.
2. Please do not leave for lunch without you get someone to replace you.
3. Jack, do you know where Myron went to?
4. One of the reporters asked her several questions in regards to the proposed government legislation.
5. All the extra paperwork will be divided between the three shift supervisors, Mike, Carolyn, and Elaine.
6. According to the announcement, the increases are retroactive from last January.

7. Did you realize that the price on this invoice is different from the price listed in the catalog?
8. We read in the company newspaper where Elliot has been made manager of our California office.
9. Todd couldn't hardly wait to leave for Puerto Rico.
10. As you can well imagine, Ms. Madison was real angry when she heard that the contract had been canceled.

Using Business Vocabulary Fill in the blanks with the correct word from those listed below.

a. approximate	f. freight
b. bankruptcy	g. irrelevant
c. chronological	h. mandatory
d. exhaustive	i. negotiate
e. extension	j. valuable

1. Stocks, bonds, and all other (?) securities must be locked in a fireproof vault overnight.
2. At tomorrow's meeting we will try to (?) a five-year loan at 12 percent interest per year.
3. All we jurors considered Mr. Martin's testimony (?) to the case.
4. Because Norton Industries has been unprofitable for three years, (?) proceedings will begin early next month.
5. Please take all these invoices and arrange them in (?) order, beginning with January invoices.
6. The (?) cost for the entire project is $10,000.
7. According to the contract, the shipper pays the (?) charges.
8. Because they could not meet the payment deadline, we have agreed to a 30-day (?) for the total balance.
9. The research department has conducted an (?) survey to discover our customers' preferences.
10. Wearing safety equipment is (?) in the laboratory because of toxic fumes.

Case Problem

Making It Clear and Simple You have been asked to revise and simplify a memorandum that contains the following paragraph. Rewrite the paragraph in everyday, clear language.

> Subsequent to April 10, Mr. Lawrence terminated his contract with this organization after completing a considerable amount of years of continuous and exemplary service. Apropos to his decision to sever relations, Mr. Lawrence stated that he had procured an infinitely superior contract that was the quintessence of betterment. We must employ perseverance in endeavoring to replace this lost contract with one of comparable caliber.

27 ABBREVIATIONS

Abbreviations provide the writer with shortcuts for expressing words and phrases, and shortcuts are certainly appropriate at times. In fact, certain abbreviations are never spelled out—*Mr.*, *Ms.*, and *Mrs.*, for example. However, abbreviations are not always acceptable. The business writer must know both how and when to use abbreviations in order to prepare communications that are concise and understandable.

ABBREVIATIONS WITH PERSONAL NAMES

Various abbreviations can be used with personal names, either before the name or after the name or both. Study the following rules for using abbreviations with personal names.

Before Personal Names

Most of the titles used before personal names are abbreviations:

Singular	Plural
Mr.	Messrs. (from the French, *messieurs*)
Mrs.	Mmes. or Mesdames
Ms.	Mses. or Mss.
Miss	Misses
Dr.	Drs.

As you see, except for *Mesdames, Miss,* and *Misses,* all these titles are abbreviations. In general, all other titles used before personal names are spelled out whether the full name or only the last name is given.

Governor Reed	Superintendent Alexandra Crespi
Senator Lewis	the Honorable Shirley Chisolm
Professor Chang	the Reverend Clarence Owens
Captain Kent	Brigadier General Harold W. Simpson

(In informal correspondence, long terms may be abbreviated; for example, *Brigadier General* may be abbreviated *Brig. Gen.*)

After Personal Names

Academic Degrees and Similar Abbreviations. Abbreviations of academic degrees, religious orders, and similar abbreviations generally have internal periods: *M.D., D.D.S., Ph.D., B.S., Ed.D.; S.J., D.D.* Check your dictionary whenever you are not sure of the abbreviation.

When such abbreviations follow a person's name, use a comma before the abbreviation. Do *not* use *Mr., Ms., Mrs., Miss,* or *Dr.* before the person's name.

> Henry Clancy, Esq. *or* Mr. Henry Clancy (Not: *Mr.* Henry Clancy, *Esq.*)
> Jane T. Prentiss, M.D. *or* Dr. Jane T. Prentiss (Not: *Dr.* Jane T. Prentiss, *M.D.*)
> Price S. Raymond, Ph.D. *or* Dr. Price S. Raymond (Not: *Dr.* Price S. Raymond, *Ph.D.*)

Other titles before the person's name may sometimes be appropriate:

> Reverend Peter Goode, S.J.
> Professor Alicia P. Stevens, Litt.D.

Note that in a sentence, any such abbreviation following a name must be set off with *two* commas, unless the abbreviation ends the sentence.

> Jane T. Prentiss, M.D., is the subject of today's "Woman in the News" column.

Jr. and Sr.   Traditionally, a comma was always placed before *Jr.* and *Sr.* when either followed a person's name. The trend now, however, is to omit the comma. Nonetheless, always write the name precisely as the person writes it.

> Mr. James K. Leonard, Jr. (Mr. Leonard prefers the comma before *Jr.*)
> Dr. P. Dale Inger Sr. (Dr. Inger does not use a comma before *Sr.*)

Use *Jr.* and *Sr.* only with a person's full name, not with the last name only.

> **Incorrect:**   Mr. Leonard, Jr.
> **Incorrect:**   Dr. Inger Sr.

When a comma is used before *Jr.* or *Sr.,* a comma is also needed after *Jr.* or *Sr.* (unless, of course, the abbreviation ends the sentence).

> According to our records, Mr. James K. Leonard, Jr., is the trustee.

☐ Checkup 1

Correct any abbreviation errors in these sentences.
1. The new executive vice president will probably be either Adam J. Pierce Jr. or Eleanor P. Higgins.
2. The keynote speaker at the fund-raising dinner was Sen. Palmer.
3. The youngest partner in this law firm is Lawrence Nesbitt Esq.
4. The property is owned by the Messrs. Deere, who are cousins.
5. Prof. Handy was a research director for a large chemical company before she joined our firm.
6. Dr. David Wells, M.D., is the head of our firm's medical department.
7. As far as I know, Mister DeWilde is planning to go to Nashville tomorrow.
8. According to the announcement, Dr. Arnold Trask, Ph.D., has been named head of the economics department.

NAMES OF COMPANIES AND ORGANIZATIONS

Always write the name of a company or organization as the firm itself prefers. Whenever possible, check the company's letterhead or some *official* source to find out whether the correct name is *Ross and Pearl* or *Ross & Pearl; Quick Contracting Co.* or *Quick Contracting Company; Hanson Bros.* or *Hanson Brothers;* and so on.

Inc. and Ltd. As with *Jr.* and *Sr.*, the trend is to omit the comma before *Inc.* and *Ltd.* in official company names. Again, however, always follow the *official* name.

> Karen works for Time Inc. in New York City.
> Write to Garden Cameras, Inc., for more information. (Note *two* commas to set off *Inc.*)

All-Capital Abbreviations Many names of organizations, associations, government agencies, and so on, are abbreviated in all-capital letters with no periods or spaces between the letters:

AAA	American Automobile Association
AFL-CIO	American Federation of Labor and Congress of Industrial Organizations
AT&T	American Telephone and Telegraph
FBI	Federal Bureau of Investigation
IRS	Internal Revenue Service
NASA	National Aeronautics and Space Administration
NEA	National Education Association
UAW	United Auto Workers
USDA	United States Department of Agriculture

In addition, the call letters of broadcasting stations are always written in all-capital letters without periods.

> WPAT-FM   WNBC-TV

When *United States* is abbreviated (before the name of a government agency, for example), periods are used.

> the U.S. Office of Education

☐ Checkup 2

Are abbreviations used correctly in the following sentences?

1. Mr. Ramirez has been employed by T.W.A. since he became an aviation mechanic.
2. Since 1979 Mrs. Klein has been an attorney for the AFL-CIO.
3. The U.S.D.A. offers several booklets that are of special interest to consumers.
4. Jason and Ruth are accountants in the headquarters office of A.T.&T.
5. Veterans are urged to write to the VA to find out about educational benefits.
6. Dr. Chester is an aerospace engineer for N.A.S.A. in Houston.
7. If you have any questions about your taxes, call the I.R.S. office nearest you.

OTHER ABBREVIATIONS

Use the following rules to guide you when using abbreviations.

Year Dates and Expressions of Time

A.D. and *B.C.* Significant historical dates are often preceded by the abbreviation *A.D.*, which means "the year of our Lord" (from the Latin, *anno Domini*), or followed by *B.C.*, which means "before Christ."

> The Roman orator Cicero was born in 106 B.C. (*B.C.* follows the year date.)
> Attila the Hun died in A.D. 453. (*A.D.* precedes the year date.)

a.m. and p.m. Write *a.m.* and *p.m.* in lowercase letters with no spacing. Always use figures with these abbreviations, and do not use *o'clock* with *a.m.* or *p.m.* Remember: *a.m.* means "before noon" and *p.m.* means "after noon."

> The meeting will be at 10:15 a.m. on Thursday. (**Not:** 10:15 o'clock a.m.)

Days and Months

The days of the week and the months of the year should be abbreviated only when space forces the writer to do so (as in tables and lists, for example). In such cases, use the following abbreviations. Note that *May, June,* and *July* are not abbreviated.

Days of the Week	Months of the Year
Sun., Mon., Tues.,	Jan., Feb., Mar., Apr.,
Wed., Thurs., Fri.,	May, June, July, Aug.,
Sat.	Sept., Oct., Nov., Dec.

Units of Measure

General Use In routine correspondence, units of measure are spelled out: *yards, pounds, kilograms, degrees, meters, gallons,* and so on. Use figures with units of measure.

> Each swatch is about 3 inches by 4 inches.
> We will need at least eight 1-gallon containers.
> The sample that we tested contained about 3 grams of zinc.

Technical Use In technical work and on invoices, units of length, weight, capacity, area, volume, temperature, and time are usually abbreviated. Among the commonly used terms are these:

yd	yard, yards	g	gram, grams
in	inch, inches	kg	kilogram, kilograms
oz	ounce, ounces	m	meter, meters
pt	pint, pints	mm	millimeter, millimeters
gal	gallon, gallons	km	kilometer, kilometers
ft	foot, feet	l	liter, liters
lb	pound, pounds	cm	centimeter, centimeters

There are many more units of measure; use a comprehensive reference manual to find the correct abbreviations.

☐ Checkup 3

Correct any misuse of abbreviations in the following sentences.
1. Because Mrs. Heeley is now in a conference, we have rescheduled the production meeting for 4:30 PM.
2. The warehouse is only 2 or 3 km from the office.
3. We signed a ten-year lease on Feb. 9, 1981, with Trenton Realty Company.
4. Our mail room suggests that packages weighing over 25 lb be shipped book rate.
5. As you can see, the diode is only about 2 centimeters long.
6. Thank you for inviting us to your grand opening on Aug. 14.

Geographical Names

City Names   Do not abbreviate the name of a city, except for the word *Saint* in *St. Paul, St. Louis,* and so on. Do not abbreviate the words *Fort, Mount, Point,* or *Port,* as in *Fort Myers, Mount Vernon, Point Pleasant,* and *Port Jefferson.*

State Names   There are two sets of abbreviations of state names: (1) the traditional abbreviations and (2) the two-letter abbreviations developed by the Postal Service for addressing envelopes. (See the chart on page 223.)

In the body of a business letter, memo, or report, spell out the names of states. In addresses, use the two-letter abbreviations or spell out the full names. In all other cases, use the traditional abbreviations. Note these examples:
1. In the body of a business letter:
   As you requested, we will ship the entire order to your Cranston, Rhode Island, warehouse before May 13.
2. In an envelope address:
   Mr. Anthony J. Candela
   1301 Rockaway Parkway
   Los Angeles, CA 90052
3. In a bibliography:
   Bullinger's Postal and Shippers Guide for the United States and Canada, Bullinger's Guides, Inc., Westwood, N.J.

Number, No., and

When the word *number* is needed before a figure, use the abbreviation *No.* (or its plural, *Nos.*). At the beginning of a sentence, however, the word *Number* should be spelled out.

ABBREVIATIONS OF STATES, TERRITORIES, AND POSSESSIONS OF THE UNITED STATES

AL	Alabama	Ala.	MO	Missouri	Mo.
AK	Alaska	. . .	MT	Montana	Mont.
AZ	Arizona	Ariz.	NE	Nebraska	Nebr.
AR	Arkansas	Ark.	NV	Nevada	Nev.
CA	California	Calif.	NH	New Hampshire	N.H.
CZ	Canal Zone	C.Z.	NJ	New Jersey	N.J.
CO	Colorado	Colo.	NM	New Mexico	N. Mex.
CT	Connecticut	Conn.	NY	New York	N.Y.
DE	Delaware	Del.	NC	North Carolina	N.C.
DC	District of	D.C.	ND	North Dakota	N. Dak.
	Columbia		OH	Ohio	. . .
FL	Florida	Fla.	OK	Oklahoma	Okla.
GA	Georgia	Ga.	OR	Oregon	Oreg.
GU	Guam	. . .	PA	Pennsylvania	Pa.
HI	Hawaii	. . .	PR	Puerto Rico	P.R.
ID	Idaho	. . .	RI	Rhode Island	R.I.
IL	Illinois	Ill.	SC	South Carolina	S.C.
IN	Indiana	Ind.	SD	South Dakota	S. Dak.
IA	Iowa	. . .	TN	Tennessee	Tenn.
KS	Kansas	Kans.	TX	Texas	Tex.
KY	Kentucky	Ky.	UT	Utah	. . .
LA	Louisiana	La.	VT	Vermont	Vt.
ME	Maine	. . .	VI	Virgin Islands	V.I.
MD	Maryland	Md.	VA	Virginia	Va.
MA	Massachusetts	Mass.	WA	Washington	Wash.
MI	Michigan	Mich.	WV	West Virginia	W. Va.
MN	Minnesota	Minn.	WI	Wisconsin	Wis.
MS	Mississippi	Miss.	WY	Wyoming	Wyo.

Use the two-letter abbreviations on the left when abbreviating state names in addresses. In any other situation that calls for abbreviations of state names, use the abbreviations on the right.

Several invoices are missing from this file: Nos. 2079, 2082, and 2091.
Number 2076 is the only outstanding invoice, according to my records.

The abbreviation *No.* may be omitted when a word such as *Invoice, Check* or *Room* precedes the figure.

We will be in Room 1104, and Tom and Roy will be down the hall in Room 1115.

However, *No.* is retained in expressions such as *License No. K-5161, Social Security No. 064-36-9848,* and *Patent No. 789,654.*

To save space, the symbol # is sometimes used on forms; it is also used in technical copy.

Compass Points

In Street Addresses   Spell out compass points that appear before the street name; abbreviate compass points that follow the street name.

> 587 North 187 Street, N.W. (Spell out *North* before the street name; abbreviate *N.W.* after the street name.)

Note that in street addresses, abbreviations such as *N.W.*, *S.E.*, and so on, are written with periods and no spacing.

In Technical Writing   In technical copy, the compass points are abbreviated with no periods and no spacing:

N (north)   NW (northwest)
E (east)   SE (southeast)

Chemical Symbols

Chemical symbols and formulas *are* abbreviations. Do not use periods with chemical symbols:

O (oxygen) H_2O (water)   Fe (iron)

Letters That Substitute for Names

Whenever letters are used to stand for names of people, the letters are not followed by periods.

> Assume, for example, that Mr. A asks Mr. B for a five-year loan at 10 percent interest a year. (No periods after *A* and *B* in this sentence)

But if the letter actually is a shortened form of a name, then a period follows the letter; for example, if Mr. Barstow were to be referred to as "Mr. B.," then a period should follow *B*.

Shortened Words

Words such as *phone, lab, gym,* and *ad* are shortened forms of *telephone, laboratory, gymnasium,* and *advertisement*. The short forms are not considered abbreviations; they are well established in our language as complete words. They are not followed by periods.

☐ Checkup 4

Are abbreviations used in these sentences? Correct any errors.

1. Mr. Allen, who is in charge of our Saint Louis office, has developed an effective procedure for handling invoices.

2. We plan to build the warehouse in the NW part of the state, where it will be easily accessible from major roadways.
3. Please pay Invoice No. R-156-874 immediately so that we may save the 2 percent discount.
4. Myrna's new jewelry store is at 12 W. 47 Street in New York City.
5. Among the regional offices that Ms. Franco will visit this month are the ones in Des Plaines, IL, and Kalamazoo, MI.
6. Apparently, two invoices were paid twice: No. 4167 and 4182.

COMMUNICATION PROJECTS

Practical Application

A. In the following sentences, correct any incorrectly written abbreviations. Write *OK* for any correct sentence.

1. The two elements in common table salt, Na. and Cl., combine to form NaCl.
2. One of the guests at tomorrow's banquet is the Rev. John Baxter DeGroat.
3. Sheila postponed our session until next Mon. a.m.
4. No. 489-56 is the only file that she signed out.
5. Send these contracts to the attention of Mister Albert J. Paul.
6. She is now applying for a position with the State Department of Education in Saint Paul, Minnesota.
7. Station W.X.Y.Z. claims to have the largest share of the daytime audience.
8. To save gas, add 16 oz of Magic Oil to every 10 gals of gas.
9. Dr. Jane T. Prentiss, M.D., corroborated the medical examiner's report.
10. Stanley Morgan, Sr. will retire at the end of this month. He will be succeeded by his son, Stanley Morgan, Jr.
11. This U.S.D.A. booklet offers consumers many helpful tips to improve nutrition and yet save money.
12. Later in the a.m. we will attend a private screening of our newest movie, which will be released on Mar. 15.
13. We moved our office to NJ only two months ago.
14. Her territory includes the NE part of the state, which is a heavily populated area.
15. Next year, our sales meeting will be held in N. Mex.
16. The marketing research project will be coordinated by Prof. Dean.
17. I have enclosed Check No. 576 in complete payment of the balance of my account.
18. An A.B.C. reporter requested an interview with Ms. Mendez.
19. One of our research chemists, Dr. L. Boyce, Ph.D., has developed a simple process for separating these chemicals.
20. While she is in Florida, she will call on one of our customers in the Ft. Myers area.

B. Correct any errors in the following sentences. Write *OK* for each correct sentence.

1. In England, a traffic circle is called a roundabout.
2. Either Suzanne or Priscilla are going to supervise the Donnelly account.
3. The balance is due on Apr. 30, but we may be able to get a 30-day extension.
4. After we leave Seattle, we will travel to Brit. Col. to meet Mr. Marshall.

5. Our company encourages us to support U.N.I.C.E.F.
6. In his office is a beautiful antique statue that dates back to 150 A.D.
7. The gift-matching policy encourages employees to donate money to selected charities; the Company will then match each employee's gift.
8. On her desk is the sales report for the first quarter and the salary-review forms.
9. We expect our new Fall fashions to sell well—very, very well.
10. Rebecca said, "I'm optimistic enough to believe that the present sales pattern will be reversed by the end of summer".
11. Does anyone know whether Ms. DeKooning has already left.
12. Prices will be increased by an average of 15 percent beginning in July; we are encouraging our customers therefore to take advantage of the current low prices and to stock up on fast-selling items.
13. Mr. Morales was selected because he is a hard-working dependable experienced copywriter.
14. Does Carole plan on attending both meetings?
15. We will need at least a doz. large cartons to ship all these materials.
16. This terminal is connected to the main computer at our N.Y. office.
17. A corp. on the West Coast has offered us an excellent price for our building in San Francisco.
18. Whom has Mr. Paulson selected to head the Honolulu office?
19. That carton has been laying there unopened for several days now.
20. Does Ms. Claxton and Mr. Orsini have copies of the latest schedules?

Editing Practice

Plurals and Possessives   Rewrite any sentences that contain errors. Write *OK* for each sentence that is correct.

1. Do you know whose going to be assigned to handle the Brancusi account?
2. Mike keeping a chronological file is an excellent idea.
3. Obviously, their are still some problems to be resolved.
4. Miss Burke's asking for a transfer surprised all of us.
5. The Paulsons home will be put up for sale as soon as the mortgage for their new home is approved.
6. Gale and Ellen's jobs are very different, even though they are both sales representatives.
7. The first two suggestions are mine; the rest of the suggestions are theirs.
8. Mrs. Chang commented on you helping others to complete their projects.
9. The doctor's lounge, which is now being redecorated, is on the second floor of the hospital.
10. In about three weeks time, we should know just how well this new product will sell.

The Word Processing Supervisor   Correct any spelling errors in the following sentences. Write *OK* if a sentence has no error.

1. The decision to make the salary increases retractive to May has been changed.
2. The attornies both agreed that we should bring suit against the Exeter Corporation.
3. The newspaper reports were clearly eroneous; there is no truth to the story.

4. We are now equiping each store with its own computerized inventory-control system to help reduce out-of-stocks.
5. Our supervisor coroborated Michele's statement concerning the sale of the Chicago property.
6. In our opinion, the value of the building and the property is overated by as much as 30 percent.
7. All of us agree that Mr. Bennett exagerated the damage that had been caused by the flooding.
8. In carefully controled experiments, we proved that our product removes stains better than any other product on the market.
9. Because Phyllis is an intelligent, compatent accountant, I'm sure that she will enjoy a successful career here at Dunn Iron and Steel Company.
10. The pronounciation of Messrs. is "messers."

Case Problem

A Ticklish Situation   Mr. Noble is one of the best customers of the Paterson Electrical Supply Company. On March 15, he sent payment for an invoice dated March 1, with terms of 2/10, n/30. Mr. Noble deducted the cash discount, to which he was not entitled. When the credit manager at the Paterson Electrical Supply Company called the matter to his attention, Mr. Noble indicated that he always makes payment within the discount period but that someone in his office slipped up and forgot to mail this month's payment on time.

1. What should the credit manager for the Paterson Electrical Supply Company do about this situation?
2. Suppose Mr. Noble made a habit of deducting the cash discount whenever he paid after the expiration of the discount period. What might you, as credit manager, write Mr. Noble in your letter refusing to accept the deduction?

28
NUMBERS

Sums of money, order quantities, discounts, expressions of time, measurements, percentages, addresses, dates—all require the business writer to express numbers. Obviously, numbers are commonly used in all business messages, and they are very, very important. Errors in number use can cause confusion and uncertainty; moreover, they can be expensive and time-consuming. Therefore, be sure to master the following principles of number use so that you will be sure to write clear and accurate business messages.

USING WORDS TO EXPRESS NUMBERS

Why is it important to know when to express numbers in figures and when to express them in words? One reason is that long-established use dictates certain rules. Another reason is that figures and words have different effects on the reader. Figures, for example, tend to emphasize a number, while words tend to de-emphasize a number: *$100* is more emphatic than *a hundred dollars.* Thus we use figures when the number is a significant statistic or deserves special emphasis, while we use words for numbers in a formal message and for numbers that are not significant and need no special attention.

The business writer must know the general rules for expressing numbers in words and for expressing them in figures and must be able to manipulate the rules when it is necessary to achieve a greater degree of formality or to provide greater emphasis. First let's see when the writer should use words to express numbers. Then we will see when the writer should use figures to express numbers.

At the Beginning of a Sentence

Use a spelled-out word, not a figure, at the beginning of a sentence. If writing the word is awkward, then rewrite the sentence so that the number does not occur first.

> Ninety-two percent of the employees whom we surveyed said that they prefer the new plan. (Not: *92 percent. . . .*)
>
> Of the employees whom we surveyed, 92 percent said that they prefer the new plan. (Better than *Ninety-two percent. . . .*)

Numbers From One Through Ten

In business correspondence, the numbers from *one* through *ten* are generally spelled out.

> Last week, nine people in our department were out of the office.
>
> Ms. Lordi began as an account executive ten years ago.
>
> Their store was formerly on Fifth Avenue. (Note that numbered streets from *first* through *tenth* are also spelled out.)

Fractions

Fractions are expressed in words in general business correspondence.

> About one-fifth of our customers account for nearly four-fifths of our business.
>
> Only one-third of our sales representatives have been with our firm for more than three years.

However, a mixed number (a whole number plus a fraction) is expressed in figures.

> Our new warehouse is at the center of $7\frac{1}{2}$ acres of a beautiful hilly region.

Indefinite Numbers

Spell out indefinite numbers and amounts, as shown in these phrases:

> a few million dollars
> hundreds of requests
> several thousand employees

Numbers in Ages and Anniversaries

Ages are spelled out—unless, of course, they are significant statistics.

> Our supervisor will be twenty-six years old tomorrow.
> She is in her early thirties.
> Angelo Russo, 27, has been appointed director of marketing.
> (A significant statistic.)

When ordinal numbers (*1st, 2d, 3d, 4th,* and so on) are used for ages and anniversaries, they are generally spelled out.

> his twenty-first birthday
> our seventeenth anniversary

But when more than two words are needed to spell the number, or when special emphasis is desired, express the numbers in figures.

> our company's 125th anniversary (Not *one hundred and twenty-fifth*)
> A 10th Anniversary Sale! (For emphasis)

Centuries and Decades

Centuries are generally expressed in words.

> the nineteen hundreds (But for emphasis, the *1900s*.)
> the twentieth century
> eighteenth-century fashions

Decades, however, may be expressed in several ways.

> the nineteen-eighties OR the 1980s OR the eighties OR the '80s

☐ Checkup 1

Find and correct any errors in number use in the following sentences. Rewrite sentences if necessary.

1. When completed, the entire report should be no more than 8 pages long.
2. 52 percent of the employees returned their questionnaires, as of today.
3. Ms. Faversham's family has owned property on Fifth Avenue since the 1890s.
4. About $\frac{1}{5}$ of our expense budget is for raw materials.

5. We should print a few 1,000 more of these brochures.
6. 19 applicants have been interviewed by Mrs. Byers this morning.
7. Model 12A brings in three and half times more revenue than Model 11.
8. Employees under the age of 35 will pay a lower premium for the optional life insurance program. (Significant statistic)

USING FIGURES TO EXPRESS NUMBERS

For Numbers Higher Than Ten

As you know, the numbers from *one* through *ten* are spelled out. Numbers higher than *ten* are expressed in figures.

> We now have 12 tellers in this branch.
> She gave each of us a copy of the 18-page report.

However, express related numbers in the same way. If any of the numbers is above 10, express all the numbers in figures.

> In Conference Room B we will need 4 tables, 24 chairs, and 2 easel stands. (Because one of the related numbers is above 10, all are expressed in figures.)

Note: Figures are more emphatic than words because figures stand out clearly (especially when they are surrounded by words). Therefore, when greater emphasis is required for a number from *one* to *ten*, use a figure to express that number. For example:

> only 5 minutes (More emphatic than *five minutes*)
> a 3-year loan (More emphatic than *a three-year loan*)

For Sums of Money

Sums of money are written in figures.

> This invoice totals $119.79.
> We have already exceeded the budget, which was $500. (Not $500.00. The extra zeros are unnecessary.)
> We spent between $4,000 and $5,000. The unit cost is estimated to be 55 cents. (Not $0.55. Use the symbol ¢ in tables and in technical copy.)

Note that words *and* figures are often used to express amounts of a million or more.

> $9 million   or   9 million dollars
> $12.5 million   or   12.5 million dollars

Be sure to repeat the word *million* in expressions such as this:

> between $2 million and $3 million (Not between $2 and $3 million)

Also be sure to treat related numbers in the same way.

> between $500,000 and $1,000,000 (Not between $500,000 and $1 million)

Remember that indefinite amounts are spelled out:

> We spent a few hundred dollars.
> They bought about a thousand dollars' worth of merchandise.

In Addresses

Use figures for house numbers except for *One*. For street numbers, spell out the numbers from *first* through *tenth*. Use figures for all other street numbers.

> The bank is located at One Wall Street. (Spell out *One* when it is a house number.)
> The book store that was at 121 West 12 Street has now been moved to 94 West 14 Street.

When the house number and the street number are not separated by *East*, *West*, or a similar word, use the ordinals *st*, *d*, and *th* with the street number.

> 2131 96th Street (The ordinal *96th* helps to prevent possible confusion.)

ZIP Code numbers are, of course, always given in figures.

> New York, New York 10020 (Note that no comma precedes the ZIP Code number.)

☐ Checkup 2

Correct the following sentences.
1. What is the typical interest rate for a ninety-day loan?
2. All twelve of us were invited to a special workshop on word processing.
3. We now have nine stores in the East, eight in the Midwest, seven in the South, and eleven in the West.
4. We estimate that the market for this product is between $4 and $5 million.
5. The newsstand price for this magazine is only 75ᶜ an issue.
6. Deliver these contracts to County Bank, 1221 21 Avenue, by noon today.
7. The list price is $150.00, but we were able to get a 20 percent discount.
8. It is important to note that this is a 2-year loan, not a 3-year loan, as had originally been requested.

With Units of Measure and Percentages

Use figures with units of measure and with percentages, as shown below:

> Each office is 10 feet by 12 feet.
> This television screen measures 19 inches diagonally.
> Each vial contains exactly 5 cubic centimeters of the serum.
> For the special sale, we have reduced our prices an average of 12 percent from the manufacturer's suggested list price.

Note: Use the symbol % only in tables and forms. In other cases, spell out *percent*.

With Decimals

Decimal numbers are always expressed in figures:

> Mix this powder with water in a ratio of 4.5 parts powder to 1 part water. (A ratio may also be expressed as follows: 4.5:1 ratio of powder to water.)

When no number appears before the decimal, add a zero to help the reader understand the number quickly.

> A very slight increase—0.5 percent—was reported for the month of March. (Without the zero, the reader might read "5 percent.")

With *a.m.* and *p.m.*

As you already learned, always use figures with *a.m.* and *p.m.*

> at 9 a.m.
> between 11:45 a.m. and 12:30 p.m.

With *O'Clock*

With the word *o'clock*, either figures or words may be used. For greater emphasis and less formality, use figures. For more formality but less emphasis, use words.

> You are invited to join us at eight o'clock on Tuesday, the thirteenth of March, to celebrate the release of our new comedy hit, "The Magician." (*Eight o'clock* is more formal than *8 o'clock*.)
> All our representatives will be in town next week, and we'd like our supervisors to join them for dinner next Thursday at 8 o'clock in our fiftieth floor dining room. (Less formal, more emphatic)

In Dates

Use figures to express the day of the month and the year in dates:

> March 19, 1982 (Not March 19th, 1982)
> April 29, 1983 (Not April 29th, 1983)

When the day is written before the month, use an ordinal figure or spell out the ordinal number.

> the 4th of June OR the fourth of June
> the 21st of April OR the twenty-first of April

Note: The ordinal figures are *1st, 2d, 3d, 4th* and so on.

Consecutive Numbers

Consecutive numbers should be separated by a comma when both numbers are in figures or when both are in words.

In 1981, 121 employees were promoted.
Of the eight, three were delayed by traffic.

But if one word is in figures and the other is in words, no comma is needed.

On May 12 two executives retired from Piedmont Industries Inc.

When one of the numbers is part of a compound modifier, write the first number in words and the second number in figures (unless the second number would be a significantly shorter word). Do *not* separate the numbers with a comma.

two 9-page booklets (But 200 nine-page booklets)
fifty $10 bills (But 100 ten-dollar bills)

☐ Checkup 3

Make any necessary corrections.
1. We are planning our Grand Opening for the first of June.
2. A shipping charge (about .2 percent of the invoice) is automatically charged to the customer.
3. Sandra scheduled the meeting for eight a.m. tomorrow morning.
4. By September 6th, we will have completed the entire project.
5. The interest rate (on an annual basis) is eighteen percent, as explained on page 3 of the credit agreement.
6. This compound, which is imported from Germany, is available only in two-liter containers.
7. For best results, mix five and a half parts Tuff-Glu to two parts water.
8. The deadline for sending the ad to the printer is either July 8th or 9th.

COMMUNICATION PROJECTS

Practical Application
A. Correct any errors in the use of numbers in the following sentences. Write *OK* for any correct sentence.
1. Our net operating profit is approximately 19%.
2. Overtime has been approved for 8 people who are working on the Freemont Hardware account.
3. The state government has appropriated $700,000,000 for the mass-transit improvement program.
4. The luncheon has been scheduled for the 6 of June, as Ms. Rafferty requested.
5. Because the manufacturing cost for these pamphlets is only $0.19, we plan to use them as handouts for our promotional campaign.
6. Our purchasing department buys general office supplies from a store on 3rd Avenue.
7. The total interest charge each month is based on one and a half percent of the outstanding balance.

8. Dr. Rosemary Hewett, twenty-nine, is the youngest executive in our company.
9. The limousines are scheduled to pick us up at exactly 11:45 a.m., so that we will be sure to reach the airport no later than 12:45 p.m.
10. All eighty-seven cars in our fleet are rented from the Able Car Rental Company.
11. Our auditorium can accommodate a few 1,000 people.
12. In 1979, Mr. McGrath accurately predicted, "We expect the 1980s to be a decade of unparalleled success for all 4 companies in our corporation."
13. If you wish, you may pay the total in monthly installments of $25.00.
14. We estimate that about $\frac{2}{3}$ of our employees will be affected by the transit strike.
15. Because the list price of this machine is so high, the commission is .75 percent of the selling price.
16. She is now seeking estimates for paving six and a half acres of land for employee parking behind our new plant.
17. Mr. Elmont said that we have already shipped two thousand five hundred samples to customers.
18. Next year's budget for sales is 12.5 percent higher than this year's sales budget.
19. When you go to the Post Office, please buy 100 eighteen-cent stamps.
20. Each life-like reproduction stands 18 inches high and weighs more than 10 pounds.

B. Correct any errors in the following sentences. Write *OK* for each correct sentence.
1. In newspaper jargon, a free-lance reporter is known as a stringer.
2. Mrs. Kitt said, "The 1st thing we must do is to find out how much it will cost to repair this machine."
3. One of our subsidiaries is the Glenn Aircraft corporation.
4. The manager of our word processing department Fran Wayborn will explain how to use the forms.
5. We discussed the advertising budget for two hours this morning but we did not find any simple ways to cut the budget.
6. Next June, *Electronics Today* magazine will publish a special issue on computer games; therefore we are preparing a two-page ad for that issue.
7. Between you and I, I have little confidence that this product will sell at this high price.
8. The President is struggling to keep the annual inflation rate under ten percent.
9. When Ms. Erickson returns from Europe on March 19th, we will reschedule the managers' meeting.
10. Kevin Smith, an executive with W.X.Y.Z., will discuss the benefits of radio advertising next Tuesday at 3 p.m. in our auditorium.
11. The governor has named our executive vice president to a panel to study critical business issues.
12. His wife Dr. Teresa DiCarlo is a researcher in the Chemical Division of Ulster Products, Inc.
13. Over the past few years, her commissions have averaged $7,500.00 a year.
14. At this morning's news conference, Clark Gifford, President of Gifford Industrial Plastics, announced plans for expanding the company.

15. Each district manager must submit their first-draft budget to the national sales manager by August 15.
16. We're meeting with the Royce Advertising Agency staff next Thurs. to discuss ways in which we can promote this product more effectively.
17. It is too late to run this ad in the March issue, the deadline was January 12.
18. Donald and Edward agree that the four-color ad is the most effective one, don't they.
19. Please check the enclosed schedules, budgets and estimates for the Benson Plumbing advertisements.
20. The procedure for getting approval of cost overruns is described in our *Policies and Procedures Manual*. (See pages 27 through 33.)

Editing Practice

The Word Processing Supervisor   Proofread the following excerpt. Correct any errors.

> Please send me 100 copies of your pamphlet, *Principals of Time Management*, which was advertised in the November issue of *Effective Management*. I have enclosed a check for fifty dollars to cover the cost of these pamphlets, including the mailing cost.
>
> I should like to have the pamphlets by Febuary 21, when we will conduct a workshop for supervisors. Therefore, I would be happy to pay any extra charge for shipping the pamphlets to me by that date.

Case Problem

The Difficult Caller   Manuel Ortiz, assistant to Richard Gibson of the Lakeland Insurance Company, receives a telephone call for Mr. Gibson from Patricia Harrow, a customer who is a representative of a business machine firm. Gibson often purchases equipment from Mrs. Harrow.

Manuel tells Mrs. Harrow that Gibson is out of the office for the day. Mrs. Harrow insists on telling Manuel her troubles. She is irate because the Lakeland Insurance Company purchased three new adding machines from a competing firm. She wonders why, since she is both a policyholder of and a supplier for the company, she was not given the opportunity to make the sale. She even threatens to cancel her insurance.

1. What should Manuel say to Mrs. Harrow?
2. What should Mr. Gibson do about the situation when he returns?

CHAPTER 5

USING WORDS FOR GREATEST EFFECT

Ideas travel best in words. No matter how clear, how fresh, how exciting the ideas in your mind, they will die unless you find the right words to express them. To communicate your ideas to others, either in writing or in speaking, you must choose your words with care.

The importance of choosing words applies to simple ideas as well as complex ones. Let us say, for example, that you have a craving for a certain dessert. This dessert appears so vividly in your mind's eye that your mouth waters. You can see and describe all the ingredients and the whole process of making the dessert. But for some reason the usual words fail you. You go to a restaurant and tell the waiter exactly what you want: a dessert consisting of an elongated, tapering, tropical fruit with soft, pulpy flesh, sliced into two parts; atop this fruit go three scoops of a sweet, frozen dairy food, each scoop a different flavor. Sprinkled on the three scoops of frozen food, you want the naturally dried fruit of a certain North American tree. Over all this you want ladles of sugary solutions of liquefied fruit from Hawaii. Finally, you want a mound of the yellowish part of milk containing butterfat, aerated through and through.

All this information might not get you anything to eat because nowhere in the long, accurate description are the *right words* for the dessert. Even knowing one of the two right words would help. If you said, "Give me a banana bifurcated!" you might not go hungry. If you said, "Give me a banana divided!" your chances of eating would improve greatly. But you wouldn't be sure of getting what you wanted unless you said, "Give me a banana split!"

Notice that the right words are not necessarily the ones with the most syllables.

The English language offers an immense choice of words. For every occasion, in business as in ordering dessert, English has a word to communicate the right meaning in a way that will be clearly understood. The most convenient place to find a needed word quickly is in your own memory. If you do not know the needed word, however, there are three excellent, quick reference books at your disposal: a dictionary, a thesaurus, and a dictionary of synonyms. Recourse to these books not only will solve the immediate problem of finding the right word for a single occasion but also will stock your vocabulary for future occasions. With practice in using the dictionary, the thesaurus, and the dictionary of synonyms, you need never settle for less than the precise word.

THE DICTIONARY

The most useful and most often *used* reference for those in search of the right word is the dictionary. Learning to use the dictionary is part of learning to use the language. Every successful writer, secretary, editor, proofreader, executive, and student keeps a dictionary within reach and is adept at using it.

The choice of a dictionary is important. A standard abridged (concise) dictionary serves most of the needs of ordinary office and school use. Pocket-sized dictionaries, however, contain too few words, give less information about each word, and lack the supplements that make a good dictionary a broad reference book.[1]

For our purposes we will divide dictionary information into two kinds: "Word Information" and "Other References."

Word Information

The main use of the dictionary is, of course, to look up information about specific words—spellings, definitions, synonyms, and the like. As an example of the extensive information provided by a good dictionary, look at the dictionary entry for *business* shown at the top of page 241.

Spelling   First the dictionary entry tells how the word *business* is spelled. Many people face a problem at this point because they do not know which letters stand for which specific sounds. Section 32, "Improving Spelling Skills," provides the hearing and seeing skills needed for finding words in the dictionary. Here are some other guideposts for good spelling:

> Be sure that you see the letters in their correct order; for example, *niece*, not *neice*.
>
> Be sure that you have not inserted letters that are not there, as *athaletic* instead of *athletic*.
>
> *Be sure that you have included all the letters that are in the word; for example, embarrass*, not *embarass*.
>
> Be sure that the word is not some other word that is spelled somewhat like the one you are seeking. *Read the definition.* Suppose you are writing this sentence: "Mr. Harris sent me a (*complementary/complimentary*) copy of his book." You need to verify the spelling of *compl?mentary*. In the dictionary you will find *complEmentary*, followed by the definition "serving to fill out or complete." This definition is not the meaning you want. But look under *complimentary* and you will find "given free as courtesy or favor." Now you know that the word you seek is *complimentary*.
>
> Many words have more than one spelling. The dictionary shows spellings that are equally correct by joining them by *or*. For example, the dictionary entry for *traveler* reads "traveler *or* traveller." This indicates that both spellings are standard, both are commonly used. When one spelling is less commonly used, the dictionary joins them by *also*: "lovable *also* loveable" shows that both spellings are used, but the second less commonly so.
>
> Pay particular attention to compound words to determine whether they are written as one word (*shortcut*), two words (*sales check*), or a hyphenated word (*left-handedness*).
>
> Be sure to include any accent marks that are part of a word. For example, *résumé* is a noun that means "a summary"; but *resume* is a verb that means "to assume or take again."

[1]The dictionary used as the source for this discussion and throughout this text (except where noted) is *Webster's New Collegiate Dictionary*, G. & C. Merriam Co., Springfield, Massachusetts, 1980.

Hyphenation   Sometimes a word must be divided at the end of a line of writing. Unless the word is divided at a certain place or places, the reader may be confused and will be delayed. Here is an example of this kind of problem:

> Please return this package and its contents promp-
> tly if you want a refund.

Dictionary entries use centered periods to indicate the correct places for hyphenating words: *col · lege; ap · pre · ci · ate*, but *ap · pre · cia · tive.*

Capitalization   The dictionary shows if a word is to be capitalized when it is not the first word of a sentence. For example, the word *south* is usually not capitalized, but when it refers to a specific region, it *is* capitalized.

Pronunciation and Division Into Syllables   Immediately after the regular spelling of a word, the dictionary shows the word's phonetic spelling. This indicates how the word, when spoken, should be broken into syllables and which syllable or syllables should be accented. If phonetic symbols are new to you, refer to the section of the dictionary that explains them. (Many dictionaries show a convenient phonetic guide on every page or on every other page.)

The dictionary shows that the pronunciation of *appreciate* is uh-pre-she-at. The hyphens indicate syllable breaks. (*Webster's New Collegiate Dictionary* and some other dictionaries show major and minor stresses by placing an accent mark *before* the stressed syllable or syllables. In this text we place an apostrophe *after* a syllable to show that the syllable is stressed; and we show only major, not minor, stresses.)

Word Origin   A word's origin, also called its etymology or derivation, is interesting and informative and often fixes the word's meaning in memory. The origin of the word *radar*, for example, is shown as "*radio detecting and ranging.*" This will help us remember the word's correct meaning and spelling. Words that are formed, like *radar*, from the initial letters of a compound term are called "acronyms." When you know their etymologies, acronyms are easy to remember.

Definition   A good dictionary lists all of a word's definitions, usually in the order in which they developed. Often the dictionary gives examples of the word's use in more than one sense. For example, see page 241, where the entry for *business* shows several examples of the word's use.

Inflectional Forms and Derivatives   The dictionary shows the irregular plural of nouns, the past tense and participial forms of irregular verbs, and the comparative and superlative forms of irregular adjectives and adverbs. After the definition of the noun *contract*, for example, are its derivative noun *contractibility* and its derivative adjective *contractible*. And the entry for the irregular verb *sell* gives its past, *sold*, and its present participle, *selling*.

Synonyms   For many entries the dictionary also lists synonyms (words that have almost the same meanings as the entry). The entry for *invent*, shown on page 241, lists three synonyms. Note that although they have what the dictionary calls a "*shared meaning element*," each synonym has its own distinct shades of meaning. Columbus did not *invent* America, but he did *discover* it. The Wrights did not *discover* the airplane, but they did *invent* it.

> **busi·ness** \'biz-nəs, -nəz\ *n, often attrib* **1** *archaic* : purposeful activity : BUSYNESS **2 a** : ROLE, FUNCTION ⟨how the human mind went about its ∼ of learning —H. A. Overstreet⟩ **b** : an immediate task or objective : MISSION ⟨what is your ∼ here at this hour⟩ **c** : a particular field of endeavor ⟨the best in the ∼⟩ **3 a** : a usu. commercial or mercantile activity engaged in as a means of livelihood : TRADE, LINE ⟨in the ∼ of supplying emergency services to industry⟩ **b** : a commercial or sometimes an industrial enterprise ⟨sold his ∼ and retired⟩; *also* : such enterprises ⟨∼ seldom acts as a unit⟩ **c** : usu. economic dealings : PATRONAGE ⟨ready to take his ∼ elsewhere unless service improved⟩ **4** : AFFAIR, MATTER ⟨a strange ∼⟩ **5** : movement or action (as lighting a cigarette) by an actor intended esp. to establish atmosphere, reveal character, or explain a situation — called also *stage business* **6 a** : personal concern ⟨none of your ∼⟩ **b** : RIGHT ⟨you have no ∼ hitting her⟩ **7 a** : serious activity requiring time and effort and usu. the avoidance of distractions ⟨immediately got down to ∼⟩ **b** : maximum effort **8 a** : a damaging assault **b** : a rebuke or tongue-lashing : a hard time **c** : DOUBLE CROSS
> **syn** BUSINESS, COMMERCE, INDUSTRY, TRADE, TRAFFIC *shared meaning element* : activity concerned with the supplying and distribution of commodities

By permission. From *Webster's New Collegiate Dictionary*, © 1980 by G. & C. Merriam Co., Publishers of the Merriam-Webster Dictionaries.

This dictionary entry provides extensive information for the word *business*.

Illustrations   A good dictionary often uses illustrations to make a word's meaning clear. Illustrations are especially helpful in understanding definitions of terms that denote complex physical forms and objects. The meanings of some of these terms, in fact, are difficult to grasp from words alone but become clear at once after looking at an illustration. Can you visualize a *toggle joint* without the aid of an illustration? A *houndstooth check*? A *saltbox*? After looking at the illustrations in a good dictionary, you will have no difficulty understanding these terms.

Other Information

A good dictionary provides much more than just word information. For instance, a good abridged dictionary contains a guide to the organization and use of the dictionary, explanatory notes about the kinds of information contained at each entry, a key to phonetic symbols, a guide to correct punctuation, a list of abbreviations used in the word entries, and more. Here are some of the extra aids you may find helpful.

Signs and Symbols   This section comprises signs and symbols frequently used in such fields as astronomy, biology, business, chemistry, data processing, mathematics, medicine, philately, physics, and weather.

Biographical Names   The names of famous people, each with the proper spelling and pronunciation, are listed under this heading. Such biographical data as dates of

> **in·vent** \in-'vent\ *vt* [ME *inventen,* fr. L *inventus,* pp. of *invenire* to come upon, find, fr. *in-* + *venire* to come — more at COME] **1** *archaic* : FIND, DISCOVER **2** : to think up or imagine : FABRICATE **3** : to produce (as something useful) for the first time through the use of the imagination or of ingenious thinking and experiment ⟨∼ a new machine⟩ — **in·ven·tor** \-'vent-ər\ *n* — **in·ven·tress** \-'ven-trəs\ *n*

By permission. From *Webster's New Collegiate Dictionary*, © 1980 by G. & C. Merriam Co., Publishers of the Merriam-Webster Dictionaries.

The last two lines of this entry offer synonyms for *invent* and explain the *shared meaning element* of the three synonyms.

By permission. From *Webster's Collegiate Thesaurus,* © 1976 by G. &
C. Merriam Co., Publishers of the Merriam-Webster Dictionaries.

birth and death, nationality, and occupation are also given. This section may be used,
for example, to check the pronunciation of names to be used in a speech or to identify
unknown names encountered in reading or conversation.

Geographical Names This section provides information about places—name, pronunciation, location, population, and so on. This section, therefore, can be helpful
when checking the spelling of places to which correspondence is to be addressed.

Handbook of Style This very useful section contains rules on punctuation, italiciza-
tion, capitalization, and plurals; sample footnotes; forms of address; and style in business correspondence.

THESAURUS

If you know a word, the dictionary will give you its meaning. The thesaurus works the
other way around: if you know the general idea that you wish to express, the thesaurus
will give you a choice of specific words to express that meaning. Thus the thesaurus
offers a selection of different expressions all related to the same idea. Look up the
general idea, and you can choose the expression that is most appropriate.

Roget's International Thesaurus and *Webster's Collegiate Thesaurus,* two popular
references, are arranged differently. *Roget's* has two sections: the main section and
the index to the main section. For example, to find a synonym for the adjective *creative,* look up *creative* in the alphabetic index. There you will find these three entries,
each followed by a key number: *productive 164.9, originative 166.23,* and *inventive
533.18.* The key numbers refer to numbered paragraphs in the main section. Thus, if
inventive is closest to the idea you wish to convey, turn to entry number 533 in the
main section and find paragraph 18 for a listing of synonyms.

Like a dictionary, *Webster's Collegiate Thesaurus* has only one list of entries that are
arranged in alphabetic order. To find synonyms for *creative,* just turn to the entry *creative:*

In this entry the capital letters for the word *INVENTIVE* indicate that more information can be found at that entry, which is also in alphabetic order.

By permission. From *Webster's Collegiate Thesaurus,* © 1976 by G. &
C. Merriam Co., Publishers of the Merriam-Webster Dictionaries.

Whichever thesaurus you choose, be sure to learn how to use it properly. The thesaurus will be especially helpful when you wish to: find the most suitable word for a given idea; avoid repeating a word; find the most specific word; or replace an abstract term.

To Find the Most Suitable Word for a Given Idea

You work in the office of an expanding small business, and all of a sudden there is more work than you can reasonably handle. Your manager is even busier than you are, and she tells you to draft a 20-word classified ad for a co-worker who will be your assistant.

You know exactly the kind of co-worker you need: someone who will come to work on time, work hard, not need to be told repeatedly how to do office tasks, not sit by idly waiting to be told what to do when you are busy and work is piling up; someone who will take his or her own initiative to deal with unforeseen problems, but will not go too far. In addition to all this, the person must be a good typist, work well with both words and numbers, and deal with all kinds of people on the telephone.

How can you squeeze so much information into only 20 words? Grab the thesaurus and take the ideas in the description one by one. First you need a shorter expression for *will come to work on time*. The idea here is time or timeliness, which leads you to the adjective *punctual*. *Punctual* is the word you need. You can solve the rest of the problem in one of the Communication Projects at the end of this section.

To Avoid Repeating a Word

After drafting the description of the ideal co-worker, you notice that you have used the word *skillful* three times. In order to avoid three occurrences of the same term in your advertisement, you look under *skillful* in the thesaurus and find synonyms such as *proficient, expert, masterful, adroit,* and *adept.*

To Find the Most Specific Word

Often you may know the general word for an object or an idea, but the word that you know may be too vague for your purpose. For example, if you needed the specific name of a particular car model, under the entry for *car* you would find *coupe, hardtop, limousine, sedan,* and others.

To Replace an Abstract Term

Imagine that you are writing a memorandum and that you wish to replace the word *precipitous* in the phrase "a precipitous decision." Among the substitutes you would find in your thesaurus are *hasty, abrupt, hurried,* and *sudden.*

A thesaurus such as *Roget's International Thesaurus* or *Webster's Collegiate Thesaurus* is a writer's tool that will increase in value as you become more adept in its use. With a good thesaurus on your reference shelf, you will not have to reach far for the flavor, color, and fresh images that will make you an effective writer.

DICTIONARY OF SYNONYMS

A single example will show the value of a dictionary of synonyms. *Roget's International Thesaurus* lists approximately a hundred types of hats. If you need only to be reminded of the exact name of a familiar type of hat (for example, *fedora*) then the thesaurus ends your search. But what if you don't know the difference between a fedora, a beret, a bowler, a busby, a derby, a homburg, a shako, a snood, and a toque? Then you have to return to the dictionary and look up each of these words until you find the definition that matches the description given you ("a felt hat with a lengthwise crease in the top"). Clearly, this will take time.

A dictionary of synonyms not only *lists* words of similar meaning (as does a thesaurus) and *defines* words of similar meaning (as does a dictionary), but both lists synonyms and gives brief definitions, pointing out what distinguishes one synonym from another—all in one place. This saves many long searches through the dictionary.

(The use of synonyms and antonyms is discussed fully in Section 31.)

COMMUNICATION PROJECTS

Practical Application

A. Using a thesaurus, complete the classified ad begun on page 244 in the text, under "To Find the Most Suitable Word for a Given Idea." In 20 words or less, describe the co-worker that fits the description.

B. For a speech she was preparing, Mildred James referred to the following people. She used a dictionary to check the pronunciation of their names. For each name, write the pronunciation and give some identifying information about the person.

1. Waldheim, Kurt
2. Wagner, Richard
3. Stokowski, Leopold
4. Chou En-lai
5. du Maurier, Daphne

C. The firm you have just joined imports goods from all over the world. You begin to jot down place names that are unfamiliar to you so that you can look them up in the dictionary, learn exactly where they are, and master their pronunciation. What do you find for the following?

1. Gloucester
2. New Delhi
3. Kuala Lumpur
4. Istanbul
5. Dubrovnik

D. The following words should be part of your vocabulary. For each, write the correct pronunciation and the most common definition. Then use each word in a sentence.

1. excise
2. ecology
3. morale
4. bankruptcy
5. depreciation
6. lien
7. mortgage
8. emanate
9. franchise
10. monopoly

E. The writer of the following sentences confused two similar words. Replace any incorrect word with the correct one. Define both the correct and the incorrect word.

1. At the reception each person will be formerly introduced to the guest of honor.
2. The speaker we have chosen is an imminent author and lecturer.
3. Should supervisors advice their subordinates?
4. The vice president notified all personal of the early closing.
5. The report on the new factory sight was submitted to the board today.

F. Are you sure which of the two spellings for each word below is the correct spelling or the preferred spelling? Check your decision against the dictionary.

1. saleable, salable
2. labeled, labelled
3. center, centre
4. envelope, envelop (noun)
5. instalment, installment
6. advisor, adviser
7. judgement, judgment
8. acknowledgement, acknowledgment

Editing Practice

Hidden Pairs   From each group of words below two can be matched because they are similar or opposite in meaning. Find each pair. Jot down the letters of your choice and indicate whether the words are synonyms or antonyms.

Example: (a) practice (b) proscribe (c) placate (d) preempt (e) retaliate

Answer: c and e; antonyms

1. (a) wield (b) procure (c) wither (d) obfuscate (e) obtain
2. (a) circumstance (b) sanitation (c) cenotaph (d) situation (e) accident
3. (a) dispense (b) depreciate (c) spend (d) disburse (e) disperse
4. (a) devalue (b) give (c) locate (d) retain (e) indicate
5. (a) unlawful (b) illegible (c) ineligible (d) unreadable (e) uncouth
6. (a) deny (b) alleviate (c) aggravate (d) solder (e) obfuscate
7. (a) wretched (b) rotated (c) obsolete (d) antiquated (e) meticulous
8. (a) imitative (b) exemplary (c) despicable (d) deplorable (e) showy
9. (a) fireplace (b) decrease (c) abundance (d) dearth (e) bravery
10. (a) preempt (b) prescribe (c) replace (d) prejudge (e) remunerate

Case Problem

Problem Solving   You are a transcription pool supervisor, and Ms. Healey, who draws on the pool for stenographic assistance, has asked you not to send her Gary or Janice. Her reason is that they change her punctuation and wording; consequently, time is wasted and nerves are frayed because she insists that they retype the letters exactly as she dictated them.

What steps would you take to solve this problem and to ensure that there will be no similar problem in the future?

30
ACHIEVING PRECISION IN WORD USAGE

Words not only communicate ideas but also stir the emotions. Words can lift spirits, inspire action, or soothe injured feelings. If chosen with less care, words can bewilder, depress, or enrage. This is clear to anyone who has ever had to say, eyes downcast, "I'm sorry—I didn't mean it *that* way."

Others judge your ideas based on the words you use, and, they also judge you yourself. The reaction to an ill-chosen word may be "She has a limited vocabulary"—or worse, "She is insensitive." Limited word resources can prevent you from showing your intelligence, imagination, and sensitivity. Achieving precision in word usage requires knowing many words, knowing their correct roles in the language, and being able to predict how listeners will interpret these words in an enormous variety of combinations. The guides below will help you toward these goals.

THE CORRECT WORD

Careful speakers and writers know the difference between correct usage and illiterate usage. This difference is not merely a matter of what some authority somewhere declares to be correct. Illiterate usage is illiterate because it does not make sense. Consider the word *irregardless*. We can break it into three parts to reveal its confused meaning: *ir regard less*. When attached to the end of a word, *-less* means "without." *Hopeless* means "without hope"; *regardless* means "without regard." Attached to the beginning of a word, *ir-* means "not" or "without." *Irrelevant* means "without relevance." *Irregardless*, then, means "without without regard." It makes no more sense than *irhopeless* does. Although your listeners or readers may understand what you mean, the illiteracy will tell something about you.

Irregardless, like some other illiteracies, probably came about as the result of combining parts of two correct expressions, *regardless* and *irrespective of*. Another cause of illiteracies is mispronunciation. If *relevant* is mispronounced, for example, we may hear the mysterious word *revelant*. Does it mean "revealing?" Does it have anything to do with revels? While the listener ponders this, the speaker may say many intelligent things that the listener will not hear.

Other illiteracies arising from mispronunciation are *irrepair'able* for *irrep'arable*, *renumeration for remuneration* (although *enumeration* is correct); *hunderd* for *hundred; strinth* for *strength; compare'able* for *com'parable*.

Mistrust and avoid any words that you cannot find in the dictionary.

HOMONYMS

Words that look or sound alike—but have different meanings—are known as homonyms. Choosing the incorrect word (although it may sound or even look correct) is one of the most frequently committed errors of word usage.

For example, the tenants of a large apartment house receive a letter urging that "All the *residence* should protest the increased tax rate." This important message might be ignored simply because the writer cannot distinguish people, *residents*, from places, *residences.* Another letter writer may request a ream of *stationary*, much to the amusement of the *stationer* supplying it.

Below are some homonyms that every business writer should know.

aisle, isle	loan, lone
allowed, aloud	mail, male
altar, alter	medal, meddle
ascent, assent	miner, minor
assistance, assistants	overdo, overdue
attendance, attendants	pain, pane
bail, bale	passed, past
brake, break	patience, patients
canvas, canvass	peace, piece
cereal, serial	presence, presents
cite, site, sight	principal, principle
coarse, course	raise, raze
complement, compliment	rap, wrap
correspondence, correspondents	right, write
dependence, dependents	sole, soul
desert, dessert	some, sum
dual, duel	stake, steak
foreword, forward	stationary, stationery
forth, fourth	strait, straight
grate, great	their, there, they're
hear, here	threw, through
instance, instants	to, too, two
intense, intents	wait, weight
lean, lien	waive, wave
leased, least	weak, week
lesser, lessor	

Pseudohomonyms

Pseudohomonyms are words that sound somewhat alike but have different meanings. They are called "pseudo" because, when pronounced correctly, these words do *not* sound exactly alike. For example, the statement "Smith, Jones, and Hill earned $300, $500, and $800, respectfully" is incorrect. The communicator has confused the word *respectfully* (meaning, "courteously") with *respectively* (meaning "in the order given"). The pseudohomonyms that give the most trouble are listed on pages 248 and 249.

accept, except	eligible, illegible
access, excess	emigrate, immigrate
adapt, adopt	eminent, imminent
addition, edition	expand, expend

adverse, averse	extant, extent
advice, advise	facilitate, felicitate
affect, effect	fiscal, physical
allusion, illusion	formally, formerly
appraise, apprise	ingenious, ingenuous
carton, cartoon	later, latter
cooperation, corporation	liable, libel
dairy, diary	our, are
decent, descent, dissent	persecute, prosecute
deceased, diseased	personal, personnel
deference, difference	precede, proceed
detract, distract	reality, realty
device, devise	recent, resent
disburse, disperse	respectfully, respectively
disprove, disapprove	statue, statute
elicit, illicit	suit, suite

Spelling

If you were a business executive, would you a hire an engineer whose résumé listed a degree in *compewter* science? You would look even less kindly on an applicant who wrote to request a position as a *fial* clerk. Poor spelling would make you doubt that these people could do the jobs that they sought. Poor spelling makes a terrible first impression because everyone has access to a dictionary. The poor speller has few excuses.

Business executives complain more about employees' poor spelling than about any other single shortcoming in the use of language. In the world of business, improving your spelling improves your prospects. You can improve your spelling by giving careful attention to the similarities and differences between homonyms or pseudo-homonyms and to the suggestions in Section 32 at the end of this chapter. The most important step to improved spelling, however, is developing the dictionary habit.

WORDS SUITED TO THE AUDIENCE

In a speech before a social club, an architect would lose the audience by discussing a new building in technical terms such as *cantilever, pendentive, corbel, interstice,* and *tenon.* But by recasting the speech in nontechnical terms such as *living space, cross ventilation, structural strength,* and *safety,* the architect could hold the audience's attention. Using a strange vocabulary before an audience is as big a mistake as using a language that is foreign to the audience. Genuine communication takes place when a speaker chooses words geared to the interests and knowledge of the listener.

WORDS WITH DIFFERENT SHADES OF MEANING

English offers many ways to describe the same basic facts with altogether different implications. A solitary person, for example, might be called a *wallflower,* a *sneak,* or a *rugged individualist.* The wrong choice of terms can distort the speaker's or writer's intentions and perhaps even offend someone.

Only an unskilled writer or speaker would use the word *cheap* to mean *inexpensive.* Certainly no salesperson would make that mistake. *Cheap* means "worthless or shoddy"; *inexpensive* refers only to cost, not to quality. Sometimes an *inexpensive* suit is a bargain; a *cheap* suit never is.

A competent host would never introduce an honored guest as "notorious for his gifts to charity." *Notorious* means "unfavorably known." *Famous* may be either favorable or unfavorable. *Infamous* does not mean "unknown" but "having a reputation of the worst kind."

Whenever in doubt about a word's meaning, check the dictionary before proceeding. If there is no time to look up the unknown word, then phrase your idea in a way that avoids the unknown and potentially damaging term.

WORDS TO AVOID

Building a successful business or a successful career requires building goodwill. Because words play a vital part in the creation of goodwill, a skilled communicator chooses words and phrases that the listener and reader can appreciate. In general, this means choosing positive rather than negative terms, presenting information directly and without repetition, and using fresh and current expressions rather than old, stale ones. The information below will help you to avoid words that will hamper your efforts to create goodwill.

Avoid Negative Words

Which of the following paragraphs is more likely to retain customer goodwill?

> You omitted to state the quantity and the colors of the slacks you ordered. We cannot ship with such incomplete order information.
>
> The size 36 slacks you ordered will be on their way to you just as soon as you tell us how many pairs you want and in what colors—tan, gray, navy, or maroon.

Although the second paragraph is the obvious selection, note that both paragraphs try to say the same thing. The second paragraph is positively worded and avoids such unpleasant expressions as "you omitted" and "cannot ship with such incomplete information." Negative words are almost sure to evoke a negative response. The customer reading these may cancel the order.

Words create negative responses when the reader feels blamed or accused. Most expert business writers consider *failed, careless, delay,* and *inexcusable* negative words, regardless of how the words are used, and recommend avoiding these words. Actually, such words are unpleasant primarily when they are accompanied by *you* ("you failed") or *your* ("your delay"). "Your oversight," "your error," "your claim" signal the reader to react negatively; but "our oversight," "our error"—though not necessarily wise choices of words—carry a different impression entirely.

The following words can sound only negative when used with *you* or *your* and thus cannot promote good business relationships.

blunder	defective	inability	regret
claim	delay	inadequate	trouble
complaint	dissatisfaction	inferior	unfavorable
criticism	error	mistake	unfortunate
damage	failure	neglected	unsatisfactory

Delete Unnecessary Words

Words that are repetitious are a waste of the reader's or listener's time. Such words clutter the message and can distract, delay understanding, and reduce emotional impact. The italicized words in the following expressions are unnecessary and should be omitted.

adequate *enough*	connect *up*
as yet	continue *on*
at about	*and* etc.
up above	*as to* whether
both alike	*past* experience
new beginner	*free* gratis
cooperate *together*	inside *of*
same identical	my *personal* opinion
lose *out*	rarely (seldom) *ever*
meet *up* with	repeat *back* or *again*
modern methods *of today*	refer *back*
over *with*	*true* facts
customary practice	

Avoid Out-of-Date Words

Words that are out of date suggest that the speaker or the writer is behind the times. Imagine the reaction to a sign that said, "ESCHEW SMOKING"! In certain uses, the words below have a similar effect.

advise or state (for *say, tell*)	kindly (for *please*)
beg	party (for *person*, except in legal work)
duly	same ("and we will send you same")
esteemed	trust (for *hope, know, believe*)
herewith (except in legal work)	via

BUILDING AN EFFECTIVE VOCABULARY

Make a list of five nouns, five verbs, five adjectives, and five adverbs. Then write an essay or a story using only those twenty words and the articles *a, an,* and *the* and common conjunctions such as *and, but,* and *or.* Try to rewrite a news story using only this restricted vocabulary, or try to describe how you spent last night. You will find these exercises the most difficult writing you have ever done. The point here is simple: The more limited a writer's vocabulary, the more difficult the job of communicating becomes.

The principle demonstrated also works the other way: The richer your vocabulary, the easier it will be for you to write, to speak, to read, and to listen. Every new word that you learn makes it easier for you to read more widely and to encounter and learn still more words. Mastering a language is like learning to walk: The first steps are the most difficult. Because you have already taken the first steps, building an effective vocabulary is now a matter of expanding your knowledge. The suggestions below will help you to do so.

Become Word-Conscious

When you hear or see an unknown word, you feel curious—you feel the urge to know what it means. Curiosity is your natural ally in building an effective vocabulary, so use it to your advantage. Remember the word (or write it down) until you can get to a dictionary. Becoming word-conscious means satisfying your curiosity every time you encounter a new word. To do otherwise is to choose ignorance.

Once you become word-conscious, you will be amazed to discover how many new and interesting words will come to you each day. You will hear new words in class, on the job, from radio, television, and movies, and in the theater. You will see new words in newspapers, magazines, textbooks, novels, advertisements, and even on package labels.

Keeping a notebook of new words will speed your progress. Write down words and their definitions and review them from time to time. If you hear a new word, be sure to note its spelling. If you read a new word, be sure to note its pronunciation. New slang expressions are worth noting too. You should always label them as slang, however, and realize that they are inappropriate in most business situations.

Learn to Use Word Tools

A good vocabulary is a vast and complex structure that must be built piece by piece. Your own inborn curiosity will give you the necessary energy to build your vocabulary, but you will also need the right tools: a dictionary, a thesaurus, and a dictionary of synonyms. Besides making the construction easier, these tools will ensure that your vocabulary will be strong and lasting. (See Section 29 for instructions on the use of these tools.)

Practice Using New Words

A new word really becomes part of your vocabulary when you first write it or speak it correctly. As soon as you are sure that you understand the meaning and shades of meaning of a new word, use it in business and social conversation or correspondence. Each new word makes possible greater variety and precision in word usage, and these in turn increase your power to express and advance your views. Practice with new words gives you the excitement of first exerting your new word power.

COMMUNICATION PROJECTS

Practical Application

A. Do you know the following words well enough to pronounce each correctly and to use it in a sentence? If not, consult the dictionary. Then try using each in a sentence.

aggravate	supersede
devise	consignment
eligible	intercede

B. From the choices in parentheses, select the word that best completes the meaning of each sentence.
1. The governor's calming speech (disbursed, dispersed) the mob.
2. As one of the signers of the contract, he is not (a disinterested, an uninterested) party to the negotiations.
3. Being trapped in the elevator for three hours had no (affect, effect) on her mood.
4. All the (fiscal, physical) assets of the company are to be sold at auction.
5. He was appointed (council, counsel) in the company's tax division.
6. The work was done without the (assistance, assistants) of the clerks.
7. Mrs. Ford was asked to prepare a (bibliographical, biographical) description to be used to introduce the speaker to the audience.
8. He waited (awhile, a while) before calling his manager.
9. Your account is long (passed, past) due.
10. The printer made a (sleight, slight) change in the style of type.

C. Recast each of the following negative sentences in positive terms.
1. Not until today did your letter reach us, too late for our special offer, which ended last week.
2. There is no excuse for misunderstanding my clear instructions, even if you were interrupted while I was talking.
3. Since you failed to state whether you want legal- or letter-size, we cannot send the filing cabinets that you ordered.
4. I will not be in the office on Tuesday, so I will be unable to help you then.
5. Do not use a transistor radio battery with this calculator because the circuitry cannot withstand such high voltage.

D. Study the following excerpts from advertisements, and write on a separate sheet of paper the descriptive words you find.
1. Tired of your world? Try ours—Australia!
    Head out to sea and see the dazzling, undersea architecture of the Great Barrier Reef. Head back to shore and bask in the soothing rays of the southern sun on our long, pristine, white beaches. Head inland and see the magnificant moun-

tains of the Mount Olga Range. Head overland and see implausible, prehistoric animals come true.

Australia...older than the Old World and newer than the New!

2. In the can't-wait world of business, there's a need for a big bank that rolls up its sleeves and gets the job done. Business lives in a microsecond world. A quick, competent, yes-or-no decision can make the difference between success and failure...for a program, for a product, even for an entire company. At _____ Bank, we've structured our whole decision-making process on quickness and competence. We've a minimum of committees and a maximum of authority for our individual bankers...and almost no room at all for corporate "formality." For instance, we've pulled together financing packages in excess of $100 million—virtually overnight—for some of the nation's top corporations. And we were able to do it because our decision makers weren't behind closed doors when the decision was needed.

3. Let's shield roadside pillars before they become killers! Too many solid concrete obstructions are being left completely unshielded, and they're taking too many lives. But there's a way to correct this deadly hazard before it results in a needless disaster. A properly placed guardrail or an energy-absorbing crash cushion shielding these pillars would give an errant motorist a good chance of survival. We'll never eliminate human error on our highways. But with enough public awareness and concern, we can reduce the number of roadside deathtraps that kill and maim thousands of Americans every year.

E. Suppose you were asked to prepare a sales promotion letter to older people announcing a "See America Now" tour service. Choose any part of the country for your "tour"—or all of it—and for each point below, write a brief paragraph using a variety of descriptive, picture-making words.

1. Be adventurous.
2. Relive American history.
3. Be economical.

Plan and present a two-minute description of a product you'd like to sell. Use specific words, utilizing all the vocabulary know-how you've acquired so far in this course.

Editing Practice

The Word Processing Supervisor   A word is missing in each of the following sentences. Study the context of each sentence and supply a suitable word.

1. Although the _____ has expired on this equipment, we are entitled to maintenance under the terms of the service contract.
2. You may give as much or as little as you like, because contributions are entirely _____.
3. Our research scientists work in the largest and most modern _____ in the industry.
4. Because word processing operators must work rotating shifts, any applicant for such a job must have a _____ schedule.
5. The representatives of management and labor were unable to reach agreement; therefore, the dispute has been referred to an impartial board for _____.

6. Although Ms. Rostropovich expressed her views clearly, Mr. Foche was less
_____.

Case Problem

Tactful Words   The office manager of the Casko Company found, when she examined letters written by Rudy Blake, that Rudy was not very tactful when he wrote to customers of the company. He frequently used expressions like *your error, you claim,* and *you failed.* In discussing this problem with Rudy, the office manager learned that Rudy did not understand that these expressions were negative and could result in the loss of goodwill—or even customer business. "After all," said Rudy, "when customers are at fault, why shouldn't we tell them so?" How should the office manager answer Rudy?

**31
ACHIEVING
VARIETY IN WORD USAGE**

Imagine that the following excerpt is from a report submitted to you by one of your staff members.

> The present machines are still *good*, but the new ones should effect a *nice* savings each year—enough to pay for themselves in just three years! Therefore, I think it is a *good* idea to replace the old machines while we still have a *good* part of our capital-expense budget left. With *good* machinery, there is no question that we'll do a *nice* job on all the work coming up in June. . . .

And so on. Did you notice the overuse of *nice* and *good*? In colorless writing, every positive description usually consists of *nice* or *good* or a similar worn-out word.

The effective writer, on the other hand, might have said, "The present machines are still *working well* (or *working efficiently*) . . . a *sizable* savings . . . a *profitable* idea . . . a *substantial* part . . . With *modern* machinery . . . an *impressive* job . . . ."

Like other overused words and phrases, *nice* and *good* carry little information and no flavor or color. Not only are trite terms weak themselves, but they also weaken other terms used with them—like water added to punch.

If you are to keep the attention of your reader or listener, then you must avoid worn-out words and phrases and strive for fresh and lively ways of stating your ideas. Your success as a business communicator depends on your imaginative use of expressions that long ago lost their strength. In other words, if you rely on such clichés, you keep your communications vivid and interesting.

WHAT TO AVOID

Avoid Overused Words

Replacing overused words with more exact and colorful terms can change a dull communication into a bright and compelling one. The adjective *good* is overused and weak: a *good* maneuver, a *good* negotiator, a *good* speech, a *good* employee. Instead, for greater interest, say: an *adroit, clever,* or *nimble* maneuver; a *patient, forceful,* or *wily* negotiator; a *thought-provoking, informative,* or *engrossing* speech; a *loyal, diligent,* or *industrious* employee.

Adjectives such as *awful, bad, fine,* and *great* are also overused. Often these adjectives have no more meaning than a grunt or a moan. The following sentences show how meaningless these words can be.

1. Friction among staff members can result in a *bad* situation.
2. The meeting last Thursday was *great* and the resolution passed was *great* too.
3. We have an *awful* backlog of orders.
4. The company gave a *fine* luncheon for him when he retired.

While these vague, dull terms deaden the sentences, the choices below impart life and zest.

> Sentence 1: *difficult, painful,* or *troublesome* situation
> Sentence 2: *important, productive,* or *memorable* meeting; *constructive, salient,* or *eloquent* resolution
> Sentence 3: *enormous, gigantic,* or *overwhelming* backlog
> Sentence 4: *delightful, fitting,* or *splendid* luncheon

By substituting more precise adjectives for the imprecise and overworked *great, awful, bad,* and *fine,* you will create fuller, more distinct descriptions. Words, like people, become less effective when overworked. Examine your own speech and writing to discover the words that you overwork.

Avoid Overused Expressions

To be *brutally frank,* if a *goodly number* of clichés are *part and parcel* of your *manner of speaking,* then it is *crystal clear* that your English is a *far cry* from *passing with flying colors* the *acid test* of *top-notch, A number 1, King's English according to Hoyle.* How can so many words say so little! Most of those words are parts of overworked expressions that long ago lost their strength. In other words, if you rely on such clichés, your English is weak.

Clichés say much about you. The use of clichés exposes a lack of imagination—the tendency to repeat the familiar, even when the familiar is not worth repeating, rather than to think of new and forceful expressions. Clichés waste time, obscure ideas, and bore readers and listeners. Your imagination is sure to provide better expressions once you resolve to avoid clichés.

Some commonly overused words and expressions, together with suggested substitutions for them, are listed below.

For	Substitute
along the lines of	like
asset	advantage, gain, possession, resource
at all times	always
by the name of	named
deal	agreement, arrangement, transaction
each and every	each *or* every
face up to	face
factor	event, occurrence, part
field	branch, department, domain, point, question, range, realm, region, scene, scope, sphere, subject, theme
fix	adjust, arrange, attach, bind, mend, confirm, define, establish, limit, place, prepare, repair
inasmuch as	since, as
input	comment, information, recommendation
in the near future	soon (or state the exact time)
line	business, merchandise, goods, stock
matter	situation, question, subject, point (or mention what is specifically referred to)
our Mr. Smith	our representative, Mr. Smith,
proposition	proposal, undertaking, offer, plan, affair, recommendation, idea
say	exclaim, declare, utter, articulate, express, assert, relate, remark, mention
reaction	opinion, attitude, impression
recent communication	letter of (give exact date)
run	manage, direct, operate

WHAT TO STRIVE FOR

Identifying and avoiding hackneyed words and expressions is like giving away worn-out clothes: now you must find something to replace them. There are reference books to help you in the search for variety in expression, but you cannot expect to find ready-made words and phrases to express every new idea. Achieving variety in word usage demands creativity. To develop creativity you need to understand, study, and apply the following suggestions.

Select Suitable Synonyms

Choosing suitable synonyms is the most direct means of achieving variety. A synonym, as you know, is a word that has the same or nearly the same meaning as another word; for example, *new, novel, modern, original,* and *fresh* are synonyms. Although synonyms have the same basic meaning, each synonym has a different shade of meaning. To select the synonym that best expresses a specific idea, you must go beyond the basic idea and learn the distinctions.

¹**bad** \\'bad\\ *adj* **worse** \\'wərs\\; **worst** \\'wərst\\ [ME] **1 a :** failing to reach an acceptable standard : POOR **b :** UNFAVORABLE
⟨make a ∼ impression⟩ **c :** not fresh or sound : SPOILED, DILAPI-
DATED ⟨∼ fish⟩ ⟨the house was in ∼ condition⟩ **2 a :** morally
objectionable **b :** MISCHIEVOUS, DISOBEDIENT **3 :** inadequate or
unsuited to a purpose ⟨a ∼ plan⟩ ⟨∼ lighting⟩ **4 :** DISAGREEABLE,
UNPLEASANT ⟨∼ news⟩ **5 a :** INJURIOUS, HARMFUL **b :** SEVERE ⟨a
∼ cold⟩ **6 :** INCORRECT, FAULTY ⟨∼ grammar⟩ **7 a :** suffering
pain or distress ⟨felt generally ∼⟩ **b :** UNHEALTHY, DISEASED ⟨∼
teeth⟩ **8 :** SORROWFUL, SORRY **9 :** INVALID, VOID ⟨a ∼ check⟩ —
bad *adv* — **bad·ly** *adv* — **bad·ness** *n*

By permission. From *Webster's New Collegiate Dictionary*, © 1980 by
G. & C. Merriam Co., Publishers of the Merriam-Webster Dictionaries.

Instead of using the overworked word *bad*, for example, you look in the dictionary
and find these synonyms: *evil, ill, wicked,* and *naughty.* These synonyms cannot be
used interchangeably. The dictionary entry is instructive:

Murderers are worse than *naughty,* and mischievous children at their worst do not
deserve to be called *evil.* But both *naughty* and *evil* are more vivid than saying, "The
murderer is very bad," or "The children aren't too bad." By using each of the synonyms for *bad* in appropriate cases, you introduce variety and color.

Sometimes a dictionary will refer you to another entry for synonyms. For example,
when looking for synonyms under the adjective *exact,* you will read "see *correct.*"
There, under the entry for *correct,* are listed the synonyms *correct, accurate, exact,
precise, nice,* and *right.* If no synonyms are listed for the word you seek and there is no
reference to another entry, you can create a phrase to achieve variety. Under the word
explore, for example, the dictionary lists no synonyms, but look at its definition: "to
search through or into; to examine minutely; to penetrate into; to make or conduct a
systematic search." Thus, instead of using *explore,* you can make a phrase to fit:
"*search* the area *thoroughly,*" "*examine* the records *minutely,*" "*systematically search*
the files."

An excellent source of synonyms, of course, is the thesaurus. With the help of the
thesaurus you can avoid trite expressions and develop variety in word usage. For instance, suppose you are preparing a report in which you claim "Capable office
workers are few and far between." You wish to avoid the expression *few and far between,* partly because it is trite and partly because it does not exactly express the
thought you would like to convey.

The dictionary will provide limited assistance here. The word *few* is defined as "not
many; consisting of or amounting to a small number." The thesaurus, on the other
hand, gives many additional similar words and phrases; for example, *sparseness,
handful, meager, small number, hardly any, scarcely any, scant, rare,* and *minority.* So
you might say, "Capable office workers are in scant supply."

USE APPROPRIATE ANTONYMS

An antonym is a word that means *exactly* the opposite of another word. For example,
light is an antonym of *dark.* Antonyms may also be "created" by using such prefixes
as *il-, in-, ir-, non-,* and *un-* before a word. For instance, *legible* becomes *illegible;
credible, incredible; trustworthy, untrustworthy; expensive, inexpensive; delivery,
nondelivery; responsible, irresponsible;* and so on.

Facility in the use of antonyms opens broad possibilities to the communicator.

While *additional* reading sounds like an added burden, *unrequired* reading sounds as if it might even be fun. It is sad when the dead are *forgotten*, but sadder still when they are *unmourned*.

Some antonyms emphasize a break from tiresome routine. *Experts* are always explaining distant *events* to us, but a *nonexpert* describing a *nonevent* might be more interesting to *noncelebrities* like us. If we didn't drink too much cola, the *uncola* wouldn't sound so refreshing.

Choose Picture-Making Words

Picture-making words make readers or listeners "see" what is being described—often with themselves in the picture. A necktie with an *intricate pattern* is difficult to visualize, but a *gold and crimson paisley* calls an image to mind. Notice that more specific words are better at picture-making. Since the thesaurus is the best aid in the search for specific terms, it is a treasure house of picture-making words as well. Let's say that you start with a vague description like a *big, hairy dog*. The thesaurus can supply more specific terms for *big* and *hairy dog* like *hulking* and *St. Bernard*. You can complete the picture by visualizing it more fully and then describing what you see: a *hulking St. Bernard leaving a trail of coarse, white hairs on the carpet*.

Advertising copywriters must make each word count since each word is costly to the client. The copywriter's language is sometimes extravagant, but it always makes pictures. A shirt has *windowpane* checks; an evening gown has *spaghetti* straps; a scarf comes in *crayon-bright* colors; a coat has a *face-framing* collar. Notice the colorful words in the following advertisements:

> This compact car will still be sipping its first drink when the gasguzzlers are lining up for a third round.
> Our down comforter will keep you toe-curling cozy all winter.
> Our new acoustical ceiling soaks up excess noise.

Read the last advertisement aloud and note that it not only creates a picture but also has enough *s* sounds to provide its own "noise."

Using picture-making words will improve your messages, whether spoken or written, but it requires much work and practice to develop this skill. You can develop it, however, if you force yourself to visualize a complete picture of what you want to describe, and then consult the thesaurus until you find the most specific descriptive terms that apply. First comes the idea, then the full picture, and finally the right words. If you see this process through, then you will be able to hold the attention of your readers and listeners in school, business, and private life.

COMMUNICATION PROJECTS

Practical Application
A. In each of the following sentences, the italicized word or phrase is weak. Substitute a more exact or vivid word or phrase.
  1. The contractor made some *great* suggestions for remodeling the office.

2. Staff members expect the new manager to be a *big* improvement.
3. The report he prepared was *not worth a dime.*
4. The victim looked *bad* after the accident.
5. Our new supervisor does a *fine* job.
6. Safety on the highway is *a good idea.*
7. The misunderstanding resulted from a *bad error.*
8. At the office picnic, *a good time was had by all.*
9. The new, high-speed photocopier collates papers *very well.*
10. Everyone agrees that Mrs. Crawford is *nice.*

B. Each of the following sentences has a question mark where a descriptive word should be. Insert a word that strengthens the whole sentence.
1. He had to be (?) to solve such a difficult problem.
2. When creativity was needed, she was always a (?) example to the rest of the staff.
3. The museum's collection was so (?) that it was the highlight of an already memorable tour.
4. Anyone who has ever had to cling to a high ledge knows how (?) it is to look down.
5. After looking for the lost papers for an hour, he lost his patience and became (?).

C. Match each word in Column I with a word or phrase from Column II that has similar meaning.

I	II	
a. hint	1. happen again	11. trustworthy
b. stubborn	2. judge	12. validate
c. procrastinate	3. supporter	
d. confirm	4. allusion	
e. reliable	5. minor	
f. adherent	6. illusion	
g. recur	7. postpone	
h. evaluate	8. obstinate	
i. precarious	9. merchandise	
j. goods	10. unsafe	

D. Substitute fresh terms for the overworked words in the following phrases.

1. fix the vending machine
2. a good meeting
3. a fine program
4. fix the letter
5. a good presentation
6. a fine supervisor
7. a good secretary
8. fix the broken space bar
9. a fine building
10. fix this error

E. Find original replacements for the clichés italicized below.

1. a worker who never *leaves you in the lurch*
2. must stop *passing the buck*
3. get it done *somehow or other*
4. *ironing out the bugs* in our procedure
5. thought about *calling it quits*
6. he *gets on his high horse*
7. she *racked her brains*
8. he *sets no store by*
9. she *made short work of* it
10. likes to *toot her own horn*

F. Write an antonym for each of the following words.

1. ethical
2. implausible
3. exorbitant
4. penalize
5. sensitive

6. fascinating
7. trivial
8. synthetic
9. accept
10. encourage

Editing Practice

Picture-Making Words   Rewrite these sentences, substituting exact, picture-making words for the italicized words.

1. The high waves *hit* the side of the ship.
2. They felt *good* sitting on the rug in front of the fireplace.
3. When he lit the cigar despite their objections, they all *looked* at him through the smoke.
4. When the bus finally arrived, they were all *very cold*.
5. His anger was *noticeable* just beneath the surface.

Case Problem

The Uninformed Employees   The Warner Paper Manufacturing Company makes cardboard boxes, as well as other paper products. The vice president in charge of production, Tom Orasco, saw a demonstration of a new machine that folds boxes more efficiently than the one now owned by the company. While this new machine would not reduce labor, it would do a better job of folding. Mr. Orasco decided to order the new machine on a trial basis. When the machine was delivered to the room where it would be used, it was not unpacked because the manufacturer's representative could not set it up until the following week. Of course, most of the employees noticed the box and could see from the markings on the crate that it was a new folding machine. Soon rumors began to spread that this new machine would replace many of the employees and that they had better start looking for new positions.

Within one week after the machine arrived, Bill Weatherill, the head supervisor, came to Tom Orasco and told him of the discontent arising in the department, all because of lack of information about the new machine. Bill emphasized that the employees had many reasonable questions about the machine and the effect it would have on their work.

1. Who should handle this problem—Bill Weatherill or Tom Orasco?
2. What can he tell the employees in order to allay their fears?
3. What should have been done to prevent this problem from occurring?

A spelling error is like a hole in the paper, an upside-down word, a grease stain on the page. The reader must pause to solve a puzzle rather than speed ahead to absorb the writer's message. Since the writer did not take time to consult the dictionary, the reader must waste time deciphering the mystery that pretends to be a word. The reader must bear a burden that belongs to the writer, and naturally the reader feels annoyed.

In business, your spelling errors will not only annoy your superiors but also make them reluctant to let you represent the company in dealings with customers and others. Poor spelling makes both you and your company look inept. As a result, spelling errors will delay or prevent your advancement.

To overcome any spelling difficulties that you may have, you should study and apply the principles presented in this section. You will learn some guides to correct spelling, and you will become alert to the spelling pitfalls that make consulting a dictionary imperative.

GUIDES TO CORRECT SPELLING

Although there are many variations in the spelling of English words, some principles almost always hold true. Every writer must know and be able to apply these principles—the basic guides to correct spelling.

Final Y

Many common nouns end in *y*: *company, industry, entry, territory, warranty, vacancy, attorney, survey, monkey*. The spelling of the plurals of these common nouns depends on whether the *y* is preceded by a consonant or a vowel. If preceded by a consonant, the *y* is changed to *i* and *es* is added: *company, companies; industry, industries; entry, entries; territory, territories; warranty, warranties; vacancy, vacancies*. If preceded by a vowel, only *s* is added: *attorney, attorneys; survey, surveys; monkey, monkeys*.

Ei and Ie Words

Among the most frequently misspelled words are these: *believe, belief, deceive, deceit, perceive, conceive, conceit, receive, receipt, relieve*, and *relief*. The word *Alice* is a clue to their correct spelling. In *Alice* we see the combinations *li* and *ce*. These combinations can help you remember that the correct spelling after *l* is *ie* (*believe*); after *c*, *ei* (*receive*).

Endings *Ful, Ous, Ally, Ily*

To spell the endings *ful, ous, ally,* and *ily* correctly, a writer needs to remember that:

The suffix *ful* has only one *l*: *careful, skillful, gainful, peaceful*. An adjective ending with the sound "us" is spelled *ous*: *previous, various, miscellaneous, gratuitous*.

The ending *ally* has two *l*'s: *financially, originally, incidentally, fundamentally*.

The ending *ily* has one *l*: *necessarily, craftily, hastily, busily*.

Doubling a Final Consonant

Knowing when to double and when not to double a final consonant is easy for the person who can determine the sound. The only rule needed is this: If the last syllable of the base word is accented, if the vowel sound in the last syllable is *short*, and if the suffix to be added begins with a vowel, double the final consonant.

compel	compelled, compelling	omit	omitted, omitting
equip	equipped, equipping	prefer	preferred, preferring
occur	occurred, occurrence, occurring	regret	regretted, regretting

In each of the following words, the accent is on the *first* syllable; therefore, in the preferred spelling, the final consonant is *not* doubled.

benefit	benefited, benefiting
cancel	canceled, canceling (*but* cancellation)
differ	differed, differing
equal	equaled, equaling
marvel	marveled, marveling, marvelous
travel	traveled, traveler, traveling

Words of One Syllable

If you can hear the difference between long and short vowel sounds, then you can tell whether or not to double the final consonant of a one-syllable word. If the vowel sound is long, do *not* double; if the vowel sound is short, double the final consonant.

hope	hoping (*long vowel*)	hop	hopping (*short vowel*)
plane	planing (*long*)	plan	planning (*short*)
pine	pining (*long*)	pin	pinning (*short*)
cause	causing		
seize	seizing		
lose	losing		

☐ Checkup 1

Correct any spelling errors in the following sentences. Write *OK* if a sentence is correct.

1. We submited the report on expired warrantys.
2. The day was peacefull except for the voidding of the purchase order.
3. We did not recieve your check, so we are cancelling the delivery.
4. The strikers are hopping for a fundamentaly different contract.
5. The planing of the sales campaign improved steadilly.
6. Do you have all the supplys you need for this project?
7. She referred the reporter to the necessarily cautious attorneys.
8. He was courteus even when his opponent was decietfull.

DICTIONARY ALERTS

Since no one can remember how every word in the English language is spelled, good spelling requires frequent use of the dictionary. On the other hand, no one has time to look up every word encountered in daily life. One of the skills of the good speller is recognizing the types of words that are most likely to be misspelled—spelling pitfalls. These pitfalls alert careful spellers to the need to consult the dictionary.

The most common spelling pitfalls are presented here so that you, too, will be alert to the tricky combinations that send even excellent spellers to the dictionary. **Remember:** Use the dictionary whenever in doubt, but especially if the word in question contains one of these prefixes or suffixes.

Word Beginnings

Words beginning with the prefixes *per, pur* and *ser, sur* present a spelling obstacle because they sound alike. If you are not absolutely certain of the correct spelling of any given word, check a dictionary. Study the following words:

perimeter	purloin	serpent	surmount
perplex	purpose	servant	surplus
persist	pursuit	service	surtax

Word Endings

The following groups of word endings are tricky because they have similar sounds or because they may be pronounced carelessly. The spellings of these endings, however, differ. Do not try to guess at spellings of words with the following ending sounds.

"Unt," "Uns"   If these endings were always clearly enunciated as *ant, ance, ent, ence,* they would present no problem. However, because they are so often sounded "unt" and "uns" and because there are so many words with these endings, they are spelling danger spots. They must be spelled by eye, not by ear. Some common words having these endings are the following:

accountant	maintenance	incompetent	existence
defendant	perseverance	dependent	independence
descendant	remittance	permanent	interference
tenant	resistance	silent	violence

"Uhble," "Uhbility"   The sound "uhble," which might be spelled *able* or *ible*, is another trap. The alert writer consults a dictionary in order to avoid misspelling this ending. Some common "uhble" and "uhbility" words are the following:

enjoyable	availability	collectible	flexibility
payable	capability	deductible	plausibility
receivable	mailability	reversible	possibility
returnable	probability	ineligible	visibility

"Shun," "Shus"   Words ending in "shun" might be spelled *tion*, *sion*, or even *cian*, *tian*, *sian*, *cion*, or *xion*. The ending "shus" might be *cious*, *tious*, or *xious*. Learn the spelling of the words listed here, but at the same time, remember never to trust a "shun" or a "shus" ending.

audition	dietitian	conscious	complexion
collision	anxious	suspicious	conscientious
connection	suspension	technician	pretentious
ignition	suspicion	statistician	propitious

"Shul," "Shent"   The ending that sounds like "shul" is sometimes spelled *cial* and sometimes *tial*. A "shent" ending might be *cient* or *tient*. Look at the following words and learn how they are spelled, but never take chances on the spelling of any word ending in "shul" or "shent."

artificial	essential	omniscient	impatient
beneficial	partial	deficient	proficient
judicial	substantial	efficient	quotient

"Ize," "Kul"   The ending "ize" might be spelled *ize*, *ise*, or even *yze* (*analyze*). A "kul" ending could be *cal* or *cle*. An expert writer, therefore, consults a dictionary for these word endings. Study the following "ize" and "kul" words:

apologize	advertise	identical	obstacle
criticize	enterprise	mechanical	particle
realize	improvise	statistical	spectacle
temporize	merchandise	technical	vehicle

Ar, Ary, Er, Ery, Or, Ory   *Stationary* and *stationery* end with the same sound, but they are spelled differently. Words that end in *ar*, *ary*, *er*, *ery*, *or*, or *ory* should be recognized as spelling hazards; you should always verify each spelling. Memorize the spellings of the following words:

calendar	grammar	advertiser	customer	debtor	realtor
customary	temporary	adviser	carpenter	inventory	advisory

"Seed" Although only a few words have "seed" endings, they are frequently written incorrectly because the ending has three different spellings. When studying the following list of "seed" words, memorize these facts: (1) The *only* word ending in *sede* is *supersede*, and (2) the *only* words ending in *ceed* are *exceed*, *proceed*, and *succeed*. All other "seed" words, then, must be spelled *cede*.

sede	**ceed**	**cede**	
supersede	exceed	accede	precede
	proceed	cede	recede
	(*but* procedure)	concede	secede
	succeed	intercede	

☐ Checkup 2

What is the correct spelling of the words in parentheses?
1. You are to (proseed) in accordance with the (preseeding) directions.
2. (Reversuhble) raincoats will be on sale next week.
3. We are all prone to (critisize) public officials.
4. Bill's outstanding characteristic is his (perseveruns).
5. We are unable to grant you any (extenshun) of time.
6. Are those signatures (identikul)?
7. The policy was a (radikul) departure from (elementuhry) principles.
8. Evelyn's promotion was certainly a (surprize) to all of us.

YOUR SPELLING VOCABULARY

Business writers cannot take the time to verify the spelling of every word. They must, therefore, take the time to learn the correct spellings of the words used most often in their communications. Knowing how to spell troublesome words requires more than memorization. You must analyze each word and fix in your mind its peculiarities, as illustrated by the analyses of the following twenty words.

accommodate (two *c*'s, two *m*'s)	occasion (two *c*'s, one *s*)
aggressive (two *g*'s, two *s*'s)	occurred (two *c*'s, two *r*'s)
believe (*ie*)	precede (*cede*)
chief (*ie*)	privilege (*vile*)
convenient (*ven, ient*)	proceed (*ceed*)
definite (*fi*)	receive (*ei*)
develop (no final *e*)	recommend (one *c*, two *m*'s)
embarrass (two *r*'s, two *s*'s)	repetition (*pe*)
forty, fortieth (only *four* words without *u*)	separate (*par*)
ninth (only *nine* word without *e*)	until (only one *l*)

COMMUNICATION PROJECTS

Practical Application

A. Without using a dictionary, write the correct forms of the words enclosed in parentheses. Then check your answers in a dictionary.

1. The construction supervisor found that the two (survey) did not agree.
2. These contracts are (original), not duplicates.
3. Our account is (pay) on the 15th of each month.
4. It would be (waste) to dispose of the contents too (hasty).
5. The contract was (advantage) to our interests.
6. Although the expansion plans were (fundamental) sound, inflation forced (manage) to cancel the project.
7. After (ride) the train home, she began (rid) her briefcase of outdated papers.
8. Thread, zippers, and (sundry) are for sale in the notions department.
9. The (defer)-payment plan makes purchasing easier for our customers.
10. The assembly line uses many overhead (pulley).
11. The applicant was nervous because the interviewer never stopped (swivel) his chair.
12. It was (presume) of the assistant director to agree to the contract in the director's absence.
13. All (warranty) are six months longer on the new models than on the old.
14. According to the contract, the manufacturer is responsible for (maintain) of the equipment.
15. They developed a storage and (retrieve) system for all our files.

B. Make any spelling corrections needed in these sentences.

1. All procedes will go to charity.
2. Engineers were called in to solve the technicle problems.
3. Competant secretaries are highly valued in our division.
4. Please seat the two parties at seperate tables.
5. Adjasent offices would be conveniant.
6. Ms. Arkin said that there is no noticable difference in quality.
7. Our sales are steadilly increasing.
8. She refered me to her assistent, who showed me the rest of the laboratory.
9. Some proceedures save time, others are wasteful.
10. Currant developments may prevent renewal of the agreement.
11. Karen is convinced that the Hotel MacElliot has superior accomodations.
12. I am afraid that this account will be uncollectible.
13. Barry ommited the revised costs in his memo to Mrs. Weems.
14. Miss Dill cordialy invited her entire staff to the special celebration.
15. The exhibitors showed many products and accesseries.

C. Correct any spelling errors you find in this letter.

Dear Ms. Vukovich:

Thank you for your letter and purchase order of August 12. We are sure that our new Polyform injection-molding machines will be sufficiant for all your needs in the manufacture of shock-proof plastic packaging.

Demand for Polyform has been contageus, and I am afraid that our backlog of orders will prevent us from delivering within ten days, as you request. In order to meet the needs of our customers, we are increasing our labor force and expanding our plant—already the largest in the industrey. We may be able to fill your order within three weeks; in any case, I can assure you that the delay will not excede 30 days.

Please let me know if this delivery schedule will satisfy your requirements. If not, we will refund your check at once. Of course, we know that we will be able to serve you more promptley in the future.

Sincerely,

Editing Practice

Why Be Trite?   Rewrite these sentences, using lively and different words for the trite italicized expressions.

1. Our new office supervisor is a *tower of strength.*
2. She advanced in the company by *the sweat of her brow.*
3. Despite heavy use, the old typewriter is *none the worse for wear.*
4. The idea came to him *like a bolt from the blue.*
5. *In this day and age,* mastery of English is essential for a business career.

Proofreading a Memo   Even though memos go to co-workers rather than to customers, the messages should be correctly written. Correct any spelling errors in the following memo.

Since we hired six new sales representatives last March, our sales have increased dramaticalley. As a result, we are now having difficultys in producing all the products that are now backordered, and we are faceing the problem of not being abel to meet all the commitmants we made to customers.

We must, therefore, act quickly to change this potentialy harmfull situation. If we cannot fill customers' orders as promised, we must then explore such possibilitys as refunding deposits and curteously cancelling orders, asking customers whether they would acept late deliverys, hireing part-time or full-time production help, and subcontracting the manufacture of some of our componants. Of course, there are other alternatives too.

Let's meet to discuss these and other possible actions on Wednesday, November 12, at 2:00 p.m. in our conferance room.

Using Business Vocabulary   Fill in the blanks with the correct word from the following list.

a. delinquent	f. personnel
b. emphasized	g. principal
c. estimated	h. principle
d. mutually	i. retrieval
e. personal	j. visualize

1. Have you compared the actual cost to the (?) costs?
2. Mr. Turner suggests that we turn over all (?) accounts to a collection agency.
3. Ms. Hall (?) the need to make the laboratory safe for all employees.
4. The slides helped us to (?) the procedures that Daniel was describing.
5. We have a sophisticated (?) system for storing all our files.

6. Granting them exclusive rights to market our products will, we hope, prove to be (?) beneficial.
7. Mr. Scanlon wrote a (?) note to Ms. Bowen to congratulate her on her promotion.
8. The president stressed that the safety of all employees was her (?) concern.
9. The (?) in our department are well-trained, experienced sales people.
10. Although we stand little to gain from the law suit, Mr. Heller feels it is a matter of (?).

Case Problem

Leading a Discussion   Alice McTavish was chairperson of the dance committee for the Business Club at Cherokee Business College. The committee was meeting to plan the annual graduation dance, and Peter Schmidt made a suggestion to get a name band to play for the dance. Alice did not think the suggestion was feasible, since a name band would cost more than they would take in through ticket sales. However, Alice, as chairperson, did not want to oppose any suggestions made by members of the committee. She hoped someone in the group would say something in opposition to the suggestion, but no one said anything except that it was a good idea.

1. What is the function of a group leader?
2. Should Alice let the group go ahead with the suggestion even though it will certainly be a failure?
3. What can Alice say to get the committee to see the misdirection of the suggestion without appearing as though she is trying to force her own opinion on the group?

CHAPTER 6

ESTABLISHING WRITING SKILL

"What's in it for me?" is our normal, automatic response to any number of suggestions, proposals, plans, and requests. This reflex cannot be dismissed as mere selfishness. By asking "What's in it for me?" we show our natural, strong instinct for self-preservation. We seldom have to ponder the question for long—the answer comes quickly. When the answer to "What's in it for me?" is attractive, then we decide to go along with the proposal or request. When it is not, we reject the offer.

In business, as in other areas, we can capitalize on this psychological principle. We can learn to build in an attractive answer whenever our communications cause someone to ask "What's in it for me?" For example, the advertising copywriter who plays up the vitality and healthy appearance of milk drinkers, overlooking the calories and butterfat in every glass of milk, is making a sales pitch and supplying the consumer with an attractive answer to that automatic question: "What's in it for me?" Answer: Milk will make you lively and healthy-looking.

Understanding that this psychological principle works in successful business writing, as well as in selling and advertising, should help you write better letters. The more you learn and understand about human behavior, the more effective your business writing will become. In the remaining sections of this textbook, you will learn various types of business writing. To prepare you, this section will teach you basic principles that apply to all the sections that follow. By studying these principles, you will progress from an untrained writer, to an average writer, and finally to a master writer. The better you understand the topics in this section the faster you will speed your improvement.

"WHAT'S IN IT FOR ME?"

Self-interest is as complex as people are, and almost everyone shares certain basic kinds of self-interest. By learning how to appeal to the kinds of self-interest discussed in this section, you will learn to write letters with built-in answers to the question "What's in it for me?"

Increasing Income Most people who work for a living are interested in earning more money. Therefore, if what you propose to a client or customer is an opportunity to make money, emphasize that in your letter. If your business is selling stocks or mutual funds, then your customers are approaching you for the explicit purpose of making money. In order to make your customers deal with you rather than your competitors, your sales letter should be equally explicit. Clients reading the following letter excerpt would appreciate such a direct, factual approach.

If in 1980 you had invested $10,000 in Eastern Motion Pictures, today your investment would be worth $21,323—more than double your money! (The figures, of course, must actually be true.)

Making Money by Saving Money   Business people know that they can make money by saving money; for example, by special discounts. If your company is a supplier that offers discounts, your writing should emphasize how these discounts save money and how *you alone* offer this particular discount. For example:

> Take advantage of our unique November discount—4 percent off!—and enjoy savings that mean higher profits for you.

In other instances, your readers might not realize how much they could save by accepting the offer in your letter. Tell them in simple, direct, and forceful terms. If you want to sell an office machine, for example, the financial-gain incentive might be:

> The Instant Business Data computer will help you take prompt action on accounts past due. Often our customers find that taking prompt action improves their collection rate on problem accounts by more than 20 percent—a significant increase in revenue and a sharp reduction of headaches.

Quoting Dollars and Cents   Whenever you quote amounts of money, apply your knowledge of psychology. Thus, when quoting income for the reader, use large dollar figures to make the offer more attractive. When asking the reader to pay out money, use smaller dollar figures. For instance, in an ad to sell a building with six apartments, each renting at $300 a month, you would quote *yearly* income figures:

> Your yearly income from this property will be a comfortable $21,600. (Not "Each apartment will bring you a monthly income of $300.")

For mortgage payment figures, however, quote *monthly*, not yearly, payments:

> The amount remaining after the down payment can be financed by a 30-year conventional mortgage that will cost you only $212.93 a month.

Health and Security

Health and security are major concerns of most people, and buying incentives that are based on these concerns appeal to people's instincts for self-preservation.

Advertisements for many products—in particular, for medicines—appeal to a common desire to preserve and to promote your own good health. Be alert for opportunities to use this incentive in your writing. If, for instance, you are promoting the sale of a water filter, you should stress facts that relate to good health, such as:

> Your water not only will taste better but also will be free of germs and other contaminants that may harm you and your children.

The appeal to people's desire for health is often used in real estate.

> Come to Sunmend Valley, where the dry, mild climate is like a balm for many kinds of respiratory and rheumatic ailments.

An appeal to people's desire for security can also be a part of your promotion efforts. Suppose, for example, you are promoting a new car, the Kiwi, and can emphasize any one of several buying incentives. Knowing the importance of security motivation, you would certainly emphasize that factor in promotional material. Your letter or ad might read:

> You and your family will be safe in a Kiwi. Built for stability and efficiency, the Kiwi grips the road when most other cars would be headed for a ditch. The press of a button on the dashboard locks all doors instantly. You will no longer fear that a child will fall out, or that anyone from outside can reach in and grab the passengers in your car.

Personal Comfort

All of us desire comfort and beauty in our daily living, both at home and at work. Thus the built-in answer to "What's in it for me?" will often be "more comfort," "more beauty," or "more relaxation." The spur to action here is a deliberate appeal to the senses and the emotions.

A moment's thought will bring to mind many goods and services that can be sold by stressing personal comfort. One example is the following ad to promote the sale of mattresses:

> Each morning you will wake up rested and refreshed, eager for an energetic and productive day.

Here is an illustration of the appeal to the desire for comfort in a business setting:

> The ExecuChair will keep you comfortable, alert, and aggressive throughout the entire working day—and even after five. No aches, no pains, no fatigue. Everyone needs support sometime; the ExecuChair will give it to you all the time.

Comfort sometimes results from making the work load easier and quicker. Consider how these picture-making sentences could make a homeowner feel like rushing out to buy a minitractor:

> In summer, your TuffJob tractor will mow your lawn quickly and evenly, freeing your weekends for poolside fun. In winter, your TuffJob tractor will shovel your snow away effortlessly and return you to your fireplace in minutes.

THE DRIVE FOR PERSONAL RECOGNITION

There are three billion people in the world, but not one of us is content to feel as small as one three-billionth of anything. We all want to be at least noticed, if not praised, admired, or even saluted. This drive for personal recognition may be partially satisfied by acquiring possessions that society recognizes as status symbols, such as a sleek car, a lavish home, or chic clothes.

Each of us yearns to be recognized and acknowledged. Whether you call the longing for personal recognition ego or dignity or self-respect, it is a powerful force. The successful business writer must understand this force and its universal appeal. Often success in writing depends largely on how well the writer can feed the reader's appetite for self-worth. The guidelines presented in the following paragraphs will help you to become skillful at appealing to the drive for personal recognition.

Focusing on the Readers

Inflate your readers' egos by emphasizing that your readers are your first concern. You can safely assume that your readers will agree that they are of primary importance—both to themselves and to you. You should strive, therefore, to flavor your communications with *you* and *your* rather than with *I* and *we*. Compare the following illustrations of *we* and *you* approaches:

> **We:** Experience has convinced us that our Instant Index Automatic Filing System is the most efficient way to keep thorough and accessible business records.
>
> **You:** You will never have to waste another minute shuffling through papers once you get your hands on the Instant Index Automatic Filing System.
>
> **We:** Please send us your check for $21.89, so that we may balance our books.
>
> **You:** Your check for $21.89 will balance your account and maintain your excellent credit rating.
>
> **We:** Take it from us: We have the best temporary office workers in town.
>
> **You:** Our temporary office workers will turn your impossible backlog into your luxurious lead time.

Using Readers' Names

One of the most pleasant ways of receiving personal recognition is to hear or see your own name mentioned favorably. Without a name, each of us is just one more faceless atom in the masses of the populous modern world. If someone forgets your address or your telephone number, you are not likely to be offended. But if someone forgets your name, you feel diminished. Having your name mentioned, by contrast, makes you feel significant in someone else's eyes as well as more confident of your own worth.

When you use the addressee's name in the body of a letter, you assert the addressee's importance. Use of the reader's name—a technique called direct address—makes a message seem warm and personal. Consider the following example:

> Answering your inquiry has been a pleasure, Ms. Delancy. I hope you will always feel free to call on me whenever you think I can help you.

Because she sees *her* name in the body of the letter, Ms. Delancy knows that to you, she is not just one more customer receiving a form letter: She is a unique, memorable person reading a letter written with her alone in mind. However, do not overdo it; once is usually enough. And be sure to spell the addressee's name correctly!

Being Courteous

Your courtesy also helps the reader feel important and respected. Readers may take courtesy for granted in business communications and hardly notice its use. On the other hand, a discourteous letter will strike the reader as impolite or even contemptuous. Even the failure to include a routine "please" and "thank you" may give offense. Where courtesy is concerned, give the reader what the reader feels is due.

Answering Letters Promptly

You should answer most letters within twenty-four hours of receiving them. Everyone resents being made to wait—especially for a simple "yes" or "no" answer. Having to wait for a reply makes you feel insignificant and often delays you unnecessarily.

Some letters, of course, cannot be answered immediately. You might need time to look up facts or policies as the basis for the reply. When you need to delay a response, you should write and say when you expect to be able to send an answer or you might have been out of town when the letter arrived. If so, be sure to tell the reader that the delay was unavoidable. When the reply is late, the reader has the right to an explanation and perhaps an apology. You must respect that right or risk further offense to the reader. The following sentence is an example of an explanation for a late reply:

> The brochure that you requested has just been revised. The new version arrived from the printer only this morning. I am sorry for the delay but hope that all your questions will now be answered by the brochure, enclosed with this letter.

When you receive an angry letter from a customer, you must first consider whether the customer's anger is justified. Were you negligent or tardy in serving the customer? If so, try quickly to apologize and put things right. If you feel, after reflection, that the customer is being unreasonable and you grow angry with the customer, delay answering the letter until you are no longer angry yourself. Your anger may pass more easily if you write a scathing letter, enjoy your "vengeance," then tear up the letter and throw it away. In business, the wastebasket is the only proper place for such foolish letters.

Suppose, for example, that a customer writes an angry, rude letter enclosing partial payment of a past due bill, denying ever having agreed to pay shipping and handling charges. You consult your files and find copies of your correspondence with him. You see not only that you told the customer about the charges but that he signed a form on which the charges are prominently displayed. You consider sending him photocopies of all the correspondence and explaining why the charges are just. You think about pointing out that the customer is either absentminded or incompetent or dishonest and that you have been competent and thorough at every stage. You consider these approaches but choose instead this more reasonable and fruitful approach.

> Thank you for your October 3 letter. I am sorry that this misunderstanding has arisen about the shipping and handling charges. I feel sure that the enclosed copies of our correspondence will clear up the misunderstanding and confirm our friendly and mutually beneficial business association.
>
> If you need further information about settlement of the amount past due, please feel free to call or write. I will be happy to assist you.

How should you respond when you receive an angry complaint and find that you *are* wrong? Restraint again is the best policy, even when the complaint is made rudely. The heat of anger might tempt you to write:

> All right, so we made a mistake. Everybody does. You don't have to get nasty about it.

But careful thought assures you that instead you should write something like this:

> Thank you for your June 17 letter, in which you explain why you deducted $12.75 from our October 1 statement. We have adjusted your account so that it now shows no balance due.
>
> We are sorry that we did not indicate that the September 15 shipment was to be sent prepaid. You may be sure that we will make every effort to prevent any such error from happening again.

Using Status Appeal

You have learned that the drive for personal recognition can sometimes be satisfied by attaining status. Usually attaining status requires doing something or owning something that the general public will notice and will perhaps admire or envy. Always remember, however, that "status" means different things to different people. The same object that is a status symbol to a reader of *Colonial Homeowner* might be a symbol of bad taste to a reader of *Nature First,* and vice versa. And both a reader of *Disco Dirt* and a reader of *Literary Quibbles* might find status appeal in objects of no interest to readers of the first two magazines.

As a business writer, you must be able to analyze the tastes and interests of your readers. Sales campaigns and other business writing today often exploit special, limited markets reached through mailing lists. Writers of such campaigns often use status as a standard sales "persuader"; this appeal may be either the main selling point or a strong supporting one. Whenever you see a sentence like the following, you will know that the writer is appealing to someone's desire for a suburban, middle-class status (the basis of many advertising campaigns):

> Be the first in your neighborhood to enclose your property with the prestigious Mayflower Colonial picket fence.

In business, your writing responsibilities can be expected to range far beyond sales letters. The appeal to status is a powerful tool in almost any type of communication. Suppose, for example, that you are writing a collection letter. You can appeal to the reader's desire to maintain his or her status as a good credit risk.

> We know that your present excellent credit rating is well earned and that you will want to maintain it. Thus we urge you to send us the overdue amount of $197.69 no later than March 15.

MAKING AND KEEPING FRIENDS

Without customers there could be no business. Building a large following of customers requires more than having a good product. As important almost as the product itself is the intangible known as goodwill—good public relations, or simply making and keeping friends. Goodwill, a psychological factor, motivates customers to do business with one particular company rather than its competitors.

We all develop skills for making friends in our private lives. In business, we can put the same skills to work for our firms. You can make friends for your firm by writing communications that *you* would enjoy receiving. The specific guidelines below will give you a fuller understanding of how to write communications that win friends for you and your employer.

Using a Conversational Tone

Suppose you go into a drugstore to buy shampoo, and the clerk, who is waiting on another customer, looks at you with earnest, dewy eyes and says, "Your entrance has been duly noted, and careful attention will be accorded you at the first opportunity." You would appreciate the thought that the clerk expressed, but you wouldn't warm up to him. You would think him strange indeed. Some business writers make the same mistake as the clerk: They use language that is outdated, stilted, and cold.

The successful business writer uses a conversational tone that talks *to*, not *at*, the reader. In the illustrations below, note the difference between the *talking at* and the *talking to* approaches.

> **At:** Please mark your reply for the attention of the writer.
> **To:** If you mark your reply for my attention, we'll be able to give you quicker service.
> **At:** Please reply at your earliest convenience.
> **To:** You would really help us by sending this information soon.

Being Cordial and Pleasant

There is nothing more irresistible than someone who meets you more than halfway, who *shows* you unmistakably that it is pleasant to be with you. Letters can express these cordial feelings on behalf of a firm almost as effectively as face-to-face meetings can express them between friends—and with equally beneficial results.

Compare the two examples below and see how the writer of one has taken the trouble to make the message cordial.

> We have approved your application for a Global Gas charge account. Your charge card is enclosed.
>
> Welcome to the select circle of Global Gas charge account friends! Your Global charge plate is enclosed. Please come in soon for a visit. If you have any questions about the many advantages of going Global, our customer service representative will be happy to answer them on the toll-free Global Friendship Line: 800-111-3287.

Which of the two messages would you rather receive?

Showing Concern for the Customer

Business is competition for customers. Although you may write to hundreds of customers, you must learn to make each customer feel important to you and your company. Otherwise your competitors will leave you behind.

Not all business communications are as businesslike as a bank statement. In fact, some communications are really social in nature—letters of appreciation, of congratulations, of sympathy. Like other social communications, these letters should reflect the writer's interest in individuals. Business writers must be alert for opportunities to send messages that show concern for the customer. First, however, the business writer must be sensitive to the customer's feelings at special times—whether times of joy or grief.

Even when writing a letter strictly for business, a skilled writer chooses words that show interest in the *reader*'s concerns. Note in the pairs of sentences below how the second version of each turns an ordinary communication into a message that shows interest and concern for the reader.

> In answer to your letter of June 5, the sale of high-intensity lamps can be increased by displaying them in the furniture department as well as in the lighting department.
>
> When we read your June 5 letter, we could see that you have a problem, all right; but we think we can help you solve it. Here's how: . . . (The letter goes on with the suggestion made in the first example.)
>
> Enclosed is a list of special discounts that we are offering you on goods purchased for your Christmas sale.
>
> We know that the Christmas sale is your biggest event of the business year, and we want to help make it bigger than ever. We have enclosed a list of special discounts on goods purchased for the holiday sale. You will find that every item on the list was chosen with you and your customers in mind.

Being Helpful

Writers who are quick to extend a helping hand, whether or not their firms will derive any profit from it, are earning dividends in goodwill and friendship. If your readers benefit from the extra time and effort you have voluntarily spent on their behalf, you are winning—for yourself and your company—steadfast and permanent friends. The following illustration shows how a request for information might be handled by an untrained writer, by an average writer, and by a master writer.

Untrained: Unfortunately we do not carry any shelving.

Average: We do not carry shelving, but we believe that the information you request can be obtained from North Side Shelving and Wall Systems.

Master: Our company does not carry shelving, but we have made some calls and have learned that you can get the information you need from North Side Shelving and Wall Systems, 233 North Almond Avenue, (343) 206-9854.

Keeping Friends

Good business writers always try to make new friends. However, *keeping* old friends is just as important as making new ones. There would be little point in gaining a new customer if, at the same time, you lost a steady, faithful customer.

All the psychological factors discussed here apply to letters written to present customers, but the real secret of keeping friends is to *tell* them occasionally how much you appreciate them and how important they are to you. The way to keep your customers is not by lavishing flattery on them, but by sharing sincere expressions with them:

Doing business with you, Mr. Gordon, is always a pleasure.

We appreciate your friendship, Miss Abrams, and we want you to feel free to call on us for help any time.

Ms. Parker, your long-time friendship is one of the things that makes us glad we're in this business.

Without good friends like you, Mr. Marotte, our business would be just a business. Sure, we like to make a profit. But there's more to it when we're providing dependable services to good friends like you.

COMMUNICATION PROJECTS

Practical Application

A. Rewrite the following sentences with a *you* point of view.

1. Next Monday we will offer outstanding bargains to charge-account customers.
2. We think that our beautiful mountain resort is unsurpassed as a vacation area.
3. Our all-leather shoes are better than the competition's because we make them better.
4. For the month of June, we will offer a 10 percent discount on our energy-efficient air conditioners.
5. We can show any dealer how to cut prices on tableware and still increase profits.

6. We are delighted to invite you along with other suppliers to an open house to tour our new research and testing lab.
7. We will let you know as soon as we complete repairs on your television.
8. Our forklifts are easy to operate and as reliable as our famous bulldozers—the industry standard.
9. Before booking your party, we need to know the size of your group, the date of arrival, and the kinds of facilities needed.
10. We know that our line of humidifiers and air cleaners can be sold in great volume and at high profit.
B. Read this letter and list the sales techniques used by the writer.

Dear Mr. Spenser:

Your Oswald Office Optimizer electronic data storage system is on the way to you now and will soon make your life in the office much more pleasant. The more you use the "OOO," the more you'll enjoy it. And your clerks and secretaries will love you for making their jobs so much easier.

In order to help you take full advantage of the Optimizer's many features, we will send an experienced Optimizer trainer. The trainer will work with your staff to make sure that they appreciate and can apply the Optimizer's many office abilities.

As a bonus to you, we are including with your Optimizer our new double-density magnetic disk. This will *double* the memory of your office record system at no additional cost to you. The Optimizer should meet your needs no matter how fast your business grows. Your efficiency will be the envy of your competitors for years to come.

We are sure that you will enjoy using the Optimizer, and we welcome you to the ranks of satisfied Optimizer users. Your growing success in the coming years will make us as happy as it does you.

Cordially yours,

C. Reword the following messages to give them a conversational tone.
1. Be cognizant that our advertising rates will be increased next January 1.
2. Only after a thorough review of credit references can we extend charge-account privileges.
3. Your interest in our undertakings is always noted and appreciated.
4. No single factor contributes more to our success than the patronage of our customers.
5. Routine owner maintenance procedures will be furnished upon receipt of a written request.
6. Your complaint has caused us to instigate a meticulous investigation.
7. Words cannot express our gratitude for your unswerving loyalty.
8. Should you desire a price list, rest assured that we will send one forthwith.
9. Procedures for placing an order are summarized in this booklet, the last section of which contains an order form.
10. This special collector's catalog contains a host of elegant yet affordable furniture treasures.

D. The Nostalgia Record Club sent inactive members a letter that began with the sentence below. Can you improve on it?

> In the past eight months, we have received no orders from you despite sending several attractive offers of all-time favorites.

Editing Practice

Plurals and Possessives   Write the correct forms, (singular possessive, plural possessive, or plural) for the words shown in parentheses.

1. The optician examined all the new (lens) with care.
2. Many (passerby) come into our store.
3. (Ms. Enderby) sales report showed outstanding effort.
4. A serious job hunter keeps several different (résumé) handy, each having (it) own slant.
5. The two (son-in-law) will open their new store in the Woodbridge Mall.
6. Not a day passes without (Peter) drinking several (cupful) of coffee.
7. The (man) department is on the ground floor.
8. Do you know (who) sales total was highest?
9. (Woman) dresses are the mainstay of the fashion industry.
10. The (Martz) have lived in this area since revolutionary times.
11. Our branch of the company is only one of many (subsidiary).
12. Barton's Appliance Center refuses all (c.o.d.)
13. All businesses have their (up) and (down).
14. The (Striblings) payment arrived ahead of time.
15. The (Jones) hardware company was founded in 1912.

Spelling Pitfalls   The paragraph below contains some of the words most often misspelled in business writing. Test yourself by finding and correcting any errors.

> We at Rodgers Tool & Die consider it a privelege to recommend Alfred Wilkins for the position of general manager of your West Coast factory. Mr. Wilkins has been out-standing from his first day of work for us. As personell director of Rodgers Tool & Die, I am responsible for the opperation of our managerial training program. I can say sincerley that we have never had another trainee who could rival the natural managerial talent of Alfred Wilkins. In the three years that Mr. Wilkins has worked for us, I have watched his progres with admiration. Since being placed in charge of our alumimum casting operation last July, Mr. Wilkins has improved both production and staff morale. Although we will find Mr. Wilkins difficult to replace, we understand that his decision to relocate to the West Coast is final. You are to be congratulated for being able to obtain his services.

Case Problem

A Compounded Error   Thomas Sparks typed a stencil, proofread it quickly, and ran off a thousand copies. Only then did Tom see the mistake—a misspelled word. Should this material with the misspelling be mailed to customers or not? What about all the paper and time wasted?

1. Should Tom say anything about the error or let the material be sent without mentioning it?
2. If he decides to say something, what should Tom say to his boss?

34
PLANNING: THE KEY TO EFFECTIVE WRITING

Businesses should plan for every contingency. Whether interest rates rise or fall, whether inflation worsens or eases, whether times bring boom or recession, businesses must be ready. The success of any business operation depends in large measure on planning and organizational skill.

Written communications are a major business activity. The vast and eager market for new word processing and electronic typewriting products shows the importance that businesses place on written communications. But recognizing this importance may not prepare you for the following statistic: Business correspondents write every year the equivalent of 300 letters for every person in the United States. This figure does not include the millions of direct-mail advertising pieces and interoffice memorandums and reports produced every year.

Like other business operations, written communications require careful planning and organization. In order to contribute to the success of your company, you will need the planning and organizational skills required by all business operations. Dashing off a letter can lead to serious mistakes in business. The purpose of this section of your textbook is to equip you with the planning and organizational skills that good business writing requires.

THE MECHANICS OF PLANNING

Writing business communications is a serious and difficult job. In order to write a successful business communication, the writer must first think through the task at hand. The writer must know *why* the communication is being written, *what* information is to be conveyed, and *how* the message can be made most effective. Only then can the writer hope to produce a clear, convincing message.

Determining Your Purpose

Every forceful business letter has a guiding purpose. Everything in the letter, from the salutation to the complimentary close, is done to achieve that purpose. Usually the purpose is simple: to persuade a supplier to extend further credit; to refuse a customer's request without causing offense; to order supplies; to promote goodwill; to sell a product. As you face each writing project, you would do well to begin by writing down the purpose of the letter or memo. You might make notations like the following:

> Request price quotation on resurfacing of company parking lot.
> Answer inquiry about our new line of infrared burglar alarms.
> Refuse Hamilton Associates extra credit requested.
> Get credit information from Dunn about RanchoRadio chain.
> Allow 30 days' credit to Merck & Columbia, rather than 90 requested.

Assembling the Information

After defining the purpose of your letter, your next step is to gather all the information necessary to achieve that purpose. Failure to do the proper research before writing a letter will force you to write another letter answering questions about the information you left out of the first letter. Although follow-up letters are sometimes unavoidable, usually the first letter should get the job done.

Suppose, for example, that you are asked to write a routine letter requesting a rush price quote on paper for the company's high-speed printer. You are told that the company will need 120,000 sheets of 16-pound paper in the next month. Knowing that 500 sheets make up a ream, you do a quick calculation and fire off this letter:

> Please quote us your best price on 240 reams of 16-pound paper.

Two days later you receive a letter from the paper supplier asking several questions: Does your printer, like most high-speed printers, feed long, continuous forms of paper to the platen? If so, are the forms packaged as rolls, or as folded and perforated sheets? How is the paper advanced—by friction-feed or pin-feed? Does your printer use traditional $8 \frac{1}{2} \times 11$ inch sheets, or the new $14 \frac{1}{2} \times 11$ inch style? Do you want plain white paper, or the more popular green-bar format? Do you really want the paper supplied in reams, or would the usual current packaging of 3,500-sheet continuous forms be acceptable? And what method of payment will you use?

Obviously, you should have assembled all the pertinent information before writing the letter, as in the following notes:

> Remind rush; request expedite (6)
> Need 35 boxes of 3,500 sheets (2)
> $14 \frac{1}{2} \times 11$ inch green-bar format (2)
> 16-lb economy bond (2)
> Request bid, not place order (1)
> Pin-feed, fan-fold (2)
> Company to open account if bid acceptable (3)
> Prefer charge paper to account unless credit review would delay delivery (4)
> Deliver loading dock on Wisner Avenue side of building (5)

Orderly Presentation

Your notes now cover all the necessary information. You have jotted them down, however, without regard to the best order for presenting the information in your letter.

The final step in assembling the information is to number your notes in the most logical order. (The numbers in parentheses after the items on page 284 illustrate how to present these topics. Note that all the paper specifications are grouped in item 2.) Now you have assembled the facts for a successful letter.

The Social Framework—The Letter As Visit

You now know *why* you are writing and *what* you must say, but something essential to a good letter is missing. It is the same thing that is missing from the following visit.

> Edward Moran walks into Lamont Office Supply and sees the proprietor, Ellen Lamont. He walks straight toward her and says, "Sixteen number two pencils, one electric pencil sharpener, twelve boxes paperclips, fourteen yellow legal pads."
> Ms. Lamont replies, "One hundred fifty-four dollars and ninety-five cents."
> Mr. Moran hands Ms. Lamont a check. Ms. Lamont hands Mr. Moran a package.
> Exit Mr. Moran.

Why is this scene so strange and unreal? Neither Edward nor Ellen acts as one human being does on meeting or visiting another. They both ignore the inescapable social framework of their business transaction.

Business letters that include only the necessary facts are lacking in the same way as the strange visit described above. Just like a visit, a good letter must contain the following social elements:

1. Greeting: "Good morning, Ms. Lamont."
2. Statement of purpose: "I stopped by because my office is almost out of supplies."
3. Business of the occasion: Edward specifies what he needs.
4. Leave-taking: "Good-bye, Ms. Lamont, and thank you for helping me so promptly."

This procedure is the outline for a personal visit. It could also be the outline for a visit by mail.

Greeting   The salutation is the greeting of a letter. If the letter is written to an individual, the salutation should be *Dear Mr. Bond* or *Dear Mrs. Baker*, not the cold *Dear Sir* or *Dear Madam.*

Purpose of the Visit   When making a personal visit, you follow the greeting with a statement of the purpose of the call. Similarly, after the salutation, the opening paragraph of a letter tells the reader what will be discussed in the letter. Here are three examples of opening paragraphs that state the purpose of the call:

> We are comparing the advantages of leasing and purchasing outright the construction equipment that we use in our major projects. Please send us financial and tax information about your leasing program.

Because a recent burglary has made us security-conscious, we would like information about your locks, alarms, and electronic surveillance systems.

We are delighted that your August 4 letter expressed interest in our company's debentures, and we have enclosed both a prospectus and some general information about our operations.

Business of the Call   This is the "meat" of your call. If, for instance, you were writing that letter ordering paper for a high-speed printer, here is where you would make the orderly presentation of the facts that the supplier will need.

Leave-Taking   Sometimes a letter has another paragraph that becomes a part of the leave-taking. Consider the following examples:

Your sales of our products have been outstanding, and we look forward to filling many more of your orders this year.

We have come to rely on the excellent sales that result from buying advertising time on your station.

Thank you for giving us an opportunity to explain our policy on discounts and back orders.

If you add another paragraph, there are two pitfalls to avoid. First, never use a participial closing, an *ing* expression, such as *Wishing you the best of luck in your new venture, we are . . .* or *Looking forward to seeing you at the conference, I am . . . .* Instead, simply write, *We wish you the best of luck in your new venture.* Or, *I am looking forward to seeing you at the conference.* Second, never offer thanks in advance. To do so would be presumptuous. Express gratitude for a favor or a service when you can acknowledge it, not before.

In all letters, the complimentary closing completes the leave-taking and affords the writer a last chance to set the tone of the communication. The choice ranges from the cold *Very truly yours* to the warm *Cordially.* An incongruous closing can be confusing, as shown in the following examples:

This is to inform you that we are seeking an eviction order to remove you from the offices in our building.

Cordially yours,

We are delighted that you have accepted our invitation to appear at the benefit dinner to be held in your honor.

Very truly yours,

BEYOND THE MECHANICS

A mastery of the mechanics of planning, although necessary for effective business writing, takes us only so far. If we stopped there, our letters would have limited influence on our readers. Planning must go beyond the mechanics if we are to influence our readers in ways more subtle than extending normal courtesies, stating the facts of our business, and presenting arguments. Courtesies, facts, and reasoned arguments are not the only ways in which a letter can guide the reader's judgment. Every letter carries with it a certain atmosphere. The techniques that follow will show you how to create an atmosphere in which your message will appear at its best.

Atmosphere Effect

All of us have had the experience of meeting someone and immediately responding with a judgment like "I'll bet he's smart" or, on the other hand, "Oh, what a bore!" If asked the reasons for our judgment, we probably couldn't offer any. We know only that something about that person registered an impression and we cannot reason it away. For want of a better term, we might call it the "atmosphere effect."

Let's see if we can make impressions, or atmosphere effect, work for us in our business writing, so that our readers will think, "I'd like to do business (or I like doing business) with this company."

First Impression   The reader's first impression on opening a letter might be "a quality firm," "a very ordinary company," or even "a shoddy operation." To create a desirable atmosphere effect, the stationery must be of good quality, the letterhead design attractive, the typing imprint uniform, the right-hand margin even, and the erasures not discernible.

Further Acquaintance   After registering the first impression created by your letter, the reader looks for confirmation. Correct and polished grammar, spelling, punctuation, word usage—all these are needed to solidify the "quality firm" first impression. Avoid using clichés like *attached hereto, the writer,* and *under separate cover;* otherwise, the atmosphere effect of your letter would be that of a stale, unprogressive business operation.

Paragraph Length   Paragraph length is a key factor in creating a good first impression. The length of paragraphs in a letter is so important to atmosphere effect that it merits special treatment (Section 37).

As you plan your letter, remember that reading can be *hard work.* You do not want your reader to open your letter, see a densely packed page, and think "What a job to wade through this!"

If you are a trained writer, your readers won't have to wade through the communications you write. Your paragraphs will not exceed eight lines. Writing more than eight lines will not be necessary if, after you have written five or six lines, you are alert to a shift in thought that would justify starting a new paragraph.

An added advantage is your command of the transitional words and phrases presented in Section 37. These expressions enable you to carry your reader smoothly from sentence to sentence and from paragraph to paragraph. For instance, where would you "break" the following overlong paragraph and how would you edit if for smoothness?

> We are sorry that you did not enjoy our Modern Magellan Nature Tour of the Amazon in Brazil last month. We feel that our literature gave you an accurate impression of what to expect. Our literature states, "Modern Magellan Nature Tours are not for the faint of heart. Our naturalist-guides take you to the most remote and primitive areas remaining on earth. You'll see all the natural wonders that the area of your choice has to offer. You'll look down from the peaks, look up at the waterfalls, and see eye to eye with birds and beasts." This does not say explicitly that you are going to wake up and find a thirty-foot anaconda in your tent. But everyone knows the anaconda is a snake native to

the Amazon. You must admit that faint of heart is exactly what you were when you discovered the snake curled around your cot. Of the forty-two members of your tour group, only one other complained. He felt the tour lacked excitement. We are now trying to arrange something more stimulating for him. I am afraid that we must refuse your request. We cannot arrange another tour for you or refund your money paid for the first tour. We clearly stated this no-refund policy in our brochures.

There are various editing possibilities for this paragraph, but one revision might go like this:

We are sorry that you did not enjoy our Modern Magellan Nature Tour of the Amazon in Brazil last month. We do feel, however, that our literature gave you an accurate impression of what to expect. As our literature states, "Modern Magellan Nature Tours are not for the faint of heart. Our naturalist-guides take you to the most remote and primitive areas remaining on earth. You'll see all the natural wonders that the area of your choice has to offer. You'll look down from the peaks, look up at the waterfalls, and see eye to eye with birds and beasts."

Although this does not say explicitly that you are going to wake up and find a thirty-foot anaconda in your tent, the anaconda is an animal native to the Amazon. Of the forty-two members of your tour group, one person said that he felt the tour lacked excitement. We are now trying to arrange something more stimulating for him.

I regret that we must refuse your request: We can neither arrange another tour for you nor refund your money paid for the first tour. As we indicated in our brochures, the price of the tour cannot be refunded.

Now that you know why you should not write long paragraphs, be careful not to overcompensate and create letters full of short, choppy paragraphs, like the following letter:

Our company sponsors a baseball team in the Little Amateur League.
We'd like an estimate on the cost of equipment for 30 players. The players are 9 to 11 years old.
We would need delivery by April.
Please include in your estimate the cost of shipping.

Unquestionably, the paragraphs are short; in fact, they are so short that the reader gets quite a bumpy ride. With minor changes, the writer could have written the letter as follows:

Our company sponsors a baseball team in the local Little Amateur League. Please quote us your best price on the cost of equipment for 30 players, aged 9 to 11. Be sure to include a home plate, bases, catchers' gloves, and first basemen's mitts.
Since the season opens in late May, we would need delivery by April 15 to our factory here in Montague. Please be sure to include the cost of shipping in your estimate.
We would appreciate receiving your quote by Friday, March 15.

Facilitating Action

We often tend to follow the course of least resistance. We do immediately the tasks that are easy and put off those that will take time and effort. Recognition of this human tendency suggests ways of increasing the chances of getting quick and favorable responses to your letters and memorandums.

Courtesy Carbon A courtesy carbon is a duplicate that is sent with the original copy of a letter. This device is effective when the reader can reply by writing answers in the margin of the carbon. The reason for its effectiveness is that the reader is relieved of the chore of planning and composing a reply.

For example, suppose you are president of a statewide photography association and are writing to give one of your colleagues a choice of dates for the annual meeting and to ask for recommendations for a speaker for that meeting. If you send a courtesy carbon, your colleague can answer your letter by writing in the margin *January 21* and *Dr. Crouch, Professor of Graphic Arts Technology at City College.* What do you think are the odds that you will get a quick answer?

When you assemble information for a letter that will be accompanied by a courtesy carbon, one of your notes should be *Call attention to courtesy carbon.* When you are composing that letter, be sure that you convey to the reader the no-work-involved idea. For example, say something like this:

> Just jot your comments in the margin of the enclosed carbon and drop it into the mail.

Enclosed Card or Return Slip Another method of bringing about a prompt and favorable response is to enclose a card or return slip with the letter. Suppose your firm, General Stamp and Record Club, is planning a new campaign for customers. Your

---

GENERAL STAMP AND RECORD CLUB
Joliet, Illinois

Yes! Please send me your latest money-saving catalog.

Name _____

Street _____

City _____ State _____ Zip _____

Positive words such as *yes* and *money-saving* help to make this return card an effective way to facilitate action.

job is to write the promotional copy that will go to thousands of people on a newly obtained mailing list. Management has decided to offer each potential new customer a free copy of the company's latest discount catalog. An addressed return card will be enclosed, postage-paid.

The psychological motivation for your letter will be financial gain—making money by saving money—and the spur to action will be a final paragraph such as this:

> You will start to save money just as soon as you fill out and return the enclosed card. No postage is necessary.

Attached Perforated Form   Still another means of facilitating action is to use a perforated return form that can be detached from the letter. This method can be just as effective as a separately enclosed slip.

When you write this type of letter, be sure to include a paragraph that calls attention to the form. For instance:

> To renew your subscription—and to receive a bonus of six free issues!—fill in the form at the bottom of this page, tear it off, and mail it *today.*

Watch That *If!*   Our readers almost always have a choice of what to say in response to our messages. When reminded of the choice, however, people are more likely to decide against a new proposal. The writer, therefore, should never remind readers that they have a choice. Always assume that the readers will act favorably. Your confidence will help make the case for your proposal.

If is the word that indicates a choice; and *if* is the word to watch. Perhaps we can best illustrate this bit of psychology by rewording the last two examples.

> If you would like to receive the latest edition of our money-saving catalog, just fill out and return the enclosed card. No postage is necessary.
> If you wish to renew your subscription—and win the bonus of six free issues!—fill in the form at the bottom of this page, tear it off, and mail it *today.*

The *if* in each of these examples suggests to your readers that they might *not* like to receive or wish to renew—and the chances are that they will go along with the *not.* Be aware that the *if* in each of these paragraphs is the word that risks losing the order.

Rereading Your Letters

Many employees never climb from the bottom of the salary heap because they do not add extra polish to the work they do. There is no future for people whose philosophy is "That's good enough."

A business writer's extra polish is the final check of each communication. After you finish your letter-writing stint for the day, reread the letters as if they were addressed *to* you, not sent *by* you. From this fresh and different viewpoint, you should be able to spot any errors you have made, either in language or in psychology. And although additional time and effort is involved, your intelligence tells you that only by spending that time can you produce a top-notch job.

COMMUNICATION PROJECTS

Practical Application

A. As a new employee of Woodtech Industries, you are answering a letter asking for safety information on Woodtech's new Treeshucker tree harvester. You have jotted the following notes; now number them in the order in which you should present them in a letter.

Mechanically strips branches
Insurance companies offer lower casualty and life charges for users
No longer a need for lumberjacks to climb trees
Strong enough to hold large tree in grasp after shearing
Bundles branches automatically
Automatic gyroscopic counterbalance keeps machine from tilting
Requires only one operator
Eliminates need for axes, rip saws
Overhead shield protects operator from falling objects
Outstanding safety record

B. Using the notes you have just arranged, write the letter.

C. Choose one business situation in which the use of a courtesy carbon would hasten a reply, and another in which it would not. Explain why for each situation. Also describe effective and ineffective situations for use of an enclosed reply card and state your reasons.

D. You work in the marketing department of the Starr Encyclopedia Company. You have been assigned to write a form letter for parents of grade school children explaining why they should buy the Starr Encyclopedia. Arrange the following notes in an order suitable for use as the outline for the letter. Then write the letter.

Encourages children to read
Provides stimulus for children's curiosity
Gives children an advantage in competing for grades
As useful and enjoyable for adults as for children
Costs less than competing encyclopedias
Easy payment plan
Edited by some of the nation's leading educators
Enables parents to say "Let's look it up" instead of "I don't know."

Editing Practice

Editing for Redundancies   Rewrite the sentences below, eliminating all unnecessary repetitions.

1. Since the game is sold out, we received a refund of our money back.
2. Please tell Cheryl that her present was funny and very unique.
3. At the next meeting, we will discuss the budget, agree on a plan, draft a contract, and etc.

4. It is the customary practice of this firm to pay all bills within ten days.
5. The new floor lamp lights and illuminates the whole room.
6. The innovative new design increased sales at once.
7. The fashion designer introduced her new line for the first time.
8. The engineer may perhaps be able to correct the malfunction.
9. Ms. Connors rarely ever arrives late for work.
10. Consumer goods depreciate in value quickly.

Making the Headlines   You are assigned to proofread the next issue of your company newsletter. Which of the following headlines would you rewrite? How?

> New Processors of Coal Speeds Production
> Engineering Chief Enjoys Redesigning Himself
> Company Soon Plans Prompt Reorganization

Case Problem

A Personal Matter   Steve Hull is writing a rush report for his supervisor when he receives a call from an old college friend, Terry Orlando. Terry wants to reminisce about college days. Steve realizes that Terry, a self-employed graphic artist, is not aware that personal calls during office hours are frowned on by management.

1. What should Steve say to Terry?
2. Why are personal calls usually taboo during office hours?

35 STRUCTURING PHRASES, CLAUSES, AND SENTENCES

In the writing of every message, words must be grouped with care; otherwise the reader will be confused. Small differences in the grouping or placement of words can make huge differences in meaning. Consider the following example.

> "Calling the meeting to order, the new toothpaste drew the praise of the marketing director."
> "When the meeting was called to order, the new toothpaste drew the praise of the marketing director."

While we can understand how a new kind of toothpaste might please the marketing director, even in this age of scientific miracles we can't expect toothpaste to call a meeting to order. In order to avoid the confusion and embarrassment that accompany such a ridiculous statement, the writer must learn to keep together words whose meanings belong together.

A combination of words that properly belong together is called a *thought unit*. When the writer correctly places the words of a thought unit, the reader can understand the meaning quickly and easily. When the writer incorrectly places the words of a thought unit, however, the reader may get a completely mistaken idea of the writer's meaning. Sometimes the mistaken idea is laughable, but in business such mistakes are more likely to cause serious problems, as in the example below.

> If our new Road Snuggler tires don't satisfy you, just fill out the enclosed warranty forms and send them back to us—we'll pay the postage.

The difference between the cost of mailing the warranty forms and the cost of mailing the tires would be considerable. Does the pronoun *them* stand for the papers or the tires? Let's hope that the writer's employer won't mind paying the postage for both.

The first step in developing your writing skill is to learn to structure phrases, clauses, and sentences in a way that makes your meaning unmistakable. This chapter will show you how.

WORDS IN THOUGHT UNITS

Sometimes a confusing, laughable, or simply false meaning is conveyed because a single word is not connected with its proper thought unit. The following advertisement is an example of a misplaced adjective.

> Gnarled women's walking sticks for sale at unbeatable prices.

Placement of the words seems to indicate that *gnarled women's* is a thought unit. But what woman wants to be described as *gnarled*? Women who answered this ad would be more likely to hit the salesclerk with a walking stick than to buy one. The correct thought unit is *gnarled walking sticks*. Therefore, the copywriter should have written the ad as shown below.

> Women's gnarled walking sticks are on sale at unbeatable prices.

Misplaced adverbs, too can lead to confusion:

> The idea for changing our sales emphasis came to me after I had opened the meeting suddenly.

The thought unit *opened suddenly* is incorrect. The idea *came suddenly,* and so the sentence should read as follows:

> The idea for changing our sales emphasis suddenly came to me after I had opened the meeting.

PHRASES IN THOUGHT UNITS

Incorrectly placed phrases, as well as incorrectly placed words, can change the meaning of a message completely. Expert writers edit their work carefully to see that they have placed phrases correctly. An expert writer would reject the following sentence:

> These repairs can be performed by anyone who has studied the technical manual in fifteen minutes.

Surely no technical manual could be studied in fifteen minutes, but someone who had spent weeks studying a technical manual might be able to perform a minor repair in fifteen minutes. The sentence on the preceding page, then, should read:

> These repairs can be performed in fifteen minutes by anyone who has studied the technical manual.

Now read the following classified advertisement and see the confusion that results from an incorrectly placed thought unit.

> **For rent:** Three-room apartment for married couple with balcony only.

This ad might bring to the real estate office only those couples who already have a balcony. But how many couples can there be who have a balcony but don't have an apartment? The ad should say:

> **For rent:** Three-room apartment with balcony for married couple only.

Two misplaced phrases can be even worse than one. Imagine receiving a direct-mail advertisement that contained the following sentence:

> Our glazed ceramic tiles are guaranteed to please you and your family without qualification in your bathroom.

The correct thought units are *tiles in your bathroom* and *guaranteed without qualification*. The following revision would be more likely to sell you the tiles:

> Our glazed ceramic tiles in your bathroom are guaranteed without qualification to please you and your family.

CLAUSES IN THOUGHT UNITS

Misplacing a car is a bigger mistake than misplacing a bicycle. We shouldn't be surprised, then, to learn that a misplaced clause can have even more devastating consequences than a misplaced word or phrase. How would the public react if the president of your company made this announcement?

> Our goal as a new company is to get the public to try our products until we become better known.

The sentence sounds as if once your company *is* better known, no one will want to try your products. Moving the *until* clause clears up the matter.

> Until we become better known, our goal as a new company is to get the public to try our products.

Because clauses pose a special hazard since they often are used to explain people's motives. Consider the statement below:

> Ms. Carr hardly noticed the flowers that were sent by her husband because she was concentrating so intensely on the labor contract she was negotiating.

Imagine the loving note that Mr. Carr must have sent with the flowers: "Thank you so much for concentrating intensely on the labor contract. I will always remember this as one of the most touching moments in our life together."

Unless Mr. Carr is a member of management or the labor union, he could hardly be expected to send his wife either the note or the flowers as described above. More likely the following sentence better describes the situation:

> Because she was concentrating so intensely on the labor contract she was negotiating, Ms. Carr hardly noticed the flowers that were sent by her husband.

Now Ms. Carr's reason for taking little notice of the flowers is easy to understand.

AMBIGUOUS *WHICH* CLAUSES

The word *which* is a pronoun that refers to another word in the sentence. If the word referred to is unclear, confusion will result. A mark of the expert writer is the ability to place a *which* clause with the word modified, explained, or amplified.

Here is an example of one misuse of a *which* clause—simple misplacement:

> We have a prospectus on gold bullion, which we send free of charge on request.

Placing *which* immediately after *gold bullion* alters the meaning of the sentence. Will the *gold* be sent without charge? The writer of the sentence above actually intended to say that the *prospectus* would be sent. Accordingly, the *which* clause should have been placed as follows:

> We have a prospectus, which we will send free of charge on request, that deals with gold bullion.

While clear and a definite improvement, the rewritten sentence would gain force and polish if the *which* clause were removed in favor of the version below:

> On request, we will send you our prospectus on gold bullion.

Another misuse of a *which* clause will be familiar to all. Although it is perfectly acceptable for *which* to refer to a broad idea rather than to a single noun, the writer must take extra care to see that the reference is clear. Pronoun reference in the sentence below is ambiguous:

> Further resistance to the board's decision will only jeopardize your position, which neither of us wants.

The problem here is that the *which* clause may refer either to the broad idea *will only jeopardize your position* or to the single noun *position*. Although most of us can guess the meaning intended, incorrect interpretations come more easily. *Which* seems at first to belong to the thought unit *your position*. If neither of the persons referred to wants the position, why should they care whether the position is jeopardized? A clearer statement of the sentence's intended meaning would be as follows.

> Further resistance to the board's decision will only jeopardize your position, and we do not want to jeopardize your position.

Here is an example of a *which* clause making clear reference to a broad idea:

> He predicted that the discussion would become heated, which is precisely what happened.

Used with care, *which* clauses perform valuable service. In the sentence below, the *which* clause achieves a degree of clarity that would be difficult to equal in as few words.

> Read clause 5, which contains the productivity standards under the new contract.

☐ Checkup 1

Look for thought-unit errors in each sentence below. Then rewrite each sentence to make its meaning clear.
1. Inflation and the trade deficit are misfortunes that will continue in the experts' opinions.
2. People often buy things with their credit cards that they don't need.
3. Blue men's jeans are on sale at fantastic prices.
4. The new cash registers are intended for new cashiers because they require little training.
5. I have found that giving the customer a chance to explain her needs while demonstrating the merchandise often helps to close the sale.

WHO DID WHAT?

In business communications, as in any other kind of communication, it is essential that the writer make it absolutely clear *who* has done or will do a specific thing. Sometimes, however, the writer confuses the thought by having the wrong person or thing connected with an action, so the meaning intended is not conveyed to the reader. Such a violation of the thought-unit principle can cause doubt or uncertainty as to *who* did *what.*

> If not satisfied, we will return your money.

Consider the thought unit *If not satisfied, we.* The meaning here is that *we* are the ones who might not be satisfied. If a customer returned the goods and asked for a full refund, the manufacturer could refuse on the grounds that the manufacturer was well satisfied with the customer's money. The correct meaning is immediately apparent to the reader when the sentence is revised.

> If you are not satisfied, we will return your money.

Occasionally, if the who-did-what principle is violated, the sentence becomes ridiculous, for an object, not a person, seems to be performing an action.

> Entering the room, the projector was seen teetering on the edge of the table.

The thought unit *entering the room, the projector* pictures the projector as entering the room. This kind of phrasing shows a serious lack of communication know-how. In this revision, a person performs the action:

Entering the room, Mr. Fosnough saw the projector teetering on the edge of the table.

Here is another illustration of this type of error:

After climbing to the top of the tower, the whole city lay spread before us.

What does the thought unit *after climbing to the top of the tower, the whole city* mean? How could a city climb to the top of the tower? Revised, the sentence would read:

After climbing to the top of the tower, we saw the whole city spread before us.

A who-did-what violation, sometimes called a *dangler,* does not necessarily occur at the beginning of a sentence. For example, note the error in the following sentence:

Mr. Paine saw the expected caller glancing up from his desk.

As written, the thought unit is *caller glancing up from his desk.* Was the caller at his own desk, and did he glance up from that desk? Was the caller glancing up from Mr. Paine's desk; and if so, what physical contortions were necessary to perform the act? Most likely, it was Mr. Paine who glanced up from his own desk. In order to eliminate the confusion, the sentence should be written like this:

Glancing up from his desk, Mr. Paine saw the expected caller.

INDEFINITE, CONFUSING PRONOUN REFERENCE

Each pronoun borrows its meaning from a noun. When the writer fails to make clear which noun a pronoun refers to, the pronoun loses its meaning or assumes an incorrect and unintended meaning. One vague or mistaken pronoun reference can garble an entire message. The careful writer checks each pronoun used in order to make certain that its reference is clear.

Confusing *He* or *She*

When you use either the pronoun *he* or the pronoun *she,* you must make certain that the antecedent is clear. If more than one man or more than one woman is mentioned in the sentence, the writer should take special care in placing the pronoun as near as possible to the person referred to. The following sentence leaves the reader wondering "Who returned from the conference?"

Mr. Mulloy sent Tom to hand-deliver the bid immediately after he returned from the engineering conference.

Does the *he* in this sentence refer to Tom, or to Mr. Mulloy? If the reference is to Mr. Mulloy, then the sentence should be revised as follows:

> Immediately after he returned from the engineering conference, Mr. Mulloy sent Tom to hand-deliver the bid.

If, on the other hand, Tom is the one who attended the conference, then the sentence should read:

> Immediately after Tom returned from the engineering conference, Mr. Mulloy sent him to hand-deliver the bid.

Indefinite *It*

Using the pronoun *it* to refer to something that is not immediately clear is a common offense. For example, read the following sentence:

> I will place the football in punt position, and when I nod my head, kick it.

Kick what? This indefinite *it* could result in a painful injury, wouldn't you say? The indefinite *it* must be replaced by the noun to which it should refer; and the revised sentence reads:

> I will place the football in punt position, and when I nod my head, kick the ball.

Inept writers tend to use the pronoun *it* as a catchall word, even if there is no antecedent to which the *it* can refer. Consider the use of *it* in this sentence:

> It is the positive sales approach that is the effective element in these letters.

In this example the *it* reference is vague and serves only to make the sentence wordy. Consider how much more effective the sentence would be if it were written like this:

> The positive sales approach is the effective element in these letters.

Other Indefinite Pronoun References

Speakers who are uncertain of their sources frequently use the careless "they say" as a reference. Writers who use the same vague reference are considered amateurish; in written communication references must be definite and exact. For example, read the following sentence:

> They say that sales will decrease during the next six months.

Who is meant by *they* in this sentence? A lack of definiteness earmarks a poorly trained writer. A precise writer would present the information this way:

> *Market News* reports that sales will decrease during the next six months.

Another type of indefinite reference that is puzzling and annoying to a reader is illustrated in this sentence:

> Although I dictated all morning on Tuesday, my secretary typed only two of them.

The slipshod *two of them* is vagueness carried to an extreme. Two of what? stories? letters? reports? news releases? A clear and explicit thought could be communicated by writing:

> Although I dictated all morning on Tuesday, my secretary typed only two of the letters.

☐ Checkup 2

Examine each sentence below. Ask yourself who did what, and look for the antecedent of each pronoun. If necessary, revise the sentence to make the meaning clear.

1. Dancing near the window, the Statue of Liberty was clearly visible from the rooftop restaurant.
2. Marie was analyzing Carolyn's production report before she left for the day.
3. Opening the office door, the elegant walnut desk made a strong impression on the visitor.
4. After revising the first two sections, the document failed to win approval.
5. John and Lois evaluated the new breakfast products while they were members of the laboratory staff.
6. They can't believe that profits are up again despite inflation.
7. Even though she conducted interviews all week, Ellen didn't hire any of them.
8. He submitted the policy and the medical form, but it was not signed.

COMMUNICATION PROJECTS

Practical Application

A. All these sentences fail to keep thought units clear. Revise the sentences as necessary.

1. Auditing is routine in business, but few of them find any irregularities.
2. To meet the sales quota, the garden tools should be displayed in the hardware department.
3. Susan told Karen that if her work did not improve, she would have to seek employment elsewhere.
4. Come to the special winter sale featuring electric women's socks.
5. After eating dinner, the clock struck two.
6. Covered with proofreader's marks, Mrs. Falstaff sent the first draft back for revision.
7. To establish a new brand name, a product should be labeled and packaged attractively.

8. The superintendent installed an electric heater near Mr. Grant's desk that used 220 volts.
9. To restore an antique to its original condition, caution must be exercised.
10. When the dispatcher talked to the messenger, he told him to deliver the package to the new address.
11. If you are a good cost analyst, teach it to the rest of the staff.
12. If damaged in normal use, you are covered for the replacement part by our guarantee.
13. She showed me the new benefits package, which sent me home in a better mood.
14. The secretary took the sales chart out of the file cabinet, which everyone had been waiting to see.
15. They claim that production will rise as soon as summer season begins.
16. In fine print, it gives many exceptions to the basic rules.
17. If allergic to antibiotics, the drug may be replaced with a sulfa formula.
18. Examined from all angles, Edward saw that the situation was not hopeless.
19. To replace the ribbon, lift the ribbon-release knob with your thumb and snap it onto the spool.
20. Our landlord owns this building and the one across the street, but he wants to sell it by the end of the year.

B. Revise any sentences as necessary to clarify thought units. Write *OK* for any correct sentences.

1. After traveling all day, our hotel was still miles away.
2. Susan will go if an emergency arises for the medicine.
3. In summer, Jane and I often take long walks near her beachhouse.
4. I could see the old office building where I used to work in the distance.
5. I only have been to Arizona once before.
6. Annette's boss will give her the promotion when she returns from the workshop.
7. Our graphics designer is only satisfied with first-class publications.
8. In your employee guidebook, it says to schedule vacation days at least three months in advance.
9. Only the regulatory board can rule on our application for a license.
10. The price of gasoline is hurting our company, which jeopardizes our salary increases.
11. The men drove out to see the warehouse in their compact car.
12. My brother has two weeks' vacation only this year.
13. While trapped in the elevator, Ms. Egmont's meeting was missed.
14. They will pay moving expenses if the company transfers me to Piedmont.
15. When writing adjustment letters, courtesy is essential.
16. She bought a gold man's wristwatch for her boss's retirement.
17. The new switchboard operator can almost handle 30 calls a minute.
18. Any product is eligible for the industry award that has not been submitted before.
19. He found the contract that he lost lying in the safe.
20. The construction superintendent rode up to the giant crane in a golf cart.

Editing Practice

Editing for Context   Some of the following sentences contain words that do not fit the context. Rewrite any such sentence. Write *OK* if a sentence is correct.

1. All of us agree that this machine has preformed very well.
2. The engineer surveyed the coarse of the new canal.
3. Please have a limousine meet Ms. Thatcher at the airport.
4. Our research center is idly designed for scientific work.
5. This invoice was dated in defiance with the new regulations.
6. Our investigation shows that the firm you inquired about is soluble.
7. Before beying a stock for speculative purposes, consider the risks.
8. Deliverance of the new desk is expected any day.
9. The salesman remonstrated the new equipment skillfully.
10. What is the deference between these two lists?

Proofreading a Memo   Although memos go to fellow employees rather than to customers or suppliers, clear and correct writing remains important. What corrections would you make in this memo?

> Renewvation of our office will be completed on December 30. New carpets will make the office both more attractive and quieter. Esculators from the lobby to the first three floors will reduce traffic in the elevators. Despite these improvements, we are certain to undergo some inconvenience in the process of adjusting to all the mollifications. I think that we could make the transition much easier if meetings were held to explain all the changes that are about to take place. I purpose that each department hold a meeting with the building supervisors to make certain that we all know what to expect. Holding these meetings now may save time and confusion in the long run.

Case Problem

The Annoyed Customer   Paula Waters is a temporary employee at Goodrum's Department Store during the holiday season. An angry customer comes in with a pair of curtains sold her by another clerk, who promised that the curtains would not fade or shrink when washed. Clearly, these care instructions were incorrect. The customer proceeds to vent her anger on Paula.

1. What should Paula say to the customer?
2. What can the store do to keep the customer's business?

A good letter flows smoothly. Unaware of sentences, clauses, and phrases, the reader moves with the continuous flow of ideas. Nothing interrupts the reader's concentration—no awkward phrases, vague references, or imbalanced constructions.

Because a good letter moves so easily for the reader, he or she may feel that the letter flowed as easily from the mind of the writer. But the letter as it first occurred to the writer was probably much the same as a first draft of anyone's writing—full of awkward phrases, vague references, and imbalanced constructions. The writer took the time, however, to look and listen for problems in the rough draft. Then the writer applied advanced writing techniques to eliminate the problems. By learning the advanced techniques presented in this section, you will learn how to take the roughness out of a rough draft. Once you master these techniques, the effort required to produce one of those "effortless," excellent letters will be greatly reduced.

WORD USAGE

Good word usage, as discussed in Chapter 5, requires knowledge and control of synonyms, antonyms, and homonyms. Trite expressions, pointless repetition, and negative words must be avoided.

Performing professionally as a writer requires enhanced control of word usage. You must learn to use planned repetition of words to emphasize important points. You must learn to listen for combinations of words in your own writing that produce harsh or awkward sounds. You must learn to find positive words to describe ideas that you want to be accepted.

Positive Words

Positive words are pleasant to hear and to read. They are words that create a receptive, pleasant glow in the mind of a reader. Consequently, the master writer deliberately uses words that produce this desirable psychological effect. The words in the following list evoke a positive response.

advancement	courage	genuine	satisfaction
agreeable	eager	gratify	success
attractive	earnest	happy	trustworthy
cheerful	easy	integrity	valued
comfortable	encourage	liberal	victory
compensation	enjoy	pleasure	warmth
confident	fortunate	profit	welcome
cordial	generosity	progress	willingness

Planned Repetition of Words

Although careless repetition of words shows lack of imagination, *planned* repetition can sometimes achieve striking emphasis of an important idea. Repeating the words *too* and *easy* in the following examples helps to emphasize each point in a unique way.

> Whether it was too little too late or too much too late doesn't matter. It was too late.
>
> He did the easy things the easy way, and he was easy to replace.

A major goal of any advertisement, of course, is to make readers remember the name and purpose of the product. Sometimes this goal is accomplished by simple repetition of the name, but clever ad writers manage to vary the order of the repeated words to prevent monotony. Consider the clever and purposeful transposition of words below.

> HEALTHTONE will add years to your life, and HEALTHTONE will add life to your years.

The Sound of Words: Neither Musical Nor Ugly

Excessive repetition of sounds can make tongue-twisters that disturb the reader. Even when reading silently, the reader cannot ignore sentences like:

> Send six Compu-Check calculators c.o.d.

Sound repetition can cause problems other than tongue-twisters. Although easy to say, the following sentence is hardly a pleasure to hear:

> When you steer your weary feet here at any time of year, you'll get a treat in the comfort of our store.

Avoid unpleasant sounds, but do not attempt to write business letters that sound musical or poetic. The letter, like everything else in business, has a job to do. For greatest effect, concentrate on that job.

Correcting the *This* or *Thus* Fault

A rather common writing fault is the use of *this* or *thus* to refer to an entire preceding thought. This lack of precision sometimes forces a reader to reread, or to recast, a sentence in order to comprehend the writer's meaning. The slipshod, inexact use of *this* and *thus* can spoil an otherwise fine writing performance.

> Our stockroom is overcrowded. This has existed since we moved to the new building on Juniper Street.

To what does the *this* refer? To the overcrowded *condition* of the stockroom. An accomplished writer would have stated the point specifically, as in the following:

> This condition has existed since we moved to the new building on Juniper Street.

Now read the following sentence, which shows another example of unclear word reference.

> Mr. Burr has passed the CPA examination, thus proving that he is competent to open a set of books for you.

Thus, as used here, is ambiguous. The thought could have been expressed more clearly and more directly as follows:

> The fact that Mr. Burr has passed the CPA examination is proof of his ability to open a set of books for you.
> Mr. Burr has passed the CPA examination and therefore is competent to open a set of books for you.

Correcting the *So* and *And So* Faults

Whenever you read a sentence that uses *so* or *and so* to introduce a clause, you can improve the sentence greatly by substituting a more meaningful conjunction. Note how weak the connection is between the two clauses in the following sentence:

> Melissa Kubek has worked for us for only one month, so we are unable to tell you much about her.

The first clause here gives the reason for the second. *Because* is a better choice for joining clauses that give causes and results. The following sentence is stronger, clearer, and more polished than the version above.

> We are unable to tell you much about Melissa Kubek because she has worked for us for only one month.

And so is not a two-word conjunction. It is two conjunctions used to form some vague connection between two clauses. Consider the sentence below:

> Mr. Quilby is an astute accountant, and so we recommend that you talk with him.

The first clause here is the reason for the second. We can make the relationship plainer by rewriting:

> Since Mr. Quilby is an astute accountant, we recommend that you talk with him.

ADVANCED BALANCING TECHNIQUES

Chapter 3, Section 19, stressed parallel structure. The basic principle presented was that parallel structure is a must for ideas of equal importance. A noun should be parallel with a noun (or a pronoun), an adjective with an adjective, and a phrase with a phrase. For example, if you say, "The new washing machines are quiet, efficient, and require little maintenance," the sentence seems to lose momentum halfway through. However, if you say, "The new washing machines are quiet, efficient, and maintenance-free," the sentence is strong to the end. Two adjectives are coordinated with a third adjective rather than with a clause. The sentence gains strength through balance.

Advanced balancing techniques apply the principle of parallel structure broadly. In the paragraphs below, you will study techniques of balancing comparisons, modifiers, verbs, prepositions, conjunctions, and clauses. Studying these paragraphs will help you to write with greater force and consistency.

Balancing Comparisons

Comparisons are balanced only if they are complete, and they can be complete only if they include all the necessary words. The omission of one necessary word can throw a comparison out of balance, as in the example below.

> Research shows that men spend more time looking at window displays than women.

As written, the sentence could mean that men spend more time looking at window displays than they do looking at women—a somewhat doubtful statement. The comparison lacks balance, as well as sense, because an essential word is omitted. One word can make the meaning of the sentence clear.

> Research shows that men spend more time looking at window displays than women *do* (or spend).

Here is another imbalanced comparison:

> Mr. Boyd's status in the Elko-Haber Corporation is more than a clerk.

This sentence lacks sense because essential words are omitted. An expert would write:

> Mr. Boyd's status in the Elko-Haber Corporation is more than *that* of a clerk.

An imbalanced comparison like the one below provides a chance for skillful revision.

> Owen can write just as well, if not better, than Allen.

Disregarding the words set off by commas, the sentence reads as follows: *Owen can write just as well than Allen.* Of course, no one would say "as well than." In the following revisions, the first is acceptable, but the expert will write the second, more polished sentence.

> Owen can write just as well as, if not better than, Allen.
> Owen can write just as well as Allen, if not better.

Balancing Modifiers

Omission of single-word modifiers can destroy balance in several ways. Such an omission can produce, for example, this illogical message:

> We need a traveling sales representative and stenographer.

Failure to write "a stenographer" makes "a traveling sales representative and stenographer" the same person. Dim, indeed, is the prospect of hiring a person who can serve in the dual capacity of traveling sales representative and of stenographer.

> The workers can't begin without a blueprint, welder, and electrical outlet.

Since the modifier is not repeated with each member of the series, a is understood as the modifier for all three members of the series. But "a electrical outlet" would never be acceptable writing. For balance, the series should read, "a blueprint, a welder, and an electrical outlet."

Do you see why the next sentence is out of balance?

> Mr. Frias speaks often of his parents, wife, and son.

The modifier his is the correct modifier for all three members of the series and is technically correct; however, a writer with a "feel" for language would repeat the modifier his to achieve a fullness and roundness of tone. See how much better the sentence reads this way:

> Mr. Frias speaks often of his parents, his wife, and his son.

Balancing Verbs

Structural balance demands that whenever the parts of verbs in compound constructions are not exactly alike in form, no verb part should be omitted. In the following sentence, this rule has been broken.

> I never have, and never will, file a dishonest tax return.

Failure to include the past participle filed with the auxiliary have causes the meaning to be "I never have file and never will file...." Since the verbs in this compound construction are not exactly alike in form, no verb part should be omitted. The sentence should read:

> I never have filed, and never will file, a dishonest tax return.

The following sentence shows the same kind of error.

> Your check was received yesterday and the machines shipped by express.

The omission of the auxiliary verb after machines structures the sentence like this: "Your check was received, and the machines was shipped." The plural noun machines requires a plural verb; therefore, the sentence must read:

> Your check was received yesterday, and the machines were shipped by express.

Balancing Prepositions

The omission of a preposition can also throw a sentence off balance. You learned in Section 18 that some words must be followed by specific prepositions. When two prepositional constructions have the same object, you must use, in each construction, the preposition that is idiomatically correct. Failure to supply the correct preposition results in a mismatch; note the following example:

Office workers should have confidence and respect for their supervisors.

In this illustration, *confidence and respect* is a compound, both parts of which are modified by the prepositional phrase *for their supervisors. For,* then, is the preposition used with both *confidence* and *respect.* But would anyone ever say or write "confidence *for* their supervisors"? The correct preposition to use with *confidence* is *in.* To be balanced, the sentence should read:

Office workers should have confidence *in* and respect *for* their supervisors.

Balancing Conjunctions

In oral communication, subordinate conjunctions, particularly *that* and *when,* can often be omitted without causing any confusion. In written communications, however, such omissions may destroy the balance of the thought units of a sentence and thus confuse the reader. Read the following example aloud:

Ms. Taft frequently talks about the time she had neither money nor position.

If this were an oral communication, the speaker could make the meaning clear by pausing slightly after the word *time.* The reader, however, might see the thought unit as "Ms. Taft frequently talks about the time she had," with the result that the words following *had* would not make sense. Therefore, the sentence should be written like this:

Ms. Taft frequently talks about the time *when* she had neither money nor position.

The following sentence may also be misread:

We investigated and found the furniture was shipped on May 2.

The reader may see "We investigated and found the furniture" as one thought unit. The subordinate conjunction *that* adds clarity and comprehension to the sentence:

We investigated and found *that* the furniture was shipped on May 2.

In informal writing, however, subordinate conjunctions may be omitted if their omission will not confuse the reader.

Yes, we do have the book you mentioned.

The omission of *that* in this sentence does not confuse the reader; therefore, the writer may omit the word.

Balancing Clauses

Another mark of writing distinction is to avoid incomplete (elliptical) clauses whenever failure to write the complete clause would confuse the reader. In the sentence "You are a better skier than I," the meaning "than I am" is clear. But listen to this:

> Did Mr. Trautman pay the bill or his accountant?

This sentence could be interpreted as follows: "Did Mr. Trautman pay the bill, or did he pay his accountant?" Both of the following revised sentences make the meaning clear; the second sentence, however, is more polished than the first one.

> Did Mr. Trautman pay the bill, or *did* his accountant pay it?
> *Who paid* the bill, Mr. Trautman or his accountant?

COMMUNICATION PROJECTS

Practical Application

A. Some of the sentences below repeat like sounds too often. Rewrite the sentences to make them sound less distracting to the reader.

1. Research shows that hodgepodge word usage produces messages that dissolve into unintelligible gibberish.
2. The coarse mesh, of course, can stand more pressure.
3. The proofreader missed the error; so, "Mr." remained misspelled.
4. A summary of some of his serious mistakes no longer seems necessary.
5. Frightening February inflation figures force us to feel that the effectiveness of the tough new price controls was only fancied.

B. Rewrite any sentence that disregards an advanced writing technique. Write *OK* for any correct sentence.

1. The manufacturer was concerned about the high cost of raw materials, so he raised the price of his merchandise.
2. Shall I report for duty next week?
3. Miss Watral never has, and never will, be able to understand the procedure that she should follow.
4. Our product is better, not equivalent, to theirs.
5. After the suit was altered, the customer would not take it nor pay for the alterations.
6. We need help with the typing, the checking, and the assembling.
7. Now that we have our manager's approval, we must think about ways to improve our present procedures.
8. The staff has great admiration and faith in Ms. Caldwell.
9. Our warehouse burned down my last visit there.
10. The order was for a television and rooftop antenna.
11. We all must work on this critical problem—and work and work and work.

12. When we transferred the files, several folders were misplaced. This was not Stephen's fault.
13. Mrs. Brando said that Peter's poster was more original than the other contestants.
14. She suggested that we retype, proofread, and all catalog copy be submitted by May 15.
15. The meeting was adjourned without our taking any action or making any decisions. This caused us to be dissatisfied.
16. Eileen ignored the whispered comments, thus proving that she had strong character.
17. Should Ms. Riordan sign the letter or Sally?
18. The company cannot afford to buy a computer, so it uses the time-sharing plan offered by the Our Time Is Yours Data Company, Inc.
19. I noticed the secretaries in the program were the same ones I had seen earlier.
20. Automation played an important role in revitalizing the company and will continue to.

C. Find and correct any sentences with weakness in thought-unit construction or in advanced writing techniques. Write *OK* for any correct sentence.
1. That's the report that I was waiting for.
2. Marilyn and Susan learned the value of setting goals and working toward them at an early age.
3. Ed was hurt in the accident, but all the others uninjured.
4. Having reached the limit on her company expense account, using her own money was the only way for Pamela to buy the ticket.
5. Did Bob get the promotion or Steve?
6. It stresses in your June 12 memo that initials must be placed on applications that have been approved.
7. Anna lives in Des Plaines, which is a suburb of Chicago.
8. Mr. Worth told Ben that he would need help to complete the company newsletter on time.
9. The cost of buying the machine would be less than renting it.
10. Having a broken lens, we returned the enlarger.
11. Anyone who works for that company is trained for just one job.
12. Did you order the cheese on rye or your assistant?
13. Terry understood the problem he had been studying suddenly.
14. They asked questions, but did not get answers, from Mr. Davis.
15. Compared with the other applicants, Alfred seems very well qualified; thus he was offered the job.
16. We have bought airline tickets from that agency ever since they first opened.
17. She appears self-possessed, but all the others panicky.
18. Mr. Whitaker shows more interest in Laura's project than he does Gary's.
19. Subtracting losses resulting from market fluctuations, the net annual profit has dropped sharply.
20. She was our most trusted adviser, so we expected more of her.

Editing Practice

Editing the News   Edit and rewrite the following excerpts from your company's "house organ."

1. Mr. Stevens became owner of the company in which Andrew Carnegie first enjoyed success in 1963.
2. The company personnel department will give its last battery of tests before beginning to interview applicants for the position.
3. The following article is one in a series written by Margaret Soames, a clinical psychologist for the *Customer Service Weekly*.
4. The auditors are on their way to the warehouse in a chartered plane.
5. Some geologists came upon signs of an unknown petroleum deposit hiking through the woods.

Spelling and Pronunciation   Can you find any spelling errors that were probably caused by mispronunciation?

> The visiting efficiency expert aired when he said that the operators waste 20 percent of their time at the terminals. There are times when the operators must wait for the central processor to complete a computation. Although the operators are idle during those periods, they have no choice. They have too little time to start any other task before the terminal is active again.

Case Problem

A Better Plan   Wilma Spencer keeps the payroll records at the Richman warehouse. Previously she had done the same work for Osmond Transfer Company. Wilma thought that the records at Osmond were set up much better and that the system of keeping records at Richman, therefore, should be changed.

1. Should Wilma present these ideas to her present employer?
2. How can she do so without being offensive?

37 WRITING WITH POWER

Some writers have the power to influence the thoughts and actions of readers. Writers who have the power to influence are always in demand in the world of business. In order to sell products, promote goodwill, and serve the needs of customers, businesses must be able to use words to influence people every day. The writer who has the power to make routine communications convincing and persuasive is invaluable to any business.

How do some writers succeed in writing with power? They master the essentials of English, use advanced writing techniques, and learn to use psychology in their writing. The most powerful writers add to these strengths the ability to recognize and eliminate major weaknesses, to control sentences and paragraphs, and to structure for emphasis. Studying this section will add these strengths to your arsenal and bring you nearer the goal of being an invaluable business writer.

THE MAJOR WEAKNESS

When a written communication is inadequate, the reason can often be traced to either of two kinds of weaknesses: (1) using the passive voice instead of the active voice; and (2) shifting in voice, tense, person, or number. The examples in the following paragraphs will help you learn to recognize and eliminate these two major weaknesses.

Active Versus Passive Voice

Voice is that property of a transitive verb that shows whether the subject acts or is acted upon. Any verb phrase composed of a past participle with a "being" verb helper is in the passive voice: *will be shipped, has been sent, was done, is frozen*. In the active voice, the subject is the doer of an action; in the passive voice, the subject is acted upon.

> Gibson sent us a message. (Active voice)
> A message was sent to us by Gibson. (Passive voice)

The active voice expresses thoughts in a stronger, livelier way than does the passive voice. Compare these two sentences:

> Your order will be shipped on Monday, July 8. (Passive voice)
> We will ship your order on Monday, July 8. (Active voice)

Both sentences state the same information, but the active voice sentence is more direct. In the following pair of sentences note that the sentence using the active voice makes a stronger selling point than does the weak, passive sentence.

> Last year our machines were sold to 75 out of every 100 business firms in Detroit. (Passive voice)
> Last year, we sold our machines to 75 out of every 100 business firms in Detroit. (Active voice)

Use the active voice to help strengthen your business communications.

Shifts in Voice, Tense, Person, or Number

In a sentence containing more than one clause, the writer can best maintain a consistent, forceful flow of information by keeping to the same voice, tense, person, and number. Clauses in the same sentence should, of course, be closely related. Any shift in voice, tense, person, or number weakens the relationship between clauses.

When a paragraph contains two or more closely related sentences—as good paragraphs do—the writer should permit no shift in voice, tense, person, or number between such sentences. Like shifts between clauses, shifts between closely related sentences weaken the writer's attempts to persuade and convince the reader.

Shift in Voice   When one verb in a compound or a complex sentence is in the active voice, the other verb or verbs must also be in the active voice. Using the active voice in one clause and then shifting to the passive voice in another clause, or vice versa, weakens the communication.

> In winter the file clerks freeze with the cold, and in summer they are stifled with the heat.

The shift from the active voice in the first clause to the passive voice in the second clause diminishes the strength of the statement. Both verbs should be in the active voice, or both verbs should be in the passive voice. Since the active voice is the stronger, the sentence should read:

> In winter the file clerks freeze with the cold, and in summer they stifle with the heat.

Shift in Tense   A verb has six principal tenses—present, past, future, and the three "perfects"—each tense showing the time of an action. Writers can make their communications stronger by avoiding a shift in tense unless an actual difference in time must be indicated.

> Edelman uses such simple language that any reader will easily understand his meaning.

This sentence shows a shift in tense, from present tense in the first clause to future tense in the second clause. The statement can be strengthened by avoiding the shift as follows: "Edelman uses such simple language that any reader easily understands his meaning."

Shift in Person   A shift in person within a sentence is such a glaring weakness that any reader notices it immediately. For example:

> I should like to know the name of a branch store where you can get service within twenty-four hours.

The first person *I* is the subject of the first clause; the second person *you* is the subject of the second clause. The shift is weak because it is illogical. Why should *I* want to know where *you* can get fast service? The sentence should read:

> I should like to know the name of a branch store where I can get service within twenty-four hours.

Shift in Number   A shift in number from singular to plural, or vice versa, weakens a message because this type of shift, like the shift in person, conveys an irrational message.

> A communicator must be well trained, or they will not be able to build goodwill.

Communicator in the first clause is singular in number, but *they,* which refers to *communicator,* is plural in number. To add strength to the sentence by avoiding this shift, you should write:

Communicators must be well trained, or they will not be able to build goodwill.

SENTENCE AND PARAGRAPH CONTROL

A sentence, in most cases, should state a single thought. In a paragraph, sentences should be joined so that the series of thoughts expressed supports a single, more general, and more important idea. If sentence structure is faulty or if paragraph organization is poor, the whole communication will fail. The reader will wonder why the writer bothered to put such a boring, scarcely related collection of words on paper.

Unless the writer can shape sentences and paragraphs to perform their tasks of asserting and supporting ideas, then the writer is wasting his or her own time as well as the reader's. Without sentence and paragraph control, the writer is powerless.

Sentence Control

Proper sentence control generates writing power. In order to exercise sentence control, the writer must learn that (1) each sentence must contain only one main thought, (2) extremely long sentences bury the main thought, and (3) a series of short sentences makes the asserted thoughts seem disconnected.

One Main Thought   In Chapter 4, Section 20, you learned not to use a comma to join two separate and distinct thoughts. From the viewpoint of writing power, the comma-for-period fault weakens a message because more than one main thought is expressed in a single sentence, as in the following example:

We are interested in your views on merchandising, we need to do some more research before we can present our own opinions.

The correct punctuation, of course, is a period. However, other alternatives for correcting the comma-for-period fault include (1) using a coordinate conjunction, (2) using a semicolon or a semicolon plus a transitional expression, and (3) using a subordinate conjunction to make one of the thoughts dependent on the other. These methods are more advanced techniques than the one of simply writing two separate sentences, and expert use of them produces more effective communications. For example, compare the following revisions of the example given above, and note how the relationship between the two thoughts is clarified in the last three revisions.

We are interested in your views on merchandising. We need to do some more research before we can present our own opinions.
We are interested in your views on merchandising, but we need to do some more research before we can present our own opinions.
We are interested in your views on merchandising; however, we need to do some more research before we can present our own opinions.
Although we are interested in your views on merchandising, we need to do some more research before we can present our own opinions.

More about the use of transitional expressions is given on page 315, and the proper subordination of thoughts is explained on pages 315 and 316.

Proper Length   Beyond a certain length, sentences seem to grow weaker with each added word. The frustrated reader may begin to struggle with an extremely long sentence and may wish that the writer had chopped something off.

> Thank you for informing us in your letter of October 30 that you have still not received the illustrated *Manual of Landscaping* that we shipped to you by parcel post on or about last October 1, but there's no need for you to worry because we are going to start inquiries with the post office and perhaps file an insurance claim, meanwhile sending you another copy of this truly spectacular textbook on the techniques of successful landscaping.

The reader has to swallow far too many words merely to learn that another copy of the desired book will be sent. The writer was correct, of course, to point out that the post office is to blame for the delay. The writer could have expressed that thought better, however, in a separate sentence. Study the following revision:

> Thank you for informing us that your copy of the *Manual of Landscaping* has not reached you. We are mailing you a new copy at once and asking the post office to make certain that this one reaches you soon.

On the other hand, a succession of short sentences weakens writing power because the reader is jerked along from thought to thought.

> We received your letter. It arrived this morning and was most welcome. All the sales representatives read it; they liked your suggestions. Your letters are always friendly. We enjoy hearing from you.

An expert would never write such a stop-and-go, stop-and-go communication. Instead, the expert would smooth out the bumps like this:

> Your letter arrived this morning, and all the sales representatives liked your suggestions. Your letters are always so friendly that we enjoy hearing from you.

In some situations, the planned use of short sentences can be very effective. Short sentences are useful to bring out a series of important facts, to emphasize a point, and to break up a series of longer sentences. The following excerpt from a sales letter illustrates the planned use of short sentences.

> The Eureka camera is made especially for quick-moving action photography. Its motorized film-advancer prepares you for your next shot a fraction of a second after you press the shutter. You just focus and shoot! And its easy-open back permits you to insert a new cartridge faster than you can in any other camera. You can reload in 15 seconds! Best of all, the Eureka is equipped with a computerized flash that works on a rechargeable battery. You have a built-in flash! See your dealer for complete details.

Paragraph Control

Achieving paragraph control requires the writer to focus on one main idea and make certain that all sentences in the paragraph help to support the main idea. In addition, the writer must avoid overlong paragraphs and make smooth transitions from one paragraph to the next.

The first sentence of a paragraph should be written with the paragraph's idea in mind. The writer must know where the paragraph is going before attempting to guide the reader there. If the writer does not know what conclusion the paragraph is to have, then the writer should stop writing and start thinking.

Proper Length   In general, a paragraph should not be longer than six to eight lines. If the development of one thought requires more than six to eight lines, the writer should carry that thought over to another paragraph. To help the reader bridge the gap between paragraphs, the writer can make use of the transitional words and expressions listed below.

Smooth Transitions   The reader of a polished business communication is carried along by interest in its message, by the rhythm and momentum of its words, and by the seamless transitions between paragraphs. The knowledgeable writer ensures the smooth flow of ideas by using appropriate transitional expressions. Here is a partial list of such expressions:

accordingly	however
after all	in addition
again	likewise
also	meanwhile
at the same time	moreover
besides	nevertheless
consequently	notwithstanding
equally important	on the contrary
for this purpose	on the other hand
further	similarly
furthermore	still
hence	therefore

STRUCTURING FOR EMPHASIS

Suppose you gave a friend a necklace of identical beads with a single, striking jewel. If, when your friend tried on the necklace, she wore the jewel at the back of her neck where no one could see it, what would you think? Undoubtedly you would think that the jewel should be displayed in the most prominent place. Your friend would be a fool not to position the jewel so as to emphasize it.

Written communications are more effective when the writer emphasizes the most important points. After identifying the most important points, the writer must structure sentences so that the reader will immediately understand which points are most important. A business writer who learns the principles of emphasis will be able to display the most important points prominently, adding power to every communication.

Proper Subordination of Ideas

Proper subordination of ideas depends on the ability to determine the difference between an important idea and a lesser idea. The important thought is expressed as a main clause, and the lesser idea is properly written as a subordinate clause. The principle can be remembered as follows: "Main idea—main clause; subordinate idea—subordinate clause." Consider the following sentence:

I had just started to write up our bids when your revised specifications arrived.

Which idea is more important, the fact that "I had just started to write up our bids" or the fact that "your revised specifications arrived"? The arrival of the revised specifications is the more important idea; therefore, it should be expressed as the main clause. The sentence should read:

Your revised specifications arrived just as I had started to write up our bids.

Coordination Versus Subordination   When a sentence contains two ideas of equal importance, divide the sentence into two main clauses. For example, consider the following:

The work is difficult, but the rewards are great.

On the other hand, writing power is diluted when the writer fails to see that the thoughts belong, not in two main clauses, but in a main clause and a subordinate clause. Note the following example:

There were other candidates, and Ruth received the promotion.

This sentence places equal stress on what the writer considers to be two main ideas. The emphasis should properly be placed on Ruth's receiving the promotion, even though there was competition. For force, as well as for clarity, the sentence should be written:

Although there were other candidates, Ruth received the promotion.

Interrupting Expressions   Unwittingly, some writers destroy the forcefulness of proper subordination by writing the lesser idea as an interrupting expression. For instance, read this sentence:

You are, considering the risks involved in such an investment, very fortunate.

The main thought, *you are very fortunate,* is interrupted by the lesser idea, *considering the risks involved.* This interference with the flow of the main thought is so distracting that the force of the statement is completely lost. Properly written, the sentence reads:

Considering the risks involved in such an investment, you are very fortunate.

Variety in Sentence Structure

Communications that lack variety lack interest. One sure way to produce a dull communication is to use only simple sentences. Equally dull is a communication with all compound sentences, or one with all complex sentences. Variation in type of sentence is another method of emphasizing important ideas. Variation in connectives and transitional expressions also helps place emphasis where it belongs. Study the following paragraph:

> Your new Megalith Motors Diesel Transport Truck costs more and offers more features. The diesel engine is durable, and you will enjoy its trouble-free operation. The engine uses less fuel while idling, and uses less fuel on the road. Diesel trucks stand up to years of wear and have high resale value. You chose the right truck, and the years will prove it.

Too many compound sentences and too many *ands* make the above paragraph dull. See what an improvement structural variety makes in the version below.

> Your new Megalith Motors Diesel Transport Truck costs more, but it offers more features too. Since the diesel engine is durable, you will enjoy years of trouble-free operation. You will use less fuel both when idling and when on the move. Furthermore, because diesel trucks stand up to years of wear, they have high resale value. The years will prove that you chose the right truck.

Emphasis by Climax

In almost any series—of words, of phrases, of clauses, or of complete thoughts—the order of presentation is vital. Unless each item in the series is of equal importance, you owe it to your reader to rank the items in importance. You should usually present the least important item first and build to the most important. Consider the contrast between the effects of the two series below:

> Evans was determined to make the project a success no matter what the price—his weekends, his career, even his life.
> Evans was determined to make the project a success no matter what the price—his life, his career, even his weekends.

Emphasis by climax is what makes the first version powerful and the second ridiculous. Whenever a piece of writing includes a series, the writer can add power by finding a sequence that builds toward the most important item.

Emphasis by Mechanical Aids

Oral communication lends itself to dramatic gestures that emphasize important points. Shouting, pounding on a desk, and stamping a foot are effective only if they are seldom-used devices that contrast with normal conversation. Even changes in tone or pitch—whispering, for example—can be used to create striking emphasis.

However, overuse of emphasis can make so much noise, can be so distracting, that the listener cannot hear the words. Thus overemphasis often makes the message incomprehensible.

Written communication, too, lends itself to ways of emphasizing important points. Because the means are entirely mechanical, the writer must decide what to emphasize—and also the degree of emphasis desired. To emphasize a point, the writer can:

> Underline.
> Tabulate.
> Use dashes or a series of dots.
> Use exclamation points.
> Set words or expressions in all-capital letters.
> Type important words in red (if available on the typewriter ribbon).

If the mechanical means of creating emphasis are used excessively, contrast—and therefore emphasis—is lost. Knowing this, expert writers rely more on writing power than on mechanical devices to shape their thoughts and to convey their messages in a clear, forceful manner.

The Danger of Power Failure

Now that you have studied writing power, a word of warning to prevent power failure: Mastery of craftsmanship techniques will not make your writing effective unless you use language that is simple, direct, and clear. The purpose of communication is to convey a message, not to parade an extensive vocabulary.

Simple language is the most powerful, as the following example from *Think* magazine (July-August 1964) shows. During World War II, America's Asian and European enemies possessed strong air forces. Because President Roosevelt was concerned about possible air attacks on Washington, one of his staff prepared a memorandum about air raid precautions:

> Such preparations shall be made as will completely obscure all Federal buildings occupied by the Federal Government during an air raid for any period of time from visibility by reason of internal or external illumination. Such obscuration may be obtained either by blackout construction or by termination of illumination. This will, of course, require that in building areas in which production must continue during the blackout, construction must be provided that internal illumination may continue. Other areas may be obscured by terminating the illumination.

Annoyed at this gobbledygook, Roosevelt revised it as follows:

> Tell them that in buildings where they have to keep the work going, they should put something across the windows. In buildings where they can afford to let the work stop for a while, they should turn out the lights.

COMMUNICATION PROJECTS

Practical Application

A. Rewrite the following items in accordance with the directions given in parentheses.

1. My plane was late, and I missed my first appointment. (Subordinate the less important idea.)
2. Gary had been warned by Mr. Foley that the excuse would not be accepted again. (Change to active voice.)
3. Ms. Rinehart occupies a spacious office. It is on the seventh floor of our building. (Combine into one forceful sentence.)
4. Is your automatic collator out of commission, and does it need some small repairs? Call us, and we will come and give it special attention. We are most thorough, and our prices are reasonable. (Rewrite and vary sentence structure.)
5. When conferring with the new reporter, the editor told her that reporters sometimes write stories they did not choose; but write each story accurately, and you will get increased skill and better assignments. (Correct any shift in voice, tense, number, or person.)
6. I was talking on the telephone at work, and I noticed smoke curling from the air vent. (Subordinate the less important idea.)
7. My Spanish is still reasonably fluent; this is my first visit to Puerto Rico in ten years. (Give major importance to the first clause.)
8. The electronic computer is a triumph of technology. They originally occupied city blocks, but today they are small enough to fit on your desktop. (Correct any shift of voice, tense, and so on.)
9. The defendant is only twenty years old and she has not been proved guilty. (Give major importance to the fact that the defendant has not been proved guilty.)
10. Filing is an essential office activity. It saves work. Accurate filing is accurate finding. (Combine into one sentence, with proper subordination.)

B. Reword the following sentences to make them more powerful.

1. Important communications must first be outlined, or it will be ineffective.
2. You asked for immediate delivery of the signed contract; we are sending it today by special messenger.
3. Our expert electronics technician removed pieces of dust from the printed circuit board, and your calculator is as good as new.
4. The customer comes into the store and orders his alarm system. Afterward, he spent an hour discussing our credit agreement.
5. The attorney expected to face arrest, conviction, and suspicion.
6. Vivian's industrious attitude was pleasing to her supervisor, and he complimented her on it.
7. This new microwave oven will be discovered to be the best improvement in your employee lunchroom.
8. Each and every one of us, being convinced that Stan is innocent, is more than willing to defend him against those charges.

9. Everyone thinks that being successful depends on getting a lucky break.
10. The recommendation having been made by Ms. Forest, she should explain it.

C. These sentences review the writing techniques presented in Sections 35 and 36. Rewrite all the sentences.

1. Office conversation is enjoyed by Ted as much, if not more, than by other accountants.
2. We interviewed a lot of secretarial help, but hired only one of them.
3. Our firm has built a beautiful office building on Lincoln Boulevard that is so bright and airy.
4. Mr. Dewitt told us that his father died before he was born.
5. Authoritarian management has and always will be notorious for its stifling of individual initiative.
6. We noticed the invoice was for the wrong model.
7. Demand for fuel-efficient vehicles will increase yearly, which is the forecast of experts in the automotive field.
8. In selling rare coins, we found that newspaper ads resulted in more leads than using direct-mail letters.
9. Before accepting delivery of a new office machine, the installation technician should give a demonstration.
10. We have all been reading and been dismayed by the increasingly serious shortage of fossil fuels.

D. Choose the word that best completes each of the following sentences.

1. From Edna's remarks, we (implied, inferred) that she will soon choose her administrative assistant.
2. Please include a postage-paid return (envelop, envelope) with the letter to Tangible Industries.
3. In our haste to (expand, expend) our operations, we overlooked some depressing economic indicators.
4. The committee will, we hope, use our recent report for (reverence, reference).
5. When I see her (poring, pouring) over her ledgers, I do my best to remain quiet.
6. Every time Felix chairs the meeting, he (waists, wastes) half an hour with his boring anecdotes.
7. The box included (through, thorough) instructions for assembling the packing carton.
8. Please make up your mind—this is no time to (waver, waiver).
9. The attorney later confided to her client her fear that the only (voracious, veracious) employee might not be believed.
10. The findings of the two independently conducted (polls, poles) were exactly the opposite.
11. A 12-foot (petition, partition) separates Donald's office from Marianne's.
12. Clara's (ingenuous, ingenious) solution to the perplexing problem was a surprise to everyone—except Clara herself.
13. After three weeks of drafting blueprints, I am thoroughly (board, bored) with straight edges and compasses.

14. Even though Ms. Olivetti is out of town, someone should (apprise, appraise) her of these shocking events.
15. The land in which we invested is on the (border, boarder) of Wesley Boulevard and Anselm Avenue.
16. Our budget for (capitol, capital) expenditure for next year has been cut in half.
17. The federal government regulates (interstate, intrastate) commerce; (interstate, intrastate) commerce comes under the authority of each state.
18. Infant (morality, mortality) is on the rise because parents neglect to have their children given the standard immunization shots.
19. Her claim is that (no body, nobody) of employees can represent her without her consent.
20. The (officious, official) version bears a distinctive logotype on the copyright page.

Editing Practice

The Correspondence Supervisor   Edit and rewrite the following paragraph.

> Only yesterday did the new edition of *Successful Management* come off the presses. Your letter of inquiry came just as I was about to mail your copy in fulfillment of your prepublication order. In answer to your other question, yes, we will be publishing books on marketing and advertising strategies. We are enclosing a catalog and price list of all our books for business executives.

Power Failure   The following sentences are an illustration of power failure. How would you have written this message?

> The annual incursion of wayfarers from other national jurisdictions has once again surfeited the metropolitan municipality with myriad legion of eager shoppers on continuous exploratory missions. Our merchants could not be more ecstatic, but everyone else is already quite enervated with directing the invading hordes to destinations of their choosing.

Case Problem

Remembering Names   How well do you remember names after an introduction? Six of your classmates will select assumed names and will introduce themselves to you. You may ask one question of each classmate as you try to fix an assumed name in your memory. Then, using the pseudonyms, introduce each student to another student.

CHAPTER 7

WRITING BUSINESS LETTERS AND MEMOS

38
STYLE
FOR MEMOS

Communications *within* organizations can be as complex and important as communications with the world outside. Often two employees in different departments of a company, for example, must agree on a position before either of them can write to one of the company's customers or suppliers. Unless they reach agreement themselves before entering into communication with an outsider, employees of a company may unknowingly make conflicting statements. Such poor internal communications are certain to confuse the outsider and embarrass the employees. When the matter is important or complex, employees within a company will want to commit to paper any decisions, agreements, and recommendations made among themselves. This is what makes the memorandum, or *memo*, as essential a part of business life as the business letter.

FORM OF THE MEMO

Printed interoffice memo forms make it easier both to write and to read memos. Most companies use memo forms printed in two sizes: $8\frac{1}{2} \times 11$ inches and $8\frac{1}{2} \times 5\frac{1}{2}$ inches. Often, printed memo forms come in convenient snap-out sets. These provide an original for the addressee, copies for two or three other intended readers, and a file copy for the writer. A few companies still choose to produce interoffice memos on the typewriter as the need arises. These companies give up the convenience of the snap-out forms but do gain the advantage of complete flexibility—preparing as many or as few copies as are needed for every occasion.

The heading of a printed memo form, such as the one on page 325, usually includes (1) the name of the company, (2) the title *Interoffice Memorandum* (or *Interoffice Memo*), and (3) the guide words *To, From, Subject,* and *Date*. In a large company, the heading may also include *Department, Location,* and *Telephone Extension*. (Other examples are shown in Sections 48, 49, 55, and 59.) A completely typewritten memo is shown on page 326.

The *To* Line

The writer fills in the *To* line with the name of the person who is to receive the original of the memo; the writer should add an appropriate courtesy title (*Ms., Miss, Dr., Mrs.,* or *Mr.*)

> TO: Ms. Marjorie DeRoulet
> TO: Mr. Alfred Wilson
> TO: Dr. Wilhelmina Kurtz

MICHELAUDIO FINE ART OF SOUND

Interoffice Memo

TO: Mr. Howard Wheeler
General Manager
SUBJECT: Need for Greater Display
Areas in Audio Centers

FROM: Carla Landmoor
Sales Supervisor
DATE: August 9, 19--

As you requested last week, I have looked into the reports from some of our local managers that display space is becoming cramped. After speaking with all 27 of our local managers and inspecting 12 of our audio centers in person, I have compiled the following data:

OPEN FLOOR AND COUNTER SPACE IN MICHELAUDIO CENTERS

No. of Centers	Open Floor Space (Sq. ft.)	Open Counter Space (Sq. ft.)
12	97	8
9	102	11
6	119	9

These figures make clear what my on-site observations confirmed: There is little available counter space for display of our merchandise. What room we have for expansion is on the floor. The only immediate way to increase our display space is to install rotary display stands or cardboard fold-out stands.

I recommend that we investigate the prices of floor display equipment as soon as possible and then proceed with purchase. I would be happy to handle this myself if you wish.

For the longer term, I believe that we will have to enlarge most of our audio centers either by construction or by moving to new buildings. The problem of limited display space is certain to become more acute when we begin to sell video recorders and cassettes next fall.

Please let me know if you agree with my recommendations and if there are any steps that you want me to take in order to implement them.

CL

lq
cc Arnold Woodward

This printed memo form, part of a three-part snap-out set, includes the company's name and the words *Interoffice Memo*, as well as the guidewords *To, From, Subject,* and *Date*.

The writer should include the addressee's job title when:
1. The writer wishes to show deference:

TO: Mr. José Martinez Fernandez, President and Chief Executive Officer

```
                    INTEROFFICE MEMORANDUM


        TO:  Mrs. Edna Botkin, Manager        FROM:  Aurelio D. Cervantes

    SUBJECT:  National Luggage Show           DATE:  September 3, 19--


    As requested in your August 19 memo, I offer these suggestions concerning
    our representation at next March's National Luggage Show in Chicago:

    1.  I recommend that we reserve a large booth as soon as possible.
        Although we have never had difficulty in reserving space at the last
        moment, reserving early would enable us to include the booth number
        in our preshow advertisements.

    2.  Most of the booths at these shows are indistinguishable from one
        another.  I suggest that we hire a designer to make ours eye-catching.

    3.  Our personnel who will work at the booth should receive special train-
        ing not only in the finer points of our product line but also in
        interpersonal relations.  It seems to me that our products are truly
        superior to all our competitors' products, and yet our sales are no
        better than theirs.  Perhaps we should do more than allow our products
        to sell themselves.  I have enclosed brochures on some of the better
        sales training programs available from independent specialists.

    Please let me know whether you would like to discuss these suggestions
    or whether I can help in any other way to prepare for the show.

                                                    ADC

    pdn
    Enclosure
```

An entirely typewritten memorandum.

2. The addressee has more than one job title, and the writer's message concerns the duties that belong with only one of the titles.

> TO: Ms. Edna Wintergreen, Chairman, Employee Committee on Community Relations
> (Ms. Wintergreen is also the director of personnel.)

3. The addressee happens to have the same name as another employee, or a very similar name, so that the writer must make clear which of the two people is intended to receive the memo.

> TO: Edwin Willis, Assistant Chief Engineer
> (Edward Willis is the production manager.)

In large companies, it may be helpful to include address information in the *To* line of an interoffice memo. For example:

> TO: Mr. Carl Pappas, Room 3301, Benefits Office
> TO: Dr. Annette Kane, Laboratory 3, Research Department

If the memo is going to more than a few people, the writer should consider typing "See Below" on the *To* line and placing the list of recipients at the end of the memo under the heading *Distribution*. Placing the distribution list at the bottom gives the memo a more balanced appearance and spares the readers the chore of reading the long list of names until after they have read the heart of the memo—its message.

> DISTRIBUTION:
> Dr. Sylvia Harcourt, General Manager
> Mr. Thomas Cefalino, Personnel Director
> Mr. Charles Broad, Purchasing Department
> Ms. Olivia Cortez, Accounting Department
> Mrs. Maureen Perry, Promotion Department
> Mr. Ingmar Jorgensen, Production Manager
> Mr. Eisaku Okakura, Chief Designer

The *From* Line

It is usual for the writer of a memo not to use a courtesy title before his or her own name. If required, the writer may include a job title, department affiliation, office room number, and telephone extension.

> FROM: Esther Weiss, Researcher, Investment Department, Room 2103, Ext. 983

The *Date* Line

In both letters and memos, the date should be written in full rather than abbreviated or given in figures only.

> DATE: October 20, 19— (*or* 20 October 19—)

The *Subject* Line

The writer should state the subject of a memo clearly and briefly. Only in exceptional cases—such as technical matters—should the subject of the memo require more than a single line. The example below says all that is necessary; the rest should be left to the body of the memo.

SUBJECT: Request for Additional Input Terminal

The Body, or Message

The memo, unlike the business letter, includes no salutation. Instead the writer leaves two blank lines beneath the subject line, then goes directly to the message. The body is single-spaced, (but if the message is unusually short, it may be double-spaced). The block paragraph style is usual, but paragraphs may be indented. Many companies decide these matters according to a style of their own; thus new employees should ask if there is a "house" style for memos.

The Signature

The writer's initials are typed on the second line below the message. (Typing or signing the full name is unnecessary because the full name appears after *From*.) Most writers also *sign* their initials on each memo (either next to the name on the *From* line or near the initials at the bottom of the memo).

Below the signature the typist includes his or her own initials and any notations (for example, enclosure notations and carbon copy notations) that may be needed. Thus the end of the memo may look like this:

TPW

CB
cc Adele Blake

For more details, see a comprehensive reference manual.

TONE OF THE MEMO

The tone of a memo depends largely on the position of, and the writer's relation to, the person to whom the memo is addressed. In some ways, the choice of tone is easier in business settings than in many social settings: Relationships are often clear between two persons on different levels within the corporation. In general, the writer of a business memo chooses a more formal tone when addressing top management than when writing to an equal or a subordinate, unless the writer knows that the addressee prefers an informal tone.

Even within clear corporate structures, of course, there will still be times when the writer is not certain what tone to use in a memo. The best course in these cases is to choose a middle way—neither too formal nor too deferential. Avoid using contractions like *you'll* and *here's* but do not resort to elevated, artificial, or stilted language either. Stick to business. For example:

Here is the report on last month's production, with the changes that you requested yesterday. The figures on Model 26 are now broken down to show the number of completed units that have received the modifications recommended by the Customer Service Department. In addition, all tables now have an added line showing production for the same period last year.

Subject matter also helps to determine the choice of tone for a memo. A memo announcing the schedule of the company's softball team would obviously have a lighter tone than a memo justifying costs that ran over budget. The more serious the topic, the more serious the tone.

ORGANIZATION OF THE MEMORANDUM

The form and the tone of a memorandum are only means to help the writer convey his or her message. The memorandum's organization is another means to the same end. A memorandum tries to "sell" its readers a point of view. This holds true whether the writer wishes to convince a superior of the need for new office equipment or to convince someone under the writer's supervision of the need to maintain high work standards. The memo is more likely to achieve its goal if it is brief and to the point without seeming brusque or incomplete. A memo is usually even more sparing in its use of words than a good letter.

The organization of a memorandum should be simple and clear. There is no need for more than these three elements: (1) a statement of purpose, (2) a message, and (3) a statement of future action to be taken.

Statement of Purpose

The subject line tells the reader what the memorandum is about but does not usually state the writer's reason for writing. Often the writer can make the purpose clear simply by referring to an earlier memo (whether written or received) or to a previous meeting or telephone conversation. Here are some examples of how a writer can state the purpose of a memo:

> At the last meeting of the Media Research staff, I was assigned to investigate and report on the comparative costs of print and broadcast advertisements in the northern part of the state. Here is a summary of what I found.
>
> I received the attached letter just this morning. I think you will agree that it shows the need for a speedy change in our procedures for taking telephone orders.
>
> As the new board of directors requested at the June 12 meeting, I am sending you a summary of the company's present provision for Individual Retirement Accounts.

Message

After the statement of purpose, the writer should go directly to the main points of the message. The object is to help the reader grasp the main points as easily and clearly as possible. Often the best approach is to list and number each important point. For example:

> At yesterday's meeting, the office library's acquisitions budget for the coming year was drastically cut. As a result, the library may be forced to impose limits or quotas for purchases on behalf of each of the company's departments. In view of this, I recommend that:
>
> 1. All the employees in our department submit within the next week a list of all books and periodicals that our department may need by year's end.
> 2. The supervisors and section chiefs review these lists and decide which publications are most important to the department.
> 3. We communicate our needs to the acquisitions librarian as soon as possible.

If the memorandum covers several important topics, side headings can help the reader to see each topic distinctly:

> The need for field engineers varies from region to region. A few offices seem to be overstaffed, but most are understaffed. Here is a breakdown of our field-engineering strength by region.
>
> **Midwest.** The Midwest is our busiest region, but our field engineers are able to keep up with demand despite a high volume of work. Each field engineer services an average of 12 customers per month and makes 4 service calls per week.
>
> **East.** Although not yet as busy as the Midwest, our regional office in the East places the greatest demands on its field-engineering staff. Each field engineer services 15 customers each month and makes 7 service calls each week. The average weekly overtime is 11 hours. This demand is probably related to recent economic growth in the East and to the performance of our Eastern sales office last year.
>
> **Far West.** Our field engineers in California and the other Western states shoulder much lighter work loads than engineers in our other regions. Each field engineer performs an average of only 3 service calls per week and services a total of 7 customers. The primary reason is simply the abundance of engineers in the West. Taking advantage of this fact in the Western employment market, we employ more engineers but our labor cost per service call is less than elsewhere. This lower cost is due to lower salaries and the complete lack of overtime and related charges.

Statement of Future Action

The memorandum should usually end with a statement of future action to be taken or with a request for further instructions, as illustrated in the following examples:

> I will send further details about the reasons for this recommendation if you wish, including a full explanation of the financial analysis provided by the research staff.
>
> Please notify me of your decision as soon as possible so that I can either start to carry out this plan or to develop a new one.

The writer of the memorandum on page 325 has organized well. The first sentence states the purpose, a table displays relevant information, and the last paragraph explains the meaning of the table. Despite such clear organization, the memorandum would be weak if the last sentence did not suggest a future action.

COMMUNICATION PROJECTS

Practical Application

A. After six months' full-time employment with your company, employees become eligible for tuition reimbursement for courses taken at local colleges in evenings and on Saturdays. In order to receive reimbursement, however, employees must show that courses are likely to improve specific job-related skills, or to increase the employee's general value to the firm in the long term. The company official who oversees this program—Personnel Evaluation Officer Julia Agee—has a reputation for reviewing each application carefully and for rejecting many applications. Ms. Agee requires each applicant to submit a memorandum showing how the applicant's successful completion of the course will benefit the company. You wish to take a course called Introduction to Electronic Data Processing. Write a memo persuading Ms. Agee to reimburse you for tuition costs.

B. You work for the Dazzle Jewelry Company, which has offices on the eighth floor of a large office building. Valuables are received every day in the receiving department and shipped out from the order-fulfillment department. Since the prices of precious metals have soared in recent years, thieves have attempted almost every week to break into the Dazzle offices at night. Concerned about the possibility of an armed robbery during office hours, you and other employees in the business office would like the company to separate the business office from the departments that actually handle valuables—the receiving department and the order-fulfillment department. Write a memo to top management expressing the employees' concerns and proposing ways of coping with the growing threat of crime.

C. You are an administrative assistant in the personnel department and you have always enjoyed travel. You hear many employees complaining about the increasing costs of travel. Some employees have even had to abandon their vacation plans for trips abroad. When you look into the costs of a two-week vacation in France, you find the amount prohibitive. Rather than simply abandoning your hopes for a European vacation, you decide to find a way to see France for less. You decide to try to form a company holiday club so that employees can take advantage of the lower group travel rates. After obtaining permission, you write a memo to all employees to see if any others are interested in forming a holiday club and organizing travel groups. You want to find out where others would like to travel, at what time of year, and in groups of what size. Write a memo describing briefly the advantages of the holiday club. Include a brief questionnaire to determine whether enough common interests exist to warrant the forming of travel groups.

D. You are an assistant to the director of a firm that imports fabrics for the fashion industry. The director has assigned you to report on the fabric choices of prominent designers for the fall season. After analyzing the collections of major designers, you have learned that the usual cold-weather fabrics—wools, cashmeres, mohairs, flannels, and corduroys—will be common. But you have also found prominent use of other fabrics—polyesters and ultrasuedes. In addition, you have noted occasional use of silks, especially silk crepe de chine. Write a memorandum that presents this information so that the director can understand it at a glance.

E. You are an administrative assistant in a large typesetting plant that has continued to use metal type while its competitors have converted to phototype. Business is slow. While the plant's manager is on vacation, the art director of one of your largest customers calls and insists on speaking to someone. Since the manager is away and the assistant manager is out to lunch, the call is referred to you. The caller tells you that she is moving her company's account to another typesetter—one of those using phototype. She says the reasons are simple economics: the same work that would cost $1,200 if done in metal type would cost only $875 in phototype. Write a memorandum relaying this information to the manager.

Editing Practice

The Correspondence Supervisor   Edit and rewrite the paragraph below.

> We are sorry to learn that the floor lamp you purchased from us is not working correctly. We test each of our lamps, extensively before shipping. Every lamp must be inspected twice and then left on for seventytwo hours otherwise it never leaves the factory. Your lamp must therefor have been damaged in transit. A replacement lamp is allready on the way to you. Please return the defective lamp freight collect. We will study the nature of the damage and try to improve our protective packaging in order to prevent recurences. We value our reputation high and thank you for calling our attention to this problem so that we can correct it at once.

Case Problem

A Confidential Matter   Rumors are sweeping the office that the new office manager will be appointed today. Will it be Helen Bullfinch, Thomas Kreps, or someone from outside the firm? Vivian Wallace, the vice president's secretary, knows who has been appointed because her boss made the selection. The vice president has asked, however, that Vivian keep the information confidential until an official announcement is made. Anita Colon, Vivian's best friend in the company, would like to know who has been chosen. At lunch Anita asks Vivian, "Please tell me who got the job; I won't breathe a word to a soul. I promise."

1. Should Vivian tell Anita?
2. What should Vivian say to Anita?

39
STYLE
FOR BUSINESS LETTERS

No two people do anything in exactly the same way. Consider an activity such as singing. Think how many different kinds of singing you have heard, ranging from rock, pop, and jazz to grand opera. In every category of music, each singer sings in a unique way. All the qualities that make one singer sound different from every other are the singer's *style*.

Within limits, there is room for individual style in writing business letters too. Business letters are not, of course, the place for extremes of style. The writer of a business letter is simply trying to state a message as clearly as possible. To accomplish this objective, the writer of a business letter uses *style* in two different meanings of the word. In the first sense, *style* refers to the way the author chooses words and constructs phrases, clauses, sentences, and paragraphs. The writer uses English well in order to write a pleasant, interesting, clear, and informative message. *Style* in this first sense is discussed later in this section.

Style's second meaning with regard to business letters is a visual concept, referring to the overall appearance of the business letter—the positioning of typewritten copy on a sheet of paper; the typeface used; the color of type; and the quality of the stationery itself. Before the reader's eyes find the first word of the message, the appearance of the letter makes an impression on the reader's mind. Whether the reader knows or not, the first impression shapes the reader's attitude toward the message and the writer—regardless of what the message is about, regardless of who the writer is.

Style in the two senses described above is as important to the success or failure of a letter as is the letter's content. By studying the suggestions of this section, you can learn to make the style of your letters—both the format and the manner of writing—influence the reader to react favorably to you and to your ideas.

THAT FIRST IMPRESSION—APPEARANCE

In Section 34 you learned that a letter's appearance can help your firm win and keep a reputation as a dependable business. Making your letters look good makes your company look good. In the paragraphs that follow, you will learn more about making your letters work for your firm, not against it.

Balanced Format

You know that an attractive letterhead printed on good-quality paper, a message typed in proportion to its balanced margins, and a pleasing format all combine to make your letter inviting to the reader. Sloppy letters, like sloppy people, have a negative effect.

White Space   The symmetry of a well-placed letter invites the reader's attention. A letter placed too high, too low, or too far to either side upsets the balance of white space that frames the picture, or message. All letters, however long they are, should have a generous margin of white space on all sides.

Typewriting Quality   No matter how attractive the paper and the letterhead, a letter will do nothing to enhance your firm's standing if the typing is sloppy. The following checklist will help you make sure that the typing of your letters is visually pleasing.

Checklist for Well-Typed Letters

Evenness of Characters
All characters should be of the same weight.
Every character should be complete—no chips or scratches.
Every character should be clear—no ink-clogged characters.

Quality of Ribbon
Ribbon should have ample ink to make clear typescript.
Color should be appropriate to color of stationery (usually black ribbon for white stationery).
Polyethylene rather than fabric ribbon should be used for highest print quality.

Neatness of Corrections
Use good typing eraser and typing shield.
Don't use liquid paper on original copy of correspondence.
Correction paper (such as Ko-Rec-Type) may be used if mistaken strokes are not visible.
Retype entire page if erasures are noticeable.

The Letterhead

Great care goes into the design and printing of letterheads. Letterheads are so important to a company's image that top management may reject many designs before adopting one. Some well-designed letterheads are displayed on page 335.

Equally important is the quality of the paper on which the letterhead is printed. The size, shape, weight, and texture of stationery contribute to the reader's first impression. Stationers, printers, and advertising agencies often advise companies about the selection of paper. When selecting stationery, keep in mind the following points.

Quality stationery suggests that the firm considers its letters—and its readers—important.

The usual letterhead size is $8\frac{1}{2}$ by 11 inches, but special sizes may be used to create special impressions. For example, physicians, lawyers, and other professional people often use the smaller, baronial ($5\frac{1}{2}$ by $8\frac{1}{2}$ inches) stationery.

Tinted paper is sometimes used for special effects. A garden shop may, for instance, select green paper.

Business people believe in the power of a picture—"a picture is worth ten thousand words." Artwork and photography are used increasingly in letterheads, especially in promotional letters. Of course, the letter's second page should be of the same quality, size, and color as the letterhead. Although many

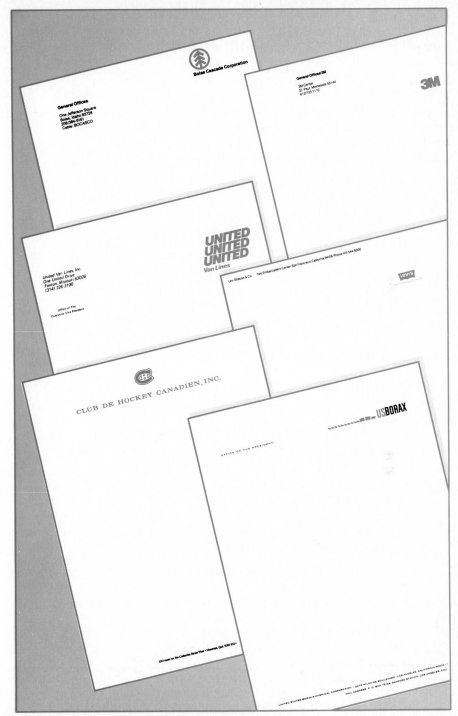

Well-designed letterheads help to project a positive image.

companies prefer that the second-page stationery be blank, without any printing, others are using a printed second page with the company name in small print. Information copies or file copies are usually typed on onionskin paper.

The Envelope

Business envelopes are usually printed with a return address designed to echo the letterhead being used. It is essential that the information contained in the envelope address be identical with that in the inside address. The following guidelines, illustrated in the envelope at the bottom of this page, should always be observed:

Begin typing the mailing address on line 14, about 4 inches from the left edge for a regular-size—No. 10—business envelope. The blocked style, single-spaced, is preferred by the U.S. Postal Service.

Always include the ZIP Code number. Leave one space between the state and the ZIP Code number.

On-arrival or addressee directions (*Please Forward, Confidential,* and so on) should be typed about three lines below the return address.

Indicate special mailing services, such as *Special Delivery* or *Air Mail,* below the stamp (about 9 lines from the top of the envelope).

The U.S. Postal Service prefers that no information be placed below the ZIP Code number.

Punctuation Styles

The two commonly used punctuation styles for business letters are (1) open and (2) standard, or "mixed."

Willard Carlton

tyro talent agency
1932 Sunshine Avenue
Hollywood, California
90069

ATTENTION MS. ROBERTA QUAYLE

Brohamer Recording Studio
108 Avenue of the Angels
Los Angeles, CA 90042

The information typed on the envelope should match the information in the inside address of the letter.

It is important to remember that the punctuation of the *message* is the same, regardless of which style is used for the other letter parts.

Open Punctuation Style   This style, shown on page 339, requires that *no* punctuation be used after any part of the letter except the message. Open punctuation is frequently used with full-blocked arrangements, as both styles are considered time-savers for the typist.

Standard Punctuation Style   In the standard punctuation style, only the salutation and the complimentary closing are followed by a mark of punctuation. The salutation is followed by a colon, and the complimentary closing is followed by a comma. The standard style, which is more commonly used, is shown on pages 338, 340, and 341.

Letter Arrangement Styles

Almost every company uses one of four long-established styles of letter arrangement. Although any of the styles is acceptable, most companies prefer that all their employees use the same style. In some cases, however, the choice of styles is left to the individual. If you are given a choice, you should use one of the styles shown and described on the following pages.

You will notice that most of the differences among styles of letter arrangement have to do with horizontal placement of the letter's parts. Vertical sequence follows the same logical order in all the styles.

Study the names for parts of the business letter, as illustrated on page 338.

Full-Blocked Letters   In the full-blocked style, letters are written with *all* the parts beginning at the left margin. This style, which is illustrated on page 339, saves typing time because the typist does not have to use the tabulator in setting up the letter. Frequently, open punctuation (see page 339) is used with the full-blocked style.

Blocked Letters   A letter in blocked style, as illustrated on page 340, follows the format of a full-blocked letter except in the position of the dateline, complimentary closing, company signature, and writer's identification. All these parts start at the horizontal center of the page.

Semiblocked Letters   A semiblocked letter, as shown on page 341 generally follows blocked style. However, first lines of paragraphs are indented five spaces (some writers indent ten spaces).

Simplified Letters   The administrative Management Society has developed and advocates the use of the simplified letter style, as shown on page 342. The arrangement of the simplified letter is the same as the arrangement of the full-blocked style. However, the simplified letter is different in the following ways:

1. The salutation and the complimentary closing are eliminated.
2. The subject line, which is standard in the simplified style, and the writer's identification line are always typed entirely in capital letters.
3. Listings in the message are indented five spaces, except when the items in the listing are numbered or lettered. Items identified by letters or numbers are blocked.

The simplified letter is designed to save time. However, efficiency is not the sole criterion in judging a business letter. Many writers consider the simplified style cold and impersonal, and as a result, they prefer to use one of the traditional styles.

tyro talent agency

1932 Sunshine Avenue
Hollywood, California
90069

2 February 12, 19--

3 Brohamer Recording Studio
108 Avenue of the Angels
Los Angeles, California 90042

4 ATTENTION MS. ROBERTA QUAYLE

5 Ladies and Gentlemen:

6 Subject: Recording Session for John Thoreson

As soon as possible, and certainly within the next two weeks, we need to
schedule a recording session for our new client, the singer John Thoreson.
I know that this request gives you less notice than usual, and we are
willing to be flexible as to both the time of the session and the fee.

Mr. Thoreson is always in demand for live appearances, of course, but now
the demand is greater than ever because of the publicity surrounding his
7 recent TV appearance. We know you professionals at Brohamer are well
acquainted with the shifting tides of publicity and will do everything
possible to squeeze in a session for Mr. Thoreson.

I have enclosed a list of the instrumentalists required for each song
that we wish to record. Also enclosed are the timings of each of these
songs at Mr. Thoreson's last performance. We hope to hear from you soon
about arrangements for the requested recording session. We plan to continue our practice of using your studio for demo recordings of all our
artists not under contract to recording companies. If you need further
information or if we can be helpful in any way, please feel free to call.

8 Cordially yours,

9 TYRO TALENT AGENCY

Willard Carlton

10 Willard Carlton
Vice President, Promotion

11 WC/rl
12 Enclosures
Timings
List of instrumentalists
13 cc Mr. Peter Petrakis

Parts of a business letter:

1. Printed letterhead
2. Date line
3. Inside address
4. Attention line
5. Salutation
6. Subject line
7. Body
8. Complimentary closing
9. Company signature
10. Signer's identification
11. Reference initials
12. Enclosure reminder
13. "cc" notation

Note that the vertical sequence in which the parts are positioned is normally not altered.

**Manhattan
Office Services Inc.**

Suite 1107
Empire State Building
New York, New York 10001
(212) 555-5000

July 19, 19--

Mr. Harold G. Lester
Lester Gourmet Foods, Inc.
499 Exeter Street
Pompano Beach, FL 33061

Dear Mr. Lester

Subject: Form of a Full-Blocked Letter

This letter is arranged in the full-blocked style. Every
line begins at the left margin. Because this style is the
fastest to type, it is considered very modern. In keeping
with the modern feeling of the full-blocked style, most
companies use the "open" style of punctuation.

This letter also illustrates a form of the subject line that
can be used with any style of letter. Like an attention
line, a subject line may be typed with underscores or capitals.
In a full-blocked letter, the subject line must be blocked
(flush left); in other letter styles, the subject line may be
blocked or centered. It always appears after the salutation
and before the body because it is considered part of the body.

Law firms and the legal departments of companies sometimes
prefer to use the Latin terms Re or In Re instead of the
English word Subject.

Yours sincerely

Sonya Hedberg

Sonya Hedberg, Director
Word Processing Department

nnt

The full-blocked letter style is vigorous and aggressive. Note that this letter uses open punctuation and includes a subject line.

USING WORDS THAT MOVE THE MESSAGE

In business, writers use words to do jobs. Words, therefore, are the tools of writing. To write forceful communications, the writer must make sure to choose words that work—words that *perform expressively,* words that move the message from the writer to the reader.

**Manhattan
Office Services Inc.**

Suite 1107
Empire State Building
New York, New York 10001
(212) 555-5000

```
                                    November 6, 19--

                                    REGISTERED

          Mr. Edward S. Swoboda
          Swoboda Rare Books, Inc.
          6864 Mercer Street
          Windsor, Ont.
          CANADA N9E 1X6

          Dear Mr. Swoboda:

          In the blocked letter style, we display quotations and similar
          special data in a special paragraph, like this:

                    The paragraph is indented five spaces on both sides
                    and is preceded and followed by one blank linespace.

                    If more than one paragraph is required for the quo-
                    tation, then another blank linespace is left between
                    paragraphs.

          We indicate the mail service (a double space below the date)
          only if we are sending the correspondence by some special
          service, such as "express mail" or "special delivery"; we do
          so in order to record on our own file copy the use of the
          special service.

                                    Yours very truly,

                                    Sonya Hedberg

                                    Sonya Hedberg, Director
                                    Word Processing Department

          EM/ptt

          P.S.  We treat postscripts like paragraphs in the body of the
          letter except that we may use the abbreviation "PS:" or "P.S."
          before the postscript.
```

The blocked letter style is the most flexible. Note the treatment of the mailing notation, the indented extracts, and the postscript.

Like other kinds of tools, some words become worn out. Some words are unnecessary when they try to repeat the same job that other words are doing. Some words are so complicated that they make a simple task difficult. And some words are like tools made especially for one specific job—in any setting other than their specialty, these

Manhattan Office Services Inc.

Suite 1107
Empire State Building
New York, New York 10001
(212) 555-5000

October 26, 19--

Sandifer, Rogers & Scotto
88 Lafollet Street
Philadelphia, PA 19123

ATTENTION PROCEDURES MANAGER

Gentlemen:

    For a letter design that is both distinctive and standard,
try the semiblocked style. One of the two most popular styles,
the semiblocked calls for indenting paragraphs <u>five</u> spaces,
but some people prefer to indent ten spaces.

    This letter also shows you an alternative arrangement
for the attention line: centered and all in capitals (instead
of being blocked at the left margin and underscored). In two
respects, however, the attention line shown here is standard:
It is followed by one of the standard salutations, such as
"Gentlemen," and it is typed <u>above</u> the salutation.

    Other noteworthy points of style in this letter are the
following: (1) the use of "standard" punctuation, which calls
for a colon after the salutation and a comma after the complimentary closing; and (2) the use of the "cc" notation at the
bottom to indicate who will receive carbon copies.

                    Yours sincerely,

                    Sonya Hedberg

                    Sonya Hedberg, Director
                    Word Processing Department

dbc
cc Ms. Gloria Trapnell
   Mr. Henry Oates

The semiblocked letter style is conservative. Many writers consider it an "executive" style. Note the attention line and the *cc* notation.

words are not only useless but they often garble the message.

    Make sure that your words are working for you. Use modern words; eliminate unnecessary and repetitious words; put your ideas in clear and simple words; and avoid using jargon or "shop talk."

Manhattan Office Services Inc.

Suite 1107
Empire State Building
New York, New York 10001
(212) 555-5000

March 26, 19--

Mr. Lawrence T. Kopay
Jarrett Market Research, Inc.
5331 Bisset Drive
Houston, TX 77058

THE SIMPLIFIED LETTER

You will be interested to know, Mr. Kopay, that several years ago the
Administrative Management Society (formerly NOMA) designed a letter form
called the "Simplified Letter." This is a sample.

1. It uses the full-blocked form and "open" (minimal) punctuation.

2. It uses no salutation and no complimentary closing. (AMS regards
    these conventional expressions as meaningless.)

3. The simplified style displays a subject line all in capitals, both
    preceded and followed by two blank lines. Note that the word "Subject"
    is omitted.

4. The simplified style identifies the signer by a line all in capitals
    that is preceded by at least four blank lines and followed by one
    blank line if further notations are used.

5. Seeking to maintain a brisk but friendly tone, the simplified style
    uses the addressee's name at least in the first sentence.

Mr. Kopay, this use of the reader's name in the body is intended to compensate for the absence of the salutation and the complimentary close.
Some say that the simplified style just does not look like a business
letter. Because of its efficiency, however, this style is worth trying,
especially where output is below standard.

Sonya Hedberg

SONYA HEDBERG, DIRECTOR
WORD PROCESSING DEPARTMENT

cc George G. Graham

The simplified letter style is the favorite of the efficiency-minded writer. Note the open
punctuation and full-blocked design.

Use Modern Expressions

Expressions, like fashions, change. Few people today would choose the cumber-
some, confining clothes worn a few generations ago. In letter writing, fashions
change, too. Some expressions are just as old-fashioned as celluloid collars and high-
buttoned shoes, but many people continue to use them in business letters. Make sure

that you know the expressions that are out of date so that you can avoid them; but also make sure that you know and use modern expressions in your letters.

Use	Do Not Use
say, tell, let us know	advise, inform
now, at present	at this time, at the present time, at the present writing
as, because, since	due to the fact that, because of the fact that
letter	favor
regarding, concerning	in re
if, in case	in the event that
please	kindly
a specific word	same
for	in the amount of
according to	in accordance with

Eliminate Redundancy

Redundancy in writing or in speech results from using words that are unnecessarily repetitious; for instance, using *free gratis* for *gratis*. Since *gratis* means "free," *free gratis* means "free free." The following list includes some common redundancies that should be avoided.

Use	Do Not Use	Use	Do Not Use
about	*at* about	converted	converted *over*
above	*up* above	enter	enter *into*
alike	*both* alike	experience	*past* experience
beginner	*new* beginner	identical	*same* identical
check	check *into*	practice	*customary* practice
cooperate	cooperate *together*	otherwise	*as* otherwise
connect	connect *up*	repeat	repeat *again*
continue	continue *on*	together	*both* together
		etc.	*and* etc.

Use Plain, Simple Words

Would you call a lamp a "visible radiation generating and distributing device"? This ridiculous, fancy expression does a poor job of saying what *lamp* says. Why bother with six fancy words, when one simple word will do the job?

The purpose of a business letter is to convey a clear message in an efficient yet polite way. The writer's purpose must be the same. If, instead, the writer is intent on showing off an extensive vocabulary, the purpose of the letter will suffer. Extensive vocabularies are valuable because they provide the exactly right word for every use. The writer should not try to force the longest, most impressive-sounding polysyllable to do the work of a common everyday word. Forcing inappropriate words into a business message is like using an air hammer to open a tin can: The job will be done clumsily, wasting much and leaving a mess behind.

For example, suppose you buy an expensive lawn mower only to find that it doesn't work. You write the following complaint to the manufacturer:

> Your lawn mower has proved to be a deleterious, nonutilitarian mechanism in my yard.

By showing off your vocabulary, you would have obscured the meaning of your own complaint. The manufacturer would be forced to consult a dictionary, then to write you and ask for more specific information. Your message would have gotten you help sooner if you had used simpler words, like the following:

> Your lawn mower has proved to be a useless piece of machinery in my yard because the engine will not start.

Avoid Jargon

Most trades develop a technical vocabulary that is likely to be unintelligible to anyone outside the trade. This vocabulary is called *jargon*. You should learn and use the special words of your trade, but remember that jargon is shop talk. It is COIK (Clear Only If Known). For example, if you are writing to shoe store managers about *findings*, they'll know that you mean the merchandise other than shoes, such as polish, shoelaces, hosiery, and accessories. This is shoe store jargon and is understandable to them. However, no manager would talk to customers about buying *findings*. Why? The term is COIK—Clear Only If Known.

WRITING SKILL

The business writer's usual goals are to win friends and, at the same time, bring about favorable action. Certain qualities have proved effective in writing friendly letters that facilitate action: conciseness, clarity, cohesiveness, and completeness. The following paragraphs tell how to give your letters these important qualities.

Be Concise

Concise messages save time—and in business, time is money. As a rule, the shorter the message the better—with one important reservation: The effective business letter should never be so short as to be abrupt, curt, or rude. As a writer of business letters, you should say what you must say, say it politely, and say no more.

The principal enemy of conciseness is repetition. Have you ever had the feeling of being told the same thing a thousand times? If so, you no doubt felt angry because needless repetition was wasting your time. Arousing such feelings in the reader of a business letter neither makes friends nor brings about favorable action. How would you react if you received the following letter?

> In reviewing your proposal—in response to which we have arrived at a decision—we considered everything fully and completely. We looked at the financial aspects of the proposal, at the practical aspects of the proposal, and at

the managerial aspects of the proposal. We don't just jump into things. It's not our way. To the best of our knowledge, ability, and belief, we overlooked nothing before reaching our decision, which is final, irrevocable, and nonnegotiable. I'm afraid that we have decided that the proposal is unworkable under present economic conditions, circumstances, regulations, and restrictions.

What the reader most wants to know is whether the proposal was accepted or rejected. In either case, the reader may want to hear the reason for the acceptance or rejection—but only once. The following abridgement of the paragraph would serve the reader better.

Thank you for sharing your proposal with us. We explored every aspect of the proposal—financial, practical, and managerial. Despite its positive features, we concluded that your proposal would not succeed in the current economic climate.

Another enemy of conciseness is irrelevancy. For instance, note how much of the following is irrelevant to the subject of the letter.

One of our best customers got pretty annoyed today because we didn't have any extension cords in stock. Usually we do, but my partner thought I had ordered them, and I thought that he had.
Now I would like to order two dozen 6-foot extension cords. And from now on, I will do the ordering . . . .

At times, whole paragraphs can be eliminated without destroying any pertinent information. Be sure that whatever you include in your letters is relevant to your purpose.

Be Clear

Clear writing is specific rather than general. Clear writing tolerates no ambiguities, such as pronouns that may refer to more than one noun. A skilled business writer would never be guilty of the confusing statement below.

We have many satisfied customers of our typewriters, and they have found that they seldom need repairs but when they do they service them quickly.

As bad as the ambiguity in the example above is the running together of ideas. Short sentences tend to be clearer than long, involved ones. See how much clearer the message is when it is written as two precise sentences.

Thousands of satisfied customers use Sayre typewriters. These customers are satisfied because seldom, if ever, do Sayre typewriters need repair.

The revised statement is not vague, as the first is. Instead of dealing in vague generalities, a clear style deals in specifics. For example, *Your order will be shipped in the very near future* is too general a statement to be clear. *Your order will be shipped on May 15* is specific and, therefore, quite clear.

Be Coherent

Coherence in style refers to the way a letter holds together. In the coherent letter, there is unity of thought—each sentence and paragraph flows smoothly into the next. The business writer should use connecting or linking words to lead the reader from one idea to another. Here are some examples of linking words and phrases:

since	as a result
naturally	on the other hand
however	nevertheless
thus	therefore
for instance	of course
for example	as a matter of fact

These linking words help to hold the message together. Keep in mind, though, that clear, orderly thinking in organizing a letter, as discussed in Section 34, is the most important factor in writing a coherent letter. Linking words simply make the logic of the letter more quickly apparent to the reader.

Be Complete

Suppose you received the following letter and nothing more.

Dear Mr. Dixon:
Send us our order.

Sincerely yours,

Besides being abrupt and rude, the letter has another major failing: It is incomplete.
A complete letter gives all necessary information: what order? whose order? when to ship it? where to ship it? how? The following letter, while still concise, is both polite and complete.

Dear Mr. Dixon:
On July 3, we placed an order with you (our Purchase Order C-2732) for two of your Model 26 Ditchdiggers. We made clear that we must have the machines by August 15 in order to complete excavation for our housing project before the autumn rains begin. Your sales representative, Ms. Hartnet, promised delivery by that date.
Since it is now August 12, we would like to know whether the Ditchdiggers have been shipped. If not, would you please ship them at once by truck rather than by rail? Please wire immediately to tell us how you plan to get the order to us in time.

Sincerely,

COMMUNICATION PROJECTS

Practical Application
A. Using the simplified letter style, write a letter to your instructor stating whether you think the simplified style is appropriate for all business letters. Include your reasons why or why not.

B. Using the letter style you prefer, write a letter to your instructor explaining how the style selected is superior to the other styles discussed in this section.

C. Modernize the following expressions.

1. In re your letter of 27th last, …
2. At the present writing we have still not received …
3. Please be advised that your payment is overdue.
4. Your order of December 3 is being processed, and we will ship same to you within the week.
5. Due to the fact that your check in the amount of $135.99 has been returned because of insufficient funds, …

D. Find and eliminate any redundancies in the following sentences.

1. Past experience shows that most businesses use the same customary practices.
2. Danforth & Company is using the same identical display.
3. Unless the whole staff cooperates together, we won't finish the report in time.
4. The requirements of the two forms are both alike.
5. The heating system has been converted over from gas to solar power.

E. Make the following sentences clearer and more forceful by using simple words.

1. From the expression on the president's face, we knew that he was engaged in deep ratiocination.
2. The general manager discommended the proposal.
3. She was the cynosure of the board meeting.
4. His dark blue suit was in every way comme il faut.
5. He attempts to get his way by hectoring his opponent.

Editing Practice

Updating Vocabulary   Rewrite these excerpts from business letters, eliminating all outmoded words and expressions.

1. I would like to make an appointment at your earliest convenience.
2. Hoping to see you soon, I remain,
   Sincerely yours,

3. Kindly advise us of your decision soon.
4. At the present writing, we are developing a new model.
5. Due to the fact that our profits are falling, we are trying to lower costs.
6. Thank you in advance for your help.
7. We have received your order for a rheostat and are shipping same today.
8. Enclosed please find our remittance.
9. In the event that you have an accident, this policy will cover your liability.
10. Finances were not part of the vice president's purview.

The Word Processing Supervisor   Are there any spelling errors in this paragraph? Tell in a single sentence the reason for each error.

> Because we specialize in the needs of attornies, our building is uniquely equipped to serve lawyers. Each suite already has a large room furnished with shelves and tables—ideal for a legal liberry. In addition, there are rooms suitable for large and small conferences, and, of course, several private offices.

Case Problem

Carbon Copies   In some firms it is a practice to make a carbon copy of a reply to a routine letter on the back of the letter being answered. Suggest some possible advantages and disadvantages of this procedure.

40
WRITING
REQUESTS

In business, time is money—and new technological methods of handling information have enabled business to take advantage of this fact as never before. Only 50 years ago, all requests for money owed were handled by writing letters. But for large companies today, billing has become entirely mechanized: In an hour, high-speed computers calculate and print thousands of requests for payment.

Now that machines can do so much, why is it still important that business people be able to write request letters and memorandums? Today many small companies continue to rely on staff members to write all letters, and not merely in order to avoid the expense of complex business machinery. Mechanized requests lack the personal touch that builds goodwill for a company. Customers and suppliers will develop no working relationship with a machine, but they often come to depend on a courteous, helpful correspondent. Small companies trade as much on such working relationships as on products and services.

Even in large companies with the most advanced computing equipment, many request letters and memorandums remain the responsibility of individual men and women. Some requests are too important and too delicate to be entrusted to a machine. It would be disastrous, for example, to send a form letter to request more time to repay a loan. Some other requests are too infrequent to mechanize. Still others arise from needs that cannot be foreseen.

Everyone in business today needs all kinds of information and services in the course of work, and often the only way to get the things needed is to write a request letter or memorandum. Typical reasons for writing requests are (1) to ask for an appointment, (2) to reserve a hotel room, (3) to obtain price lists, catalogs, reports, magazines, and books, (4) to seek technical information about products and services, (5) to order merchandise, (6) to ask one division of a company to coordinate efforts with another division of the same company, (7) to ask for information missing from a letter, (8) to ask a favor—permission to use a restricted library or to quote from copyrighted materials.

Writing request letters and memorandums is often considered a routine matter. If the writer shows interest in a product or service, the reader will be happy to grant the request because it offers an opportunity to make a sale. Even in this case, however, the writer should not assume that the request will be granted. A vague, confused, or discourteous request may be ignored or denied.

When the request is extraordinary, the writing of the request letter or memorandum demands especially careful thought and planning. The quality of the writing may sway the reader to grant or refuse the request. Therefore, observe the following guidelines in all written requests, whether they are of a routine nature or are more complicated.

Give complete information.
Give accurate information.
Be sure the request is reasonable.
Be courteous.
Be brief.

Note how these guidelines are followed in the request memorandum on page 351.

GIVE COMPLETE INFORMATION

The ideal written request would not require the reader to send back a letter asking for further information. There are exceptions to this rule, of course. Some requests, for example, contain many parts or options and require further communication. Nevertheless, the writer should always be able to foresee and include the most important facts. As a rule, the request contains the necessary information if it answers the following questions: Who? What? How many? When? Where? Why?

Note how the letter on page 352 answers these questions.

Letters of this type are nearly always on company letterheads, which help to answer the questions *Who?* and *Where?* In addition, the writer may need to give the department and perhaps the floor and room numbers as well. If the return address differs from the letterhead, that must, of course, be included.

The writer should leave ample time for the supplier to handle the request. If the writer is not sure that there is time enough, he or she should express willingness to pay added shipping or handling costs to speed things along.

It is not necessary to say why a request is being made, but sometimes the reader can serve you better if your purpose is clear. If the supplier knows only that you need booklets, then he or she will make an effort to send them. But if the supplier knows that the booklets are for a *conference*, then the booklets might arrive with additional information about displays, slides, and audio and video cassettes that could make the difference between a dull conference and a successful one. The supplier will also rush the reply because you may no longer need the products after the conference ends.

In the letter that follows, the writer explains the intended uses for hotel accommodations. The hotel manager has experience in hosting all kinds of meetings and may be able to suggest enhancements: perhaps the service of coffee outside the large conference room rather than at the table, so that everyone can stretch and be refreshed. Although a request for a hotel reservation is often routine, details must be given to assure that all special requirements are met.

Dear Mr. Syms:

Please reserve a suite for Ms. Helen C. Ryan for October 10–13. Ms. Ryan, executive vice president of Larwex Enterprises, Inc., will arrive at the hotel at approximately 4:45 p.m. on October 10.

During her stay, Ms. Ryan will be conducting a series of seminars for eight regional sales managers. Therefore, she would like to have a suite with an adjoining conference room large enough for a table and nine chairs. She will also need a portable chalkboard. If an appropriate suite is not available, then please reserve a large double bedroom for Ms. Ryan and a small conference room in which luncheon may be served on both October 11 and 12. The conference room will be needed on October 13 as well; but the meeting will end at 11 a.m., so luncheon will not be required.

Please confirm this reservation and let us know what type of accommodations you are holding. Would you also send some sample luncheon menus.

Very truly yours,

A letter requesting an appointment must stress not only why the request is being made but also why the reader should grant the appointment. The writer must spell out the facts in a way that draws the reader's interest. If possible, the letter should show what the reader stands to gain from consenting to see the writer, as in the letter below.

Dear Mr. Carstairs:

Would you like to show the antiques from your shop to thousands of buyers around the world? I can offer you an opportunity to do exactly that—at no cost to you.

My firm is creating a catalog of the world's privately owned antiques. Because the catalog will be stored on magnetic tape, it can be transmitted to any city in the world that has international telephone lines. Transmission will include high-resolution photographs. This catalog will enable buyers to see almost every piece of interest to them. Monthly updates will keep this electronic catalog current. Clearly, this will revolutionize the market for antiques.

Next month I will be in Chicago visiting antique dealers in order to photograph their collections. I hope that you will let me photograph your inventory too.

Prospective antique buyers will pay a fee for use of the catalog, but there will be no charge to dealers. All we ask is the opportunity to photograph your inventory in order to put it on display before thousands of potential customers who would otherwise never see it. I will photograph after business hours if you prefer. The process will take only one full day or two evenings.

If you would like to take advantage of this new service, please let me know as soon as possible so that we can arrange a date convenient to you.

Sincerely,

INTEROFFICE MEMORANDUM

TO: Charles Hiller, Office Manager

FROM: Dorothy Monroe, Mailroom Supervisor

SUBJECT: January 23, 19--

DATE: Need for Another Postage Meter

Our use of postage has increased more than twofold in the last six months. The volume of outgoing first-class letters has risen from an average of 390 a day to almost 1,000. The increase in second-class mailings has been almost as great. In the same period, postal rates have gone up 18 percent. It is no wonder that our postage meter seems to run out of postage every day.

Simply putting more postage in the meter would help but would not solve the problem. It is company policy never to leave the mailing of a completed first-class letter until the next day. Since most outgoing first-class letters reach the mailroom between 3 p.m. and 5 p.m., there are only two hours available for processing approximately 800 letters. Using a single meter, we simply do not have enough time to place postage on every item.

The result, I am afraid, has been late delivery of some company mail. During the past week, we have received three complaints about this from outside the company and two complaints from within.

I am sure that you will agree that another meter is needed. I have obtained a purchase order and filled it out for your signature, and I would be grateful if you would authorize the purchase as soon as possible. I will send a member of my staff to get the second meter as soon as I receive authorization.

DM

Whether a request is of a routine nature or is more complicated, it should give complete and accurate information. In addition, it should be reasonable, courteous, and brief.

GIVE ACCURATE INFORMATION

Before signing a request, the writer should check the accuracy of every item of information. This is especially true when ordering goods or services. A typographical error may bring an unwanted delivery of 100 calculators rather than the 10 that are needed.

BURTON-FERNANDEZ INSURANCE, INC.

2201 North Arbor
Dallas, Texas 75203

November 8, 19--

Mr. Warren McGiver
Education for Insurance, Inc.
9532 McLemore Boulevard
Brockton, Massachusetts 02402

Dear Mr. McGiver:

Your announcement in the October issue of <u>Insurance America</u>
describes a new training booklet, "Making Sure About Insurance."
Burton-Fernandez will hold a training conference for new personnel here in Dallas during the week beginning December 8,
and your booklet sounds well suited to our needs.

I have enclosed a check to cover the cost of 100 copies of
the booklet, postage included, $2.25 left over. The extra
money is to pay airmail costs for a dozen copies. I will
need these by November 12 so that our training staff will
have time to prepare a good program based on the booklet.

If you find any difficulty in supplying the booklets by the
dates required, please let me know at once. If necessary, you
may rush all the booklets by airmail and bill me for the
additional cost.

Very truly yours,

Stanley Olson

Stanley Olson
Personnel Director

jr

A request letter should answer the questions "Who?" "What?" "How many?" "When?" "Where?" and "Why?"

Whether ordering by purchase order or letter, the writer should present the information in a way that displays it clearly and makes it easy to check. Sometimes figures
have a way of blending into the text of a letter. The use of simple tables avoids this
problem, enabling both writer and reader to check the most important facts with less
chance of error.

Note the use of the table in the example below.

Dear Ms. Pendergast:
Please send the following calculators by airfreight:

Model No.	Quantity	Description	Unit Price	Total
HT-19	6	Programmable engineering calculator	$27.00	162.00
TP-371	4	Basic financial calculator	22.00	88.00
Total Cost:				$250.00

It would be helpful if we could receive these calculators within a week. Please let us know if that will not be possible.

Sincerely,

MAKE REASONABLE REQUESTS

No one sets out to make an unreasonable request. Yet people make unreasonable requests every day. Why?

Sometimes people do not know that what they are asking is extremely difficult to do. Sometimes people know, but find it easier to ask the impossible of others than to attempt it themselves.

Unreasonable requests, of course, are seldom granted. They are, therefore, usually a waste of the writer's time. Even worse, they make a terrible impression on the person who receives them.

What would you think if you were an employee of a chemicals manufacturer and you received the following request?

Please send me the chemicals needed to make polyethylene. Also enclose a complete set of instructions.

You would see at once that the writer of the request knew too little about chemistry to be trusted with any chemicals. He has not even learned enough about chemistry to ask a sensible question. If you had spent years studying chemistry and would have to spend hours answering the request, you would feel that the request was unreasonable. It asks too much.

Requests are unreasonable when they ask too much. Often the unreasonable request asks too much of someone's time, as in the example above. It is equally possible to ask too much of someone's influence or money or patience or good nature. It asks too much of someone's influence, for example, to request a character reference from someone who hardly knows you.

How much is too much? This depends on not only what you are asking but also of whom. The closer the relationship between two persons, the more one might reasonably expect of the other. Judging whether a request is reasonable is difficult to reduce to a simple formula, but often the answer comes in the form of a feeling: the uncomfortable feeling that you may be imposing on someone. When that feeling arises, consider with care whether the request that you are writing is clear, specific, pertinent, and possible within the bounds of the effort that you feel entitled to expect from the reader. If you still feel that you are imposing, then don't ask.

BE COURTEOUS

Like the unreasonable request, the discourteous one may stem from a misunderstanding of the relationship between writer and reader. The writer seems to think that making a request somehow places the writer above the reader. The writer may think, "Since I may buy products from her, she will go to a lot of trouble for me." Or perhaps the writer thinks, "It's part of her job to be polite to me, but I don't get paid to be polite to her."

The result of such attitudes may be a letter that does the writer more harm than good. The letter below, for example, is discourteous enough to lower the reader's opinion of the writer.

> Oliver O'Reilly
> Adorno Office Supply
> 146 East Rutherford
> Denver, Colorado 30043
> Dear Sir:
> Send your price list, your catalog, and a box of No. 2 pencils right away.
> Yours truly,

In this instance the discourtesy is a matter of what the writer has left out. *Mr.* does not appear in the inside address. At that point the writer does at least know Mr. O'Reilly's name, but Mr. O'Reilly becomes nameless four lines later in the salutation. The simple request that forms the basis of the letter is delivered with all the grace of a shoe on the table. After this, the complimentary close sounds almost sarcastic. Mr. O'Reilly will probably send the things requested, but he should not be expected to go out of his way to be helpful.

Often the writer's courtesy benefits the writer as much as it does the reader. One example of this mutual benefit is the courtesy carbon (described in Section 34), which makes it easier for the reader to reply. The benefit to the writer is that the response may come sooner.

Another courteous technique is the simple one of numbering the questions or requests when there are several. The numbered items serve as a checklist for the reader's convenience. Use of the checklist will reduce the chances of any of the writer's inquiries being overlooked. The letter below is an example of this technique.

> Dear Ms. DePaul:
> I have seen your advertisement about electronic banking and the apparent convenience is appealing. The use of a "debit card" to replace the writing of checks seems certain to save time.
> I am concerned, however, about what may happen if the card is ever stolen. I also wonder whether payment by card is acceptable to everyone. Before applying for a card, therefore, I need answers to the following questions:

1. How great is my liability if a thief gets and uses the card?
2. How soon must I notify the bank in event of theft?
3. Who will and will not accept payment by debit card? Will retail stores? The telephone and power companies? Will federal, state, and local governments accept electronic payment of taxes?
4. What regulations, if any, apply to these cards that do not apply to checking accounts?

I must say that I am quite satisfied with your services now, both checking and savings. I appreciate your high standards of service and know that you will answer the questions above with your usual thoroughness. Thank you for your assistance.

Sincerely,

BE BRIEF

Brevity has several virtues. It is courteous because it does not waste the reader's time with needless or irrelevant details. Brevity is efficient since it eliminates rambling observations that would only distract the reader from the request itself. Brevity is also prudent, since it reduces the chances of writing something foolish. A request letter or memorandum is long enough if it gives the reader enough information to serve you and acknowledges that the reader is performing a service. The letter or memorandum is too long if it hinders the reader's efforts to serve you quickly.

COMMUNICATION PROJECTS

Practical Application

A. Write a letter to Whitesmith's Business Supply, 1199 Memorial Boulevard, Des Plaines, Illinois 46043, to order a desk. Before writing the letter, jot down answers to each of the following questions:

> *Why* are you writing?
> *What* kind of desk are you ordering?
> *How* do you want to pay for and receive the desk?
> *When* do you want the desk?
> *Where* do you want the desk delivered?

B. Find in magazines or newspapers two advertisements that invite you to write for additional information about products and services. Write a letter to each company to ask for a catalog, sample, brochure, or other descriptive information.

C. Write a letter notifying your favorite magazine that you have changed your address and would like to have your subscription transferred to the new address.

D. Write a letter to the Superintendent of Documents, U.S. Government Printing Office, Washington, D.C. 20402, asking for a list of publications about an occupation that interests you.

E. An advertisement for Rhenish Business Machines has interested you in a new high-speed copier. Write the company asking for the names and addresses of Rhenish dealers in your area.

F. At a meeting of the Consumer Awareness Club, someone proposes subscribing to the periodical *Consumer Reports,* published by Consumers Union, Mount Vernon, New York 10962. One club member has heard that a group of people can subscribe to the magazine and the *Annual Buying Guide* at reduced cost. You volunteer to request information from Consumers Union about group subscriptions. Write the request letter on behalf of the club.

G. A valuable oil painting was given to you as a gift. One morning you notice a crack in the painting. Write the Fine Arts Museum requesting its booklet *Care and Preservation of Oil Paintings.*

H. How many ways can you express "please" and "thank you" without using the actual words? Consider yourself *good* if you find five ways; *excellent* if you find eight; *expert* if you find ten.

Editing Practice

The Word Processing Supervisor   Edit and rewrite the following paragraph, correcting all errors.

> Please send me the compleat two-volume set of *Marketing and Distribution.* I understand that for the price of $39.95 I will also receive a one-year subscription to *American Business Today,* along with a callendar for business executives. Please refrane, however, from placing my name on any mailing lists.

Rewrite Desk   Improve the following first lines from request letters.
1. You are hereby informed that your warranty has expired. Please read the company service regulations herewith before requesting any maintenance hereafter.
2. Here is the booklet.
3. We have not received your scheduled payment and want it now.
4. Your letter of October 9 fails to make clear which model you own.
5. We could surely use the advice of a management consulting firm like yours.

Case Problem

Positively Friendly   Positive statements are more likely to win goodwill and to promote business than are negative ones. Rewrite these statements to make them sound more friendly.
1. Nothing is more frustrating than a customer who fails to understand the instructions that go with your blender. There isn't much we can do to fix the blender now.
2. I'm sorry, but you can't very well expect us to replace damaged merchandise when you are responsible for dropping the typewriter.

41
ANSWERING REQUESTS

Because request letters usually seek information about a product or service, they present an opportunity to make a sale. Expensive advertising campaigns elicit some requests for products or services. Other letters of request come through the efforts of sales personnel. And some, of course, come because someone "chanced" to hear about a product, perhaps from a satisfied customer. Whatever prompted a request letter, the business writer answering the request has an important opportunity.

Requests vary, of course, and so must responses. A skilled business writer, however, will treat the writing of almost all responses as an opportunity to make a sale or to promote goodwill. Consider response letters written for the following common reasons:

1. To transmit printed materials, such as a catalog, a price list, or a booklet.
2. To answer questions about products or services.
3. To acknowledge an order received and to give the date and method of shipment and the terms of payment.
4. To agree to or to confirm a meeting or appointment.
5. To express regret that an appointment cannot be made or kept, and perhaps to suggest another date.
6. To explain a delay in shipping or an accounting error.
7. To acknowledge receipt of information, materials, money, or merchandise.
8. To follow up on decisions reached at meetings and during conversations.

A moment's reflection will show how a letter written for any of these eight reasons could be used to promote sales or goodwill.

MAKING LETTERS RESPONSIVE

In its first sense, *responsive* simply means "giving a response." The second and more specific sense, however, is the one intended here: "quick to respond or react appropriately or sympathetically."[1] What qualities would we expect to find in a letter that is responsive in this sense? To begin with, the letter would be prompt. The letter would be appropriate to the questions asked—it would provide complete and specific information. The letter would be sympathetic to the needs stated in the request and would, therefore, be helpful. In addition, the response letter would seek to take advantage of the opportunity to promote goodwill or make a sale. In a word, the response letter would be *sales-minded*.

We can now state five basic rules to guide the writer of response letters:

1. Be prompt.
2. Be helpful.

[1]*Webster's New Collegiate Dictionary*, G. & C. Merriam Co., Springfield, Mass., 1980, p. 987.

3. Be sales-minded.
4. Be specific.
5. Be complete.

Be Prompt

Every inquiry, every request, and every favor should be acknowledged promptly. Many companies require that every letter be answered within forty-eight hours of its receipt; some organizations allow only twenty-four hours for a response.

Even when an inquiry cannot be answered in detail, common business courtesy dictates that some kind of reply be sent promptly. The letter of inquiry should be acknowledged, and the inquirer should be given some specific indication of when to expect the information sought. For example:

> Dear Ms. Cargill:
> Your request for a price quote on bulk orders of No. 223X Bohemian lead crystal is being handled by Mr. Stanley Merritt. He is contacting the importer to determine how soon the crystal could be obtained in the quantity needed, and at what price. Mr. Merritt expects to have a response by September 12 and will write you as soon as he has the information you requested.
> Sincerely yours,

The writer of this letter has acknowledged the request and has told the customer that a specific person is acting on it. The response also lets the customer know to expect another, fuller response a short time after September 12. Of course, the writer would send Mr. Merritt a carbon of this letter and place another copy in a "tickler" file—a daily reminder—for September 12.

Writers who handle many similar requests each day must look for shortcuts that will enable them to write many replies promptly. Whenever possible, therefore, writers will take advantage of word processing equipment.

Modern word processing equipment has a memory feature that will store many letters permanently. For example, to send 100 original copies of the same letter to 100 different people, the operator enters the correct codes (to tell the machine which letter is needed) and types the date line and the 100 addresses and salutations. (Many machines will automatically type salutations.) The equipment will automatically do the rest! Such equipment obviously saves a tremendous amount of typing time, even if only a few words or a paragraph must be changed from letter to letter.

The letter shown on page 360 was prepared on a word processor. The operator typed the date line, the inside address, and the salutation and stopped the machine at the end of the third paragraph. The operator typed the last paragraph. The machine then completed the letter.

Another way to handle a large volume of requests quickly is to print a card or letter with blanks that can be easily filled in as necessary for each specific request. For example, Good Health Publications uses the following printed letter to answer requests for any publications that are out of stock. Besides the date line and the inside address, the typist merely includes the name of the out-of-stock publication and the date by which the customer will receive a copy.

Structured Business Programmers Inc.

89 Dunhill Drive
Bellevue, Washington 98005

April 14, 19--

Mr. Perry Eaton
Quarry Water Filtration Inc.
88 West State Street
Boulder, Colorado 80302

Dear Mr. Eaton:

We are delighted to comply with your request for additional
information about computer programs for your business.

Whether you need systems to handle General Ledger, Payroll,
Accounts Receivable, Accounts Payable, Inventory, or mailing
lists and correspondence, we can supply programs that do the
job for less than you imagined possible. You owe it to
yourself to visit our local dealer and see some of our soft-
ware in action. Structured Business Programs will make your
computer the hardest worker on your staff.

We have a complete line of off-the-shelf, tested programs for
all major minicomputers and microcomputers on the market.
For most businesses, these tested programs will do any major
business function--from recordkeeping to word processing and
forecasting--and at less than $800 each. The enclosed folder
describes each program in detail, with illustrations of
printouts and run-times. In addition, we can tailor programs
exactly to your needs.

If you would like a list of SBP users in your area, or if you
need additional information, please call our representative
in Boulder, Georgia Dunleavy, at 555-9182. Ms. Dunleavy will
be happy to make an appointment at your convenience to
demonstrate our products and answer your questions.

Cordially yours,

Michael A. Southwick

Michael A. Southwick
Sales Manager

dq
Enc.

Word processing equipment makes it easier for writers to answer requests promptly. To complete this letter, the operator typed only the date line, the inside address, the salutation, and the last paragraph.

Dear
Thank you for requesting a copy of _____.
Because demand for this booklet has been much greater than we expected,
we are temporarily out of stock. A second printing has been ordered and

should be delivered soon. In fact, you should have your booklet by
_____.

We appreciate your interest in Good Health Publications.

Sincerely yours,

An alternative approach is to prepare a card or letter that is entirely printed; no information must be added to it. Printed responses are discussed on pages 367–371.

Promptness is especially important when acknowledging a favor. A tardy note of thanks, no matter how well written, seems to show a lack of appreciation. Prompt acknowledgments need not be long, but they should be sincere and cordial, like the one below:

Dear Mr. Carbo:

Thank you for your hospitality during my visit to Cleveland. When I got home last night, I couldn't help thinking that the Edmonds contract would never have been signed without the help of you and your well-managed staff. I appreciate your thoughtfulness in foreseeing the protracted negotiations and providing for every comfort of the negotiators.

You may be sure, Mr. Carbo, that I would welcome the opportunity to return your hospitality if business or pleasure should bring you to Phoenix.

Cordially,

Since customers and potential customers are pleased and impressed by prompt responses, capitalize on your promptness by mentioning how quickly you have acted. Usually you need only indicate when you received the letter you are answering, as shown by the following illustration:

When I received your letter in today's mail, I checked immediately into the availability of a private banquet room for your May 30 dinner meeting, and I am pleased to report that ....

When you go out of your way to give prompt service, you should let the reader know what you have done; otherwise, the reader simply cannot be impressed by the special effort. Note how the following letter does this.

Dear Miss Eyre:

Usually our volume of business makes it impossible for us to send a surveyor on less than two weeks' notice.

Because construction of your house has been halted, however, pending the results of a new survey, we have made you our first priority. One of our surveyors will visit your lot tomorrow morning and will make every effort to complete the survey before nightfall.

Sincerely yours,

Be Helpful

Response letters should show a sympathetic understanding of the needs expressed in a request and should, if possible, make more than the minimum effort to help. An answer that is grudging or indifferent is not really responsive and will surely annoy the recipient. The thoughtful writer remembers that behind every request is someone who has pinned hopes—great or small—on the response.

Going beyond the minimum to help does not mean merely writing a longer letter. It means, for example, being aware of a customer's needs and designing a letter to satisfy those needs if possible. The writer of the letter on page 360 has responded by enclosing a folder, by describing the suitability of the computer programs for performing major business functions, and by telling the reader where to obtain additional information. The writer of the following letter not only fills the request but also anticipates the inquirer's interest in a closely related product. Going beyond the minimum in helpfulness did not, however, require writing a long response.

> Dear Ms. Kroll:
>
> It's good to know that you are considering ImageMaker, our telephone facsimile transmitting system. One of our most popular items, the ImageMaker will enable you to send any graphic design 24 by 24 inches or smaller to any office in the world equipped with an ImageMaker and a telephone. The ImageMaker should be particularly valuable to you and your partner-architects in other cities. Now you won't have to wait days to react to one another's latest sketches.
>
> A wonderful complement to ImageMaker is our reducing, high-resolution photocopier, the ImageReducer. With no discernible loss in precision, the ImageReducer will reduce graphic designs as large as 48 by 48 inches to 24 by 24 inches—small enough to transmit using the ImageMaker. The combination of ImageMaker and ImageReducer will save not only the transit time of mailing or of shipping by airfreight but also the cost.
>
> We very much appreciate your interest in our products and would be happy to demonstrate them for you soon.
>
> > Sincerely,

Even though you may not always be able to provide what the reader desires, you should be as courteous and as helpful as possible. For example, the letter below probably won a friend for the writer's company, even though the correspondent could not give the customer what she wanted.

> Dear Mr. Preston:
>
> I wish we could send you the copies of the collector's limited edition of *Middlemarch* that you requested, but I'm afraid we have sold out. As you know, we pledged that we would print only 800 copies of the leatherbound, gilt-edged limited edition. We owe it to earlier purchasers to honor our pledge. We can offer you some equally beautiful limited editions of George Eliot's other books, as well as splendid limited editions of most nineteenth century English novelists. If any of these items interest you, please let us know soon so that we can reserve copies for you.
>
> > Sincerely,

Be Sales-Minded

Most products in the American marketplace are of high quality. Occasionally one manufacturer makes a product markedly better than competing products, but other manufacturers are quick to catch up. When products are similar in quality, what makes one a success and another a failure? **Answer:** The quality of service.

Everyone employed by a company today—the sales representative, the receptionist, the secretary, the messenger, the manager, the mail clerk, the switchboard operator, the correspondent, the president—has a part to play in serving customers. Every employee is expected to treat the public in a manner that will make and keep friends for the company. The company must both provide good service and project the image of providing good service.

Since service is so important to sales, sales-minded people must convey the idea that they are more interested in having satisfied customers than in just making a sale. Sales-minded people do not allow their letters to sound routine. Each letter is individualized as time permits; each one shows interest in the particular person to whom it is addressed. If a hundred letters must go out, the sales-minded writer will make each letter sound special.

One way of making response letters seem special is by varying the expressions used. If each day you must respond to many requests, you may be inclined to make them all sound alike; for example:

> This is to acknowledge receipt of your request for ....

The danger does not lie in the fact that two customers may find out that they have received exactly the same letters. The danger is that the writer becomes bored, and this boredom results in a mechanical indifference that shows in the letters. On the other hand, if the writer tries to create different letters, correspondence will become more interesting to write and more interesting to read. In how many different ways can you express "This is to acknowledge receipt of your request for ..."? Here are a few:

> Thank you for your order for ....
> Your order for the Smokecleaner is being ....
> This morning I had the pleasure of sending you ....
> I know you will be pleased with the new Smokecleaner ....
> We are grateful for your interest in Smokecleaner, and ....
> Your request for Smokecleaner arrived this morning, and I ....
> The Smokecleaner you asked for is being ....
> You made a wise choice when you ....

You, of course, can add to this list. The point is that you shouldn't allow your letters to sound like a broken record. By varying your wording of the same ideas, you will make your letters sound fresh, and you will give the reader the feeling that you are writing especially for that reader alone.

Of course, the ultimate purpose of every business activity is to make a sale. Most response letters, if they are well written, give the writer an opportunity to accomplish this goal. Unlike most sales letters, however, the letter of response is in answer to a direct request. In other words, it is in answer to an invitation to sell something to the reader!

As you read the following effective response letter, don't you get the feeling that the writer is sales-minded?

Dear Mr. Carlisle:

Thank you for asking about FINANCE WEEKLY, the publication prepared especially for business executives like you.

As a subscriber to FINANCE WEEKLY, you will receive every Friday valuable information about significant business changes throughout the nation. The enclosed form will bring you three months of this helpful financial service on a special introductory basis. The fee? A very low $5 for three months, or 12 issues—less than 50¢ an issue.

FINANCE WEEKLY not only keeps you abreast of present trends and developments in the financial world but also provides you with the kind of information you need from the world of politics and government...the world of banking...the world of stocks and bonds...the world of foreign trade...everything that affects the financial picture in *your* world—in your business and in your personal life.

To take advantage of this special introductory offer and to benefit from FINANCE WEEKLY's keen judgment and helpful advice, complete and return the enclosed form today. You need not send any money now. If, after reading the first issue, you don't agree that FINANCE WEEKLY will help you save much more money than the cost of a subscription, just let us know and we will cancel your order without charging you one cent!

Remember, too, your fee for this informative service is a tax-deductible business expense. This introductory offer is a huge saving over the annual subscription rate of $48—the rate at which 9 out of 10 regular FINANCE WEEKLY readers renew our service year after year.

We start your service just as soon as we hear from you. Once you learn to depend on FINANCE WEEKLY to help you make business and personal decisions, we know that you will look forward eagerly to receiving each Friday's issue.

Sincerely yours,

Note the chatty narrative style of the letter. Adding ellipses (. . .) in this instance contributes to the easy flow of the letter. This device is not recommended for all response letters, but it can be used effectively in some letters.

Remember that the good response letter offers an excellent opportunity to be of service as well as to make a sale. You can see these points in action in the following response letter.

Dear Music Lover:

Here is the brochure on quadraphonic sound that you recently requested. It describes this outstanding, new, four-channel music system that you may own and enjoy in your home for just slightly more than you might spend on an ordinary stereo system.

Quadraphonic sound does more than just add two speakers to your present two-channel, twin-speaker stereo system. It is as close to concert-hall realism as any home system can hope to be. Plan an early visit to our showroom in your city to hear a demonstration of this miracle of sound.

To broaden our market for quadraphonic records, the Classic Music Library has made it possible for you and your family to enter this fascinating new world of sound. And you don't have to make any of the time-consuming and costly mistakes that many people make when they buy stereophonic equipment and records.

We have taken care of all details for you in this superb Classic Quadraphonic system, assembled by the world's leading sound engineers. These artists of sound have created and assembled for you a finely engineered and matched set of stereophonic components; a complete 50-record library of the world's best music; a remarkable 10-record audiovisual encyclopedia of music, the first of its kind; a full set of beautiful library cases; and a custom-designed, handrubbed hardwood cabinet for displaying the entire library.

Yes, simply because Classic wants to broaden the market for these new quadraphonic records, you can now have the Classic Music Library installed in your home for only $50 down and $16.50 a month until the low total price of $875 is paid. This price is only a few dollars more than you would pay for ordinary stereo records and an ordinary stereo system. Look—and listen to—how much more you get for just a little more money!

To order your Classic Music Library, simply fill out the enclosed postage-paid card and mail it today. It will bring you a selection of records to choose from and samples of wood finishes to match the type of cabinetry that will best suit the decor of your home.

Sincerely yours,

Even though Classic's letter may be a printed form letter, it has been written with the personal touch that combines all the essential qualities of the well-written response. Note the effective use of the *you* attitude, the use of word-picture images, and the logical presentation of benefits that the product has for the reader. This letter of response, therefore, provides an excellent opportunity to persuade a customer to buy.

Be Specific

In all letters of response, the writer should specifically identify the subject of the letter being answered. In the examples given here, notice how the writer has taken pains to be specific.

In acknowledging receipt of money, you should refer to the amount and to the purpose for which the money was paid. For example:

Thank you for your check for $82.90, which we will apply to the balance of your account.

We appreciate receiving your check for $196.88 in payment of Invoice No. 50402.

In confirming appointments, repeat the time and place of the meeting so that there will be no misunderstanding. Note these examples:

We are pleased to accept your invitation to attend the Market Sales Conference on November 10–12 in the Santa Ana Room of the Chancellor Inn.

I was delighted to have the opportunity of chatting with you this afternoon. As we discussed, I shall meet you in Anaheim at 2:30 next Tuesday afternoon in the lobby of the Ramsdale Hotel.

When acknowledging the receipt of important business papers (and they should always be acknowledged), the paper or the document should be specifically named—contracts, policies, checks, stocks, bonds, and so on. For example:

The Letter of Agreement for drilling an exploratory well on the Hendershot lease reached us today. Our counsel will review the agreement's final amendments as quickly as possible. If there are no unforeseen problems, we expect that our officers will sign the agreement and return it to you by Thursday.

The San Antonio Municipal Bond certificates, Nos. 11,211-12,974, have been received and are now stored in a safe-deposit box at the Holloway Trust Company.

Frequently orders for merchandise are acknowledged by letter. These acknowledgments should specify the date of the order and the purchase order number. The acknowledgment should also refer to the date and method of shipment, as well as to any special instructions concerning the order. For example:

We are delighted that you are taking advantage of our end-of-year sale on furniture. Your Order 437, dated December 18, will be shipped by United Parcel this afternoon. As you requested, we will deliver to your Sansone Street store.

Another form of response letter is the follow-up letter, which should always be written to thank a customer for an order, to confirm a meeting date, to formalize a business agreement, or to verify information exchanged during a telephone conversation. Follow-up letters must be specific in enumerating the major points of the agreement or conference, as shown by the following letter:

Dear Clarence:

I am writing to confirm our telephone conversation of this afternoon regarding the first Estes Stores Celebrity Amateur Golf Tournament. We reached agreement on the following points:

1. Susan McDowell will handle liaison with the charities that will benefit from the tournament's proceeds.
2. You will be responsible for recruiting celebrities to play in the tournament alongside local amateurs.
3. I will coordinate plans with both the Amateur Golfers' Group and the Stebbing Golf Club.
4. The tentative date for the tournament is June 23, 19--.
5. A Coordinators' Committee will be formed of Estes Stores' management, with full charge of financial arrangements for the tournament.

Please let me know if you see the need for further arrangements of any kind. Thanks for your help in organizing this important public-service event.

Cordially,

Be Complete

An important quality of every business letter is completeness, and the letter of response is no exception. "Have I included all the information the reader needs?" is the question everyone must ask before mailing a response letter. The writer who is not able to answer all the questions asked should direct the inquirer to a source where the answers can be found.

To make sure that complete answers are included in response letters, some writers underline the important points in the letter of inquiry; others jot comments in the margins of the letter. These underscored words and marginal notes then serve as an outline to help the writer prepare a complete response letter.

This technique is illustrated by the letter of inquiry shown on page 368 and the response to that letter shown on page 369. Note how the writer, in responding to the questions, answers them in the order they were asked and uses the same numbering system. Note, too, that *every* question is answered, even though the folder enclosed will answer the same questions. By personalizing the letter in this way, the writer has made it more effective.

USING PRINTED RESPONSES

One advertisement in a national magazine can cause a deluge of request letters, especially if a free booklet or a free sample is offered. Such an advertisement may draw hundreds of thousands of pieces of mail, all of which must be answered. Obviously, this many requests cannot be promptly or efficiently answered by writing individual letters; individual letters would be impractical, much too costly, much too time-consuming.

When such a great response is anticipated, form letters or cards are printed in advance, before the advertisement appears, and are ready to be mailed as requests are received. The copy is carefully written so that it will answer most of the inquiries prompted by the advertisement and will keep to a minimum the number of individual responses that will be needed. If the printed response is too specific, its use will be limited; if it is too vague, it will not be useful in answering most of the requests. Its planning, therefore, is a major consideration. (See the printed form on page 370.)

The writer's first step is to try to anticipate the questions that will be asked; the next is to answer each one clearly. The form letter may itself provide the information, or it may simply refer to an enclosed booklet or pamphlet that answers the questions. But no matter how well the writer anticipated the readers' queries, some individual replies will usually have to be written to answer questions not covered in either the form letter or the booklet.

A reply card may be included (usually postage paid), to facilitate the reader's ordering the product, asking for a free demonstration, requesting inclusion on a mailing list, making an appointment with a sales representative, and so on.

The printed response form shown on page 370 was accompanied by a "handy postpaid card" and an explanatory booklet. This response card is not too specific; its use will not be limited. On the other hand, hotel reservation confirmation forms and

1783 Lincoln Boulevard
Westwood, Virginia 23205
April 2, 19--

Ms. Marion Lemaster
Sales Manager
Electrostatic Cleaner Company
896 Kingston Avenue
Chicago, Illinois 60613

Dear Ms. Lemaster:

I am very much interested in the Electrostatic electronic
air cleaner that was advertised in the March issue of Home
Products. There are some questions I would like answered
about your air cleaner to help me decide whether yours is
the make that best suits my needs.

  1. Under what principle does your air cleaner work? *agglomerate*

  2. Where does the unit have to be mounted? *Vertical, horizontal, underneath*

  3. How often does the collecting cell have to be
      washed? *18 mos.*

I should appreciate your answering these questions in time
for me to make a decision by May 10.

                          Very truly yours,

                          James A. Daughtrey
                          James A. Daughtrey

Jotting comments in the margin of a request letter help the recipient to answer the request
completely.

similar special-use responses are very specific, but because they fit highly standardized situations they suit their purposes very well.

   A word of caution about printed responses: Make sure that the letter sent really answers the request. In the rush to respond to a large number of requests, you can easily

Electrostatic Cleaner Company 896 Kingston Avenue • Chicago, Illinois 60613

April 24, 19--

Mr. James A. Daughtrey
1783 Lincoln Boulevard
Westwood, Virginia 23205

Dear Mr. Daughtrey:

Thank you for your interest in the Electrostatic electronic air cleaner. I am delighted to answer the questions you have asked about the model advertised in Home Products.

    1. This model, FL-190-A, operates on the agglomerator principle. The dirt particles are charged and collected on the cell plates in the conventional way, but as they build up on the cell, they "agglomerate" or break off in chunks, which are easily retained by the special pad on the clean-air side of the cell. This method of air cleaning, used successfully for many years in commercial installations, eliminates the need for frequent washing of the cell.

    2. The unit may be mounted either horizontally or vertically in any forced-air system, or it may be placed underneath a furnace.

    3. The cell may have to be removed and washed in a good nonsudsing detergent once every 18 months or so. This procedure will be necessary only if the cell is especially sticky or greasy.

I am enclosing a folder that describes the unit in more detail, gives price information, and lists the dealers in your area who carry this model. You will find that there is no finer air filter on the market, that its installation is flexible, and that its price is competitive.

Please let us know if you have any further questions.

Very sincerely yours,

Marion Lemaster

Marion Lemaster
Sales Manager

rej
Enclosure

By answering each of the reader's questions in the same order as they appeared in the original request, the writer has made this response more effective.

make errors, either because you read the request carelessly or because you are not thoroughly acquainted with the contents of the form letter.

For example, suppose that a dealer who now obtains service independently requests information about costs of factory repair service from the manufacturer,

Semaphore Industrial Products
4445 Sandusky Road
Ridgefield, Connecticut 06877

Here's the information you requested.

We hope that you'll find ideas to solve your business problems. That's what Semaphore is all about--making products that solve your problems.

If you see a role in your business for any of our products, use the handy enclosed postpaid card today. The sooner you contact us, the sooner we can start solving your problems. You can count on us for a prompt response.

Thank you for your interest.

Sincerely yours,

E. F. Hopewell
Vice President, Sales

A printed form is useful for answering many similar requests promptly.

Predmore Drycleaning Machines. How will the dealer react if he receives the following reply?

To Service Engineers of Predmore:
The Predmore service and parts manual that you requested is enclosed.
The manual describes normal repair procedures for each subassembly. If you

have any problems, however, you may either write to or telephone our Service Department (555-3838, Extension 112).

Please note that factory repair service is also available to dealers and their customers—and at minimum cost. For information about factory repair services and prices, please request Predmore Factory Service Manual PD1985.

Best Regards,

The dealer, of course, is not a service engineer and was not asking for a manual of service and parts. What the dealer wanted was information about the cost of factory service. Someone at Predmore sent an inappropriate response letter without reading the response letter or the dealer's request letter carefully. The response letter even gives the number of the manual that the dealer needs. But instead of sending that manual, someone simply stuffed the wrong form letter into an envelope. Lost: one potential customer because of an inappropriate form letter.

COMMUNICATION PROJECTS

Practical Application

A. Steven Crowell, 23 Saltway Drive, Saltway, Florida 33596, requested from your company, Allword Publishing Inc., a copy of your new magazine *Microwave Chef*. Demand has exceeded expectations, and the first issue has sold out. Write an appropriate response to Mr. Crowell.

B. Patricia Thompson, Sales Manager for Bermuda Beauty Lawn Products, 1132 South Market Avenue, Claremore, Minnesota 54335, has received an order from the Howard House and Garden Shop, 853 Wallace Street, Dearfield, Illinois 62705. The order, dated March 1, is large and is the first received from Howard House and Garden. Terri Sturz, the manager of Howard, wants to know the terms of payment and how and when the merchandise will be shipped. Write Ms. Thompson's reply to Ms. Sturz.

C. Alice O'Toole, Director of Public Relations for Smithton Typewriter Manufacturers, 332 Phillips Avenue, Manchester, New Hampshire 03110, has telephoned Gerald Maurice, Chief Advertising Consultant for New England Best Business Consulting, 212 Crofts Street, Peterborough, New Hampshire 03484, and asked him to make a presentation on "Advertising in the Electronic Age" at the convention of the New England Advertising League. The presentation is to take place on June 24 at the Merrick Hotel in Cambridge, Massachusetts 02138, starting at 4:30 p.m. Mr. Maurice is to make a 40-minute presentation and then participate in a 20-minute discussion period. The meeting will be held in the Peerless Ballroom and will be followed by dinner from 5:30 to 7 p.m. Mr. Maurice is invited to the dinner as a guest of the Advertising League. Write the letter that Ms. O'Toole should send to Mr. Maurice to confirm all the details of his participation in the convention.

D. Suppose that Mrs. Andrea Childs, 2224 Humbolt Street, Akron, Ohio 44313, owner of an Infinite Video Computer Game System, made by Infinite Video, 833 West San Pedro, Mountain View, California 94041, has sent a defective unit to the factory for repair. Unfortunately there is a shortage of a usually abundant silicon integrated circuit, or "chip," needed to repair the game system. Integrated circuits have been ordered from Japan but are not expected for two weeks. Write a letter explaining the delay and telling Mrs. Childs when to expect the return of her repaired unit.

E. As a correspondent for GleamGold Healthful Shoes, 3558 Layton Street, Monroe, Maryland 20810, you have been asked to write a form letter that will accompany a brochure, "The Health of Your Feet: Our Way and Theirs." Requests for the brochure are expected to come from a coupon advertisement that will appear in *The Elegant Gentleman* magazine. Remember that a good response letter offers an excellent opportunity to be helpful as well as to make a sale. Be sure to mention that the brochure lists local GleamGold dealers and includes a reply card for other free informative brochures from GleamGold.

Editing Practice

Updating Correspondence   Rewrite these excerpts from letters, replacing any dated expressions.

1. The information in your application has been duly noted.
2. We wish to extend our thanks to you for taking the time to complete the questionnaire.
3. I have before me your letter of October 10.
4. Up to the present writing, we have not received your payment for last month.
5. We will be sending the service manuals to you under separate cover.
6. I am enclosing an invoice in the amount of $210.98.
7. In the event you will be unable to accept the offer, please advise.
8. I am sending herewith the annual report for last year.

Case Problem

Right Meeting—Wrong Report   Mark Maxwell works in the sales department of the Rapier Razor Company. His supervisor asked him to attend an important meeting of the advertising department staff to explain how the two departments can work together more effectively to increase sales in the year ahead. Mark misunderstood the subject he was to discuss and, instead, prepared a talk on the function of the sales department. Listening to the introduction, Mark realized that he had misunderstood the topic.

1. What should Mark do when he is called upon?
   a. Give the report he prepared.
   b. Admit his mistake and ask that the meeting be rescheduled if necessary.
   c. Blame his supervisor for giving him the wrong information.
   d. Bluff his way, hoping that no one will notice.
2. How could this situation have been prevented?

42
ANSWERING
PROBLEM REQUESTS

We cannot always give people what they want. Some requests are unreasonable; in addition, circumstances force us to refuse many reasonable requests. The bald fact is that we sometimes have to say "No."

Few of us like giving "No" for an answer. Most of us, in fact, find saying "No" so unpleasant that we put off saying it when it must be said. We hope that someone else will do the dirty work or that the passage of time will say "No" by implication. But ultimately the bad news must reach the person whose request is being refused.

With the bad news, inevitably, comes disappointment. When you must give a "No" answer, keep this key fact in mind: Refusing a request always disappoints someone. No matter how unreasonable the request, the person who made it hoped for a positive answer. Business writers must be sensitive to the person who has pinned hopes on the answer to a request and faces disappointment. A clumsy refusal may deepen the disappointment into anger and resentment. In business terms, this means that poor handling of an answer to a request destroys goodwill.

TYPES OF PROBLEM REQUESTS

If a personnel officer interviews ten applicants for one new job, then the officer must say "No" nine times and "Yes" only once. When buying a new carpet, the consumer says "Yes" to the salesperson in one store and "No" to salespeople in all the others. Companies have to say "No" to the credit applications of persons who habitually fail to pay bills.

These common types of request hardly scratch the surface of the many that must be turned down. Consumers constantly ask wholesalers to sell products directly at the wholesale price. Manufacturers are often asked to sell their products directly to the consumer or to unauthorized retailers. Sometimes people ask a company for information that could be revealed only at great risk to the company—a product formula, a trade secret, or a marketing strategy for a new product.

Answering some requests would take too much time and money. Granting requests to endorse political figures or controversial ideas might damage a company's standing in the marketplace. Requests for confidential information about employees are nearly always refused.

Every business, furthermore, receives more requests than it can honor for donations to charities, educational institutions, religious groups, service clubs, and other worthy causes. Most businesses, as good citizens, do contribute generously to such causes, but there is a limit to the amount that can be budgeted for such contributions.

All too often, then, businesses must say "No" to requests. But when businesses do find themselves forced to say "No," they must be sure to state good reasons—reasons that will not offend the person or company making the request. Indelicate answers to problem requests can endanger the goodwill that a business has built up in a community.

WRITING ANSWERS TO PROBLEM REQUESTS

How can businesses answer problem requests without jeopardizing goodwill? Correspondents must be sensitive to the feelings of the people who have made the requests. A skillful writer can say "No" gracefully without causing ill feeling. The following five guidelines for answering problem requests will help you acquire the skills necessary for writing this difficult kind of communication:

> Be positive.
> Show appreciation.
> Distinguish between the person and the request.
> Don't place blame.
> Give reasons.

Be Positive

People tend to reflect toward others the attitudes displayed toward them. If you are negative in your approach to others, they are likely to be negative toward you. If you are positive in your approach, people are likely to react toward you in a positive manner. For example, if you frown when you meet someone, the chances are that the other person will frown too. On the other hand, put a pleasant smile on your face, and the odds are that the other person will respond with a smile. Psychologically, then, if you want your reader to respond in a positive manner, you must write in a positive manner—even when you are saying "No." Consider the contrast between the following examples of negative and positive statements:

Negative	Positive
Your product does not meet our specifications.	Our engineers believe that the brand we selected is closest to our specifications.
You do not meet our standards for this particular job.	Although your qualifications are excellent, we feel that we must continue to search for someone who meets all the unique qualifications for this job.
In view of your poor payment record, we are unable to grant you credit.	We shall be glad to evaluate your credit record after you have settled some of your obligations.
We must say "No."	Unfortunately, we cannot give you a "Yes" at this time.
Your prices are too high.	Perhaps, when you have adjusted your prices to make them more competitive, we shall be able to do business with you.
We cannot give you the information you want.	We should like to send you the information you request, but we know you will understand why this is not possible.

The letter on page 376 illustrates how positive words and a positive attitude may soften a refusal and help to retain the goodwill of the customer.

Show Appreciation

Often requests, even though they cannot be granted, require considerable effort on the part of the person or company making the request. Showing appreciation for such effort is one way to create or preserve friendly relations.

If a charity, for example, requests a donation when no funds are available, the correspondent who answers "No" must remember to show appreciation for the charity's previous good works. See, for example, the letters illustrated on pages 376 and 379.

Showing appreciation can also help when one business must say "No" to another. Manufacturers often purchase components from other firms for use in assembling a complex product. Dozens of companies may compete for the opportunity to supply the components. Competition involves not only the quality of the components but also delivery schedules and service arrangements. Notice how the following letter shows appreciation despite having to say "No."

> Dear Mr. Fountain:
> Thank you very much for the time, the effort, and the ingenuity that you and your staff devoted to developing a prototype air-filter for our new model Z-999 helicopter engine. The filter that you developed performs well in tests and has many superior design features.
> The decision was difficult, but we have decided in this instance to adopt the filter submitted by Filtrex Aviation Products Inc. Large-scale production of the Filtrex filter seems slightly nearer at hand, and you know how important speed is in introducing a new engine to the aviation market.
> Let me assure you, however, that we are impressed by the quality of your design team. We appreciate your interest in doing business with us, and we would welcome further proposals for use with our many other products.
> > Sincerely,

Distinguish Between the Person and the Request

Make clear that rejection of a request does not mean rejection of the person or the company who made the request. Final refusal of one proposal need not rule out consideration of a later proposal on another matter. Leaving the door open to future proposals may soften the blow of a present refusal.

Here are some phrases that offer future hope:

> Perhaps at some future time we shall . . . .
> Maybe, when our needs expand . . . .
> We are keeping your application on file for . . . .
> We wish that we were able to consider your request, but . . . .
> It is possible that next year . . . .
> We shall certainly keep your proposition in mind when . . . .

Global Industrial Enterprises, Inc.

993 Wichita Drive
Houston, Texas 77052

May 11, 19--

Ms. Eleanor Rote
Confederation for Good Works
Corporate Gifts Committee
296 Belweather Lane
Houston, Texas 77058

Dear Ms. Rote:

Your eloquent letter of May 9 has reminded us once again of
the many worthy activities of the Confederation for Good Works.
Your contributions to the community are unsurpassed.

GIE must budget for donations to charities, and since we
receive many deserving solicitations, we prefer to review all
these requests at the same time. We make decisions about
charitable gifts during the month of September. We will
keep your request on file and give it careful consideration
at that time.

We very much appreciate your thinking of GIE, and we wish you
continued success in all the Confederation programs.

Very sincerely yours,

Baxter H. Taranto

Baxter H. Taranto
Vice President

BHT:tn

Showing appreciation is especially important when the writer must say "no" to a request for a donation to a worthy cause. Note that the writer leaves the door open for the future.

The following letter illustrates the gentle art of leaving the door open.

Dear Ms. Sanders:

We appreciate your interest in working for McDougald Industries. Thank you for taking the time to prepare an application for the position of newsletter editor.

Although your credentials are impressive, we have decided to adhere to our requirement of a minimum of four years' journalistic experience. Your career shows promise, but we feel that we require someone who has had more experience.

Your qualifications are excellent as a reporter, and we will keep your résumé on file against future openings in that position if you are interested. In any case, we know that you have a bright future, and we wish you the best.

Very sincerely yours,

On the other hand, encouraging false hopes may only lead to further heartbreak. If you cannot see any use in encouraging future proposals, neither invite them nor forbid them. Show appreciation for the person making the request. Offer reasons for refusal that will save face for the person making the request. Be friendly and be tactful. Although you may have to walk a thin line, be careful neither to hurt feelings nor to lead anyone on. The following letter shows both honesty and delicacy in meeting a difficult problem.

Dear Mr. Ricupero:

Thank you for expressing an interest in working for McDougald Industries and for taking the time to prepare an application for the position of newsletter editor.

Competition for the position has been keen, and we have had to refuse many worthwhile applicants. We very much regret that we cannot offer you the position.

We do appreciate your letting us see your résumé. Please accept our best wishes for your continuing contributions to our community.

Very sincerely yours,

As an applicant, you would not be so disgruntled by this gentle refusal, nor would you blame the company, for it has given you a face-saving reason for the refusal. Remember that applicants may also be customers or friends of customers, so it is to the advantage of the company to retain their goodwill even when turning them down for a job.

Don't Place Blame

Even worse than rejecting the person who makes a request is blaming that person for the "No" decision you must make. Little can be gained by blaming your reader for sins, sins that cause your refusal. Basic kindness should prevent any but the most naive writer from writing the following:

Under no circumstances would we ever make a purchase from your company. The last order we gave you arrived a month late, despite the fact that you promised faithfully to get it to us on time.

You will help your reader save face when you avoid statements that suggest fault or blame. Here are additional examples of placing blame:

> Because of your mistake, we cannot . . . .
> Since we were dissatisfied with your previous service . . . .
> You neglected to let us know that . . . .
> Because of your unsatisfactory repair of . . . .
> Since you failed to . . . .

Suppose that bidders for a contract had been notified that the bids would be opened at 3 p.m. on June 5. Suppose that one contractor did not submit a bid until the following morning. You have heard from business associates that this contractor has in the past submitted bids after the deadline to undercut the lowest bidder. For ethical reasons, you cannot accept the late bid. However, you should certainly not write a letter like the following.

> Dear Ms. Teele:
> You failed to submit your bid at or before 3 p.m. on June 5. You have been known in the past to follow such a practice in order to undercut the bids of your competitors. Submitting bids after the deadline is unethical and unfair to other bidders. We cannot, therefore, condone such unethical procedures.
> It goes without saying that we must reject your bid.
> > Very truly yours,

Instead, the letter to the unsuccessful bidder should be worded something like this:

> Dear Ms. Teele:
> Your bid on our proposed office building was received at 11 a.m. on June 6. Since all bids were opened at 3 p.m. on June 5, the deadline indicated, we are returning your bid unopened.
> We know that you will understand why the bid must be returned to you.
> > Sincerely yours,

Such a letter should cause this contractor to make sure that she submits future bids on time.

Give Reasons

Good reasons make refusals easier to take. Since most refusals are in fact based on good reasons, stating reasons is an important part of saying "No." The reasons should be true, should be convincing, and should be objective, not personal. Here are some good reasons for having to refuse requests.

> Because our margin of profit is so small, a further reduction in our selling price would result in a loss to us.
> Our budget for charitable donations for this year has been exhausted.
> Our dealer agreement gives Marlin's the exclusive right to sell our products in your city.
> To collect the information you request would require several weeks, and we simply cannot afford to devote so much time to doing the job.
> The All-Aide line we are now carrying has proved to be a very successful item for us, and we do not think a change at this time would be a wise decision.

**STERNHAUS
TRUCKING COMPANY INC.**
80760 VARICK AVENUE
MINNEAPOLIS, MINNESOTA 55430

August 30, 19--

Mr. Theodore de Vries
President
Center for Public-Affairs Studies
390 Hamilton Avenue
Minneapolis, Minnesota 55445

Dear Mr. de Vries:

Thank you for your letter of August 28 requesting a contribution to the Center for Public-Affairs Studies. We have
long admired the work of the Center, and we applaud your
service to the nation.

Sternhaus has for the past decade made a practice of matching
our employees' gifts to worthy causes. Through these matching
donations, we feel that we not only contribute to the public
good but also reaffirm our commitment to the well-being of
our employees and to the things they value.

Our program of matching gifts--the Sternhaus Gift-Matching
Program--fully consumes the budget that we are able to devote
to philanthropic efforts. We do hope that among our employees
there is an interest in supporting institutions like yours,
and we will certainly match any gifts that our employees make
to your program.

We very much appreciate your thinking of Sternhaus. Although
we can contribute to your fund-raising drive only through the
matching arrangement described above, we do want to emphasize
our respect for the Center's work.

Cordially yours,

Lorinda Stanhope

Lorinda Stanhope
Vice President-Public Relations

LS:kb

By giving the reasons why the request must be refused, Ms. Stanhope has written a convincing, objective reply.

If you must refuse a specific request, sometimes you can propose another course of action that may bring a favorable response. Notice the attempt to achieve such a goal in these communications.

> I regret that another engagement makes it impossible for me to speak at your April meeting. However, I would be happy to speak at your May or June meet-

ing. I would appreciate your giving me a month's notice.

Why not put your suggestions in writing and send them to us? After we have had an opportunity to carefully consider your suggestions, we can get together to discuss them further.

Note how the writer of the letter illustrated on page 379 has carefully explained why the request must be refused. Note also that the policy of the company has a built-in alternative: If the employees contribute, the company will match their contributions.

Now assume that you work for a wholesaler who sells only to retail outlets. A consumer (not a retailer) has sent you a rather large order. You must refuse because it would not be fair to your retail-store customers for you to sell directly to consumers at wholesale prices. Note how the reasons given in the following letter soften the refusal because they show that the writer's decision is factual and objective.

> Dear Ms. Morrow:
>
> Thank you for your letter requesting a pair of Dance Designer Model 121 ballet slippers. We appreciate your interest in our products, and we are forwarding your order with a copy of this letter to Harlequin Dance Shop, 332 West Brinker Street, Wichita, Kansas 67202. Harlequin is the Dance Designer retailer serving the Wichita area.
>
> Besides Harlequin's expertise in serving dancers, we refer you to Harlequin for the following reasons:
>
> 1. Harlequin has an exclusive franchise to sell Dance Designer products in your area.
> 2. Harlequin carries the complete line of Dance Designer products.
> 3. The franchise agreement prohibits Dance Designer from selling directly to the public in the Harlequin area.
>
> We are confident that Harlequin Dance Shop can serve you every bit as well as we could ourselves, and we recommend that you visit Harlequin soon.
>
> Yours very sincerely,

The writer of this letter has stated sound reasons for refusing Ms. Morrow's request. In addition, the writer has extended a courtesy by forwarding the order to a local retailer. Ms. Morrow will receive her slippers almost as quickly as she would have if Dance Designer had shipped the slippers directly. Here is a refusal performed entirely in positive terms—appreciation, explanation, and assistance.

COMMUNICATIONS PROJECTS

Practical Application

A. The Association of Women for Charity has asked you to speak at its monthly meeting on January 15. The topic is to be "Organizing the Office." Since you received the invitation only on January 8, however, you do not feel that enough time remains for you to prepare a good speech. Write a note of refusal to the chairperson, Mrs. Blanche Ludlum, 8788 North Filmore, Blacksburg, Virginia 24060.

B. You are a new employee in the sales office of a manufacturer of motion picture projectors, screens, and accompanying audio equipment. Your predecessor has been fired, leaving behind a stack of half-finished correspondence. How would you revise the following draft of a letter left in the "out" basket?

Mr. Geoffrey Boole
1100 Davona Drive
Indianapolis, Indiana 46226

Dear Sir:

Your order for a Zapamattic movie outfit has reached us. As manufacturers, we do not deal directly with the buying public. Therefore, we cannot fill your order as requested. Contact Hagen Camera Retailers, 668 Northpoint Street, Indianapolis, Indiana 46221. Let us know how you make out.

Yours truly,

C. The Knobhill College Foreign Affairs Club has written you, president of Mendez & Swan, Inc., asking the company to contribute $250 to help pay expenses for ten club members to visit three South American capitals. You are happy, as an individual, to contribute $50; but Mendez & Swan has a policy of contributing only to national charities and community-wide local causes. Write the letter that you will send, along with your personal check, to the club's president, Ms. Audrey Caxton, 334 Dormitory 2 East, Knobhill College, 227 East Kelly, New Orleans, Louisiana 70140.

D. You work for Smithson & Maddox, Inc., publishers of science textbooks for junior high schools and high schools. The Stinson Teachers Association has written asking your firm to exhibit books at the next meeting of the city teachers. Expected attendance is 300 teachers, only 70 of whom will be science teachers. The exhibit fee is $50. Your company's policy is to exhibit only at national and statewide meetings at which there will be at least 400 science teachers in attendance. Write the letter of refusal to Mr. Conrad Blakely, President of the Stinson Teachers Association, 2945 Westlake Road, Stinson, New Mexico 87101.

E. A representative of the Super Cola Company wrote the answer below to a request from Susan McNeil, a junior high school student, for the formula of the company's popular soft drink. Rewrite the letter as you think it should be written.

Dear Miss McNeil:

The formula of our unsurpassed soft drink is a closely guarded secret. Over the years our competitors have tried again and again to pilfer the formula —without success. Few of our own employees know the formula, and those who do have signed a nondisclosure agreement. We are not about to release the formula to you. At your age, you should be learning the hard facts about competition in the business world.

Very truly yours,

Editing Practice

The Editing Desk   Edit and rewrite the following paragraph, correcting all errors.

We regret that, washing in accordance with the care label caused your dress to shrink. Other customers have made the same complaint since we introduced the dress only last week. We have spoken to the manufacturer, who has already completed an investigation. The manufacturer acknowledges that: the wrong care labels were sewn into these dresses because of a mistake on the production line. A check refunding the full purchase price, of $75, should reach you within two weaks.

Case Problem

The Chronic Complainer Myoshi Tora works at the desk next to Paul Thebes. Paul complains ceaselessly about everything—the poor lighting, the bad ventilation, the unfairness of the supervisor, the shortcomings of other employees, and all Paul's own personal problems. Myoshi sees little justice in the complaints. Myoshi tries to overlook Paul's incessant complaints, but the constant interruptions make Myoshi's own work more difficult.

1. What should Myoshi do about the situation?
2. What, if anything, should Myoshi say to Paul?

43 WRITING CLAIM AND ADJUSTMENT LETTERS

Despite the most rigorous quality-control programs, flaws do sometimes occur in both goods and services that reach customers. Customers are quick to point out such flaws. Since businesses succeed in the long term by keeping customers satisfied, most businesses give customer complaints a fair hearing and try to settle them.

The handling of customer complaints is a normal and important part of business. Most of these complaints concern purchased merchandise that fails to work, purchased services that fail to meet acceptable standards, or promised refunds or credits that fail to appear. A customer's letter reporting such a complaint is called a "claim letter" because the customer claims to have received less than what he or she is entitled to. A company's response to a claim letter is called an "adjustment letter" because the company often attempts to make an adjustment satisfactory to the customer.

This section teaches you the important skills needed to write both claim and adjustment letters. Why must the business writer be capable of writing both kinds of letters? Because every business has customers, and at the same time every business is a customer.

THE NATURE OF CLAIMS

A claim is an assertion that the customer has received less than his or her due. While many claims are founded on fact, some arise from misunderstandings. Sometimes customers are right in saying something is amiss but wrong in blaming the seller of the goods or services in question; a third party for example, a shipping company may be responsible for the problem. Occasionally a customer is simply mistaken. The point to keep in mind is this: When a business receives a claim letter, someone will have to judge whether there is a basis for the claim. When a business writes a claim letter, the claim must be able to stand up to the examination of a judge in another company. Consequently, the major task in writing a claim letter is to make the most convincing case possible for the claim asserted.

MAKING THE CASE FOR YOUR CLAIM

If you order and are billed for merchandise but do not receive it, you have a just claim against the company that sold you (or your firm) the merchandise. The inconvenience resulting from the failure to deliver the merchandise may annoy or anger you. As you write the claim letter for the merchandise not received, you may feel an impulse to express your annoyance or anger, as did the writer of this letter:

Mr. Alfred Bonner
Billing Department
Mendenhall Plastics Corporation, Inc.
4338 Columbus Avenue
Trenton, New Jersey 08629

Dear Mr. Bonner:

We have received your invoice for twenty-five 100-pound bags of polypropylene resins of injection-molding grade. When we placed this order 17 days ago, we stressed the need for speedy delivery of the resins and were promised delivery within 10 days. Your invoice for 25 bags arrived on the tenth day. On the fifteenth day, we got a shipment of five 100-pound bags of resins.

We are still awaiting the remaining 20 bags of resins that we need to complete a rush custom-molding operation. You probably knew all along that you couldn't deliver the goods as promised. If the resins are not here by Friday, we are prepared to go to court.

Yours truly,
Bertrand Copeland
Manager, Purchasing Department

Although Mr. Copeland may be the "injured party" under the law, he was mistaken to let his injured feelings dominate the claim letter. Approximately 98 percent of the situations leading to claims are accidental, not intentional. Furthermore, most businesses recognize just claims and try to settle them fairly. By sending the threatening letter above, however, Mr. Copeland may actually have decreased his chances of receiving the needed plastic resins. The angry letter is likely to make the reader want to fight the claim rather than settle it.

Belligerent claim letters are often ineffective because they fail to take into account the human feelings of the reader. **Remember:** It is the reader who must pass judgment on your claim and decide upon any action in response. Suppose the reader of the angry letter above investigates and discovers that all 25 bags of resins were shipped on time, that the shipping company is responsible for the delay. Rather than shipping an additional 20 bags right away, the reader is more likely to reply:

> Dear Mr. Copeland:
> Investigation reveals that all 25 bags were shipped on time. Copies of the shipping papers are enclosed. Take up your problem with the shipping company.
>
> Yours truly,

If Mr. Copeland had written the following—more reasonable—letter in the first place, he would probably have received the needed plastics sooner.

> Dear Mr. Bonner:
> We have received your invoice for twenty-five 100-pound bags of polypropylene resins of injection-molding grade. When we placed this order 17 days ago, we stressed the need for speedy delivery of the resins and were promised delivery within 10 days. Your invoice for 25 bags arrived on the tenth day, but we received none of the resins until the fifteenth day, when we received only 5 bags.
>
> We would appreciate your checking your records to make sure that all the resins have been shipped. If so, please check with the shipping company at once. Our customer desperately needs the items to be made from these resins and is understandably upset that we have not delivered them as promised. We are counting on you to help us make up for lost time.
>
> Please let us know the minute you find out what has happened to this vital shipment of resins. We will hold your invoice until we receive all 25 bags of resins. Then, of course, we will be happy to send payment.
>
> Sincerely yours,

This letter is firm in asserting a claim but takes a positive attitude toward the reader—who is, after all, the judge of the claim. Rather than attempting to bully the reader, this letter makes a good case for the claim. The letter is factual, reasonable, and persuasive. In most instances, this kind of approach will bring good results.

WRITING CLAIM LETTERS

The example discussed above suggests some rules for writing your claim letters. In addition to maintaining a positive attitude toward the business or person addressed in your claim letter, you should also:
1. Be sure of your facts.
2. Describe your claim completely and concisely.
3. Suggest reasonable solutions.

4. Avoid threats and demands.
5. Avoid accusations.

Be Sure of Your Facts

The successful claim must state clearly all the facts about the claim. If, for example, part of your order is missing, it is important to establish that the portion of the order was missing on arrival. You must be certain that every item has been weighed, counted, checked, and rechecked so that you know exactly what was received and what was not received. Many slipups can happen on your side, the claimant's side—errors in ordering, misplacing a shipping or acknowledgment copy, miscalculating extensions on bills, misunderstanding verbal instructions on an order—even errors made at the receiving dock or in the storeroom. As the claimant, you will be doubly embarrassed to find that the error is yours! Be sure of your facts before writing a claim letter.

Describe Your Claim Completely and Concisely

Give the details necessary to establish your claim, such as dates, styles, catalog order numbers, and purchase order, invoice, or check numbers. Only then can the recipient of your claim determine how the error occurred. More important, only in this way can the recipient determine the source of the error and try to prevent similar mistakes from recurring.

Suppose, for example, that the insurance company that handles your automobile insurance notifies you that your policy is no longer valid because you have failed to pay your premium. You recall that you wrote the company a note on the back of their notice stating that your policy would be canceled if your premium was not paid within 10 days. In that note, you explained that your check (No. 186) had been mailed January 4 for the full amount of the premium. Since you had no further word from the insurance company, you assumed that they had located the check and that everything was all right. Now the claim letter that you write might read as follows:

> Dear Ms. Higgins:
> I was distressed to receive your notice of March 1 indicating that you have canceled my automobile insurance policy No. AZ1843687 for failure to pay the premium of $350 due on January 15.
> On January 4, I mailed Check 186 for $350. On January 17, the check, endorsed by your company and stamped "Paid," was returned to me. I reported this information to you on the back of a notice of cancellation mailed to me January 30. Since I received no further word from you, I assumed that the matter had been straightened out satisfactorily.
> I am enclosing a photocopy of the front and back of my canceled check. Would you please send me a notice of the reinstatement of my insurance.
> Very truly yours,

Note that the letter gives *all* details, completely but concisely, so that the insurance company can quickly rectify the situation.

Suggest Reasonable Solutions

The claim letter that suggests a reasonable solution strengthens your chances of gaining a just settlement. For example, if you placed an order and received only part of it, one solution might be to indicate that you will accept the missing portion if it arrives by a specific date, as shown by the following statement:

> We shall be happy to accept the 6 lamps if they reach us before February 5, the first day of our Anniversary Sale.

Or suppose that you were overbilled $50 on an order. In this case, you might say:

> Our records indicate that we were billed $250 for the merchandise on our Purchase Order 3290, dated July 7. The figure should have been $200. Therefore, please credit our account for $50 and send us a credit memorandum for this amount.

It is usually best to suggest the kind of solution that you consider acceptable. If you received defective merchandise, for example, you might request replacement of the merchandise, cancellation of the order, a credit of the amount to your account, or substitution of a similar item that meets your needs. By suggesting a solution, you will let the company know what kind of action you want taken. When your suggestion is reasonable, there is a good chance that the company will follow your suggestion.

Avoid Threats and Demands

Give the receiver of your claim the benefit of the doubt. Of course, no courteous person would use such phrases as *you must, I want you to, I demand, unless you,* or *I must insist.* Furthermore, a claimant who makes threats and demands will only alienate the reader. Rather than use such strong language, a good writer uses a positive approach and gives the reader sound reasons to support the claim. The chances are that this approach will result in a faster settlement of the claim.

Suppose that the letter you write to the insurance company is not answered within a reasonable length of time. You may want to send a follow-up claim to the president of the agency that handles your insurance. Here is an example of the kind of letter you could write:

> Dear Ms. McDonald:
> I am enclosing a photocopy of a letter I wrote to the main office on March 5. My letter has not yet been acknowledged, and I am concerned about whether my automobile insurance is in force.
> I should very much appreciate your looking into this matter for me and providing written notification regarding the status of my automobile insurance.
> Very sincerely yours,

By selecting and addressing the follow-up claim to a higher official, you indicate you are concerned about a reply, yet your letter doesn't threaten or blame or accuse.

After you, as claimant, have exhausted all your letter-writing resources, your attorney may want to write in a more threatening tone.

Avoid Accusations

The goal of a claim letter is to receive a fair adjustment, *not* to place blame or gain revenge. Accusations make receiving a fair adjustment less likely. Suppose, for example, that you are the manager of a shoe manufacturer selling wholesale to many shoe stores. You allow a 2 percent discount on payments received within 15 days of the date of an invoice. One month a customer, Mr. Norris, mails a check 30 days after the invoice date—much too late to qualify for the discount—but deducts 2 percent. The letter happens to reach you on a particularly negative day. In the frustration of the moment, you fire off the following letter:

> Dear Mr. Norris:
>
> You know full well that you mailed your check this month too late to qualify for our 2 percent discount. Trying to get away with a thing like this is no better than picking our pocket. We have to pay our bills on time in order to receive discounts, and so must you. Don't try to pull a fast one like this again. You will not receive next month's order until you pay the balance of this month's bill.
>
> Yours truly,

Perhaps Mr. Norris does realize that he has mailed his check too late to qualify for the discount but hopes that no one will notice. Mr. Norris is, of course, prepared to pay the extra 2 percent. He is guilty of nothing more than wishful thinking. Receipt of the accusing letter above may cause Mr. Norris to take his business elsewhere.

Here is a more effective claim letter to Mr. Norris:

> Dear Mr. Norris:
>
> Thank you for your check for $456, dated June 30, in payment of our invoice of June 1 for $465.12. You are one of our most valued customers, Mr. Norris, and we hope that you found the merchandise up to our usual high standards. We understand how hectic a business office can be. With so many records to process, nothing could be easier than misreading a date or forgetting a deadline. As you know, our terms of 2/15, n/30 are more generous than most businesses allow. We do try to overlook it when a payment arrives a day or two late to qualify for the discount. But if we permit the discount on a check that arrives 15 days late, then we will effectively destroy the incentive for all our customers to pay promptly. With today's finance charges and interest rates at such high levels, prompt payment is more vital than ever.
>
> We can resolve the matter simply in whichever of two ways you prefer. We can either credit your account $456 and carry over to your next statement the unpaid balance of $9.12, or, if you find it more convenient, you can mail us the $9.12 to complete this month's payment.
>
> Next month we will be introducing our new fall line of women's shoes. (We will have all items in stock by July 24.) We have enclosed an advance-release brochure for you, and we will be eager to hear your reaction to this new designer collection.
>
> Cordially yours,

This letter meets the test of an effective claim letter. It is positive in tone, and the facts are clearly and concisely presented. Two acceptable solutions are suggested to the customer. Instead of accusing, the writer is courteously appreciative; in addition, the writer tries to develop goodwill.

In writing claim letters, remember that you're writing to people—people who are just as human and just as reasonable as you are. Calmly explain your facts; suggest reasonable alternatives; and avoid any discourteous threats, demands, or accusations. A claim letter written in this manner is likely to produce a favorable and prompt adjustment.

MAKING SATISFACTORY ADJUSTMENTS

Here are some everyday business situations involving dissatisfied customers: (1) An order for printed personal stationery is filled with the address incorrectly printed. (2) A customer makes a claim against an out-of-town retailer for overbilling, forgetting that the account also showed a previous unpaid balance. (3) A customer seeks damages from an appliance manufacturer for a defect in a newly purchased electric blender. In each instance, the customer feels justified in writing a claim letter to ask the appropriate person for an adjustment.

To handle adjustment letters satisfactorily, you, the writer, must use language skillfully; you must also have a sound understanding of the psychology involved in handling and settling claims. Because all claims are somewhat distasteful and irritating to the claimant, the adjustment-letter writer should soothe the claimant's feelings. To the extent possible, you should try to retain or rebuild the claimant's goodwill as a future customer. Finally, within the limits of company policy, you must provide an adjustment that is equitable.

Any person responsible for making adjustments must be familiar with the company's policies. Policies, of course, are the guide rules for the actions of a business. Such rules ensure that a business will act in a consistent manner in all its transactions. These rules provide guidelines for arriving at adjustments that are fair both to the customer and to the company.

Equitable Adjustments

Equitable adjustments mean reasonable, right, fair, honest, and impartial decisions in dealing with claims. As a writer of adjustment letters, you must act as a judge. You must collect all the facts for and against the claim, weigh the evidence, and arrive at a decision that is right both for your business and for the customer. Therefore, before replying to a claim letter, you must consider all aspects of the situation and be satisfied that your decision is equitable.

Making the Right Decision

Even the most clever writer of adjustment letters will be unable to write a letter to retain goodwill and future sales if the basic adjustment decision is unfair or unjust to the customer. The writer of adjustment letters can, however, rely on certain guides in weighing the evidence and arriving at wise decisions. Three sources of evidence that the adjuster should tap are the company, the claimant, and the transaction itself.

The Company   Your company, like most other companies, is ethical in its dealings. (You would not want to be associated with a company that is not.) Ask yourself the following questions to determine the extent of your company's responsibility in causing the claim. Do you know, without a doubt, that the company is not at fault? Could anyone in the company have made a misleading statement? Could the advertising be misinterpreted? Could your records be at fault? Is it possible that someone in the company made a mistake? If such questioning reveals an element of blame on the part of the company, you, the adjuster, will probably decide to honor the claim, at least in part.

The Claimant   To help you evaluate the claimant's share in causing the claim, ask questions like these: Could the claimant be mistaken? Is the claim, if true, the kind that a reasonable person would make? Has the claimant provided all the information you need to check the claim and fix responsibility for it? Does the claimant have a record of fair dealings with your company?

The Transaction   The answers to the following questions will help you arrive at an equitable decision about the transaction. Did your company carry out all its obligations—both explicit and implied—to the customer? Has your company made any claims with reference to this product such as, "Double your money back if you are not absolutely satisfied"? Were any misleading statements made to the customer by your sales personnel? Is there evidence of faulty materials or workmanship in the product? Were the instructions for use of the product clear and complete? If you find a defect either in the product or in the handling of the transaction, you should decide in favor of the claimant. This is just one more application of the almost universal business rule of trying to please the customer.

Sometimes you will have to seek further information before you can answer the above questions. You may need to question some of your fellow employees or to write the claimant before you have all the facts at your disposal. The following letter is an example of an inquiry addressed to the claimant.

> Dear Mrs. Slezak:
>
> Thank you for your October 17 letter reporting a malfunction of your Ralston 299 aquarium filter. We are sorry that you are having problems with the filter, a product that is usually quite reliable.
>
> We have looked in vain for a copy of your warranty agreement, which should be on file here. The period of the warranty is normally six months. If you could send us the number from the top right corner of your receipt, we could date the purchase. If you do not have the receipt, then please give us the name of the dealer from whom you made the purchase and the approximate date of purchase.
>
> As soon as we receive the information, we will be happy to make an adjustment.
>
> > Sincerely yours,

When you receive the necessary information, you will be able to make an equitable decision on the claim.

WRITING ADJUSTMENT LETTERS

Arriving at a just decision is one matter; communicating this decision in a way that will satisfy the claimant is another. The easiest adjustment letter to write is one allowing the claim. The most difficult is a letter for a claim that must be disallowed. The letter for the claim in which some compromise is found equitable lies between these extremes.

An Allowable Claim

Mistakes occur even in the best-regulated businesses. When the fault is your company's or your own, admit the error freely. The claimant will respect you if you are big enough to admit a mistake, especially if you have erred for the first time. You should accept the responsibility of correcting your error without quibbling over the added cost or effort caused by it. Remember that the writer's aim is to keep the claimant as a customer. Note how the writer of the following letter attempts to retain the customer's goodwill.

> Dear Dr. Fowler:
>
> Thank you for your December 9 letter reporting a problem with your new barometer.
>
> From your description of the problem, we believe that your aneroid barometer was mistakenly calibrated for use as an altimeter. We manufacture altimeters and aneroid barometers using the same mechanism—only the calibrations are different. Somehow our normally efficient production staff and inspectors must have placed the wrong model number and name plate on the mechanism that you received. We are reviewing our procedures in an effort to prevent this kind of mistake from happening again.
>
> We are very sorry for our mistake, and we have shipped you a new barometer by airfreight. We hope our error did not spoil any of your weather forecasts. If we can be of further assistance to you, Dr. Fowler, please don't hesitate to write or call.
>
> Sincerely yours,

Provided the cost is small, some companies will allow a customer's claim—even when evidence for the claim is doubtful. The object is to keep the customer. The hope is that future sales will compensate for any loss that results from settling a doubtful minor claim.

A Partially Allowable Claim

Letters seeking a compromise solution to a claim require more delicacy. If the item in question is of great value, the company may want to send an adjuster to negotiate a compromise in person.

Suppose, for example, that a recent purchaser of a commercial automatic film processor wants to exchange the processor. The customer states that the processor is no good because the developed film comes out wet instead of dry. You feel certain that the problem is caused by failure of the small fan under the drying hood. Replacement of the fan will take one of your service technicians ten minutes and cost you only $25. Exchanging the entire processor, which weighs 200 pounds and is valued at $9,000, will be expensive because of shipping costs. Moreover, the customer will have to wait at least three weeks for arrival of a new processor. You decide to seek a compromise adjustment.

How much of an adjustment a company makes in a case like this depends on company policy. You believe that the customer will be satisfied with the processor after the fan is replaced. You are also willing to offer the customer a $50 discount toward the purchase price as compensation for the inconvenience caused by the failure of the fan. Your letter describing this proposed adjustment might read as follows:

> Dear Ms. Hammond:
> We very much regret the news that your new SuperSpool Rapid Film Processor is not working properly. The problem sounds to us as if the fan under the drying hood is at fault. Although we thoroughly test each processor before it leaves our plant, the machines are sometimes damaged by rough handling in transit.
> Exchanging your processor for a new one would require subjecting another unit to the hazards of shipping. In addition, you would be without a processor for at least three weeks. We seriously question the wisdom of exchanging the entire unit when only one small component is the cause of all the trouble.
> We realize that the fan's failure has inconvenienced you, Ms. Hammond, and we want you to be satisfied with our products and our service. We believe that the following adjustment would serve you well. We can send a service technician to your plant with a new drying fan. Replacement of the defective fan should take only 10 minutes, and you can test the processor immediately to make sure that everything is working properly. In addition, we have included a $50 discount certificate.
> If this adjustment is satisfactory, please call our service center at 555-2243 to make an appointment at your convenience. We will make sure that someone answers your call promptly.
> We are also confident that your SuperSpool Rapid Film Processor will provide good service for years to come.
> Sincerely yours,

The writer of the letter above must be prepared to negotiate with Ms. Hammond. She may wish to be compensated, for instance, for all film wasted as a result of the fan's failure.

A Nonallowable Claim

Perhaps the most difficult letter to write is the one in which you must refuse to grant an adjustment. Sometimes the refusal is necessary just to avoid setting a precedent for allowing unjustified claims. The cost of settling one such claim might be small, but a business cannot afford the cost of settling many unjustified claims.

For example, assume that you are a fabric manufacturer. Unless you handle fabrics on consignment, you cannot permit every retail outlet to return yard goods just because the goods don't sell. Suppose, however, that you receive a request from Mr. Trevino to return the unsold goods. Of course, you must disallow the claim; but you should do so in such a way that you will retain Mr. Trevino as a customer. Your letter to him should protect your company's position and, at the same time, should show interest in the customer's point of view. For example:

> Dear Mr. Trevino:
>
> Thank you for writing us about the summer suiting materials you wish to return for credit. We checked our records and we find that you received the goods on March 1, in plenty of time for your presummer sales.
>
> Of course, we can see why the fabric weights that you bought must be sold during a particular season. We wish we were in a position to absorb your materials into our stock. Unfortunately, we have no outlet for them and our warehouse space is limited.
>
> May we recommend that you cut your price to 10 percent above cost and include them in your midsummer clearance sale. Most stores do this most successfully when a fashion item fails to move. Hobart's Department Store used a novel way of disposing of similar materials last year—they featured the fabrics as drapery materials rather than as suiting.
>
> Our Mr. Aikin will be in your store on August 1 to show you our new winter and spring patterns. If you have not sold the material by that time, Mr. Trevino, Mr. Aikin may have some additional suggestions for you.
>
> Sincerely yours,

Note that this letter accomplishes the following purposes:

1. It starts with a positive tone, and the tone throughout the letter is friendly and courteous.
2. It acknowledges Mr. Trevino's claim and sympathizes with his problem.
3. It offers suggestions that Mr. Trevino may follow, and gives as an example the name of a well-known department store that was successful in solving a similar problem.
4. It helps maintain goodwill and good public relations by indicating that there will be follow-up by a company representative.

COMMUNICATION PROJECTS

Practical Application

A. The City-Wide Newspaper Delivery Service, 322 Oxford Street, Detroit, Michigan 48226, has billed you for a month's delivery of both daily and Sunday newspapers. You ordered only the daily newspaper, however, and that is all you received. The delivery service has charged you $7.20 for 24 issues of the daily newspaper and $3.40 for 4 issues of the Sunday newspaper. For an adjustment to your bill, write to Ms. Sylvia Ferrer, the customer service representative for the City-Wide Newspaper Delivery Service.

B. Sylvia Ferrer receives your letter seeking an adjustment to your monthly bill (see A above). Her records confirm your claim that you ordered and received only daily newspapers. Compose the adjustment letter that Ms. Ferrer should send in response to your claim.

C. Review the letter of adjustment addressed to Ms. Hammond (page 391) concerning the problem film processor. Assume that Ms. Hammond is not satisfied with your offer to replace the fan and to send a $50 discount. Instead, Ms. Hammond agrees to accept replacement of the fan, but she also wants full compensation for all film wasted as a result of the defective fan. You decide to write Ms. Hammond offering to send a claims adjuster to her photography business to examine the wasted film and determine its value. But you also decide not to commit yourself at this point, to pay for all film wasted. Write the letter.

D. After visiting Ms. Hammond's photography business (see C above), your adjuster tells you that five 100-foot rolls of 12-inch-wide film were ruined because the fan failed. Since the film is valued at $.50 per foot, the cost of the film wasted is $250. Your adjuster says that the fan is definitely the immediate cause of the wastage. The adjuster adds, however, that Ms. Hammond should have stopped running the processor and called for service after the first roll or two of film was ruined. Decide how much compensation Ms. Hammond is entitled to, and write a letter to her either accepting or denying her claim to compensation for all 500 feet of wasted film.

E. Write a letter for William Steiner, the manager of Le Crepuscule, a French restaurant located at 665 Darien Street, Omaha, Nebraska 68108. Today Mr. Steiner has received a new, heavy-duty commercial food processor, but his chef shows him that it does not slice foods as precisely as advertised. Write the manufacturer, Whirling Wonder Kitchen Aids, One Bluegrass Way, Lexington, Kentucky 40506, requesting replacement of the food processor.

F. You work in the Claims and Adjustments Department of Whirling Wonder Kitchen Aids. You receive a letter from the manager of Le Crepuscule (see E above) requesting replacement of a food processor that is not slicing evenly. You know from experience that uneven slices usually result from a damaged slicing disk. Write Mr. Steiner, the manager of Le Crepuscule. First, ask whether the food processor performs correctly with other attachments, such as the two-bladed knife and the shredding disk. If the machine does correctly dice, chop, grate, grind, and shred, you explain, the problem is definitely the damaged slicing disk. Offer to replace the slicing disk at no cost if this is the problem.

Editing Practice

Applied Psychology Rewrite the following sentences so that each promotes goodwill.

1. There is no chance that we will be able to deliver your order on time because a number of smarter consumers placed their orders before you.
2. Since you were careless and failed to sign your Check 210, we are returning it.
3. You must be too lazy to open your mail, because we have already written you once about this matter.
4. Your October 3 letter fails to explain satisfactorily your delay in paying.
5. Your failure to reply has made the problem even worse.

6. We will repair the chair that you claim was damaged in transit.
7. You are the only person who ever found our football helmets unsatisfactory.
8. You neglected to indicate the number on our invoice.
9. You complained that Order 977 did not arrive on time.
10. You made a mistake of $27 on our March 15 invoice.

Case Problem

Attending to Customers   Charles Winthrop is a sales representative in the men's furnishings department of Lambert's Department Store. Early on Saturday morning his supervisor came by and said, "Charles, see if you can get your new merchandise marked and put on the shelves as quickly as possible. It's going to be a busy day, and I have several special things for you to do." While Charles was rushing to complete the job, a customer, Mr. Casey, entered the department. Even though Charles was the only available sales representative, he continued marking the merchandise and let the customer wait. Just as Charles finished his marking and went to wait on the customer, Mr. Casey walked out.

1. Was Charles justified in ignoring Mr. Casey in order to finish marking the new merchandise? Why or why not?
2. What should Charles have said to Mr. Casey as soon as he saw him?

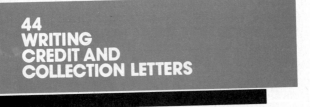

44 WRITING CREDIT AND COLLECTION LETTERS

Imagine a new company that sells a very expensive product. The product has taken two years to develop, and because it is expensive, each sales representative may work months to sell one item to a client. When a sale is made, the profit is substantial; but until it starts making profit on a regular basis, how much money must this company have in order to meet its payroll, to purchase supplies, and to pay its rent, taxes, and other business expenses?

Not many companies can finance such a new operation using cash on hand. Most must rely on credit. Indeed, even established, successful business firms must often rely on credit to help them meet day-to-day expenses, expand their operations, or take advantage of a unique opportunity that suddenly arises. Just as businesses cannot operate without money, businesses cannot operate without credit.

Individuals, too, rely on credit to improve their personal lives. The average person buys a home, a car, and many other items on credit; finances a vacation on credit; uses credit to pay for emergency bills; and so on.

Indeed, for businesses and for individuals credit is a most valuable tool when it is used wisely.

Today, the use of credit is widely encouraged by business firms and retail stores as an incentive to buy their products. Rare is the adult who does not have at least one credit card for charging such purchases as gasoline, hotel accommodations, airline tickets, car rentals, restaurant bills, and other kinds of merchandise and services. Businesses make use of the credit privilege for similar reasons.

The most common type of credit is open-account credit, which usually means that the customer has 30 days in which to pay for purchases. Consumers buy on open account from those who deliver their daily newspapers, from utility companies, and from retail stores. Business firms also buy on open account from many of their suppliers. To encourage prompt payment of an account, suppliers often grant retail stores and other large-buying customers a discount when an invoice is paid within a certain period. Typical terms are 2/10, n/30, which means that 2 percent may be deducted from the total amount of the bill if it is paid within 10 days of the date of the invoice; otherwise, the entire amount is due in 30 days. Retail customers do not generally enjoy this discount privilege.

THE THREE C'S OF CREDIT

Both consumers and business people receive credit on the basis of character, capacity, and capital—the three C's of credit.

Character

People of good character feel all their obligations strongly. With respect to financial obligations, people of good character feel a strong desire to pay what they owe. Evidence of such a responsible attitude in a borrower makes getting credit much easier.

Capacity

Capacity is the ability of people or businesses to meet their financial obligations. Even a person of the most upright character cannot repay a loan if he or she lacks the necessary money. Most critical in evaluating capacity is income. In a broader sense, *capacity* refers to the ability to earn income and to manage it wisely.

Capital

Capital refers to personal or business assets—cash, securities, real estate, and personal property. Creditors consider capital assets the most important of the three C's because these assets determine whether the business has the ability to pay if legal action to obtain payment should be required.

INVESTIGATING CREDIT APPLICATIONS

When asked questions about character, capacity, and capital, most of us give honest answers. Some people, unfortunately, do not. Applicants for credit fill out forms that ask for information about their assets, debts, income, and character references. Applicants may also be interviewed. A handful of people not only give dishonest answers but also are quite convincing at it. Extending credit to dishonest people would

Edson Wholesale Produce Inc.

1201 Great Market Street
Montgomery, Pennsylvania 17752

September 12, 19--

Mrs. Margaret Farrell
Credit Manager
Montgomery Commercial Bank
343 Franklin Street
Montgomery, Pennsylvania 17752

Dear Mrs. Farrell:

Ms. Annette Connor, owner of Connor Gourmet Greenery, 3229 Wilson
Avenue, Montgomery, Pennsylvania 17752, has filed an application for
credit with our firm. Ms. Connor has listed your bank as a reference.

In order to reach a judgment on Ms. Connor's application, we need
answers to the following questions about her record with you. We will
hold in confidence any information that you give us.

1. What is the average monthly balance in Ms. Connor's checking
    account(s)? What is the balance in her savings account(s)?

2. Have you extended credit to Ms. Connor on a secured or unsecured
    basis? Is any amount outstanding? On what basis?

3. Has your lending experience with Ms. Connor been satisfactory? Has
    she ever written an overdraft? Have there been any drawings against
    uncollected funds? What has been the maximum amount of loans that
    you have made to her?

We are considering extending credit up to $4,500 on terms of 2/10, n/30.
We would be grateful for your advice as to whether this credit limit is
a reasonable one for Ms. Connor's firm.

Very truly yours,

Steven Dana

Steven Dana
Credit Manager

SD:oz

For greatest effect, credit inquiries should ask specific questions.

raise interest rates for the rest of us, because the lender would have to make up for losses somehow. Consequently, credit managers are faced with the problem of determining which applicants for credit are telling the truth.

Investigations of applicants for credit rely on various sources—firms and stores with which the applicant has done business, banks where the applicant has accounts, and bureaus that specialize in credit rating. The letter on page 396 asks a bank for information about an applicant for credit. On page 398 is the bank's reply to the credit inquiry. Note that the bank is careful to provide accurate answers to the questions asked without divulging the actual account or loan balances.

Letters sent to the other business references supplied by the credit applicant would be similar to the one illustrated; of course, the questions asked would vary. For example:

1. Approximately how many years has the credit applicant had an account with you?
2. What is the maximum amount owed you at any one time?
3. What is the maximum amount of credit you would be willing to grant the applicant?
4. How would you consider the applicant as a credit risk? (Please check) Excellent_____Average_____Questionable_____

GRANTING CREDIT

Most applicants for credit are granted the privilege (although in inflationary times the government may restrict the granting of credit). When an investigation reveals that an applicant is a good risk, the business firm or store writes a letter of welcome. In this letter the seller should explain the terms of credit and should encourage the customer to use the new charge privileges. Because the granting of credit signals a new source of business, the welcoming letter is frequently signed by an officer of the company. The letter granting credit provides an excellent opportunity to establish a good business relationship with a new customer. For this reason, many large businesses resist the temptation to send form letters to new charge customers.

Business people recognize that an individually typed letter, even one that is prepared by automatic typewriter, provides a desired personal touch that will lead to good customer relations.

The letter shown on page 399 grants credit to the Connor Gourmet Greenery, whose owner is Annette Connor. The letter states both the credit terms and the personal services that Ms. Connor can expect to receive.

There is now a great variety of retail credit arrangements. Revolving accounts are common, as are various types of installment plans. Consumers should receive and read carefully a specific description of the terms of a charge account. The letter illustrated on page 400 grants credit to a customer of a retail store.

REFUSING CREDIT

Refusing credit requires writing a tactful and delicate letter. Some credit managers think refusing credit is such a sensitive task, in fact, that they prefer to handle it in person rather than by mail. Other credit managers prefer not to refuse credit explicitly,

Montgomery Commercial Bank

343 Franklin Street
Montgomery, Pennsylvania 17752

September 17, 19--

Mr. Steven Dana
Credit Manager
Edson Wholesale Produce Inc.
1201 Great Market Street
Montgomery, Pennsylvania 17752

Dear Mr. Dana:

I am pleased to reply to your inquiry of September 12, 19--, concerning
Ms. Annette Connor, owner of Connor Gourmet Greenery. We have had
dealings with Ms. Connor for the past nine years and are happy to answer
your questions.

Ms. Connor maintains both a regular checking account and a savings account
here. The balance of the checking account averages in the high four
figures, and the balance of the savings account averages in the low five
figures.

Unsecured loans reached a yearly high last October of high four figures.
Nothing is now outstanding. Our experience in lending to Ms. Connor has
been satisfactory in every way. We extended seasonal credit in April 19--,
on a secured basis up to a high of low five figures. All payments have
always been made promptly and according to terms.

We hold Ms. Connor's character and her business ability in the highest
regard. We think that you will experience no difficulty as a result of
extending Ms. Connor credit up to $4,500 on the terms you indicated.

If you have any further questions about Ms. Connor's financial capacity,
please let us know. We will be happy to supply additional information.

Yours very sincerely,

Margaret Farrell

Margaret Farrell
Credit Manager

MF:htt

Responses to credit inquiries do not divulge the actual amounts of account balances or loan balances.

but not to grant credit "at this time." The sentence below is an example of this tactic of saying "No" by virtue of not saying "Yes":

> Based on the information we have received regarding your credit standing, we feel we cannot make a decision on your application at this time.

Edson Wholesale Produce Inc.
1201 Great Market Street
Montgomery, Pennsylvania 17752

September 24, 19--

Ms. Annette Connor
Connor Gourmet Greenery
3229 Wilson Avenue
Montgomery, Pennsylvania 17752

Dear Ms. Connor:

Thank you for your recent request for open account credit
with us. We are pleased to extend you credit to a maximum
of $4,500, with terms of 2/10, n/30.

We anticipate a long, congenial business relationship with
you, Ms. Connor. Our service representative for your account
will be Charles Whitson. He will contact you every week to
make sure that you are getting produce in the quantity and
the quality that you need. If you have any questions about
produce or service, please feel free to contact Mr. Whitson
at any time.

Best wishes for the continued growth of Connor Gourmet
Greenery. Please let us know if we can be of service to you.

Yours very truly,

Steven Dana
Steven Dana
Credit Manager

SD:oz

A letter granting credit to a business firm should state the specific terms of credit and should develop a rapport with the customer.

Still other credit experts believe that the refusal can be handled effectively by letter without serious injury to the customer's pride. For example, the following letter of refusal was written by a credit person who believes in "leveling" with the customer. To avoid a negative response on the part of the rejected customer, however, the writer

Medley Moore & Company

One Whiteplains Place
Salt Lake City, Utah 84106

February 9, 19--

Mrs. Frederick Landy
455 Indian Way
Ogden, Utah 84401

Dear Mrs. Landy:

   Medley Moore & Company is delighted to add you to our list of credit
customers. We sincerely believe that our association will be long and
mutually pleasant.

   As one of our charge customers, you will enjoy many privileges. You
will receive advance notice of all special sales and will therefore be
able to take advantage of some wonderful bargains before they are
announced to the general public. You will automatically become a member
of the Medley Moore Travel Club, which entitles you to special rates on
more than a dozen European and Asian tours planned each year.

   Your status as a charge customer will also make it easier for you to
enjoy the many conveniences and amenities of shopping at Medley Moore.
You can charge meals in the Medley Moore Revolving Restaurant, charge
beauty treatments in Monsieur Hercules' Medley Moore Salon, and charge
instruction fees in the Medley Moore Crafts Studio.

   On the 10th of each month, you will receive an itemized statement
of all purchases made through the last day of the preceding month; purchases made after that date will appear on the following month's bill.
Payments are due on the 25th of each month.

   Please feel free to make regular use of your new charge card. Medley
Moore hopes to have many opportunities to serve you.

                                    Cordially yours,

                                    Melissa Moore

                                    Melissa Moore
                                    President

MM:gk
Enclosure:
   Charge card

A letter granting credit to an individual, like a letter granting credit to a business firm, should
specify the terms of the credit agreement and should help to build good customer relations.

has presented the factual, nonemotional information that caused the application to be
rejected. Also, the writer has counterbalanced the refusal by adding positive statements.

Dear Mr. Knapp:

We appreciate your requesting credit at Dyer's.

As is always the case in considering credit applications, Mr. Knapp, we have carefully investigated your ability to handle additional credit. Since your present credit obligations are substantial, we feel you should not endanger your credit reputation by taking on additional obligations.

Please let us continue to serve you on a cash basis until you have had time to reduce your present obligations. When the circumstances are more favorable, we will welcome your renewed application.

Sincerely yours,

The credit manager who refuses credit to an applicant, whether in person or by letter, has one objective—to persuade the customer to buy on a cash basis. This effort calls for the highest form of communication skill. Note how this is done in the above letter to Mr. Knapp and in the letter shown on page 402.

COLLECTION LETTERS

The more thorough the credit investigation, the fewer the losses from bad accounts. However, even the best regulated credit department will grant credit to some customers who will not pay their bills. Charge customers who do not meet their obligations must be reminded to make payment.

Collecting an overdue account is not an easy task. No one likes to ask for money. Yet businesses must ask—or lose money. The trick is to get customers to pay without losing their goodwill. The collection of overdue accounts will be greatly simplified if the following rules are observed.

Be Sure Customers Understand Your Credit Terms

The terms of credit should always be explained to the customer at the time credit is granted. (In fact, the law requires doing so.) In commercial credit (between wholesaler and retailer), it is also advisable to review credit terms pleasantly, but firmly, when you acknowledge a new customer's first order. If your terms are 30 days net, you expect your money in 30 days. Do not hedge with weak statements like *We hope you will send your check in 30 days.* You should instead say, *Our terms are 2 percent discount if you pay within 10 days; the net amount is due in 30 days.*

Assume That Customers Will Pay

When a customer fails to pay a bill on the date the payment is due, you should assume that this failure is an oversight. Most of your customers are honest, but they may tend to forget or to procrastinate. And psychologically, a distasteful task such as separating oneself from money tends to be delayed to the last moment. If the usual monthly statement does not produce results, send the customer a second statement a week or ten days later. You can write or stamp *Second reminder* or *Please remit* on

Lancelot Marine Supplies & Services
99 Ocean Front
Long Beach, California 90802

September 18, 19--

Mr. Anthony D'Alessio, President
Pacific Miracle Fishing Company
223 Seaview Road
Long Beach, California 90810

Dear Mr. D'Alessio:

We wish that we could grant open-account credit to Pacific
Miracle Fishing Company, but our credit investigation indicates
that we will be unable to do so at this time.

Like everyone else in the marine industries, we face the
problem of high receivables and operating costs. We feel that
we cannot increase our open accounts if there is an indication
that our terms of 30-day payments could not be met.

We would like, for the present, to handle Pacific Miracle Fishing Company on a c.o.d. basis. You are a valued customer, and
this decision in no way reflects your integrity and that of
your associates. After six months, we will be glad to review
credit references in the hope that we can then put your account
on an open basis.

We sincerely hope that you will not be discouraged from dealing
with Lancelot. We handle many companies on a c.o.d. basis and
pride ourselves on prompt shipping and delivery. We will do
our very best to give you first-rate service at every
opportunity.

Sincerely yours,

Stephanie Travis

Stephanie Travis
Credit Department

ST:abt

The objective of this letter refusing credit is to convince the customer to buy on a cash basis.

the statement. Some credit departments use a rubber stamp with a humorous reminder, such as a drawing of a finger with a string tied around it or a cartoon face drawn with a very sad expression. Some companies use impersonal printed forms such as the form shown on page 403; others use humorous forms. Most customers will respond to gentle hints that their accounts are overdue and that you want your money. Remember, the first follow-up is not an attack; it's a gentle nudge and is highly impersonal.

Send Additional Reminders Frequently

If a customer does not respond to the second statement, it's time to go into action. An account that is 120 days overdue is usually much more difficult to collect than one that is only 40 days overdue. Therefore, if you haven't received payment within ten days after sending a second statement, you should write a letter to the customer. Thereafter, send frequent reminders until the account has been paid.

THE COLLECTION SERIES

You have sent both a monthly statement and a reminder to Michael Wise, a charge customer. Ten days after the reminder was mailed, you have still received no response. Your first follow-up letter, though clear and firm, should still give Mr. Wise the benefit of the doubt.

First Follow-Up Letter

Dear Mr. Wise:

To date you have not responded to two statements mailed to you. We must remind you that the balance due on your account is $225.80.

If your records differ from the balance shown, please let us know at once. If your records and ours agree, please send us your check for $225.80 to clear your account.

                              Sincerely yours,

Just a Reminder . . .

Perhaps you've overlooked sending us the minimum payment due on your most recent credit card statement.

Your payment for the amount due below will be appreciated. Has it already been mailed?

  Credit Card No.: 126–07–9845

  Minimum Amount Due: $39.

Royal Department Store
Duluth, Minnesota 55801

This impersonal printed form is a gentle hint that an account is overdue.

What if Mr. Wise fails to respond to the first follow-up letter? Practice varies from company to company. In general, however, the second follow-up letter should go out not later than 15 days after the first. The tone of the second letter should remain friendly and courteous, but should be firmer and more insistent than the first.

Second Follow-Up Letter

Dear Mr. Wise:

We have still not received the $225.80 balance that you owe us, and we do not understand why we have not received that sum or at least a word of explanation for the delay in payment.

To remind you of the facts: The net amount was due on June 20. We did not hear from you by that date. We sent a second statement on July 1. When we had still received no reply as of July 12, we sent another letter asking if there was an error or some other problem hindering you from making payment. As of today, August 1, we still have had no word from you. In all fairness to us—and to yourself, Mr. Wise—please let us hear from you by return mail.

Sincerely yours,

How long will the company wait before taking legal action against Mr. Wise? Again, practice varies from one company to another, but most companies will send from three to five letters before turning the account over to a lawyer or a collection agency. Either of these steps is expensive and time-consuming, and companies prefer to take every possible step before resorting to legal action.

In a five-letter follow-up series, the third letter to Mr. Wise will be more insistent and forceful than the second. The fourth letter will frankly demand payment. The fifth letter will state that legal action will be taken if the delinquent customer fails to take advantage of this last opportunity to pay. Note how each of the letters that follow is sterner than the one before.

Third Follow-Up Letter

Dear Mr. Wise:

Help us save your reputation.

We have been very patient—your account is now 75 days overdue. You have ignored two statements and two previous letters. Your unpaid balance remains $225.80.

Knowing our credit terms, you purchased merchandise on account. You have received the merchandise. You have not, however, sent your check for $225.80.

You are placing your credit standing and your reputation in jeopardy.

Help save your credit rating and your reputation. Send us your check for $225.80 now.

Sincerely yours,

Fourth Follow-Up Letter

Although the tone of the fourth letter in this series is still more severe, the writer is still trying to appeal to the delinquent customer's self-interest.

> Dear Mr. Wise:
>
> As you must know, this letter is the sixth reminder that you owe us $225.80. You answered neither of two statements and none of four letters. Your account is now *90* days overdue.
>
> The fact that we have sent six reminders shows, Mr. Wise, that we have exercised great patience for your benefit. But our patience is not endless. The fact remains that you have not only failed to pay the balance due us, but you have also failed on all six occasions to send us a reply of any kind.
>
> You have forced us to set a deadline, Mr. Wise. If we are to save your credit rating and your reputation, you must send us your check for $225.80 within seven days.
>
> > Sincerely yours,

Fifth Follow-Up Letter

One more letter might be sent before turning over Mr. Wise's account to a collection agency or a lawyer. The following is an example of the very last letter in a collection series:

> Dear Mr. Wise:
>
> This is truly your last chance. If we do not receive your check for $225.80 within ten days, we will turn this account over to our attorney for collection.
>
> We have taken every possible step to avoid this action, but we can avoid it no longer. This letter is the seventh reminder of your overdue balance. The $225.80 is now 100 days overdue.
>
> We want our money, of course, but we do not want to embarrass you with a legal action. Nor do we want to add legal fees to what you now owe us. But what other recourse do we have?
>
> All we want is the $225.80 that you owe us for goods received. Please help us avoid legal action and help yourself maintain a good reputation and credit standing.
>
> > Sincerely yours,

Each of these collection letters had two objectives: (1) to collect the money due and (2) to retain the goodwill of the delinquent customer. As it becomes clearer and clearer that the customer is not "playing fair" with the creditor, however, the tone of each succeeding letter becomes more and more insistent and, finally, demanding. By the time the last collection letter in the series is sent, it is obvious that the customer is not going to pay. The principal function of this final letter is to scare the reader into paying the bill in order to avoid legal action.

COMMUNICATION PROJECTS

Practical Application

A. You are an employee in the credit department of Old World Wholesale Meats and Sundries, a large supplier of meats and other foods to restaurants. The Food Right chain of restaurants has been a customer for five years. Although the chain has always paid its bills, often the payments have come 45 to 60 days late. When the Food Right chain applies for an increase in its credit limit from $5,000 to $10,000, you are assigned the task of writing a letter refusing the request for an increase but retaining the customer's goodwill. Write the letter.

B. You are credit manager for a large electrical appliance retailer. It is your responsibility to review and approve every piece of correspondence related to credit and collection. The following letter reaches your desk. First criticize this letter, then rewrite it as you think it should be.

> Dear Ms. Donner:
> This is to inform you that your application for credit has been approved. Thank you.
>
> Very truly yours,

C. As credit manager of Beam & Company, a clothing manufacturer, you find one of your oldest and most reliable customers, Very, Very Chic Boutique, is behind 60 days in making payment for a lot of dresses. The balance due is $4,500. You have already sent two statements and one letter pointing out that the account is past due. Write the next letter to be sent to Estelle Regine, the owner of the boutique.

D. MacDowell Department Store employs you in its collection department. You are assigned to write a series of three form letters. The first letter is a reminder to be mailed 15 days after the second statement has been mailed. The remaining letters are to be mailed at 15-day intervals. You are instructed to include in the third letter a warning of legal action. Write the letters.

E. You work in the credit department of a large chain of retail stores. You are given the task of drafting three different first reminders that a bill is past due. Since the first reminder that an account is overdue is usually a gentle nudge, you are told to make one letter humorous and in another letter to ask whether there has been a mistake. Choose your own approach for the third gentle reminder.

Editing Practice

Editing the News   Edit and rewrite the following excerpts from copy submitted by the police court reporter.

1. An automobile reported stolen yesterday morning by Jack Desmond was found this morning abandoned on Route 99.
2. The defendant pleaded guilty to the reduced charge through his attorney.
3. The sheriff caught the bandits who attempted to rob the First National Trust Company within a week.

4. The officer hurried to the amusement park where the thief was last seen on his motorcycle.
5. Police found the man who had been injured in a hunting accident in the Worldclass Hotel.

Case Problem

Social Graces in the Office   What would you say to each of the following people under the circumstances indicated?

1. Maria Torres asks you to have lunch with her, but you have already promised to have lunch with Kathy Thomas, who doesn't get along well with Maria.
2. Neal Schwartz has just returned to the office after a long illness.
3. Tina Gibson, an attorney with the firm of Gibson and Masters, has recently died. Her surviving partner, Tim Masters, will now handle your firm's legal work.
4. Stella Conrad has just been promoted to the position of supervisor of your department.

45 WRITING SALES LETTERS

In the age of radio and television, letters remain a major force in the art of selling. Why? For one thing, the sales letter enjoys the advantage over electronic messages of giving recipients something they can put their hands on. The sales letter also is more direct and personal than a television or radio commercial intended for millions of people.

We all receive sales letters—invitations to join a book club or a record club, to subscribe to a magazine, to buy insurance, or to try a new product. Businesses spend millions of dollars on sales letters every year, and they highly value people who can write effective sales letters. Since many companies keep records of the responses and the sales resulting from every sales letter, a writer's effectiveness can be measured precisely. To succeed under such rigorous conditions, a writer must develop special skills. Among the skills particularly useful in writing sales letters are using language that is appropriate to the target audience; understanding buying motives; attracting the reader's attention; setting up a close relationship with the reader; appealing to specific buying motives; persuading the reader to act; and giving the reader an opportunity to act.

Although you may not become a specialist in sales letters, you should strive to learn the guidelines for this kind of writing. Most business letters are intended to promote sales of goods or services, whether directly or indirectly. A response letter sells goodwill. A claim letter sells its claim. An adjustment letter may try to sell the idea that a claim is ill-founded. Indeed, techniques used in writing sales letters will prove helpful in writing all business communications.

THE TARGET AUDIENCE

Next to the face-to-face visit of a sales representative, the sales letter is the most effective direct contact with the customer. Radio, television, and newspaper advertisements are necessarily appeals to a mass audience. Sales letters, on the other hand, are aimed directly at a carefully picked audience.

Marketing specialists choose the target audience after studying the product to be sold. If the new product is a drug or medical instrument, the target audience will consist of physicians. If the product is construction equipment, the target audience will be contractors. Choosing the target audience is usually more difficult than in the two preceding examples. Companies wishing to sell a new product for businesses, such as a photocopier, may have to do extensive research to determine the best target audience—whether small businesses, large businesses, or both.

The target audience for some products, of course, is the general public. Here the problem confronting market researchers and writers is to determine the buying motives most likely to appeal to the reader. A further discussion of buying motives follows.

The Mailing List of the Target Audience

After identifying the target audience, the next step is to seek a mailing list of its members. Mailing lists are obtained from various sources. The most valuable for any firm are its own customer files, prospects reported by sales representatives, inquiries that have come in by mail, and other correspondence. Printed materials such as telephone directories, credit-rating books, and professional directories are also good sources. Other sources of mailing lists include names of subscribers to certain magazines, business associations, civic clubs, alumni groups, and social clubs.

Businesses also rent or buy mailing lists from firms that specialize in compiling or acquiring such lists. Usually a list is rented for one or two mailings. If the list chosen is large, firms may rent only a portion of it for a trial mailing before renting the entire list.

Thanks to modern market research and the availability of selective mailing lists, the writer of sales letters almost always knows who the target audience is. The writer must take care to adopt a tone that will appeal to the target audience. Different approaches are required, for example, when writing to motorcyclists and when writing to gardeners. The writer must determine the buying motives of the target audience before writing an effective sales letter.

Understanding Buying Motives

Identifying Wants and Needs   In general, we can say that people buy products and services to satisfy needs or wants. People's true needs are relatively simple—food, housing, clothing, transportation. People's wants, by contrast, are endless. People want not just any food, but delicious food; not just four walls, but a comfortable house. They want smarter clothing and an efficient or elegant or prestigious car. People also want security, status, the approval of friends and loved ones, health, money, and personal attractiveness. People's wants are not all so serious, of course. They also include conveniences, recreation, and entertainment.

While people are aware that they want the general things described above, people are often not aware of how particular products may fulfill their wants. This is especially true with respect to new products and services. The writer's job is to convince people that a specific product, or service will satisfy one or more of their wants.

Satisfying Wants and Needs   To become interested in a particular product or service, the reader must recognize that the product or service can satisfy a want or a need. The writer must, therefore, show how purchasing the item will bring the reader prestige, good health, fun, beauty, savings, security, romance, freedom from drudgery, and so on.

The following list indicates the kinds of personal wants and needs that can be satisfied by the products and services shown:

Product or Service	Want or Need
Reclining rocker	Comfort
Stocks or bonds	Profit
Insulation	Savings, comfort
Electronic oven	Convenience
Mouthwash	Health and attractiveness
Stereo	Enjoyment
Burglar alarm	Security
Cologne	Personal attractiveness
Pastry	Satisfying appetite
Contribution	Enhancing reputation
Power mower	Convenience
Laundry and cleaning delivery service	Convenience
Shampoo	Personal attractiveness
Exclusive dress	Prestige

QUALITIES OF SALES LETTERS

After identifying the target audience's motives for buying a particular product or service, the writer can proceed to writing the sales letter itself. There is no such thing as a "standard" sales letter. Sales letters vary in length, in organization, and in content. Generally speaking, however, an effective sales letter has these five qualities:

It attracts the reader's attention.
It sets up a close relationship with the reader.
It appeals to one or more specific buying motives.
It persuades the reader to act.
It gives the reader an opportunity to act.

Although achieving these qualities might sound easy, no sure-fire formula for writing a successful sales letter has been found. The wastebaskets that are filled daily with thousands of unread sales messages attest to that fact. Yet sales letters are used successfully and extensively by thousands of business organizations. Probably no two sales letters written about a product are alike; business is always experimenting with different approaches, different appeals, different want-satisfying devices.

Attracting the Reader's Attention

A sales letter is like a door-to-door sales representative—it is seldom invited to call. As a caller without an invitation, the sales letter must attract favorable attention immediately. As in door-to-door selling, a favorable appearance and approach can create the proper sales atmosphere.

The appearance of sales letters makes the difference between whether they are read or tossed into the wastebasket. Appearance starts with the envelope. Sales letters often come in envelopes that promise big prizes, valuable certificates, and great savings inside. Recently, creative ad writers have taken advantage of word processing equipment by adding personalized, attention-getting questions to the envelope, such as the one shown on page 411: "How can Nora J. Smithson increase the productivity of her present staff by 15 percent?" The reader generally reacts by opening the envelope and reading the message.

Once the reader opens the envelope, other factors come into play. Superior stationery and an engraved letterhead give an appearance of importance. A newsletter format prepares the reader to take the information seriously. An enclosed free sample is another good way of getting the reader's attention.

Setting Up a Close Relationship With the Reader

The writer must keep the sales prospect reading. The best way to achieve this goal is to set up a close relationship with the reader, for example, by referring to the reader as *you* as often as possible. Another good device for establishing intimacy is to start the letter with a rhetorical question. Combining these two devices, we might write an opening sentence like:

> How many dos and don'ts of great cooking do you know?

or:

> Who *wouldn't* love you when you're wearing irresistible Alphonse Cloucheau perfume?

Other techniques that can be used in the first paragraph to establish a close relationship with the reader include: (1) using imperative verbs; (2) using informal punctuation (dashes, exclamation points, underscores, ellipses, and parentheses); (3) using contractions; (4) using short, informal sentences; (5) repeating the reader's name in text; and (6) complimenting the reader.

Manhattan
Office Services Inc.
Suite 1107
Empire State Building
New York, New York 10001
(212) 555-5000

```
"How can Nora J. Smithson in-        Ms. Nora J. Smithson
crease the productivity of her       Office Manager
present staff by 15 percent?"        Campbell & Reed Inc.
                                     1221 Avenue of the Americas
                                     New York, New York 10020
```

Word processing equipment makes it simple to attract the reader by using a personalized, attention-getting question on the envelope.

Here are more opening lines illustrating these techniques:

Opening	Product or Service
Will your family sleep safely tonight?	Insurance
Very frankly, we're worried about *your* complexion.	Cosmetics
Up-to-the-minute enjoyment at a very old-fashioned price. That's what you get . . . and you deserve it.	Magazine
Are *your* child's grades just "satisfactory"?	Encyclopedia
Now! You can look *ten years younger.*	Exercise machine

Appealing to One or More Specific Buying Motives

Now comes the time to take advantage of market research and other knowledge about the target audience of the sales letter. The writer seeks to make a connection between the features of the product or service being sold and the presumed buying motives of the reader. The goal, of course, is to induce the reader to buy. Inducements to buy are called *sales appeals,* and sales appeals are the main act of the sales letter. The envelope, the stationery, and the opening line only set the stage.

See how the following excerpts use sales appeals to stimulate the reader's buying motives.

Sales Appeal	Buying Motive
Your family will give you *rave notices* when you serve Venezio Spaghetti. This zesty dish helps *you* put all the color and vigor of the Italian Riviera on your family's table.	Approval of family

Thousands of small businesses have replaced outmoded stamp sticking with this compact, low-cost, desk-model postage meter.	Convenience, economy
The *Star* is more interesting— and *you* will be too.	Personal status
Let music take *you* on a world tour of beauty, romance, and adventure.	Enjoyment
Frame your home and grounds in *intimate privacy* and *safety.*	Security, comfort
Be good to *your* dog. TASTY is now *flavor-primed.* Makes your dog an eager eater.	Care of pet

If the target audience consists of gardeners, the writer might choose to appeal to the reader's desire for status, for tranquil and beautiful surroundings, and for fresh, wholesome vegetables. The following sales appeals would be effective.

> Using the techniques in *Roses, Roses,* you can produce a new species of rose and give it *your own name.*
>
> Natives say the Brazilian Beauty Gardenia brings with it the peace of the dark, untraveled rain forest.
>
> Be sure *your* family's food is free of harmful pesticides.

The sales appeal brings the reader to the point of wanting to buy a product. The writer must then nudge the reader just a little further, by persuading the reader to act on the desire to buy.

Persuading the Reader to Act

From the beginning, the sales letter tries to put the reader in an agreeable frame of mind. Immediately after the sales appeal, however, the writer should step up the campaign of persuasion. The techniques used to develop a close relationship between writer and reader are now employed to make the reader say, "Yes, I want to buy this!"

The most effective technique in inducing the reader to say "Yes" is the rhetorical question. A sales letter may contain several rhetorical questions at various points, but a rhetorical question is most effective after the sales appeal. After describing the virtues of the product and making the sales appeal, what could be more effective than questions like the following?

> Do you want to bring some joy into the life of a loved one?
>
> Wouldn't you feel better if you knew your family was truly safe?
>
> Do you want your child to earn better grades in school?

After answering "Yes" to rhetorical questions like these, the reader is as ready to act as he or she will ever be. But the writer's job is not over.

LISTENER'S
HIGHLIGHT RECORDS
6877 56TH AVENUE DETROIT, MICHIGAN 48210

Ms. Jane Sturbridge
939 Manzanita Circle
Reno, Nevada 89509

Dear Ms. Sturbridge:

Did you know that...

      ...psychologists claim that people who listen to classical music
        "get more out of life"?

      ...lovers of classical music control stressful situations better
        than people who do not listen to classical music?

      ...listening to good music is considered one of the least expensive
        yet most highly rewarding pleasures?

Yes, you probably do know these facts, Ms. Sturbridge, because you have
purchased several classical record albums in the past year. For you and
all the other people who appreciate the great classics, we have assembled
more than 1,000 of the world's favorite classical albums and packaged them
in sets of four long-playing records, all of the highest quality. The
price of each set of four records? A remarkable $12.95.

That's right. For only $12.95 you can select any of the four-record
sets described in the enclosed brochure. If this sounds as if it is an
exceptional opportunity to add to your collection or to purchase superb
gifts for friends and loved ones--well, you're right.

Does the enclosed brochure include any favorites that you've been meaning
to buy? Probably. But don't look too long, because we expect our limited
supply to be depleted very, very quickly.

We won't say any more, because we know that the brochure--and the $12.95
price--will sell these fantastic records for us. To reserve your sets,
just check off the appropriate boxes on the enclosed return card and mail
it to us. That's all you must do. We will bill you later.

                Sincerely,

                Edwin Thornsberry

                Edwin Thornsberry
                Classical Records Department

This sales letter makes it very easy for the reader to respond to the offer. All she must do is
check off her selections; her name and address are already on the postage-paid return card.

Giving the Reader an Opportunity to Act

The prospective buyer may read mail in the evening, after the stores have closed.
What happens if—after reading the sales appeal—the reader feels the urge to buy

your product but cannot do so at that moment? Chances are good that the reader will lose the urge before morning and forget all about the product. To prevent loss of sales in this manner, writers of sales letters make sure to include an opportunity for the reader to act *now*.

There are many ways of giving readers an opportunity to act. Enclosing postage-paid reply cards, order forms, and coupons, or giving a toll-free telephone number will make it easy for the reader to take immediate action. Note how the letter on page 413 gives the reader a simple opportunity to act. The examples below show some other ways to give the reader an opportunity to act—and conveniently.

> Just write your initials in the box on the postpaid reply card and drop it in the mail now.
>
> Just print your name and address on the coupon—SEND NO MONEY.
>
> To receive the SuperSlimmer for *seven* days *free* trial, just slip the entry form—which we have already made out in your name—into the postpaid YES envelope enclosed.

THE SALES LETTER CAMPAIGN

A series of sales letters will often be written to prospective customers, particularly to sell higher-priced items. In such follow-up letters, professional writers sometimes use a different appeal in each letter, with the hope that one of the appeals may ultimately persuade the reader to take action to buy the product or service.

In the sales campaign, as many as eight letters may be sent, depending upon the nature of the product, its cost, and the nature of the market. The letters in such a series should be spaced about ten days apart, and they should be kept relatively short.

COMMUNICATION PROJECTS

Practical Application

A. After looking through magazines, newspapers, and catalogs, list at least ten different sales appeals you find. Prepare your list under these three headings: (1) Type of Product, (2) Trade Name, and (3) Sales Appeal.

B. You are employed to write a sales letter for a company specializing in products for infants. List the various buying motives that you think mothers and fathers of infants might have.

C. Write three different opening lines that attract the reader's attention. Then write three lines that help to establish a close relationship between you and the reader. In each line, use different techniques for establishing a close relationship.

D. Select any product that you would love to own. Now, pretending that you are a dealer who sells this product, write a sales letter for the product. Find a way to make it easy for readers of the letter to agree to come to your place of business for a free demonstration of the product.

E. Write a sales letter—including an attention-getting envelope—that asks young married couples to buy life insurance. Be sure to attract the reader's attention, to set up a close relationship with the reader, to appeal to a specific buying motive, to persuade the reader to act, and to give the reader an opportunity to act.

Editing Practice

Applied Psychology   Change the following letter excerpts into sentences that will promote good public relations.

1. You claim that the television was not tested after it was repaired.
2. Your failure to pay the bill at once shows faulty business judgment.
3. Since you failed to give us your warranty number, we cannot do anything to help you.
4. Because you neglected to send us the coupon with your check, we cannot send you the desired product.
5. You cannot expect us to deliver free of charge to someone who has never bought anything from us before and may never buy anything again.

Case Problem

Etiquette for Social-Business Situations   Analyze the following statements to see whether you think they represent good social-business etiquette. If you need help, consult a book of etiquette.

1. To place a call, always have your secretary get the other party on the telephone.
2. At a luncheon, if the host orders an alcoholic drink, so must the guest.
3. At a large formal dinner, you should not begin eating until the host begins.
4. When introducing an older person to a younger one, the older person's name is mentioned first.
5. The person being called on the telephone is the one to terminate the conversation.

The dictionary defines *public relations* as "the business of inducing the public to have understanding for and goodwill toward a person, firm, or institution."[1] Indeed, whether an organization sells a product or a service or whether it is a nonprofit organization, it benefits from good public relations.

Favorable public relations means that the public has a positive attitude toward the organization. In the long run, businesses know that such favorable public opinion promotes the success of the organization. If, for example, the Jordan Meat-Packing Company has a favorable image among consumers, a new product marketed by Jordan will probably be more readily accepted by the meat-buying public. Advertising campaigns for Jordan's products may be more effective because the meat-buying public already has a good opinion of the Jordan Company. They will have faith that Jordan sells high-quality products at fair prices.

Unfavorable public opinion, on the other hand, can ruin a firm. If a newspaper report states or implies that the Jordan Company has been labeling nonbeef products "100 percent beef," public opinion of that company will almost surely drop—even if the report is later proved false. Consumers who remember the negative report may start buying another brand if they doubt the integrity of the company.

Knowing the benefits of good public relations, all businesses strive to create—and to keep—a favorable image of their organizations in the eyes of the public. An oil company may televise a short film showing the public that the company strives to protect the environment wherever it drills for oil. A well-known, reputable person narrates the film to lend it additional credibility. At no time does the narrator say "Buy your oil and gas from _____." Instead, the narrator points out all the good things the company is doing for the public.

Letters are a primary means for creating favorable public relations. Public relations letters are primarily sales letters in that they try to convince or persuade the reader, although no specific product is mentioned. The goal of public relations letters is *indirectly* to make a sale. In essence, public relations letters lay the groundwork for future sales. They make it easy for the buyer to say "yes" at a later date because the buyer considers the company fair, reliable, prestigious, or efficient. Such favorable images do indeed spur sales.

In this section, we will look at four major aspects of public relations writing: creating a favorable company image, promoting a new business, recognizing and exploiting promotional opportunities, and thanking customers for patronage. Careful studying of this section will give you a solid introduction to public relations writing. Since almost every business communication has among its goals the creation of a favorable

[1]*Webster's New Collegiate Dictionary*, G. & C. Merriam Co., Springfield, Mass., 1980, p. 932.

image and the promotion of goodwill, you can apply the lessons of this section in many areas.

CREATING A FAVORABLE COMPANY IMAGE

Many companies spend millions of dollars each year to favorably influence public attitudes toward their enterprises and toward the people who work for them. Some companies sponsor special television shows, on which the only advertising is a mention of the company's name. Some firms run newspaper and magazine ads that are intended primarily for public enjoyment or enlightenment. Large grants for research are given to medical and educational groups by some companies. Others make large endowments to universities and colleges and offer scholarships to worthy students. Although nearly all companies feel an obligation to offer such services for the benefit of society, they are at the same time very much aware of the public relations value of such actions.

In an effort to create a favorable company image, many large organizations employ public relations specialists whose function is to see that the company has its "best foot forward" at all times. PR specialists are trained to use all communication media—letters, newspapers, radio, television, magazines, films—to influence public opinion. They prepare countless news releases, radio announcements, and articles; they arrange for press conferences, speaking engagements for top executives of the company, public receptions, and so on. They seize every opportunity to develop a favorable feeling toward the organization for which they work. For example, when a downtown building is being remodeled or expanded, causing some inconvenience to shoppers and pedestrians, the alert PR specialist arranges to install colorful signs such as the one shown below.

The public relations person is also likely to be the one to see to it that peepholes are

PARDON OUR APPEARANCE!

Please excuse the noise and dust
as we hurry to complete a bigger
and brighter housewares department.
Come to our grand opening party
on September 1!

Clark's. . .
Growing to Serve You Better

By explaining a temporary inconvenience to shoppers, this sign helps to build a favorable feeling toward Clark's.

installed at strategic points so that "sidewalk superintendents" may observe the progress of the construction.

Every business is judged daily in the courts of public opinion. And public opinion is powerful! If opinion is favorable, the way is usually smooth; if it is unfavorable, the going can be rocky indeed. Following are typical situations in which public relations specialists seek to influence public opinion.

1. A commuter railroad is operating at a deficit. Although fares have increased 200 percent in the past five years, the company is still losing money and must ask for another increase. Of course, the railroad is sensitive to the opinions of its customers; it needs their understanding and their support. The PR department of the railroad may place advertisements in newspapers, may purchase radio time, may issue circulars to riders, and may write letters to leading citizens in order to explain why the railroad has found it necessary to seek authority to raise fares.

2. A private water main on the grounds of a manufacturing plant bursts, submerging a low stretch of a nearby public road in two feet of water. The company provides a detour road on its own grounds, posts large signs with directions to drivers and apologies to the community, and employs someone to direct traffic until repairs are complete. In addition, the company publishes apologetic letters in the local newspapers, explaining how the accident happened and what steps are being taken to prevent a recurrence.

3. The manager of the local airport writes to homeowners who live near the landing field to apologize for the noise created by the jet engines and to assure these people that improvements will be made soon.

4. A large public school system plans to use modular scheduling in all its schools starting next fall. A news release is issued to newspapers, and a letter is written to parents and to various civic organizations to inform the public of this new development.

5. A growing university has changed its name from Bowdark Teachers College to Bowdark University of Arts and Sciences. The university's PR department writes a special letter to the alumni of the institution in order to inform them of the school's new name.

6. A newspaper reports that several accidents have been caused by defective XYZ-77 tires. The XYZ Corporation prepares a news release helping customers to identify the specific tires in question and outlining how they may then be checked or replaced. In addition, XYZ writes to its retailers and to all customers who have bought its "77" model tire.

The public relations office of a department store located in a business district handled a difficult situation by (among other things) mailing its customers the letter below.

Dear Ms. Winter:

We wanted you, as one of our privileged charge customers, to be the first to know about some changes that are taking place at Mandrake's Department Store. We think these changes will suit your changing shopping needs.

You have probably noticed that Mandrake's is aboutely jammed late in the afternoon on weekdays and during our evening hours on Thursdays. We are the largest department store in the downtown area. People who have jobs in the city have begun to do all their shopping on weekdays.

The reason for this change in shopping habits is simple: As gasoline costs have risen, people have avoided driving downtown on Saturdays. Since there are few Saturday buses, Mandrake's has come to be almost as quiet on Saturdays as it is bustling on weekdays.

Mandrake's is now making a major change in hours in order to serve our customers best under these new conditions. Starting May 1, Mandrake's will be open every weeknight until 8:30 p.m. and Thursdays till 10:00 p.m. Shoppers will no longer have to cram their increased weekday shopping needs into the old ten-to-six schedule.

Unfortunately, we must close Mandrake's on Saturdays until further notice. We hope that the energy situation will improve, enabling us to reopen on Saturdays soon. In the meantime, we know that most of our customers have been asking for a change in hours. We hope that the change will not inconvenience you. If you do feel inconvenienced, please send us a note suggesting another solution to this scheduling problem. We are investigating every possibility from arranging for chartered Saturday buses to opening suburban branches.

We appreciate your business, Ms. Winter, and we pledge to continue giving you the very best in merchandise and service. We look forward to seeing you at Mandrake's soon.

Sincerely,

PROMOTING A NEW BUSINESS

Promoting a new business requires a combination of public relations and sales techniques. Suppose you work in the sales promotion department of the Tres Chic Boutique, which manages a chain of women's specialty shops. Tres Chic has recently opened a new boutique in Chalon Hills and has hired Colleen Gregus as manager of this shop. As part of the promotional efforts—and to help Colleen get off to a good start—you want to create an atmosphere in the community that will bring customers to the new store. In addition to running a number of newspaper ads, sponsoring spot announcements on the local radio station, and distributing thousands of circulars, you write the following letter that will be duplicated and mailed to a list of two thousand telephone subscribers in Chalon Hills. The image that is being created for this new business is built around Colleen Gregus—local resident who made good.

MAY WE INTRODUCE YOU TO—
Colleen Gregus,
manager of Chalon Hills' newest and most unusual specialty shop for women:
TRES CHIC BOUTIQUE
located in El Camino Real Shopping Square, Devonshire Road and Pillar Drive. Perhaps you already know Colleen and her husband, Ron. Both of them grew up in your city and were graduated from local schools. They both attended Southeastern University, where Colleen majored in Fashion Arts and Ron in

Business Administration. Colleen and Ron represent a winning team, with her original ideas in dress designing and his business expertise.

You may recall that Colleen is past president of the Parent-Teacher League of the Chalon Hills Elementary School, where her 6-year-old Jason and 8-year-old Lisa attend school. Colleen was instrumental in our civic drive to save the trees along Highway 7, and she recently was appointed Den Mother for Cub Scout Pack 540. She plans to continue in this capacity and to continue taking an active role in community affairs. For the past two years, Colleen has served as buyer for the Fashion Court Department at Manderville's Department Store, in addition to participating in community activities.

Many of the new fashions you will find at TRES CHIC BOUTIQUE were designed by Colleen herself. Her staff of seamstresses will be on hand at all times to ensure that you always get the proper fitting and the styling that most becomes you. You'll also find a large selection of ready-made fashions in the latest styles to suit every occasion.

Do drop by to say hello to Colleen at TRES CHIC BOUTIQUE. She will be glad to see her old friends and to meet new ones at Chalon Hills' loveliest new shopping spot.

Cordially yours,

Of course, the PR image this letter is trying to create will not emerge unless Colleen and her staff give customers excellent merchandise and service. Customers must find at TRES CHIC BOUTIQUE the quality merchandise and friendly service that the letter promises.

Building an Image

The first months for Colleen Gregus are crucial. Once the image has started to emerge, she must keep building it. The TRES CHIC BOUTIQUE chain wants to help Colleen get firmly established, because her success will, of course, benefit the company as well. In your campaign to build an image, you prepare this form letter to mail to everyone who visits the shop.

Dear_____:

Thank you for visiting TRES CHIC BOUTIQUE this week. We are pleased to welcome you as a new customer, and we are delighted that you gave us an opportunity to show you some of the newest designs in women's wear.

Whatever your needs in women's wear, be assured that your choices from TRES CHIC will always be of superior quality. Careful attention by an efficient, courteous staff, including expert seamstresses, ensures you of clothes that fit you perfectly. Whatever your needs—a street dress, a pants suit, or an exclusive gown for a special occasion—we are prepared to cater to your every fashion wish.

Stop by frequently and browse. You will see new selections each time you visit, for only by moving our stock quickly can we keep one step ahead of the fashion market.

Cordially,

Recognizing a PR Moment

Timing the PR letter is important; the precise time when the public will listen to and accept an idea is a *PR moment*. Obviously, the PR moment for creating a business image occurs when the business first opens. Another PR moment is immediately after a new customer's first visit. The two letters illustrated at the bottom of page 419 and on page 420 are examples of good timing.

A new item or service in a business can also provide a PR moment. Suppose that TRES CHIC BOUTIQUE has, by popular demand, started daily fashion showings at the Larkspur Restaurant in Chalon Hills. Colleen and Ron take advantage of this public relations moment to announce this new feature. The opening paragraph of their announcement might start like this:

> In response to popular demand, TRES CHIC BOUTIQUE is pleased to announce a daily fashion showing of its latest creations. While dining at the Larkspur Restaurant in Chalon Hills, between 12 and 2 p.m., watch the lovely models who will circulate throughout the dining room, showing the newest TRES CHIC fashions.

Anniversaries and special dates also provide important PR moments. For example, at the end of one year of operation, a 24-hour variety store might take advantage of the occasion by writing an "anniversary" letter that begins like this:

> From unknown to indispensable—that's the story of the Pit Stop Store during the past twelve months.
>
> We opened our 24-hour roadside variety store only one short year ago, on May 10. Now we're your number one choice for late-night and rush purchases. Why? Because we've learned to stock merchandise the way you like it, and we provide you the quick, courteous service that you need when you're in a hurry. You know that at the Pit Stop you'll walk out fast with what you need.

PUBLIC RELATIONS—OTHER PROMOTION OPPORTUNITIES

The opportunities for writing letters to friends and customers of a business are limited only by the imagination. Of course, many such letters have a definite sales objective. Yet they also enhance the image of the firm. The following are typical subjects for promotion letters:

> An invitation to open a charge account.
> An announcement of a special privilege or service to preferred customers.
> An incentive to charge customers to use their accounts more frequently.
> A welcome to new residents and visitors.
> A congratulatory message.
> An invitation to a demonstration, lecture, or reception.
> A reminder of a holiday or special occasion.
> A thank-you for business patronage.

Inviting Charge Accounts

A cash customer of a store or a firm is often invited to open a charge account. The charge-account invitation includes an application form. On selected days, employees may hand invitations to customers as customers enter the store. All a customer needs to do is fill in the form, fold and seal it, and drop it in the mail.

Giving Charge Customers Special Privileges

Charge customers are usually loyal patrons. They buy more than cash customers, and they return to the store again and again. In order to serve and to keep charge customers, most stores create special occasions to which only charge customers are invited. Here is a PR letter inviting a charge customer to such an occasion:

> Dear Mrs. Ferrara:
>
> You are invited to a special courtesy shopping day at Bender's next Friday, April 7. As a valued charge customer, you will enjoy double privileges. In the splendor of the Tropical Promenade on the fourth floor, you will sip complimentary lemonade while you see a preview showing of the latest Paris fashions. You will also be entitled to make purchases in every department at special bonus savings not advertised to the public.
>
> The fashions to be modeled will not be placed on our selling floors until April 22. We want you, a valued charge customer of Bender's, to have first choice. Your Bender Charge Card is your ticket to this spectacular shopping event. Tell your friends about this exclusive event if you must—but come alone. This special show and sale is just for YOU from your friends at Bender's.
>
> Cordially yours,

Encouraging Charge Customers to Use Their Accounts

Stores take note of customers who have seldom used their charge accounts. A clever letter to such inactive customers may bring them and their purchasing power back to the store. Here is a letter that may prove irresistible to the inactive charge customer:

> Dear Customer:
> You've
> Earned
> 10¢   Is it worth 10 cents a line to you to read this
> 20¢   letter?
> 30¢   We'll gladly pay you that amount—but only if
> 40¢   you read the entire letter.
> 50¢   Now, we reason this way: You really are a valued
> 60¢   customer. But lately you haven't been in even
> 70¢   to say "Howdy." We would like you to come back;
> 80¢   we would like to see you often; we would like

90¢	you to reopen your account. We think that it is
$1.00	better for us to have a long-time customer like
$1.10	you on our books than a new customer whom we
$1.20	don't know. And since it would cost us at least
$1.30	$2.50 to open a *new* account, we would rather pass
$1.40	this amount to you.
$1.50	So we say, "Here is a $2.50 check on the house."
$1.60	Come in and select anything you wish, to the value
$1.70	of $25 or more, from our extensive stock of nation-
$1.80	ally advertised clothing and shoes for the entire
$1.90	family. Invest in that household appliance—pop-
$2.00	up toaster, steam iron—you have been dreaming
$2.10	about. Or do your gift shopping early for such
$2.20	items as diamonds, watches, radios.
$2.30	The enclosed check, worth $2.50, is your down
$2.40	payment.
$2.50	Why not come in tomorrow?

Cordially yours,

Welcoming New Residents and Visitors

Hotels, department stores, and various businesses often obtain lists of the visitors who are expected to attend conventions in their city in order to write them letters of welcome. The letter illustrated on page 424 is an example of such a welcome.

When a new family moves into a community, many alert business firms write a letter of welcome. Naturally, the purpose of the letter is to win friends and customers. Note the technique employed in this letter:

Dear Neighbor:

Dolan's—Boise's favorite cleaning establishment—welcomes you to the community. We hope that you will like our friendly people, our modern stores, our lovely city parks and playgrounds, and our exciting cultural and entertainment centers. We are definitely a proud, growing, and bustling community.

Dolan's has grown up with Boise. We were the first cleaning establishment in the city, having opened our doors for the first time in 1902. As a family-owned business, we have been serving the cleaning needs of the community ever since. Our cleaning plant was remodeled with the most modern equipment just two years ago, and we now have five pickup outlets throughout the city for your convenience. But best of all, we have the friendliest, most efficient staff of employees.

We are enclosing a certificate entitling you to a 20 percent discount on your first cleaning order. We would like to show you why Dolan's is Boise's most popular cleaning establishment. There IS a reason!

Sincerely yours,

101 East Adams
Chicago, Illinois 60603
(312) 555-1234

```
WELCOME TO CHICAGO!

        While you are attending the annual meeting of the
National Magazine Publishers' Association, you are cordially
invited to visit The Sports Shop--one of the world's largest
and best-known centers for sporting goods.

        Whenever your schedule permits, you and your family will
find a welcome here at The Sports Shop.  We are open from
9 a.m. until 10 p.m. from Monday to Saturday, and we feature
a complete line of sporting clothes and equipment for men,
women, and young adults.  Whether your love is fishing or
golf, lacrosse or Ping-Pong, you'll probably find items you've
not seen in other stores.  To encourage you to visit us, we
will give you our Giant Sports Catalog free as soon as you
enter the store.  This prized catalog is recognized as one
of the most complete mail-order sporting goods catalogs avail-
able, and you will surely want to take it home with you.

        We look forward to meeting you!

                              Sincerely,

                              Lorraine Bentley

                              Lorraine Bentley
                              Manager

PS:  Yes, we do accept all major charge cards.
```

Welcoming visitors—in this case, conventioneers—helps to win friends for The Sports Shop.

Writing Congratulatory Letters

Any occasion for congratulations is a PR moment. For example, some businesses write letters to congratulate parents on the arrival of a new baby. The list of names is usually obtained from hospital notices in the local newspaper.

Enclosed with the following letter is a pair of miniature long trousers.

Dear Mark:

You're a mighty discerning young man to have chosen the parents you did, and that's why I'm writing this letter to you instead of them. Congratulations!

Here's your first pair of long pants. A little early, perhaps, but I want you to get used to coming to Hayden's for all your clothing needs. Your dad has been a friend of ours for some time now. We like to think he is well satisfied with his purchases, and we hope you'll bring him in to see us often.

Tell you what: If you'll come in with your dad one year from now (I'll remind you), I'll have a present for you that you can really use.

Sincerely,

Sending Special Invitations

The following letter is typical of those that are used to invite customers to special demonstrations or receptions. Note that such a letter may also serve a sales function.

Dear Mrs. Simpson:

Artist Norman Wyeth, who paints some of the most widely acclaimed seascapes, will be at Maximo's Art Shop on Saturday, April 10, from one until three in the afternoon. Prints of his "Storm on the Shore" will be on sale. A limited number of copies, only 50, will be available for sale at our shop exclusively, and each copy will be numbered and signed personally by Mr. Wyeth.

You are invited to come and meet Mr. Wyeth and, if you are among the lucky, to purchase one of these prints of his most famous work. While you are here, you might want to look around our gallery for other paintings and prints that may "catch your eye."

Cordially yours,

Writing Letters for Special Occasions

Holidays and other special occasions provide opportunities to build goodwill and to promote sales. Study the techniques employed in the following examples:

Dear Dad:

Mind if we slip a small string around that middle finger of your left hand?

Not that we think you're absentminded. Far from it. But just in case the press of business has made you suffer a temporary lapse of memory, we thought it would be helpful to remind you that May 12 is Mother's Day. You hadn't forgotten? Good.

We know you'll also remember that Peterson's is the store where Mother would purchase her own gift if she were doing the shopping. We have all those lovely things that women appreciate—jewelry, boudoir sets, manicure sets, leather-crafted desk sets, luxurious handbags, elegant luggage.

Drop in this week for a chat with our Mrs. Mendez. From years of experience, Mrs. Mendez knows the gifts that women cherish forever. She can help you choose the perfect gift for this occasion.

Cordially yours,

Dear Mrs. Amundsen:

Let's talk about golf. Yes, I know that there's snow on the ground and not a leaf on the trees. The fairways aren't fair, and the temperature is unmerciful.

But January is golden weather at The Sport Shop. The floor is abloom with the most fantastic selection of golf balls, clubs, bags, shoes, carts, jackets, caps—everything you can imagine. Come stand under our palm tree and see our fresh white rows of golf balls, the roll-a-away BermudaRug putting green, the warm, gleaming woods, and the sunny golf fashions. Once the golfers in your family get their hands on these, can spring be far behind?

To make The Sport Shop even warmer, we've slashed prices by 25 percent. Why not come down and get a little bit of spring right now, at our fabulous Spring-in-January sale.

Sincerely yours,

THANKING CUSTOMERS FOR THEIR PATRONAGE

There is a saying that "the squeaky wheel gets the grease." Some customers, too, feel that they will get attention only if they complain and make trouble for a firm with whom they are doing business. Loyal customers who never complain and who quietly and promptly pay their bills may receive no attention at all. An increasing number of business firms, however, are trying to remedy this situation. The letter illustrated on page 427 is an excellent example of how one hotel attempts to show its appreciation to its loyal customers.

Another way to show appreciation to customers is this letter, thanking a customer for making prompt payment.

Dear Mrs. Crane:

Congratulations—your Chevrolet sedan is all yours as of today. The enclosed canceled note is evidence that you've made all the payments.

You don't owe us any more payments, but we feel we owe you this one last statement—a statement of how pleased we are with you as a customer. You made every payment right on time. We hope you'll call on us again whenever you need financing.

The enclosed certificate entitles you to preferred credit privileges at the lowest available rates. Just present this certificate to any of our branch banks for fast service on loans of any kind. As long as we have money to lend, we'll be pleased to help you.

Cordially yours,

Note that the writer of this letter not only thanks the customer but also uses this letter to serve a sales function by encouraging future business.

The Ashland Hotel

220 SW 5 Avenue
Portland, Oregon 97204
(503) 555-5000

June 13, 19--

Ms. Helen Redford
Sales Manager
Bartlett Equipment Corp.
711 SW Alder
Portland, Oregon 97205

Dear Ms. Redford:

Thank you for thinking of the Ashland Hotel as the place to
hold your meetings.

For several years now, you have used our facilities to host
your special dinners, to demonstrate products to customers,
to train your new representatives, and to lodge your employees
and guests whenever they are in our city. We do, indeed,
make special efforts to make all your meetings successful,
because your appreciation of our efforts always shows.

Well, we appreciate your business, Ms. Redford, and we sincerely enjoy serving you, your employees, and your customers.
Thank you for doing business with us.

Cordially yours,

Thomas Hilton

Thomas Hilton, Manager
Corporate Sales Department

The Ashland Hotel thanks loyal customers for their patronage by sending letters like this.

COMMUNICATION PROJECTS

Practical Application

A. Suppose that you are a college graduate with five years of business experience either as (a) a secretary in an attorney's office, (b) a travel agent in a large agency, or (c) a tax accountant in a public accounting firm.

You decide to set up your own (a) public stenographer's office, (b) travel agency, or (c) tax accounting business. You choose to begin promoting your new business by writing a letter and sending it to 100 businesses in the community. You wish to emphasize both your business experience and your excellent college education. Write a letter that includes all the details that will improve your chances of succeeding in your own new business.

B. Develop a letter that encourages charge customers of a retail store to use their charge accounts. Use your ingenuity in making the letter different from others you have seen.

C. You are the manager of Trendy's Department Store. Trendy's has always provided charge cards without charging any fee other than interest. Extremely high interest rates and tight credit force you to introduce a $10 annual fee for charge cards in order to cover Trendy's own increased borrowing costs. Write a letter explaining this new store policy tactfully. **Remember:** Your customers have for years been accustomed to paying no fee, and you are imposing the fee through no fault of the customers.

D. You work for Newlook Decorators, an interior decorating firm that is introducing a new line of furniture and decorations this spring. A special preview showing of the new line is planned for charge customers, including family and friends, at the Newlook showroom, 657 Woodside Avenue, March 21, from six until nine in the evening. You are assigned to write a letter of invitation. Admission will be by ticket only, and you are enclosing a ticket with each invitation. The general public will not see the new line until March 28. Write a letter that makes the most of this occasion.

E. You are manager of Rexroth's Hardware Store, an established firm on the outskirts of a large city. Traditionally your customers have come from the city. New towns and neighborhoods are springing up beyond city limits, however, and you are looking for a way to develop business with the residents of these new areas. You decide to write a letter, enclosing a discount coupon worth $5, that invites each resident of the new areas to visit your store. Write an appealing invitation addressed to new residents.

Editing Practice

Editing to Improve Writing Techniques Edit the following sentences to improve any poor writing techniques.

1. Arriving at 10 a.m., I told Tim that he should allow more travel time in order to avoid being late again.
2. Did you learn why the charge customers returned their monthly statement?
3. Ellen borrowed the stapler which was on my desk.
4. Judy said she couldn't find any stamps for the letters after looking in the desk drawers.
5. You may use either of these four calculators to help with the bookkeeping.
6. In order to prepare the invoice, all the figures will be needed by you.
7. Within two days after I sent my complaint to Ms. Carruthers, a reply was received from her.
8. There is no future for the business communicator who is careless or indifferent to the techniques of writing.
9. The mail would lie in the out-basket for hours and sometimes days.

10. Our engineers have made many improvements in design, and so we shall be able to produce a better product.
11. The committee must complete the research, assembling of facts, and writing the report.
12. In his writing, Ed consistently used unnecessarily big words, thus making his communications ineffective.
13. Perry always has and always will be late for meetings.
14. Sylvia is one of the best if not the best secretaries in the office.
15. He felt the facts should determine his reply.

Plurals and Possessives   Indicate the correct plural or possessive forms of the words enclosed in parentheses.

1. The Wood Building has only (attorney) offices on the first 20 floors.
2. (Marie and Laura) telephone, which they share, is on Marie's desk.
3. All the (secretary) in this company speak Spanish fluently.
4. The two (general manager) reports were in agreement.
5. My (boss) desk is always cleared at the end of the day.
6. Each employee received a box of (handkerchief) at Christmas.
7. All the (analysis) that have been submitted support this recommendation.
8. Each choir member sang two (solo).
9. The (President-elect) room was provided as a courtesy by the hotel.
10. For good investments, buy stock in public (utility).
11. (Children) excess energy often gets them into trouble.
12. Dr. Knowles is a man (who) experience is highly regarded.
13. All notices of employment opportunities in the department are posted on (it) bulletin board.
14. Many (chintz) are used for making curtains.
15. The (Lynch) are not remodeling their downtown store.

Case Problem

Making Statistics Meaningful   As an employee of the public relations department, Nora Nadel is responsible for taking visitors through the company plant and for telling them facts and figures about the company. Here is part of the talk she uses on her tours: "Five years ago, we had only 127 production workers. Today, we have 1,270. Five years ago, we produced 19,550 clocks each year. Today, the workers produce 247,000 clocks annually. Five years ago, we were losing $1,000 a week. This year, our profits will be about $250,000." These facts are an important part of Nora's presentation, but they are difficult for visitors to grasp because of the way in which Nora presents them.

Can you present the facts in such a way that visitors will grasp them more readily?

Business people maintain social lives apart from business. In their private lives, they belong to such organizations as college alumni associations and civic or religious groups. Business people also develop social lives in connection with business. They develop relationships with co-workers, customers, and suppliers; with neighbors in an office building or an industrial park; with fellow members of professional organizations such as the American Institute of Certified Public Accountants, the National Sales Executives Association, and the Administrative Management Society; and so on. Although most of these social activities are only indirectly related to jobs, many companies encourage their employees to participate because active, outgoing employees help to build a favorable company image.

Their professional and personal relationships require business people to write many communications of a semisocial nature: congratulatory letters to friends and business associates who have been promoted; thank-you letters for favors, gifts, hospitality, and special services; condolence letters to those who have suffered misfortunes; letters involving the affairs of professional, social, and civic organizations; and formal social communications.

Belonging part to business and part to private life, these communications may be called *social-business messages.* In some cases, social-business messages are simply natural expressions of feelings between persons who happen to have met through business. In some cases, however, social-business messages are, in effect, public relations letters of individuals who are employed by business organizations.

FORMAT OF SOCIAL-BUSINESS LETTERS

For social-business letters, a smaller-size stationery—baronial or monarch—is preferred by most executives. Of course, the regular company stationery also may be used.

Basically, the format of a social-business letter is the same as the format of a regular business letter. However, the salutation in a social-business letter is often followed by a comma, rather than by a colon. In addition, the inside address may be written at the foot of the letter, like this:

Cordially yours,

Ms. Laura Desmond, President
Bank of Commerce and Trust
1735 Lincoln Boulevard
Cincinnati, Ohio 45202

LETTERS OF CONGRATULATION

Job promotions, honors bestowed by groups or organizations, appointments or elections to office, and other achievements of a business or of its employees are all appropriate occasions for writing congratulatory messages. In fact, such occasions are excellent PR opportunities. Since everyone wants to be respected and admired, a cordial letter of congratulation on such important occasions will always build the reader's goodwill toward the writer, and such goodwill, of course, is a valuable asset to businesspeople.

Congratulating Individuals

Many social-business letters are written to congratulate someone on an important career achievement. For example, suppose that you are a business executive and you read in the local newspaper that a fellow member of the Administrative Management Society has just been promoted to an important position in her company. As a thoughtful person, you might write a congratulatory letter like this one:

> Dear Meg,
>
> I was delighted to see in yesterday's *Times* the story about your promotion to Chief Engineer at Continental Shelf Mining Company. I know that you earned the promotion through years of hard work. I also know that such good things couldn't happen to a nicer person.
>
> It is always a pleasure to see someone's true ability win recognition. Congratulations and best wishes for continued success.
>
> Sincerely,

An astute businessperson should take advantage of the opportunity to promote goodwill on any occasion when a friend, a business associate, or an acquaintance has been honored by a group or an organization. Of course, the warmer and more friendly the letter, the more effective it will be. However, the wishes expressed must be sincere if the reader is to accept the gesture as something more than just a means of promoting business. The following letter sincerely expresses the writer's pleasure in the honor bestowed upon a friend:

> Dear Ethel,
>
> The Soroptimists made a wise choice in naming you "Business Teacher of the Year." I know that this recognition is well deserved. Over the many years of our friendship, I know how dedicated you have been to your work and to the welfare of the students in your classes. Please accept my sincere congratulations.
>
> This occasion also provides an excellent opportunity for me to offer my personal thanks for your many expressions of friendship over the years. May I thank you, too, for your many hours of work serving on several committees and particularly for your leadership and accomplishments on the Education Committee. I am always confident that a committee's work will be done efficiently and promptly when you are its leader. It is indeed a pleasure knowing you and working with you.
>
> Cordially,

Sometimes, however, the businessperson wishes to write to extend congratulations to someone only casually known or perhaps to someone not known at all. Such a letter will necessarily be somewhat more formal in tone than one written to a friend, but nevertheless it should be cordial and sincere. Because such letters are often used to build valuable business contacts, they require extra care and skill in writing. Letters like the following should achieve the desired purpose without offending the reader:

Dear Mr. Koontz:

Please allow me to express my best wishes on your election as president of the City Council. Your dedication to the improvement of our community is an inspiration to us all.

You ran for office on a platform that every citizen can endorse. I know that you will work hard to honor your campaign pledges and to make this city a better one for every business and every resident.

I sincerely wish you a productive, successful, and memorable term of office.

Cordially yours,

Some occasions call for letters of congratulation that are more personal in nature. For example, a social honor, an important anniversary, special recognition, or some other personal achievement usually calls for congratulatory letters to be written. Here is a letter that could be written on one such occasion:

Dear Carolyn:

It was such a pleasure for me to be in attendance last night at the Chamber of Commerce Awards Banquet when you received the "Executive of the Year" award. Your business record has been one of consistent success. You have single-handedly demonstrated that this community is again an excellent place to do business.

I think your achievement is all the more remarkable because your outstanding business performance is matched by your record of constant civic service. Somehow you find time and energy, even when no one else can, to tackle the toughest problems facing our community.

Please accept my congratulations on the recognition that you have earned by your superb performance as a business executive.

Cordially yours,

Another excellent opportunity for a personal letter of congratulation is any important achievement by the children of friends or business associates. Such a letter may be written to the parents or, especially if the writer knows the family, directly to the son or daughter of the business associate. Note the example below.

Dear Richard,

I was happy to learn from your father today that you have been selected as the valedictorian of your high school graduating class. I know that you have worked very hard over the past four years to achieve this distinction and that your parents are very proud of you, and justly so. I have taken much personal pleasure in watching you grow into such a fine young man over the many years I have enjoyed the friendship of you and your family.

My sincere best wishes, Richard, for continued success during your college career.

Sincerely,

Not only are letters of congratulation written to customers and friends outside the organization, but they are also frequently sent to fellow employees in the company. In fact, some executives consider these letters among the most important they write. There are, of course, many occasions to write letters of congratulations to co-workers; one obvious occasion for such a letter is a job promotion. Here is an example:

Dear Miss Hatachi:

I was both pleased and proud to learn of your promotion to the position of administrative assistant to the president. This position is one of the most important in the company, and I know that no one is better qualified than you to fill it. How long has it been since you and I first joined this company? We were among the first employees, as I recall, shortly after it was formed more than ten years ago. I have very much enjoyed our association, and I look back with pleasure at what has often been a very close working relationship.

Even though your new position will reduce the opportunities for such a working relationship, I hope that you will call on me if there is any way in which I may be of assistance to you. I also hope that we will get to see each other from time to time at some of the company social functions. Good luck to you!

Cordially yours,

An important anniversary with the company provides another occasion for writing a congratulatory letter, as illustrated here:

Dear Stan,

Congratulations on your twentieth anniversary with Finecraft. I remember your first day of work here, as a draftsman in the design department. Your progress at every stage has been an example for us all. Those of us in the production department know that when we work with you, our projects are bound to succeed.

I look forward to congratulating you on your twenty-fifth anniversary as well. Of course, by then you will have designed furniture so ingeniously that it will be able to build itself, leaving the production department with nothing to do but inspection!

Best wishes for continued success, health, and happiness.

Sincerely yours,

A letter of congratulation may also be appropriate when an employee retires. The tone of such a letter, however, depends primarily on the attitude of the person retiring. Some look forward to retirement; others do not. If you don't know the feelings of the retiree, use a style similar to that used in the following example:

Dear Mrs. Lopez:

I, among several hundred other employees here at Robinson's, will miss your pleasant smile and cheerful voice over the telephone. It hardly seems possible that you have been with us 18 years and that after next week you will be retiring.

It will be difficult finding a replacement who will contribute as much as you have to the friendly feeling among employees and customers.

All good wishes to you in your retirement. I hope you will enjoy many, many years of good health and happiness with your friends and family. Please visit us whenever you have the opportunity and the desire to do so.

Sincerely,

Congratulating Other Companies

A letter written by one business firm to congratulate another requires slightly different handling. Such a letter often has sales overtones.

> Dear Mr. Moritz:
>
> Congratulations on the completion of your new Family Fare Theater at Longwillow. I drove past the new building yesterday afternoon and stopped to watch as the workers put on the finishing touches. I think the Longwillow theater is going to be the most handsome and most successful in your chain.
>
> Please let me know if you would like to make any special arrangements for delivery of supplies for the concessions. Although yours will be the only theater in the Longwillow area, we will be happy to make special arrangements to provide prompt and convenient service to you there.
>
> We would welcome the opportunity to extend our service and our help to this newest member of the Family Fare family.
>
> Cordially yours,

THANK-YOU LETTERS

Occasions that call for thank-you letters often arise; for example, to acknowledge receipt of a gift, to express appreciation for thoughtfulness, for special favors, and so on. Thank-you letters in business are just as necessary as the "bread and butter" notes sent to friends who have entertained you in their homes or who have done something especially nice for you. In fact, failure to write a thank-you when it is called for can lose goodwill, because people expect their gifts and special efforts to be appreciated and are displeased when appreciation is not shown.

Promptness in sending a thank-you note is as important as what is said, because any delay in sending the letter may be taken to imply a lack of sincere appreciation.

Writing Thanks for a Gift

Business executives often receive gifts from suppliers and from others with whom they do business. Although some business firms deplore this practice, it nevertheless exists. Some companies prohibit the acceptance of gifts by individuals, as indicated tactfully in the following example:

> Dear Mr. Strang:
>
> Thank you very much for the thoughtfulness you showed in sending the beautiful graphite fly-fishing rod and other equipment that arrived in my office this af-

ternoon. I am indeed an avid fly fisherman, and I know that the rod you chose is the best made.

I am forwarding the equipment to our company lodge at Trout Hollow, for use of our employees and our guests whenever they visit. I have already completed arrangements to have labels placed on every piece of equipment saying, "Gift to Bogwell International from Industrico Distributing."

On behalf of all those who will enjoy the use of this magnificent fishing equipment, let me express our deepest appreciation. You will have to be our guest for a weekend of fishing at Trout Hollow some weekend this spring.

                              Sincerely yours,

Writing Thanks for Hospitality

When hospitality has been extended to you, common courtesy calls for a thank-you. For example, suppose that you visit a supplier's factory in another city to discuss the purchase of his product. He makes reservations for you at a hotel, takes you to dinner, and in other ways looks after your physical comfort—he even entertains you in his home. Of course, a "bread and butter" note is a must.

Dear Mrs. Erickson:

Thank you for the many courtesies extended to me on my recent visit to Mill Valley. My stay was certainly much more pleasant because of your thoughtfulness in arranging for my comfort.

The high spot of the entire visit was the evening spent in your beautiful home. You and Mr. Erickson are most gracious hosts. The food was excellent; the conversation, stimulating; the people, delightful. The time passed so quickly that I was embarrassed to find that I had stayed so long—so engrossed and comfortable was I in being part of such good company.

I have mailed you a small package as a little token of my appreciation for the many kindnesses shown me. I shall not soon forget my visit to Mill Valley.

                              Sincerely yours,

Writing Thanks for Courtesies

When you receive a letter of congratulation upon a promotion, a special recognition, or an achievement, you should acknowledge it with a thank-you letter. For example:

Dear Roger:

You were very thoughtful to write me about my recent promotion. One of the most satisfying things about being promoted is that one often gets such pleasant letters from the nicest people! I already like my new job very much, and I know that I will enjoy it even more after I have really become accustomed to this completely different work.

Thank you, Roger, for all your good wishes and your thoughtfulness. About that offer to be of assistance—I may be calling on you sooner than you expect, so be prepared!

                              Sincerely,

Writing Thanks for Special Favors

Often friends or business acquaintances go out of their way to do a favor. Someone, for example, may recommend a friend for membership in a club, another may recommend a particular firm to a customer, or still another may be of special service in a business situation. A special favor of this kind deserves a thank-you; for example:

Dear Mr. Martinez:

This morning we visited Mr. Bruce Stargell of Bruce's Goodies, Inc. Mr. Stargell mentioned your recommendation when he placed an order for display and storage equipment for his chain of ten new candy stores that he will open this fall.

We thank you, Mr. Martinez, for recommending us to Mr. Stargell. We appreciate the order immensely, but not one bit more than we appreciate your confidence in us. You have paid us a compliment of the highest order.

Please accept our thanks for this favor. I assure you, we will repay your kindness at the earliest opportunity, which we hope will be soon.

Cordially yours,

FORMAL INVITATIONS AND REPLIES

From time to time, business people receive formal invitations to such events as an open house, a special reception to honor a distinguished person, a special anniversary, or a formal social gathering. Such invitations are usually engraved or printed and are written in the third person.

The illustrations on pages 437 and 438 show the formal printed invitation, the formal handwritten invitation, the handwritten acceptance, and the handwritten refusal. An acceptance or a refusal is occasionally typewritten; however, this practice is not recommended. Handwritten invitations and replies are written on personal stationery or special note-size stationery. Plain white notepaper may also be used.

LETTERS OF CONDOLENCE

Just as you would write a note or send a card of sympathy to someone who has suffered the loss of a close relative or friend, so do business executives write letters to friends and associates upon learning of misfortunes and tragedies in their lives. Naturally, letters of condolence should be genuinely sympathetic. It is not easy to comfort those who have suffered losses; letters of condolence, therefore, are among the most difficult letters to write. Although handwritten condolence letters are preferable, typed letters are acceptable. If you are unable to write a really personal note of sympathy, you may send a printed sympathy card. Following is a letter of condolence.

Dear Carl:

The news of your brother's untimely death yesterday has stunned and saddened me. I know that you have suffered a great loss. Please accept my sincere sympathy.

When my mother died last year, a friend sent me a copy of Dylan Thomas's

> # The Sales Executives' Club
>
> requests the pleasure of your company
> at a formal showing
> of its new film
> "Selling the American Dream"
> Tuesday, the tenth of May
> at eight o'clock
> Cavalier Room of the Century Hotel
>
> R.S.V.P.

A formal printed invitation.

poem, "And Death Shall Have No Dominion." I found the poem a source of consolation again and again. I hope the poem will serve you as well as it did me. My heart goes out to you and your family in your time of grief.

Sincerely yours,

> *Mr. and Mrs. Delbert Anderson*
> *request the pleasure of*
> *Mr. and Mrs. Peter De Merrit's company*
> *at a dinner party*
> *on Saturday, the Fourth of July*
> *at eight o'clock*
> *5208 Lupin Drive*
>
> *R.S.V.P.*   *Telephone 555-7116*

A formal handwritten invitation.

Ms. Audrey Brennan
accepts with pleasure
the kind invitation of
The Sales Executive Club
for Tuesday, the Tenth of May

A handwritten acceptance to an invitation.

You do not have to wait until you enter the world of business to take advantage of the suggestions made in this section. Because of the personal nature of the correspondence discussed, much of the material will apply to you even now.

Mr. and Mrs. Peter De Merrit
regret that a previous engagement
prevents their accepting
Mr. and Mrs. Anderson's
kind invitation
for the Fourth of July

A handwritten refusal to an invitation.

COMMUNICATION PROJECTS

Practical Application

A. You are president of a medium-sized company, Starbuckle Decorative Metals. When informed that one of the company's oldest employees, bookkeeper Carl Wickford, is retiring after thirty years with Starbuckle, you genuinely want to thank him for such long service. You decide to write a letter thanking Mr. Wickford for his years with the company and to enclose a check for $200. Write the letter.

B. Marianne Mullinix was a classmate of yours in college. You read in the newspapers that Marianne, after only three years at Destry Investing, has been chosen Outstanding Financial Analyst. Marianne's reward is twofold: a promotion to Assistant Director of Financial Analysis and an expense paid tour of the Orient. Write a letter of congratulation to Marianne on her achievements.

C. You have just returned from a business trip to Louisville, Kentucky. During your three-day stay in Louisville, you were the house guest of Barbara and Peter Lembo, long-time friends of your family. Barbara even met you at the airport and insisted on personally driving you to your business appointments, rather than having you experience the difficulty of getting around a strange city in a rented car. (Taxi drivers were on strike during the time you were in Louisville.) Write a note of thanks to the Lembos, who live at 87 Mark Twain Drive, Louisville, Kentucky 40204. Today you ordered a gift to be sent them as a small token of your appreciation.

D. You have just learned of the illness and death of Mrs. Frederick Olson, the wife of one of your company's suppliers who has become a friend of yours. In addition to Mr. Olson, Mrs. Olson (Helga) leaves a married daughter (Anne) and three young grandchildren, Tom, Alex, and Inga. Write a letter of condolence to Frederick Olson, Director of Marketing for Ludlow Manufacturing, 668 West Ludlow, St. Louis, Missouri 63399.

Editing Practice

Editing for Redundancies   Eliminate all unnecessary repetitions in the sentences below.

1. We are planning to revert back to personal contact as our main sales strategy.
2. The expense accounts submitted by Lois and Maury are both alike.
3. The report was supplied free, gratis.
4. By the time I arrived, the inspection was over with.
5. The manager refused to repeat his remarks again for the employees who arrived late.
6. The desk will fit just inside of the entrance.
7. Past experience shows that Fred is habitually late.
8. Clean your typing element daily, as otherwise you will not get sharp copy.

Case Problem

Listening for Essential Ideas   Your instructor will read an article to you. Listen carefully; then summarize the article in as few words as possible.

CHAPTER 8

PREPARING REPORTS AND SPECIAL COMMUNICATIONS

48 MEMORANDUM REPORTS

In business, a report is probably the primary method for providing information. Executives, supervisors, managers, department heads, and many others receive reports that provide them with essential information to help them perform their duties. Likewise, many of these people write reports to supply others with essential business information.

A report is almost always written, but it may, of course, be given orally. If the information is important enough to report, it is important enough to put in writing—even if only for the record. Anything worth reporting is important; therefore, "Put it in writing" is the basic principle behind all reports.

The values of a written report, compared with an oral report, are obvious. An oral report may be misunderstood. Much of an oral report may be quickly forgotten, especially statistical data. Even a forceful oral report will grow weaker and weaker each day. A written report, however, can be referred to again and again, so that the reader reinforces the message with each reading. Moreover, a precise and permanent record exists in the report itself.

One way of classifying reports is according to length—*informal* (shorter reports) or *formal* (longer reports). Because formal reports usually require extensive research, documentation, investigation, and analysis, the style of presentation is usually different from the style used for a short report. You will learn how to prepare a formal report in Section 49. But first you will learn how to prepare an informal report, the type you will probably prepare most often.

MECHANICS OF INFORMAL REPORTS

In Section 38, you learned to use a memorandum as a means of corresponding with other employees within an organization. The same memorandum form is used for writing informal reports, hence the name *memorandum report.*

The memorandum report begins with the same information that was included in the memorandum you learned to use for interoffice correspondence, as follows:

> To:
> From:
> Date:
> Subject:

Whether you use this exact form or whether you adapt it will depend upon the circumstances under which you are working at the time you are preparing the report. *How* you use the above outline will depend on a number of variables. These are discussed on pages 443–444.

To

The way you address the person to whom the report is going depends primarily upon the degree of formality or informality of your office atmosphere. For instance, if everybody addresses the boss by his or her first name and the boss approves, and if the report is of a personal nature, you might write:

To: Fran Wilson

But suppose you know that the report will be read by other persons, as well as by the boss, or that the report will be filed for future reference. Then it would be better to write:

To: Ms. Frances Wilson

From

The *From* line should match the tone of the *To* line. For example, the first two lines of a very informal memorandum report written only for the personal information of the boss would appear as:

To: Fran Wilson
From: Ted King

For a report that is not for the exclusive information of the boss or that is to be filed for future reference, a different *From* line would be used. You should keep in mind that all readers are likely to know the boss, but they may not know who you are. Therefore, you might write:

To: Ms. Frances Wilson
From: Ted King, Assistant Regional Manager

Subject

The *Subject* line should be a comprehensive, yet clear and precise, statement that will prepare a reader for rapid assimilation of the information given in the report. Composing a good subject line, therefore, requires a high degree of skill. Let's look at some illustrations. Here is a subject line for a credit manager's report to the vice president in charge of credit.

Subject: Credit

Of course, such a subject line would be meaningless to the vice president. One could not tell what the report is really about without reading the report itself. The following line, however, would orient the reader immediately.

Subject: Credit Applications Handled During April, 19—

Suppose that you are a personnel director and receive a report with a subject line like this one:

> Subject: Employee Absenteeism

Possibly you have forgotten that you asked for a report on some phase of employee absenteeism. If that is the case, the above subject line will not refresh your memory or prepare you to quickly grasp the facts presented in the report. Wouldn't the following subject line be more helpful?

> Subject: Causes of Employee Absenteeism, January-March, 19—

Date

Because conditions change so rapidly that facts presented on one date may not be valid at a later date, every report should contain the date on which it was written. And how frustrating to search for a report in the files, a report that could prove very valuable if only you knew when it was written!

Wherever dates are given in the body of a report, those dates must be specific. Instead of writing, "Last Tuesday, we sent...," you would write, "On Tuesday, March 5, 19—, we sent...."

Adapting the Memo Form

Although the memo form we have been using is the one most frequently used, there are variations that may sometimes be more appropriate. For example:

> Carmen Mendoza
> October 13, 19—
> Causes of Employee Absenteeism, January-March, 19—

This adaptation shows that Carmen Mendoza wrote the report and gives the date; but it states the subject as a heading, or title. The assumption is that this report would go only to the person requesting the report and, therefore, requires no additional name. However, if an addressee's name is necessary, the body of the report could start like this:

> Mrs. Alvarez: The causes of employee absenteeism from January through March, 19—, are as follows:

File Copies

Whenever you write an informal report, even if you think it is not important, be sure to make a copy for your own files. Anything important enough to put in writing is important enough to be retained. You may never need to refer to your file copy, but you cannot be certain that you or someone else in the company will not need some of the information contained in the report sometime in the future. The best precautionary measure against lost or misaddressed reports is to have in your files a folder marked "Reports," which contains a copy of every report you write.

PLANNING AND WRITING INFORMAL REPORTS

Many people, including some correspondents, think that writing involves merely sitting down and dashing off a few words. This is a false notion that largely accounts for the fact that good business writers are scarce and therefore very much in demand.

Actually, a topnotch writing effort of any kind represents hard work and is the result of much thought, careful planning, and excellent training. For the know-how that will enable you to write informal reports of the very best quality, you need to study, think about, and apply the following principles.

Being Clear, Complete, Correct, and Concise

As you know, writing that is *concise* is not writing that is incomplete. To be concise, you must say everything that needs to be said, but you must say it in the fewest possible words.

You are also well aware that your writing must be clear and complete. You would not write a "fuzzy" sentence like this:

> Ms. Olsen told Mrs. Wertz about the overtime situation in the mail room, and she said she would have the report on her desk in a few days.

Instead, you would write a clear, complete, specific message, such as this one:

> Ms. Olsen reported to Mrs. Wertz that she would have the report on mail room overtime on Mrs. Wertz's desk on Wednesday, May 18, 19—.

All reports must be correct in every detail. Perhaps we should use the stronger term *accurate,* because any information important enough to be reported must be more than substantially correct; it must be completely accurate. For example, if you are asked to report the number of free-sample requests that come in on a given day, you'd better be sure that you give an exact, not an approximate, count.

Wording

The wording of reports differs from that of letters. A letter is designed to do more than convey a message, for its accompanying purpose is to win new customers or clients for the company and to retain old ones. Therefore, the tone of a letter is warm and friendly. A report, on the other hand, is a straightforward, factual presentation—and it should be worded as such.

As an illustration, read the following opening paragraph of a letter answering a request for information about your company's free tuition program for employees.

> In response to your May 14 request, we are pleased to tell you that we do provide free tuition for employees taking work-related courses in local schools

under the following circumstances:....(Then you would itemize and explain the circumstances under which your company pays the tuition for its employees.)

Now, note how the wording changes when the same information is given in a report.

Employees taking work-related courses in local schools will be reimbursed for tuition when the following requirements have been met:
1. The course has been approved in advance by the employee's supervisor.
2. The employee earns a grade of "C" or better.
3. The employee has been with this company for six months or more.

FORMS OF PRESENTATION

How brief or how detailed should your informal report be? Should you give the requested information in a single paragraph? Should you present the information in outline form? For the most effective presentation, should you tabulate the information?

Because you are preparing the report, no one but you can answer these questions. Only you are close enough to the situation to know why the report was requested, to be able to project the probable uses of the information, and so on. To be able to make a wise decision about the form your report should take, though, you must know the types of presentations and the purposes that each best serves.

Paragraph Form

The paragraph form is used for the presentation of a simple fact. For example, if your boss has requested that you report how many hours of overtime were paid the previous month—and you are certain that the only statistic your boss wants is the total number of hours—you might write the following in a memo-style report:

In the month of February, 19—, the total number of hours of overtime in the Accounting Department was 10 hours.

Or, if you would like to give a little extra information, you might add to the above statement:

There are 24 employees in the department, and 6 employees (25 percent) accounted for the 10 hours of overtime.

Outline Form

If, however, you know that your boss has a personal interest in the staff, you might corrrectly believe that you should list the names of the persons who worked overtime. You could present all the information necessary in outline form, as follows:

Information regarding overtime in the Accounting Department during February, 19—, is as follows:

1. Total employees in department: 24
2. Total hours of overtime: 10
3. (25 percent) Employees working
   overtime: 6

James Miles, $1\frac{1}{2}$ hours
Doris Tyson, 2 hours
Kenneth Ulrich, $\frac{1}{2}$ hour
Ina West, 3 hours
Robert Williams, 1 hour
Nicholas Zorba, 2 hours

Note how the outline form is used to highlight the suggestions in the memo shown on page 448.

Table Form

In some cases, the most effective way to present information is in table form. The advantage of a tabulated presentation is that the reader can more easily see the total situation at a glance without wading through a great many words. Obviously, the decision to tabulate should be influenced by the amount and the kind of information to be included and also by the writer's projection regarding the uses to which the information is likely to be put. In table form, the previously discussed overtime report would look like this:

Accounting Department Overtime
Month of February, 19—

Employee	Overtime Hours	Reason
Miles, James	$1\frac{1}{2}$	To complete January billing
Tyson, Doris	2	To prepare expense statement
Ulrich, Kenneth	$\frac{1}{2}$	To complete checking cost estimates
West, Ina	3	To complete January billing
Williams, Robert	1	To check travel expenses
Zorba, Nicholas	2	To post expenses

Total employees: 24 Overtime Hours: 10
Total employees working overtime: 6
Percent: 25

INTEROFFICE MEMORANDUM

TO: Ms. Lillian Pine   FROM: Carlos Ortiz

SUBJECT: Increasing Credit Card Use   DATE: June 9, 19--

Our firm has issued 4,567 credit cards to customers during the past three years. However, a survey made recently by our credit department indicates that only 46 percent of these credit card holders have made purchases exceeding $25 during this same three-year period. The average charge is $75.

A national study recently made by the American Association of Credit revealed that the average purchase by credit card holders is $150. This figure would seem to indicate that we are not getting the maximum benefits from the credit cards we issue and that we should be able to increase our volume of credit business by encouraging greater use of credit cards by our customers.

I am therefore recommending that we undertake a campaign to encourage customers who hold credit cards to make greater use of their cards. The initial steps of this campaign should include the following:

1. Preparing folders encouraging new customers to apply for credit cards. An application form should be a part of this folder, which would be available not only in the credit office but also at numerous locations within the store.

2. Placing full-page advertisements in both the morning and evening newspapers, explaining how customers can more widely use their credit cards and not get into economic difficulties by overcharging.

3. Buying television time for spot announcements with a theme similar to that of the newspaper advertisements.

I would suggest that representatives from the both the credit and the marketing departments form a committee to plan the strategies of this program not later than the end of this month.

I will be happy to discuss any aspects of these suggestions with you at your convenience.

CO

Ideas for increasing efficiency, productivity, or profitability are always welcomed. Note how the subject line in this unsolicited report appeals to the reader's interest.

UNSOLICITED REPORTS

An unsolicited report is, quite simply, one that you make on your own initiative rather than one you are asked for. In business, any idea that you might have for increasing efficiency, productivity, or profit-making will usually be welcome. And more than likely you will want to put your idea in writing so that you may present it in the most complete, logical, and generally effective manner. See the unsolicited report shown on page 448.

How do you go about preparing and submitting an unsolicited report? Here are some details that you should consider before you begin to write.

To

You will want to direct your suggestion or idea to the person who has the authority to put it into effect. Usually this person will be your boss; but even if it happens to be someone else, courtesy and protocol demand that the suggestion be routed *through* your boss *to* that other person. For example:

> To: Ms. Olive Steep (your boss)
>   Mrs. Audrey Harris (the "authority" person)

Subject

In any report, the subject line should tell the reader what the report is about. In an unsolicited report, though, you should slant the wording of the subject so that it will appeal to the reader's particular interest. For example, if you know that your boss is particularly interested in increasing customer use of credit cards, your subject line might read:

> Subject: Suggestions for Increasing Credit Card Use

COMMUNICATION PROJECTS

Practical Application

A. In memorandum report form, addressed to your instructor, report on your vocational plans following graduation.

B. Select two stocks that are listed in your local newspaper's New York Stock Exchange report. From the information provided in the newspaper, write an informal report about these two stocks. Address the memorandum report to your instructor.

C. Write an informal report on changes that you feel would be desirable in the registration process at your school. Address the report to the registrar.

D. Prepare a tabulation report, similar to the one on page 447, for the following information:

> Sources of Employees Hired During the Year 19—: The state employment service referred 36 candidates; 16 were hired. Local college placement offices referred 27 candidates; 19 were hired. Private placement services referred 41 candidates; 17 were hired. Newspaper advertising resulted in 53 candidates; 10 were hired. Unsolicited applicants included 6 candidates; 1 was hired. Notices in employee service magazines resulted in 12 candidates; 7 were hired.

E. From *one* of the following areas—accounting, secretarial, marketing, management, or economics—indicate three subject lines that would be likely for short reports. For example, in accounting, a possible subject for a short report might be: Sources of New Clients.

Editing Practice

The Word Processing Supervisor   Can you find any spelling or homonym errors in the following excerpts from a Circulation Department report?

> Newsstand sales plus subscription sales acceded 1.5 million copies in the month of February. Clearly, the principle reason for this sharp increase is that our radio and television advertising in December and January was well planned. In fact, we expect our March addition to reach 1.6 million copies; sales should then level off in April and May and (as usual) decrease over the summer months.

Case Problem

To Ask or Not to Ask Questions   One of the most important things new employees must learn is when to ask for help and when to use their own judgment in trying to solve a problem. People who solve their own problems are appreciated only when their work is correct. On the other hand, new employees who make mistakes because they are afraid or hesitant to ask questions may very well find themselves in serious trouble. What would you do in the following situations?

1. Jean's boss asks her to make six copies of a report. On the list of those who are to receive a report is "Ms. Lincoln." There are two Ms. Lincolns in the company—one is the supervisor of the word processing center and the other is the office supervisor. Because the report concerns the purchase of new typewriters, Jean decides that the supervisor of the word processing center is the one who should receive the report. Without asking the boss, Jean sends the report to the supervisor of the word processing center.
2. Bob has just started work as an order-editor and finds on his desk an order for an item that he has not heard of. He knows that recently many items were declared out of stock, and he assumes that this is one of them; therefore, he notes this information on the order.
   a. Do you agree with Bob's action?
   b. Should he have checked further?
   c. What could be the consequences of his action?

49
FORMAL
BUSINESS REPORTS

In the previous section, you learned how to prepare a memorandum report, which is generally limited to one or two pages. In this section, you will learn how to prepare longer, more formal business reports. Formal business reports, in addition to being longer than informal memorandum reports, are usually concerned with complex problems or questions necessitating investigation, analysis, research, and documentation. For example, here are some typical formal report subjects: an analysis of the methods of marketing a company's products; a feasibility study to determine whether to change a method of operating a particular aspect of a business, such as a study to determine whether to change to computer accounting and billing; an experiment to test the qualities of a new product.

The writing of a formal business report may require weeks or even months of extensive research and reading related to the topic of the report, and the completed report could contain anywhere from several pages to more than a hundred pages. Regardless of its length, a formal report must be expertly written because often the report is the basis upon which a company decides whether or not to spend many thousands of dollars.

Who generally does the actual writing of a report? The writing may not be done by the person who conducts the research. Not everyone is capable of writing an effective formal report, so even though an executive or an engineer or other technician may actually conduct the research, often a secretary or administrative assistant will be closely involved in the actual preparation of the report itself. So here is still another way of increasing your value to your boss and to your company—being able to prepare an effective formal business report. In Section 59, there is a discussion on "Research Activities" that will prove very helpful to you in assisting executives with their research.

Some companies conduct a considerable amount of research and write many reports concerning these research projects. Such companies often employ specialists (sometimes called "technical writers") whose sole function is to take the material assembled by the researcher and put it into report form. If the researcher writes the report, the technical writer assists the researcher in preparing the report. Technical writers are, of course, in top salary brackets because of their expertise, which is in short supply.

You already have a head start in learning how to write the longer formal report. In Section 48 you learned how to write informal memorandum reports, and this knowledge will serve as an excellent background for learning how to write the more complex formal report.

PREPARING TO WRITE FORMAL REPORTS

There are some variations in the style and form used for preparing formal reports, usually determined by the nature of the subject being investigated. A technical report, such as one that specifies the requirements for manufacturing computer components, may be organized in outline form with very little text. Similarly, the reports of chemists, engineers, and other scientists are likely to include many tables, charts, and graphs with a relatively small amount of written interpretation. On the other hand, many business reports are mainly narrative, with a small amount of tabular matter. Despite this variation in the style and form of reports, most formal reports include these main sections:

> Introduction
> Summary
> Body
> Conclusions and Recommendations
> Supplementary Material

Before commencing the actual writing of the formal report, the writer-investigator must first determine the purpose and the scope of the report. To make this determination, the investigator must gather reliable facts, assemble and analyze those facts, draw conclusions from the factual analysis, and, finally, make recommendations that are reasonable in view of company needs.

Defining Purpose and Scope

Why is the report being written? The answer to this question should appear in the introductory section of the report. For example, in a study to determine whether a company should establish a word processing center (instead of letting each department handle its own communication using conventional methods), the purpose of the report might be stated as follows:

1. To determine current methods of preparing communications.
2. To determine the efficiency of these methods.
3. To determine the feasibility of establishing a word processing center to handle correspondence and report writing activities.

A report writer must avoid selecting a topic that is too large to be handled effectively. The experienced report writer, therefore, clearly defines the scope of the problem and sets boundaries that keep the research within reason. For example, think how difficult it would be to do research involving "Telephone Techniques of Office Workers." This topic is much too broad in scope to be treated in one report, if it could be treated at all. The topic needs to be limited to a more specific group. A revision that would be more practical might read: "Telephone Techniques of Stenographers and Secretaries of the Thompson Insurance Company."

Gathering Information

"No report is stronger than the facts behind it." Computer specialists, in speaking of the preparation of reports by machine, emphasize this statement vividly with their term *GIGO* (pronounced *GUY-GO*), standing for "garbage-in, garbage-out." The value of any report depends on the quality of the material going into its production. If "garbage" goes in, "garbage" is bound to come out. With reliable facts behind it, a reliable report can be written; with questionable data, only a questionable report can result.

In gathering information and documenting it, writers should be familiar with the authoritative references in their fields. There are, of course, many general references that everyone needs. Such standard sources as the *Writer's Guide to Periodical Literature*, *The Business Periodicals Index, Facts on File, The World Almanac,* and *The New York Times Annual Index* are invaluable helps to nearly any writer.

In each field of business, such as accounting, marketing, or office administration, there are basic references as well as current periodicals that should be reviewed frequently by report writers. Naturally, anyone doing research must first learn how to find and use books, periodicals, card catalogs, and various indexes. Section 59 suggests additional basic references and specialized references. In addition, it suggests ways to use the library for research activities.

When data are to be obtained in other ways, such as through the use of questionnaires or personal interviews, other research techniques must be mastered.

Working Bibliography In consulting the various reference works pertinent to the subject, the writer should make up a list of the books, periodicals, reports, and other sources to be used as references in the report. This preliminary list of sources is called the *working bibliography*. If the writer makes each entry of the working bibliography on a separate card (5 by 3 or 6 by 4 inches), the cards will make it easier to assemble the final bibliography of sources actually used. The writer will also find the bibliography cards useful when footnoting material in the report.

A book card for a working bibliography should contain all the following information:

> Author's full name (last name first)
> Title (and edition, if there is more than one)
> Name and location of publisher
> Date of publication (latest copyright date)

In addition, it is helpful to include for the writer's own use the library's call number for the reference.

The following illustration shows a bibliography card that has been prepared for a book reference. Note the library's call number in the upper right corner.

When consulting a magazine, newspaper, or other periodical, the writer prepares a bibliography card like the one on page 454. This card should show the full name of the author, the title of the article (in quotation marks), the name of the publication (and location, if a newspaper), the date, volume, and number of the publication, and the page numbers.

> Pryor, Margaret J.
>
> Financial Management
> _____
>
> McGraw-Hill Book Co., Inc.
> New York, 1982

Note-Taking The writer also uses cards for taking notes. Cards are much more practical for this purpose than sheets of paper because cards are sturdy and can be sorted and resorted easily.

The ease with which material can be organized and a report can be written depends to a large extent on how well notes have been made from reading. Most good writers take more notes than they need. This practice gives them a great deal of information, which they can "boil down" to the essentials before writing the report.

> Gregg, Andrew C.
> "Setting Goals for
> Business Success,"
> The Manager's Journal,
> July 1982, pp. 87-96
> Vol. 10, No. 7

When you take notes from your reading, be sure to carefully identify each source. Always use a new card for each new source or topic. Normally, summary statements or phrases with page references are sufficient for note cards. Whenever you use a quotation, however, be sure to copy the statement exactly, enclose it in quotation marks, and list the number of the page from which the quotation was taken. Later, when you are organizing the material for writing, you may find it helpful to include a brief subject reference at the top of each card; for example, if you are tracing the development of a product, you might identify references by "year," "developer," or "site of development."

ORGANIZING THE REPORT

After all the material related to the topic has been collected and studied, the writer can begin to organize the report. At this time, the note cards should be revised, sorted by topic, and tentatively organized into a logical sequence for the report.

Outline

Using organized note cards as a guide, the writer next makes an outline to serve as the structure, or framework, of the report. The outline should be kept as simple as possible. While determining the outline, the writer should keep in mind the kinds of topic headings the report requires. If outline entries are carefully thought out, many of them can be used as topic headings in the final report. The writer should keep in mind the following points in making the outline:

The purpose of the report is to convey information efficiently.
A good report structure gives the reader a sense of movement; one thought naturally reads into another.
The outline is a time-saver when the writer starts writing.
The outline should be arranged to present material in logical units and in logical sequence.

Headings

Most books, articles, and business reports utilize headings to indicate the organization of the material. Headings of equivalent weight should be styled alike. For example, the main divisions of an article, a report, or a chapter in a book may be centered, and the subdivisions of each main heading may be typed as paragraph headings. When there are more than two divisions, however, the following arrangement of headings should be used:

CENTERED FIRST-ORDER HEADING
Centered Second-Order Heading
BLOCKED THIRD-ORDER HEADING
Blocked Fourth-Order Heading
Indented Fifth-Order Heading

If the report writer is consistent in the use of headings, the reader will better understand the report's organization and content. Consistency should be observed in the form as well as in the style of the headings. In general, a topic form is preferred to a sentence form. For example, "How to Write Reports" is preferable to "This Is How to Write Reports."

WRITING THE REPORT

There are considerable differences between the informal writing style of business letters and memorandums and the writing style commonly found in formal reports. These differences will be pointed out in the following discussion.

Style

Long business reports are important documents upon which management bases many of its high-level decisions. Consequently, such reports tend to be written in a serious, formal style, usually in the third person. The impersonal style helps the writer avoid interjecting a personal tone, which might weaken a report by making it seem merely a statement of one person's opinions and beliefs, instead of a sound evaluation of the data gathered for the report. Of course, usually only one person, the writer, is evaluating the facts, but the more the writer can de-emphasize the *I* and cite facts to back the evaluation, the more objective and more persuasive the report will sound.

A poor report writer presenting a report on letter-writing practices might make these statements:

> It seems to *me* that the semiblock style of letter takes too much time to type. *Personally*, *I* would *prefer* to use the simplified letter for all company correspondence.
> Even though most of the other departments prefer mixed punctuation, *I* have a strong *preference* for open punctuation, which *I* feel we should adopt.

Even though the facts may provide a sound basis for the evaluations given in the examples above, these sentences do not seem objective because the writer has used so many personal references. In addition, the writer has shown how judgments are drawn from the data gathered.

On the other hand, the good report writer knows that merely stating a judgment will not persuade anyone to accept it, no matter how soundly based on fact and reason the judgment may be. Therefore, the expert writer uses an impersonal style and relates all evaluations to the facts found in the study. This writer carefully avoids any expressions that may imply that the evaluations are based on personal opinions instead of sound reasons and facts. Instead of the sentences given above, the expert writer would write the following:

> The evidence revealed by this survey indicates that the semiblocked style of letter takes 15 percent more typing time than the simplified style.
> Use of the simplified letter style would be appropriate for the Thompson Insur-

ance Company because the style has the modern look of simplicity and is also faster and easier to type.

Three of the five departments studied use mixed punctuation; however, adoption of open punctuation would have the following advantages: . . . .

(Explanation of these advantages would follow.)

The same impersonal writing style illustrated above should characterize every section of the report. Remember that making it possible for the reader to reason from the facts presented is an important factor in the success of any business report.

Title Page

The title page usually includes the complete title of the report, the name and title of the author, the name of the person for whom the report is prepared, and the date the report is submitted. Each of these items should be attractively arranged on the page. A typical title page is illustrated on page 458.

Table of Contents

This section is prepared after the report has been completed. One commonly accepted form is illustrated below.

TABLE OF CONTENTS

Introduction

The introductory section of a long report is designed to tell the reader why the report was written, how the data were gathered, and what the report does (or does not) do.

Suppose that Irene Fox, a vice president of the Thompson Insurance Company, has asked John Kraft, office administrator, to investigate the feasibility of establishing a word processing center, with a view toward improving the company's correspondence function and also cutting costs. In such a report, Mr. Kraft would include in

```
                    THE FEASIBILITY OF ESTABLISHING

                    A WORD PROCESSING CENTER

                              AT

                    THOMPSON INSURANCE COMPANY










                              May 15, 19--

                              Prepared for:   Irene Fox

                              Prepared by:    John Kraft
```

This title page shows the complete title of the report, the name of the author, the name of the person for whom the report is prepared, and the date the report is submitted.

the introductory section the *purpose* and *scope* of the report and the *procedures* followed to collect and analyze data.

Purpose and Scope   First, the writer should explain why the report was written. Next he should clearly enumerate the basic objectives of the report.

This report was prepared at the request of Ms. Fox, vice president of the Thompson Insurance Company. The purposes of the report are:

1. To determine what practices are used in preparing communications in each department of the company.
2. To determine what equipment is used in preparing communications in each department of the company.
3. To determine the costs involved in preparing communications.
4. To determine whether the establishment of a word processing center would improve company communications and/or decrease the cost of producing company communications.

In addition, a brief statement of the scope of the investigation may be included in this section.

This investigation is limited to the communication practices in the home office of the Thompson Insurance Company in Springfield, Illinois.

Procedures   The introductory section of the report should describe the methods that were used to collect and analyze the data. Here is an example:

To collect valid information for this report, all supervisors responsible for correspondence in each department and all technical writers were interviewed. The questionnaire shown in Appendix C of this report was sent in advance and was completed by each supervisor and technical writer. The questionnaires were reviewed carefully and were analyzed during the final interview conducted by Ms. Perez. Major manufacturers of word processing equipment were contacted, and each manufacturer presented a demonstration of its equipment. In addition, current periodicals were consulted so that the results of this company survey could be compared with recommended practices for handling communications in other companies.

Summary

For the busy executive, the summary is placed early in the report (following the introduction). This section contains the most significant information in capsule form, which is helpful to the reader who cannot take time to read the entire report. When time permits, the reader can complete the reading of the report. The length of the summary may range from one paragraph to four or five pages, depending on the material that has been gathered. The following example is the opening paragraph of the summary of the feasibility study to determine whether a word processing center should be established at the Thompson Insurance Company:

SUMMARY
This study recommends that a word processing center be established at the home office of the Thompson Insurance Company and shows that such a center would improve correspondence practices and decrease correspondence costs. The specific data gathered during this investigation resulted in the following conclusions that led to the above recommendation:

1. More time than is necessary is expended in both the dictation and the transcription processes.
2. There is a great variation in letter styles used throughout the company.
3. Correspondence often is not answered for as many as two to three days after it is received.
4. Many letters that are individually written could well be form letters.

Body

The body is the report proper. In this section the writer tells what was done, how it was done, and what the writer found. Writing this section should present no great difficulties if the writer follows a carefully prepared outline and has good notes. The writer should stick to accurate, verifiable facts and present them in a clear, concise manner. The suggestions given in Chapter 6 for forceful, clear writing apply to the writing of reports.

Conclusions and Recommendations

This section can easily be the most important one in any report, for it is here that the real results of the report appear. The writer's conclusions tell the busy executive, on the basis of the most reliable data available, "Here is what the report shows."

Personal observations should be reduced to a minimum—conclusions should be drawn from the facts only. In the light of the conclusions and from experience with the company, the writer can make recommendations. (**Note:** As a guide to making worthwhile recommendations, the writer should glance back at the listed purposes of the report. As a rule, there could well be at least one recommendation for each stated purpose.)

By referring to the purposes stated in the introduction of the report on the feasibility of establishing a word processing center at the Thompson Insurance Company, the writer might include the following conclusions and recommendations:

CONCLUSIONS AND RECOMMENDATIONS
From an analysis of the data gathered in this study, the following conclusions are drawn:
1. Current dictation and transcription practices waste time.
2. Almost half the letters that are individually written could be form letters or could make use of form paragraphs.
3. Little use is made of available dictation equipment.
4. Most of those who dictate do not know how to dictate properly.
5. Secretaries are never permitted to compose letters.
6. A variety of letter styles is used, depending upon each dictator's preference.

With these conclusions in mind, the following action is recommended:
1. Establish a word processing center, using one text-editing typewriter and two automatic typewriters.

2. Make dictation equipment available to each dictator.
3. Provide each dictator with instruction in how to dictate properly and how to properly use dictation equipment.
4. Adopt the simplified letter as the standard letter style to be used throughout the company.
5. Keep comparative communication costs as a basis for determining whether word processing centers should be established in the various branch offices of the company.

Supplementary Information

Supplementary information, which is given after the conclusions and recommendations, provides substantiating data for the report. One or both of the parts discussed below may be included.

Bibliography   This section is an alphabetic listing of all the references used in the report. Bibliographical entries are listed in alphabetic order by author. Forms for book and periodical entries are shown below.

> **Books**
> Lawrence, Harold F., *Communication Procedures*, Eastern Book Company, New York, 19—.
> Williams, Jane, and Alex Holmes, *How to Dictate*, Hyatt Books, Inc., Chicago, 19—.
> **Periodicals**
> Goldstein, Arnold, "Word Processing Centers," *The Office Worker*, Vol. XV, No. 6, 19—, pp. 89-100.
> Utrillo, Anthony, "Cutting Communication Costs," *The Executive*, Vol. IV, No. 3, 19—, pp. 34-38.

Appendix   The appendix consists mainly of supporting information to back up the material in the body of the report. Long tables, charts, photographs, questionnaires, letters, and drawings are usually placed in this section. By including such material at the end of the report, the body of the report is freed from the kinds of detail that make reading difficult.

Letter of Transmittal

A short letter of transmittal (see page 462), composed after the report has been completed, accompanies the report. It is written in the form of a memorandum and usually contains such information as:

> A reference to the person who authorized the report.
> A brief statement of the general purpose of the report.
> Appropriate statements of appreciation or acknowledgment.

THOMPSON INSURANCE COMPANY

INTEROFFICE MEMORANDUM

To: Ms. Irene Fox, Vice President

From: John Kraft, Office Administrator

Date: February 5, 19--

Subject: Attached Report on the Feasibility of
         Establishing a Word Processing Center

On December 10, 19--, you authorized a feasibility study concerning the establishment of a word processing center. This
study is now completed. The results of the study, together
with my conclusions and recommendations, are contained in the
attached report.

The results are significant, and I hope that they will be of
value to you. Much credit should be given to Carmen Perez,
my assistant, who conducted several of the surveys and helped
a great deal with the organization and writing of this report.
If you wish, I shall be glad to discuss the report with you
at your convenience.

                         JK

cp
Enclosure

Written in the form of a memorandum, a letter of transmittal generally accompanies a formal report.

Progress Reports

As indicated earlier, it sometimes takes months to complete an investigation and prepare the finished product, the written report. When such is the case, it is a good idea to keep the person who requested the investigation informed as to the progress being made. How frequently such progress reports are made depends upon how much time has elapsed since the original request was made.

A progress report generally is made in memorandum form. Suppose that you were requested on December 10 to make an investigation of the feasibility of establishing a word processing center at the Thompson Insurance Company home office. On January 15, you might prepare the following memorandum:

> As you know, you asked me on December 10 to investigate the feasibility of establishing a word processing center. As of today, I have completed all the preliminary investigation and am ready to analyze the data I have gathered. I am in the process also of investigating word processing equipment available from the leading manufacturers. I expect to complete all my investigation and analysis by January 31 and to have the completed report on or before February 5.

MECHANICS OF REPORT WRITING

An immaculate physical appearance, expert placement, and meticulous attention to the mechanics of English, spelling, and punctuation emphasize the importance of the finished report. For this reason, mechanics, as well as organization and writing style, are important in preparing the report.

Of course, all the mechanics of English, spelling, and punctuation discussed in earlier chapters apply to report writing. Some suggestions for setting up a report are also necessary, and they are presented in the following paragraphs.

1. Use common sense and show variety in paragraphing; take care to avoid too many long and too many short paragraphs. Keep in mind that the topic sentence, telling what the paragraph is about, very frequently appears first. Also, the closing sentence is often used to summarize the meaning of the paragraph.

2. Be generous in using headings. Take care to leave plenty of white space around major headings, tables, and other display materials. Be sure that all headings of the same value within a section are parallel in wording. For example:

Nonparallel	Parallel
Writing the Introduction	Writing the Introduction
The Body	Writing the Body
How to Write the Closing	Writing the Closing

3. Use footnotes to give credit when the ideas of others are used, either verbatim or modified. A footnote may be placed at the bottom of the page carrying the footnoted item, or all the footnotes may be listed at the end of the report. Footnotes should always be numbered consecutively, whether they appear at the bottom of each footnoted page or are grouped at the end of the report. The information usually given in a footnote includes the footnote number, author, book or periodical title, publisher, place and date of publication, and page numbers. Since footnote styles may vary, it is advisable to consult the company's reference manual or a standard reference manual.

4. Select carefully any tables, charts, diagrams, photographs, drawings, and other illustrated materials used to supplement the writing. To promote better under-

standing of the contents, choose the items that contribute most to the report. Try to eliminate any items that are not pertinent.

5. Bind the report attractively. Many types of binding, from the single staple to an elaborate sewn binding, can be used. Reports that are subject to frequent, rigorous use should be placed inside a special hardback report folder for protection. Do not rely on a paper clip to bind the report; the chances of losing part of the report are very high.

6. Observe these rules of good manuscript form:
   a. Type all reports on standard $8\frac{1}{2}$- by 11-inch paper. Legal-size paper will not fit standard office files.
   b. Use double spacing except for long quotations (usually three or more lines), for which single spacing is preferred. Of course, type on only one side of the sheet. Consult a standard style manual for other spacing details.
   c. Leave ample margins. Commonly accepted are these:
   Left margin: $1\frac{1}{2}$ inches to allow for side binding
   Other margins: 1 inch
   First page only: When it contains the title, allow a 2-inch top margin.
   d. Always prepare at least one carbon copy.
   e. Traditionally, the first page is not numbered when it contains the title. All other pages, beginning with 2, should be numbered in the upper right corner.
   f. Follow this pattern for any material presented in outline form:
   I.
     A.
       1.
         a.
           (1)
             (a)

COMMUNICATION PROJECTS

Practical Application

A. Select a topic related to some aspect of school life, family life, or your job that you feel would be suitable for a formal report.

1. Indicate the title of your report.
2. What would be the purpose and scope of this report?
3. What procedures would you use in gathering data?

B. Develop a questionnaire that would be suitable for a report on "Study Habits of College Students."

C. You have been asked by your supervisor, Donald Revson, to attend a meeting on employee turnover and to write a report as a result of what you learn from the meeting. From the notes you took, prepare a report, supplying other data that you think might be appropriate. Here are your notes:

1. Annual turnover rate: Manufacturing employees, 28%; office, 12%.
2. Reasons given for leaving the company (in order of frequency): Manufactur-

ing—Working conditions undesirable, higher salary in another company, friction with supervisors, no opportunity for advancement. Office—Better salary, no opportunity for further advancement, working conditions disliked, friction with managers, difficulty of commuting, inadequate employee benefits.

3. Recommended actions: Improve facilities by (1) redecorating offices and installing air conditioning and (2) replacing old furniture and equipment with modern and efficient articles; encourage frequent departmental meetings that will give employees an opportunity to express their opinions; institute training program for supervisors; initiate a salary survey of similar businesses; study promotion policies; obtain services of a management consultant to make recommendations concerning employee benefits; consider the possibility of designating a personnel relations counselor to handle grievances.

4. Department managers are to consider the turnover problem with reference to their experiences with employees under their supervision, are to be prepared to discuss the problem further, and are to make recommendations at a special meeting to be held on September 15. Prior to this meeting, by September 8, managers should submit a memorandum on morale in their departments.

5. In the discussion, it was brought out that there seems to be an atmosphere of unrest and that morale is generally low. It was also pointed out that the commuting problem may be eased shortly, when the proposed new bus route (direct from the Riverside area) goes into effect.

D. You are the assistant to the sales manager of the Cen-Vac Corporation, manufacturers of central vacuum cleaner systems. Each week the company's thirty-five sales representatives send your boss handwritten notes on the number of calls they made during the week, the number of call-backs (return calls), the actual sales made, the referrals received from customers, and their own comments, including customers' comments. Create a standardized report form that all representatives can use to send in sales information. Then prepare a memorandum for your boss suggesting the new form be used and explaining why it is an improvement over the present system.

Editing Practice

Editing for Writing Power Edit and rewrite these sentences for the purpose of improving writing power.

1. Desiring to improve conditions, an employee lounge was created by the company.
2. Mr. Thomas is our new manager, and he is a specialist in sales.
3. The ideas suggested in your report have been carefully considered.
4. We liked your report. It was complete. We hope to use many of your suggestions.
5. One of the products was discontinued, when all plans for our advertising campaign had to be dropped.
6. We specialize in quality; but price, too, receives our consideration.
7. Visit Myron's, and there one can find many good values.
8. Not having been able, through banks or agencies at his disposal, to obtain any information concerning loans; and as he did not know the rules for making such loans, the new manager decided we must pay cash.

9. Although she couldn't really spare time away from the job, but wanting to start her vacation now, Jaclyn's plans were incomplete.

10. The report to the executives about the new accounting system that was started recently for the office in Chicago, was very long and complicated so then the accounting manager had to call a special meeting to explain it.

Vocabulary and the Report Writer   Identify and correct the vocabulary errors that weaken the effectiveness of this report writer's opening paragraph.

> This report on sight possibilities for the construction of a new plant was authorized by Carl Sampson, vice president, on August 1, 19—. The information presented hear is the result of frequent conferences with the ten leading reality agents in this city. A personal inspection trip was made to every lot offered for sale, and each parcel was evaluated in terms of its suitability for the location of our plant.

Case Problem

The Avid Conversationalist   Jack Williams, the mail clerk at Clark, Inc., is supposed to complete his daily delivery of mail by 10:45 a.m. and then return to the mail room in time to process the outgoing mail for a 12:15 p.m. pickup. However, when Jack gets to the sales department, Bill Sachs usually engages him in a lengthy, one-sided conversation. As a result, in several instances Jack has not completed processing all the outgoing mail on time. Today Jack is late starting his deliveries, and Bill tries to engage him in another lengthy conversation.

1. What can Jack say to Bill without offending him?
2. What should Jack do if Bill persists in talking?

50 SPECIAL BUSINESS COMMUNICATIONS

In addition to short memorandum reports and long formal business reports, there are two other types of business reports that you should know how to prepare. One of these communications, called a "news release," is used to report newsworthy events to newspapers, with the expectation that the newspapers will prepare an article for publication from this report. Another special type of report that you should learn to write is one that summarizes everything that happens at a meeting. This report is called the "minutes" of the meeting. Knowing how to prepare either or both of these special reports is another way of making yourself valuable to your employer.

A very special type of communication used by many businesses comes under the category of telecommunications. Telecommunications messages are dispatched either by teleprinter or by some other form of telegraphy. Two factors characterize the special quality of these communications: A special form is used to transmit the message (a telegram, a cablegram, a radiogram, or a telex), and the message is written in as few words as possible. Since the charge for telecommunications is based upon the number of words used, you must develop the skill of conveying a clear and complete message with a minimum number of words.

First let us consider the news release.

NEWS RELEASES

Publicity, advertising, public relations, goodwill—all these terms denote the effort of a business to get its name, its reputation, and its product before the public. In fact, large companies—even schools and colleges—today employ publicity directors whose job is to attract favorable public attention to their organizations.

An important means of getting the planned publicity of business into the hands of the public is the news release. Whenever a business plans an event that it considers newsworthy or capable of enhancing its public image, its public relations personnel prepare and submit a news release to various news outlets for publication. Such a news announcement may concern the appointment of a new company president after a meeting of the board of directors; it may tell of a large local expansion in a company's plant, which will increase the work force and have a great impact on the economy of the community; it may publicize the introduction of a new line or new product; or it may concern the awarding of some honor (perhaps for long, faithful service) to a member of the organization; and so on. Any item that will interest the public and create goodwill for the organization is an appropriate subject for a news release.

Any news story sent by a company must, of course, be approved for publication. In large companies, the director of public relations would have this responsibility. In small companies, individual department heads might handle their own news and distribute it in keeping with company policy, or releases might be issued from the office of the president or of one particular executive.

In order to be published and thereby serve its purpose, the release must be newsworthy; that is, the contents of the release must be of sufficient interest to the public to justify being published. Naturally, the writing style of the news release, as well as the form in which it appears, will have a strong effect on the newspaper editor who decides whether or not the news is published.

Form of the News Release

With hundreds of releases coming to their desks each week, newspaper editors will select for publication the items that require the least amount of rewriting, everything else being equal. Therefore, the news release must give complete, accurate information in a "news style" of writing that presents the facts in a clear and interesting way.

News releases may be typewritten, duplicated, or printed, but carbon copies should never be sent. A carbon copy suggests that the original copy was sent to someone more important.

Many organizations use a special form for issuing news releases. These forms are arranged so that editors can get to the heart of the story without wasting time. Like a letterhead, a news release form usually contains the name and address of the company or organization and the name, address, and telephone number of the person responsible for issuing the release to the public.

A well-written news release is illustrated on page 470. Observe the following points about the preparation of this release and of longer news releases as well.

1. The news release is double-spaced and has generous margins for possible changes by the newspaper editor.
2. The writer includes a tentative headline to identify the story. An editor, of course, may change this title to fit the style and space requirements of the publication.
3. The news release indicates the time when a story may be published. In the example, note the prominence of the phrase *For Immediate Release*. A release may be sent to newspapers before an event occurs so that news will reach the public at almost the same time the event takes place. For example, if a company plans to announce a million-dollar gift to a local hospital at a banquet on Saturday, June 25, the release might read *For Release after 6 p.m., Saturday, June 25.*
4. In a long release, subheads may be inserted between parts of the release to relieve the reading monotony and to guide the editor who wants to scan the story.
5. If there is more than one page to the release, the word *MORE* in parentheses is added at the end of each unfinished page. At the end of the last page of the release, the symbol -×××-, ###, o0o, or -30- (adapted from the telegrapher's abbreviation *30*, which means "the end") is typed to indicate the end of the release.

Writing the News Release

However good the form of a written communication, it is its words that determine whether it will be read and used. In writing a news release—just as in writing letters, memorandums, and reports—certain guides will help the writer develop an effective writing style and will improve the chances of getting the release printed. Especially important is the arrangement of paragraphs in the news release.

The opening paragraph of a news release should summarize the entire story and should present the most newsworthy information first. In this opening section, the writer should give the *who, what, why, how, when,* and *where* of the news story in such a form that this paragraph can stand by itself. If, for example, an announcement is to be made of the appointment of Gloria Atwater as personnel director of the Exeter National Bank, a poor lead paragraph might read:

> Marion Edwards, president of the Exeter National Bank in Louisville, announced today the appointment of Ms. Gloria Atwater as personnel director.

Marion Edwards is not the person the article is about, therefore the lead paragraph should read:

Gloria Atwater has been named personnel director of the Exeter National Bank in Louisville by its president, Marion Edwards.

Each succeeding paragraph should supply background facts in the order of decreasing importance. In this way, editors who need to shorten the release because of space limitations can easily "kill" the story from the bottom up. For example, notice that the first two paragraphs in the news release illustrated on page 470 make a complete news story by themselves. The remainder of the copy provides additional details.

MINUTES OF MEETINGS

Nearly every business has a number of committees that meet periodically, perhaps weekly, biweekly, or monthly. In addition, special meetings are called from time to time for the purpose of settling important matters that arise. In most cases, a written record—called *minutes*—of the proceedings is required. The minutes serve as a permanent record of the decisions reached and the actions that are to be taken and inform those who were not present at the meeting about what took place. Nearly every business employee, at one time or another, may serve as secretary to a group or committee and thus be responsible for keeping an accurate set of minutes.

Recording the Minutes

The accurate recording of the proceedings of all meetings is an important function, for the minutes usually serve as the only historical record of a meeting.

There is probably no one best way to record what happens at a meeting. The secretary of the meeting must be the judge of what is unimportant (and hence not worth recording). If an agenda of the meeting has been prepared beforehand, the secretary should receive a copy. The agenda lists briefly the business to be transacted and acts as a guide to the person who presides at the meeting. The agenda also helps the secretary check to be sure that all scheduled items are accounted for in the minutes. Much of the success of good note-taking revolves around the personal efficiency of the secretary. However, any secretary preparing to record the proceedings of a meeting should find the following general guides helpful:

1. Record the time and place of the meeting.
2. List the persons attending and those absent. In a small group, actual names can be given; in a large group, however, it is usually sufficient either to state the number of people present, such as "Forty-five members were present," or to list the names of the absentees only.
3. In the opening section of the minutes, mention the fact that the minutes for the previous meeting were read and approved, amended, or not approved.
4. Develop the art of recording the important points in the discussion of each item on the agenda. Why? Sufficient supporting facts are required so that those who were present can recall the discussion from reading the minutes and those who were not present can be informed. Papers read during the meeting are often attached to

NEWS RELEASE

Emanuel Gomez
Director of Public Relations

1678 STATE STREET
LOUISVILLE,
KENTUCKY
40202

```
          Ralph Greene
          Manager
          Louisville News Bureau
          (606) 555-7500


For Immediate Release                    June 30, 19--

            GLORIA ATWATER NAMED PERSONNEL DIRECTOR

               OF EXETER NATIONAL BANK


     Louisville, June 30, 19--.  Gloria Atwater has been named

personnel director of Exeter National Bank in Louisville by

its president, Marion Edwards.

     Ms. Atwater succeeds Arno Polczy, who retired from the

bank on June 15 after serving for 30 years.

     The new personnel director joined the Exeter National

Bank in Covington a year ago as a training director.  Prior

to that, she was a business education teacher and guidance

counselor at Lexington High School.  Ms. Atwater is a graduate

of the University of Kentucky and a member of the Louisville

Chamber of Commerce.

                         -xxx-
```

A news release must give complete, accurate information in a "news style" of writing. Note the special form used by Exeter for its news releases.

the final typewritten minutes, because it is usually not possible for the secretary to record verbatim all such information.

5. Record verbatim all resolutions and motions, as well as the names of the persons who introduced and seconded the motions. If there is difficulty in getting such in-

formation when the motion is first made, the secretary should request that the motion be repeated or even put in writing so that the exact motion is recorded.

6. Type the minutes first in draft form so that they can be edited before being typed in final form. Sometimes, too, the secretary may want to get another person's approval before typing the minutes in final form. The secretary signs the minutes, thus certifying their accuracy. Sometimes the presiding officer countersigns them.

7. Normally, make one copy of the minutes and file it in the folder, notebook, or binder used for this purpose. Usually minutes are duplicated and sent to each person present at the meeting or to designated officers who would be interested in the business of the meeting.

Format of Minutes

Various formats are used for the minutes of a meeting. The secretary's main job, however, is to make sure that all the essential information appears in a neat, well-arranged form. Some organizations prefer to emphasize the main points on the agenda by using a standardized format.

The minutes on page 472 illustrate on acceptable format. Notice the standard pattern and the topical headings that are used for all meetings of this group and the way in which the motions and discussion are concisely summarized.

Other groups use a more traditional format in which the proceedings of the meeting are written out in rather complete detail. The example on page 473 illustrates this style.

TELECOMMUNICATIONS

Telecommunications are messages that are used when both speed and a written record of the message are required. In addition, this type of message is often superior to a letter because people associate telecommunications with important and urgent messages. Therefore, they are likely to give more attention to a telecommunication than they would to a letter. Furthermore, telecommunications can be sent from ships and airplanes directly without waiting until the carrier reaches land.

As discussed in Section 2, the basic types of telecommunication include the telegram (for domestic use), the cablegram or telex (for overseas use), and the radiogram (for ship-to-shore or airplane-to-shore use). The two aspects of telecommunications that distinguish them from other types of written communications are: (1) they are transmitted on a special form and (2) the style of writing the message differs from that used in letters. Each of these aspects is explained and illustrated below.

Composing Telecommunication Messages

Brevity in telecommunications is important because the cost of sending a message is based on the number of words. Therefore, any redundancy in the messages should

EMPLOYEES' ASSOCIATION OF MIDWEST PRODUCERS, INC.

MINUTES OF MEETING OF MARCH 15, 19--

TIME, PLACE, ATTENDANCE	The regular monthly meeting of the Employees' Association of Midwest Producers, Inc., was held in the Board of Directors' room at 5:30 p.m. The president, Jan Dixon, presided. All members and officers were present, with the exception of Ila Torgeson, vice president.
MINUTES	The minutes of the last meeting, February 15, 19--, were read and approved.
OFFICERS' REPORTS	Treasurer: The treasurer reported receipts of $450, disbursements of $150, and a balance of $967 as of March 1, 19--. Tony Valenti moved the acceptance of the report. Anne Terry seconded the motion. Motion carried.
COMMITTEE REPORTS	Chairperson William Ferris presented the report of the nominating committee. The nominees are:

President:	Alice Foster
Vice President:	George McFee
Secretary:	Andrew Scott
Treasurer:	Harriet Sorga

The president called for nominations from the floor. Since no additional nominations were made, Rosa Sanchez moved that nominations be closed and that a unanimous ballot be cast for the slate of officers presented by the committee. The motion was seconded by Yamen Abdulah. Motion carried.

UNFINISHED BUSINESS	Preliminary plans for the Annual Retirement Dinner to be held June 30 were discussed. Tory's Inn and Edwin's were suggested for this event. The president is to appoint a committee to look into the possibility of holding the dinner at either of these places and to report to the group at the next meeting.
NEW BUSINESS	The president reported that the Board of Directors is considering a policy change regarding tuition reimbursement to employees for college courses taken. The change would involve getting approval for the course in advance. There was considerable discussion regarding this change, some of the group feeling that sometimes it is not possible to get the approval in advance. The feeling of the group was to recommend to the board that the words, "unless prior approval is not feasible," be added to this change in policy.
ADJOURNMENT	The meeting adjourned at 7:20 p.m.

Respectfully submitted,

Karen Mateyak

Karen Mateyak

This format for minutes uses topical headings.

be avoided. The word *redundancy* has a special meaning here; it includes not only repetitiveness but also *any* part of a message that could be omitted without loss of meaning.

It would, of course, be false economy to sacrifice completeness and clarity for brevity; that is, it would be a waste of money to write a 15-word message that might be misunderstood if just three additional words would ensure its clarity. The skilled com-

```
                    MINUTES OF THE MEETING

                           of the

                    Board of Directors

                    Midwest Producers, Inc.
                        March 1, 19--


    Presiding:     Rita Chambers

    Present:       Frank Kapa
                   Andrea Maez
                   Theresa Morgan
                   Lawrence Rogers
                   Morgan Yang

    Absent:        Louis Ulrich

    The meeting was called to order at 10 a.m. by Ms. Chambers.
    The principal topics for discussion concerned recommended
    changes in two company policies, one related to donations to
    charitable organizations and the other related to reimbursing
    employees for tuition for college courses.

    With reference to donations to charitable organizations,
    Ms. Morgan proposed that all donations be limited to a maxi-
    mum of $250.  After some discussion, the Board concurred and
    voted unanimously to add this limit to the present policies
    concerning charitable donations.

    Mr. Rogers proposed that tuition reimbursement should be made
    only if the employee has received prior approval of the course
    submitted for tuition reimbursement.  The present policy does
    not require that approval be given in advance.  Mr. Yang was
    opposed to the change and suggested that this proposal be
    tabled until the next meeting.  In the meantime, employee
    opinion regarding the change should be sought.  The Board
    voted to table the proposal until the April meeting and asked
    Mr. Yang to consult with the Executive Board of the Employees'
    Association regarding pros and cons of this change.  The
    meeting adjourned at 11:15 a.m.

                        Respectfully submitted,

                        Frances R. Post
                        Frances R. Post, Secretary
```

The proceedings of the meeting are written out in complete detail in this format for minutes.

poser of telecommunications, however, can usually express a thought in surprisingly few words by eliminating unnecessary words.

The composer of the teletype message, unlike the letter writer, does not always need to use complete sentences and may dispense with some typical courtesies of the business letter. Contrast the following paragraph from a letter with a telegram that means the same thing.

Letter	Telegram
We would like to have you check our letter of June 15 and the accompanying purchase invoice, Number 632A. We requested that you deliver the furniture to our store to reach us by September 1. However, we have planned a summer sale that is to begin on July 15 and would like to advertise this furniture if we can be certain that it will be in stock when we announce the sale. Please let us know promptly.	Confirm immediately if order 632A can be available for sale July 15.

Note that the telegram expresses in 12 words the essentials of what the letter says in 77 words. Furthermore, the telegram is likely to get special attention.

Often telegrams are sent because of a change in travel plans. For example:

> American flight 183 was grounded because of the bad weather. Instead, I will arrive on Amtrak at Pennsylvania Station at 1:20 p.m. on Wednesday.

While the message is concise, it contains 24 words. Suppose your base charge is for 15 words; how can you reduce the word count? By eliminating such redundant words as *was, because of the bad, instead, I will, on, at, at,* and *on,* you can reduce the word count to only 12 words without loss of meaning. The message would then read:

> Weather grounded flight 183. Arrive Amtrak Pennsylvania Station 1:20 p.m. Wednesday.

Another common means of saving time and money in sending teleprinted messages is through the use of abbreviations and codes; for example, LA for Los Angeles, ATL for Atlanta, DTR for Detroit. Standard lists of such address abbreviations are used by telephone and telegraph companies, airlines, and other organizations. Some companies develop common code abbreviations that are used to exchange teleprinted messages within the company. However, the cost to encode or decode a message of nonstandard language is a deterrent to the frequent use of codes unless the code is a computer language.

From a study of telecommunication messages, you can see that considerable difference exists in purpose—and thus writing style—between business letters and telecommunication messages. As a rule, the well-written telecommunication message has these features:

1. Only necessary words are included. In the telegram regarding the change in travel plans, 12 words were easily eliminated without any loss of meaning.
2. Explanatory information is usually omitted. In the telegram about the change in delivery date of the furniture, the reason for requesting the change was not stated. Only vital information was included.

Telegram

western union

NO. WDS.–CL. OF SVC.	PD. OR COLL.	CASH NO.	CHARGE TO THE ACCOUNT OF	☐ OVER NIGHT TELEGRAM
			Sender	UNLESS BOX ABOVE IS CHECKED THIS MESSAGE WILL BE SENT AS A TELEGRAM

Send the following message, subject to the terms on back hereof, which are hereby agreed to

October 25   19 – –

TO **Fasano Industries** CARE OF OR APT. NO.

STREET & NO. **910 Washington Street** TELEPHONE **(312) 555-2339**

CITY & STATE **Chicago, IL** ZIP CODE **60602**

Accept telephone quotation of $915 each for 16 Model
H150 units. Purchase order to follow.

Earle Metzger
Bazant and Company

SENDER'S TEL. NO. **(608) 555-8967** NAME & ADDRESS **Bazant and Company
1404 Wauwatosa Avenue
Milwaukee, WI 53213**

Western Union provides this form for sending telegrams. Note that the message in this telegram contains only the most essential information.

3. Information that can be taken for granted by both sender and receiver is omitted. For example, the phrase *because of the bad* preceding the word *weather* is not necessary to the meaning. The flight was delayed, and it makes no difference whether the delay was due to bad weather or engine breakdown.

Message Forms for Telecommunications

For telecommunications, details regarding the sending of the message, the word count, and the charge for each word vary according to the type of service used and the company providing the service. Obtain current costs for the different kinds of telecommunication services from Western Union or some other telecommunication company.

Details about format remain rather constant, however, and should be understood by anyone who is responsible for preparing a teletype message.

Teletype forms may vary slightly from one company to another, but you should usually fill out the form in the following manner, as shown by the properly completed telegram on page 475.

1. Make at least one carbon copy. Additional copies may be made so that a confirmation copy can be sent to the addressee and copies can be sent to other departments as needed.
2. Single-space the message and use ordinary punctuation as you would in any other business writing. (For many years, typists attempted to simulate teleprinter type by typing the message in all-capital letters and by spelling out punctuation; for instance, using the word *STOP* to indicate a period. Such practice is now obsolete.)
3. Type the signature of the sender and the name of the company.

4. Follow instructions for filling in appropriate sections on the form. Thus, in the sample telegram on page 475, since the message is to be charged to *Dover and Company*, the word *Sender* is typed in the box titled *Charge to the Account of*. If the telegram were to be charged to a telephone number, that number would replace the word *Sender*. Were the telegram to be sent collect, the word *Collect* would be typed under *Pd. or Coll.* In addition, the class of service should be checked.

COMMUNICATION PROJECTS

Practical Application

A. The organizational meeting of the EPA (Environmental Protection Association) held its first meeting on your campus last evening. Margot Hayden was elected president and you were elected secretary-treasurer. The faculty sponsor is Professor Andre Petit, chairperson of the Science Department. The group plans to meet bimonthly on the first and third Wednesday of each month. Its aims are to publicize instances of local pollution, to investigate possible conservation measures in the community, to recommend publicity to make the college community more conservation-oriented. Write a news release about the organization—its officers, aims, plans—for your local newspaper. Supply any additional facts that you feel are needed.

B. Write the minutes for the second meeting of the EPA (see Practical Application A). Assume that various projects were proposed at the meeting—a recycling drive for newspapers and metals, bikeways throughout the city, field trips to local industrial plants to see how they handle waste products, a film on "The Water We Drink," and a poster contest for high school students. Also, add any other worthwhile activities that you would recommend. Supply all the specifics, such as motions passed or defeated, and so on.

C. Your boss, George Theopolus, Vice President of Brandt Paper Manufacturing Company of Portland, Oregon, requests that you write a news release for the *Portland Sentinel* announcing the retirement of the company president, Tito Alvarez, at the end of this year. The newspaper may make the announcement immediately since the board of directors has already regretfully accepted Mr. Alvarez's notice of retirement. Alvarez has been with the company for 25 years, serving as president for the last 10 years. He started his career with the company as a shop foreman and then became factory manager within 2 years. Alvarez became a vice president shortly thereafter and remained in that position until 10 years ago, when the board of directors elected him president. Following his retirement, Mr. Alvarez will serve as chairman of the board of directors. Alvarez lives in Seacrest with his wife. They have two married sons and one married daughter, all of whom live in Portland. Alvarez is a graduate in accounting from Youngstown College, where he was class president during his senior year. Alvarez has served on the Portland Chamber of Commerce for 5 years, is a member of both Rotary and Kiwanis, and headed the City Beautification Committee for the last three years. Using an acceptable format, write a news release. Supply any information that should be included.

D. Assume that you are the secretary of the Staunton Employees' Association, charged with the responsibility for taking minutes at all meetings and distributing copies to each member. From the following information, prepare in concise form the minutes of the latest meeting:

1. The meeting, held in Room 5A, Tyler Building, was called to order by President Karl Swensen at 5:30 p.m., March 15, 19—.
2. Correction in minutes of preceding meeting (February 15) approved: Ina Singer, not Rita Singer, was appointed chairperson of the Welfare Committee.
3. Karen Bjorn reviewed employee suggestions for January. Awards of $100 each for two accepted suggestions were approved. Bjorn to make arrangements for presenting the awards at the spring banquet.
4. Revised written procedure for handling employee suggestions presented by Jack Carlson. Accepted with editorial revision to be made by appropriate committee.
5. Meeting adjourned at 6:15 p.m., with the understanding that the next meeting would be a dinner meeting at Jackson's Restaurant, April 21, to begin at 6:30 p.m.
6. The following members were absent: Holden, Reardon, Witmer.

E. Your employer, Reva Quimby, will speak at the June 15 meeting of the Women Executives Club at the Hotel Washington in Kansas City. She has asked you to wire the hotel for reservations for June 14, 15, and 16 and to request a two-room suite with bath. (While in Kansas City, Ms. Quimby will be interviewing candidates for positions as sales representative for your company.)

1. Find out the fastest telegraphic service available in your community, the rate, and the base word count.
2. Staying within the base word count, compose the message, asking for confirmation of the reservation. Also ask for information regarding the availability of a chalkboard, an overhead projector, and a screen to be used during Ms. Quimby's presentation.

F. Revise the following telecommunications so that none exceeds 15 words. Aim for brevity, clarity, and completeness.

1. We are shipping by airfreight today the 4 parts you ordered for our calculator #34AC, except for part #YC14, which will be shipped to you next Thursday, also by airfreight.
2. Proposed contract for reconstruction of flood-damaged Plant 156 received. Must also have target dates for completion of each section of contract. Wire dates in time for our board meeting Tuesday afternoon.
3. Phillip Goetz expects to arrive in Boston on Eastern Flight 67 on Friday morning. Please arrange to pick him up at the airport and brief him on Tracy-Phelps contract en route to board meeting.
4. Our Purchase Order 7683 for four executive desks and matching executive chairs has not arrived and our inventory is depleted. If the order has not yet been shipped, arrange shipment for six of each by fastest method.
5. The computer printout of the March sales forecast was lost and never reached us. Please airmail two copies immediately.

Editing Practice

Supply the Missing Words   Indicate a word that you think would make sense if inserted in the blank space within each sentence.

1. If this booklet does not give you the ... you desire, please write us again.
2. Thank you for being so ... in filling our order.
3. We are happy to tell you that your ... has been established at the Hotel Essex.
4. We hope that we shall have the pleasure of serving you whenever you have ... to use hotel facilities.
5. Once you know the ... of a charge account, you will never shop without your charge account plate.
6. Please sign the original copy and return it to us in the enclosed envelope, retaining the ... for your files.
7. We understand that you will probably ... to purchase as much as $1500 worth of merchandise monthly on your account.
8. We hope that your clerical staff will ... some means of checking purchases made by persons of the same name but of different addresses.
9. We have taken steps to see that there is no ... of this type of mistake.
10. We hope that our business dealings will be ... pleasant and profitable.
11. The report ... the data that had been gathered by the newly elected subcommittee.
12. The new inventory system was ... just before the spring rush began.
13. An office worker's ... is judged not only by the volume of work completed but also by the accuracy of the work.
14. All the payroll ... were noted on the check stub.
15. Government ... are available to many different groups to assist in making up for losses.

Proofreading for Homonym Errors   Identify and correct any homonym errors you find in the following paragraph.

The principle task of report writing is not the report itself; it is the assembling of facts that are the bases for statements made therein. The value of a report, then, depends upon the thoroughness with which all aspects of the situation have been studied. Any supervisor can sight numerous instances of poor reports that were due solely to a superficial job of assembling facts.

Spelling Alert!   Check the following paragraph for spelling errors. How many can you find?

Enclosed are the comparisons of the estimated and the actual expenses for the period from January 1 thorough June 30 of this year.

As you will see, the actual expenses for this period total $27,500, which is $2,500 (or 10 percent) over the estimated expanses for this period. (Most of this $2,500 was spent on temporary help during the month of Febuary, when we needed to process a backlog of orders.)

For the next six-month period, we are confident that we will be able to make up this $2,500 and keep our total actual expenses for the year within the total anual budget of $52,000.

Case Problem

To Bluff or Not to Bluff   During an interview for a position as assistant office manager, George Accore was asked to express his feelings about word processing. Unfortunately, George knows very little about word processing.

1. Should George bluff his way through or admit that he knows very little about word processing?
2. What should he say that will not make him look bad during this interview?
3. What risks does he take if he should bluff?

CHAPTER 9

COMMUNICATING ORALLY

As you enter the reception area of the multistoried building occupied by the Corliss Insurance Company, you are greeted by a warm smile and friendly voice of the receptionist asking, "May I be of help to you?" You reply, "I have a nine-thirty appointment with Ms. Gonzales." The receptionist tells you, "Ms. Gonzales' office is on the twelfth floor, Suite 1241C. May I please have your name so that I can telephone to let Ms. Gonzales know that you are on your way up to see her?" After you tell the receptionist your name, she directs you to an express elevator that stops on the twelfth floor. You are already favorably impressed with the Corliss Insurance Company, based on this initial encounter with one of its employees.

As you step from the elevator on the twelfth floor into a tastefully furnished office, you observe a number of employees busily engaged in a variety of activities. A young man approaches you. "Good morning; I'm Mr. Black, Ms. Gonzales' administrative assistant. She will see you just as soon as she completes a long-distance telephone call that came in while you were on your way up. Please make yourself comfortable here, and I would be happy to bring you a cup of coffee."

As you glance around the busy office, you notice several employees quietly engaged in telephone conversations. In a corner of a partitioned section, someone is explaining and demonstrating how to operate a duplicating machine. In a glass-enclosed conference area, a small group is gathered around a table listening to an explanation of some figures on a flip chart. A young executive in another office is using a dictation machine. You notice on a nearby bulletin board an announcement of a sales training conference; another announcement indicates that there will be a meeting of the Office Employees' Federation next Thursday afternoon.

Your communication instructor was right—oral communication *does* play an important role in the daily activities of every office employee! Then, as you are shown into Ms. Gonzales' office, you realize how fortunate you are to have had some training in oral communication. Why do you consider yourself so fortunate? Well, you are in Ms. Gonzales' office to be interviewed for a position that you very much want. You are about to make your training in oral communication work for you.

THE IMPORTANCE OF ORAL COMMUNICATION IN BUSINESS

Even before you began to work in the business world, you were convinced of the importance of oral communication in all business activities. This conviction will grow stronger each day. From the receptionist who greeted you in the lobby to the president on the top floor, information is continually being transmitted orally from one employee to another, from employees to customers and vendors on the outside, and from these and other outsiders to employees of the firm. The success enjoyed by any business organization depends, to a very large degree, upon the success of its members in making themselves understood and in persuading others to accept their ideas.

Though written communication is important in transacting business, oral communication is used more often and by more people. Some business positions require the use of oral communication almost exclusively, and the people who fill these jobs are hired on the strength of their ability to speak well. The sales representative, the office receptionist, the switchboard operator, the person who handles customer service or complaints—all these people must be highly skilled in oral communication. The office or factory supervisor, the public accountant, the personnel manager, the bank teller, the business executive, and the secretary are only a few of the other workers who make extensive use of oral communication in carrying out the responsibilities of their positions.

If you aspire to a position of leadership in business, your ability to speak forcefully, persuasively, and convincingly will play a vital role in helping you achieve your goal. At meetings and conferences, speakers will include all levels of employees, top management people, and outside consultants. On many occasions, you will do much of the talking. You will seek to solve grievances of employees; you will conduct meetings and small group discussions; you will give talks to employees, to the public, and to business and professional groups. In your daily contacts with supervisors and co-workers, you will use oral communication for reporting, instructing, reprimanding, giving information, and asking for information. This power to communicate orally is important to every business leader.

THE ROLE OF ORAL COMMUNICATION IN BUSINESS

Business uses oral communication in a variety of ways and in a variety of settings. Here are some examples of how business employees depend on oral communication:

To sell goods and services. All salespeople, whether they are selling goods or services, rely on their oral communication ability to help them make sales. Whether it is an insurance agent who canvasses you at home or the retail salesperson who asks, "Would you like a tie to go with that shirt?" both use their oral communication abilities to sell. Even the airline ticket agent uses oral communication to assist you in arranging your proposed business or vacation trip.

To give instruction to an individual or to a group. The teacher, whether he or she performs in a school situation or in special business or industrial classes on the job, is dependent on oral communication; the sales manager who conducts special training classes for sales representatives must be an effective oral communicator; even the computer programmer who must instruct a new assistant relies heavily on oral communication.

To explain or report to supervisors, to subordinates, and to those on the same level. The sales manager may report orally to the vice president in charge of sales; the supervisor in the office interprets a new company policy for employees; an employee explains a grievance to the supervisor; the general manager's secretary tells the file clerk to pull all correspondence with the Chang Equipment Company.

To give information to customers and potential customers. A customer calls a department store for information about the sizes, colors, and prices of vinyl tile; another customer telephones for advice about the best method of cleaning recently purchased rugs.

To give formal speeches before groups. The president of a company is asked to give a speech before the members of the Rotary Club; an accountant is asked to talk to a college class in advanced accounting; the secretary to the president of a large manufacturing firm is asked to address a group of college students on "The Advantages of Becoming a Secretary."

To participate in social-business conversation. The office manager telephones the secretary of Kiwanis to cancel a reservation for the luncheon meeting tomorrow; a sales representative congratulates two former associates who have gone into partnership.

To interview employees and prospective employees. The personnel manager and the section supervisor interview applicants for an accounting position; the supervisor discusses an employee's merit rating at the end of the probationary period.

To acquire information necessary to conduct the everyday affairs of business. The credit manager of a department store calls the local credit bureau to determine the credit rating of a new customer; the mail clerk telephones the post office to find out which class of mail to use for a special mailing the company is planning; the accountant visits the Internal Revenue Service office to discuss methods of figuring depreciation on equipment; a secretary telephones a travel agency to get information about hotel accommodations in Portland.

To purchase goods and services. A homeowner asks a department store sales person many questions about a rug she would like to buy; the purchasing agent telephones a local stationer to order file folders; the manager of a truck fleet inquires about a truck-leasing plan.

To provide service for customers and potential customers. The credit manager explains to a customer the procedure for opening a charge account; the section manager in the bedding department tells a customer why bedding can't be returned for exchange or refund.

To participate in meetings. A sales manager conducts a meeting of the Sales Executives Club; a secretary contributes ideas for the convention of the National Secretaries Association to the members of the planning committee.

To participate in informal discussion with fellow employees. The receptionist takes up a collection to buy a gift for a fellow employee who is in the hospital; the mail-room supervisor organizes a committee to plan the office Christmas party; the sales promotion manager gets all the employees in the office together for lunch.

These are just a few examples of oral activities that may be observed every day in business—activities that rely for their success almost wholly upon effective oral communication.

FORMS OF ORAL COMMUNICATION IN BUSINESS

Businesses use oral communication in a variety of ways, some ways more frequently than others. Among the most commonly used methods of communicating orally are the following:

Face-to-face conversation—interviews, sales, social-business situations, informal discussions between supervisors and employees.

Telephone conversation—with another office, with customers, with suppliers.

Conversation via interoffice communication devices—between executive and secretary-receptionist, between sales representative on selling floor and clerk in stockroom.

Dictation and recording—dictating a letter to a secretary, using a dictating machine for dictating letters, recording meetings electronically.

Radio and television appearances—giving interviews or reporting information.

Formal speeches—debates; panels; addresses to employees, the public, customers, or professional groups.

Leadership of, or participation in, group discussions or meetings—leading employee group discussions, participating in stockholders' meetings and in meetings of business and professional organizations.

Instruction—teaching training classes for sales representatives and retail store employees.

Each of these methods of communication requires a slightly different technique. The difference may be in the amount and kind of prior preparation, the manner in which the voice is projected, or the style in which the speaker makes the presentation. For example, speaking over the telephone requires a knowledge of how far the telephone mouthpiece should be held from the lips and how much the speaker's voice should be projected. A radio or telephone presentation may be read from copy and, therefore, requires a knowledge of how to read without giving the impression that you *are* reading. Leading a meeting requires a knowledge of parliamentary procedure. Teaching a class requires that the teacher know how to ask questions properly. Participating in a panel or in a group discussion requires the ability to think quickly and to put thoughts into understandable language without hesitation.

ORAL COMMUNICATION AND EFFECTIVE BUSINESS RELATIONSHIPS

Regardless of the type and level of position you hold in business, oral contact with people both inside the company and outside the company will be an important influence on your job success. Furthermore, these oral contacts will influence the success of the company that employs you. When employees get along with each other—with those functioning on the same job level as well as those on levels above or below them—they are likely to be more productive employees. Moreover, satisfactory internal relationships among employees will also contribute to better relationships with those outside their company. The result of effective public relations is almost certain to be increased business.

In business, how does oral communication help develop the most desirable atmosphere for effective employee relationships? By establishing an environment that provides for a free flow of information and ideas between management and employees. When employees have frequent and easy means to discuss and express their ideas and concerns, morale is likely to be high. And when morale is high, work efficiency is greater. Personal conferences with employees, committee meetings, group conferences, and informational speeches that provide for question-and-answer sessions are some of the primary situations in which oral communication contributes to improved relations among employees and between management and employees.

How does oral communication contribute to effective public relations? By ensuring that every spoken communication with a customer is a positive experience. Although business spends considerable time and money to plan and create carefully worded letters and advertising copy to keep customers and to win new ones, often the oral contacts are overlooked. Successful businesses do not neglect the importance of oral communication and, therefore, train their employees in areas such as public speaking, correct telephone techniques, and group discussion leading. The manner in which a customer is treated on the telephone or in person is just as important in developing goodwill as is the written communication—sometimes even more important. *All* employees—salespersons, secretaries, receptionists, accountants—create a public image of the company they represent by the manner in which they speak to customers and potential customers. A curt or rude employee can cause a business to lose many sales—and even to lose customers of long standing. Every employee a customer comes in contact with *is* the company. Therefore, the telephone conversation or the face-to-face conversation must, through the words and tone used by the employee, make these customers feel that their interests are important and that the company wants them to be satisfied.

AN ORAL COMMUNICATION
IMPROVEMENT PROGRAM

At the beginning of this section, you became aware of how oral communication helped you to develop an initial impression of the company you visited. The receptionist who greeted you the moment you entered the building certainly contributed to your positive impression. Also, during your visit, you observed how a variety of oral activities played an important role in the performance of many employees' daily tasks. Finally, as you were about to participate in a job interview, you became even more appreciative of the need for effective oral communication.

The manner in which you use your oral skills on the job can either help or hinder you in performing your everyday activities and advancing to higher positions. The remaining sections of this chapter provide you with the opportunity to learn techniques for improving your oral communication skills when dealing with both co-workers and the public.

COMMUNICATION PROJECTS

Practical Application

A. For each of the following business positions, indicate the oral communication activities that you think would be typical in that position:

1. Accountant
2. Retail salesclerk
3. Secretary
4. Personnel interviewer
5. Receptionist

B. Be prepared to discuss each of the following topics:

1. The Importance of Communication Skills for Success in College
2. The Importance of Communication Skills for Success in Business
3. How Ineffective Communication Leads to Problems

C. Be prepared to take the affirmative or negative side in a debate on this topic: *Resolved: That beginning business employees do not need effective communication skills as much as more experienced business employees.*

D. Under three headings—Home, School, Business—list as many oral communication activities as you can.

E. Practice reading aloud the following instructions for talking on the telephone so that you do not sound as though you are reading the material or have memorized it.

> Clear enunciation is extremely important if you wish to be understood by the listener. Each word and each syllable must be pronounced distinctly. Your voice should be well modulated, and you should move your lips, tongue, and jaw freely. Hold the mouthpiece about an inch from your mouth, speaking directly into the transmitter. Keep your mouth free of gum, candy, and other objects that could affect your pronunciation or cause you to slur your words. Often, you can tell if your words are being heard clearly by the number of times the listener asks you to repeat what you have said.

F. Without using gestures or written diagrams, *orally* give directions for the following:

1. How to reach the nearest department store by automobile or by walking.
2. How to reach the school library (or cafeteria) from the classroom in which this subject is taught.
3. How to fold a letter for mailing in a No. 10 envelope.

G. Be prepared to describe an object orally without telling the class what the object is. If you have described the object clearly, the class should be able to identify it from your description.

Editing Practice

Spelling and Vocabulary Some of the following sentences contain spelling errors; some test vocabulary; some are correct. For each correct sentence, write *OK* on your paper. Correct each incorrect sentence.

1. What advise will you give the new employee?
2. Joan was not effected by the salary increase.

3. The company benefitted from the purchase of new typewriters.
4. The employee was presented formerly to the president today.
5. Ms. Lightner's position in the company precludes any argument.
6. The company will celebrate the occassion with a storewide sale.
7. Our office is equiping each floor with new telephones.
8. The specifications for the building are accurate.
9. Even the rich do not like to waist money.
10. Do not breath a word about the change in procedures.

Editing for Context   Rewrite any sentences containing words that do not fit the context. Write *OK* for any correct sentence.

1. Please sign the affidavit before August 10.
2. We must addend to a set of rules established by the committee.
3. To countenance serious inflation, drastic cuts must be made in budgets.
4. We did not receive the article listed on the manifest.
5. We are affiliated with the largest manufacturer of electronics in the country.
6. Your failure to make prompt payment demented our confidence in your integrity.
7. Harold purchased an annuity policy for his own protection.
8. Your actions do not ward our taking any steps to improve the situation.
9. We purchased the goods at a tremulous saving, which we are passing on to our customers.
10. We hope you will not comply us to consult with our attorney.

Case Problem

Who's Rude?   Ms. Ulrich's secretary, Anne, picked up the ringing telephone. The voice at the other end asked to speak to Ms. Ulrich. Anne responded by asking, "May I ask who is calling?" The voice at the other end abruptly said, "No, you may not," and hung up.

"What a rude person," thought Anne, with a perplexed expression on her face.

1. Was the caller rude or was Anne rude?
2. What should Anne have asked the caller in order to get the information she wanted? Why?

Let's eavesdrop on two supervisors who are discussing the candidates for a promotion to a very important and well-paying position. Perhaps you are one of the people they are considering for this position.

"Both Marguerita and Anna have similar backgrounds and experience. How can we decide which one to select?"

"Well, we need to consider the most important aspects of the work to be performed. A heavy part of the work involves conducting meetings to train sales representatives as well as meetings with buyers and customers."

"Yes, that's true. Furthermore, a great deal of business is conducted over the telephone. And we mustn't overlook the monthly community consumers' meeting, where this candidate will have to give a formal presentation and lead the group discussion following the presentation."

"It seems quite obvious, doesn't it, that the person we select must have outstanding oral skills? Which of the two do you feel is the more qualified in this respect?"

"Marguerita has demonstrated that she can do a superior job in making presentations and in talking over the telephone. Remember how well she led that group discussion on human relations last month."

"She certainly speaks very effectively; she has a large vocabulary; and she impresses people favorably with her personal appearance. Since Anna is weak in her oral communication skills, I guess we should select Marguerita to fill this position."

Would you agree with their choice? Undoubtedly, you would have to feel that the right decision was made. It is unfortunate that so many candidates for good positions eliminate themselves for consideration because they are weak in oral communication. In most business positions, oral communication is probably used more frequently than written communication. Furthermore, obtaining a good position and succeeding in it depend so heavily upon persuasive oral communication. That is why it is so important that you become aware of the two major factors that determine a person's effectiveness in communicating orally—physical appearance and speech qualities.

APPEARANCE

With the exception of the person talking on the telephone or using dictating equipment, the speaker can be seen by the listeners. Because speakers are seen before they are heard, listeners form some kind of impression even before the speaker utters a word. And this impression often influences the listeners' interpretation of the speaker's words. This first impression is based primarily on posture, the use of the speaker's hands, eye contact that the speaker makes with the listeners, body and head movement, and the speaker's overall personal appearance—dress, grooming, and so on.

A speaker's physical appearance often sets the stage for the acceptance or nonacceptance of the speaker's words. A speaker who makes a good physical impression quickly gains the interest of listeners. (But a speaker must have something interesting and worthwhile to say—and must say it in an effective manner—to hold the attention of the listeners for any length of time.) The first barrier to effective oral communication will be overcome if the speaker has good posture, is dressed appropriately, is well groomed, and knows how to make each listener feel that the listener is being spoken to directly.

Posture

Many speakers make the serious mistake of underestimating the importance of good posture to overall good physical appearance. Regardless of how short or tall you may be, you should always stand up to your full height. You'll find that good posture will help you develop better breath control. Good posture will also make you appear more confident and give your audience the impression that you know what you are talking about and that your message is really important. Of course, no speaker should appear stiff or pompous and all-knowing. Instead, you should develop a natural posture, constantly reminding yourself to stand erect, with shoulders back and stomach in. Such posture helps improve your voice quality and gives you the appearance of authority.

Hands

While you are speaking, do not distract your audience by pulling at your clothing, putting your hands to your face or hair, or toying with something you are holding. Listeners will automatically direct their attention to your physical maneuvers and will soon lose track of what you are saying to them. If you are standing, it is probably best to place your arms and hands in a relaxed position at your sides (rather than behind your back or folded in front of you). From time to time, make natural gestures. If there is a lectern in front of you, you may wish to place your hands on either side of it. However, remember *never* to lean on the lectern!

When you are talking from a sitting position, you will be heard better if you sit slightly forward in your chair. You may rest your arms and hands in your lap, on the arms of the chair in which you are sitting, or partially on the edge of the table or desk in front of you. However, never use the desk or table as a place to rest your head and elbows. A lazy-looking speaker encourages apathy on the part of the audience.

Facial Expressions

A speaker's facial expression influences the listeners' impressions. A relaxed, pleasant, interested expression will create a better atmosphere for communicating, of course, than a wrinkled brow and turned-down mouth. As you look in a mirror from time to time, see whether you can capture your personality as others see it. Are your facial muscles relaxed? Is your smile natural, pleasant, and genuine? What characteristics in your facial expression are appealing to those around you? See if you can develop animation and show enthusiasm in your facial expression. Above all, you must look alert and interested if you want to impress your listeners.

Eye Contact

One of the best ways to appear interested is to look at your audience, whether that audience is composed of just one person or of more than a hundred. Everyone likes to feel directly addressed by the speaker. Therefore, your eyes should never leave your audience for any extended period of time; it's hard for your listeners to stay interested when you are looking constantly at your notes, the wall, the ceiling, or out the window. When talking to one or two persons, look squarely into the faces of your listeners (without, of course, staring them down) unless you are directing their attention to an object such as a chart. When speaking to a large audience, move your eyes over the entire audience; look into the faces of your listeners and not over the tops of their heads.

Body Movement

Body movement also contributes a great deal to the physical effect created by a speaker. The effective speaker never paces back and forth because excessive movement will distract an audience. It is permissible to move your body from the hips in order to turn from side to side or to move your body in a forward motion to add emphasis to a remark. Of course, if you are using a chart or other illustrative material, you must move from time to time to the visual device. However, when speaking, you should try to face the audience as much as possible and to stay in one place as long as you can.

Grooming and Dress

Personal appearance—grooming, cleanliness, and attire—is also an important factor in effective communication. How a speaker looks and dresses expresses personality just as much as speech and conduct do. There are so many factors involved in personal appearance that not all of them can be considered here in depth. But if you are interested in better oral communications you should be aware that you communicate best when you appear your best. Good appearance breeds confidence. Appearing clean, being dressed neatly and conservatively, avoiding extremes in personal grooming and clothing styles, and selecting attire and accessories that are tasteful and in harmony with one another and with your personality are some of the factors of personal appearance that you should consider. A speaker who ignores any one of these suggestions cannot hope to be very persuasive as an oral communicator.

SPEECH QUALITIES

Although a speaker's physical appearance creates the first impression on the audience, the quality of speech may have an even greater influence on the audience. The quality of speech is determined by the following factors:

Force or volume of voice   Rate or tempo of speech
Pitch or level of voice   Enunciation
Tone   Pronunciation

The force of a speaker's voice and the pitch and the tempo of speech depend, to a great extent, on the speaker's breath control. The volume of air that is taken into the lungs and breathing control help determine how much force a speaker's voice will have; both factors also affect the voice pitch. The rate of speaking will be determined by how frequently a speaker must breathe more air into the lungs. The speaker should talk only when breathing air out—never when taking air into the lungs. Good posture can help a speaker breathe in the maximum amount of air and can help to control the amount of air expended.

Force (Volume)

In order for oral communication to be effective, the message must be heard and heard clearly. Sufficient volume, therefore, is required; and good breath control is important to achieve sufficient volume. If your voice is too soft and you have trouble being heard, you should practice breathing deeply and controlling your breath with your diaphragm and abdominal muscles, just as a singer does. The large abdominal cavity should be used to store a supply of air that can be released evenly to produce a clear, sustained tone. How much force you must use will, of course, be determined by such factors as how good the acoustics are in the room in which you are speaking, how large your audience is, and whether or not you are using a microphone or other electronic device to amplify your voice.

Pitch (Voice Level)

A speaker's voice will be more audible if it has a pleasing pitch. *Pitch* refers to the level of a sound on a musical scale. Practice can help correct the shrillness of a voice that is pitched too high or the excessive resonance of a voice that is pitched too low. Equally in need of correction is the constant pitch that results in a monotone. An effective speaker varies the pitch. The rising and falling of voice pitch is called *intonation*. Intonation can indicate that a statement is being made, that a question is being asked, or that a speaker is pausing. A drop in pitch indicates finality or determination and is, therefore, used at the end of a declarative sentence. For example, in reading the following sentence you should close with a drop in pitch.

I cannot *possibly* attend the dinner meeting, especially on Monday. (Emphasize the word *possibly*.)

You should raise your pitch when you ask a question or when you wish to express suspense, doubt, or hesitation. Read the following sentences, closing with a rise in pitch.

What *more* can I do? (Emphasize *more*.)

I'm *so* sorry I can't go with you today, but I will *definitely* go next week. (Emphasize the words *so* and *definitely*.)

Gliding the pitch up and down or down and up usually expresses sarcasm or contempt, as in the slang expression "Oh, yeah?"

The most important aspect of pitch is variation. Variation of pitch not only helps hold the audience's attention but also helps listeners know the exact meaning intended. Important words can be stressed by a rise in pitch. Comparisons can be stressed by using the same pitch for each element; contrasts, on the other hand, can be made by pitching the first element high and the second low.

Notice the different shades of meaning that emerge as you read the following sentences and emphasize the italicized words.

> *Antony* gave her the book.(Antony did, not someone else.)
> Antony *gave* her the book.(It was a gift.)
> Antony gave *her* the book.(Only she was given the book.)
> Antony gave her *the* book.(The particular book or special book)
> Antony gave her the *book*.(He gave her the book, not something else.)

Tone

The tone of your voice often reveals your attitudes and feelings. Naturally, a pleasant and cheerful tone is more desirable because it will have a better effect on your audience. On the telephone, the tone of your voice must substitute for your facial expression. Hence, the observation, "The voice with the smile." In addition, variation in tone, as well as in volume and pitch, can be used to add interest to your speaking voice. The kind of tone you use should be appropriate for the words and ideas you are expressing.

Speaking Rate (Tempo)

The rate at which you speak should be varied, too, to avoid extremes in either direction. You should not speak so rapidly that words are not understood, but neither should you speak so slowly that the audience does not pay close attention to what is being said. You should regulate your rate of speaking so that you are able to enunciate each word clearly so that the listener will hear each word without difficulty. A good speaking rate is 125 words a minute; oral reading rates and radio speaking tend to run slightly faster—about 150 words a minute. To determine what a rate of 125 words a minute sounds like, read aloud the paragraph below in a half minute. Reread the paragraph as many times as necessary until you achieve the desired rate. At the end of a quarter minute, you should be at the diagonal line. Use this line as a guide to either increase or decrease your speaking rate.

> A good speaker talks slowly enough to be understood by the listeners and speaks in a pleasant voice, articulating and pronouncing each word correctly and distinctly. To develop a good / speaking voice, you must spend sufficient

time practicing the elements of good speech. An effective speaker is a definite asset to business and will usually find more opportunities for advancing in the job. (63 words)

Changing the rate contributes to variety, as well as to clarity. Important words may be spoken slowly; unimportant words or phrases, more rapidly.

Try to speak in thought units so that you can assist the listener in interpreting your words. If the sentence is short, obviously the thought unit will consist of the entire sentence, as in "My office is very pleasant." When there are several thought units within a sentence, then the speaker should pause slightly after each thought group, as in "My office is very pleasant; / but I must agree, / some days are much more hectic than others."

Use pauses to stress major points. By pausing between major points or after important statements, you add variety and emphasis to the points you want the audience to remember.

Enunciation and Pronunciation

Because good enunciation and pronunciation are such important aspects of effective business speaking, they receive separate treatment in Section 53.

COMMUNICATION PROJECTS

Practical Application

A. Reread the first two pages of this section. Assume that you are also a candidate for the position discussed. How would you compare your oral communication skills with those of the other two candidates? List your strengths and weaknesses, including such factors as your overall personality, the first impression you make on others, your personal appearance, your facial expressions, and your mannerisms. Briefly comment on each of these factors.

B. Select three prominent individuals (in politics, sports, or the arts) who frequently appear before the public in some type of speaking role. List the factors—pro and con—that affect their speaking effectiveness.

C. Read each of the following sentences in three ways so that the meaning is changed by your emphasis.

1. Walter mailed the card yesterday afternoon.
2. I enjoyed Paris more than any other city on my trip.
3. Will Jimmie be at the party again this year?
4. If it is possible, please get here earlier on Wednesday.
5. Please forgive me; I really didn't expect to be this late.

D. Read the following sentences twice. Then, standing before the class, read them aloud. Try to keep your eyes on the audience as much as possible as you read the material.

1. Olive is never late for work, if she can help it.
2. I doubt very much that I will be able to come to the office picnic next week.

3. No, they do not perform with great efficiency, in my opinion.
4. What difference does it make whether or not I attend the meeting tomorrow?
5. Do you really believe that she will be able to complete the assignment on time?

E. Read the following paragraphs twice. Then, standing before the class, read them aloud. Try to keep your eyes on the audience as much as possible as you read the material.

1. To be an effective speaker, you must be aware of your audience at all times, not only in selecting and preparing your topic but also in giving your speech. Audiences respond favorably only to speakers who talk directly to them and who smile occasionally. The speaker who looks at the ceiling, at notes, or into space quickly loses rapport with the audience.

2. Nearly every speech of any length is brightened considerably by touches of humor and by human-interest narratives. Of course, such stories should not dominate the speech. Observe the following rules: Use stories and jokes that add interest to the subject or illustrate a particular point. Before telling a joke to an audience, test it on friends to make sure it has a punch line. Make sure that stories and jokes do not offend or embarrass the audience. And time your stories to make sure that they are not too long.

3. When you are talking to an audience, pretend that you are carrying on a face-to-face conversation with just one person. Remember that the audience is just as eager for you to perform well as you are to do so. Don't be upset if you are nervous—even experienced speakers and actors are! Feeling nervous is a result of anxiety about doing a good job, and most authorities feel that a little stage fright provides needed tension.

4. Most people take telephone usage for granted—and this is one of the reasons why so many office workers are ineffective telephone communicators. Too many employees assume that a business telephone conversation is the same as a personal telephone call. Actually, the telephone is one of the most important communication media in business; and it must be used with great skill, especially when talking with outside callers and with superiors in the office.

F. Present a three-minute (approximately) talk to the class on a topic of your choice. Try to make each person in your audience feel as though you are talking individually to that person.

Editing Practice

Synonyms or Antonyms? In each item below, two words are synonyms or antonyms. For each item, identify the pair by letter and indicate whether the words are synonyms or antonyms.

1. (a) slander (b) reference (c) equality (d) disparity (e) excellence
2. (a) opener (b) glamor (c) candor (d) hypocrisy (e) sagacity
3. (a) hunt (b) perform (c) discipline (d) start (e) chasten
4. (a) estranged (b) reconciled (c) old (d) erudite (e) odd
5. (a) affable (b) garrulous (c) gracious (d) loquacious (e) joyous
6. (a) blissful (b) clever (c) happy (d) boisterous (e) busy

7. (a) respiratory (b) sordid (c) involuntary (d) stolid (e) phlegmatic
8. (a) excusing (b) modest (c) faultless (d) extraneous (e) pretentious
9. (a) convex (b) solid (c) harrowing (d) cadaverous (e) concave
10. (a) contrive (b) death (c) action (d) undershirt (e) demise

Editor's Alert   Thoroughly examine the following sentences for needed corrections. Make those corrections, rewriting any poorly worded sentences.

1. All secretarys desks should be locked at the close of business.
2. There's no reasons for you to be late so often.
3. Paul ordered 20 reams of paper at $5.25 each, making a total of $105.
4. Will you and him be at the meeting tonight?
5. Please continue on as though nothing were said.
6. Complete the questionaire as soon as possible.
7. Please follow-up the requests made in each peice of correspondents.
8. Our company has always in the past—and always will—be noted for prompt delivery.
9. The assignment was only given to Ina and I last Monday.
10. 100 candidates applied for the position we advertised.

Case Problem

Who's to Blame?   Janet Yost and Leonard Marks both type for Mr. Allen. One morning Mr. Allen came to Janet with a typed letter in which there were many errors. He was most irritated because of the careless proofreading and requested that the letter be retyped. Janet noted that the reference initials were "lm."

1. If you were Janet, what would you do about the situation?
2. What suggestions would you make to prevent a similar situation from happening again?

53 ENUNCIATION AND PRONUNCIATION

Maria Lopiano, a typist for the Perez Wholesale Furniture Company, handed her boss the attractive finished copy of a letter she transcribed from a dictated cassette and then returned to her desk to continue with her next task. In a few minutes, her boss came rushing out of his office, a frown on his face, obviously disturbed about something.

"Maria, you're gonna havta type this letter over. You made a terrible error that wudda cost us a lotta money if I hadna caught it—and, darn it, I was in a hurry to get this letter in the mail."

"What did I do wrong?" asked the distressed Maria.

Her boss explained, "See here, where you have 'forty tables for $14,000'? It's supposta be *fourteen* tables for $14,000."

"I'm sorry," apologized Maria, "but that's what you said on the tape, *forty*."

"I couldna said that. Play that part of the tape again."

When the tape reached the word in question, it became apparent that Maria's boss so poorly enunciated the *fourteen* that anyone would have mistaken the word for *forty*.

The boss apologized, but regardless of who was at fault, Maria had to take the time—and additional stationery—to retype the letter. However, it was indeed fortunate that the error was caught before the letter was mailed and resulted in a large monetary loss to the company.

One could cite many other instances in business—and even in social situations—where poor enunciation has led to costly delays, unnecessary expense, and the loss of goodwill. That is why it is so important for all business employees, particularly those who have face-to-face or telephone contact with customers and venders and those who use dictation equipment, to both enunciate and pronounce words clearly and correctly.

ENUNCIATION VS. PRONUNCIATION

Although the terms *enunciation* and *pronunciation* are closely related, they do have slightly different meanings. Understanding the difference between the two terms and making a strong effort to eliminate the barriers to effective enunciation and pronunciation will contribute greatly to improved speech.

Enunciation

Enunciation refers to the distinctness or clarity with which you articulate or sound each part of a word. For instance, saying "walkin" for *walking* or "gonna" for *going to* are examples of careless enunciation. Careless enunciation often occurs in *ing* words, such as "willin" for *willing* and "askin" for *asking*. Also, whenever we speak rapidly, most of us have a tendency to run our words together, dropping some of the sounds. Saying "dijago" for *did you go* and "meetcha" for *meet you* are examples. A person who slurs too many words is likely to be misunderstood or not heard at all, particularly over the telephone or on transcribing equipment. It is annoying for both the listener and the speaker if the listener must ask the speaker to repeat something several times. With transcribing equipment, errors may be made if the speaker cannot be reached for verification. Such difficulties can often be avoided if we simply speak more slowly.

Pronunciation

Pronunciation refers either to the sound that the speaker gives to the various letters or combination of letters that make up a word or to the way in which the speaker accents the word. A person who says "pronounciation" instead of "pronunciation" is guilty of a pronunciation error. Should you say "libary" or "library," "com' · par · able" or "com · par' · able"? The dictionary indicates that the pronunciations are *library* and *com' · par · able*; and these are the pronunciations used by careful speakers.

Of course, there are regional differences in pronunciation; and, in addition, a number of words have more than one acceptable pronunciation. In the latter case, the dictionary lists the preferred pronunciation first.

Many difficulties in pronunciation arise because some letters or combinations of letters are pronounced one way in some words and another way in others. For example, the combination *ow* is given a long "o" sound in *know* but an "ow" sound (as in *ouch*) in *now*. Other difficulties in pronunciation arise because a letter may be sounded in some words while in other words the same letter is silent; for example, *k* is sounded in the word *kick*, but it is not sounded in such words as *know* and *knee*. Because of these inconsistencies in our language, it is essential to consult the dictionary whenever you are in doubt about the pronunciation of a word.

Though errors in pronunciation are less likely to cause misunderstandings than errors in enunciation—you would know what was meant if someone said "com · par'· able" instead of "com'· par · able"—such errors tend to distract the listener and may even cause the listener to consider the speaker careless or uneducated. The business employee who is eager to succeed does not wish to be branded with either of these labels.

Furthermore, since so many words are written according to the way they sound, you can improve your spelling ability by carefully and correctly pronouncing and enunciating each word you use. Many words are misspelled because letters that should be sounded are overlooked. Those who repeatedly say "goverment" instead of "government" probably overlooked the *n* in this word. Some words, on the other hand, are misspelled because extra sounds are inserted where they do not belong; for example, pronouncing "athaletic" instead of "athletic." In still other instances of mispronunciation, the sequence of letters in the word may be rearranged. How many people do you know who say "irrevelant" when they really mean "irrelevant"? You can easily see how taking sufficient care in pronunciation will help prevent other errors, such as "quite" for *quiet* and "praps" for *perhaps*.

Most business employees have to give and to receive information and instructions over the telephone or in face-to-face conversation. To prevent the costly misunderstandings that are often caused by improper pronunciation and enunciation, you should make every effort to develop and practice intelligible speech.

IMPROVING ENUNCIATION AND PRONUNCIATION

Follow this four-step plan to help you improve your enunciation and pronunciation:
1. Use the dictionary to determine the preferred pronunciation of words about which you are uncertain.
2. Speak slowly enough, and with sufficient care, so that each letter in a word is sounded as it is supposed to be sounded and so that words are not run together.

3. Learn to use your jaw, your lips, and your tongue (the physical organs of speech) properly.
4. Practice frequently the correct enunciation and pronunciation of words that are frequently mispronounced or poorly enunciated.

You have already learned how to use the dictionary to determine the preferred pronunciation of words, and you have also learned how to control your speaking rate. Now you will learn how to use effectively the speech organs that assist in correct enunciation and pronunciation. Also, you will practice enunciating and pronouncing words that frequently cause difficulty.

DEVELOP A FLEXIBLE JAW

A rigid jaw results in muffled speech. Many sounds need to be vocalized and should, therefore, be made by movement of the mouth. If such sounds are forced through a locked jaw, a jaw that does not move up and down on its hinges, these sounds are certain to be muffled and indistinguishable. Keeping your jaws locked tight, try to pronounce these words—*neither, capable, try*. Can you understand what you are saying? Obviously you cannot, and you could not expect any listener to understand words that are pronounced in this manner.

To be an intelligible speaker, you must move your jaw freely between an open and a closed position. Say each of the vowels and notice the different positions of your jaw as you say *a, e, i, o, u*. Compare your jaw positions as you say first the sound "ow," as in *how*, and then the sound "oo," as in *room*. When you say "ow," your jaw is dropped. However, when you say "oo," you move your jaw only slightly if at all.

Practice will help give you the free-moving feeling of a flexible jaw. First, stand before a mirror and practice the following words to be certain that your jaw is unlocked.

only	winning	about	seventy-five
try	capable	arrive	nine eight one
fine	evening	idea	reporting

Practicing the phrases below will exercise your jaw and help make it flexible.

going to go	down and out	up and around
around and away	sky high	down, up, and out
I've been	you've been	I've seen

Finally, practice saying these sentences to prove that your jaw is flexible enough so that each word is clearly enunciated and pronounced.

Shirley placed the pencil on the table.
Many men and women have power, prestige, and financial ability.
Please telephone 964-7850 right away.
My flexible jaw contributes to better speech, I know.

DEVELOP MOBILE LIPS

As you were practicing the preceding words, phrases, and sentences, you probably noticed that in addition to your jaw moving up and down, your lips were assuming many different positions. Six consonant sounds are made by action of the lips. The lips are closed for the sounds of "m," "b," and "p." The lower lip touches the edges of the upper front teeth for the sounds of "v" and "f." The lips are rounded for the sound made by *w*, as in *woman*.

Poor enunciators do not move their lips very much; as a result, their speech is often unintelligible. The good speaker, on the other hand, uses a variety of lip positions. In addition to the lip movements for the six consonants previously mentioned, the "oo" sound in *who, lose, shoe,* and *do* requires rounded lips. The lips are widely stretched for the "e" sound in *me, we, key,* and *see.* In words like *few, boys, use,* and *how,* the speaker is required to use two different lip positions. The sound for "ow," as in *how* and *now,* requires that the jaw be dropped and the lips be rounded to form a circle.

While using proper lip positions, practice these words. First read across and then read down the columns.

wasting	mine	voice	very	wonder	pension
vocal	very	wary	file	victory	violent
winter	when	why	food	cost	careful
cool	mister	many	time	meaning	forceful

Now practice the following phrases, making certain that you avoid lazy lip movements.

office manager	readily available	answer the telephone
lose the money	when we go	empty the basket now
many men may	very fine work	what we wear

Are your lips sufficiently mobile, so that you can enunciate clearly each word in the sentences given below? Practice the sentences until every sound is clear.

Peter Piper picked a peck of pickled peppers.
She sells seashells by the seashore.
How, now, brown cow?
The rain in Spain falls mainly on the plain.
Which witch was the wickedest witch?
Hickory dickory dock, the mouse ran up the clock.
The whistling west wind whipped the whispering trees.
Who picked up the bale of mail this morning?

DEVELOP A LIVELY TONGUE

Repeat several times: *The tip of my tongue moves lively in my mouth.* Do you feel the lively movement of your tongue as you say these words? Try saying the same sentence with your tongue held loosely in your mouth, using a minimum of movement. Do you notice the lack of clarity? In order to enunciate precisely, to make your speech clear, you must move your tongue to several positions—the front of your mouth, the back of your mouth, the roof of your mouth, and even between the top and bottom rows of teeth for the "th" sound heard in *either, this,* and *that.*

Now that you know how a lively tongue feels, stand in front of a mirror as you practice the following words.

feel	forward	seal	sadly	saw	suit
main	many	some	sight	peace	mail
twine	train	later	legal	poster	port

Did you feel the lively movement of your tongue? Now practice these words that require your tongue to be placed between your teeth.

think	thought	either	neither	loath	thorough
then	the	with	whether	through	wrath

Using the lively tongue that you have learned to develop, practice the following phrases and sentences until each sound is clearly enunciated.

health, wealth, and happiness
actually colder than yesterday
the attempted assault and battery
through thick and thin
this, that, those, them, and these
seesaw at three thirty-three
Linger a little longer, lovely lady.
The thirty-three discounts are listed on page three.
There were thirty thousand thermos bottles sold there.
Nothing gained, nothing lost, and nothing accomplished either.
Their number over there is 333-1237, but there is no one there now.

You have practiced sufficiently the several suggestions for improving your enunciation and pronunciation which have been presented in this section. However, it is important that you continue to be conscious of the way in which you enunciate and pronounce words, to use your dictionary to determine the correct pronunciation of words about which you are in doubt, and to continue to practice good speech habits. If you follow these suggestions, you will find that your speaking will improve and that improved speech will quickly become easy and natural for you.

COMMUNICATION PROJECTS

Practical Application

A. The following phrases are frequently run together even though each word should be enunciated separately and distinctly. Practice saying these phrases properly, first in isolation and then in an original sentence that you create for each phrase.

give me	did you	going to	do you	got to
being there	want to	kind of	come here	will you
have been	didn't you	don't know	going to go	have to

B. From one of your textbooks, select a paragraph that you think will be of interest to the class. Read the paragraph aloud to the class, and be careful to enunciate words clearly and to pronounce them correctly. Each member of the class will list every word you enunciate poorly or mispronounce.

C. You wish your secretary to place a number of long-distance telephone calls for you. Dictate the following names and telephone numbers, making certain that the names and numbers are intelligible. Spell the difficult or unusual names; for example, "Irvine (I-r-v-i-n-e) Insurance Company of Nashua (N-a-s-h-u-a), Minnesota. I want to talk with Mrs. Phillips. The number is (612) 555-7814."

Person to Be Called	Company and City	Telephone Number
1. Karl Frosch	County Employment Service Worcester, Massachusetts	(617) 123-9876
2. Credit Manager	Poughkeepsie Manufacturing Co. 101 Smith Street Poughkeepsie, New York	(914) 455-6389
3. Will speak with anyone	Marcy & Yates Associates Oxnard, California	(805) 488-3770
4. Ms. Carolyn Lehr	Lehr Advertising Agency New York, New York	Don't know the number
5. Dr. Grace Bohlander	Riverside Hospital Albuquerque, New Mexico	(505) 111-8347 Extension 183

D. You wish to send the following message by telegraph to one of your customers. You telephone the message to the telegraph office. You will be called on in class to read all the information as you would read it over the telephone.

> **To be sent to:** Mr. Stephen Weisenthal, Moderne Lampshade Manufacturers, Inc., 2122 Cherry Drive, Elizabeth, New Jersey 07202.
> **The message:** Returning 189 assorted lampshades. Replace with models 89, 96, and 97 in white and beige only.
> **Sender:** Your name and address.

E. As office manager, you find it necessary to order a number of items from a local stationer. Since you need the items in a hurry, you telephone the information to the stationer. Assume that you have dialed the number and that the person at the other end says, "Torrance Stationers; may I help you?" Pick up the conversation from this point, and place the order for the following items.

1. 6 boxes of medium-hard carbon paper, No. 880, $8\frac{1}{2}$ by $11\frac{1}{2}$, Stock No. 2-105-19
2. 4 boxes 20-lb white typewriting paper, $8\frac{1}{2}$ by 11, Stock No. 13-1276
3. 2 quire stencils, Stock No. ABD-1379
4. 1 dozen No. 2 pencils, Stock No. 54-927

Editing Practice

States, Capitals, Principal Cities   In each item below, there are two states, capitals, or principal cities that are misspelled. Spell them correctly.

1. Lincoln   Colombus   Cheyanne   Pierre   Jefferson City
2. Racine   Laramie   Pittsburg (Pa.)   Bethlahem   Portsmouth
3. Michigen   Idaho   Arizona   Montanna   New Jersey
4. Honalulu   Albeny   Richmond   Charleston   Indiannapelis
5. Seattle   Spokane   Hoboken   Scenectady   Cincinatti
6. Wichita   Clevland   Agusta   Duluth   Butte
7. Olympia   Providence   Topeka   Frankfourt (Ky.)   Helana
8. Minnesota   Colarado   Pensylvania   Virginia   Rhode Island
9. Minnapolis   Juneau   Trenton   Charleston   Jeferson City
10. Brooklyn   Pasedena   Brockton   Levenworth   Lowell

Editors' Alert   In each of the following sentences, make any changes that will correct or improve the sentence. Carefully check *every* detail.

1. The portible typewriter is to heavy to lift.
2. The number of people in attendence were large.
3. You can type the letter however it must be done today.
4. All us employees are covered by insurance.
5. We did consider the investment a year ago and decided against it at that time but perhaps the situation is different now and you can tell us how the venture would now be profitable for us.
6. I do not like to type, filing, and being given dictation.
7. 12 men and women worked from seven to eight p.m. for over-time pay.
8. It was not feasable to install the equipment at the present time.
9. On February 15 245 items disappeared before they could be loaded on the trucks, which we are at a loss to explain.
10. John spoke to Bill about the error he made.

Case Problem

The Helpful Busybody   Brady Owens has been working at the Ulster Accounting Services for only a month, but his boss, Ira Keogh, asked Brady to prepare a special report for him and gave very specific instructions regarding the preparation of the report. Marvin Kelsey, a long-time employee, observed Brady preparing this report and indicated that it was being prepared incorrectly. Said Marvin, "I've been with the company over ten years and I've prepared many similar reports. You are not doing your report correctly."

1. If you were Brady, how would you handle the situation?
2. Was Marvin entirely at fault in his actions?

54 ONE-TO-ONE COMMUNICATION

High on the list of communication activities of most business employees—if not at the very top—is communicating orally on a one-to-one basis. Business workers talk with colleagues in their own departments, with their supervisors and various department heads, with top management, and with such service employees as messengers and custodians many times during each working day.

In addition, many employees talk either on the telephone or face-to-face with individuals outside the company—customers, sales representatives, suppliers, visitors, and various people soliciting or giving information. As a matter of fact, many business employees depend to a great extent on their oral communication skill to earn their living—sales representatives, switchboard operators, and receptionists are just a few examples. Every business worker who has contact with the public plays an important role in developing and promoting the company image. When the agent of an insurance company speaks to customers, it is not as an individual but as a representative of the company. The same is true of a receptionist, a secretary, a credit clerk, or a switchboard operator. In one sense, those who speak for the company *are* the company to those people who do business with that firm.

GUIDELINES FOR ONE-TO-ONE COMMUNICATION

The following suggestions should serve as guidelines for communicating effectively on a one-to-one basis, whether communicating face-to-face or over the telephone.

Listen Attentively

The ability to listen attentively is one of the most important skills connected with effective oral communication. Being attentive and showing interest in the other person are just two attributes of the good listener that lead to more effective communication. For example, if you are attacked verbally by an irate customer for something over which you have no control, you can go a long way toward soothing the customer by merely listening attentively. Often, you need not say anything, because what the customer most wants is an attentive and sympathetic listener.

Use the Person's Name

Be certain that you clearly hear the name of the person whom you have met or talked with on the telephone for the first time. Repeat the name right after it is given to you: "I'm happy to meet you, Mr. Cole." If you aren't absolutely sure of the person's name, ask that it be repeated; you can say, "I didn't hear your name clearly," or "How do you pronounce (or spell) your name?" Then, after hearing the name, pronounce it aloud in order to fix it in your mind. Whenever appropriate, use the name once or twice during the conversation. "Yes, I understand, Mr. Cole." Finally, always be sure that you say the person's name in your good-bye: "Good-bye, Ms. Gonzales; I was happy to talk with you."

Permit Others to Talk

Don't do all the talking. Give the other person a chance to talk, while *you* listen attentively. Watch for signs that the other person wants to say something or is becoming bored and not listening carefully. No matter how interesting you think the conversation is or how well informed or articulate you think you are, you must give your listener a chance to speak. Otherwise, you will not keep your listener's attention and respect.

Encourage Others to Talk

Sometimes the other person seems to prefer listening to talking. Remember, however, that a good conversationalist is one who not only talks well but also encourages the listener to contribute to the conversation. Ask frequent questions to let the other party know that you are interested in listening too. And prove your interest by listening attentively.

Look at the Speaker

Of course, this guideline applies only to face-to-face conversation. A speaker likes to have the listener's complete attention. When you speak, you like to feel that your listeners are focusing on what you are saying and not being distracted by objects or sounds coming from other directions—conversations in another part of the office or something that is happening outside the building, for example. So when you listen, make eye contact with the speaker; look at the person who is talking.

Compliment When Suitable

Many people with whom we come in contact are seeking approval. Compliments are always welcome, so compliment whenever the occasion is suitable. Paying a compliment is especially effective during tense situations. If a valued employee or a customer has a complaint that you cannot justify or remedy, you can put that person in a better frame of mind for a "No" answer by paying a compliment. Compliment the employee for work well done or for loyalty. Compliment the customer for paying promptly or for his or her good taste. In all conversations, be generous with praise when it is timely and when it is deserved. But never pay a compliment unless you can do so honestly and convincingly. Insincerity is easily detected.

Keep Conversations Concise

Since you should not prolong conversations unduly, you should keep your conversation to the point. If you are asked for opinions, give them quickly and clearly. However, being concise does not mean you must be brusque. Try to sense what the situation calls for and act accordingly. Most people do not want to hear unnecessary details or to listen to prolonged excuses for your inability to do something they have requested. Tell them enough to satisfy them; and if you are in doubt, the best rule to follow is to keep your conversations short.

Establish the Best Atmosphere

It is said that Napoleon had his desk raised so that he could look down upon everyone who came to see him. Some executives sit behind a huge desk when they talk to visitors for the same reason. These executives feel that they appear more important, more courageous, and more dominating.

The trend today for good relations with colleagues and customers is to create a conversational atmosphere that is more relaxed. Executives who are effective communicators move from behind their desks and face their visitors without a barrier between them. This type of atmosphere makes possible a better give-and-take situation and, therefore, more effective communication.

RECEIVING THE PUBLIC

Although in most companies the receptionist greets all visitors, many employees also have contact with the public. In small offices and in most retail establishments, this situation applies to every employee. You should, therefore, be familiar with the basic procedures for meeting the public.

Give Prompt Attention to Visitors

Recognize a visitor's presence immediately. Even if you are busy, you can interrupt your work for as long as it takes to smile and say to the new arrival, "I'll be with you in a moment. Won't you sit down?"

Greet Visitors Pleasantly

Greet visitors with a pleasant smile and voice, and show friendliness by using their names in your greeting whenever possible. Add a personal touch to your greeting, such as "Good afternoon, Dr. Ward. It's a pleasure to see you again." Such friendly greetings make callers feel that they are getting special treatment and put them in a better frame of mind to do business with your company.

Be Courteous to All Visitors

Every visitor should receive friendly and courteous treatment, regardless of the purpose of the visit. Even if the visitor is obviously upset about something and acts accordingly, you must overlook any discourtesy and show that you are understanding. It may be that your visitor is annoyed about what he or she feels is "unfair treatment" from your company. There may be some justification for this feeling, so you now have an opportunity to mend a business rift. Even if you can do nothing about the situation, you can listen understandingly to the complaint. Treating an annoyed customer discourteously will only tend to make the situation worse. Usually a person responds well to pleasant treatment, and your courteous attitude will help to calm the visitor and will give your company a chance to make amends.

Apologize for Delays

If an appointment cannot be kept promptly by the person who is to receive the visitor, you should tell the visitor why ("I'm sorry, Mr. Dallas, Miss Mercado has been delayed at a meeting with the president"); and you should tell him about how long he may have to wait ("Miss Mercado should be able to see you about 11:30"). Make the visitor comfortable (a selection of current magazines and today's newspaper should be available, or offer a cup of coffee if it is available). You might ask, "Shall I telephone your office and tell your secretary that you will be delayed a half hour?"

You may have some visitors whose shabby appearance leads you to believe they could not possibly have business of interest to one of the company executives. Don't be too sure! Sometimes the one who scorns that well-groomed look is a VIP— perhaps even the most important stockholder in the company. Everyone is, of course, entitled to your most courteous treatment.

Find Out the Purpose of the Visit

Almost every caller will have an appointment with an executive or other member of the company. For example, a visitor may say to you, "I am Mary O'Neill; I have an appointment with Miss Mercado," and you will usher her to the appropriate office or telephone the executive that her visitor has arrived. If you do not know, however, whether the visitor has an appointment, you must ask, "May I help you?" or "Whom do you wish to see?" If the visitor has no appointment, take his or her name, the name of the company he or she represents (if any), and the purpose of the call. Relay this information to the person who you think can be of most help to the caller. After getting permission to show the visitor in, invite the visitor to follow you to the appropriate office. Then present the visitor like this: "Miss Mercado (hostess), this is Ms. Mary O'Neill (visitor)."

Be Discreet and Tactful

Protect both your employer's and the company's interests by being discreet in your comments to visitors. For example, if your employer is late coming to the office in the morning or returning from lunch, it is not necessary to supply unnecessary details to the visitor. Instead of saying, "Mrs. Stein is late getting in this morning," say, "I expect Mrs. Stein about 9:15." If she is late returning from lunch, you might say, "Mrs. Stein had an important luncheon meeting and should return shortly." Avoid making conversation about company business or personnel. If the subject comes up, be noncommittal and change the topic of conversation as quickly as you can. Never engage in negative statements, such as "Hasn't business been poor lately?" or "We have a terrible time getting good secretaries."

Be discreet in giving any opinions solicited by the visitor. The person the visitor will see may have a different opinion from your own. For example, the visitor may want to show you certain products and ask whether you think your company might be interested in buying them. Unless you are responsible for company purchases, however, you should not give an opinion about the company's possible interest in buying the products. Of course, you should not be rude even though you are pressured for comment. Simply say pleasantly, "I am sorry, but I do not purchase our company's supplies."

COMMUNICATING BY TELEPHONE

Communicating by telephone requires techniques that are quite different from those used in one-to-one conversation. Since those engaged in telephone conversations are unable to see one another, they must depend entirely upon their voices to communicate friendliness, interest, and a willingness to be helpful.

Since most people assume they know how to use the telephone properly, when as a matter of fact they do not, many office workers are ineffective telephone communicators. Furthermore, too many employees assume that a business telephone conversation requires the same treatment as a personal telephone call. Actually, the telephone is one of the most important communication media in business; so it must be used with great skill, especially in conversations with callers from the outside and with superiors in the office.

The following suggestions may seem elementary to you. Nevertheless, you should read them carefully and follow them whenever you use the telephone for either personal or business use:

> Talk directly into the mouthpiece.
> Talk slowly and naturally. Exaggerate your enunciation slightly. Shouting is never necessary.
> If a caller must be transferred to someone else in the company, say, "If you will hold on just a moment, I will have your call transferred." Then depress the telephone plunger twice, very slowly, and repeat until the operator returns to the line. Then say, "Will you please transfer this call to Rod Campbell on extension 4103."
> If, while talking, you must put down the receiver, place it on a book or magazine rather than drop it on a hard surface. In this way, you will protect the caller's ear from irritating noises.
> Place the receiver gently in the cradle when you hang up.

Guidelines for Effective Telephone Communication

Courtesy is the key to effective telephone communication. Greet all callers pleasantly. This pleasantness is achieved by the words you use and the tone of your voice. If you know who the caller is, you might say something like this: "Good morning, Ms. Alvarez," or "Hello, Bill." If you do not know who the caller is, identify yourself first—"Mrs. Rossi speaking" or "Johnny Low." When answering the telephone for a department, be certain to identify both the department and yourself—"Accounting Department, Ms. Park" or "Word Processing Center, Jerry Asher." A secretary usually answers the employer's telephone like this: "Miss Bertrand's office" or "Miss Bertrand's office, Ms. Gomez speaking."

Your voice should be friendly and your manner courteous, regardless of who is calling. This manner is *especially* important when talking to outside callers. Remember that the impression created by your voice should be that of a friendly smile. Show the caller that you want to be helpful; always listen attentively, and don't interrupt. So that the caller will know you are listening, occasionally acknowledge comments with a "Yes" or with some other simple verbal response. Use the caller's name at least once before hanging up, and conclude the call with a remark like "Thank you for calling us, Dr. Goldstein," or "We will look into the matter for you right away, Ms. Koch."

Originating Calls

The telephone company makes the following suggestions for originating calls:
1. Plan the conversation before you call. A little forethought will save both time and money. If your conversation will be an involved one, jot down notes in advance.
2. Place your own calls. Not only is it faster and easier to do so, but it is also more courteous. No busy executive likes to be greeted with "Hold on, Mr. Gomez, I have Mr. Carpenter on the line." Mr. Gomez then has to wait until Mr. Carpenter gets on the line. Since Mr. Gomez is the person being called, it is discourteous to keep him waiting.
3. To avoid delays, identify yourself promptly and state the purpose of your call. For example, say, "This is Janet Archer of Litton and Warren. I would like to speak to the person in charge of adjustments."

Receiving Calls

To ensure efficient use of the telephone when you receive a call, observe the following suggested procedures:
1. Answer promptly and identify yourself immediately. You should answer at the first ring, if possible, and not later than the second ring.
2. Respond to inquiries graciously, take appropriate notes, and verify important details. "Yes, we shall be glad to send you a duplicate copy of last month's statement. You want the December, 19—, statement; is that correct?"

3. At the close of the conversation, take the required action. Be certain that you keep all promises you make to the caller.
4. Allow the caller to hang up first.
5. If you are going to be away from your telephone, let someone know; and indicate how you would like calls handled that are directed to you during your absence.

Answering for Others

Two special suggestions are appropriate when you are answering telephone calls for other people in your firm.
1. If the person called is not available, offer to be of help or to transfer the call to someone who can help.
2. If the caller wishes to speak to only one individual and that person is not available, obtain the caller's name and telephone number and record the caller's message, if any.

Handling Complaints

The true test of your ability to effectively handle telephone calls will be revealed when you must deal with an annoyed customer who has a complaint. You must remember that you represent your company and that little or nothing is to be gained by allowing yourself to become angry. Your task will be made much easier if you follow these suggestions when you are required to handle complaints on the telephone.
1. Listen carefully to the caller's complaint. Take careful notes of all important details.
2. Express interest in and an understanding of the caller's problem. "Yes, I can see why you were annoyed by the mistake in your bill, Mr. Hayakawa, but I am sure we can correct it right away."
3. Tell the caller what action you will take. If you cannot make the adjustment yourself, refer the caller to someone who can. Don't make the caller repeat the entire story to someone else; each time the message must be repeated to another person, the caller becomes angrier.

COMMUNICATION PROJECTS

Practical Application
A. You are the administrative assistant to Oliver Malcolm, president of Malcolm Electronics Inc. Mr. Malcolm will be holding a very important conference in his office for the next two hours and has told you that he does not want to be disturbed under any circumstances. The following situations occur during the hours Mr. Malcolm does not want to be disturbed. What would you say to each of the individuals involved in the following situations?

1. The plant manager, Fred Yates, telephones and says that it is urgent that he speak with Mr. Malcolm.
2. Mrs. Malcolm, the president's wife, telephones and asks to speak with her husband.
3. Mr. Graves, an important customer from out of town, arrives an hour early for an appointment he has with Mr. Malcolm.
4. The chairman of the board of directors, Y. C. Potts, telephones and asks to speak with Mr. Malcolm.

B. The administrative services manager, Marcella Kingston, has requested that you prepare a one-page memorandum on "Improving Telephone Usage."

C. Indicate how a receptionist should respond to the following visitors who approach the reception desk and say:
1. "Hello."
2. "I want to see Mr. Jackson."
3. "Do you think there is anyone in this company who can help me get this stupid bill straightened out?"
4. "I have a 10 a.m. appointment with Mr. Clark." (Mr. Clark has not yet arrived at the office.)
5. "I am from Roberts Cleaning Products, and I would like to demonstrate some of our products." (The building superintendent is the only person who is responsible for making such purchases.)

D. How would you handle a caller with whom your boss does not wish to speak? Your boss calls this person a "time waster."

E. What are the qualities of a good listener?

F. Suggest three greetings a receptionist might use to find out the purpose of a caller's visit.

Editing Practice

Editing to Improve Writing Techniques   Rewrite the following sentences, and correct all evidence of poor writing techniques.
1. Harriet will continue on with the work she started yesterday.
2. I know that you can handle the situation as well, if not better, than me.
3. I left work a hour early.
4. Is this stock generally considered a "Blue Chip?"
5. Mr. Todd told Fred that his brother has been asked to join the staff.
6. Our receptionist recognized the caller looking up from the desk.
7. Mrs. Abbate told Rachel that she would be promoted soon.
8. Did you loose the contract that was in this envelope?
9. The defendant was persistent.
10. The jury reached its decision, and its not a happy one.

Case Problem

The Unqualified Employee   Gloria Harris, head of the sales department, received the following written report from Daniel Friedman, a supervisor.

I cannot recommend Helen Anderson, my secretary, for a salary increase at this time. During her first six months on the job, she tried very hard to do good work, but she soon lost interest. Now my work is taking second place to her long coffee breaks and her personal visits and telephone calls. Yesterday, for example, it took three hours to get three short letters typed.

Accordingly, Gloria must talk with Helen about the quality of Helen's work and the reason for her not getting a salary increase. What should Gloria say to Helen in the discussion?

55 GROUP DISCUSSION

If you were to ask most business executives how many meetings they attend in the course of a week, the typical answer is likely to be "Too many!" Such responses are based on the fact that many executives attend from two to as many as twelve or more meetings every week. As a result, these executives have to extend their working day or take work home to complete. Although group conferences are among the most important media for exchanging ideas and reporting information within business, the frequency of meetings is decried by almost everyone. Such might not be the case if meetings were organized and conducted more efficiently and if more were accomplished than is usually accomplished.

As a responsible business employee, you are likely to have frequent opportunities to participate in a variety of capacities in many types of group conferences. You might be selected as a member of a *standing* (permanent) committee that meets regularly, such as a planning committee, a publicity committee, or a finance committee. You may also be called upon to serve on a committee formed for a particular purpose only, such as a committee appointed to study employee grievances or to plan the company's 25th anniversary celebration. These temporary committees, formed for a special purpose and then disbanded after the purpose has been achieved, are called *ad hoc* (pronounced "ad hock") committees. You may even be selected as chairperson of one of these committees, with the responsibility of planning and conducting the meetings.

Because meetings consume so much time and talent in the typical business organization, they should be organized and conducted efficiently. The time spent on meetings adds up to many thousands of dollars every year for the typical business organization. In addition to attending meetings during business hours, the business worker often goes to many meetings and serves on a number of committees outside the company—for example, in professional, social, religious, political, and civic groups.

PARTICIPATING IN MEETINGS

Everyone who is invited to join a group discussion has an obligation to contribute his or her best thinking and suggestions. Time and money are wasted because employees take meetings for granted and do not contribute their maximum efforts to the discussion. They often come to a meeting unprepared, uninterested, and uninspired. The six basic rules for participating effectively in a meeting are explained in the following discussion.

Prepare for the Meeting

The first rule for effective participation in a meeting is to come prepared. Find out in advance all that you can about the topics to be discussed at the meeting. If there is an agenda (see page 517), study each item carefully and learn more about those topics you are not familiar with. For example, if the subject of personnel evaluation is to be discussed, be sure that you know what the current company procedures are for evaluating personnel and the advantages and disadvantages of these procedures. You may wish to refer to books or articles dealing with this topic or to examine company forms that are currently in use. In addition, it is often useful to get the opinions of knowledgeable people who will not be present at the meeting. If there is to be a discussion of a revision of the evaluation form, study the form thoughtfully, try it out, and ask various people who use the form what they like and do not like about it.

Being prepared also means coming to a meeting with a set of well-founded opinions. Opinions that are worth listening to in a business meeting are the ones backed up by facts. People are often opposed to a new idea merely because they don't know enough about it. The old saying, "You're down on what you're not up on," applies to participation in a meeting. Make certain that this saying never applies to you.

Express Opinions Tactfully

When someone asks you for your opinion or when you volunteer an opinion, be tactful in expressing yourself. Often, opposing points of view can cause strong disagreement. No matter how strongly you may feel that you are right and that the other person is wrong, your chances of winning that person's support are no better than your tactfulness in presenting your views. For example, don't say, "You're wrong, and here's why." Instead, you might say, "Your point of view certainly has merit, Frank, but I have doubts because . . ." Never tell someone that he or she is wrong—*wrong* is a strong term, and your right to use it requires indisputable evidence. In selling your point of view, the "Yes, but . . ." technique is effective; that is, acknowledge the other person's point of view and show your respect for it. Then present your own ideas. For example, "Yes, I agree that the solution seems simple and that your idea represents one way to approach the problem, but..."

In expressing yourself, separate facts from opinions. Label as facts only those statements for which you have solid evidence. Opinions should be signaled by such words as "it seems to me," "as I understand it," or "in my opinion."

Make Positive Contributions

One of the most unwelcome participants in a group meeting is the person who thinks "No." This person's primary mission seems to be that of killing the ideas and proposals that others voice. Such a participant seldom presents a positive idea but is always quick to say of someone else's idea, "That won't work."

Most meetings are held for the purpose of solving problems, and problems cannot be solved in a negative atmosphere. Participants must be willing to approach a problem with the attitude that the only way to solve it is to present as many ideas as possible. No one immediately vetoes an idea someone else has presented; instead, each person tries to see the idea's merits and to enlarge upon the idea's possibilities, no matter how weak it may seem at first. To smother ideas before they are fully aired is not only rude but also extremely disheartening to those who are genuinely trying to reach intelligent decisions.

Be Courteous

The ideal meeting is one in which everyone participates freely. The overaggressive speaker who monopolizes the discussion will discourage the participation of others. Even though you may be more knowledgeable about the topic than anyone else in the group, you should never display your knowledge in an offensive, overbearing manner. You may win the skirmish and lose the battle—the too-sure, know-it-all person often does.

More victories have been won in group discussion by modesty and tact than will ever be achieved by overaggressiveness. Don't jump in while others are speaking; wait your turn patiently. Show interest in what others are saying. You will win more friends by listening and taking notes on remarks by others than by interrupting their remarks—regardless of how inane the remarks may seem to you. Acknowledge that others may have as much information as you have or perhaps even more.

Courteous group members do not (1) resort to sarcasm when they disagree with someone, (2) interrupt the person who is talking, (3) fidget, (4) gaze into space, or (5) carry on side conversations with other members of the group while someone else has the floor.

Keep Remarks Concise and Pertinent

Some participants in a meeting take a roundabout route to reach the point they want to make. They ramble endlessly. If you have something to say, get to your point quickly. Meetings become boring and unproductive mainly because some participants insist on relating personal preferences, experiences, and opinions that have little or no bearing on the discussion at hand.

Take Notes

It is a good idea to develop the habit of taking notes at meetings because the act of taking careful notes (1) keeps you alert, (2) tells speakers that you consider their remarks are worth remembering, and (3) provides a valuable reference source both during and after the meeting. Take notes not only on what the speaker is saying but also on what *you* want to say when it is your turn to speak. Jot down your key remarks in advance so that your comments are well organized and complete.

LEADING GROUP DISCUSSIONS

The success or failure of a group meeting is very often determined by the leader of the group. By skillful direction, the leader can turn an ordinary meeting into an extremely profitable experience for each participant. Without good leadership, the most promising meeting can result in a waste of time for everyone concerned. To become a good discussion leader, follow the suggestions outlined here.

Prepare Thoroughly

A successful meeting or conference requires that the leader prepare thoroughly far enough in advance to make all the necessary arrangements and to contend with any problems that may arise. The discussion leader needs to know the time the meeting is to begin, the length of the meeting, and the place in which it is to be held. The leader also needs to know the names of those who are to attend and the objectives that should be accomplished at the meeting. Notification of a meeting of a standing committee usually takes the form of an agenda (a list of the topics to be discussed and the names of the persons who are to lead the discussion). The agenda should be sent as far in advance of the meeting as possible to allow the participants ample time to prepare for their role in the meeting. For a monthly meeting, the agenda should be sent at least a week ahead of the meeting date. For a weekly meeting, the agenda should be received a day or two prior to the meeting. The sample agenda on page 517 shows the topics in the order in which they will be discussed. Under new items, those that are most important should be listed first in the event that there is not sufficient time to discuss them all.

Prepare the Meeting Facilities

All the arrangements for the meeting facilities must be planned in advance so that the room, the furniture, and the equipment to be used are available and properly set up in time for the meeting. It is the responsibility of the group leader to see that the job is

```
                    ANCET REAL ESTATE COMPANY

                 Meeting of Regional Sales Managers

                      May 15, 19--, 9:00 a.m.
                        at State Street Office


                              AGENDA

        1.  Call to order by Chairperson Mendoza.

        2.  Approval of the minutes of the last meeting.

        3.  Approval of the agenda.

        4.  Announcements.

        5.  Unfinished Business:

                A.  Report of the employee welfare committee.

                B.  Continuation of discussion of hiring problems.

        6.  New Business:

                A.  Recommendations for new office locations.

                B.  Change in advertising policies.

                C.  Proposals for new property listings.

                D.  Other items.

        7.  Adjournment.
```

An agenda lists the topics to be discussed at an upcoming meeting. Under "New Business," this agenda lists the most important items first.

done properly and on time. Otherwise, there may be an insufficient number of chairs, there may be no ashtrays (or overflowing ashtrays), the room may be poorly ventilated, the audiovisual facilities may not be available, refreshments may not arrive in time for the break, and so on.

In order to make certain that the meeting starts promptly, it is best to check at least forty-five minutes prior to the meeting that everything in the meeting room is in order. This prior checking, such as making sure that audiovisual equipment is on hand and is in working order, makes it possible to take care of any problems before the meeting begins. If an operator for projection equipment is required, the meeting date should be confirmed the day before the meeting. Also, make certain that the film is available, that there is an electrical outlet, and that the extension cord is long enough. Problems can be more easily resolved if they are discovered sufficiently in advance of the meeting.

Arrive Early

The chairperson of the meeting should be at the meeting place a few minutes early to check the facilities and to set an example for the others. Arriving early also gives the leader a chance to distribute the agenda. (Even though everyone has received an advance copy of the agenda, not everyone will remember to bring it to the meeting.) The leader or the leader's secretary should also bring along a few extra pencils and pads (there will be some participants who will have neither) and extra copies of reports or other papers to be discussed, even though copies may have been distributed in advance.

Establish a Businesslike Atmosphere

The chairperson sets the tone of the meeting. If the leader begins late or is apathetic about getting the proceedings under way, the participants are likely to lose whatever enthusiasm they may have had when they entered the room. Generally it is best to start a meeting precisely at the hour for which it is scheduled, even though there probably will be latecomers. If the members of a group realize that the meeting will start without them, they are likely to make an effort to be punctual.

Guide the Discussion

The good leader talks as little as possible and draws out the opinions of the participants. Unfortunately, some people think that *leader* and *talker* are synonymous terms when it comes to running a meeting. The skillful leader brings out each participant's best thinking. The leader's function is not to show how much he or she knows but to steer the discussion in the proper direction. The experienced leader knows that the greater the participation—that is, the more minds at work on a problem—the better the chances are of accomplishing the objective of the meeting.

Encourage Participation

Everyone invited to a meeting should be able to make some contribution to the discussion. However, some people are shy and will not say anything unless they are encouraged to speak. Call on these people in a manner that will offer them encouragement; for example, "Lillian, you have had a lot of experience in advertising. What do you think of Carl's layout for next week's ad?" or "Frank, we would be interested in having the benefit of your experience in the word processing center. Do you think we need to change the facilities to make for a more conducive environment?"

A leader encourages positive participation by saying something complimentary after a speaker has made a worthwhile contribution; for example, "Thank you, Isaac, for that very time-saving suggestion," or "That's an excellent idea, Ms. Goldberg. Could you tell us a little more about how you think that plan will function?" Such types of comments are effective when they are obviously sincere. Negative comments, on the other hand, discourage participation and should, therefore, be kept to a minimum and be presented so tactfully that they do not discourage others from making suggestions. "That idea would work beautifully if. . ."

Discourage Excessive Talkers

In any group there will always be one or two people who want to do all the talking. Certainly they have a right to be heard, but unless they are listed on the agenda as the principal contributors, they should not be permitted to monopolize the discussion. Only a strong leader can prevent a loudmouth from taking over the meeting. The chairperson should be tactful but firm. "That's very interesting, Joe, but I think we ought to hear from Eileen," or "Let's get back to you a little later, Irene. I think we would all be interested in having as many points of view as we can get."

Keep the Discussion Pertinent

Meetings sometimes tend to get off the track, and if the chairperson permits the discussion to wander for too long, the principal problems to be resolved at the meeting will be bypassed entirely. All too often, a subject comes up that is of genuine personal interest to all those present at the meeting but has little or no bearing on the main topic. People just naturally like to tell about their personal experiences, likes and dislikes, and amusing anecdotes. These digressions should be permitted now and then because they lighten the discussion; we can't be completely serious all the time. However, when side issues begin to waste valuable time, they must be cut off tactfully by the leader and the discussion must be brought back on track. "That certainly was an interesting experience, Len, but let's get back to our discussion of the employees' handbook. Terry, what changes do you think are necessary in the section on retirement?" Usually you can keep the discussion on the track without being rude to anyone, but bluntness is sometimes necessary as a last resort. "Jerry, time is getting away from us, and we want to avoid having to call another meeting to settle this problem. Do you have any specific solutions?"

Summarize Periodically

It is neither necessary nor desirable for the chairperson of a group discussion to evaluate everyone's remarks as soon as they are presented. The group leader should al-

INTEROFFICE MEMORANDUM

To   Mrs. Lola Peterson   From   Karl Seltzer

Subject   Retirement Section of   Date   June 13, 19--
          Employees' Handbook

This memorandum is to remind you that at the meeting yesterday of
the Handbook Revision Committee you volunteered to conduct a survey of all retired employees to determine their suggestions for
changes in the retirement program.

You also indicated you would set up a subcommittee to work on the
revision of this section of our handbook and would report to the
parent body at its July 16 meeting any suggestions for changes
that result from your survey and the discussion at your subcommittee meeting.

Thank you, Lola, for agreeing to assist in this most worthwhile
project.

                                        KS

After a meeting, the chairperson should remind each person of his or her assignment.

ways listen attentively but does not need to comment except, perhaps, to stimulate
further discussion. "Excellent, Fred. That's an interesting point of view. I gather that
you think this plan will be more effective than the one we have been following. Is that a
correct assumption?" Above all, the discussion leader does not tear down ideas or

argue with participants; doing so will only discourage others in the group from expressing themselves. Since the leader of the meeting is only one member of the group, it is usually poor practice to judge every idea expressed instead of letting other members of the group participate.

From time to time, the chairperson should summarize the major points that have been presented. "We all seem to agree that we should not add more branch stores at the present time. Instead, you feel we should enlarge the existing branches and increase our advertising budget. Is that correct? Well, let's discuss which branches should be enlarged and how we should make use of an increased advertising budget. Nora, do you have any suggestions regarding which branch stores should be enlarged?"

Know How to Conclude

If the chairperson has prepared the agenda carefully and has conducted the meeting efficiently, the meeting should end fairly close to the time scheduled for adjournment. If the discussion seems likely to extend beyond the closing hour and it is important to continue, get the approval of the group; for example, "Ladies and gentlemen, it is five minutes of twelve, and it looks as though we won't get out of here by noon. Shall we continue the discussion, or would you rather schedule another meeting for this afternoon?"

After the meeting, the secretary should write up the minutes and distribute them as soon as possible. Memorandums should be written to those who are assigned special responsibilities at the meeting. Such a memorandum is illustrated on page 520.

Know How to Conduct Formal Meetings

Many groups conduct their meetings on a formal basis, following parliamentary rules. If you are elected to office in such a group, you should read *Robert's Rules of Order*, the standard guide to parliamentary procedure.

COMMUNICATION PROJECTS

Practical Application
A. Evaluate the following statements made by group discussion leaders. If the statement is not an appropriate one, what should have been said?
1. "I don't think that idea would work."
2. "We'd like to hear more about the plan."
3. "Jack, what has been your experience with this problem?"

B. Prepare an interoffice memorandum to all supervisors, calling a meeting at which you and they will discuss the orientation program for all new employees. You want the supervisors to evaluate the present program, to talk with new employees hired since January 1 of this year, and to do some research regarding orientation programs used in other local businesses. These aspects will be discussed at the meeting, and the supervisors will draw up a revised program that will be put into effect September 1. Supply any other information you feel would be helpful in preparing for this meeting.

C. Evaluate your ability to conduct a meeting in terms of your previous experience, if any, and the qualities necessary for an effective leader of group discussions.

D. How does one establish a businesslike atmosphere at a meeting?

E. Make a list of the steps you would take to prepare a meeting room for an all-day discussion.

F. Prepare an agenda for an ad hoc committee for which you are to act as chairperson. Select a discussion topic of your own choice. Then develop a list of topics concerned with phases of this subject and assign them to individuals in your class.

G. At a meeting of the Fiftieth Anniversary Celebration Committee of the Foster Publishing Company, Arnold Pierce was given the responsibility of gathering information regarding facilities for Family Picnic Day and the Founder's Dinner-Dance. Write a follow-up memorandum to Mr. Pierce to remind him of the assignment. Supply all the details for the memorandum.

Editing Practice

Applied Psychology   The wording of the following letter excerpts does nothing to cement good human relations. Revise the sentences.

1. We are unable to accept your application for credit because investigation reveals that you are a "poor payer."
2. We have gone to a great deal of trouble to get the merchandise to you on the date you requested.
3. We fail to understand why you say the shade does not match the lamp.
4. You made an error of $15 in the total of our last statement.
5. You claim that you mailed your check to us on March 15, but we have not received it yet.

Case Problem

The Poor Chairperson   As chairperson of the social committee, Lucille was greatly discouraged after the first meeting. She couldn't understand why so many committee members were late. Hadn't she telephoned all the members that very morning to ask if they could meet at 2 p.m.? She waited until 2:30 before enough members were there to start the meeting. When she asked the group what social activities they wanted to discuss, she got little response. Those ideas suggested did not seem practical to Lucille, and she quickly discouraged them. The meeting adjourned at 4 p.m. with nothing decided other than that another meeting would be called soon. What went wrong with Lucille's meeting?

How much speech making you are likely to do as a business employee depends upon many factors: the kind of position you hold, the degree of responsibility that comes with your position, and your effectiveness as a speaker. For many business executives, the ability to speak effectively before groups may be an important requirement of that position. For example, the responsible business executive may be expected to represent the company before professional organizations and before many different civic, religious, and educational groups. These outside speaking duties are beyond those duties involved in speaking to members of one's own company at employee meetings or in making presentations at board meetings or at stockholders' meetings.

However, even those who are not top executives often are called upon to participate in activities involving speeches before either large or small groups—introducing a speaker, explaining a new company policy to a group of employees, greeting a group of visitors, or presenting an award at a meeting of company employees and their families.

A speech, like a letter, reflects an image of the company that employs the speaker. An effective speech, like an effective letter, should convey a message clearly and convincingly and, at the same time, build an image of goodwill. And since nearly everyone is called upon at one time or another to "say a few words" to an audience, every business employee should be prepared to represent his or her company in a way that will reflect favorably on the company.

In order to deliver an effective speech—whether it is a two-minute introduction, a five-minute commentary, or an hour's discourse—the first step the speaker should take is to plan the speech carefully. Planning involves previewing the speaking assignment, gathering and organizing the material, outlining the speech, and rehearsing the presentation.

PREVIEWING THE SPEAKING ASSIGNMENT

Regardless of whether the speech topic has been selected for the speaker or whether the topic is the speaker's own choice, every speaker must answer three basic questions before gathering and organizing material: (1) What is the purpose of the speech? (2) To whom is the speech to be given? (3) How much time is allowed for the speech?

What Is the Purpose of the Speech?

Every speech should have a very specific purpose—to *explain* something, such as a new company policy; to *describe* something, such as the features of a new product or the steps in a new procedure; or to *report* on something, such as the results of a market survey. The principal goal of a speech may be to present a point of view, to inspire, to inform, or to win support for a proposal. Whatever the purpose, every speech must be organized to fit its purpose.

Assume that you have been asked to tell the company sales representatives about the sales promotion plan for your new slim-line pocket calculator. If your talk is entitled "Sales Promotion for the Slim-Line Pocket Calculator," obviously, you are not expected to dwell on how the product is made or how much it costs to transport the raw materials to the factory. The purpose of the talk is to tell the sales representatives how the company plans to promote the sale of the product through advertising and any other promotional efforts the company plans to make. Your remarks should center on these activities and convince the sales representatives that they will receive sufficient support to help make the selling job easier.

To Whom Is the Speech to Be Given?

The effective speaker finds out as much as possible about the audience before gathering material for the speech. If you are to discuss word processing techniques before a group of executives, your emphasis will be quite different from the one you would use in discussing the same topic with a group of secretaries. If your speech is one of several that are to be given, you should inquire about the rest of the program so that you can put your topic in perspective with the others. You should find out as much as you can about the interests, occupations, and age level of the audience. In addition, it is helpful to know the expected audience size and the general background of the people. The program chairperson can supply this and other useful information. With this help, you can find out what the audience already knows about the subject and what the audience expects to learn from the presentation. With such knowledge at hand, you can avoid rehashing facts already known and can give particular emphasis to areas of most interest to the audience.

How Much Time Is Allowed for the Speech?

The speaker must know precisely how much time is allowed for the speech. Obviously, you should not try to crowd into thirty minutes a topic that requires an hour. Therefore, once you know the amount of time you have been allotted, you should plan your speech so it can be adequately presented in this time period.

The clever speaker, when assigned forty-five minutes, takes only thirty-five or forty minutes. This leeway makes certain that the speech will not run overtime and, if there are five or ten minutes left, the time may be used to answer questions from the audience.

If you have been assigned a very broad topic like "Word Processing," you should select the phase of the subject that best fits the audience. For example, your speech may deal with "Improved Dictation Methods" for an audience composed of executives, or it may deal with "How to Proofread Efficiently" for an audience composed of typists who work in word processing centers.

GATHERING AND ORGANIZING DATA

There is no substitute for preparation. Even the most gifted speakers always prepare carefully beforehand, whether they are to speak for only a few minutes or for an hour. If your topic is one that you can prepare for by reading, read as widely as possible. Find a good library that has up-to-date magazines, books, and bulletins on your topic, and get as many points of view as you can. Check and double-check on facts—especially statistical information. Take notes—more than you can possibly use in your speech. Put the notes on cards and start a new card for each new subject or source. Identify on the card the source of your information in case you want to refer to it later.

The advantage of writing notes on cards is that it is easy to discard unwanted material and to arrange and rearrange the remaining material in the best order for the preparation of your speech outline. In fact, if your notes are prepared well, your final arrangement of the cards will represent an outline.

For many topics, valuable and interesting information can be obtained from talking with people who are involved in the subject of your speech. For example, if you are going to speak on "Requirements for Success in Accounting," you might talk with a number of successful accountants to determine what they feel led to their success in the profession. Take notes on your findings, and use this information in preparing your speech. First-hand information makes any presentation more interesting.

OUTLINING AND ORGANIZING THE SPEECH

After selecting the topic and gathering and organizing the data, the speaker is ready to begin outlining the speech. The following is a guide to preparing an outline:

1. Speech Title—   Time Allotted—
2. Purpose of Speech—
3. Introduction (arouse interest and give purpose)—
4. Body of Speech—Principal ideas to support purpose
   a. Principal idea No. 1
      Supporting information and material
   b. Principal idea No. 2
      Supporting information and material
   c. Principal idea No. 3
      Supporting information and material
5. Conclusion
   a. Summary of principal ideas
   b. Plea for action (if applicable)

The Introduction

The introductory remarks should be brief and should arouse the interest of the audience in the speaker and in the subject. Various methods of introducing the talk may be used; for example:

1. A direct statement of the subject and of the importance of that subject to each member of the audience.

> The title I have selected for my talk to you is "The Computer and You—Assistant or Replacement?" Each of you has a stake in the computer revolution because your future as an accountant may depend upon how well you understand the function of the computer in the operation of your business.

2. An indirect opening that is of vital interest to the audience, with a statement connecting the subject with this interest.

> Tomorrow, your job may be abolished or changed so drastically that you won't recognize it. Why? Because so many of the things that you are now doing by hand can be done much more efficiently by computer.

3. A striking example or comparison that leads up to the purpose or subject of the speech.

> Recently, a well-known computer expert compared the costs of computers to the costs of automobiles. She said that if in the last 15 years the cost of automobiles had decreased proportionally to the cost of computers, today a Rolls Royce would sell for about two dollars!

4. A strong quotation relating to the subject.

> "Computer technology must be understood by every certified professional accountant, whether or not he or she makes first-hand use of the computer," declared A. E. Troy, Chief Examiner of the Professional Accountancy Board of Examiners.

5. Important statistics related to the subject.

> A recent survey revealed that more than two hundred office workers were replaced by some type of machine in 198–.

6. A brief anecdote.

> Last week my secretary handed me a clipping from a local newspaper. It was about experiments that are now being made with a "machine stenographer." The manufacturers hope to perfect it so that the dictator merely dictates into the machine, and the letter comes out all transcribed, ready for mailing. My secretary never once thought about being replaced by such a machine but was worried only about whether it could straighten out the grammar and punctuation that I insist on mangling!

The Body of the Speech

Once audience interest is aroused, you are ready to provide the principal ideas that will support the purpose you have established for your speech. How many ideas you will present and develop will depend wholly upon the amount of time you have been allotted for the speech. It is better to develop each idea fully enough to be convincing than to present many ideas that are weakly developed and therefore not fully accepted or understood by the audience.

How is an idea communicated? First, it must be stated in a brief but clear and interesting way. Then the idea should be developed by explanation and illustration. Finally, the idea should be summarized.

Among the techniques available to the speaker for developing ideas are those in the following list. Which techniques the speaker selects will depend upon the nature of the data to be presented.

Giving examples.
Making comparisons.
Quoting statistics.
Quoting testimony of a recognized authority.
Repeating the idea in different words.
Defining terms used in stating the idea.
Using descriptive language that makes the listener "see" the situation.
Using narration to relate a story connected with the idea.
Using audio and/or visual aids.

Here is an example of how one idea used in a speech might be communicated, following several of the suggestions that have been presented. Suppose a speech is intended to convince an audience of business executives that their companies should purchase their own small airplanes for business use.

Principal Idea: A business saves both time and money by owning its own airplane.

Development: 1. Tell the story of two business firms in the same city whose executives frequently travel by air from their place of business to cities about 200 to 300 miles away. One executive used the local airline service and had to spend two nights in a hotel away from home to complete the business transaction. The other executive had her own plane and was able to return home the same day as she left.

2. Show on a comparative chart the cost of using public air transportation over a one-year period as compared with the cost of using one's own plane for the same period of time and covering about the same total mileage.

3. Give several examples of travel time between your city and another heavily visited city nearby, making comparisons in time using public airline service and one's own private plane.

4. Quote executives of leading companies in your area who own their own planes and who are convinced that the convenience, as well as the saving of time and money, makes it essential that every company conducting business hundreds of miles away have its own plane.

Audiovisual Materials Many speakers use such audiovisual materials as charts, slides, filmstrips, overhead projectors (transparencies), and motion pictures to enrich their presentations. Before deciding to use a visual aid, be certain that you have determined whether or not the material will be visible to the entire audience. The size of the audience and the type of room in which you make your presentation will be the principal determinants. Good visual aids can make your presentation more interesting by providing a change of pace. Talks dealing with figures can be made clearer and much more effective by using well-prepared charts and diagrams. If the situation is such, however, that mechanical means would prove ineffective, then consider the possibility of using duplicated handout materials.

Motion pictures should be previewed to determine whether they are appropriate. Above all, facilities and equipment should be checked prior to the presentation so that there will be no delays after the talk has started.

The Conclusion

The conclusion of a speech should be brief and to the point. A summary of the major points made in the speech and a plea for action, if applicable, are all that is needed. The summary may repeat key words or expressions already used or may restate the principal ideas in different words. Sometimes an example, a comparison, or an effective quotation serves as an appropriate summary. In any case, the final statement should tell the listeners very specifically what they should do, believe, or understand as a result of the presentation.

PRACTICING THE SPEECH

The inexperienced speaker should write out the entire speech from the outline developed, *not* for the purpose of reading the speech but for refining expressions, improving the choice of words, and timing the presentation. By recording this preliminary speech and then playing it back, the speaker can determine how the words will sound to the audience. Appropriate changes can then be made.

After you have refined the speech, have read it through several times, and have timed the reading, you should prepare an outline on index cards. This outline should include phrases, quotations, and statistics. If possible, it should be prepared in large, clear handwriting or in jumbo typewriter type so that you can refer to the notes casually from a distance of two or three feet. Supplementary materials should be keyed into the outline in some way (underlined, solid capitals, or color) that will make them stand out.

Using the final outline, you should practice delivering your speech and should try to anticipate the conditions of the actual talk. A beginning speaker often finds the following practice suggestions helpful. Stand erect—before a mirror if possible—and imagine your audience before you. Watch your posture, facial expressions, and gestures as you deliver the speech. If you can practice before an audience of family or friends who will be sympathetic but frank in their analysis, so much the better. If you can record your presentation, you will be able to hear how clearly you speak and to judge the overall effectiveness of your presentation.

DELIVERING YOUR SPEECH

Though *what* you say in your speech is extremely important, *how* you say it is equally important. The best talk ever written can put an audience to sleep if it is poorly delivered. On the other hand, an average speech can bring an audience to its feet if the speaker is poised, dynamic, and persuasive. To deliver a speech effectively, you must possess the following important characteristics: confidence in your ability to deliver an effective message, a pleasing personal appearance, and good stage presence and delivery.

Confidence

"I don't have a knack for public speaking." "Speakers are born, not made." "I'll make a fool of myself if I try to give a speech." "I'll get stage fright and forget everything I'm supposed to say." These are typical reactions of a novice speaker. If you believe any of these statements, then you, like so many other people, underestimate yourself. You're better than you think!

When you are talking to an audience, pretend that you are carrying on a face-to-face conversation with just one person. Remember that the audience is just as eager for you to perform well as you are to do so. Don't be upset if you are nervous—even experienced speakers and actors are! Feeling nervous is a result of anxiety about doing a good job, and most authorities feel that a little stage fright provides needed tension. However, try not to show the audience any signs of your nervousness.

One way to develop confidence is to make sure that the conditions under which you are going to speak are as favorable as you can make them. Try to arrive fifteen or twenty minutes before you are scheduled to speak. If you speak best standing behind a lectern—and most people do—ask your host to provide one. Even an improvised lectern, such as a cardboard box covered with a cloth and set on a table, is better than no lectern at all. If possible, get the feel beforehand of the space you are going to occupy when you do address the group. Know in advance how you will approach the podium. If you think your approach will be awkward for you or for others on the stage or distracting to the audience, ask your host to change the arrangement. Check the ventilation, the lighting, the public address system, and the seating arrangement. In short, make all the advance preparations you can to assure a feeling of familiarity with your surroundings. This is another big step in building confidence.

Appearance

One of the most important elements that will contribute to your confidence as a speaker is your appearance. If you can eliminate any concern about how you look to the audience, then you can concentrate on other aspects of your presentation. In preparing for your speech, spend a little extra time on personal grooming and the selection of clothing to assure yourself that your appearance will be as good as it can be. Clothing should be freshly cleaned and pressed, and shoes should be polished and in good repair.

Special advice to women speakers:

> Choose jewelry that is tasteful and that will not be distracting. Above all avoid jewelry that makes a distracting jangling noise when you move your hands and arms.
>
> Choose makeup suitable to your appearance, and apply it skillfully.
>
> Although a touch of bright color is appropriate—even desirable—be careful not to overwhelm your audience with bizarre color combinations or dazzling prints or stripes. You want the audience's attention on what you are saying—not on what you are wearing.

Special advice to men speakers:

> Wear a dress shirt and appropriate tie. Make certain that the style and color are currently acceptable.
>
> At least one button of the suit coat should be fastened, whether or not a vest is worn.
>
> Because in most cases the speaker is seated before the audience while waiting to be introduced, wear long socks, even if you do not ordinarily wear them, so that at no time are bare shins visible.
>
> Don't be too conservative with the necktie you choose—some experts recommend bright flecks of color. Make sure that your socks harmonize with your suit.

Knowing that you are immaculately and tastefully groomed builds confidence in yourself and establishes the audience's confidence in you.

Good Stage Presence and Delivery

Speak Out   You have a responsibility to make sure that you are heard by each person in the audience. Any person who can't hear will become uninterested, bored, and annoyed. If possible, before you deliver a speech, check the volume of your voice in the room where you will speak.

Keep your chin up when speaking so that your words will be directed out to the audience rather than down to the floor. Vary the pitch of your voice so that the audience is not lulled to sleep by a monotone. When you want to emphasize a point, raise your voice; when you wish to stir emotions, drop your voice so that it is barely audible to the audience. Either extreme of tone, of course, will lose its desired effect if prolonged.

Be Poised   If you have stage fright, take a deep breath before you begin to speak; this will relax your vocal cords. Stand with your weight distributed evenly on both feet, and don't shift from one foot to the other excessively. Don't stand too stiffly or too leisurely—appear alert but at ease. If your listeners think that *you* are comfortable, then they are more likely to be comfortable.

Reveal Awareness of the Audience   An effective speaker must be aware of the audience at all times, not only in selecting and preparing the topic but also in giving the speech. This audience awareness must be transmitted in some way to the listeners. They respond much more favorably when the speaker talks directly to them or smiles at them occasionally. The speaker who looks at the ceiling, at notes, or into space throughout much of the speech, on the other hand, quickly loses rapport with the audience.

As you speak, look slowly back and forth over the entire audience, and pause here and there to "take in" a particular segment of the crowd. Smile frequently. Train yourself to watch the audience carefully and to be sensitive to its changing moods. If, as you are talking, you see blank or uninterested expressions on the faces of your listeners, you will know that your talk is dragging and that the audience has tuned you out. This situation may call for an amusing story, a personal anecdote, or merely a change in the pitch of your voice. If you are using visual aids, you might direct the audience's attention to a chart or other illustration when the talk seems to pall.

If your audience seems tired because the hour is late or too many speakers have preceded you, be quick to sense its boredom. If you aren't sure you can reawaken its interest with a sparkling performance, cut your talk to the bare essentials. Usually it is better to omit a portion of your speech than to run the risk of boring an already weary audience. The audience will be grateful to you.

Avoid Objectionable Mannerisms A good speaker avoids objectionable mannerisms. When you talk, for example, do you toy with an object such as a paper clip, rubber band, or watch? Do you clear your throat, wet your lips, or remove your eyeglasses frequently? Do you punctuate your remarks frequently with an "uh," "ya know," "okay," or "anda"? Do you have pet expressions or slang that you overuse? If you are not aware that you have any such mannerisms, ask some of your friends to listen to a rehearsal and to criticize. A speaker who has even one annoying habit cannot give a completely successful talk, for mannerisms distract an audience.

Don't Read or Memorize Never recite your speech from memory or read it to the audience. Only a gifted actor or actress can make a memorized speech sound natural, and nothing is more boring to an audience than a singsong recitation. In addition, if you memorize your speech, you may become so flustered when you forget a line that you will find it difficult to continue. A memorized speech often does not follow a logical order because a speaker has omitted something important or has mixed up the parts.

Reading a speech so that the ideas sound convincing is also difficult. If you try to read your speech, you will lose eye contact with your audience every time you refer to your notes.

Instead of reciting or reading your speech, become sufficiently familiar with your material so that all you need is a brief outline with key words and phrases to make your speech flow in logical sequence. Use a conversational tone. Imagine that you are conversing with your audience, not giving an oration. Your voice should reflect the warm, easy tone that you would use if you were talking to a group of very good friends.

Use Notes Most speakers—even the most experienced—rely on notes to guide them in their presentations. There is nothing wrong with using notes. It is a greater crime for a speaker to dispense with notes and to give a rambling, disorganized speech than to use notes and to present an organized speech. Even if the notes are not actually used, having them on hand gives you confidence because you know you have something to fall back on if you should have a temporary lapse of memory.

Look at your notes only when absolutely necessary, and return your attention quickly to your audience after each glance at your notes. Keep your notes out of sight as much as possible while you are giving your talk, and turn the pages or cards as inconspicuously as you can. An audience is quickly discouraged by a large, slowly dwindling stack of notes.

Plan Distribution of Material Often the speaker will have duplicated material to distribute to the audience. As a general rule, such material should not be distributed at the beginning of a speech. If it is, the audience will be too busy examining the "giveaway" to pay attention to the speaker. The important points of a speech should be made before any material is distributed to the audience.

Use Stories and Anecdotes Discreetly Nearly every speech of any length is brightened considerably by touches of humor and by human-interest narratives. Of course, such stories should not dominate the speech. Observe the following rules in using humor and human-interest stories:

1. Make sure they are relevant. Use stories and jokes that are related to the topic, that add interest to the subject, or that illustrate a particular point.
2. Make sure they have a punch line. The story you tell should have a point. Before telling a joke to an audience, test it first on friends. Many stories and jokes fall flat because they are too subtle for a mass audience, because they are told poorly, or because they have weak punch lines.
3. Make sure they are in good taste. You should make certain that any story or joke you tell will not offend or embarrass the audience. Avoid risqué stories or jokes that make fun of physical handicaps, religious convictions, or ethnic groups.
4. Make sure they are short. A story or joke that lasts more than a minute or two is likely to fall flat because the audience loses interest or forgets the details that lead up to the punch line. Only the most skillful storyteller can get by with longer tales. Rehearse stories carefully before delivering them, and time them to make sure that they are not too long.

INTRODUCING A SPEAKER

One of the most important speaking assignments is introducing a speaker. A good introduction sets the stage for the main address. If the introducer does an outstanding job, the main speaker's task is greatly simplified. In introducing a speaker, observe the following points.

Make the Introduction Brief

The audience has come to hear the speaker, not the person who is introducing the speaker. Therefore, keep the introduction short—not more than two or three minutes in length.

Set the Stage for the Speaker

Do some research on the speaker. Find out from the speaker's friends, associates, or secretary some personal traits or achievements that do not appear in the usual sources. A human-interest story about the speaker's hobby, family, or generosity will warm the audience. Although you should have complete details about the speaker's experience, education, and attainments, you do not need to use them all. An audience is quickly bored, and sometimes a speaker is embarrassed, by a straight biographical presentation, no matter how impressive the speaker's background is. Only the most significant dates, positions, and accomplishments should be given. You need only to convince the audience that the speaker is qualified to speak on the topic assigned, is worth knowing, and has something important to say.

Avoid Trite Openings

When you are introducing a speaker, avoid such trite expressions as "The speaker for this evening needs no introduction," "I give you Ms. Lily Roberts," or "Without further ado, I present Dr. Adam King."

Keep Your Eyes on the Audience

Do not turn away from the audience to face the speaker you are introducing—always face the audience and keep your eyes on them. Then, after you have made the introduction, wait until the speaker has reached the lectern before seating yourself.

End With the Name

Many successful toastmasters recommend that you not mention the speaker's name until the very end of the introduction. During the introduction itself refer only to "our speaker." Then, at the end of the introduction, say something like: "It is my pleasure to present Professor Anne Lincoln."

Closing Remarks

At the end of the speaker's remarks, someone on the platform or at the speaker's table should assume the responsibility for closing the meeting. If the speech was a particularly effective one, you may say with sincerity, "Thank you, Professor Lincoln, for your most enlightening and inspiring message. We are most appreciative. Ladies and gentlemen, the meeting is adjourned." On the other hand, if the speech has been average or even disappointing, as indicated by the audience reaction, you may close by merely saying, "Thank you, Mr. Jones, for giving us your ideas on how to improve office procedures. Thank you for coming to our meeting tonight, ladies and gentlemen, and good night."

Under no circumstances should you prolong the closing remarks. If the speech was a good one, there is nothing more you can contribute to its effectiveness. If the speech was a poor one, the audience is probably tired and is anxious to leave.

COMMUNICATION PROJECTS

Practical Application

A. List three topics on which you feel qualified to speak. For each topic, give two reasons you feel qualified to speak on this topic. Indicate one audiovisual aid that you might use in presenting each topic before a group. For each topic, suggest one attention-getting title for a twenty-minute speech.

B. Select one of the topics you listed in Practical Application A for a five- or six-minute presentation before the class. Prepare an outline for this speech, and follow the format suggested on page 525.

C. After your outline has been approved by the instructor, write your speech in full. Then read, refine, and time the speech. Finally, following the suggestions made in the text, make an outline of the speech on no more than four 5- by 3-inch index cards.

D. Suggest two ways that a beginning public speaker can overcome the common problems enumerated below:

1. Excessive verbalizing (using "uh," "ya know," "okay," "anda," and so on).
2. Nervousness.

E. You will be serving as master of ceremonies at your college convocation next month. The principal speaker will be the president of your college, whom you will introduce. Gather as much information as you can about the president's background and compose a unique introduction. You may supply any additional details about the speaker that you feel will add interest to the introduction.

F. Compose two different closing statements you might make after the president's speech.

G. Based upon your ultimate career goal, prepare an outline for a five-minute talk on "Why a Career in the Field of _____ Is a Wise Choice for the Eighties." Be prepared to give this talk to the class.

Editing Practice

The Editorial Supervisor   Edit and rewrite the following paragraph.

> Enclosed please find a copy of the minutes of the last meeting. I am also enclosing a check herewith in the amount of $150. Kindly acknowledge same to the writer due to the fact that often mail is lost. Please advise at an early date if their will be a change in rates due to the fact that you stated all costs will be increasing.

Case Problem

Playing Fair   Annie, a co-worker and friend, confides to you, "I don't think Ms. Gordon likes me. I was late twice this week and only fifteen minutes each time, but she warned me that if I'm late just one more time, she will deduct an hour's wages from my salary check." Your experience with Ms. Gordon (who is also your supervisor) has led you to believe that she has always been fair to the employees and that she was merely carrying out her responsibility in seeing that employees report to work on time. In discussing the matter with your friend, however, you don't want to appear to be an "apple polisher."

1. Do you think Ms. Gordon played fair with your co-worker?
2. What would you say to Annie?

CHAPTER 10

COMMUNICATING FOR CAREER SUCCESS

Your college education has prepared you with the appropriate skills and knowledge in a particular business field, such as accounting, secretarial work, marketing, or management. In addition, this course in communication and your mastery of the materials in this textbook have prepared you to handle the reading, writing, listening, and speaking requirements of any job in the business world. Among your first uses of these communication skills will be exploring the various sources of jobs.

SOURCES OF JOBS

When you are ready to obtain a position in your chosen field or to advance yourself within that field, how do you determine what jobs are available?

Family and Friends

Through members of your own family and from your own friends who are employed in business, you may find out what job opportunities are available in their firms. Businesses often feel that their own employees are good sources of job applicants for new positions. Therefore, when you are in the market for a job, check with members of your own family, their friends, and your own friends.

Newspaper Advertisements

The classified advertisement sections of newspapers are usually filled every day with announcements of job openings in many types of business positions. When you locate a position that sounds appealing to you and for which you meet the stated requirements, you should follow up on that advertisement to find out more about the available position. Your follow-up will either be in the form of a telephone call arranging for a personal interview or in the form of a letter of application accompanied by a résumé (see pages 542 and 544).

You may also use the classified advertisement section of a newspaper in another way. If you are seeking a position, you may advertise your availability in the "Situations Wanted" section of the newspaper. In preparing such an advertisement, you should clearly indicate the type of position you seek and briefly state the most important qualifications you possess. Above all, make it easy for employers to contact you. The following is an example of a "Situations Wanted" advertisement:

ADMINISTRATIVE ASSISTANT, dictation 140 wam, typing 65 wam, 6+ yrs. exper., supervise 3 employees, wd. proc. exper., wants position dwntn, 1100+ mo., 555-4366 after 5 p.m.

Interested employers will ask you to come for a personal interview or may request first that you write them a letter of application, with a résumé. Some employers will send you one of their application forms and will ask you to complete it and return it to them before they ask you to come in for a personal interview.

Employment Agencies

Most vocational educational institutions have a placement office in which they maintain files of student applicants. If your school has a placement office, you should complete an application form and supply a list of three references—people who know about your education, your personal character, and your business experience. The procedure for acquiring references is discussed on page 543.

In addition to school placement services, your state employment office may be a good source for jobs. Check your telephone directory for the state employment office near you; then call to find out the procedure for registering your name and to ask any questions that you may have.

Private employment agencies are numerous in most cities. They may place applicants in part-time as well as in full-time positions. For placing an applicant in a full-time position, the agency charges a fee, which varies according to the annual salary for each particular position. The fee may be paid by the applicant, or it may be paid by the employer. Many private agencies focus on only one area of employment—secretarial, accounting, editorial, production, and so on. Do some research to find out which agencies in your area specialize in your field of interest.

Direct Application

If you wish to work for a particular firm, you may apply for a position directly, either by calling in person at the firm's employment or personnel office (and completing an application form) or by sending a letter of application and a résumé. If your application makes a good impression and you possess the qualifications for a position the firm has available, you may then be called in for a personal interview.

USING YOUR COMMUNICATION SKILLS
TO ACQUIRE A JOB

You can readily see that you will use all your communication skills in seeking a position. Your communication skills will prove of even greater importance in actually acquiring the position you desire. The impression made by the application form you complete or by the letter of application and résumé you send will determine whether you reach the next step—the personal interview. Therefore, follow the advice in the remainder of this section regarding application forms, application letters, résumés, and other employment letters.

THE APPLICATION FORM

To complete an application form, you will need pertinent information (dates, names, addresses, and telephone numbers) regarding your educational background and experience. Therefore, whenever you apply for a job, carry with you a "pocket résumé." Don't rely on your memory. Also, carry one or two pens with you to complete the application. Complete the form neatly (use a typewriter if available), leaving no blank unanswered. Either write *n/a* (meaning "not applicable") or insert a dash (—) to indicate that you have not accidentally overlooked the item. Always reread your application before submitting it to make certain that it is correct and complete.

THE RÉSUMÉ

A résumé is an outline or summary of a job applicant's background and qualifications for a job. The way in which it is prepared and the information it supplies help determine whether the applicant will be requested to appear for a personal interview. Poorly prepared résumés usually wind up in the wastebasket. Therefore, your résumé should be prepared with great care and should emphasize your qualifications that best meet the requirements of the job you are seeking. During the interview, the résumé may serve as an agenda of topics to be discussed. Prepare a cover letter or letter of application to mail with your résumé. (The letter of application is discussed later in this section.)

Because you may apply for several job openings, it may not be practical to type an original copy of a résumé for each job. On the other hand, a carbon copy or a mimeographed or dittoed copy does not look professional and will give the reader a poor impression of you. However, you may inexpensively reproduce as many copies as you need through the offset process (which looks like professionally printed copies), using good-quality bond paper. In every city fast copy services are available that will print copies at a very reasonable cost. All you have to do is prepare the original copy exactly as you wish it reproduced. Suggestions are provided in the next paragraph.

Format

Although one résumé may vary from another in organization and layout, most are commonly divided into these sections: (1) work experience, (2) education, (3) personal information, and (4) references. Each section should be arranged to show clearly the qualifications of the applicant. The typing should be clean and even, the margins should be well balanced and uncrowded, and the headings should stand out. In choosing a format, try to select one that best fits the information you will include. In doing so, keep in mind these points:

1. State the facts; leave interpretation of these facts to the reader.
2. Be sure the facts are complete. For example, say *when* you were graduated and from *where*; *when* you resigned from a position and *why*.
3. Be neat and orderly; there should be no typographical errors, smudges, or other evidence of sloppy work. Within each section of your résumé, list the most recent information first.

4. Use brief phrases rather than complete sentences. For example, say "Took legal dictation" rather than "I took legal dictation each day from Mrs. Lopez, an attorney."
5. Limit the résumé to one page if possible. By doing so you will be forced to organize well and to list only important details.

An effective résumé is illustrated on page 542. Notice the prominence of the name, address, and telephone number of the applicant. Notice also the use of capitalized side headings and the use of underscoring to make certain aspects of the résumé stand out clearly.

Work Experience

Although the most important job qualification for a new graduate is educational preparation, do not underestimate the value of any kind of work experience, part-time or full-time. Almost everyone has held some type of job during vacations or on a part-time basis after school. Such jobs as paper carrier, soda jerk, filling-station attendant, filing clerk, gardener, or even baby-sitter are experiences that speak well for the young man or woman seeking a job. Such experiences should be reported; they demonstrate that the applicant is industrious, has initiative, and is dependable. If you worked to pay for your education, state this fact.

In organizing the work-experience section of your résumé, list the latest work experience first; that is, list work experience in reverse chronological order. For each job give inclusive dates, as well as the reason for leaving. For example, an applicant might write "Carter Shoe Store, 1976–1978, Assistant Manager; left for advancement." On the other hand, a lack of experience in the area of work for which you are applying should not be emphasized on the résumé. Rather, it might be better to take the positive approach and say, "While attending school, I had a number of part-time jobs, such as babysitting and soda-fountain clerking, to help earn my tuition." When you write your letter of application, you can then show how your knowledge *of* the job for which you are applying will more than compensate for your lack of experience *on* the job.

Education

Your educational background will count very heavily in job hunting. Make the most of your presentation by including the following facts. First, list any colleges you have attended and the dates of attendance. List any degrees or diplomas you have obtained. Detail here information such as the following:

Your major course of study (accounting, secretarial administration, advertising).

Special subjects you have had that will enhance your value as an employee. For example, a course in office management or business communication will be of interest to the prospective employer even though you are applying for a job in the accounting department. Be specific about subject titles. "Accounting IV" tells the employer nothing; "Corporation Accounting" is more specific.

```
                              Mary Lafredo
                              1789 Andrews Place
                              Louisville, KY 40201
                              Telephone (606) 555-3446


POSITION APPLIED FOR    Secretary, with opportunity for advancement to
                        Executive Secretary or Administrative Assistant.

EXPERIENCE

July, 1978, to          Canter Furniture Manufacturing Company, 17 Main
Present                 Street, Louisville, Kentucky--Secretary

                        Duties:  General secretarial work in sales depart-
                        ment, including taking and transcribing dictation;
                        accounting; filing; operating transcribing machine;
                        switchboard.

                        Reason for leaving:  Company going out of business

                        Starting salary:  $175        Present salary:  $225

October, 1976, to       St. Joseph's Hospital, 89 Liberty Avenue, Louisville,
June, 1978              Kentucky--Part-time Office Clerk

                        Duties:  Worked afternoons and evenings while
                        attending school.  Typing, filing, transcribing,
                        and switchboard; occasionally served as receptionist.

                        Salary:  $4.50 an hour

EDUCATION               Washington Community College, Louisville, Kentucky--
                        1976-1978.  Awarded Associate in Secretarial
                        Science degree.

                        Louisville High School, Louisville, Kentucky--1972-
                        1976.  Graduated with honors, business education
                        major.

PERSONAL                Birth date:  March 1, 1958
                        Birthplace:  Louisville, Kentucky
                        Hobbies:  Reading, tennis

REFERENCES              Mr. Harold Canter, President
(with permission)       Canter Furniture Manufacturing Company
                        17 Main Street
                        Louisville, Kentucky 40202
                        Telephone:  555-5400

                        Dr. Marvin Brody, Chairperson
                        Secretarial Administration Department
                        Washington Community College
                        Louisville, Kentucky 40203
                        Telephone:  555-1200
```

The format of à résumé helps to make it more effective. Note how the side headings and underscoring emphasize various aspects of this résumé.

Second, name the high school from which you were graduated and the date of graduation. If you took subjects that relate to your qualifications for the position, list them.

Stress leadership qualifications, extracurricular activities, and special honors. Business managers want employees with a wide range of interests; they want people with social poise and with leadership potential. Therefore, in listing both hobbies and interests, show that you have varied interests and that you have developed social graces and leadership qualities through extracurricular activities.

Personal Information

Federal law prohibits employers from asking the age, sex, marital status, religion, or race of applicants for positions. Therefore, whether you voluntarily supply such information is optional. If you consider any of this data an asset, you should provide the information on your résumé. To decide, try to view yourself through the eyes of an employer.

References

To avoid making your résumé too long, limit your references to three persons. You should be prepared to supply additional references should the prospective employer request them. If you have had little or no job experience, include the names of instructors who know your potential as a business employee. However, if you have had any kind of work experience, list former employers who can attest to the quality of your work. Always include the job title of each person you list. For instance, write "Ms. Arlene McFee, Office Manager," or "Dr. C. Jay Raymond, Professor of English," Give the complete address and telephone number of each person, as illustrated in the résumé on page 542.

If you are registered with a school placement office, you may not need to list your references on your résumé. Instead, you can assemble a reference file for the placement office and, at the bottom of your résumé, state "References on file with City College Placement Office are available upon request." In this way, a prospective employer need contact only one source for references. In addition, your references will not be bothered by telephone calls and letters; they will complete one letter for your file. Of course, you benefit too: you save space on your résumé, and you can easily keep an up-to-date reference file.

You should always obtain permission—in person, by telephone, or by letter—from each person whose name you use as a reference. Answering inquiries for prospective employers is a time-consuming task, and the people who agree to perform this task on your behalf do so because they have confidence in you, like you, and want you to succeed. Therefore, you owe them the courtesy of keeping them informed about your progress in getting a job.

THE LETTER OF APPLICATION

After you have prepared your résumé and you can see clearly how your qualifications fit the job you seek, you are in a good position to organize a cover letter or letter of application. The letter of application is your sales message. However, when the résumé accompanies the application letter, the letter should not merely repeat the data in the résumé. The function, then, of the letter is to highlight your most important qualifications to make the employer eager to learn more about you and grant you a

```
                                                  134 Post Street
                                                  Duluth, MN 55801
                                                  June 15, 19--


          Mr. William Isozaki, Editor
          Readers Review Magazine, Inc.
          1450 Park View Drive
          Duluth, MN 55802

          Dear Mr. Isozaki:

               I am applying for the position of administrative assistant that was
          called to my attention by the Placement Office of Tremona College.  I am
          confident that you will find my qualifications for this position merit
          your serious consideration.

               A summary of my qualifications is enclosed.  You will find that my
          college training provides an excellent foundation for the position for
          which I am applying.  I have always been interested in writing, and you
          will see from my résumé that I have concentrated heavily on English and
          the communication arts.  I have held editorial positions in both high
          school and college.  Furthermore, my skill in shorthand and typewriting
          has been used in these positions, as well as in part-time jobs I held
          while attending college.

               As an administrative assistant, I would welcome the opportunity to
          assist in an editorial capacity as well as to use my secretarial skills
          in performing my duties as your assistant.  I have had experience in both
          proofreading and layout.  My secretarial skills are well above average,
          and I enjoy working with others.  You will find that I am eager to learn
          and happiest when I keep busy.

               If you wish to telephone me to arrange a personal interview, you can
          reach me at 555-8700, Extension 34, between 3 and 5:30 p.m. any weekday.
          I can make arrangements to come to your office at your convenience.

                                             Sincerely yours,

                                             Gloria Hanson

                                             Gloria Hanson


          Enclosure
```

The letter of application is a personalized sales message.

personal interview. The résumé will help the employer determine whether you have the education and skills required for the job; the letter should convince the employer that you should get the job because you will be an asset to the company. In other words, the résumé is factual and rather formal; the application letter is a personalized sales message. Study the letter on this page and the following guidelines to help you in writing a letter of application.

Get to the Point Immediately

The first paragraph of the application letter should state the following:

Your intent to apply for the position.
The position for which you are applying.
The source from which you learned about the vacancy (if it is not a "blind" application).

There is no one "best" opening for a letter of application. The following opening sentences are suggestions that have been used successfully.

For Newspaper Ads

Please consider me an applicant for the position of management trainee, as advertised in the June 25 issue of the *Herald*.

I am applying for the position of accounting clerk that was advertised in the *Kansas City Star* on Sunday, May 15.

The position of assistant buyer, which you advertised in the April 1 issue of the *Examiner*, is one for which I feel well qualified. Please consider me an applicant for this position.

I am interested in the position of word processing supervisor advertised in the Help Wanted section of the June 12 *New Orleans Times*. I should like to apply for that position.

For Referrals

A mutual friend, Harold West, has suggested that I write you concerning a position as secretary in your company.

Your company has been recommended to me by Mrs. Anita Flores, the placement director of Royal College, as one with exceptional opportunities for those interested in advertising. I should like to inquire about a possible opening in the copy department.

Attorney Dorothy Friedman, a friend of my family, has told me of an opening as associate editor of your company magazine. May I be considered an applicant? (Ms. Friedman is a member of the law firm used by the employer.)

For "Blind" Applications

I believe my qualifications for a position as insurance adjuster will interest you. May I tell you what they are?

I have chosen your company's personnel department as one in which I would like to work. Therefore, I hope you will be interested in my skills and abilities.

Here are five reasons why I think you will be interested in interviewing me for the position of traffic supervisor in your company.

Tell Why You Should Be Considered

The second paragraph of your letter should convince the employer that you are a desirable candidate for the position referred to in the first paragraph. For example:

> Undoubtedly, Mr. Kaplan, you want a secretary who can take dictation and transcribe rapidly and accurately, a secretary who has a thorough grasp of secretarial procedures—filing, telephone duties, letter writing, and mail routines. My training at Atlantic College (detailed on the enclosed résumé) has prepared me to handle all aspects of secretarial work competently and confidently. You will be proud to sign the letters I place on your desk.

Here is another example of a second paragraph in which you demonstrate your qualifications.

> A summary of my qualifications is enclosed. As you will see, my training at Carlton Business College was very comprehensive. Not only did I complete all the accounting courses offered by the college, but I also studied personnel management, economics, business psychology, office supervision and management, typewriting, and statistics. In all my courses, I consistently ranked in the upper 25 percent of the class.

Of course, the nature of the second paragraph will depend on what you have to sell. If your business experience is limited and unlikely to impress the employer, you will have to emphasize your educational background. In such a case, you might follow the above paragraph with a statement such as this:

> Of particular interest to me in the accounting course was machine accounting. In this class we learned the applications of accounting theory to automated procedures and equipment. I am especially eager to work in a large organization, such as yours, where EDP is used on a wide scale.

Here is another example of capitalizing on achievements in school:

> You will notice from my résumé that English and business communication were among my favorite subjects. In addition, I was a member of the debating team, was on the journalism staff, and was president of our speech club. You will find my written and oral communication skills well above average.

The writer of the following paragraph admits lack of business experience but compensates for this with her interest and enthusiasm.

> I must admit that I do not have first-hand experience as a bank teller, Mr. Vitt. Compensating for this lack of experience is my deep interest in your bank and in the work your tellers do. Several times during the past year, I have talked with Larry Hamilton, who started his teller training with you a year ago, about the interesting duties he performs and the pleasant working conditions. He is very enthusiastic about the opportunities for advancement. These discussions make me even more certain that banking is the kind of work I want to do and that your bank is the one in which I would like to work. I know that within a short

period of time, I can learn to perform effectively as one of your tellers. Won't you give me an opportunity to try?

If you have had business experience that is related to the position for which you are applying, make the most of it.

I am particularly interested in machine accounting in which automated equipment and procedures are employed. Last summer I was a temporary employee in the systems department of Laskey-Brent Corporation, where I had an opportunity to become acquainted with EDP techniques. This experience was valuable, and I have decided to do further study in the field in evening school after I have obtained a position.

Show Willingness to Work and Learn

The employer who hires you is taking a risk—a risk that you may not be fitted for the position. One of the best assurances you can give that you are a safe risk is your willingness to learn and your genuine interest in the job. For example:

Obviously, there will be many routines and procedures that will be new to me. You will find me eager to learn and to improve.
I shall bring to the job a willingness to work and an eagerness to improve. Let me prove that statement to you.
I am not afraid of hard work; in fact, I enjoy it.
I have no illusions about my lack of experience; yet I am quick to learn and I enjoy learning.
I pride myself on my punctuality, accuracy, and dependability.
I learn fast and I remember what I learn.

Make It Easy for the Employer to Ask You for an Interview

The last paragraph of your letter of application should be the action-getting paragraph—aimed at obtaining an invitation for an interview. Make it easy for the employer to contact you.

I can come to your office for an interview between 9 a.m. and 5 p.m. on any weekday. My telephone number is 555-7613. If you would prefer to write, please use the address at the top of this letter.

Some job-hunters are more direct; they prefer to follow up on the letter rather than wait for the employer. For example:

I can come to your office for an interview between 9 a.m. and 5 p.m. any weekday. After you have had a chance to review my qualifications, I shall call your secretary for an appointment.

Some successful applicants enclose a postage-paid return card for employers to complete. For example, see the card illustrated at the top of page 548.

```
Dear Ms. (Applicant's Name):

Please come to my office on _____
                                          (Date)


at _____ for an interview.
              (Time)


                                    Very truly yours,


                                    _____
                                    (Employer's Name)
```

If a postal card is enclosed, you might include the following statement in your letter.

> Just complete the enclosed postal card and ask your secretary to drop it in the mail. I am available at any time that is convenient for you. If you would prefer to telephone, my number is 555-2518.

Send the application letter in an envelope of the same good quality bond paper as that on which the letter is written. Here again, the rules for neatness, good style, and placement apply. Choose a plain (unprinted) white business envelope such as a No. 10 ($4\frac{1}{8}$ by $9\frac{1}{2}$ inches). Include your return address in the upper left corner of the front of the envelope.

OTHER EMPLOYMENT LETTERS

Requesting Permission to Use Someone's Name as Reference

You should never use someone's name as a reference without first requesting permission to do so. Although permission may be requested by telephone or in person, it is often requested in writing:

> As you may know, I was recently graduated from the City College of Business; and I am making application at several firms in the Baltimore area for a position as legal secretary. May I list your name as a reference on my application forms? I should be most grateful for this privilege.
>
> You may answer at the bottom of this letter and return your reply in the enclosed envelope.
>
> Thank you.

Thanking Your References

After you accept a job, you should personally thank each person who helped you to get the job—and you should do so by writing a letter or a brief note.

> You will be pleased, I am certain, to learn that I have accepted a position as legal secretary with Mumford, Hayes, and Richards, one of the largest law firms in Baltimore. I start to work next week, and I am looking forward eagerly to my new position. The job is exactly what I was looking for.
>
> Thank you very much for allowing me to use your name as a reference. I am sure that your recommendation was instrumental in my being hired.

Interview Follow-Up Letters

After you have been interviewed, it is good strategy (as well as courtesy) to write to the interviewer, especially if you have reason to expect that a decision will not be made in a short time. Your thank-you letter gives you another opportunity to do a selling job. The letter might follow this form:

> I enjoyed meeting you and talking with you on Tuesday. Certainly, I came away with a much clearer picture of the work of a mail-room supervisor in the Corporation. The work sounds very exciting and challenging, and I am more convinced than ever that it is something I would like to do.
>
> Thank you for your time and the many courtesies you showed me. I was especially glad to meet Mrs. Wallin; please convey my best wishes to her.

Accepting the Position

If you have been notified that you have been chosen for a position, it is wise to accept in writing, especially if the firm is out of town or if your reporting date is a week or two away. You might use the style illustrated in the following letter.

> I am pleased to accept the position as your secretary. I know that I shall enjoy working with you in the field of public relations and communications. The salary of $150 a week, plus benefits, is quite satisfactory to me.
>
> As you requested, I shall report to work on Monday, July 5, at 8:30 a.m. Thank you for giving me this opportunity.

Declining a Position

Occasionally it is necessary to decline a job after it has been accepted. Naturally, you need solid, justifiable reasons for doing so. In such an event, give the reasons for your action. The following example illustrates a letter giving an acceptable reason for declining a job.

> This morning I received some news that distresses me. My husband has been transferred to Atlanta, effective the first of next month.

Although I am pleased that this transfer means a promotion for my husband, I am distressed that I must decline the very fine position that you offered me. I was looking forward to working with you. It was a wonderful opportunity, and I shall always be grateful to you for your kindness.

COMMUNICATION PROJECTS

Practical Application

A. For the career field of your choice, what are likely to be the best sources of information regarding job openings?

B. For each of the sources you indicated in Practical Application A, write an appropriate opening paragraph for a letter of application.

C. From the "Help Wanted" advertisements in your local newspaper, select a position that appeals to you and for which you are qualified (or will be upon graduation). Write a letter of application answering the ad, and attach a résumé you have prepared specifically for this job.

D. Write a letter to one of the people listed as a reference on your résumé (Practical Application C) to ask permission to use his or her name.

E. As a result of your application for the position in C above, you have been called for a personal interview. Write an appropriate interview follow-up letter, supplying all the necessary information.

F. Assume that you have accepted the position for which you applied in C above. Write a letter of notification and thanks to one of the people who served as a reference for you.

G. Although you accepted the position for which you applied in C above and are scheduled to start work next week, yesterday you were offered a better position with the firm's chief competitor. This position has greater potential for advancement, a higher starting salary, and considerably better fringe benefits. Therefore, you decide to accept the better offer. Write a letter to the other employer, whose position you had already accepted, explaining why you must decline the position.

Editing Practice

Editors' Alert   Here are more sentences on which you can sharpen your editing skills. Try to develop an all-seeing eye that doesn't miss a detail. If necessary, rewrite the sentences.

1. The office manuel, upon which we have been working the passed 2 years, will be reddy next week.
2. Having done every thing to expidite the delivery, the merchandise will reach you on the date promised.
3. The acknowledgment, in my judgement, lead to the development of the new procedure.
4. Its well-known that our company treats it's customers good thats why are sales are high.
5. Who's book received the most publicity, your's or mine?

Case Problem

Practical vs. Ethical   Reread Practical Application G. Be prepared to discuss your feelings, pro or con, regarding the applicant's rejection of an offer that had already been accepted.

58
HANDLING
EMPLOYMENT INTERVIEWS

The job interview is probably the most important aspect of the job-seeking process—and the critical determinant as to whether you are hired. Thus, it is essential that you go to each interview very well prepared and with your oral communication skills perfected. Regardless of how skillful and knowledgeable you may be, how impressive your résumé, or how persuasive your letter of application, all may fail you if you cannot sell yourself when you meet a prospective employer face to face.

In an interview, every time you speak you have an opportunity to sell yourself. Your response to questions, your description of experiences and situations, your explanation of procedures and methods—all contribute either favorably or unfavorably to the interviewer's impression of you. Therefore, you must prepare adequately for the interview and make plans far in advance. As a result of the type of planning you do, the interview may either be a frightening or an enjoyable experience.

HOW TO PLAN FOR THE INTERVIEW

Although you were not conscious of it at the time, preparation for the interview actually began quite some time ago. A number of years ago you had to choose the type of work you wanted to do. Then you had to obtain the necessary education and training required in this type of work. Ahead of you lies the job of selecting the type of company for which you want to work, compiling a résumé, writing a letter of application, and obtaining the interview. Such long-range planning is necessary, of course. The following discussion will be helpful in preparing for the job interview itself.

Know What You Have to Offer

Good sales representatives know their products thoroughly—better than anyone else does. They have analyzed their products from every conceivable angle; they know their strengths and their weaknesses. They understand fully what features of their

---

products are most likely to appeal to prospective buyers, and these are the features they emphasize in their sales presentations.

As a job applicant, you are a sales representative, and your product is yourself. Preparing a résumé gives you an opportunity to put down on paper what you have to sell—to see your strong points and compare them with those that your competitors for the position may have. The items emphasized on the résumé are those every employer is interested in—education, experience, and special interests and abilities. You should know these qualifications so well that you can communicate them orally without hesitation.

The first step in planning for the interview, therefore, is to anticipate questions that you may be asked about your education, experience, and personal qualities. Here are examples of some of these questions:

> What subjects did you concentrate on while attending college?
>
> Which of these subjects did you like best? Why?
>
> Tell me something about your course in _____ (personnel administration, business communications, office management, or other subjects).
>
> I see by your application that you worked at Randolph's for two summers. What kind of work did you do? What did you like most about your job? What did you like least?
>
> What do you most enjoy doing outside of working hours—hobbies and other activities?
>
> Were you active in school organizations? Which ones?
>
> Do you consider your skills (a) about average? (b) above average? (c) below average?
>
> Do you like to write? Do you consider yourself strong in English?

Answers to such probing questions will tell the interviewer a great deal about you and about how well you would fit the position, how quickly you would adjust to the job and to the people around you, and what your potential is for growth. In preparing for a job interview, then, you might ask yourself this question: What would I want to know about me if I were the interviewer?

Make a Positive First Impression

As you plan for the interview, ask yourself, "What can I do to make a positive first impression upon the interviewer?" First, you must be on time for the interview. Arise early enough to allow sufficient time to perform all the necessary grooming chores and to provide for any delays in traveling to the interview. Wouldn't it be better to arrive a half hour early for the interview than to arrive five minutes late?

On no other occasion is it more important to look your best than at an employment interview. The impression you make when you walk into the room will very likely influence the interviewer's attitude toward you throughout the entire interview. Plan ahead, therefore, to make the most of your appearance. Furthermore, *knowing* that you look well will help to make you feel more at ease. If possible, determine in advance if there are any company rules regarding grooming and dress; for example, ask any employees whom you know. If you really want to be employed by this firm, prepare accordingly.

Regardless of any specific grooming and dress rules that may exist, there are two characteristics that you can be certain will affect that first impression you make—neatness and cleanliness. Clean hair, clean hands, clean fingernails, clean shoes, and clean clothing are "musts." Clothing should be pressed, should be clean, should be color coordinated, and should lean more toward the conservative than the bizarre. Remember, you are trying to give the interviewer the impression that you are businesslike and that you will convey a businesslike impression to the customers of that business. Will wearing casual clothing convey that impression?

Plan What You Will Say

Interviewers operate in different ways. Some will do most of the talking and will ask only a few questions about your education and experience. Others will draw you out as much as possible and say very little. Be prepared for such general statements or questions from the interviewer as these:

> Tell me about yourself. (This request will give you a chance to emphasize your most salable features. The interviewer doesn't want to know about your childhood but wants you to answer such questions as these: What do you do best? What do you like best?)
> Review your college work and your experience. (Here you will emphasize the college courses that will best implement your qualifications for this particular job. The same is true of your experience.)
> What do you think your strongest points are? your weakest?
> Tell me why you think you should be hired for this position.
> What job will you have five years from now?

Anticipate also some personal questions, such as:

> What kind of person do you think you are?
> Do you like to work?
> What do you enjoy doing in your leisure time?
> Do you read a great deal?
> Where do you live?
> What salary do you expect?
> Are you punctual in your appointments?
> Do you have any financial obligations?

Although you should anticipate the questions you are likely to be asked, it's a good idea also to think of questions you would like to ask the interviewer. Not only will you receive information, but your asking questions will also show the interviewer that you have given careful thought to the position. Be prepared, therefore, to ask such questions as:

> What duties are required in this position?
> Does the company provide opportunities for further education?

What are the opportunities for advancement?
What type of insurance is available through the company?
What about employee social and recreational facilities?

Anticipate the Salary Question

More often than not, the salary paid for a position—at least the general range—is known to the applicant before the interview. If the salary is not known, however, and the interviewer has not mentioned it, you should say, near the end of the interview, "I understand that the beginning salary for this position is $_____ a month. Is this correct?" (Base the figure you mention on knowledge, not whim. Find out from employment agencies or newspaper ads what the salary is for the jobs you apply for—before you apply.)

Sometimes information about the salary is withheld, or the salary is listed as *open*. This means that the company has set a general salary range for the job, but the specific amount paid will depend upon the qualifications of the applicant.

If the interviewer asks you, "What salary do you expect?" be prepared to give an honest, straightforward answer. Find out in advance what similar jobs are paying; then say something like this: "I understand that similar jobs in this area range from $_____ to $_____ a month. I had expected to receive about $_____." (Mention a figure somewhere in the middle or, if you consider yourself unusually well qualified, near the top.)

Plan What You Will Take With You

Every applicant for a position should bring the following items:

> A good pen.
> A pencil with a good eraser.
> A résumé. (This may be put in a plain folder, in a large envelope, or in a special acetate folder. The résumé should never be folded and put in a pocket or purse.)
> A small pad on which to take notes.

Applicants for stenographic positions are usually given a typewriting and shorthand test. In addition to the items listed above, they should also take a clean stenographer's notebook, a good typewriter eraser, and possibly an eraser shield. Although these items are usually supplied by the company, it is well to be prepared in case they are not.

If you are applying for a position in which samples of your work would be helpful, take some along. Put them in a folder or in a clean envelope.

On the day of the interview, give yourself plenty of time to arrive at the interviewer's office on schedule. Take no chances on traffic jams and delayed trains, taxis, or buses; start early. Last-minute dashes to make an appointment are likely to find you disheveled and breathless. Plan your schedule so that you can walk into the receptionist's office with calm assurance.

You'll usually be asked to fill out an official application form, and arriving ten or fifteen minutes early will give you a head start on this task. You will want to complete the application blank slowly and carefully (it will be part of your permanent record if you get the job). Try to get a copy of this application blank before arriving for the interview. In this way, you can be sure to give it the attention it deserves.

Find Out All You Can About the Company

There are two main reasons for finding out in advance all you can about the company. First, knowing something about the organization will help you to decide whether it is a place in which you would like to work. Second, you should have a strong answer to the often-asked question, "Why did you choose our company?" Too many applicants have no ready answer to that question beyond the weak "I just heard it is a nice place to work," or "It's close to my home." It is much more effective to say, "I have always been interested in investments, and I know that your company is one of the leading investment firms in this area."

How should you research facts about a company? You might talk to the person, such as your placement counselor, who referred you to the organization. You might ask this person or an instructor for the name of an acquaintance who works there; then talk to the employee. If you have an opportunity, pick up copies of employee magazines, booklets, or advertising brochures. Above all, learn the exact spelling of the name of the person who is to interview you. If you are not absolutely sure, telephone the interviewer's secretary or speak to the company receptionist.

THE INTERVIEW

When you arrive at the office, you will be greeted by a receptionist. Give your name and the purpose of your visit. "I'm (your name). I have an appointment at nine with Mr. Chan." If you have to wait a few minutes, review your résumé, check over the completed application blank, read the literature that will probably be available in the reception office, or otherwise occupy yourself. Don't engage in conversation with the receptionist unless you are invited to do so.

When you are ushered into the interviewer's office, try to be relaxed (though not casual or arrogant) and to look pleasant. Do not extend your hand unless the interviewer does so first. It is enough to say, "How do you do, Mr. Chan." You do not need to give your name; the secretary or receptionist will have announced your arrival.

Seat yourself only when you are invited to do so. Keep with you the materials you have brought. Don't place anything on the interviewer's desk unless you are invited to do so. The interviewer may or may not ask to see the application blank and the résumé. The moment will come, however, when you are asked about your education and experience. This is the time to give the interviewer your résumé if you haven't already done so. Say something like this: "Here is my résumé, on which that information is summarized. I also have completed the application blank." (Hand both to the interviewer.) Wait for the interviewer to make the first move. You will know at once how the interview will be conducted—whether the interviewer is going to ask most of the questions or prefers that you take the initiative. Usually the interviewer will direct the proceedings.

Don't smoke. Even if you are a smoker, it is probably best to refuse a cigarette if it is offered to you. Say simply, "No, thank you; not just now." If you are a nonsmoker, you merely decline with "No, thank you."

Face and speak directly to the interviewer. Don't stare at the floor or out of the window while either of you is talking. Of course, you should take your eyes from the interviewer's occasionally, but leave no doubt that you are talking and listening to him or her. Speak slowly and enunciate carefully. Give your answers and statements in a straightforward manner; show that you have thought them through and that you can speak with precision. Give short answers; the interviewer doesn't want your life story or your complete personal philosophy in answer to every question. At the same time, a mere "Yes" or "No" is not sufficient. For example, if you are asked this question, "I see you had one course in accounting. Did you like it?" it is not enough simply to say "Yes" (assuming that is how you actually feel). You might add, "I enjoyed the course very much, and I plan to take more accounting in evening school."

Be specific about your special qualifications. If you are asked about your skills in shorthand and typewriting, give the results of your last tests. Say something like this: "I can write shorthand at 100 words a minute fairly consistently on new material. My typing speed on the last few tests was in the upper 60s." Or "My accounting courses consisted of principles, cost, intermediate, and departmental. In the departmental course we were introduced to automation as it relates to accounting, and I especially enjoyed that." Or "I consistently made top grades in communications courses, and I particularly liked writing credit and collection letters." Or "One of the most interesting things I did during my summers at Randolph's was to verify cash balance each day. It wasn't easy to make everything balance, since we had so many people handling the cash, but I was successful at it and learned a lot from the experience."

On the other hand, be noncommittal about controversial matters. If you are asked what you thought of Randolph's as a place to work and your opinion isn't especially favorable, say something like this: "My work there gave me some valuable experience, and I enjoyed much of it." If you are asked for your opinions about people for whom you have worked and for whom you feel no special fondness, say something like this: "Ms. Lincoln was often helpful to me; I believe I profited from working with her."

The interviewer will usually be interested in why you left other positions, especially when you have indicated on your application blank that you left because of unsatisfactory working conditions or for other negative reasons. If you complain to the interviewer about the people or about the company policies, however, you may give the impression that you are a chronic complainer. Try to be objective and to say something like this: "I found it difficult to adjust to some of the procedures and to the unusual hours at Randolph's. Many of the people were extremely pleasant and helpful. There were some with whom I didn't have much rapport, but I'm sure some of the fault was mine." The interviewer will appreciate your frankness as well as your discretion.

Try to be at ease; smile occasionally. Remember that the interviewer needs someone to fill a position that is open and is just as eager to make a decision in your favor as you are to get the job. Most interviewers are pleasant, friendly, and understanding. Try to display an air of confidence. Above all, don't fidget. Nervousness often shows up in such habits as brushing imaginary lint off clothing, straightening and re-straightening a tie, fussing with hair, toying with an object such as a purse or a paper clip, and putting hands to the face. Avoid such habits; give your attention to the interviewer.

The interviewer will let you know when the interview is over. The usual sign is to rise. As soon as the interviewer does so, you should also rise. The exchange that takes place might be something like the following conversation.

> *Interviewer (rising):* I enjoyed meeting and talking with you.
> *You (rising):* Thank you, Mr. Chan. I appreciate the time you have given me.
> *Interviewer:* We have your telephone number, and we will call you just as soon as we have reached a decision.
> *You:* Thank you. I shall look forward to hearing from you.
> *Interviewer:* Good-bye.
> *You:* Good-bye.

Leave quickly and thank the secretary and the receptionist as you leave.

FOLLOWING UP THE INTERVIEW

As soon as possible after the interview, make a written summary from notes and memory of the facts you learned in the interview and the opinions you have formed about the company and about the job for which you were interviewed. If you are being interviewed for jobs in several different companies, this written summary will prove an excellent way to refresh your memory about the interview when you are trying later to make your final job choice.

Whether or not you follow up the interview with a thank-you letter to the interviewer will depend on how much you want the job. If the position is an especially desirable one, you will want to thank the interviewer for his or her time and to reemphasize some of your special qualifications. For other suggestions relating to follow-up letters after interviews, refer to Section 57.

COMMUNICATION PROJECTS

Practical Application

A. Prepare written answers to each of the following questions and statements likely to come up in an employment interview.

1. Why do you wish to work for our company?
2. What kind of work do you enjoy doing most?
3. What kind of work do you enjoy doing least?
4. What salary do you expect?
5. What are your job goals for the next ten-year period?
6. Why have you selected this type of work?
7. Tell me about yourself.

8. Why did you leave your last position?
9. How do you spend your spare time?
10. What do you do in the summer?

B. List ten suggestions (in the form of "Dos" and "Don'ts") for *preparing* for a job interview. Then list ten suggestions to be observed *during* the interview.

C. Make a list of the questions you might like to ask the interviewer about the position for which you are applying or the company for which you will be working.

D. Assume your interviewer says, "I notice that your department supervisor at Landow's was Harry Wilson. I've heard that Wilson is a tough person to get along with. Did you like working with him?" Compose the answer you would give your interviewer. (Assume that what he heard about Harry Wilson is true, insofar as you are concerned.)

E. Answer the following questions:

1. Why do you think that you should thank the secretary and the receptionist when you leave the interviewer's office?
2. It is suggested that you take a small notebook along with you to the interview. What notes might you want to make?
3. Why is it important to choose carefully the company for which you would like to work?
4. In large companies, the applicant for a position is interviewed at least twice; first by a personnel specialist, and later on by the person for whom the applicant will work. What do you think is the main purpose of the first interview? How might the two interviews differ?

F. Assume that you have been interviewed for a position with the Bruxton Insurance Company (a position in which you are very much interested and for which you are well qualified). The interviewer, Mrs. Roberta Peterson, was very pleasant and favorably impressed with your qualifications. However, she told you that she plans to interview several other applicants before making a decision. Write a letter to Mrs. Peterson to thank her for the interview. Emphasize special qualifications you possess or present additional facts that may improve your chances for getting the job.

Editing Practice

The Rewrite Desk   Edit and rewrite the following paragraph.

> We hope you will except our apolegy for sending our payment so late. Rather then to have the same thing occurr next month, we will note on our calender the date the payment should be mailed so as to reach you on time.

Case Problem

Introductions and Courtesy   Yolanda Estrella is a new secretary who has been assigned the desk next to Morgana Holden's. When Yolanda first reported for work, the office administrator was involved in a meeting in the president's office and, therefore, was unavailable to introduce Yolanda to Morgana or to any of the other employees in the office.

1. What could Morgana do to make Yolanda feel welcome?
2. If Morgana does nothing, what might Yolanda do?

59 HANDLING COMMUNICATION DUTIES EFFECTIVELY

As you already know, communication is fundamental to any business operation. Little if anything would be accomplished in business without communicating information. Among those business workers whose duties are almost exclusively concerned with communications are secretaries, executive secretaries, and administrative assistants. Without them, the flow of information would cease in most offices.

It is, therefore, especially important for all business workers to understand the duties of these specialists, and these duties are discussed in the remainder of this section. If you plan to pursue a secretarial career, then this section will be of obvious interest to you. But even if you do not plan to pursue a secretarial career, you should pay special attention to this section, because it will help you to work more effectively *with* your secretary.

RESPONSIBILITIES RELATED TO INCOMING MAIL

Most executives give the mail their first attention each day. Therefore, the efficient secretary gets to the office early enough to open and sort the mail so that it is on the executive's desk when he or she arrives.

Opening the Mail

Use a letter opener. Never rip mail open or cut it open with scissors, because the contents might be damaged. Check each envelope carefully for enclosures.

If the mail contains checks or other important papers, slit open the envelope on three sides (so that it opens as flat as a sheet of paper) to make sure that you do not overlook enclosures. Also, because addresses are frequently given only on the envelope, make sure that you have a record of the address before destroying the envelope.

Sorting the Mail

In a small office, all incoming mail may be picked up and distributed by whoever arrives at the office first: the secretary, the receptionist, an office assistant, even the boss. In a large office where a great deal of mail is received, the mail is picked up and distributed by a special staff in a central mail room. In either case, letters addressed to individuals or to departments are usually delivered unopened. Letters addressed to the company without specific reference to individuals or to departments are opened, read, and then distributed to the appropriate persons.

Usually, the secretary is responsible for receiving and opening the employer's mail. The mail is handled in the following manner:

Letters marked "Personal" are placed *unopened* in the executive's IN basket or on the desk.

All other letters are opened, read carefully by the secretary, and placed on top of the executive's desk or in the IN basket. If passersby can look into the office, place the letters inside a folder so that they cannot be seen.

The mail should be arranged in order of importance. A commonly accepted arrangement is as follows (in order from top to bottom):

Telegrams
Letters marked "Personal"
Other first-class mail
Circulars and advertisements
Magazines and newspapers

If there is a great deal of mail, it may be separated into three folders marked "Telegrams," "First-Class Mail," and "Other Mail." Some secretaries separate the mail according to the urgency with which it must be handled (some telegrams are not important, while a particular newspaper item or a circular may be). In this case, folders are labeled "First Priority," "Second Priority," "For Reading Only—No Action," and so on. Of course, the secretary must know enough about the employer's business to know which pieces of mail are in most urgent need of attention.

In addition to opening and sorting the daily mail for the executive, the administrative assistant usually takes on the following duties.

Reading the Mail

Usually the administrative assistant is expected to read the mail before placing it on the employer's desk. There are two important reasons for reading the mail: (1) to keep informed of matters that have a bearing on the executive's work and (2) to make the executive's job of answering the mail an easier one.

Suppose an executive receives a letter from Lee Jackson, a business acquaintance in another city. Mr. Jackson writes that he will be visiting the city on a certain date and hopes to see the executive. The assistant reads the letter, checks the executive's calendar, and makes the following notation on Mr. Jackson's letter: "You will be in New Orleans that week." Or suppose the executive receives a letter from Ms. Eileen McGee, a supplier, in which Ms. McGee refers to a specification sheet she received from the executive. The assistant attaches to Ms. McGee's letter a copy of the specification sheet referred to so that the executive will have on hand the information needed to reply to Ms. McGee. The assistant may also be called on to perform the following tasks in order to ease the load of the executive:

Underline important dates, amounts, or statements on incoming letters. Place notations in the margin of incoming letters, such as "I will answer this request" or "He refers to a telephone call from Mr. Allison" or "She means June 11 (instead of June 10)."

Place a routing slip on letters that probably should be handled by another department. Of course, if the letter is addressed to the executive, he or she should be given the opportunity to read it even though someone else will reply. The routing slip, however, makes it easier to handle the letter if the executive agrees with the recommendation to route it elsewhere.

Read and flag for the executive's attention magazine or newspaper articles of special interest. This may be done by clipping to the publication a memo slip containing a notation such as "See pages 43, 44, and 76."

Digesting the Mail   The busy executive who receives a large amount of correspondence may expect an assistant to prepare digests (summaries) of important messages. An executive who is planning to be away on an extended business trip may ask the assistant to send summaries once a week or perhaps more often.

Digest of Important Mail Received February 15

Mr. K. T. Stephens	Wants you to speak at the Boston meeting of the Executive's Association on May 10. Send him the topic of your own choosing.
Ms. Terri Alborn (A-1 Interiors)	Wishes to make several changes in plans for refurbishing your office. Wants your reaction after you have studied changes.
Mr. Karl Alden	Can you visit the Atlanta branch in March? Will have visitors from France observing our operations. Would like you to host a dinner in their honor.
Mrs. Rita Lopez	Outlines advertising program for summer. Wants your reactions by end of this month.

RESPONSIBILITIES RELATED TO OUTGOING MAIL

Since busy executives have many communication responsibilities related to outgoing mail, secretaries should be able to accept some of these duties to free their bosses for other tasks. By taking responsibility for as many of the following outgoing mail duties as possible, secretaries will be valuable to the firm—and to their bosses!

Dictation and Transcription

Techniques of taking and transcribing dictation are not within the scope of this book. Certainly the secretary prepared to enter the business world has acquired and perfected these skills. Most employers look for more than these basic skills; they expect their secretaries to know the finer points of grammar, punctuation, capitalization, and spelling. Many executives rely on their secretaries to edit and correct their dictation; some also expect their secretaries to verify the facts, figures, and names used in their dictation.

Editing   How much editing should the secretary do on the letters the boss dictates? That depends almost entirely on the boss. Some administrators dictate very methodically, indicating punctuation, unusual spellings, and new paragraphs. Usually these executives are so sure of themselves that they want very little editing done. Others dictate only the barest outline of a letter and say to the secretary, "Fix it up." Most bosses, however, are somewhere between these two extremes; if the dictator makes errors in grammar and punctuation, the secretary usually can feel free to make the necessary changes. Obviously, the secretary must be positive of the correction before proceeding. If not, the secretary may say to the executive, "You mentioned April 11 as the first day of the meeting. Did you mean April 12?" or "In my notes I have 'I don't want to set any precedents in this decision.' I believe you actually said, 'I don't want to set a *precedent.*' "

Finished Letters   After transcribing the letters, the secretary should proofread them carefully while they are still in the typewriter. In this way, errors can be corrected without running the risk of misaligning the correction. A letter that is not correct or that contains unclear sentences should not be placed on the employer's desk for signature. The secretary should never try to pass over an error or a garbled sentence.

Transcribed letters should be accompanied by the addressed envelope and the enclosures when the letters are presented for signature. Place the envelope over the letterhead so that the flap faces the letterhead; by so doing, you won't obscure the message. If the executive is not in the office when the letters are brought in to be signed, the letters should be placed on the desk, face down or inside a folder.

Preparation for Mailing   The secretary's responsibility for outgoing letters does not end when the letters are placed on the executive's desk for signature. First, the secretary should make certain that the executive knows that the letters *are* ready to be signed so that they will be mailed that day. Check to see that every letter is signed and that any enclosure mentioned in a letter is actually with that letter. And, double-check to see that each letter goes into its proper envelope. Nothing is more embarrassing than to have one person receive a letter that should have gone to someone else.

After preparing the letters for mailing, the secretary should make sure that the mail goes out on that day. If the outgoing mail collection has been missed, the secretary should either deliver the mail to the mail room or drop it into a mailbox after the office closes.

Letter Writing

Your preparation in this course should enable you to lighten your employer's work load by taking the responsibility for writing routine letters. Tactfully suggest that you undertake the job of writing routine letters: reservation letters, requests, referrals, thank-yous and acknowledgments, letters about appointments, and transmittal letters. Many of these letters are discussed in Chapter 7. However, some are so important to the secretary and administrative assistant that they receive additional emphasis here.

Reservation Letters   For letters making hotel and travel reservations, either the employer's signature or the secretary's signature may be used. Refer to Chapter 7 for additional information on writing reservation letters. The letter that follows has been written for the employer's signature.

> Please reserve a single room with bath for me for November 15 and 16, at a rate not to exceed $45.
>
> I shall arrive about 5 p.m. on November 15 and expect to check out before 2 p.m. on November 17. Please send me a confirmation of this reservation.

Request Letters   Request letters, too, may be written either for the employer's or for the secretary's signature. Here is an example of a request letter written for the secretary's signature.

> Ms. Irene Tyson, the supervisor of our word processing center, attended your session on word processing at the convention of the American Executive's Institute last week in Denver.
>
> Ms. Tyson indicated that your firm has available a unique layout for your center that contributes to a very efficient operation. She indicated that attendees interested in this layout would receive a copy of the layout and a description of the procedures followed if they would write a letter making their request known.
>
> We should very much like to have a copy of the layout and procedures. We should also like permission to reproduce a sufficient number of copies for our branch offices. We would be happy to pay for any expenses incurred in sending a copy to us.

Referral Letters   Often executives may not be able to give personal attention to letters sent to them but really meant for someone else. In such cases, secretaries usually write an acknowledgment letter for their own signature and attend to any necessary follow-through. The following letter would be sent in answer to the request; at the same time, a copy of the original letter and a carbon copy of the reply would be sent to the person who can fulfill the request.

> Thank you for requesting 100 copies of our booklet, *Job Application Advice*, for distribution to the seniors in your school. We are pleased that you feel our booklet will be useful to your students.
>
> Unfortunately, our supply of this booklet has been depleted. Therefore, I am referring your request to our Detroit office, where this booklet was prepared. You should receive your 100 copies within two weeks.

Letters While the Boss Is Away   Even though the secretary may not be requested to write letters while the boss is in the office, while the boss is away the secretary may be expected to acknowledge important letters received and to explain any delays caused by the boss's absence. Letters written for these reasons are usually brief, courteous, and noncommittal—that is, the letter does not reveal private company business such as where the boss is or why the boss is away.

Sometimes the correspondence cannot await your employer's return. Such letters are referred to someone else in the company. Only urgent or highly important letters are routed in this way.

Thank you for your April 5 letter to Mrs. King.

Since Mrs. King will be out of the office for a month, I am referring your letter to Mr. Cary Yates, our credit manager. Mr. Yates will write you just as soon as he has had an opportunity to review your request.

After writing this reply, the secretary should write a memorandum to Mr. Yates, transmitting the letter to him.

TO: Mr. Cary Yates   FROM: Carol West
                                            Secretary to Mrs. King
SUBJECT: Attached letter   DATE: April 7, 19—
               from Lee Sims

The attached letter requires a decision by April 15, and as you know, Mrs. King is on vacation until May 2. I have also attached a copy of my letter to Mr. Sims. I know Mrs. King would want you to handle Mr. Sims' request.

I would be grateful if you will send me a blind carbon of your letter to Mr. Sims for our files.

CW

When you answer a letter for your employer, do not express opinions that could disagree with those of your employer or that may prove embarrassing. For example, if a letter applying for a job was sent to a personnel director who will be away from the office for some time, the personnel director's secretary would *not* write:

Thank you for your application for a management trainee position.

Your qualifications are excellent, and I know Mrs. Gordon will be favorably impressed.

The personnel director may feel differently about the applicant or may not have an opening at the present time. Therefore, a noncommittal letter like the following would be more appropriate.

Thank you for your application for a management trainee position. Mrs. Laura Gordon, the personnel director, is out of the office until June 15. She will write you shortly after she returns.

This letter makes no commitment beyond indicating that a reply will be forthcoming. Note, too, that the letter does not provide any confidential information regarding Mrs. Gordon's whereabouts.

Here is a summary of procedures to follow while the executive is away.

1. If the boss will be away for more than two or three days, acknowledge all letters to which a correspondent might reasonably expect a prompt answer. An example of such an acknowledgment letter is the letter above.
2. Forward mail to a knowledgeable person in the company if the incoming letter indicates that some action must be taken immediately.
3. If the employer is on an extended trip, send copies of letters requiring action before he or she is expected to return to the office. Be certain to send any necessary supporting materials.

4. Answer all letters that you would be expected to handle if your boss were in the office.
5. Place in folders all mail received—letters awaiting the executive's attention, photocopies of letters forwarded to others for reply, carbon copies of letters that you or others have answered, advertising mail, newspapers, and so on.

Other Letters In addition to the preceding letters, the secretary or administrative assistant may compose other letters on behalf of an executive or follow up on those that require future action. The initiative for writing letters for the executive may come from the assistant or from the employer, who might write on an incoming letter a notation such as "Tell him I'll see him next week." The assistant who takes the initiative may do one of the following:

1. Write a rough-draft reply and attach it to the incoming letter placed on the employer's desk.
2. Make such notations on incoming letters as "I'll answer" or "Will send today" or "Will say you'll be away that week."

There is no hard-and-fast rule about the duties of the administrative assistant in handling the employer's correspondence. Whether the assistant writes letters for the employer depends entirely on the executive's wishes and the assistant's ability. In any event, the assistant should never be presumptuous. The assistant should turn over *all* incoming letters, routine or not, until the employer decides that the assistant is able to originate correspondence.

Communication Follow-Up The efficient administrative assistant assumes responsibility for following up on the employer's communication activities. For example, if certain letters must be answered by a specific date, the assistant should remind the employer when an answer is due. The assistant can either maintain a tickler file or record reminder notes on a desk calendar pad.

Follow-up is needed, for example, for incoming letters that arrive with enclosures omitted, for outgoing letters that request appointments and that have not been answered, for materials requested that have not arrived, or for some other action referred to in incoming or outgoing correspondence that has not materialized after a reasonable time. Here are some examples of such follow-up letters:

We received your April 3 letter indicating that you will be glad to accept the speaking assignment at the convention of the International Executives' Society in London on June 14.

We would appreciate your sending by the end of this month the title of your presentation, a brief biographical outline, and a list of any equipment you would like to use in conjunction with your presentation.

Mr. Hajas left this morning on an extended trip to our major marketing centers. He would like to arrange a meeting with you for about an hour while he is in Washington on October 15. Would anytime between 11 a.m. and 2 p.m. be convenient for you?

I must telephone Mr. Hajas before he leaves New York City on October 13. Therefore, would you please wire or telephone me collect (555-8798) before that date to let me know if you can see Mr. Hajas, and at what time?

Signing Letters

When your boss is away or is in a hurry to leave the office, you may be asked to sign his or her name to dictated letters. Or you may be asked to sign all routine correspondence, even when your boss is in the office. If such is the case, write your initials immediately below your boss's "signature," as shown here:

Cordially yours,

James R. Riley

BK

James R. Riley

Some employers prefer that their signatures be imitated when the letter is written to people whom they do not know personally.

An administrative assistant sometimes writes letters for his or her own signature, as shown in the following examples:

Very truly yours,

(Ms.) Anne Roth

Administrative Assistant

to James A. Torgeson

Cordially yours,

Gerald M. Hoover

Assistant to the President

Messages

Whenever the employer is out of the office or in conference, the secretary should make written notations of all telephone calls received or in-person visits. Written messages do not rely on the secretary's memory but do remind the employer to follow through. By keeping a copy of all messages, the secretary can advise the employer in advance if a telephone call is to be returned or if some other task is to be performed.

The illustration shown below is typical of the message forms used in most offices. Notice that only a few words are used in the message, yet the message is clear and complete.

MEETINGS AND CONFERENCES

Although a very informal meeting may require little preparation, the success of most meetings depends upon careful planning. To prepare for meetings, an assistant should be able to attend to these details: (1) reserve and set up the meeting room and restore it to order after the meeting; (2) prepare an agenda (a list of topics to be discussed at the meeting); (3) make definite assignments for each participant; and (4) take notes and prepare minutes of the meeting.

The Meeting Room

Make certain there is a sufficient number of chairs for participants and a few extra chairs for unexpected guests. If possible, conference members should be seated

Telephone Message

To: *Ms. Esther Greene*

Here is a Message for You

Mr. Otto Haspel

of *Haspel Interior Design*

Phone No. *555-3770*   Ext. *923*

☑ Telephoned	☐ Will Call Again
☐ Returned Your Call	☐ Came To See You
☑ Please Phone	☐ Wants To See You

Furniture is ready.
When do you want delivery?
Need to give two days' notice.

Taken By	Date	Time
T. Z.	*8/25*	*11:30*

51-50540 (Rev 7/78)

Writing clear, brief messages contributes to productivity and good relations with customers, suppliers, and co-workers.

around an oval table in order to take the stiffness out of a meeting and to give everybody an opportunity to see, hear, and concentrate on the contributions of each participant.

Place a copy of the agenda, several pencils, and a writing pad on the table for each participant. Don't forget to provide ashtrays and drinking water. If audiovisual aids are to be used, make certain that the proper facilities are available, including an operator if one is needed to run the equipment.

After the meeting is over, make certain that all equipment and unused supplies are returned and that the meeting room is restored to its original order. Report any problems involving borrowed equipment. Check all seating locations to be sure that no personal possessions have been left behind.

The Agenda

An agenda of a meeting is usually sent in advance to all participants of a meeting so that they will have time to prepare their comments, suggestions, or questions. A copy of the agenda should be available for each participant at the meeting room in case someone misplaces an agenda or forgets to bring it to the meeting. The agenda below is typical for an informal meeting.

Agenda

Committee on Word Processing Feasibility
September 1, 19—
10:15 a.m.—Room 14A

1. Call to Order.
2. Minutes of Previous Meeting.
3. Discussion of Word Processing Procedures—Frank Exeter.
4. Film Presentation—Anne Radcliff.
5. Examples of Word Processing Centers—George Tyler and Margaret Olsen.
6. Plans for Feasibility Study—Russell Potter.
7. Assignment of Committee Responsibilities—Ula Simms.
8. Selection of Next Meeting Date.
9. Adjournment.

The Notes and Minutes

A record should be made of what took place at the meeting, preferably in a stenographic notebook because the center rule on each page separates the names of the speakers from their remarks. The notes should be transcribed as soon as possible. Section 50 gives specific suggestions for preparing minutes.

RESEARCH ACTIVITIES

Executives often are required to do some kind of research and usually expect a secretary or administrative assistant to help with this research. The research work may consist merely of looking up information in the department's own files, of telephoning and writing to other departments to gather facts and figures, or of consulting one or more periodicals or reference books. On the other hand, some executives are engaged in activities that require more formal research or serve as editors of company publications. Many executives write articles for magazines—some may even write books. Furthermore, executives are often asked to deliver speeches. You can make yourself useful to your boss in these research capacities. Therefore, you should be able to make use of library facilities, since your responsibilities may encompass referring to basic reference books and reading current periodicals.

Basic References

Every assistant to an executive should be familiar with such basic reference resources as the following;

A Good Dictionary   The dictionary is probably the most important reference source. For most writing purposes, a dictionary such as *Webster's New Collegiate Dictionary* (G. & C. Merriam Company) or *The American Heritage Dictionary of the English Language* (American Heritage Publishing Co.) is sufficient. Executives who do a great deal of writing or editing should have available an unabridged dictionary.

A Business Writer's Handbook   A business writer's handbook contains such information as the following: rules for the use of English grammar, capitalization, spelling, punctuation; guides for transcribing, mailing, and filing business correspondence; aids to proofreading; styles and formats for typing; and information relating to postal, express, and telegraphic services.

Such handbooks provide useful sources for secretaries. Several are available. Among the most popular are *Standard Handbook for Secretaries*, by Lois Hutchinson, and *The Gregg Reference Manual*, 5th Edition, by William A. Sabin (both, McGraw-Hill Book Company).

A Reliable Fact Book   Most assistants find frequent use for a fact book such as *The World Almanac* (Newspaper Enterprise Association Inc.). This fact book contains such varied information as names and addresses of colleges and universities, population figures, baseball records, names of members of congress, senators, Academy Award winners, and much, much more.

Special References

An executive assistant needs special references that pertain to the business of the executive. For example, the assistant who works for a lawyer may need a good law dictionary, such as *Black's Law Dictionary* (West Publishing Company), and a handbook for the legal secretary, such as *Legal Office Procedures*, by Marjorie Dunlap Bate and Mary C. Casey (McGraw-Hill Book Company). Other examples of special references follow:

Administrative Assistant to a Doctor. A medical dictionary, such as *Blakiston's Gould Medical Dictionary*, edited by A. Osol and C. C. Francis (McGraw-Hill Book Company); a medical secretary's handbook, such as *Medical Office Procedures*, by Miriam Bredow (McGraw-Hill Book Company).

Administrative Assistant to a Publisher. Various stylebooks, such as *A Manual of Style*, University of Chicago Press Staff (University of Chicago Press); *Writer's Guide and Index to English*, by Porter G. Perrin (Scott, Foresman and Company); *The New York Times Style Book for Writers and Editors*, edited and revised by Lewis Jordan (Quadrangle); *Words Into Type*, by Marjorie E. Skillin and Robert M. Gay (Prentice-Hall, Inc.); *Roget's International Thesaurus*, by P. M. Roget (Thomas Y. Crowell Company).

Administrative Assistant to a Chemist. *Lange's Handbook of Chemistry*, compiled and edited by J. A. Dean (McGraw-Hill Book Company).

Administrative Assistant to an Accountant. *Accountant's Handbook,* edited by R. Wixon (Ronald Press Company); *Office Management Handbook,* edited by H. L. Wylie (Ronald Press Company).

Use of the Library

To use library facilities efficiently, you should become acquainted with the librarian and should seek the librarian's help. The librarian will be able to point out the available sources of information and special reference works as well as the library's auxiliary services, such as the interlibrary loan system and the library's reference services. Often, too, when you are not acquainted with the titles of books or articles or the names of authors, the librarian's help is a great time-saver.

Once you have found all the references you need, you should follow these practical suggestions for recording the information.

1. Be systematic and orderly in all note-taking. Most researchers use cards for this purpose.
2. Always check to make sure you have the latest edition of the book.
3. Be careful to record, for each reference, the author's full name, the title of the book or periodical, the title of the article (if a periodical reference), the volume and number (if applicable), the publisher's name, the date and place of publication, and all page numbers referred to.
4. Write on only one side of the card and limit each card to one subject. (See Section 49 for further suggestions for taking notes.)

Reading and Writing Reports

Because your boss may spend a large portion of the day reading reports, you should be prepared to read and summarize reports. Be skillful in summarizing so that no important aspects are omitted and no facts misrepresented. To avoid misinterpretation, cite the page of important items.

> Powers offers three important ways to reduce the communication costs of our company. (See page 23.)

Using the training provided in Sections 48 and 49, you should be able to write a report if you are called upon to do so.

Contributing Ideas

To be promoted to higher levels of management, you must be someone with imagination, someone who can make constructive suggestions. The illustration on page 571 is a proposal for saving time and materials that might well come from a secretary or administrative assistant.

LISTENER'S HIGHLIGHT RECORDS

To: Mr. Terry Wolfe, Vice President   From: Carla Worth

Subject: Word Processing Equipment   Date: October 15, 19--

I would like to suggest that we purchase a word processing machine similar to the A-111 described in the enclosed brochure. As you will see from this description, the A-111 machine can handle many of our routine projects in much less time than we now spend on these projects. Among the routine tasks with which the A-111 can help us are the following:

1. The revision of our Product Information Sheets. Over the past ten months we have paid more than $2,500 to Allied Typing Service for revising our Product Information Sheets. Although a sheet may have only a minor correction, the entire sheet is always retyped. With a machine similar to the A-111, we could update our Product Information Sheets daily right here in our office. Each correction would take only a few minutes, and we would always have up-to-date Product Info Sheets.

2. The updating of our Weekly Production Status Report. The average length of the Production Status Report is 30 pages every week. Of course, it is critical that we complete the report and send it to headquarters on time. With the A-111, we could revise our Weekly Production Status Report in less than one hour.

In addition, there are many more projects for which we could use the A-111 advantageously. The machine would pay for itself within one year; more importantly, we could be sure that our Product Information Sheets are always up to date and that our production reports are sent to headquarters on time.

There are other word processing machines on the market. Some may be even less expensive and/or better suited to our needs than the A-111. In any case, I think that we should explore the possibility of improving our productivity with an efficient word processor.

If you would like to discuss this suggestion further, please call me on extension 4555.

                                        CW

Enclosure

Sharing constructive suggestions with management often helps employees to advance on the job.

GETTING ALONG WITH OTHERS

Anyone who works with an executive reflects the "voice, mind, and personality" of that executive because other workers look upon this assistant as a representative of the employer's point of view. By observing the following guides to good human relations, you will help set a desirable tone in the office and contribute to the morale of your co-workers. As a result, you will reveal your ability to supervise others and place yourself in a better position for promotion.

Be Discreet

Because you are working with an executive, you will be in a position to learn about many confidential matters regarding salaries, personal feelings about employees, company plans for changes in policies or procedures, and personal family matters. Information regarding these confidential matters should never be revealed to other employees, regardless of their rank. Statements like "That's a confidential matter I can't reveal," "I'm not free to reveal such information," or "You'll have to ask ———(your boss)" will help you to keep confidences.

Be Impartial

An executive's assistant can't afford to show partiality. Your actions and attitudes toward other employees must, therefore, be based on facts rather than on emotions. By not becoming too friendly with others in the same department and by not gossiping, you will find it easier to remain impartial.

Be Loyal

Keeping confidences is one way of demonstrating loyalty. If your boss is being criticized, whether justly or unjustly, you can demonstrate loyalty by coming to the executive's defense or by saying nothing.

It is equally important that you show loyalty to employees. Because of your position, they may share many confidences with you regarding such matters as their health, pet dislikes, love affairs, feeling toward the company, or family arguments. These confidences should be kept—even from the boss. You will jeopardize office morale if you carry everything to the boss, and teamwork will then be difficult to obtain.

Be Businesslike

A higher degree of morale exists in offices where there are satisfied, productive workers. By being businesslike in your attitude toward the job and toward all other workers, you will indicate that you are aware that there is a job to be done and that the job demands hard work and efficient methods. The following "don'ts" will contribute to your businesslike attitude:

1. Don't visit among employees for social purposes. Stay at your desk unless you have business to attend to elsewhere.
2. Remember that the telephone is a business instrument—not a social one. If friends persist in calling you at the office, tell them that you are too busy to talk and that you will telephone them in the evening.

3. Don't joke about business matters or about office "characters." It is easy to take business matters—and some employees—lightly. Joking about company matters destroys purpose and takes away the genuine satisfaction that employees receive from doing their jobs well.
4. Don't let employees monopolize your time. Some employees like to visit and are constantly finding excuses to come to the assistant's desk (they may really want to see what the boss is doing). Show by your businesslike attitude that employee visits should be completed quickly.
5. Avoid extremes in clothing and accessories. Dress for business.

But Be Pleasant

Following the suggestions for getting along with others does not mean that you have to be disagreeable or even indifferent. You should smile easily and should be friendly toward everyone. Never let a bad mood show. Be cool, calm, and collected in all situations. Remember, you often set the tone for the atmosphere of the whole office as well as for job performance. Being pleasant and friendly is just as important to good human relations as being businesslike is to productivity.

COMMUNICATION PROJECTS

Practical Application

A. Assume that you are the administrative assistant in each of the following situations. Write the appropriate letters for your boss.

1. A letter from Roger Hinton to your employer requests a decision within ten days regarding Mr. Hinton's proposed study of the company's billing procedures. Your employer, Audrey Dixon, is out of the country and can't be reached. Since you are unable to make any commitment, you refer this letter to Erwin Bentley, the auditor, for a reply. Write an appropriate letter to Mr. Hinton to let him know what you are doing.
2. Your boss, Milton Metzger, was called out of town on an emergency and is not expected to return for about two weeks. On the day he left, a letter arrived from Opal Earhart, president of the Chamber of Commerce, asking permission to submit Mr. Metzger's name as a candidate for vice president of the Chamber. A reply is needed within one week, since the ballots will be sent to the printer at that time. You telephone Mr. Metzger, and he informs you that he will be unable to accept at the present time because of pressing business problems that require his full attention. Write to Ms. Earhart.

B. Your employer, John Deitz, is the public relations director of the Solar Power Company. Mr. Deitz and the advertising staff have written a colorful informational brochure, *How to Get the Most From Solar Power*, the first in a series of publications that have been made available to the general public in limited quantities. Since the announcement of this publication appeared, you have received the following requests, and Mr. Deitz has asked that you send a personal letter (for his signature) and a copy of the brochure to each inquirer.

1. "Please send me information on solar power." Marcus Tegner, 15 King's Road, Covington, KY 41018.
2. "I have seen a copy of your excellent booklet on solar power and would like 150 copies to send to my customers." Ronald Ewing, Ewing Heating and Air Conditioning, 17 Peachtree Street NW, Atlanta, GA 30301. (This request must be refused because of a limited supply. The maximum you can send is 10 copies.)
3. "May I have permission to duplicate pages 23-26 of your brochure on solar power. I want to make this information showing comparative costs of power sources available to my customers. I will give you credit for authorship." Ralph Ingersoll, I & K Corporation, 2 Oliver Street, Bridgeport, CT 06611. (Permission is granted.)

C. Compose a memorandum for your employer, Constance Romano, Director of Personnel, addressed to all department heads of the Tremont Furniture Company. Recently, the company purchased a 30-minute color motion picture film entitled *Improving Production and Increasing Profits.* You are to coordinate the use of this film and preview it for department heads only at 1:30 p.m. on Tuesday, January 15, in the company auditorium. This showing is to be followed by a discussion as to how best to use the film as a means of achieving greater productivity from the employees.

Editing Practice

The Supervising Editor   The following sentences lack writing polish. Edit and rewrite them.

1. The reason I did not finish the report today is because I had to check some information in the library.
2. Nothing must go wrong. Our business is to see it doesn't.
3. The book which I read did not give me the information I need.
4. Many young business executives hope to become Rotarians because of the prestige they have.
5. Under the last line of the letterhead is to be printed my name and title.

Case Problem

Signing for the Boss   Sometimes employers are not available to sign letters when the letters are ready to be mailed. Three different suggestions for handling this situation were made by the following employers to their secretaries:

Employer A says: "Sign my name and put your initials below the signature."

Employer B says: "Just sign my name; don't bother to initial because no one will know the difference."

Employer C says: "Do not sign my name but instead type below the typewritten signature, 'Dictated but not read.'"

What are the pros and cons of each of these methods?

INDEX

Abbreviations, 218—225
  in dictionary, 218
  of personal titles, 186, 218—219
  punctuation of, 186, 218—220
  rules for, 221—225
Accent marks, 239, 240
Acronyms, 240
Active voice, 311—312
Addresses
  abbreviations for, 222, 224
  numbered streets in, 230
  street and number in, 211, 230
  ZIP Codes for, 231
Adjectives, 113—120
  absolute, 116
  or abverbs, confusion with, 125—126,
     128—129
  articles as, 113
  with "being" verbs, 125
  comparison of, 114—115, 117
  compound, 114, 117—118
  definition of, 113
  descriptive, 114
  with linking verbs, 125—126
  Memory Hook, 126
  modifying
    commas with, 191
    omission of, 116
  numerical, 113
  in parallel structure, 149
  for picture making, 113
  pitfalls in use of, 116—120
  possessive, 113
  proper, 113, 210
Administrative assistant's duties, 560—561,
    565—573
  communication follow-up and, 565—566
  human relations and, 571—573
  letter writing and, 565—566
  mail handling and, 560—561
  meetings and conferences and, 566—568
  research and, 568—570
Administrative Management Society, 337
Adverbs, 122—129
  or adjectives, confusion with, 125—126,
    128—129
  conjunctive, 123—124
  definition of, 122
  double negative, 126—127
  Memory Hooks, 126, 128, 129
  in parallel structure, 149
  pitfalls in use of, 126—128
  position of, 126
  simple, 122—123
  types of, 122—124

Advertising copy, 15, 293, 294, 303, 467
Afterthought, dash with, 169
Agendas for meetings, 514, 516, 568
Ages, forms of expressing, 229
agree with, agree to, 135
Agreement, 95—99, 101—104, 107—110
  basic rule of, 95, 101
  and collective nouns, 102
  and compound subjects, 107—110
  and foreign-noun forms, 69—70
  and indefinite-word subjects, 99
  and inverted sentences, 97
  with *number* as subject, 104
  with part, portion, or amount as subject, 103
  and predicate nominative, 80
  of pronoun and antecedent, 109—110
  of pronoun with subject, 96, 109—110
  and relative-pronoun clauses, 109—110
  and sentence order, 97—98
  and simple subject, 101—103
  and singular or plural verbs, 96
  of subject and predicate, 95—98, 101—103,
    107—110
  and *there* at beginning of sentence, 97
all, any, 117
all of, 139
almost, most, 129
a.m. and *p.m.*, 221, 232
among, between, 138
Ampersand in company names, 177
and, 82, 144, 191
  or *but*, 146
  with independent clauses, 174—175
and so, 304
angry with, angry at, 135
Antecedents, 109—110, 297—229
Antonyms, 258—259, 302
any, all, 117
any, any one, 119
any one, 119
Apostrophe, 72—75, 196—197, 204—205
  with an appositive, 75
  in contractions, 204
  omission of, 76—77
  for omission of figures, 205
  in plurals, 65, 204
  in the possessive case, 72—75, 204
  to show joint or separate ownership, 74—75
Appositives
  apostrophe with, 75
  commas with, 88, 185
  definition of, 185
  pronouns and, 88—89
are, our, 97
Articles, 113, 209